# THE
# POLICE FUNCTION

### FIFTH EDITION

By

## FRANK W. MILLER
James Carr Professor of Criminal Jurisprudence,
Washington University

## ROBERT O. DAWSON
Bryant Smith Chair in Law,
University of Texas

## GEORGE E. DIX
A.W. Walker Centennial Chair in Law,
University of Texas

## RAYMOND I. PARNAS
Professor of Law, University of California, Davis

*Reprinted from*
Miller, Dawson, Dix and Parnas'
Cases and Materials
on
Criminal Justice Administration
(Fourth Edition)

**Westbury, New York**
**THE FOUNDATION PRESS, INC.**
**1991**

Reprinted from

Miller, Dawson, Dix and Parnas'

Cases and Materials on Criminal Justice Administration
(Fourth Edition)

Pages 1 to 637

*Library of Congress Catalog Card Number*: 91–366

**ISBN** 0–88277–881–1

# PREFACE

These materials are a complete extract of the Introduction and Chapters 1 through 10 of Miller, Dawson, Dix, and Parnas, Criminal Justice Administration (Fourth Edition 1991).

The focus of these materials is upon the police role in the modern criminal justice process and the difficult legal issues that are raised by modern policing methods. Criminal defendants' right to have certain evidence excluded from trial where a violation of the defendants' rights occurred in the gathering of evidence, of course, is a consideration that runs throughout the materials.

In each chapter we have endeavored to present legal issues in the context in which they are raised in the criminal justice process. This, we hope, enables the student to gain some appreciation of the extent to which the legal system deals realistically with police practices and of the impact, if any, of various legal norms on police activities.

Footnotes retained from material reprinted have been renumbered. Footnotes added by the editors have been identified by number. Footnotes and textual citations to authority have been deleted from principal opinions without specific indication of the omissions. Editors' footnotes are indicated by letters. We have noted omitted opinions in principal cases only when, in our view, the existence of such opinions is useful in understanding the procedural or precedential significance of the opinion reprinted.

FRANK W. MILLER
ROBERT O. DAWSON
GEORGE E. DIX
RAYMOND I. PARNAS

January, 1991

# SUMMARY OF CONTENTS

## SUMMARY OF CONTENTS

# TABLE OF CONTENTS

# TABLE OF CASES

Principal cases are in italic type. Non-principal cases are in roman type. References are to Pages.

*

# THE
# POLICE FUNCTION

*

# INTRODUCTION: CRIME AND THE CRIMINAL JUSTICE PROCESS

*Analysis*

## A. PERSPECTIVES ON THE CRIMINAL JUSTICE PROCESS

FINAL REPORT OF THE NATIONAL COMMISSION ON THE CAUSES AND PREVENTION OF VIOLENCE, TO ESTABLISH JUSTICE, TO INSURE DOMESTIC TRANQUILITY 149–156, 159–160, December 1969

### The Criminal Justice Process

\* \* \* It is commonly assumed that these three components—law enforcement (police, sheriffs, marshals), the judicial process (judges, prosecutors, defense lawyers) and corrections (prison officials, probation and parole officers)—add up to a "system" of criminal justice.

A system implies some unity of purpose and organized interrelationship among component parts. In the typical American city and state, and under federal jurisdiction as well, no such relationship exists. There is, instead, a reasonably well-defined criminal *process*, a continuum through which each accused offender may pass: from the hands of the police, to the jurisdiction of the courts, behind the walls of a prison, then back onto the street. The inefficiency, fall-out and failure of purpose during this process is notorious.

According to the 1967 report of the President's Crime Commission, half of all major crimes are never reported to the police. Of those which are, fewer than one-quarter are "cleared" by arrest. Nearly half of these arrests result in the dismissal of charges. Of the balance, well over 90 percent are resolved by a plea of guilty. The proportion of cases which actually go to trial is thus very small, representing less than one percent of all crimes committed. About one quarter of those convicted are confined in penal institutions; the balance are released under probation supervision. Nearly everyone who goes to prison is eventually released, often under parole supervision. Between one-half and two-thirds of all those released are sooner or later arrested and convicted again, thereby joining the population of repeater criminals we call recidivists.

\* \* \*

\* \* \* The police see crime in the raw. They are exposed firsthand to the agony of victims, the danger of streets, the violence of lawbreakers. A major task of the police officer is to track down and arrest persons who have committed serious crimes. It is discouraging indeed for such an officer to see courts promptly release defendants on bail and permit them to remain free for extended periods before trial, or prosecutors reduce charges in order to induce pleas of guilty to lesser offenses, or judges exclude incriminating evidence, or parole officers accept supervision of released prisoners but check on them only a few minutes each month.

Yet the police themselves are often seen by others as contributing to the failure of the system. They are charged with ineptness, discourtesy, dishonesty, brutality, sleeping on duty, illegal searches. They are attacked by large segments of the community as being insensitive to the feelings and needs of the citizens they are employed to serve.

Trial judges tend to see crime from a more objective position. They see facts in dispute and two sides to each issue. They may sit long hours on the bench in an effort to adjudicate cases with dignity and dispatch, only to find counsel unprepared, or weak cases presented, or witnesses missing, or warrants unserved, or bail restrictions unenforced, or occasional juries bringing in arbitrary verdicts. They find sentencing to be the most difficult of their tasks, yet presentence information is scanty and dispositional alternatives are all too often thwarted by the unavailability of adequate facilities.

Yet criminal courts themselves are often poorly managed and severely criticized. They are seriously backlogged; in many of our major cities the average delay between arrest and trial is close to a year. All too many judges are perceived as being inconsiderate of waiting parties, police officers and citizen witnesses. Too often lower criminal courts tend to be operated more like turnstiles than tribunals. In some jurisdictions, many able jurists complain that some of their most senior colleagues refuse to consider or adopt new administrative and managerial systems which could improve significantly the quality of justice and the efficiency of the court and which would also shorten the time from arrest to trial.

Corrections officials enter the crime picture long after the offense and deal only with convicted persons. Their job is to maintain secure custody and design programs which prepare individual prisoners for a successful return to society. They are discouraged when they encounter convicted persons whose sentences are either inadequate or excessive. They are frustrated by legislatures which curtail the flexibility of sentences and which fail to appropriate necessary funds. They are dismayed at police officers who harass parolees, or at a community which fails to provide jobs or halfway houses for ex-offenders.

Yet, with a few significant exceptions, the prisons and correctional facilities operate in isolation and reject public scrutiny. Programs of rehabilitation are shallow and dominated by greater concern for punishment and custody than for correction. Prison inmate work assignments usually bear little relationship to employment opportunities outside. Internal supervision is often inadequate  *   *   *.

[J]ails—institutions for detaining accused persons before and during trial and for short misdemeanor sentences—*   *   * are notoriously ill-managed and poorly staffed.  *   *   * Cities are full of people who have been arrested but not convicted, and who nevertheless serve time in facilities worse, in terms of overcrowding and deterioration, than the prisons to which convicted offenders are sentenced. Accused first offenders are mixed indiscriminately with hardened recidivists. In most cases, the opportunities for recreation, job training or treatment of a nonpunitive character are almost nil. These deficiencies of jails might be less significant if arrested persons were detained for only a day or two, but many unable to post bail or meet other conditions of release are held in jail for many months because the other components of the legal system do not provide for speedy trials.

In the mosaic of discontent which pervades the criminal process, public officials and institutions, bound together with private persons in the cause of reducing crime, each sees his own special mission being undercut by the cross-purposes, frailties or malfunctions of others. As they find their places along the spectrum between the intense concern with victims at one end, and total preoccupation with reforming convicted lawbreakers at the other, so do they find their daily perceptions of justice varying or in conflict.

These conflicts in turn are intensified by the fact that each part of the criminal process in most cities is overloaded and undermanned, and most of its personnel underpaid and inadequately trained.  *   *   *

Under such circumstances it is hardly surprising to find in most cities not a smooth functioning "system" of criminal justice but a fragmented and often hostile amalgamation of criminal justice agencies. Obvious mechanisms for introducing some sense of harmony into the system are not utilized. Judges, police administrators and prison officials hardly ever confer on common problems. Sentencing institutes and familiarization prison visits for judges are the exception rather than the rule. Usually neither prosecutors nor defense attorneys receive training in corrections upon which to base intelligent sentencing recommendations.

Nearly every part of the criminal process is run with public funds by persons employed as officers of justice to serve the same community. Yet every agency in the criminal process in a sense competes with every other in the quest for tax dollars. Isolation or antagonism rather than mutual support tends to characterize their intertwined operations.

*   *   *

## Toward a Criminal Justice System

\* \* \*

The pervasive fragmentation of police, court and correctional agencies suggests that some catalyst is needed to bring them together. An assumption that parallel and overlapping public agencies will cooperate efficiently can no longer suffice as a substitute for deliberate action to make it happen in real life.

\* \* \*

A full-time criminal justice office is basic to the formation of a criminal justice system. Its optimum form, i.e., line or staff, and its location in the bureaucracy, need to be developed through experimentation.

\* \* \*

Whatever its form, the basic purposes of the criminal justice office would be to do continuing planning, to assure effective processing of cases, and to develop better functioning relationships among the criminal justice subsystems and with public and private agencies outside the criminal justice system.

## B.  THE PROCESSING OF A CRIMINAL CASE

---

### NATIONAL ADVISORY COMMISSION ON CRIMINAL JUSTICE STANDARDS AND GOALS, COURTS 11–15 (1973)

\* \* \*

#### ARREST

The first formal contact of an accused with the criminal justice system is likely to be an arrest by a police officer. In most cases, the arrest will be made upon the police officer's own evaluation that there is sufficient basis for believing that a crime had been committed by the accused. However, the arrest may be made pursuant to a warrant; in this case, the police officer or some other person will have submitted the evidence against the accused to a judicial officer, who determines whether the evidence is sufficient to justify an arrest. In some situations, the accused may have no formal contact with the law until he has been indicted by a grand jury. Following such an indictment, a court order may be issued authorizing police officers to take the accused into custody. But these are exceptional situations. Ordinarily, the arrest is made without any court order and the court's contact with the accused comes only after the arrest.

\* \* \*

#### INITIAL JUDICIAL APPEARANCE

In all jurisdictions, a police officer or other person making an arrest must bring the arrested person before a judge within a short period of time. It is at this initial appearance that most accused have their first contact with the courts. This initial appearance is usually

before a lower court—a justice of the peace or a magistrate.    * * *
Often by the time of the initial appearance, the prosecution will have
prepared a formal document called a complaint, which charges the
defendant with a specific crime.

At the initial appearance, several things may occur.  First, the
defendant will be informed of the charges against him, usually by
means of the complaint.  Second, he will be informed of his rights,
including his constitutional privilege against self-incrimination.  Third,
if the case is one in which the accused will be provided with an attorney
at State expense, the mechanical process of assigning the attorney at
least may begin at this stage.  Fourth, unless the defendant is convicted
of an offense at this point, arrangements may be made concerning the
release of the defendant before further proceedings.  This may take the
traditional form of setting bail, that is, establishment of an amount of
security the defendant himself or a professional bondsman whom he
may hire must deposit with the court (or assume the obligation to pay)
to assure that the defendant does appear for later proceedings.  Pretrial release, in some jurisdictions, also may take the form of being
released on one's own recognizance, that is, release simply upon the
defendant's promise to appear at a later time.   *   *   *

In addition to these matters collateral to the issue of guilt, it is at
the initial appearance that judicial inquiry into the merits of the case
begins.  If the charge is one the lower court has authority to try, the
defendant may be asked how he pleads.  If he pleads guilty, he may be
convicted at this point.  If he pleads not guilty, a trial date may be set
and trial held later in this court.

However, if the charge is more serious, the court must give the
defendant the opportunity for a judicial evaluation to determine whether there is enough evidence to justify putting him to trial in the higher
court.  In this type of case, the judge at the initial appearance ordinarily will ask the defendant whether he wants a preliminary hearing.  If
the defendant does, the matter generally is continued, or postponed to
give both the prosecution and the defense time to prepare their cases.

The matter will be taken up again later in the lower court at the
preliminary hearing.  At this proceeding, the prosecutor introduces
evidence to try to prove the defendant's guilt.  He need not convince
the court of the defendant's guilt beyond a reasonable doubt, but need
only establish that there is enough evidence from which an average
person (juror) could conclude that the defendant was guilty of the crime
charged.  If this evidence is produced, the court may find that the
prosecution has established probable cause to believe the defendant
guilty.

At this preliminary hearing the defendant may cross-examine
witnesses produced by the prosecution and present evidence himself.  If
the court finds at the end of the preliminary hearing that probable
cause does not exist, it dismisses the complaint.  This does not ordinarily prevent the prosecution from bringing another charge, however.  If
the court finds that probable cause does exist, it orders that the
defendant be bound over to the next step in the prosecution.  As a

practical matter, the preliminary hearing also serves the function of giving the defendant and his attorney a look at the case the prosecution will produce at trial. It gives a defense attorney the opportunity to cross-examine witnesses he later will have to confront. This informal previewing function may be more valuable to defendants than the theoretical function of the preliminary hearing.

### FILING OF FORMAL CRIMINAL CHARGE

Generally, it is following the decision of the lower court to bind over a defendant that the formal criminal charge is made in the court that would try the case if it goes to formal trial. If no grand jury action is to be taken, this is a simple step consisting of the prosecutor's filing a document called an information. But in many jurisdictions the involvement of the grand jury makes the process more complex. There, the decision at the preliminary hearing simply is to bind the defendant over for consideration by the grand jury. In these areas, the prosecutor then must go before the grand jury and again present his evidence. Only if the grand jury determines that there is probable cause does it act. Its action—consisting of issuing a document called an indictment—constitutes the formal charging of the defendant. If it does not find probable cause, it takes no action and the prosecution is dismissed.

In some jurisdictions, it is not necessary to have both a grand jury inquiry and a preliminary hearing. In most Federal jurisdictions, for example, if a defendant has been indicted by a grand jury he no longer has a right to a preliminary hearing, on the theory that he is entitled to only one determination as to whether probable cause exists.

Although the defendant is entitled to participate in the preliminary hearing, he has no right to take part in a grand jury inquiry. Traditionally, he has not been able to ascertain what went on in front of the grand jury, although increasingly the law has given him the right, after the fact, to know.

Following the formal charge—whether it has been by indictment or information—any of a variety of matters that require resolution may arise. The defendant's competency to stand trial may be in issue. This requires the court to resolve the question of whether the defendant is too ill mentally or otherwise impaired to participate meaningfully in his trial. If he is sufficiently impaired, trial must be postponed until he regains his competency.

The defendant also may challenge the validity of the indictment or information or the means by which they were issued. For example, he may assert that those acts with which he is charged do not constitute a crime under the laws of the jurisdiction. Or, if he was indicted by a grand jury, he may assert that the grand jury was selected in a manner not consistent with State or Federal law and, therefore, that the indictment is invalid.

A defendant also may—and in some jurisdictions must—raise, before trial, challenges to the admissibility of certain evidence, especially evidence seized by police officers in a search or statements obtained from him by interrogation. In view of the rapid growth of legal doctrine governing the admissibility of statements of defendants and evidence obtained by police search and seizure, resolution of the issues raised by defendants' challenges to the admissibility of such evidence may be more complex and time-consuming than anything involved in determining guilt or innocence.

\* \* \*

## ARRAIGNMENT

In view of the potential complexity of pretrial matters, much of the significant activity in a criminal prosecution already may have occurred at the time the defendant makes his first formal appearance before the court that is to try him. This first appearance—the arraignment—is the point at which he is asked to plead to the charge. He need not plead, in which case a plea of not guilty automatically is entered for him. If he pleads guilty, the law requires that certain precautions be taken to assure that this plea is made validly. Generally, the trial judge accepting the plea first must inquire of the defendant whether he understands the charge against him and the penalties that may be imposed. The judge also must assure himself that there is some reasonable basis in the facts of the case for the plea. This may involve requiring the prosecution to present some of its evidence to assure the court that there is evidence tending to establish guilt.

## TRIAL

Unless the defendant enters a guilty plea, the full adversary process is put into motion. The prosecution now must establish to a jury or a judge the guilt of the defendant beyond a reasonable doubt. If the defendant elects to have the case tried by a jury, much effort is expended on the selection of a jury. Prospective jurors are questioned to ascertain whether they might be biased and what their views on numerous matters might be. Both sides have the right to have a potential juror rejected on the ground that he may be biased. In addition, both have the right to reject a limited number of potential jurors without having to state any reason. When the jury has been selected and convened, both sides may make opening statements explaining what they intend to prove or disprove.

The prosecution presents its evidence first, and the defendant has the option of making no case and relying upon the prosecution's inability to establish guilt beyond a reasonable doubt. He also has the option of presenting evidence tending to disprove the prosecution's case or tending to prove additional facts constituting a defense under applicable law. Throughout, however, the burden remains upon the prosecution. Procedurally, this is effectuated by defense motions to dismiss, which often are made after the prosecution's case has been presented and after all of the evidence is in. These motions in effect assert that the prosecution's case is so weak that no reasonable jury could conclude beyond a reasonable doubt that the defendant was guilty. If the judge grants the motion, he is in effect determining that no jury could reasonably return a verdict of guilty. This not only results in a dismissal of the prosecution but also prevents the prosecution from bringing another charge for the same crime.

After the evidence is in and defense motions are disposed of, the jury is instructed on the applicable law. Often both defense and prosecution lawyers submit instructions which they ask the court to read to the jury, and the court chooses from those and others it composes itself. It is in the formulation of these instructions that many issues regarding the definition of the applicable law arise and must be resolved. After—or sometimes before—the instructions are read, both sides present formal arguments to the jury. The jury then retires for its deliberations.

Generally, the jury may return only one of two verdicts: guilty or not guilty. A verdict of not guilty may be misleading; it may mean not that the jury believed that the defendant was not guilty but rather that the jury determined that the prosecution had not established guilt by the criterion—beyond a reasonable doubt—the law imposes. If the insanity defense has been raised, the jury may be told it should specify if insanity is the reason for acquittal; otherwise, there is no need for explanation. If a guilty verdict is returned, the court formally enters a judgment of conviction unless there is a legally sufficient reason for not doing so.

The defendant may attack his conviction, usually by making a motion to set aside the verdict and order a new trial. In his attack, he may argue that evidence was improperly admitted during the trial, that the evidence was so weak that no reasonable jury could have found that it established guilt beyond a reasonable doubt, or that there is newly discovered evidence which, had it been available at the time of trial, would have changed the result. If the court grants a motion raising one of these arguments, the effect generally is not to acquit the defendant but merely to require the holding of a new trial.

## SENTENCING

Sentencing then follows. (If the court has accepted a plea of guilty, this step follows acceptance of the plea.) In an increasing number of jurisdictions, an investigation called the presentence report is conducted by professional probation officers. This involves investigation of the offense, the offender and his background, and any other matters of potential value to the sentencing judge. Following submission of the report to the court, the defendant is given the opportunity to comment upon the appropriateness of sentencing. In some jurisdictions, this has developed into a more extensive court hearing on sentencing issues, with the defendant given the opportunity to present evidence as well as argument for leniency. Sentencing itself generally is the responsibility of the judge, although in some jurisdictions juries retain that authority.

## APPEAL

Following the conclusion of the proceeding in the trial court, the matter shifts to the appellate courts. In some jurisdictions, a defendant who is convicted of a minor offense in a lower court has the right to a new trial (trial de novo) in a higher court. But in most situations—and in all cases involving serious offenses—the right to appeal is limited to the right to have an appellate court examine the record of the trial proceedings for error. If error is found, the appellate court either may take definitive action—such as ordering that the prosecution be dismissed—or it may set aside the conviction and remand the case for a new trial. The latter gives the prosecution the opportunity to obtain a valid conviction. Generally, a time limit is placed upon the period during which an appeal may be taken.

## COLLATERAL ATTACK

Even if no appeal is taken or the conviction is upheld, the courts' participation in the criminal justice process is not necessarily ended. To some extent, a convicted defendant who has either exhausted his appeal rights or declined to exercise them within the appropriate time limits can seek further relief by means of collateral attack upon the conviction. This method involves a procedure collateral to the standard process of conviction and appeal.

Traditionally this relief was sought by applying for a writ of habeas corpus on the ground that the conviction under which the applicant was held was invalid. Many jurisdictions have found this vehicle too cumbersome for modern problems and have developed special procedures for collateral attacks. * * *

# A general view of The Criminal Justice System

This chart seeks to present a simple yet comprehensive view of the movement of cases through the criminal justice system. Procedures in individual jurisdictions may vary from the pattern shown here. The differing weights of line indicate the relative volumes of cases disposed of at various points in the system, but this is only suggestive since no nationwide data of this sort exists.

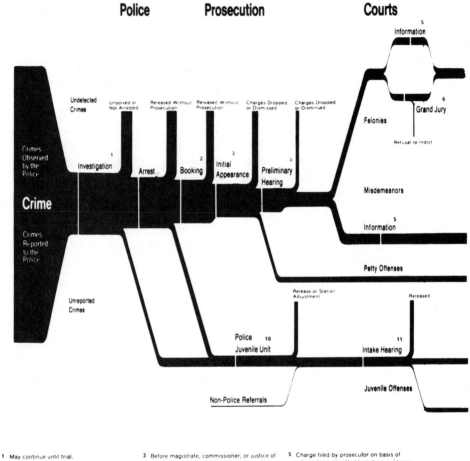

**Police**   **Prosecution**   **Courts**

1 May continue until trial.

2 Administrative record of arrest. First step at which temporary release on bail may be available.

3 Before magistrate, commissioner, or justice of peace. Formal notice of charge, advice of rights. Bail set. Summary trials for petty offenses usually conducted here without further processing.

4 Preliminary testing of evidence against defendant. Charge may be reduced. No **separate preliminary hearing for misdemeanors** in some systems.

5 Charge filed by prosecutor on basis of information submitted by police or citizens. Alternative to grand jury indictment; often used in felonies, almost always in misdemeanors.

6 Reviews whether Government evidence sufficient to justify trial. Some States have no grand jury system; others seldom use it.

Source: The President's Commission on Law Enforcement and Administration of Justice, The Challenge of Crime in a Free Society (1967).

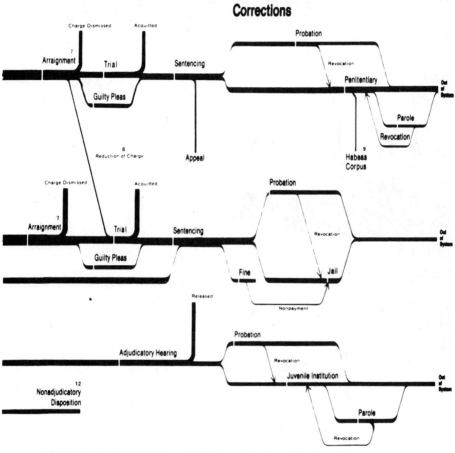

**Corrections**

Arraignment — Trial — Sentencing

Charge Dismissed — Acquitted

Guilty Pleas

Probation — Revocation — Penitentiary — Parole — Revocation

8 Reduction of Charge — Appeal — 9 Habeas Corpus — Out of System

Arraignment — Trial — Sentencing

Charge Dismissed — Acquitted

Guilty Pleas — Fine — Nonpayment — Probation — Revocation — Jail — Out of System

Released

Adjudicatory Hearing — Probation — Revocation — Juvenile Institution — Parole — Revocation — Out of System

12 Nonadjudicatory Disposition

7  Appearance for plea; defendant elects trial by judge or jury (if available); counsel for indigent usually appointed here in felonies. Often not at all in other cases.

8  Charge may be reduced at any time prior to trial in return for plea of guilty or for other reasons.

9  Challenge on constitutional grounds to legality of detention. May be sought at any point in process.

10  Police often hold informal hearings, dismiss or adjust many cases without further processing.

11  Probation officer decides desirability of further court action.

12  Welfare agency, social services, counselling, medical care, etc., for cases where adjudicatory handling not needed.

*

# Part One

# INVESTIGATION OF CRIME

## EDITORS' INTRODUCTION: FEDERAL AND STATE CONSTITUTIONAL PROVISIONS AFFECTING LAW ENFORCEMENT CONDUCT

Law enforcement conduct, and the admissibility of evidence developed by such conduct, is affected by law emanating from numerous sources other than the United States Constitution. Nevertheless, because of the United States Supreme Court's "constitutionalization" of criminal procedure, several provisions of the federal document—applicable to the states by virtue of the Fourteenth Amendment—have taken on immense significance for law enforcement activity. Much of the material in Part One of this book is devoted to exploring the content of these provisions.

## United States Constitution

### AMENDMENT IV

The right of the people to be secure in their persons, houses, papers, and effects, against unreasonable searches and seizures, shall not be violated, and no Warrants shall issue, but upon probable cause, supported by Oath or affirmation, and particularly describing the place to be searched, and the persons or things to be seized.

### AMENDMENT V

No person * * * shall be compelled in any criminal case to be a witness against himself, nor be deprived of life, liberty, or property, without due process of law * * *.

### AMENDMENT VI

In all criminal prosecutions, the accused shall enjoy the right * * * to have the Assistance of Counsel for his defense.

### AMENDMENT XIV, SECTION 1

No State shall * * * deprive any person of life, liberty, or property, without due process of law; nor deny to any person within its jurisdiction the equal protection of the laws.

———

State constitutions usually have provisions analogous and sometimes identical to those provisions. Article 1 of the Utah constitution, for example, contains the following provisions:

13

Section 12. Right of accused persons

In criminal prosecutions the accused shall have the right to appear and defend in person and by counsel  *  *  *.  The accused shall not be compelled to give evidence against himself.

Section 14. Unreasonable searches forbidden—Issuance of warrant

The right of the people to be secure in their persons, houses, papers and effects against unreasonable searches and seizures shall not be violated; and no warrant shall issue but upon probable cause supported by oath or affirmation, particularly describing the place to be searched and the person or thing to be seized.

Other state provisions differ more significantly from their federal counterparts.  Article 1, Section 4 of the Washington Constitution, for example, provides:

No person shall be disturbed in his private affairs, or his home invaded, without authority of law.

The state constitutional convention that proposed the Washington provision had been presented with language identical to that used in the Fourth Amendment to the United States Constitution but rejected it in favor of that finally used.  See State v. Ringer, 100 Wn.2d 686, 690, 674 P.2d 1240, 1243 (1983).

Obviously, a state cannot—by constitutional provision or otherwise—deprive its citizens of rights which they have by virtue of the United States Constitution.  But it is equally obvious that states can—by constitutional provision or otherwise—give their citizens more protection than those citizens are afforded by the federal Constitution. Even if a state constitutional provision is phrased similarly or identically to an analogous federal constitutional provision, the state courts need not construe the state provision as having the same content as the United States Supreme Court has given to the federal provision.  State judicial willingness to "independently" construe state constitutional provisions has become widely labeled "new federalism."  See, e.g., Wilkes, The New Federalism in Criminal Procedure: State Court Evasion of the Burger Court, 62 Ky.L.J. 421 (1974).  The state tribunals may, of course, construe state provisions as conferring no more rights upon citizens, suspects or defendants than the Supreme Court construes the federal provisions as providing, and in fact many state courts do so.

Nevertheless, an attorney representing a state criminal defendant must, after identifying a potential constitutional issue, consider both federal and state constitutional grounds.  Some courts have complained that lawyers ignore, or at least do not adequately address, such state constitutional law questions.  The Utah Supreme Court, for example, commented that "despite our willingness to independently interpret Utah's constitution in other areas of law, the analysis of state constitutional issues in criminal appeals continues to be ignored."  State v. Earl, 716 P.2d 803, 806 (Utah 1986).  Justice Souter of the New Hampshire Supreme Court has bemoaned the failure of counsel to offer sound and specific reasons why, in particular situations, the state court should construe state constitutional provisions more broadly than analogous federal provisions have been read. His court, he argued, should regard state constitutional issues as raised by briefs only if those briefs state them "directly" and develop "supporting arguments premised on policy and authority." State v. Bradberry, 129 N.H. 68, 81, 522 A.2d 1380, 1388 (1986) (Souter, J., concurring).

These materials emphasize the federal constitutional provisions and their construction. But full treatment of these issues in state litigation cannot ignore "new federalism" and state law arguments independent of federal constitutional ones.

# Chapter 1

# THE EXCLUSIONARY SANCTION

*Analysis*

---

## EDITORS' INTRODUCTION: EXCLUSIONARY RULES

The most dramatic development in American criminal procedure has been the "constitutionalization" of the area in general and, in particular, the "constitutionalization" of evidence matters by federal constitutional exclusionary requirements. To a significant extent, the requirements imposed by local statutes, case law and court rules have been eclipsed by the development of federal constitutional requirements.

The major federal constitutional requirements affecting law enforcement conduct and the admissibility in a criminal trial of evidence obtained by law enforcement efforts are set out above. These are, of course, binding on the states because of the Fourteenth Amendment. This chapter considers the enforcement of these provisions and other legal requirements by rules excluding evidence obtained in violation of their terms. The substance of these provisions is considered throughout much of the remainder of Part One; the basic contours of the Fourth and Fifth Amendments are addressed in Chapter 2.

Requirements that evidence offered by the prosecution at a criminal trial be rejected because of impropriety in the process of gathering it are often referred to as "exclusionary rules." In one sense, of course, any legal requirement that results in evidence being held inadmissible is an "exclusionary" rule. But in common legal usage, the phrase "exclusionary rule" has come to mean a legal requirement that mandates such exclusion of evidence because of the illegal manner in which it was obtained. This is usually without regard to whether that illegality affects the reliability of the evidence. The traditional requirement that out-of-court confessions given by defendants be "voluntary" (discussed in Chapter 7, infra) is in some sense an exclusionary rule

16

under this definition. But at least in its original form, the prohibition against the use of involuntary confessions appears to have been based more upon a perception that coercion rendered confessions unreliable than upon the desirability of responding to illegality in the interrogation process by holding the fruits of that illegality inadmissible as evidence.

Discussions are often conducted in terms of what is assumed to be "the exclusionary rule," as if only one doctrine or legal requirement was involved. This is simply not the case. "[T]he exclusionary rule" is usually used to describe the requirement—announced in Mapp v. Ohio, reprinted in this chapter—that evidence obtained in violation of the Fourth Amendment be excluded from state criminal trials. But this is not the only legal requirement mandating exclusion of evidence because of impropriety in the manner in which it was obtained. Other federal constitutional provisions also require exclusion of evidence obtained in violation of their requirements. Moreover, the exclusionary requirements attaching to the various federal constitutional provisions are not necessarily the same. As is developed later in these materials, for example, the extent to which evidence derived from a violation must be excluded may differ significantly depending upon whether the underlying violation is of the Fourth Amendment's requirements or, instead, of judicially-developed rules based upon the Fifth Amendment.

Evidence obtained by conduct that violates state legal requirements but no federal constitutional provision may be inadmissible as a matter of state law. If state law imposes such a requirement, the details of that requirement—as, for example, the number and scope of exceptions that sometime permit the use of illegally seized evidence—may not be the same as the details of the Fourth Amendment federal constitutional exclusionary rule.

Conceptually, then, it is best to regard exclusionary requirements as a category consisting of a number of potentially quite different exclusionary demands imposed by various legal requirements. There could be as many exclusionary rules as there are legal requirements that might be violated in the obtaining of evidence.

The Fourth Amendment exclusionary rule announced in Mapp v. Ohio has generated the most debate and controversy. Consequently, these materials emphasize that holding and its development. But it is important to keep in mind that whether and when the admissibility of evidence in a criminal trial is affected by showings that it was obtained in violation of other legal requirements presents distinguishable although related issues.

Exclusionary rule concerns are presented throughout Part One of these materials. Chapters 2 through 6 address a variety of issues concerning law enforcement authority to make searches and seizures. Action taken beyond this authority, of course, may invoke exclusionary sanctions. While exclusionary rule considerations are less pervasive in the material addressed in Chapters 6 through 10, they are nevertheless present and still important. Chapter 1 limits itself to the exclusionary sanction itself and procedural aspects of it: When, if ever, is it appropriate? If it applies, when does it require the exclusion of challenged evidence? What exceptions to the general rule of exclusion do and should exist?

## A. ADOPTION OF THE FEDERAL CONSTITUTIONAL EXCLUSIONARY SANCTION

It is clear that the United States Supreme Court did not originate the notion that those violating the law in the gathering of evidence might appropriately be penalized by a rule of evidence holding the proof inadmissible because of the manner in which it was obtained. But the Court did vigorously embrace this approach as a matter of federal judicial policy and as a mandate of federal constitutional law. This is largely responsible for the pervasive impact that exclusionary rules have upon modern criminal procedure.

The Court's attitude toward exclusionary sanctions reflects both a break from tradition and a shift in the Court's position. In Adams v. New York, 192 U.S. 585, 24 S.Ct. 372, 48 L.Ed. 575 (1904), the state defendant urged that certain evidence had been seized in violation of the Fourth Amendment and improperly used in his state criminal trial. The Court noted, however, that the evidence was clearly competent as tending to show the defendant's guilt of the crime charged. "In such cases," it continued, "the weight of authority as well as reason limits the inquiry to the competency of the proffered testimony, and the courts do not stop to inquire as to the means by which the evidence was obtained." 192 U.S. at 594, 24 S.Ct. at 374, 48 L.Ed. at 579. This traditional position—that the manner in which otherwise competent evidence was obtained does not affect its admissibility—was supported by two major considerations. One was the need to have all available relevant evidence bearing on the issues in a case. The other was the inconvenience, disruption, and other costs involved in making the often-complex and collateral inquiries necessary to determine whether challenged evidence was in fact improperly obtained. See generally, McCormick on Evidence 446 (3rd ed. 1984).

### MAPP v. OHIO
Supreme Court of the United States, 1961.
367 U.S. 643, 81 S.Ct. 1684, 6 L.Ed.2d 1081.

Mr. JUSTICE CLARK delivered the opinion of the Court.

Appellant stands convicted of knowingly having had in her possession and under her control certain lewd and lascivious books, pictures, and photographs * * * though "based primarily upon the introduction in evidence of lewd and lascivious books and pictures unlawfully seized during an unlawful search of defendant's home * * *."
* * *

On May 23, 1957, three Cleveland police officers arrived at appellant's residence in that city pursuant to information that "a person [was] hiding out in the home, who was wanted for questioning in connection with a recent bombing, and that there was a large amount of policy paraphernalia being hidden in the home." * * * [B]ut appellant, after telephoning her attorney, refused to admit them without a search warrant. * * *

The officers again sought entrance some three hours later when four or more additional officers arrived on the scene. When Miss Mapp did not come to the door immediately, at least one of the several doors to the house was forcibly opened and the policemen gained admittance. Meanwhile Miss Mapp's attorney arrived, but the officers, having secured their own entry, and continuing in their defiance of the law, would permit him neither to see Miss Mapp nor to enter the house. It appears that Miss Mapp was halfway down the stairs from the upper floor to the front door when the officers, in this highhanded manner, broke into the hall. She demanded to see the search warrant. A paper, claimed to be a warrant, was held up by one of the officers. She grabbed the "warrant" and placed it in her bosom. A struggle ensued in which the officers recovered the piece of paper and as a result of which they handcuffed appellant because she had been "belligerent" in resisting their official rescue of the "warrant" from her person. * * * The obscene materials for possession of which she was ultimately convicted were discovered in the course of [a] widespread search.

At the trial no search warrant was produced by the prosecution, nor was the failure to produce one explained or accounted for. * * * The Ohio Supreme Court believed a "reasonable argument" could be made that the conviction should be reversed "because the 'methods' employed to obtain the [evidence] were such as to 'offend "a sense of justice," ' " but the court found determinative the fact that the evidence had not been taken "from defendant's person by the use of brutal or offensive physical force against defendant."

* * *

The State says that even if the search were made without authority, or otherwise unreasonably, it is not prevented from using the unconstitutionally seized evidence at trial, citing Wolf v. People of State of Colorado, 1949, 338 U.S. 25, at page 33, 69 S.Ct. 1359, at page 1364, 93 L.Ed. 1782, in which this Court did indeed hold "that in a prosecution in a State court for a State crime the Fourteenth Amendment does not forbid the admission of evidence obtained by an unreasonable search and seizure." On this appeal * * * it is urged once again that we review that holding.

## I.

Seventy-five years ago, in Boyd v. United States, 1886, 116 U.S. 616, 630, 6 S.Ct. 524, 532, 29 L.Ed. 746, considering the Fourth and Fifth Amendments as running "almost into each other" on the facts before it, this Court held that the doctrines of those Amendments

"apply to all invasions on the part of the government and its employes of the sanctity of a man's home and the privacies of life. It is not the breaking of his doors, and the rummaging of his drawers, that constitutes the essence of the offence; but it is the invasion of his indefeasible right of personal security, personal liberty and private property * * *. Breaking into a house and opening boxes and drawers are circumstances of aggravation; but any forcible and compulsory extortion of a man's own testimony or of his private papers to be used as evidence to convict him of crime or to forfeit his goods, is within the condemnation * * * [of those Amendments]."

\* \* \*

Less than 30 years after *Boyd*, this Court, in Weeks v. United States, 232 U.S. 383 (1914) * * * [s]pecifically dealing with the use of * * * evidence unconstitutionally seized, * * * concluded:

"If letters and private documents can thus be seized and held and used in evidence against a citizen accused of an offense, the protection of the Fourth Amendment declaring his right to be secure against such searches and seizures is of no value, and, so far as those thus placed are concerned, might as well be stricken from the Constitution. The efforts of the courts and their officials to bring the guilty to punishment, praiseworthy as they are, are not to be aided by the sacrifice of those great principles established by years of endeavor and suffering which have resulted in their embodiment in the fundamental law of the land."

* * * Thus, in the year 1914, in the *Weeks* case, this Court "for the first time" held that "in a federal prosecution the Fourth Amendment barred the use of evidence secured through an illegal search and seizure." Wolf v. People of State of Colorado, supra, 338 U.S. at page 28, 69 S.Ct. at page 1361.

* * * There are in the cases of this Court some passing references to the *Weeks* rule as being one of evidence. But the plain and unequivocal language of *Weeks*—and its later paraphrase in *Wolf*—to the effect that the *Weeks* rule is of constitutional origin, remains entirely undisturbed. * * *

## II.

In 1949, 35 years after *Weeks* was announced, this Court, in Wolf v. People of State of Colorado, supra, again for the first time, discussed the effect of the Fourth Amendment upon the States through the operation of the Due Process Clause of the Fourteenth Amendment. It said:

"[W]e have no hesitation in saying that were a State affirmatively to sanction such police incursion into privacy it would run counter to the guaranty of the Fourteenth Amendment." * * *

Nevertheless, after declaring that the "security of one's privacy against arbitrary intrusion by the police" is "implicit in 'the concept of ordered liberty' and as such enforceable against the States through the Due Process Clause," * * * and announcing that it "stoutly adhere[d]" to the *Weeks* decision, the Court decided that the *Weeks* exclusionary rule would not then be imposed upon the States as "an essential ingredient of the right." * * * The Court's reasons for not considering essential to the right to privacy, as a curb imposed upon the States by the Due Process Clause, that which decades before had been posited as part and parcel of the Fourth Amendment's limitation upon federal encroachment of individual privacy, were bottomed on factual considerations.

While they are not basically relevant to a decision that the exclusionary rule is an essential ingredient of the Fourth Amendment as the right it embodies is vouchsafed against the States by the Due Process Clause, we will consider the current validity of the factual grounds upon which *Wolf* was based.

The Court in *Wolf* * * * stated that "[t]he contrariety of views of the States" on the adoption of the exclusionary rule of *Weeks* was "particularly impressive" * * *; and, in this connection that it could not "brush aside the experience of States which deem the incidence of such conduct by the police too slight to call for a deterrent remedy * * * by overriding the [States'] relevant rules of evidence." * * * While in 1949, prior to the *Wolf* case, almost two-thirds of the States were opposed to the use of the exclusionary rule, now, despite the *Wolf* case, more than half of those since passing upon it, by their own legislative or judicial decision, have wholly or partly adopted or adhered to the *Weeks* rule. * * * Significantly, among those now following the rule is California, which, according to its highest court, was "compelled to reach that conclusion because other remedies have completely failed to secure compliance with the constitutional provisions * * *." People v. Cahan, 1955, 44 Cal.2d 434, 445, 282 P.2d 905, 911, 50 A.L.R.2d 513. In connection with this California case, we note that the second basis elaborated in *Wolf* in support of its failure to enforce the exclusionary doctrine against the States was that "other means of protection" have been afforded "the right to privacy." 338 U.S. at page 30, 69 S.Ct. at page 1362. The experience of California that such other remedies have been worthless and futile is buttressed by the experience of other States. The obvious futility of relegating the Fourth Amendment to the protection of other remedies has, moreover, been recognized by this Court since *Wolf.* See Irvine v. People of State of California, 1954, 347 U.S. 128, 137, 74 S.Ct. 381, 385, 98 L.Ed. 561.

\* \* \*

It, therefore, plainly appears that the factual considerations supporting the failure of the *Wolf* Court to include the *Weeks* exclusionary rule when it recognized the enforceability of the right to privacy against the States in 1949, while not basically relevant to the constitutional consideration, could not, in any analysis, now be deemed controlling.

### III.

Some five years after *Wolf*, in answer to a plea made here Term after Term that we overturn its doctrine on applicability of the *Weeks* exclusionary rule, this Court indicated that such should not be done until the States had "adequate opportunity to adopt or reject the [*Weeks*] rule." Irvine v. People of State of California, supra * * *. Today we once again examine *Wolf's* constitutional documentation of the right to privacy free from unreasonable state intrusion, and, after

its dozen years on our books, are led by it to close the only courtroom
door remaining open to evidence secured by official lawlessness in
flagrant abuse of that basic right, reserved to all persons as a specific
guarantee against that very same unlawful conduct. We hold that all
evidence obtained by searches and seizures in violation of the Constitution is, by that same authority, inadmissible in a state court.

## IV.

Since the Fourth Amendment's right of privacy has been declared
enforceable against the States through the Due Process Clause of the
Fourteenth, it is enforceable against them by the same sanction of
exclusion as is used against the Federal Government. Were it otherwise, then just as without the *Weeks* rule the assurance against unreasonable federal searches and seizures would be "a form of words",
valueless and undeserving of mention in a perpetual charter of inesti-
mable human liberties, so too, without that rule the freedom from state
invasions of privacy would be so ephemeral and so neatly severed from
its conceptual nexus with the freedom from all brutish means of
coercing evidence as not to merit this Court's high regard as a freedom
"implicit in 'the concept of ordered liberty.'" * * * In short, the
admission of the new constitutional right by *Wolf* could not consistently
tolerate denial of its most important constitutional privilege, namely,
the exclusion of the evidence which an accused had been forced to give
by reason of the unlawful seizure. To hold otherwise is to grant the
right but in reality to withhold its privilege and enjoyment. Only last
year the Court itself recognized that the purpose of the exclusionary
rule "is to deter—to compel respect for the constitutional guaranty in
the only effectively available way—by removing the incentive to disregard it." Elkins v. United States [1960, 346 U.S. 206, 217, 80 S.Ct.
1437, 1444, 4 L.Ed.2d 1669].

* * *

## V.

Moreover, our holding that the exclusionary rule is an essential
part of both the Fourth and Fourteenth Amendments is not only the
logical dictate of prior cases, but it also makes very good sense. There
is no war between the Constitution and common sense. Presently, a
federal prosecutor may make no use of evidence illegally seized, but a
State's attorney across the street may, although he supposedly is
operating under the enforceable prohibitions of the same Amendment.
Thus the State, by admitting evidence unlawfully seized, served to
encourage disobedience to the Federal Constitution which it is bound to
uphold. Moreover, as was said in *Elkins*, "[t]he very essence of a
healthy federalism depends upon the avoidance of needless conflict
between state and federal courts." * * *

Federal-state cooperation in the solution of crime under constitutional standards will be promoted, if only by recognition of their now
mutual obligation to respect the same fundamental criteria in their
approaches. "However much in a particular case insistence upon such

rules may appear as a technicality that inures to the benefit of a guilty person, the history of the criminal law proves that tolerance of shortcut methods in law enforcement impairs its enduring effectiveness." Miller v. United States, 1958, 357 U.S. 301, 313, 78 S.Ct. 1190, 1197, 2 L.Ed. 2d 1322. Denying shortcuts to only one of two cooperating law enforcement agencies tends naturally to breed legitimate suspicion of "working arrangements" whose results are equally tainted.     *     *     *

There are those who say, as did Justice (then Judge) Cardozo, that under our constitutional exclusionary doctrine "[t]he criminal is to go free because the constable has blundered." People v. Defore, 242 N.Y. at page 21, 150 N.E. at page 587. In some cases this will undoubtedly be the result. But, as was said in *Elkins*, "there is another consideration—the imperative of judicial integrity."     *     *     *     The criminal goes free, if he must, but it is the law that sets him free. Nothing can destroy a government more quickly than its failure to observe its own laws, or worse, its disregard of the charter of its own existence. As Mr. Justice Brandeis, dissenting, said in Olmstead v. United States, 1928, 277 U.S. 438, 485, 48 S.Ct. 564, 575, 72 L.Ed. 944: "Our government is the potent, the omnipresent teacher. For good or for ill, it teaches the whole people by its example.     *     *     *     If the government becomes a lawbreaker, it breeds contempt for law; it invites every man to become a law unto himself; it invites anarchy." Nor can it lightly be assumed that, as a practical matter, adoption of the exclusionary rule fetters law enforcement. Only last year this Court expressly considered that contention and found that "pragmatic evidence of a sort" to the contrary was not wanting. Elkins v. United States, supra. The Court noted that

> "The federal courts themselves have operated under the exclusionary rule of *Weeks* for almost half a century; yet it has not been suggested either that the Federal Bureau of Investigation has thereby been rendered ineffective, or that the administration of criminal justice in the federal courts has thereby been disrupted. Moreover, the experience of the states is impressive     *     *     *.     The movement towards the rule of exclusion has been halting but seemingly inexorable."     *     *     *

The ignoble shortcut to conviction left open to the State tends to destroy the entire system of constitutional restraints on which the liberties of the people rest. Having once recognized that the right to privacy embodied in the Fourth Amendment is enforceable against the States, and that the right to be secure against rude invasions of privacy by state officers is, therefore, constitutional in origin, we can no longer permit that right to remain an empty promise. Because it is enforceable in the same manner and to like effect as other basic rights secured by the Due Process Clause, we can no longer permit it to be revocable at the whim of any police officer who, in the name of law enforcement itself, chooses to suspend its enjoyment. Our decision, founded on reason and truth, gives to the individual no more than that which the Constitution guarantees him, to the police officer no less than that to which honest law enforcement is entitled, and, to the courts, that judicial integrity so necessary in the true administration of justice.

The judgment of the Supreme Court of Ohio is reversed and the cause remanded for further proceedings not inconsistent with this opinion.

Reversed and remanded.

[The concurring opinions of JUSTICES BLACK and DOUGLAS and the dissenting opinion of JUSTICE HARLAN, joined by JUSTICES FRANKFURTER and WHITTAKER, are omitted.]

## NOTES

1. Following *Mapp*, the Supreme Court virtually without discussion assumed that the federal constitution requires exclusion of evidence obtained in violation of the defendant's Fifth Amendment privilege against compelled self-incrimination, Miranda v. Arizona, 384 U.S. 436, 86 S.Ct. 1602, 16 L.Ed.2d 694 (1966), the Sixth Amendment right to counsel, Brewer v. Williams, 430 U.S. 387, 97 S.Ct. 1232, 51 L.Ed.2d 424 (1977), and the Sixth Amendment right to counsel during certain pretrial identification procedures, Gilbert v. California, 388 U.S. 263, 87 S.Ct. 1951, 18 L.Ed.2d 1178 (1967).

2. In the post-*Mapp* case law, the Supreme Court has somewhat refined its view as to the policy considerations that support the Fourth Amendment exclusionary rule developed in that case. In Stone v. Powell, 428 U.S. 465, 96 S.Ct. 3037, 49 L.Ed.2d 1067 (1976), the Court stated:

> The *Mapp* majority justified the application of the rule to the States on several grounds, but relied principally upon the belief that exclusion would deter future unlawful police conduct.
>
> Although our decisions often have alluded to the "imperative of judicial integrity," they demonstrate the limited role of this justification in the determination whether to apply the rule in a particular context. * * * While courts, of course, must ever be concerned with preserving the integrity of the judicial process, this concern has limited force as a justification for the exclusion of highly probative evidence. * * *
>
> The primary justification for the exclusionary rule then is the deterrence of police conduct that violates Fourth Amendment rights. Post-Mapp decisions have established that the rule is not a personal constitutional right. It is not calculated to redress the injury to the privacy of the victim of the search or seizure, for any "[r]eparation comes too late." Linkletter v. Walker, 381 U.S. 618, 637, 85 S.Ct. 1731, 1741, 14 L.Ed.2d 601 (1965). * * *

428 U.S. at 484–86, 96 S.Ct. at 3047–48, 49 L.Ed.2d at 1082–83. In regard to whatever remains of the need to preserve "judicial integrity," the Court has commented:

> Judicial integrity clearly does not mean that the courts must never admit evidence obtained in violation of the Fourth Amendment. * * *
>
> The primary meaning of "judicial integrity" in the context of evidentiary rules is that the courts must not commit or encourage violations of the Constitution. In the Fourth Amendment area, however, * * * the violation is complete by the time the evidence is presented to the court. The focus therefore must be on the question whether the admission of the evidence encourages violations of Fourth Amendment rights. * * * [T]his inquiry is essentially the same as the inquiry into whether exclusion would serve a deterrent purpose. * * *

United States v. Janis, 428 U.S. 433, 458 n. 35, 96 S.Ct. 3021, 3034 n. 35, 49 L.Ed.2d 1046, 1063 n. 35 (1976).

In Stone v. Powell, the Court also elaborated on the manner in which the exclusionary rule might be expected to prevent future violations of the Fourth Amendment:

> [W]e have assumed that the immediate effect of exclusion will be to discourage law enforcement officials from violating the Fourth Amendment by removing the incentive to disregard it. More importantly, over the long term, this demonstration that our society attaches serious consequences to violation of constitutional rights is thought to encourage those who formulate law enforcement policies, and the officers who implement them, to incorporate Fourth Amendment ideals into their value system.

428 U.S. at 492, 96 S.Ct. at 3051, 49 L.Ed.2d at 1086–87.

3. The Fourth Amendment exclusionary rule adopted in *Mapp* was significantly limited in Stone v. Powell, 428 U.S. 465, 96 S.Ct. 3037, 49 L.Ed.2d 1067 (1976). In both of the cases before the Court, the petitioners had been prosecuted in state courts. They had each moved to suppress certain evidence offered against them, urging that the evidence was obtained in violation of their Fourth Amendment rights. In both cases, the state courts held that the challenged evidence had not been obtained in violation of the Fourth Amendments. Both defendants then petitioned a United States District Court for habeas corpus relief, arguing that their state custody pursuant to their convictions was in violation of the United States Constitution because those convictions rested upon evidence obtained in violation of the Fourth Amendment. In both cases, the lower federal courts concluded that the state courts had erred in finding that the evidence had been properly obtained and held that the state court convictions were consequently invalid.

The Supreme Court reversed. Since in each case the state courts had provided an opportunity for full and fair litigation of the petitioners' Fourth Amendment claims, the petitioners were not entitled to federal habeas corpus relief on the ground that evidence obtained in an unconstitutional search or seizure was introduced at their trials. If the state proceeding provided a fair forum for raising the claims, the petitioners were not entitled to another forum—federal habeas corpus—even if the claims were incorrectly resolved in the state proceeding. In explanation, the Court stated that the matter turned upon a balancing of "the utility of the exclusionary rule against the costs of extending it to collateral review of Fourth Amendment claims." 428 U.S. at 489, 96 S.Ct. at 3050, 49 L.Ed.2d at 1085. Addressing one side of the balance, it noted:

> The costs of applying the exclusionary rule even at trial and on direct review are well known: the focus of the trial, and the attention of the participants therein, are diverted from the ultimate question of guilt or innocence that should be the central concern in a criminal proceeding. Moreover, the physical evidence sought to be excluded is typically reliable and often the most probative information bearing on the guilt or innocence of the defendant. * * * Application of the rule thus deflects the truthfinding process and often frees the guilty. The disparity in particular cases between the error committed by the police officer and the windfall afforded a guilty defendant by application of the rule is contrary to the idea of proportionality that is essential to the concept of justice. Thus, although the rule is thought to deter unlawful police activity in part through the nurturing of respect for Fourth Amendment values, if applied indiscriminately it may well have the opposite effect of generating disrespect for the

law and administration of justice. These long-recognized costs of the rule persist when a criminal conviction is sought to be overturned on collateral review on the ground that a search-and-seizure claim was erroneously rejected by two or more tiers of state courts.

428 U.S. at 489–91, 96 S.Ct. at 3050–51, 49 L.Ed.2d at 1085–86. The Court then reviewed the policy considerations that support the Fourth Amendment exclusionary rule and continued:

> We adhere to the view that these considerations support the implementation of the exclusionary rule at trial and its enforcement on direct appeal of state-court convictions. But the additional contribution, if any, of the consideration of search-and-seizure claims of state prisoners on collateral review is small in relation to the costs. To be sure, each case in which such claim is considered may add marginally to an awareness of the values protected by the Fourth Amendment. There is no reason to believe, however, that the overall educative effect of the exclusionary rule would be appreciably diminished if search-and-seizure claims could not be raised in federal habeas corpus review of state convictions. Nor is there reason to assume that any specific disincentive already created by the risk of exclusion of evidence at trial or the reversal of convictions on direct review would be enhanced if there were the further risk that a conviction obtained in state court and affirmed on direct review might be overturned in collateral proceedings often occurring years after the incarceration of the defendant. The view that deterrence of Fourth Amendment violations would be furthered rests on the dubious assumption that law enforcement authorities would fear that federal habeas corpus review might reveal flaws in a search or seizure that went undetected at trial and on appeal. Even if one rationally could assume that some additional incremental deterrent effect would be presented in isolated cases, the resulting advance of the legitimate goal of further Fourth Amendment rights would be outweighed by the acknowledged costs to other values vital to a rational system of criminal justice.

428 U.S. at 493–94, 96 S.Ct. at 3051–52, 49 L.Ed.2d at 1087–88. Rejecting the argument that state court judges could not be relied upon to fairly and accurately apply defendants' Fourth Amendment rights, the Court responded:

> Despite differences in institutional environment and the unsympathetic attitude to federal constitutional claims of some state judges in years past, we are unwilling to assume that there now exists a general lack of appropriate sensitivity to constitutional rights in the trial and appellate courts of the several States. State courts, like federal courts, have a constitutional obligation to safeguard personal liberties and to uphold federal law.

428 U.S. at 493 n. 35, 96 S.Ct. at 3052 n. 35, 49 L.Ed.2d at 1087 n. 35. Of course, a defendant in state court whose conviction is affirmed on appeal may seek direct review of the decision of the highest available state tribunal by the United States Supreme Court. This is generally accomplished by application to the Supreme Court for the writ of certiorari. See Mincey v. Arizona, 437 U.S. 385, 98 S.Ct. 2408, 57 L.Ed.2d 290 (1978).

May a defendant convicted in state court seek federal habeas corpus relief on the ground that evidence was used despite a showing that it was obtained in violation of his federal constitutional rights other than his Fourth Amendment right to be free from unreasonable searches and seizures? Or is it necessary in these cases as well that the defendant show that the state proceeding failed to provide him with an opportunity for full and fair litigation of his claim? The

Court, over the vigorous objection of the Chief Justice, has failed to address whether a claim that evidence was obtained in violation of a state defendant's Sixth Amendment right to counsel is, when raised in federal habeas corpus, subject to Stone v. Powell's requirements. See Brewer v. Williams, 430 U.S. 387, 427, 97 S.Ct. 1232, 1254, 51 L.Ed.2d 424, 454–55 (1977) (Burger, C.J., dissenting).

4. As was indicated in the Editors' Introduction to Part One of these materials, most states have state constitutional provisions similar or identical to the Fourth, Fifth, and Sixth Amendments to the United States Constitution. Those state provisions may be construed by state courts as giving criminal suspects or defendants greater rights than are afforded by the federal provisions; see generally Chapter 2, infra. If evidence is obtained in violation of a state constitutional provision, is exclusion required?

First, is exclusion required under *Mapp* or otherwise as a matter of federal constitutional law? In California v. Greenwood, 486 U.S. 35, 108 S.Ct. 1625, 100 L.Ed.2d 30 (1988), officers had examined Greenwood's trash without a warrant. The California courts had held previously that such police activity was impermissible as a matter of state constitutional law. But in 1982, California voters had passed an amendment to that state's constitution which provided that evidence was not to be excluded because it had been obtained in a manner that violated the State's constitution. The Supreme Court rejected Greenwood's argument that the Due Process Clause of the Fourteenth Amendment barred the state from depriving him of an exclusionary remedy for police misconduct violating state but not federal constitutional law:

> California could amend its constitution to negate the holding ∗  ∗  ∗ that state law forbids warrantless searches of trash. We are convinced that the State may likewise eliminate the exclusionary rule as a remedy for violations of that right. At the federal level, we have not required that evidence obtained in violation of the Fourth Amendment be suppressed in all circumstances. Rather, our decisions concerning the scope of the Fourth Amendment exclusionary rule have balanced the benefits of deterring police misconduct against the costs of excluding reliable evidence of criminal activity. ∗  ∗  ∗
>
> The States are not foreclosed by the Due Process Clause from using a similar balancing approach to delineate the scope of their own exclusionary rules. Hence, the people of California could permissibly conclude that the benefits of excluding relevant evidence of criminal activity do not outweigh the costs when the police conduct at issue does not violate federal law.

486 U.S. at 44–45, 108 S.Ct. at 1631, 100 L.Ed.2d at 39–40.

Second, is exclusion required as a matter of state law? This usually depends upon whether state courts are willing to construe state provision as the Supreme Court construed the Fourth Amendment in *Mapp*. Generally, state tribunals have done so. See, e.g., State v. Dukes, 209 Conn. 98, 547 A.2d 10 (1988); State v. Novembrino, 105 N.J. 95, 519 A.2d 820 (1987). Of course, the fact that a state constitutional search and seizure provision is read as having a *Mapp*-like exclusionary remedy does not necessarily mean that the state courts must or will define the detailed requirements of that exclusionary requirement as identical to those of the Fourth Amendment's exclusionary rule.

5. When evidence had been obtained in violation of a nonconstitutional legal requirement—such as a federal or state statute—whether exclusion is possible or required presents a more difficult question. Clearly, there is no federal or state constitutional right to have evidence excluded because of a statutory violation. A few states have statutory provisions or court rules

requiring exclusion in many such situations. E.g., Vernon's Ann.Tex.Code Crim.Pro. art. 38.23 (evidence obtained in violation of "any provisions of the Constitution or laws of the State of Texas" must be excluded); Alaska Evid.R. 412 (evidence "illegally obtained" is not to be used in a criminal prosecution). Sometimes statutory requirements explicitly direct exclusion.

Courts differ in their willingness to find unexpressed legislative "intentions" that violations of statutes are to result in exclusion of evidence. The Supreme Court has held without explanation that violation of a federal statute requiring prior announcement before entering premises to execute a warrant required exclusion. Miller v. United States, 357 U.S. 301, 78 S.Ct. 1190, 2 L.Ed. 2d 1332 (1958). In addition, the Supreme Court has held that it has a "supervisory power" giving it authority to sometimes require exclusion of evidence obtained in violation of nonconstitutional legal requirements. McNabb v. United States, 318 U.S. 332, 63 S.Ct. 608, 87 L.Ed. 819 (1943). State courts may have a similar power. See People v. Dyla, 142 A.D.2d 423, 536 N.Y.S.2d 799 (1988). The Supreme Court has in recent cases been unwilling to exercise its supervisory power to create or develop "new" exclusionary requirements. See United States v. Payner, 447 U.S. 727, 100 S.Ct. 2439, 65 L.Ed.2d 468 (1980); United States v. Caceres, 440 U.S. 741, 99 S.Ct. 1465, 59 L.Ed.2d 733 (1979).

See generally, Dix, Nonconstitutional Exclusionary Rules in Criminal Procedure, 27 Am.Crim.L.Rev. 53 (1989).

## B. "STANDING," FRUIT OF THE "POISONOUS TREE," AND ATTENUATION OF THE TAINT

A determination that law enforcement officers engaged in improper activity during the preparation of the prosecution's case against the defendant, of course, does not end the exclusionary rule inquiry. In fact, the post-*Mapp* years have seen an increase in the complexity of deciding the two subissues that must be addressed: (1) what evidence is rendered inadmissible by demonstrated law enforcement misconduct; and (2) what persons are entitled to invoke the exclusionary remedy?

The principal case in this section demonstrates the interrelationship between these issues. The propriety of the arrests of the defendants was in dispute. Four members of the Court, in a dissent authored by Justice Clark, took the position that neither arrest was constitutionally impermissible. For present purposes, however, assume that the arrests were invalid; the validity of arrests such as those at issue in the principal case will be addressed in detail in Chapter 4. Consider now what effects the arrests—assuming they are invalid—have upon the admissibility of what evidence offered by the prosecution against each of the defendants.

### WONG SUN v. UNITED STATES
Supreme Court of the United States, 1963.
371 U.S. 471, 83 S.Ct. 407, 9 L.Ed.2d 441.

MR. JUSTICE BRENNAN delivered the opinion of the Court.

The petitioners were tried without a jury in the District Court for the Northern District of California under a two-count indictment for violation of the Federal Narcotics Laws, 21 U.S.C. § 174, 21 U.S.C.A. §

174. They were acquitted under the first count which charged a conspiracy, but convicted under the second count which charged the substantive offense of fraudulent and knowing transportation and concealment of illegally imported heroin. The Court of Appeals for the Ninth Circuit, one judge dissenting, affirmed the convictions. 288 F.2d 366. We granted certiorari. 368 U.S. 817, 82 S.Ct. 75, 7 L.Ed.2d 23. We heard argument in the 1961 Term and reargument this Term. 370 U.S. 908, 82 S.Ct. 1254, 8 L.Ed.2d 403.

About 2 a. m. on the morning of June 4, 1959, federal narcotics agents in San Francisco, after having had one Hom Way under surveillance for six weeks, arrested him and found heroin in his possession. Hom Way, who had not before been an informant, stated after his arrest that he had bought an ounce of heroin the night before from one known to him only as "Blackie Toy," proprietor of a laundry on Leavenworth Street.

About 6 a. m. that morning six or seven federal agents went to a laundry at 1733 Leavenworth Street. The sign above the door of this establishment said "Oye's Laundry." It was operated by the petitioner James Wah Toy. There is, however, nothing in the record which identifies James Wah Toy and "Blackie Toy" as the same person. The other federal officers remained nearby out of sight while Agent Alton Wong, who was of Chinese ancestry, rang the bell. When petitioner Toy appeared and opened the door, Agent Wong told him that he was calling for laundry and dry cleaning. Toy replied that he didn't open until 8 o'clock and told the agent to come back at that time. Toy started to close the door. Agent Wong thereupon took his badge from his pocket and said, "I am a federal narcotics agent." Toy immediately "slammed the door and started running" down the hallway through the laundry to his living quarters at the back where his wife and child were sleeping in a bedroom. Agent Wong and the other federal officers broke open the door and followed Toy down the hallway to the living quarters and into the bedroom. Toy reached into a nightstand drawer. Agent Wong thereupon drew his pistol, pulled Toy's hand out of the drawer, placed him under arrest and handcuffed him. There was nothing in the drawer and a search of the premises uncovered no narcotics.

One of the agents said to Toy "* * * [Hom Way] says he got narcotics from you." Toy responded, "No, I haven't been selling any narcotics at all. However, I do know somebody who has." When asked who that was, Toy said, "I only know him as Johnny. I don't know his last name." However, Toy described a house on Eleventh Avenue where he said Johnny lived; he also described a bedroom in the house where he said "Johnny kept about a piece" [1] of heroin, and where he and Johnny had smoked some of the drug the night before. The agents left immediately for Eleventh Avenue and located the house. They entered and found one Johnny Yee in the bedroom. After a discussion with the agents, Yee took from a bureau drawer several tubes containing in all just less than one ounce of heroin, and surrendered them.

---

[1] A "piece" is approximately one ounce.

Within the hour Yee and Toy were taken to the Office of the Bureau of Narcotics. Yee there stated that the heroin had been brought to him some four days earlier by petitioner Toy and another Chinese known to him only as "Sea Dog."

Toy was questioned as to the identity of "Sea Dog" and said that "Sea Dog" was Wong Sun. Some agents, including Agent Alton Wong, took Toy to Wong Sun's neighborhood where Toy pointed out a multi-family dwelling where he said Wong Sun lived. Agent Wong rang a downstairs door bell and a buzzer sounded, opening the door. The officer identified himself as a narcotics agent to a woman on the landing and asked "for Mr. Wong." The woman was the wife of petitioner Wong Sun. She said that Wong Sun was "in the back room sleeping." Alton Wong and some six other officers climbed the stairs and entered the apartment. One of the officers went into the back room and brought petitioner Wong Sun from the bedroom in handcuffs. A thorough search of the apartment followed, but no narcotics were discovered.

Petitioner Toy and Johnny Yee were arraigned before a United States Commissioner on June 4 on a complaint charging a violation of 21 U.S.C. § 174, 21 U.S.C.A. § 174. Later that day, each was released on his own recognizance. Petitioner Wong Sun was arraigned on a similar complaint filed the next day and was also released on his own recognizance. Within a few days, both petitioners and Yee were interrogated at the office of the Narcotics Bureau by Agent William Wong, also of Chinese ancestry. The agent advised each of the three of his right to withhold information which might be used against him, and stated to each that he was entitled to the advice of counsel, though it does not appear that any attorney was present during the questioning of any of the three. The officer also explained to each that no promises or offers of immunity or leniency were being or could be made.

The agent interrogated each of the three separately. After each had been interrogated the agent prepared a statement in English from rough notes. The agent read petitioner Toy's statement to him in English and interpreted certain portions of it for him in Chinese. Toy also read the statement in English aloud to the agent, said there were corrections to be made, and made the corrections in his own hand. Toy would not sign the statement, however; in the agent's words "he wanted to know first if the other persons involved in the case had signed theirs." Wong Sun had considerable difficulty understanding the statement in English and the agent restated its substance in Chinese. Wong Sun refused to sign the statement although he admitted the accuracy of its contents.

Hom Way did not testify at petitioners' trial. The Government offered Johnny Yee as its principal witness but excused him after he invoked the privilege against self-incrimination and flatly repudiated the statement he had given to Agent William Wong. That statement was not offered in evidence nor was any testimony elicited from him identifying either petitioner as the source of the heroin in his possession, or otherwise tending to support the charges against the petitioners.

The statute expressly provides that proof of the accused's possession of the drug will support a conviction under the statute unless the accused satisfactorily explains the possession. The Government's evidence tending to prove the petitioners' possession (the petitioners offered no exculpatory testimony) consisted of four items which the trial court admitted over timely objections that they were inadmissible as "fruits" of unlawful arrests or of attendant searches: (1) the statements made orally by petitioner Toy in his bedroom at the time of his arrest; (2) the heroin surrendered to the agents by Johnny Yee; (3) petitioner Toy's pretrial unsigned statement; and (4) petitioner Wong Sun's similar statement. The dispute below and here has centered around the correctness of the rulings of the trial judge allowing these items in evidence.

The Court of Appeals held that the arrests of both petitioners were illegal because not based on " 'probable cause' within the meaning of the Fourth Amendment" nor "reasonable grounds" within the meaning of the Narcotic Control Act of 1956. The court said as to Toy's arrest, "There is no showing in this case that the agent knew Hom Way to be reliable," and, furthermore, found "nothing in the circumstances occurring at Toy's premises that would provide sufficient justification for his arrest without a warrant." 288 F.2d at 369, 370. As to Wong Sun's arrest, the court said "there is no showing that Johnnie Yee was a reliable informer." The Court of Appeals nevertheless held that the four items of proof were not the "fruits" of the illegal arrests and that they were therefore properly admitted in evidence.

The Court of Appeals rejected [an] additional [contention] of the petitioners. [This] was that there was insufficient evidence to corroborate the petitioners' unsigned admissions of possession of narcotics. The court held that the narcotics in evidence surrendered by Johnny Yee, together with Toy's statements in his bedroom at the time of arrest corroborated petitioners' admissions. * * *

We believe that significant differences between the cases of the two petitioners require separate discussion of each. We shall first consider the case of petitioner Toy.

## I.

The Court of Appeals found there was neither reasonable grounds nor probable cause for Toy's arrest. Giving due weight to that finding, we think it is amply justified by the facts clearly shown on this record. * * *

## II.

It is conceded that Toy's declarations in his bedroom are to be excluded if they are held to be "fruits" of the agents' unlawful action.

In order to make effective the fundamental constitutional guarantees of sanctity of the home and inviolability of the person, Boyd v. United States, 116 U.S. 616, 6 S.Ct. 524, 29 L.Ed. 746, this Court held nearly half a century ago that evidence seized during an unlawful search could not constitute proof against the victim of the search. Weeks v. United States, 232 U.S. 383, 34 S.Ct. 341, 58 L.Ed. 652. The exclusionary prohibition extends as well to the indirect as the direct products of such invasions. Silverthorne Lumber Co. v. United States, 251 U.S. 385, 40 S.Ct. 182, 64 L.Ed. 319. Mr. Justice Holmes, speaking for the Court in that case, in holding that the Government might not make use of information obtained during an unlawful search to subpoena from the victims the very documents illegally viewed, expressed succinctly the policy of the broad exclusionary rule:

> "The essence of a provision forbidding the acquisition of evidence in a certain way is that not merely evidence so acquired shall not be held before the Court but that it shall not be used at all. Of course this does not mean that the facts thus obtained become sacred and inaccessible. If knowledge of them is gained from an independent source they may be proved like any others, but the knowledge gained by the Government's own wrong cannot be used by it in the way proposed." 251 U.S. at 392, 40 S.Ct. at 183.

The exclusionary rule has traditionally barred from trial physical, tangible materials obtained either during or as a direct result of an unlawful invasion. It follows from our holding in Silverman v. United States, 365 U.S. 505, 81 S.Ct. 679, 5 L.Ed.2d 734, that the Fourth Amendment may protect against the overhearing of verbal statements as well as against the more traditional seizure of "papers and effects." Similarly, testimony as to matters observed during an unlawful invasion has been excluded in order to enforce the basic constitutional policies. McGinnis v. United States, 1 Cir., 227 F.2d 598. Thus, verbal evidence which derives so immediately from an unlawful entry and an unauthorized arrest as the officers' action in the present case is no less the "fruit" of official illegality than the more common tangible fruits of the unwarranted intrusion. Nor do the policies underlying the exclusionary rule invite any logical distinction between physical and verbal evidence. * * * [T]he danger in relaxing the exclusionary rules in the case of verbal evidence would seem too great to warrant introducing such a distinction.

The Government argues that Toy's statements to the officers in his bedroom, although closely consequent upon the invasion which we hold unlawful, were nevertheless admissible because they resulted from "an intervening independent act of a free will." This contention, however, takes insufficient account of the circumstances. Six or seven officers had broken the door and followed on Toy's heels into the bedroom where his wife and child were sleeping. He had been almost immediately handcuffed and arrested. Under such circumstances it is unreasonable to infer that Toy's response was sufficiently an act of free will to purge the primary taint of the unlawful invasion.

* * *

### III.

We now consider whether the exclusion of Toy's declarations requires also the exclusion of the narcotics taken from Yee, to which those declarations led the police. The prosecutor candidly told the trial court that "we wouldn't have found those drugs except that Mr. Toy helped us to." Hence this is not the case envisioned by this Court where the exclusionary rule has no application because the Government learned of the evidence "from an independent source," Silverthorne Lumber Co. v. United States, 251 U.S. 385, 392, 40 S.Ct. 182, 183, 64 L.Ed. 319; nor is this a case in which the connection between the lawless conduct of the police and the discovery of the challenged evidence has "become so attenuated as to dissipate the taint." Nardone v. United States, 308 U.S. 338, 341, 60 S.Ct. 266, 268, 84 L.Ed. 307. We need not hold that all evidence is "fruit of the poisonous tree" simply because it would not have come to light but for the illegal actions of the police. Rather, the more apt question in such a case is "whether, granting establishment of the primary illegality, the evidence to which instant objection is made has been come at by exploitation of that illegality or instead by means sufficiently distinguishable to be purged of the primary taint." Maguire, Evidence of Guilt, 221 (1959). We think it clear that the narcotics were "come at by the exploitation of that illegality" and hence that they may not be used against Toy.

IV.

It remains only to consider Toy's unsigned statement. We need not decide whether, in light of the fact that Toy was free on his own recognizance when he made the statement, that statement was a fruit of the illegal arrest. Cf. United States v. Bayer, 331 U.S. 532, 67 S.Ct. 1394, 91 L.Ed. 1654. Since we have concluded that his declarations in the bedroom and the narcotics surrendered by Yee should not have been admitted in evidence against him, the only proofs remaining to sustain his conviction are his and Wong Sun's unsigned statements. Without scrutinizing the contents of Toy's ambiguous recitals, we conclude that no reference to Toy in Wong Sun's statement constitutes admissible evidence corroborating any admission by Toy. We arrive at this conclusion upon two clear lines of decisions which converge to require it. One line of our decisions establishes that criminal confessions and admissions of guilt require extrinsic corroboration; the other line of precedents holds that an out-of-court declaration made after arrest may not be used at trial against one of the declarant's partners in crime.

It is a settled principle of the administration of criminal justice in the federal courts that a conviction must rest upon firmer ground than the uncorroborated admission or confession of the accused. We observed in Smith v. United States, 348 U.S. 147, 153, 75 S.Ct. 194, 197, 99 L.Ed. 192, that the requirement of corroboration is rooted in "a long history of judicial experience with confessions and in the realization that sound law enforcement requires police investigations which extend beyond the words of the accused." * * * Wong Sun's unsigned confession does not furnish competent corroborative evidence. The second governing principle, likewise well settled in our decisions, is that an out-of-court declaration made after arrest may not be used at trial against one of the declarant's partners in crime. While such a statement is "admissible against the others where it is in furtherance of the criminal undertaking * * * all such responsibility is at an end when the conspiracy ends." Fiswick v. United States, 329 U.S. 211, 217, 67 S.Ct. 224, 227, 91 L.Ed. 196. * * *

## V.

We turn now to the case of the other petitioner, Wong Sun. We have no occasion to disagree with the finding of the Court of Appeals that his arrest, also, was without probable cause or reasonable grounds. At all events no evidentiary consequences turn upon that question. For Wong Sun's unsigned confession was not the fruit of that arrest, and was therefore properly admitted at trial. On the evidence that Wong Sun had been released on his own recognizance after a lawful arraignment, and had returned voluntarily several days later to make the statement, we hold that the connection between the arrest and the statement had "become so attenuated as to dissipate the taint." Nardone v. United States, 308 U.S. 338, 341, 60 S.Ct. 266, 84 L.Ed. 307. * * *

We must then consider the admissibility of the narcotics surrendered by Yee. Our holding, supra, that this ounce of heroin was inadmissible against Toy does not compel a like result with respect to Wong Sun. The exclusion of the narcotics as to Toy was required solely by their tainted relationship to information unlawfully obtained from Toy, and not by any official impropriety connected with their surrender by Yee. The seizure of this heroin invaded no right of privacy of person or premises which would entitle Wong Sun to object to its use at his trial. Cf. Goldstein v. United States, 316 U.S. 114, 62 S.Ct. 1000, 86 L.Ed. 1312.

However, for the reasons that Wong Sun's statement was incompetent to corroborate Toy's admissions contained in Toy's own statement, any references to Wong Sun in Toy's statement were incompetent to corroborate Wong Sun's admissions. Thus, the only competent source of corrobation for Wong Sun's statement was the heroin itself. We cannot be certain, however, on this state of the record, that the trial judge may not also have considered the contents of Toy's statement as a source of corroboration. Petitioners raised as one ground of objection to the introduction of the statements the claim that each statement, "even if it were a purported admission or confession or declaration against interest of a defendant * * * would not be binding upon the other defendant." The trial judge, in allowing the statements in, apparently overruled all of petitioners' objections, including this one. Thus we presume that he considered all portions of both statements as bearing upon the guilt of both petitioners.

We intimate no view one way or the other as to whether the trial judge might have found in the narcotics alone sufficient evidence to corroborate Wong Sun's admissions that he delivered heroin to Yee and smoked heroin at Yee's house around the date in question. But because he might, as the factfinder, have found insufficient corroboration from the narcotics alone, we cannot be sure that the scales were not tipped in favor of conviction by reliance upon the inadmissible Toy statement. This is particularly important because of the nature of the offense involved here.

Surely, under the narcotics statute, the discovery of heroin raises a presumption that someone—generally the possessor—violated the law. As to him, once possession alone is proved, the other elements of the offense—transportation and concealment with knowledge of the illegal importation of the drug—need not be separately demonstrated, much less corroborated. 21 U.S.C. § 174, 21 U.S.C.A. § 174. Thus particular care ought to be taken in this area, when the crucial element of the accused's possession is proved solely by his own admissions, that the requisite corroboration be found among the evidence which is properly before the trier of facts. We therefore hold that petitioner Wong Sun is also entitled to a new trial.

The judgment of the Court of Appeals is reversed and the case is remanded to the District Court for further proceedings consistent with this opinion.

It is so ordered.

Judgment of Court of Appeals reversed and case remanded to the District Court.

[The concurring opinion of JUSTICE DOUGLAS and the dissenting opinion of JUSTICE CLARK, joined by JUSTICES HARLAN, STEWART and WHITE, are omitted.]

### NOTES

1. The requirement that a confession be corroborated is discussed in Chapter 7 at page 415, infra.

2. The doctrine which precluded Wong Sun from successfully objecting to the introduction of the heroin on the same grounds as were successful for Toy has traditionally been described as a requirement of "standing." Application of the requirement in search situations is explored further in Part B(3) of Chapter 2.

In Rakas v. Illinois, 439 U.S. 128, 99 S.Ct. 421, 58 L.Ed.2d 387 (1978) (reprinted in part at page 116, infra), however, the Supreme Court appeared to "dispens[e] with the rubric of standing." 439 U.S. at 140, 99 S.Ct. at 429, 58 L.Ed.2d at 399. Instead, it explained, the cases that contain standing discussions in fact simply apply the principle that Fourth Amendment rights are personal in nature:

> Analyzed in these terms, the question is whether the challenged search or seizure violated the Fourth Amendment rights of a criminal defendant who seeks to exclude the evidence obtained during it. That inquiry in turn requires a determination of whether the disputed search and seizure has infringed an interest of the defendant which the Fourth Amendment was designed to protect. ∗ ∗ ∗ [T]his aspect of the analysis belongs more properly under the heading of substantive Fourth Amendment doctrine rather than under the heading of standing ∗ ∗ ∗.

439 U.S. at 140, 99 S.Ct. at 429, 58 L.Ed.2d at 399. The majority emphasized that the abandonment of standing "rubric" would not change either the basic inquiry or the outcome of cases. But the shift, it explained, should focus

concern on "the extent of a particular defendant's rights under the Fourth Amendment, rather than on any theoretically separate, but invariably intertwined concept of standing," 439 U.S. at 139, 99 S.Ct. at 428, 58 L.Ed.2d at 398, and result in particular decisions resting on "sounder logical footing," 439 U.S. 140, 99 S.Ct. at 429, 58 L.Ed.2d at 399.

The requirement of "standing" was defended on its merits in Alderman v. United States, 394 U.S. 165, 89 S.Ct. 961, 22 L.Ed.2d 176 (1969):

> * * * Fourth Amendment rights are personal rights which, like some other constitutional rights, may not be vicariously asserted. * * * There is no necessity to exclude evidence against one defendant in order to protect the rights of another. No rights of the victim of an illegal search are at stake when the evidence is offered against some other party. The victim can and very probably will object for himself when and if it becomes important for him to do so. * * * [None of our cases] hold that anything which deters illegal searches is thereby commanded by the Fourth Amendment. The deterrent values of preventing the incrimination of those whose rights the police have violated have been considered sufficient to justify the suppression of probative evidence even though the case against the defendant is weakened or destroyed. We adhere to that judgment. But we are not convinced that the additional benefits of extending the exclusionary rule to other defendants would justify further encroachment upon the public interest in prosecuting those accused of crime and having them acquitted or convicted on the basis of all the evidence which exposes the truth.

394 U.S. at 174–75, 89 S.Ct. at 966–67, 22 L.Ed.2d at 187.

In *Rakas*, the Court rejected a proposal that it permit any criminal defendant at whom a search was "directed" to challenge the admissibility of evidence obtained as a result of that search. It explained that it was unwilling to increase the amount of reliable evidence that would be rendered unavailable by the exclusionary rule. 439 U.S. at 137–38, 99 S.Ct. at 427, 58 L.Ed.2d at 397. It also quoted with approval Justice Harlan's argument in *Alderman* that such a "target" rule would involve excessive administrative costs in the form of lengthy hearings to determine whether particular defendants were or were not the "targets" of particular police action. 439 U.S. at 136–37, 99 S.Ct. at 427, 58 L.Ed.2d at 396–97, quoting Alderman v. United States, 394 U.S. 165, 188–89, 89 S.Ct. 961, 974, 22 L.Ed.2d 176, 195 (1969) (Harlan, J., concurring and dissenting).

3. In holding that Toy's bedroom statements were inadmissible, *Wong Sun* applied what is often called the "fruit of the poisonous tree" rule. Once a defendant establishes a violation of his constitutional rights, he is entitled to suppression of all "fruit of [that] poisonous tree." Nardone v. United States, 308 U.S. 338, 341, 60 S.Ct. 266, 268, 84 L.Ed. 307, 312 (1939). This is sometimes stated as the "derivative evidence" rule—all evidence derived from a violation of the defendant's rights must be suppressed. The "core rationale" for this rule, the Court has explained, is "that this admittedly drastic and socially costly course is needed to deter police from violations" of the protections involved. Nix v. Williams, 467 U.S. 431, 442–43, 104 S.Ct. 2501, 2508, 81 L.Ed. 2d 377, 386–87 (1984).

The "fruits" rule is not applied in some situations where the police illegality consists of a violation of *Miranda* requirements. This is developed in subsection B(4) of Chapter 7, infra.

A defendant seeking to invoke the "fruits" doctrine must establish that the challenged evidence was obtained by police as a factual result of a violation of his rights. Murray v. United States, 487 U.S. 533, 108 S.Ct. 2529, 101 L.Ed.2d 472 (1988). If evidence is obtained by police after they violated a defendant's rights but not as a consequence of that violation, the evidence is said to have an "independent source" and is admissible despite the intrusion upon the defendant's rights. Murray v. United States, 487 U.S. at 537, 108 S.Ct. at 2533, 101 L.Ed.2d at 480. Obviously, evidence obtained by law enforcement officers *before* they violated a defendant's rights is not the "fruit" of the violation and hence not subject to challenge. See Waller v. Georgia, 467 U.S. 39, 104 S.Ct. 2210, 81 L.Ed.2d 31 (1984).

*Murray* illustrates the difficulty sometimes involved in showing the factual causation required. Federal officers conducting a drug investigation observed several suspicious vehicles enter and leave a warehouse in South Boston. About 2:30 p.m. and without a search warrant, the officers went to the warehouse, forced open the door, and entered. While inside, they observed burlap-wrapped bales. They then, without seizing or disturbing those bales, left the warehouse. Later, the officers applied for a search warrant for the warehouse. The application relied upon other information possessed by the officers at the time of their first entry and did not mention that they had already entered the structure. The warrant issued about 10:45 p.m. Pursuant to that warrant, the officers entered the warehouse and seized 270 bales of marijuana—including the bales observed during the earlier entry—as well as other incriminating items. Murray and Carter were charged with conspiracy to possess and distribute the marijuana. Before trial, they moved to suppress the evidence obtained from the warehouse on the ground that it was the "fruit" of the officers' first and unreasonable warrantless entry of the warehouse. The Court of Appeals held that this motion should have been granted. By a 4–3 vote, with two justices not participating, the Supreme Court vacated and remanded. Knowledge that the marijuana was in the warehouse, Justice Scalia wrote for the majority, was obtained in the first and presumably-unreasonable search of the warehouse. But such knowledge as well as the actual marijuana itself were also acquired in the second and reasonable search pursuant to the warrant. If the search pursuant to the warrant was "genuinely independent" of the first search, the evidence would be admissible. This "independent source" rule, he explained, is based upon the need to limit the exclusion of evidence to those situations in which rejecting it is necessary to deter improper police activity. Deterrence is adequately accomplished by placing the police in the position they would have occupied had the illegal search not occurred. It does not require placing them in a *worse* position than that. To exclude evidence that has an independent source would be to unjustifiably place the police in such a worse position; they would be deprived of evidence that they in fact obtained independently of their improper conduct. 487 U.S. at 537, 108 S.Ct. at 2533, 101 L.Ed.2d at 480. But this doctrine requires that the manner in which the evidence was obtained be "genuinely independent" of the illegal search. "This would not have been the case," Justice Scalia explained, "if the agents' decision to seek the warrant was prompted by what they had seen during the initial entry, or if information obtained during that entry was presented to the Magistrate and affected his decision to issue the warrant." 487 U.S. at 541–42, 108 S.Ct. at 2535–36, 101 L.Ed.2d at 483–84. The lower courts had determined that the officers had not revealed to the magistrate who issued the search warrant any information from the illegal entry. But no finding had been made as to whether or not the officers would have sought a warrant for the warehouse if they had not earlier entered it. The matter was therefore remanded to the District Court for a determination as to whether the search pursuant to the warrant was an independent source of the challenged evidence in the sense that the opinion defined independent source.

4. In New York v. Harris, ___ U.S. ___, 110 S.Ct. 1640, 109 L.Ed.2d 13 (1990), officers had probable cause to believe Harris had committed a homicide but obtained no warrant. They nevertheless entered Harris' home and placed him under arrest. This warrantless entry violated the Fourth Amendment; see text at pages 187–90. Harris was warned of his rights and admitted the killing. He was taken to the stationhouse, warned again, and signed a written incriminating statement. Later, ignoring Harris' expressed desire to remain silent, police videotaped an interview with him. The trial court suppressed the oral statement made at his home and the videotaped statement, but admitted the written statement despite the earlier violation of his Fourth Amendment rights. The Supreme Court held this was proper, applying what the dissenters characterized as a "newly-fashioned *per se* rule." No need existed to inquire whether the taint of the improper entry became attenuated, Justice White reasoned for the majority, because that analysis is necessary only if the challenged evidence is the product or fruit of the Fourth Amendment violation. The illegality of the officers' entry and arrest of Harris in his home, he explained, did not render unlawful Harris' continued custody once he was removed from the house:

> Harris's statement taken at the police station was not the product of being in unlawful custody. Neither was it the fruit of having been arrested in the home rather than someplace else.   *   *   *   [T]he police had a justification to question Harris prior to his arrest; therefore, his subsequent statement was not an exploitation of the illegal entry into Harris' home.

___ U.S. at ___, 110 S.Ct. at 1644, 109 L.Ed.2d at 21. Therefore:

> [W]here the police have probable cause to arrest a suspect, the exclusionary rule does not bar the State's use of a statement made by the defendant outside of his home, even though the statement is taken after an arrest made in the home in violation of [the Fourth Amendment].

___ U.S. at ___, 110 S.Ct. at 1644–45, 109 L.Ed.2d at 22.

Its decision, the Court explained further, was implementing the principle that penalties, including exclusion of evidence, must bear some relation to the purposes the law is to serve. The underlying rule requiring a warrant for arrests in the home was designed to protect the physical integrity of the home. "[I]t was not intended to grant criminal suspects, like Harris, protection for statements made outside their premises where the police have probable cause to arrest the suspects for committing a crime." ___ U.S. at ___, 110 S.Ct. at 1643, 109 L.Ed.2d at 20. Once incriminating evidence gathered from arresting the suspect in his home rather than elsewhere has been suppressed, the purpose of the rule has been vindicated. Moreover, the threat of suppression of such evidence retains the principal incentive for officers to comply with the warrant requirement. Suppression of statements obtained after the suspect had been removed would provide only "minimal" incremental deterrence. ___ U.S. at ___, 110 S.Ct. at 1644, 109 L.Ed.2d at 22.

Justice Marshall, joined by Justices Brennan, Blackmun and Stevens, dissented, expressing concern regarding the consequences of the majority's holding. "[An] officer knows that if he breaks into the house without a warrant and drags the suspect outside, the suspect, shaken by the enormous invasion of privacy he has just undergone, may say something incriminating." Previously, such admissions could be used only if the taint of the improper entry and arrest was attenuated; now they are automatically available for use.

___ U.S. at ___, 110 S.Ct. at 1650–51, 109 L.Ed.2d at 29–30 (Marshall, J., dissenting).

Did *Harris* do anything beyond enforce the requirement that challenged evidence be shown to have been obtained as a factual result of the demonstrated police illegality?

5. One qualification to the general rule that "fruit of the poisonous tree" must be excluded is that the defendant's physical presence for trial and punishment is never the excludable "fruit" of improper law enforcement conduct. Illegal police activity, the Supreme Court has made clear, will affect only the admissibility of evidence; it will not affect the jurisdiction of the trial court or otherwise serve as a basis for dismissing the prosecution. Ker v. Illinois, 119 U.S. 436, 7 S.Ct. 225, 30 L.Ed.2d 421 (1886). In United States v. Blue, 384 U.S. 251, 86 S.Ct. 1416, 16 L.Ed.2d 510 (1966), the Court explained its adherence to this approach despite *Mapp* and the "constitutionalization" of the exclusionary rule:

> So drastic a step [as barring the prosecution altogether] might advance marginally some of the ends served by the exclusionary rules, but it would also increase to an intolerable degree interference with the public interest in having the guilty brought to book.

384 U.S. at 225, 86 S.Ct. at 1419, 16 L.Ed.2d at 515.

6. As the principal case makes clear, the "fruit of the poisonous tree" doctrine is subject to the qualification that "fruit" of a violation of the defendant's rights becomes admissible if the prosecution establishes that the "taint" of the constitutional violation was "attenuated" when the challenged evidence was obtained. Determining whether attenuation has occurred is sometimes a difficult task. The issue has arisen in a number of post–*Wong Sun* Supreme Court cases, many involving defendants' claims that their confessions were the excludable fruit of an earlier improper arrest or detention. Perhaps the leading case is Brown v. Illinois, 422 U.S. 590, 95 S.Ct. 2254, 45 L.Ed.2d 416 (1975), in which the Court held that compliance with Miranda v. Arizona, 384 U.S. 436, 86 S.Ct. 1602, 16 L.Ed.2d 694 (1966) (reprinted at page 427, infra), would not alone attenuate the taint. Moreover, a finding that the statement was "voluntary" (see page 408, infra), while a "threshold requirement" for a finding of attenuation of taint, does not resolve the matter. Taylor v. Alabama, 457 U.S. 687, 690, 102 S.Ct. 2664, 2668, 73 L.Ed.2d 314, 319 (1982). Instead, events intervening between the unlawful detention and the making of the statement must be examined to determine whether the statement was a sufficient act of free will to purge the taint. In *Brown*, the Court explained:

> No single fact is dispositive. * * * The *Miranda* warnings are an important factor, to be sure, in determining whether the confession is obtained by exploitation of an illegal arrest. But they are not the only factor to be considered. The temporal proximity of the arrest and the confession, the presence of intervening circumstances, and, particularly, the purpose and flagrancy of the official misconduct are all relevant.

422 U.S. at 603–04, 95 S.Ct. at 2261–62, 45 L.Ed.2d at 427.

Application of this approach was illustrated in Rawlings v. Kentucky, 448 U.S. 98, 100 S.Ct. 2556, 65 L.Ed.2d 633 (1980). Six officers arrived at a residence with a warrant for the arrest of one Marquess. Two of the occupants and four guests, including Rawlings and Cox, were present. During the search for Marquess, the officers smelled marihuana smoke and observed marihuana seeds. Two officers left to obtain a search warrant and the other four officers remained. The officers who remained on the scene permitted any occupant who would submit to a body search to leave; two did. About 45 minutes later, the two officers returned with a search warrant. The warrant and the *Miranda* rights were read to the remaining occupants. One officer then approached Cox and ordered her to empty her purse. 1,800 tablets of LSD and a variety of other controlled substances were found in the contents. After pouring these items on a table, Cox turned to Rawlings and told him "to take what was his." Rawlings immediately claimed ownership of the controlled substances. At Rawlings' trial for trafficking in and possession of the controlled substances, his claim of ownership was admitted against him over his objection that it was the "fruit" of an illegal detention.

The Supreme Court upheld the admission of the statement. Assuming without deciding that the detention was invalid, the Court held that the statement was not tainted by this detention. Several factors were considered relevant. First, the *Miranda* warnings were given; this was "important" but not "dispositive." Second, the atmosphere during the period of detention was "congenial." This outweighed the short 45 minute duration of the period between the detention and the making of the statement, which under more "strict" conditions would not be long enough to purge the taint of the detention. Third, the discovery of the drugs in Cox's purse and Rawlings' apparent desire to assume responsibility for them was a "circumstance" which "intervened between the initial detention and the challenged statements." Fourth, the police misconduct "[did] not rise to the level of conscious or flagrant misconduct." Finally, the statement was "voluntary," i.e., it was shown to have been an act of free will unaffected by any illegality in the detention. 448 U.S. at 106–10, 100 S.Ct. at 2562–64, 65 L.Ed.2d at 642–45. Justice Marshall, joined by Justice Brennan, reasoned that Rawlings' statement claiming ownership of the substances was a direct response to Cox's demand that he take what was his. Her statement was the direct product of the illegal search of her purse, which was made possible only by the illegal detention of the occupants of the house. "Under these circumstances," he concluded, "[Rawlings'] admissions were obviously the fruit of the illegal detention and should have been suppressed." 448 U.S. at 120, 100 S.Ct. at 2569, 65 L.Ed.2d at 652 (Marshall, J., dissenting).

In regard to the nature of the illegal detention, contrast *Taylor* in which the Court found no attenuation of taint. The detention in that case was characterized as "an investigatory arrest without probable cause" followed by the involuntary transportation of the defendant to the station "for interrogation in the hope that something would turn up." 457 U.S. at 693, 102 S.Ct. at 2668, 73 L.Ed.2d at 321.

7. When, if ever, should the fruits of the poisonous tree doctrine include the testimony of a witness whose identity was discovered in violation of a defendant's constitutional rights? In United States v. Ceccolini, 435 U.S. 268, 98 S.Ct. 1054, 55 L.Ed.2d 268 (1978), Biro, a local police officer, entered Ceccolini's place of business to talk with Lois Hennessey, a friend and an employee of the shop. During the course of the conversation he noticed an envelope with money sticking out of it lying on the drawer of the cash register behind the counter. Biro picked up the envelope and, upon examining its contents, discovered that it contained not only money but policy (gambling) slips. He placed the envelope back on the register and, without telling his friend what he had seen, asked her to whom the envelope belonged. She replied that the envelope belonged to Ceccolini and that he had instructed her to give it to someone. The officer related what he had observed and been told to local police detectives, who, in turn gave the information to an FBI agent. Ceccolini had already been the subject of an FBI gambling investigation. An agent interviewed Ms. Hennessey at her home and she agreed to provide information about the envelope to the agent. Ceccolini was subpoenaed before

a grand jury, where he denied any knowledge of a policy operation being run from his shop. Ms. Hennessey testified about the envelope and the grand jury indicted Ceccolini for committing perjury in his grand jury testimony. The District Court and the Court of Appeals concluded that the police officer acted illegally when he examined the envelope and that the trial testimony of the store employee was a fruit of that illegality. The Supreme Court disagreed. Writing for the Court, Justice Rehnquist concluded that although there was a causal connection between the initial illegality and the testimony of the employee, the taint had been dissipated:

> * * * [W]e hold that the Court of Appeals erred in holding that the degree of attenuation was not sufficient to dissipate the connection between the illegality and the testimony. The evidence indicates overwhelmingly that the testimony given by the witness was an act of her own free will in no way coerced or even induced by official authority as a result of Biro's discovery of the policy slips. Nor were the slips themselves used in questioning Hennessey. Substantial periods of time elapsed between the time of the illegal search and the initial contact with the witness, on the one hand, and between the latter and the testimony at trial on the other. While the particular knowledge to which Hennessey testified at trial can be logically traced back to Biro's discovery of the policy slips both the identity of Hennessey and her relationship with the respondent was well known to those investigating the case. There is in addition, not the slightest evidence to suggest that Biro entered the shop or picked up the envelope with the intent of finding tangible evidence bearing on an illicit gambling operation, much less any suggestion that he entered the shop and searched with the intent of finding a willing and knowledgeable witness to testify against respondent. Application of the exclusionary rule in this situtation could not have the slightest deterrent effect on the behavior of an officer such as Biro. The cost of permanently silencing Hennessey is too great for an even-handed system of law enforcement to bear in order to secure such a speculative and very likely negligible deterrent effect.

> Obviously no mathematical weight can be assigned to any of the factors which we have discussed, but just as obviously they all point to the conclusion that the exclusionary rule should be invoked with much greater reluctance where the claim is based on a causal relationship between a constitutional violation and the discovery of a live witness than when a similar claim is advanced to support suppression of an inanimate object.

435 U.S. at 279–80, 98 S.Ct. at 1062, 55 L.Ed.2d at 279. Justices Marshall and Brennan dissented.

## C.   GOOD FAITH AND OTHER EXCEPTIONS

To the extent that *Mapp* and *Wong Sun* recognized a general rule—that all evidence that would not have been obtained "but for" police illegal conduct must be excluded—it is immediately apparent that this rule is subject to exception. *Wong Sun* itself recognized and applied an exception for situations in which the "taint" is shown to have been "attenuated." This section considers other exceptions to the general rule of exclusion.

## UNITED STATES v. LEON

Supreme Court of the United States, 1984.
468 U.S. 897, 104 S.Ct. 3405, 82 L.Ed.2d 677.

JUSTICE WHITE delivered the opinion of the Court.

This case presents the question whether the Fourth Amendment exclusionary rule should be modified so as not to bar the use in the prosecution's case-in-chief of evidence obtained by officers acting in reasonable reliance on a search warrant issued by a detached and neutral magistrate but ultimately found to be unsupported by probable cause. * * *

I

In August 1981, a confidential informant of unproven reliability informed an officer of the Burbank Police Department that two persons known to him as "Armando" and "Patsy" were selling large quantities of cocaine and methaqualone from their residence at 620 Price Drive in Burbank, Cal. The informant also indicated that he had witnessed a sale of methaqualone by "Patsy" at the residence approximately five months earlier and had observed at that time a shoebox containing a large amount of cash that belonged to "Patsy." He further declared that "Armando" and "Patsy" generally kept only small quantities of drugs at their residence and stored the remainder at another location in Burbank.

On the basis of this information, the Burbank police initiated an extensive investigation focusing first on the Price Drive residence and later on two other residences as well. Cars parked at the Price Drive residence were determined to belong to respondents Armando Sanchez, who had previously been arrested for possession of marihuana, and Patsy Stewart, who had no criminal record. During the course of the investigation, officers observed an automobile belonging to respondent Ricardo Del Castillo, who had previously been arrested for possession of 50 pounds of marihuana, arrive at the Price Drive residence. The driver of that car entered the house, exited shortly thereafter carrying a small paper sack, and drove away. A check of Del Castillo's probation records led the officers to respondent Alberto Leon, whose telephone number Del Castillo had listed as his employer's. Leon had been arrested in 1980 on drug charges, and a companion had informed the police at that time that Leon was heavily involved in the importation of drugs into this country. Before the current investigation began, the Burbank officers had learned that an informant had told a Glendale police officer that Leon stored a large quantity of methaqualone at his residence in Glendale. During the course of this investigation, the Burbank officers learned that Leon was living at 716 South Sunset Canyon in Burbank.

Subsequently, the officers observed several persons, at least one of whom had prior drug involvement, arriving at the Price Drive residence and leaving with small packages; observed a variety of other material activity at the two residences as well as at a condominium at

7902 Via Magdalena; and witnessed a variety of relevant activity involving respondents' automobiles. The officers also observed respondents Sanchez and Stewart board separate flights for Miami. The pair later returned to Los Angeles together, consented to a search of their luggage that revealed only a small amount of marihuana, and left the airport. Based on these and other observations summarized in the affidavit, Officer Cyril Rombach of the Burbank Police Department, an experienced and well-trained narcotics investigator, prepared an application for a warrant to search 620 Price Drive, 716 South Sunset Canyon, 7902 Via Magdalena, and automobiles registered to each of the respondents for an extensive list of items believed to be related to respondents' drug-trafficking activities. Officer Rombach's extensive application was reviewed by several Deputy District Attorneys.

A facially valid search warrant was issued in September 1981 by a state superior court judge. The ensuing searches produced large quantities of drugs at the Via Magdalena and Sunset Canyon addresses and a small quantity at the Price Drive residence. Other evidence was discovered at each of the residences and in Stewart's and Del Castillo's automobiles. Respondents were indicted by a grand jury in the District Court for the Central District of California and charged with conspiracy to possess and distribute cocaine and a variety of substantive counts.

The respondents then filed motions to suppress the evidence seized pursuant to the warrant. The District Court held an evidentiary hearing and, while recognizing that the case was a close one, granted the motions to suppress in part. It concluded that the affidavit was insufficient to establish probable cause, but did not suppress all of the evidence as to all of the respondents because none of the respondents had standing to challenge all of the searches. In response to a request from the Government, the court made clear that Officer Rombach had acted in good faith, but it rejected the Government's suggestion that the Fourth Amendment exclusionary rule should not apply where evidence is seized in reasonable, good-faith reliance on a search warrant.

* * * [A] divided panel of the Court of Appeals for the Ninth Circuit affirmed. * * *

The Government's petition for certiorari expressly declined to seek review of the lower courts' determinations that the search warrant was unsupported by probable cause and presented only the question "[w]hether the Fourth Amendment exclusionary rule should be modified so as not to bar the admission of evidence seized in reasonable, good-faith reliance on a search warrant that is subsequently held to be defective." We granted certiorari to consider the propriety of such a modification. * * *

We have concluded that, in the Fourth Amendment context, the exclusionary rule can be modified somewhat without jeopardizing its ability to perform its intended functions. Accordingly, we reverse the judgment of the Court of Appeals.

## II

Language in opinions of this Court and of individual Justices has sometimes implied that the exclusionary rule is a necessary corollary of the Fourth Amendment, Mapp v. Ohio, 367 U.S. 643, 651, 655–657, 81 S.Ct. 1684, 1689, 1691–1692, 6 L.Ed.2d 1081 (1961); Olmstead v. United States, 277 U.S. 438, 462–463, 48 S.Ct. 564, 567, 72 L.Ed. 944 (1928), or that the rule is required by the conjunction of the Fourth and Fifth Amendments. Mapp v. Ohio, supra, at 661–662, 81 S.Ct., at 1694–1695 (Black, J., concurring); Agnello v. United States, 269 U.S. 20, 33–34, 46 S.Ct. 4, 6–7, 70 L.Ed. 145 (1925). These implications need not detain us long. The Fifth Amendment theory has not withstood critical analysis or the test of time, see Andresen v. Maryland, 427 U.S. 463, 96 S.Ct. 2737, 49 L.Ed.2d 627 (1976), and the Fourth Amendment "has never been interpreted to proscribe the introduction of illegally seized evidence in all proceedings or against all persons." Stone v. Powell, 428 U.S. 465, 486, 96 S.Ct. 3037, 3048, 49 L.Ed.2d 1067 (1976).

### A

The Fourth Amendment contains no provision expressly precluding the use of evidence obtained in violation of its commands, and an examination of its origin and purposes makes clear that the use of fruits of a past unlawful search or seizure "work[s] no new Fourth Amendment wrong." United States v. Calandra, 414 U.S. 338, 354, 94 S.Ct. 613, 622, 38 L.Ed.2d 561 (1974). The wrong condemned by the Amendment is "fully accomplished" by the unlawful search or seizure itself, ibid., and the exclusionary rule is neither intended nor able to "cure the invasion of the defendant's rights which he has already suffered." Stone v. Powell, supra, at 540, 96 S.Ct., at 3074 (White, J., dissenting). The rule thus operates as "a judicially created remedy designed to safeguard Fourth Amendment rights generally through its deterrent effect, rather than a personal constitutional right of the person aggrieved." United States v. Calandra, supra, at 348, 94 S.Ct. at 620.

Whether the exclusionary sanction is appropriately imposed in a particular case, our decisions make clear, is "an issue separate from the question whether the Fourth Amendment rights of the party seeking to invoke the rule were violated by police conduct." Illinois v. Gates, [462 U.S. 213, 223, 103 S.Ct. 2317, 2324, 76 L.Ed.2d 527 (1983)]. Only the former question is currently before us, and it must be resolved by weighing the costs and benefits of preventing the use in the prosecution's case-in-chief of inherently trustworthy tangible evidence obtained in reliance on a search warrant issued by a detached and neutral magistrate that ultimately is found to be defective.

The substantial social costs exacted by the exclusionary rule for the vindication of Fourth Amendment rights have long been a source of concern. "Our cases have consistently recognized that unbending application of the exclusionary sanction to enforce ideals of governmental rectitude would impede unacceptably the truth-finding functions of judge and jury." United States v. Payner, 447 U.S. 727, 734, 100 S.Ct. 2439, 2445, 65 L.Ed.2d 468 (1980). An objectionable collateral consequence of this interference with the criminal justice system's truth-finding function is that some guilty defendants may go free or receive reduced sentences as a result of favorable plea bargains.[2] Particularly when law enforcement officers have acted in objective good faith or their transgressions have been minor, the magnitude of the benefit conferred on such guilty defendants offends basic concepts of the criminal justice system. Stone v. Powell, supra, at 490, 96 S.Ct., at 3050. Indiscriminate application of the exclusionary rule, therefore, may well "generat[e] disrespect for the law and the administration of justice." Id., at 491, 96 S.Ct., at 3051. Accordingly, "[a]s with any remedial device, the application of the rule has been restricted to those areas where its remedial objectives are thought most efficaciously served." United States v. Calandra, supra, at 348, 94 S.Ct., at 620.

## B

Close attention to those remedial objectives has characterized our recent decisions concerning the scope of the Fourth Amendment exclusionary rule. The Court has, to be sure, not seriously questioned, "in the absence of a more efficacious sanction, the continued application of the rule to suppress evidence from the [prosecution's] case where a Fourth Amendment violation has been substantial and deliberate

[2] Researchers have only recently begun to study extensively the effects of the exclusionary rule on the disposition of felony arrests. One study suggests that the rule results in the nonprosecution or nonconviction of between 0.6% and 2.35% of individuals arrested for felonies. Davies, A Hard Look at What We Know (and Still Need to Learn) About the "Costs" of the Exclusionary Rule: The NIJ Study and Other Studies of "Lost" Arrests, 1983 A.B.F.Res.J. 611, 621. The estimates are higher for particular crimes the prosecution of which depends heavily on physical evidence. Thus, the cumulative loss due to nonprosecution or nonconviction of individuals arrested on felony drug charges is probably in the range of 2.8% to 7.1%. Id., at 680. Davies' analysis of California data suggests that screening by police and prosecutors results in the release because of illegal searches or seizures of as many as 1.4% of all felony arrestees, id., at 650, that 0.9% of felony arrestees are released because of illegal searches or seizures at the preliminary hearing or after trial, id., at 653, and that roughly 0.5% of all felony arrestees benefit from reversals on appeal because of illegal searches. Id., at 654. See also K. Brosi, A Cross-City Comparison of Felony Case Processing 16, 18–19 (1979); Report of the Comptroller General of the United States, Impact of the Exclusionary Rule on Federal Criminal Prosecutions 10–11, 14 (1979); F. Feeney, F. Dill & A. Weir, Ar-

rests Without Convictions: How Often They Occur and Why 203–206 (1983); National Institute of Justice, The Effects of the Exclusionary Rule: A Study in California 1–2 (1982); Nardulli, The Societal Cost of the Exclusionary Rule: An Empirical Assessment, 1983 A.B.F.Res.J. 585, 600. The exclusionary rule also has been found to affect the plea-bargaining process. S. Schlesinger, Exclusionary Injustice: The Problem of Illegally Obtained Evidence 63 (1977). But see Davies, supra, at 668–669; Nardulli, supra, at 604–606.

Many of these researchers have concluded that the impact of the exclusionary rule is insubstantial, but the small percentages with which they deal mask a large absolute number of felons who are released because the cases against them were based in part on illegal searches or seizures. "[A]ny rule of evidence that denies the jury access to clearly probative and reliable evidence must bear a heavy burden of justification, and must be carefully limited to the circumstances in which it will pay its way by deterring official unlawlessness." Illinois v. Gates, 462 U.S., at 257–58, 103 S.Ct., at 2342 (White, J., concurring in the judgment). Because we find that the rule can have no substantial deterrent effect in the sorts of situations under consideration in this case, we conclude that it cannot pay its way in those situations.

* * *." Franks v. Delaware, 438 U.S. 154, 171, 98 S.Ct. 2674, 2684, 57 L.Ed.2d 667 (1978); Stone v. Powell, supra, at 492, 96 S.Ct., at 3051. Nevertheless, the balancing approach that has evolved in various contexts—including criminal trials—"forcefully suggest[s] that the exclusionary rule be more generally modified to permit the introduction of evidence obtained in the reasonable good-faith belief that a search or seizure was in accord with the Fourth Amendment." Illinois v. Gates, supra, at 255, 103 S.Ct., at 2340 (White, J., concurring in the judgment).

* * *

As yet, we have not recognized any form of good-faith exception to the Fourth Amendment exclusionary rule. But the balancing approach that has evolved during the years of experience with the rule provides strong support for the modification currently urged upon us. As we discuss below, our evaluation of the costs and benefits of suppressing reliable physical evidence seized by officers reasonably relying on a warrant issued by a detached and neutral magistrate leads to the conclusion that such evidence should be admissible in the prosecution's case-in-chief.

## III

### A

Because a search warrant "provides the detached scrutiny of a neutral magistrate, which is a more reliable safeguard against improper searches than the hurried judgment of a law enforcement officer 'engaged in the often competitive enterprise of ferreting out crime,'" United States v. Chadwick, 433 U.S. 1, 9, 97 S.Ct. 2476, 2482, 53 L.Ed.2d 538 (1971) (quoting Johnson v. United States, 333 U.S. 10, 14, 68 S.Ct. 367, 369, 92 L.Ed. 436 (1948)), we have expressed a strong preference for warrants and declared that "in a doubtful or marginal case a search under a warrant may be sustainable where without one it would fail." United States v. Ventresca, 380 U.S. 102, 106, 85 S.Ct. 741, 744, 13 L.Ed.2d 684 (1965). Reasonable minds frequently may differ on the question whether a particular affidavit establishes probable cause, and we have thus concluded that the preference for warrants is most appropriately effectuated by according "great deference" to a magistrate's determination. Spinelli v. United States, 393 U.S. [410 (1969)], at 419, 89 S.Ct., at 591.

Deference to the magistrate, however, is not boundless. It is clear, first, that the deference accorded to a magistrate's finding of probable cause does not preclude inquiry into the knowing or reckless falsity of the affidavit on which that determination was based. Franks v. Delaware, 438 U.S. 154, 98 S.Ct. 2674, 57 L.Ed.2d 667 (1978). Second, the courts must also insist that the magistrate purport to "perform his 'neutral and detached' function and not serve merely as a rubber stamp for the police." Aguilar v. Texas, [378 U.S. 108, 111, 84 S.Ct. 1509, 1512, 12 L.Ed.2d 723 (1964)]. A magistrate failing to "manifest that neutrality and detachment demanded of a judicial officer when presented with a warrant application" and who acts instead as "an adjunct law enforcement officer" cannot provide valid authorization for an otherwise unconstitutional search.  Lo-Ji Sales, Inc. v. New York, 442 U.S. 319, 326–327, 99 S.Ct. 2319, 2324–2325, 60 L.Ed.2d 920 (1979).

Third, reviewing courts will not defer to a warrant based on an affidavit that does not "provide the magistrate with a substantial basis for determining the existence of probable cause."  Illinois v. Gates, supra, at 239, 103 S.Ct. at 2332.  *  *  *  Even if the warrant application was supported by more than a "bare bones" affidavit, a reviewing court may properly conclude that, notwithstanding the deference that magistrates deserve, the warrant was invalid because the magistrate's probable-cause determination reflected an improper analysis of the totality of the circumstances, or because the form of the warrant was improper in some respect.

Only in the first of these three situations, however, has the Court set forth a rationale for suppressing evidence obtained pursuant to a search warrant;  in the other areas, it has simply excluded such evidence without considering whether Fourth Amendment interests will be advanced.  To the extent that proponents of exclusion rely on its behavioral effects on judges and magistrates in these areas, their reliance is misplaced.  First, the exclusionary rule is designed to deter police misconduct rather than to punish the errors of judges and magistrates.  Second, there exists no evidence suggesting that judges and magistrates are inclined to ignore or subvert the Fourth Amendment or that lawlessness among these actors requires application of the extreme sanction of exclusion.[3]

Third, and most important, we discern no basis, and are offered none, for believing that exclusion of evidence seized pursuant to a warrant will have a significant deterrent effect on the issuing judge or magistrate.  Many of the factors that indicate that the exclusionary rule cannot provide an effective "special" or "general" deterrent for individual offending law enforcement officers apply as well to judges or magistrates.  And, to the extent that the rule is thought to operate as a "systemic" deterrent on a wider audience, it clearly can have no such effect on individuals empowered to issue search warrants.  Judges and magistrates are not adjuncts to the law enforcement team;  as neutral judicial officers, they have no stake in the outcome of particular criminal prosecutions.  The threat of exclusion thus cannot be expected significantly to deter them.  Imposition of the exclusionary sanction is not necessary meaningfully to inform judicial officers of their errors, and we cannot conclude that admitting evidence obtained pursuant to a warrant while at the same time declaring that the warrant was somehow defective will in any way reduce judicial officers' professional incentives to comply with the Fourth Amendment, encourage them to repeat their mistakes, or lead to the granting of all colorable warrant requests.[4]

[3] Although there are assertions that some magistrates become rubber stamps for the police and others may be unable effectively to screen police, * * * we are not convinced that this is a problem of major proportions.  * * *

[4] Limiting the application of the exclusionary sanction may well increase the care with which magistrates scrutinize warrant applications.  We doubt that magistrates are more desirous of avoiding the exclusion of evidence obtained pursuant to

## B

If exclusion of evidence obtained pursuant to a subsequently invalidated warrant is to have any deterrent effect, therefore, it must alter the behavior of individual law enforcement officers or the policies of their departments. One could argue that applying the exclusionary rule in cases where the police failed to demonstrate probable cause in the warrant application deters future inadequate presentations or "magistrate shopping" and thus promotes the ends of the Fourth Amendment. Suppressing evidence obtained pursuant to a technically defective warrant supported by probable cause also might encourage officers to scrutinize more closely the form of the warrant and to point out suspected judicial errors. We find such arguments speculative and conclude that suppression of evidence obtained pursuant to a warrant should be ordered only on a case-by-case basis and only in those unusual cases in which exclusion will further the purposes of the exclusionary rule.

We have frequently questioned whether the exclusionary rule can have any deterrent effect when the offending officers acted in the objectively reasonable belief that their conduct did not violate the Fourth Amendment. * * * [5]

This is particularly true, we believe, when an officer acting with objective good faith has obtained a search warrant from a judge or magistrate and acted within its scope. In most such cases, there is no police illegality and thus nothing to deter. It is the magistrate's responsibility to determine whether the officer's allegations establish probable cause and, if so, to issue a warrant comporting in form with the requirements of the Fourth Amendment. In the ordinary case, an officer cannot be expected to question the magistrate's probable-cause determination or his judgment that the form of the warrant is technically sufficient. "[O]nce the warrant issues, there is literally nothing more the policeman can do in seeking to comply with the law." [Stone v. Powell, supra] at 498, 96 S.Ct. at 3054 (Burger, C.J., concurring). Penalizing the officer for the magistrate's error, rather than his own, cannot logically contribute to the deterrence of Fourth Amendment violations.[6]

warrants they have issued than of avoiding invasions of privacy.

Federal magistrates, moreover, are subject to the direct supervision of district courts. They may be removed for "incompetency, misconduct, neglect of duty, or physical or mental disability." 28 U.S.C. § 631(i). If a magistrate serves merely as a "rubber stamp" for the police or is unable to exercise mature judgment, closer supervision or removal provides a more effective remedy than the exclusionary rule.

[5] We emphasize that the standard of reasonableness we adopt is an objective one. Many objections to a good-faith exception assume that the exception will turn on the subjective good faith of individual officers. * * * The objective standard we adopt, moreover, requires officers to have a reasonable knowledge of what the law prohibits.

[6] To the extent that Justice Stevens' conclusions concerning the integrity of the courts, rest on a foundation other than his judgment, which we reject, concerning the effects of our decision on the deterrence of police illegality, we find his argument unpersuasive. * * * Our cases establish that the question whether the use of illegally obtained evidence in judicial proceedings represents judicial participation in a Fourth Amendment violation and offends the integrity of the courts

## C

We conclude that the marginal or nonexistent benefits produced by suppressing evidence obtained in objectively reasonable reliance on a subsequently invalidated search warrant cannot justify the substantial costs of exclusion. We do not suggest, however, that exclusion is always inappropriate in cases where an officer has obtained a warrant and abided by its terms. * * * [T]he officer's reliance on the magistrate's probable-cause determination and on the technical sufficiency of the warrant he issues must be objectively reasonable, and it is clear that in some circumstances the officer [7] will have no reasonable grounds for believing that the warrant was properly issued.

Suppression therefore remains an appropriate remedy if the magistrate or judge in issuing a warrant was misled by information in an affidavit that the affiant knew was false or would have known was false except for his reckless disregard of the truth. Franks v. Delaware, 438 U.S. 154, 98 S.Ct. 2674, 57 L.Ed.2d 667 (1978). The exception we recognize today will also not apply in cases where the issuing magistrate wholly abandoned his judicial role in the manner condemned in Lo-Ji Sales, Inc. v. New York, 442 U.S. 319, 99 S.Ct. 2319, 60 L.Ed.2d 920 (1979); in such circumstances, no reasonably well-trained officer should rely on the warrant. Nor would an officer manifest objective good faith in relying on a warrant based on an affidavit "so lacking in indicia of probable cause as to render official belief in its existence entirely unreasonable." Brown v. Illinois, 422 U.S. [590], at 610–611, 95 S.Ct. [2254], at 2265 [, 45 L.Ed.2d 416 (1975) ] (Powell, J., concurring in part). Finally, depending on the circumstances of the particular case, a warrant may be so facially deficient—i.e., in failing to particularize the place to be searched or the things to be seized—that the executing officers cannot reasonably presume it to be valid.

In so limiting the suppression remedy, we leave untouched the probable-cause standard and the various requirements for a valid warrant. Other objections to the modification of the Fourth Amendment exclusionary rule we consider to be insubstantial. The good-faith exception for searches conducted pursuant to warrants is not intended

"is essentially the same as the inquiry into whether exclusion would serve a deterrent purpose. * * * The analysis showing that exclusion in this case has no demonstrated deterrent effect and is unlikely to have any significant such effect shows, by the same reasoning, that the admission of the evidence is unlikely to encourage violations of the Fourth Amendment." United States v. Janis, [428 U.S. 433 (1976) ], at 459, n. 35, 96 S.Ct., at 3034, n. 35.

Absent unusual circumstances, when a Fourth Amendment violation has occurred because the police have reasonably relied on a warrant issued by a detached and neutral magistrate but ultimately found to be defective, "the integrity of the courts is not implicated." Illinois v. Gates, 462 U.S., at 245, n. 14, 103 S.Ct., at 2343, n. 14 (White, J., concurring in the judgment).

[7] References to "officer" throughout this opinion should not be read too narrowly. It is necessary to consider the objective reasonableness, not only of the officers who eventually executed a warrant, but also of the officers who originally obtained it or who provided information material to the probable-cause determination. Nothing in our opinion suggests, for example, that an officer could obtain a warrant on the basis of a "bare bones" affidavit and then rely on colleagues who are ignorant of the circumstances under which the warrant was obtained to conduct the search.

to signal our unwillingness strictly to enforce the requirements of the Fourth Amendment, and we do not believe that it will have this effect. As we have already suggested, the good-faith exception, turning as it does on objective reasonableness, should not be difficult to apply in practice. When officers have acted pursuant to a warrant, the prosecution should ordinarily be able to establish objective good faith without a substantial expenditure of judicial time.

Nor are we persuaded that application of a good-faith exception to searches conducted pursuant to warrants will preclude review of the constitutionality of the search or seizure, deny needed guidance from the courts, or freeze Fourth Amendment law in its present state. There is no need for courts to adopt the inflexible practice of always deciding whether the officers' conduct manifested objective good faith before turning to the question whether the Fourth Amendment has been violated. * * *

If the resolution of a particular Fourth Amendment question is necessary to guide future action by law enforcement officers and magistrates, nothing will prevent reviewing courts from deciding that question before turning to the good-faith issue. Indeed, it frequently will be difficult to determine whether the officers acted reasonably without resolving the Fourth Amendment issue. Even if the Fourth Amendment question is not one of broad import, reviewing courts could decide in particular cases that magistrates under their supervision need to be informed of their errors and so evaluate the officers' good faith only after finding a violation. In other circumstances, those courts could reject suppression motions posing no important Fourth Amendment questions by turning immediately to a consideration of the officers' good faith. We have no reason to believe that our Fourth Amendment jurisprudence would suffer by allowing reviewing courts to exercise an informed discretion in making this choice.

### IV

When the principles we have enunciated today are applied to the facts of this case, it is apparent that the judgment of the Court of Appeals cannot stand. * * *

In the absence of an allegation that the magistrate abandoned his detached and neutral role, suppression is appropriate only if the officers were dishonest or reckless in preparing their affidavit or could not have harbored an objectively reasonable belief in the existence of probable cause. * * * Officer Rombach's application for a warrant clearly was supported by much more than a "bare bones" affidavit. The affidavit related the results of an extensive investigation and, as the opinions of the divided panel of the Court of Appeals make clear, provided evidence sufficient to create disagreement among thoughtful and competent judges as to the existence of probable cause. Under these circumstances, the officers' reliance on the magistrate's determination of probable cause was objectively reasonable, and application of the extreme sanction of exclusion is inappropriate.

Accordingly, the judgment of the Court of Appeals is reversed.

[The concurring opinion of JUSTICE BLACKMUN is omitted.]

JUSTICE BRENNAN, with whom JUSTICE MARSHALL joins, dissenting.

\* \* \* I have witnessed the Court's gradual but determined strangulation of the [exclusionary] rule. It now appears that the Court's victory over the Fourth Amendment is complete. \* \* \*

I

\* \* \*

At bottom, the Court's decision turns on the proposition that the exclusionary rule is merely a " 'judicially created remedy designed to safeguard Fourth Amendment rights generally through its deterrent effect, rather than a personal constitutional right.' " \* \* \* This reading of the Amendment implies that its proscriptions are directed solely at those government agents who may actually invade an individual's constitutionally protected privacy. The courts are not subject to any direct constitutional duty to exclude illegally obtained evidence, because the question of the admissibility of such evidence is not addressed by the Amendment. \* \* \*

Such a reading appears plausible, because \* \* \* the Fourth Amendment makes no express provision for the exclusion of evidence secured in violation of its commands. A short answer to this claim, of course, is that many of the Constitution's most vital imperatives are stated in general terms and the task of giving meaning to these precepts is therefore left to subsequent judicial decision-making in the context of concrete cases. \* \* \*

A more direct answer may be supplied by recognizing that the Amendment, like other provisions of the Bill of Rights, restrains the power of the government as a whole; it does not specify only a particular agency and exempt all others. The judiciary is responsible, no less than the executive, for ensuring that constitutional rights are respected.

When that fact is kept in mind, the role of the courts and their possible involvement in the concerns of the Fourth Amendment comes into sharper focus. Because seizures are executed principally to secure evidence, and because such evidence generally has utility in our legal system only in the context of a trial supervised by a judge, it is apparent that the admission of illegally obtained evidence implicates the same constitutional concerns as the initial seizure of that evidence. Indeed, by admitting unlawfully seized evidence, the judiciary becomes a part of what is in fact a single governmental action prohibited by the terms of the Amendment. \* \* \* The Amendment therefore must be read to condemn not only the initial unconstitutional invasion of privacy \* \* \* but also the subsequent use of any evidence so obtained. \* \* \*

\* \* \* [I]t is clear why the question whether the exclusion of evidence would deter future police misconduct was never considered a relevant concern in the early cases \* \* \*. In those formative decisions, the Court plainly understood that the exclusion of evidence was compelled not by judicially fashioned remedial purposes, but rather by

a direct constitutional command.  *  *  *  [T]he Court  *  *  * has
gradually pressed the deterrent rationale for the rule back to center
stage.  The various arguments advanced by the Court in this campaign
have only strengthened my conviction that the deterrence theory is
both misguided and unworkable.  First, the Court has frequently be-
wailed the "cost" of excluding reliable evidence.  In large part, this
criticism rests upon a refusal to acknowledge the function of the Fourth
Amendment.  *  *  *  [O]fficial compliance with Fourth Amendment
requirements makes it more difficult to catch criminals.  *  *  *  [I]t
is not the exclusionary rule, but the Amendment itself that has imposed this cost.

In addition, the Court's decisions over the past decade have made
plain that the entire enterprise of attempting to assess the benefits and
costs of the exclusionary rule in various contexts is virtually an
impossible task for the judiciary to perform honestly or accurately.
Although the Court's language in those cases suggests that some
specific empirical basis may support its analyses, the reality is that the
Court's opinions represent inherently unstable compounds of intuition,
hunches, and occasional pieces of partial and often inconclusive data.
*  *  *  Rather than seeking to give effect to the liberties secured by
the Fourth Amendment through guesswork about deterrence, the Court
should restore to its proper place the principle framed 70 years ago in
*Weeks* that an individual whose privacy has been invaded in violation of
the Fourth Amendment has a right grounded in that Amendment to
prevent the government from subsequently making use of any evidence
so obtained.

*  *  *

III

Even if I were to accept the Court's general approach to the
exclusionary rule, I could not agree with today's result.  *  *  *
[S]uch a result cannot be justified even on the Court's own terms.

At the outset, the Court suggests that society has been asked to pay
a high price—in terms either of setting guilty persons free or of
impeding the proper functioning of trials—as a result of excluding
relevant physical evidence in cases where the police, in conducting
searches and seizing evidence, have made only an "objectively reasonable" mistake concerning the constitutionality of their actions.  But
what evidence is there to support such a claim?

Significantly, the Court points to none, and, indeed, as the Court
acknowledges, recent studies have demonstrated that the "costs" of the
exclusionary rule—calculated in terms of dropped prosecutions and lost
convictions—are quite low.  Contrary to the claims of the rule's critics
that exclusion leads to "the release of countless guilty criminals,"
Bivens v. Six Unknown Federal Narcotics Officers, 403 U.S. 388, 416, 91
S.Ct. 1999, 2014, 29 L.Ed.2d 619 (Burger, C.J., dissenting), these studies
have demonstrated that federal and state prosecutors very rarely drop
cases because of potential search and seizure problems.  For example, a
1979 study prepared at the request of Congress by the General Account-

ing Office reported that only 0.4% of all cases actually declined for prosecution by federal prosecutors were declined primarily because of illegal search problems. Report of the Comptroller General of the United States, Impact of the Exclusionary Rule on Federal Criminal Prosecutions 14 (1979). If the GAO data are restated as a percentage of *all* arrests, the study shows that only 0.2% of all felony arrests are declined for prosecution because of potential exclusionary rule problems. See Davies, A Hard Look at What We Know (and Still Need to Learn) About the "Costs" of the Exclusionary Rule: The NIJ Study and Other Studies of "Lost" Arrests, 1983 Am.Bar Found.Res.J. 611, 635. Of course, these data describe only the costs attributable to the exclusion of evidence in all cases; the costs due to the exclusion of evidence in the narrower category of cases where police have made objectively reasonable mistakes must necessarily be even smaller. The Court, however, ignores this distinction and mistakenly weighs the aggregated costs of exclusion in *all* cases, irrespective of the circumstances that led to exclusion, against the potential benefits associated with only those cases in which evidence is excluded because police reasonably but mistakenly believe that their conduct does not violate the Fourth Amendment. When such faulty scales are used, it is little wonder that the balance tips in favor of restricting the application of the rule.

What then supports the Court's insistence that this evidence be admitted? Apparently, the Court's only answer is that even though the costs of exclusion are not very substantial, the potential deterrent effect in these circumstances is so marginal that exclusion cannot be justified.

\* \* \*

The flaw in the Court's argument, however, is that its logic captures only one comparatively minor element of the generally acknowledged deterrent purposes of the exclusionary rule. To be sure, the rule operates to some extent to deter future misconduct by individual officers who have had evidence suppressed in their own cases. But what the Court overlooks is that the deterrence rationale for the rule is not designed to be, nor should it be thought of as, a form of "punishment" of individual police officers for their failures to obey the restraints imposed by the Fourth Amendment. See United States v. Peltier, 422 U.S. 531, 556–557, 95 S.Ct. 2313, 2327, 45 L.Ed.2d 374 (Brennan, J., dissenting). Instead, the chief deterrent function of the rule is its tendency to promote institutional compliance with Fourth Amendment requirements on the part of law enforcement agencies generally. Thus, as the Court has previously recognized, "over the long term, [the] demonstration [provided by the exclusionary rule] that our society attaches serious consequences to violation of constitutional rights is thought to encourage those who formulate law enforcement policies, and the officers who implement them, to incorporate Fourth Amendment ideals into their value system." Stone v. Powell, 428 U.S., at 492, 96 S.Ct., at 3051. It is only through such an institution-wide mechanism that information concerning Fourth Amendment standards can be effectively communicated to rank and file officers.

If the overall educational effect of the exclusionary rule is considered, application of the rule to even those situations in which individual police officers have acted on the basis of a reasonable but mistaken belief that their conduct was authorized can still be expected to have a considerable long-term deterrent effect.  If evidence is consistently excluded in these circumstances, police departments will surely be prompted to instruct their officers to devote greater care and attention to providing sufficient information to establish probable cause when applying for a warrant, and to review with some attention the form of the warrant that they have been issued, rather than automatically assuming that whatever document the magistrate has signed will necessarily comport with Fourth Amendment requirements.

After today's decision, however, that institutional incentive will be lost.  Indeed, the Court's "reasonable mistake" exception to the exclusionary rule will tend to put a premium on police ignorance of the law. Armed with the assurance provided by today's decision that evidence will always be admissible whenever an officer has "reasonably" relied upon a warrant, police departments will be encouraged to train officers that if a warrant has simply been signed, it is reasonable, without more, to rely on it.  Since in close cases there will no longer be any incentive to err on the side of constitutional behavior, police would have every reason to adopt a "let's-wait-until-it's-decided" approach in situations in which there is a question about a warrant's validity or the basis for its issuance.  *   *   *

Although the Court brushes these concerns aside, a host of grave consequences can be expected to result from its decision to carve this new exception out of the exclusionary rule.  A chief consequence of today's decision will be to convey a clear and unambiguous message to magistrates that their decisions to issue warrants are now insulated from subsequent judicial review.  Creation of this new exception for good faith reliance upon a warrant implicitly tells magistrates that they need not take much care in reviewing warrant applications, since their mistakes will from now on have virtually no consequence: If their decision to issue a warrant was correct, the evidence will be admitted; if their decision was incorrect but the police relied in good faith on the warrant, the evidence will also be admitted.  Inevitably, the care and attention devoted to such an inconsequential chore will dwindle.  Although the Court is correct to note that magistrates do not share the same stake in the outcome of a criminal case as the police, they nevertheless need to appreciate that their role is of some moment in order to continue performing the important task of carefully reviewing warrant applications.  Today's decision effectively removes that incentive.

Moreover, the good faith exception will encourage police to provide only the bare minimum of information in future warrant applications. The police will now know that if they can secure a warrant, so long as the circumstances of its issuance are not "entirely unreasonable," all police conduct pursuant to that warrant will be protected from further judicial review.  The clear incentive that operated in the past to establish probable cause adequately because reviewing courts would examine the magistrate's judgment carefully, has now been so completely vitiated that the police need only show that it was not "entirely unreasonable" under the circumstances of a particular case for them to believe that the warrant they were issued was valid.  The long-run effect unquestionably will be to undermine the integrity of the warrant process.

*  *  *

IV

When the public, as it quite properly has done in the past as well as in the present, demands that those in government increase their efforts to combat crime, it is all too easy for those government officials to seek expedient solutions.  In contrast to such costly and difficult measures as building more prisons, improving law enforcement methods, or hiring more prosecutors and judges to relieve the overburdened court systems in the country's metropolitan areas, the relaxation of Fourth Amendment standards seems a tempting, costless means of meeting the public's demand for better law enforcement.  In the long run, however, we as a society pay a heavy price for such expediency, because as Justice Jackson observed, the rights guaranteed in the Fourth Amendment "are not mere second-class rights but belong in the catalog of indispensable freedoms."  Brinegar v. United States, 338 U.S. 160, 180, 69 S.Ct. 1302, 1313, 93 L.Ed. 1879 (1949) (dissenting opinion). Once lost, such rights are difficult to recover.  There is hope, however, that in time this or some later Court will restore these precious freedoms to their rightful place as a primary protection for our citizens against overreaching officialdom.

I dissent.

JUSTICE STEVENS, *  *  * dissenting.

*  *  * It is probable, though admittedly not certain, that the Court of Appeals would now conclude that the warrant *  *  * satisfied the Fourth Amendment if it were given the opportunity to reconsider the issue in the light of [Illinois v.] Gates [462 U.S. 213, 103 S.Ct. 2317, 76 L.Ed.2d 527 (1983), reprinted at page 130, infra].  *  *  * Yet if the Court's assumption is correct—if there was no probable cause—it must follow that it was "unreasonable" for the authorities to make unheralded entries into and searches of private dwellings and automobiles.  The Court's conclusion that such searches undertaken without probable cause can nevertheless be "reasonable" is totally without support in our Fourth Amendment jurisprudence.

*  *  * [I]f *  *  * there is no probable cause here, then by definition—as a matter of constitutional law—the officers' conduct was unreasonable.  *  *  *

The majority's contrary conclusion rests on the notion that it might be reasonable for a police officer to rely on a magistrate's finding. Until today that has plainly not been the law; it has been well-settled that even when a magistrate issues a warrant there is no guarantee that the ensuing search and seizure is constitutionally reasonable. *  *  *

The notion that a police officer's reliance on a magistrate's warrant is automatically appropriate is one the Framers of the Fourth Amendment would have vehemently rejected. The precise problem that the Amendment was intended to address was *the unreasonable issuance of warrants.* \* \* \* The fact that colonial officers had magisterial authorization for their conduct when they engaged in general searches surely did not make their conduct "reasonable." The Court's view that it is consistent with our Constitution to adopt a rule that it is presumptively reasonable to rely on a defective warrant is the product of constitutional amnesia.

\* \* \* I would vacate the judgment \* \* \* and remand the case to the Court of Appeals for reconsideration in light of *Gates.* \* \* \*

## NOTES

1. In Massachusetts v. Sheppard, 468 U.S. 981, 104 S.Ct. 3424, 82 L.Ed.2d 737 (1984), a companion case to *Leon,* the Court held that evidence obtained during a search pursuant to a warrant should have been admitted where the judge issuing the warrant incorrectly assured the officer that he had modified the warrant form to incorporate by reference the list of items to be searched for. Although the warrant may have been inadequate for failure to specify the items for which the officers could search, see Part 3 of Chapter 3, infra, the officer reasonably believed it was valid.

The "good faith" exception was extended to warrantless searches made pursuant to an invalid statute in Illinois v. Krull, 480 U.S. 340, 107 S.Ct. 1160, 94 L.Ed.2d 364 (1987). A Chicago police officer made a warrantless inspection of a junkyard, believing that the Illinois statute authorizing such inspections was valid. But the statute authorizing inspections of this sort was later held to be invalid. Nevertheless, the Supreme Court held, the evidence was admissible because of the officer's reliance on the statute. This extended *Leon* to at least certain searches conducted without warrants. *Leon's* analysis, Justice Blackmun explained for the majority in *Krull,* indicated a *Leon*-like exception covering the facts before it should be recognized:

> The application of the exclusionary rule to suppress evidence obtained by an officer acting in objectively reasonable reliance on a statute would have as little deterrent effect on the officer's actions as would the exclusion of evidence when an officer acts in objectively reasonable reliance on a warrant. Unless a statute is clearly unconstitutional, an officer cannot be expected to question the judgment of the legislature that passed the law.
>
> \* \* \*
>
> Any difference between our holding in *Leon* and our holding in the instant case \* \* \* must rest on a difference between the effect of the exclusion of evidence on judicial officers and the effect of the exclusion on legislators. \* \* \* We noted in *Leon* as an initial matter that the exclusionary rule was aimed at deterring police misconduct. Thus, legislators, like judicial officers, are not the focus of the rule. \* \* \*
>
> There is no evidence suggesting that Congress or state legislatures have enacted a significant number of statutes permitting warrantless administrative searches violative of the Fourth Amendment. \* \* \* Thus, we are given no basis for believing that legislators are inclined to subvert their oaths and the Fourth Amendment and that "lawlessness among these actors requires application of the extreme sanction of exclusion." \* \* \* There is nothing to indicate that applying the exclusionary rule to evidence seized pursuant to [an invalid] statute prior to the declaration of its invalidity will act as a significant, additional deterrent.

Moreover, to the extent that application of the exclusionary rule could provide some incremental deterrent, that possible benefit must be weighed against the "substantial social costs exacted by the exclusionary rule." When we indulge in such weighing, we are convinced that applying the exclusionary rule in this context is unjustified.

480 U.S. at 352–53, 107 S.Ct. at 1169, 94 L.Ed.2d at 376–77. But, the Court continued, the *Krull* exception is subject to certain constraints:

A statute cannot support objectively reasonable reliance if, in passing the statute, the legislature wholly abandoned its responsibility to enact constitutional laws. Nor can a law enforcement officer be said to have acted in good-faith reliance upon a statute if its provisions are such that a reasonable officer should have known that the statute was unconstitutional. As we emphasized in *Leon*, the standard of reasonableness we adopt is an objective one; the standard does not turn on the subjective good faith of individual officers.

480 U.S. at 355, 107 S.Ct. at 1170, 94 L.Ed.2d at 378–79.

Turning to the case before it, the majority concluded that any such defects as existed in the Illinois statute were not so obvious that an objectively reasonable police officer would have realized the statute was unconstitutional. The officer "relied, in objective good faith, on a statute that appeared legitimately to allow a warrantless administrative search of [Krull's] business," and the evidentiary products of his actions were therefore admissible against Krull. 480 U.S. at 366, 107 S.Ct. at 1176, 94 L.Ed.2d at 382. The majority assumed that the officer had acted within the scope of the statute, but indicated that on remand whether this assumption was correct could properly be examined:

At this juncture, we decline the State's invitation to recognize an exception for an officer who erroneously but in good faith believes he is acting within the scope of a statute. * * * [S]uch a ruling * * * does not follow inexorably from today's decision. As our opinion makes clear, the question whether the exclusionary rule is applicable in a particular context depends significantly upon the actors who are making the relevant decision that the rule is designed to influence. The answer to this question might well be different when police officers act outside the scope of a statute, albeit in good faith. In that context, the relevant actors are not legislators or magistrates, but police officers who concededly are "engaged in the often competitive enterprise of ferreting out crime."

480 U.S. at 360 n. 16, 107 S.Ct. at 1175 n. 16, 94 L.Ed.2d at 382 n. 16.

Justice O'Connor, joined by Justices Brennan, Marshall and Stevens, dissented:

I see a powerful historical basis for the exclusion of evidence gathered pursuant to a search authorized by an unconstitutional statute. Statutes authorizing unreasonable searches were the core concern of the Framers of the Fourth Amendment. * * * [H]istory also supplies the evidence that *Leon* demanded for the proposition that the relevant state actors, here legislators, might pose a threat to the values embodied in the Fourth Amendment. * * * [T]he history of the Amendment suggests that legislative abuse was precisely the evil the Fourth Amendment was intended to eliminate. In stark contrast, the Framers did not fear that judicial officers, the state actors at issue in *Leon*, posed a serious threat to Fourth Amendment values. * * * The distinction * * * is sound. * * * A judicial officer's unreasonable authorization of a search affects one person at a time; a legislature's unreasonable authorization of searches may affect thousands or millions * * *. Certainly the latter poses a greater threat to liberty. * * * [Moreover,] [l]egislators by virtue of their political roles are more often subjected to the political pressures that may threaten Fourth Amendment values than are judicial officers.

Finally, * * * [p]roviding legislatures a grace period during which the police may freely perform unreasonable searches in order to convict those who might have otherwise escaped creates a positive incentive to promulgate unconstitutional laws. * * * [I]t cannot be said that there is no reason to fear that a particular legislature might yield to the temptation offered by the Court's good faith exception.

480 U.S. at 362–66, 107 S.Ct. at 1174–76, 94 L.Ed.2d at 383–86 (O'Connor, J., dissenting).

2. A number of efforts have been made to enact legislation providing for "good faith" exceptions to various exclusionary rules. On the federal level, numerous legislative proposals have been made but none have been enacted into law. President Bush, for example, sent Congress a proposed "Comprehensive Violent Crime Control Act of 1989." Title V, called the "Exclusionary Rule Reform Act of 1989," would add the following section to title 18 of the United States Code:

§ 3508. Admissibility of evidence obtained by search or seizure

(a) EVIDENCE OBTAINED BY OBJECTIVELY REASONABLE SEARCH OR SEIZURE.—Evidence which is obtained as a result of a search or seizure shall not be excluded in a proceeding in a court of the United States on the ground that the search or seizure was in violation of the fourth amendment to the Constitution of the United States, if the search or seizure was carried out in circumstances justifying an objectively reasonable belief that it was in conformity with the fourth amendment. The fact that evidence was obtained pursuant to and within the scope of a warrant constitutes prima facie evidence of the existence of such circumstances.

(b) EVIDENCE NOT EXCLUDABLE BY STATUTE OR RULE.—Evidence shall not be excluded in a proceeding in a court of the United States on the ground that it was obtained in violation of a statute, an administrative rule or regulation, or a rule of procedure unless exclusion is expressly authorized by statute or by a rule prescribed by the Supreme Court pursuant to statutory authority.

A Draft of Proposed Legislation Entitled The "Comprehensive Violent Crime Control Act of 1989," H.R.Doc. No. 101–73, 101st Cong., 1st Sess. (1989). The substance of this proposal was introduced. See S. 87, 101st Cong. 1st Sess. (1989). See also, H.R. 3119, 101st Cong. 1st Sess. Title III (1989).

Some state legislatures have acted. Colorado, for example, passed the following statute in 1981:

16–3–308. Evidence—admissibility * * *.

(1) Evidence which is otherwise admissible in a criminal proceeding shall not be suppressed by the trial court if the court determines that the evidence was seized by a peace officer * * * as a result of a good faith mistake or of a technical violation.

(2) As used in subsection (1) of this section:

(a) "Good faith mistake" means a reasonable judgmental error concerning the existence of facts which if true would be sufficient to constitute probable cause.

(b) "Technical violation" means a reasonable good faith reliance upon a statute which is later ruled unconstitutional, a warrant which is later invalidated due to a good faith mistake, or a court precedent which is later overruled.

1981 Colo.Sess.Laws, ch. 188, p. 922, § 1, codified as Colo.Rev.Stat. § 16–3–308. See also, Ariz.Rev.Stat. § 13–3925.

3. In United States v. Calandra, 414 U.S. 338, 94 S.Ct. 613, 38 L.Ed.2d 561 (1974), the Supreme Court declined to extend the Fourth Amendment exclusionary rule to grand jury proceedings. The court below had held that Calandra need not answer certain questions it was likely he would be asked by a grand jury if those questions were based upon evidence the court had determined to have been obtained in violation of Calandra's Fourth Amendment rights. Reversing, the Supreme Court stressed that applying the exclusionary rule in this context might well delay and impede grand jury investigations. Further, any increase in deterrence of police misconduct would be "speculative and undoubtedly minimal ∗ ∗ ∗." 414 U.S. at 349–50, 94 S.Ct. at 620–21, 38 L.Ed. 2d 572–73.

4. An exception for evidence offered to impeach a testifying defendant was developed prior to *Mapp*. In Walder v. United States, 347 U.S. 62, 74 S.Ct. 354, 98 L.Ed. 503 (1954), Walder took the witness stand and denied the narcotics sales for which he was being tried. He further, still on direct examination, denied ever selling or illegally possessing narcotics. The government was then permitted to ask Walder whether on a prior occasion heroin capsules had not been seized from his possession and, when he denied this, to prove that in fact heroin had been found in a search of Walder's home several years earlier. This heroin had been suppressed in an earlier prosecution on the ground that it was obtained in an illegal search and seizure. The trial judge instructed the jury that the evidence of Walder's prior possession of heroin was not to be considered as tending to prove his guilt of the offenses for which he was on trial, but rather solely as bearing upon his credibility as a witness. He was convicted. The Supreme Court affirmed. After noting that a defendant "must be free to deny all the elements of the case against him without thereby giving leave to the Government to introduce ∗ ∗ ∗ evidence illegally secured," the Court concluded that the exclusionary rule should not be applied so as to permit a defendant to resort to perjurious testimony to support his credibility without giving the government an opportunity to challenge that testimony by means of even illegally seized evidence. 347 U.S. at 65, 74 S.Ct. at 346, 98 L.Ed.2d at 507. *Walder* was widely regarded as permitting the use of illegally obtained evidence to impeach a defendant who took the witness stand at trial, but only if the defendant went beyond denying guilt of the offenses charged and testified to "collateral matters." There was substantial doubt, however, that this exception survived Mapp v. Ohio and subsequent cases applying the exclusionary rule with increased rigor and enthusiasm.

In a series of cases beginning with Harris v. New York, 401 U.S. 222, 91 S.Ct. 643, 28 L.Ed.2d 1 (1971), the Supreme Court made clear that the impeachment exception is not only alive and well but has grown. Evidence seized in violation of a defendant's Fourth Amendment rights can be used for impeachment if he takes the stand at trial, United States v. Havens, 446 U.S. 620, 100 S.Ct. 1912, 64 L.Ed.2d 559 (1980), and at least some illegally obtained confessions can be used for impeachment, Harris v. New York, supra; Oregon v. Hass, 420 U.S. 714, 95 S.Ct. 1215, 43 L.Ed.2d 570 (1975). The defendant in *Harris* was impeached concerning matters not "collateral" but "bearing more directly [than was the case in *Walder*] on the crimes charged," but the Court found that this created "no difference in principle." 401 U.S. at 225, 91 S.Ct. at 645, 28

L.Ed.2d at 4. Thus the requirement that the defendant testify to matters "collateral" to guilt or innocence is eroded, if not eliminated. Nor is the impeachment exception limited to evidence that contradicts statements made on direct examination. In United States v. Havens, supra, the Court held that illegally seized evidence could be used to contradict a defendant's testimony on cross examination, as long as that testimony was in response to questions "plainly within the scope of the defendant's direct examination." 446 U.S. at 627, 100 S.Ct. at 1916, 64 L.Ed.2d at 566.

In support of the revitalized impeachment exception, the Court's majority has stressed the offensiveness of permitting defendants to give possibly perjurious testimony, the fact that the evidence to contradict this testimony satisfied legal standards of "trustworthiness," and the purely "speculative" nature of the possibility that the exception will encourage impermissible law enforcement conduct:

> Assuming that the exclusionary rule has a deterrent effect on proscribed police conduct, sufficient deterrence flows when the evidence in question is made unavailable to the prosecution in its case in chief.

Harris v. New York, supra, 401 U.S. at 225, 91 S.Ct. at 645, 28 L.Ed.2d at 4, "reaffirmed" in United States v. Havens, supra, 446 U.S. at 627, 100 S.Ct. at 1917, 64 L.Ed.2d at 566. Dissenters have urged that the impeachment exception "will seriously undermine the achievement of [the exclusionary rule's deterrent] objective," and is inconsistent with the exclusionary rule's objective of preserving the courts from the taint of aiding and abetting the law-breaking police officer. Harris v. New York, supra, 401 U.S. at 232, 91 S.Ct. at 649, 28 L.Ed.2d at 8–9 (Brennan, J., dissenting). The majority's approach has been described as one of simply declaring, on a case-by-case basis and without evidence, that "so much exclusion is enough to deter police misconduct," and as hardly conforming to "the disciplined analytical method * * * through which judges endeavor to formulate or derive principles of decision that can be applied consistently and predictably." United States v. Havens, supra, 446 U.S. at 633–34, 100 S.Ct. at 1920, 64 L.Ed.2d at 570 (Brennan, J., dissenting).

In Michigan v. Harvey, ___ U.S. ___, 110 S.Ct. 1176, 108 L.Ed.2d 293 (1990), the Court held by a 5 to 4 vote that a confession could be used to impeach a testifying defendant if it was obtained in violation of the Sixth Amendment holding in Michigan v. Jackson, 475 U.S. 625, 106 S.Ct. 1404, 89 L.Ed.2d 631 (1986), discussed at page 525, infra. Justice Stevens, writing for the four dissenters, argued that the requirement of exclusion under the Sixth Amendment was a part of the constitutional right itself and therefore barred the use of evidence even for impeachment use. ___ U.S. at ___, 110 S.Ct. at 1186, 108 L.Ed.2d at 309 (Stevens, J., dissenting). The *Harvey* majority stressed that *Jackson* applied a *Miranda* -like prophylactic rule designed to discourage police officers from badgering a defendant into waiving his previously-invoked right to counsel. Under *Jackson,* confessions are sometimes rendered inadmissible in order to discourage certain police conduct even though the defendants' waivers are, on their facts, sufficiently voluntary and intelligent to meet Sixth Amendment standards. The *Harvey* Court left open the possibility that a confession might be inadmissible even for impeachment if it was subject to the Sixth Amendment right to counsel and that right was violated because the defendant's waiver of counsel was ineffective because he had made no voluntary and intelligent waiver of counsel. In such a situation, the case might present a violation of "the 'core value' of the Sixth Amendment's constitutional guarantee," and render the confession inadmissible for all purposes. ___ U.S. at ___, 110 S.Ct. at 1182, 108 L.Ed.2d at 304–05.

The Court's continuing insistence that the impeachment exception be limited to situations in which "the trustworthiness of the evidence satisfies legal standards," Harris v. New York, supra, 401 U.S. at 224, 91 S.Ct. at 645, 28 L.Ed.2d at 4; Oregon v. Hass, supra, 420 U.S. at 722, 95 S.Ct. at 1221, 43 L.Ed.2d at 577, has resulted in some limitation of the exception. In Mincy v. Arizona, 437 U.S. 385, 98 S.Ct. 2408, 57 L.Ed.2d 290 (1978), the state had been permitted to impeach Mincy with a statement obtained while Mincy, undergoing medical treatment for a serious gunshot wound, was wavering back and forth into consciousness and despite his repeated requests that interrogation be delayed until he could obtain legal counsel. This confession was held to be involuntary and Due Process was violated by even its use for impeachment at the defendant's trial. 437 U.S. at 402, 98 S.Ct. at 2418, 57 L.Ed.2d at 306.

5. The Supreme Court has refused to expand the impeachment exception into one that permits use of unconstitutionally obtained evidence to rebut defense evidence in general. In James v. Illinois, ___ U.S. ___, 110 S.Ct. 648, 107 L.Ed.2d 676 (1990), James was tried for murder. Witnesses described the perpetrator as having "reddish" hair, worn shoulder length in a slicked-back "butter" style. At trial, James' hair was black and worn in a "natural" style. He had been arrested, however, sitting under a hair dryer at his mother's beauty parlor; his hair was black and curly. In response to questions, he reported that his hair had previously been reddish-brown, long, and combed straight back and that he had gone to the beauty parlor to have his hair dyed black and curled to change his appearance. Upon proof that the arrest was unreasonable, the trial court suppressed his statements. James himself did not testify at trial, but the defense introduced the testimony of a James' family friend, Jewel Henderson, that on the morning of the offense, she had taken James to school and at that time his hair was black. After determining that James' statements had been made voluntarily, the trial court permitted them to be introduced to impeach the credibility of Henderson's testimony. The Illinois Supreme Court affirmed, holding that the impeachment exception ought to be expanded to allow the prosecution to introduce illegally obtained evidence to impeach the testimony of defense witnesses other than the defendant himself.

The Supreme Court reversed, reasoning that the balancing approach of *Walder* and its progeny did not support this expansion of the exception. The expansion might deter some perjurious testimony, the Court conceded, but it would also discourage defendants from producing even legitimate defenses. Nondefendant witnesses can often not be "controlled" by defense counsel, so calling them might often accidentally result in rendering impeachment testimony admissible. Defendants, then, would refrain from presenting defense testimony even where it was legitimate. ___ U.S. at ___, 110 S.Ct. at 653–54, 107 L.Ed.2d at 685–86. Moreover, law enforcement officers, once they learned of an expanded exception, would have a significant incentive to proceed in violation of suspects' rights because the increased use that might be made of the fruits of their actions would make such activity worthwhile. Thus the proposed expansion would significantly weaken the exclusionary rule's deterrent effect on police misconduct. ___ U.S. at ___, 110 S.Ct. at 654–55, 107 L.Ed.2d at 686–87.

Four members of the Court disagreed. The impact of an expanded exception on legitimate defense cases, Justice Kennedy argued, could be minimized by limiting impeachment use of illegally obtained evidence to situations in which there is "direct conflict" between the evidence and the testimony of a nondefendant witness, "which is to say where, within reason, the witness' testimony and the excluded testimony cannot both be true." ___ U.S. at ___, 110 S.Ct. at 658, 107 L.Ed.2d at 691–92 (Kennedy, J., dissenting). Moreover, he acknowledged that the prosecution might properly be limited to impeaching assertions made by nondefendant witnesses during their direct examinations. ___ U.S. at ___, 110 S.Ct. at 660, 107 L.Ed.2d at 693. In addition:

> The potential for harm to the truth-seeking process resulting from the majority's new rule in fact will be greater than if the defendant himself had testified. It is natural for jurors to be skeptical of self-serving testimony by the defendant. Testimony by a witness said to be independent has the greater potential to deceive. And if a defense witness can present false testimony with impunity, the jurors may find the rest of the prosecution's case suspect, for ineffective and artificial cross-examination will be viewed as a real weakness in the State's case. Jurors will assume that if the prosecution had any proof the statement was false, it would make the proof known. The majority does more than deprive the prosecution of evidence. The State must also suffer the introduction of false testimony and appear to bolster the falsehood by its silence.

___ U.S. ___, 110 S.Ct. at 658, 107 L.Ed.2d at 691. Officers are unlikely to decide to engage in illegal behavior because the fruits of such actions could be used to impeach defense witnesses: "It is unrealistic to say that the decision to make an illegal search turns on a precise calculation of the possibilities of rebuttal at some future trial." ___ U.S. at ___, 110 S.Ct. at 660, 107 L.Ed.2d at 694.

6. Another exception to the exclusionary sanctions attaching to violations of federal constitutional rights was recognized in Nix v. Williams, 467 U.S. 431, 104 S.Ct. 2501, 81 L.Ed.2d 377 (1984). Williams was convicted of the murder of a young girl. Following his first trial, the Supreme Court determined that he had been interrogated in violation of his Sixth and Fourteenth Amendments right to counsel and consequently the statements he made during this interrogation had been improperly admitted into evidence at his trial. Brewer v. Williams, 430 U.S. 387, 97 S.Ct. 1232, 51 L.Ed.2d 424 (1977), discussed at page 523, infra. In addition, however, Williams had revealed to the interrogating officers the location of the victim's body. Using this information, officers found the body. At Williams' second trial, the prosecution did not offer into evidence Williams' incriminating statements nor did it attempt to show that Williams had directed police to the body. It did, however, offer evidence of the condition of the body as found, articles and photographs of clothing found on the body, and the results of medical and chemical tests performed on the body. In support of its offer of this evidence, the prosecution showed that at the time of Williams' interrogation a search for the body was underway and that 200 volunteers were involved. This search was called off when Williams began to cooperate with law enforcement officers. But, the state's witness testified, had the search not been called off it would have resulted in discovery of the body after three to five additional hours of searching. The trial judge admitted the prosecution's offered evidence on the ground that the prosecution had shown that if Williams had not been improperly interrogated, the victim's body would nevertheless have been found and therefore evidence resulting from discovery of the body was admissible. Williams was then convicted and later sought invalidation of that conviction in federal habeas corpus litigation.

The Supreme Court found no violation of Williams' federal constitutional rights in the use of the evidence at issue. All nine members of the Court agreed that the exclusionary sanction attaching to the violation of Williams' Sixth and Fourteenth Amendments right to counsel is subject to an "ultimate or inevitable discovery" exception:

> [W]hen * * * the evidence in question would inevitably have been discovered without reference to the police error or misconduct, there is no nexus

[between the error and the evidence] sufficient to provide a taint and the evidence is admissible.

467 U.S. at 448, 104 S.Ct. at 2511, 81 L.Ed.2d at 390. The rationale for this exception, Chief Justice Burger explained for the Court, is the same as that for the "independent source" rule discussed in *Wong Sun.* The need to deter unlawful police conduct is sufficiently met if police who have engaged in misconduct are put in the same position they would have been in had the misconduct not occurred. This need does not, however, justify putting law enforcement in a worse position than it would have been in had no misconduct been committed. Society's need for reliable evidence of offenders' guilt, on the other hand, strongly argues against any aspect of the exclusionary rules that would put law enforcement agencies in a worse position than they would have been in had misconduct not taken place. Both the "inevitable discovery" exception and the "independent source" doctrine serve the purpose of assuring that misbehaving law enforcement agencies are not put in any worse position than they would have been in had they avoided the misbehavior. While the case involved the exclusionary penalty for a violation of the Sixth Amendment right to counsel, the Court's discussion strongly suggests that identical exceptions will be recognized with regard to other exclusionary rules, including that adopted in *Mapp* for violations of the Fourth Amendment.

Apparently all members of the Court also agreed that the inevitable discovery exception should not be qualified by requiring the prosecution, as a condition of invoking it, to show that the officers acted without "bad faith." Such a condition, the Court reasoned, would in no way further the purpose of the inevitable discovery exception. The members of the Court did split, however, on the appropriate burden of proof. Justice Brennan, joined by Justice Marshall, reasoned:

> The inevitable discovery exception necessarily implicates a hypothetical finding that differs in kind from the factual finding that precedes applica- tion of the independent source rule. To ensure that this hypothetical finding is narrowly confined to circumstances that are functionally equiva- lent to an independent source, and to protect fully the fundamental rights served by the exclusionary rule, I would require clear and convincing evidence before concluding that the government had met its burden of proof on this issue.

467 U.S. at 459, 104 S.Ct. at 2517, 81 L.Ed.2d at 397 (Brennan, J., dissenting). The Court, however, rejected this:

> "[I]nevitable discovery involves no speculative elements but focuses on demonstrated historical facts capable of ready verification or impeachment and does not require a departure from the usual burden of proof [by a preponderance of the evidence] at suppression hearings."

467 U.S. at 444 n. 5, 104 S.Ct. at 2509 n. 5, 81 L.Ed.2d at 388 n. 5.

# Chapter 2

# CONSTITUTIONAL DOCTRINES RELATING TO LAW ENFORCEMENT CONDUCT

*Analysis*

---

Exclusionary sanctions of the sort considered in Chapter 1 come into operation, of course, only if there has been a violation of the underlying legal requirements. In constitutional terms, challenges to law enforcement conduct usually rest on provisions guaranteeing protection from compelled self-incrimination, rights to privacy and to be free from unreasonable searches and seizures, a right to the assistance of counsel, and general rights to due process of law. The major federal provisions and illustrative state provisions are set out in the Editors' Introduction at the beginning of Part One of these materials.

This chapter develops the basic content of the major federal constitutional provisions. Part A provides an opportunity to compare several of these provisions as they might apply to the extraction of a sample of a suspect's blood. Part B then focuses upon the Fourth Amendment. The Fifth Amendment privilege against compelled self-incrimination applies primarily to law enforcement efforts to obtain confessions and other self-incriminating admissions; this is the subject of Chapter 7, and the Fifth Amendment privilege is considered at length in that chapter.

## A.  SCOPE OF THE BASIC DOCTRINES

Before considering in detail the impact of the major doctrines, it is important to consider the framework for analyzing situations under these doctrines.  The principal case in this Section addresses the relevance of these doctrines to a single police activity—the extraction from a suspect of a sample of the suspect's blood.  It is important to distinguish two matters.  First, what are the "threshold" issues that determine whether the doctrine applies?  Second, *if* the doctrine applies, what requirements does it impose upon law enforcement conduct?

## SCHMERBER v. CALIFORNIA

Supreme Court of the United States, 1966.
384 U.S. 757, 86 S.Ct. 1826, 16 L.Ed.2d 908.

MR. JUSTICE BRENNAN delivered the opinion of the Court.

Petitioner was convicted in Los Angeles Municipal Court of the criminal offense of driving an automobile while under the influence of intoxicating liquor.  He had been arrested at a hospital while receiving treatment for injuries suffered in an accident involving the automobile that he had apparently been driving.  At the direction of a police officer, a blood sample was then withdrawn from petitioner's body by a physician at the hospital.  The chemical analysis of this sample revealed a percent by weight of alcohol in his blood at the time of the offense which indicated intoxication, and the report of this analysis was admitted in evidence at the trial.  Petitioner objected to receipt of this evidence of the analysis on the ground that the blood had been withdrawn despite his refusal, on the advice of his counsel, to consent to the test.  He contended that in that circumstance the withdrawal of the blood and the admission of the analysis in evidence denied him due process of law under the Fourteenth Amendment, as well as specific guarantees of the Bill of Rights secured against the States by that Amendment:  his privilege against self-incrimination under the Fifth Amendment;  *  *  *  and his right not to be subjected to unreasonable searches and seizures in violation of the Fourth Amendment.  The Appellate Department of the California Superior Court rejected these contentions and affirmed the conviction.  In view of constitutional decisions since we last considered these issues in Breithaupt v. Abram, 352 U.S. 432, 77 S.Ct. 408, 1 L.Ed.2d 448—see Escobedo v. State of Illinois, 378 U.S. 478, 84 S.Ct. 1758, 12 L.Ed.2d 977; Malloy v. Hogan, 378 U.S. 1, 84 S.Ct. 1489, 12 L.Ed.2d 653, and Mapp v. State of Ohio, 367 U.S. 643, 81 S.Ct. 1684, 6 L.Ed.2d 1081—we granted certiorari.  382 U.S. 971, 86 S.Ct. 542, 15 L.Ed.2d 464.  We affirm.

I.

### THE DUE PROCESS CLAUSE CLAIM

[In Rochin v. California, 1952, 342 U.S. 165, 72 S.Ct. 205, 96 L.Ed. 183, officers lacking probable cause had entered Rochin's house through an open door.  Forcing open the door to Rochin's second floor room, they found Rochin partly dressed and sitting on a bed, upon which his wife was lying. When they asked about two capsules which were on a night stand next to the bed, Rochin grabbed the capsules and swallowed them despite the efforts of the three officers to prevent this. Rochin was then taken to a hospital, where a doctor forced an emetic solution through a tube into his stomach, causing him to vomit. In the vomited matter were found the two capsules which were used in evidence in his later prosecution for possession of the morphine in the capsules. The Supreme Court held that the resulting conviction violated due process:

> This is conduct that shocks the conscience. Illegally breaking into the privacy of [Rochin], the struggle to open his mouth and remove what was there, the forcible extraction of his stomach contents— this course of proceeding by agents of government to obtain evidence is bound to offend even hardened sensibilities. They are methods too close to the rack and screw to permit of constitutional differentiation.

342 U.S. at 172, 72 S.Ct. at 209–10, 96 L.Ed. at 190. Petitioner argues that *Rochin* controls here. Editors.]

*Breithaupt* was also a case in which police officers caused blood to be withdrawn from the driver of an automobile involved in an accident, and in which there was ample justification for the officer's conclusion that the driver was under the influence of alcohol. There, as here, the extraction was made by a physician in a simple, medically acceptable manner in a hospital environment. There, however, the driver was unconscious at the time the blood was withdrawn and hence had no opportunity to object to the procedure. We affirmed the conviction there resulting from the use of the test in evidence, holding that under such circumstances the withdrawal did not offend "that 'sense of justice' of which we spoke in *Rochin*." 352 U.S., at 435, 77 S.Ct. at 410. *Breithaupt* thus requires the rejection of petitioner's due process argument, and nothing in the circumstances of this case or in supervening events persuades us that this aspect of *Breithaupt* should be overruled.

II.

THE PRIVILEGE AGAINST SELF-INCRIMINATION CLAIM

*Breithaupt* summarily rejected an argument that the withdrawal of blood and the admission of the analysis report involved in that state case violated the Fifth Amendment privilege of any person not to "be compelled in any criminal case to be a witness against himself," citing Twining v. State of New Jersey, 211 U.S. 78, 29 S.Ct. 14, 53 L.Ed. 97. But that case, holding that the protections of the Fourteenth Amendment do not embrace this Fifth Amendment privilege, has been succeeded by Malloy v. Hogan, 378 U.S. 1, 8, 84 S.Ct. 1489, 1493, 12 L.Ed. 2d 653. We there held that "[t]he Fourteenth Amendment secures against state invasion the same privilege that the Fifth Amendment guarantees against federal infringement—the right of a person to remain silent unless he chooses to speak in the unfettered exercise of his own will, and to suffer no penalty * * * for such silence." We therefore must now decide whether the withdrawal of the blood and admission in evidence of the analysis involved in this case violated petitioner's privilege.  We hold that the privilege protects an accused only from being compelled to testify against himself, or otherwise provide the State with evidence of a testimonial or communicative nature,[1] and that the withdrawal of blood and use of the analysis in question in this case did not involve compulsion to these ends.

It could not be denied that in requiring petitioner to submit to the withdrawal and chemical analysis of his blood the State compelled him to submit to an attempt to discover evidence that might be used to prosecute him for a criminal offense.  He submitted only after the police officer rejected his objection and directed the physician to proceed.  The officer's direction to the physician to administer the test over petitioner's objection constituted compulsion for the purposes of the privilege.  The critical question, then, is whether petitioner was thus compelled "to be a witness against himself."

If the scope of the privilege coincided with the complex of values it helps to protect, we might be obliged to conclude that the privilege was violated.  In Miranda v. Arizona, 384 U.S. 436, at 460, 86 S.Ct. 1602, at 1620, 16 L.Ed.2d 694, at 715, the Court said of the interests protected by the privilege: "All these policies point to one overriding thought: the constitutional foundation underlying the privilege is the respect a government—state or federal—must accord to the dignity and integrity of its citizens.  To maintain a 'fair state-individual balance,' to require the government 'to shoulder the entire load,' * * * to respect the inviolability of the human personality, our accusatory system of criminal justice demands that the government seeking to punish an individual produce the evidence against him by its own independent labors, rather than by the cruel, simple expedient of compelling it from his own mouth."  The withdrawal of blood necessarily involves puncturing the skin for extraction, and the percent by weight of alcohol in that blood, as established by chemical analysis, is evidence of criminal guilt.  Compelled submission fails on one view to respect the "inviolability of the human personality."  Moreover, since it enables the State to rely on evidence forced from the accused, the compulsion violates at least one meaning of the requirement that the State procure the evidence against an accused "by its own independent labors."

As the passage in *Miranda* implicitly recognizes, however, the privilege has never been given the full scope which the values it helps to protect suggest.  History and a long line of authorities in lower courts have consistently limited its protection to situations in which the State seeks to submerge those values by obtaining the evidence against

---

[1] A dissent suggests that the report of the blood test was "testimonial" or "communicative," because the test was performed in order to obtain the testimony of others, communicating to the jury facts about petitioner's condition.  Of course, all evidence received in court is "testimonial" or "communicative" if these words are thus used.  But the Fifth Amendment relates only to acts on the part of the person to whom the privilege applies, and we use these words subject to the same limitations.  A nod or headshake is as much a "testimonial" or "communicative" act in this sense as are spoken words.  But the terms as we use them do not apply to evidence of acts noncommunicative in nature as to the person asserting the privilege, even though, as here, such acts are compelled to obtain the testimony of others.

an accused through "the cruel, simple expedient of compelling it from his own mouth. * * * In sum, the privilege is fulfilled only when the person is guaranteed the right 'to remain silent unless he chooses to speak in the unfettered exercise of his own will.'" Ibid. The leading case in this Court is Holt v. United States, 218 U.S. 245, 31 S.Ct. 2, 54 L.Ed. 1021. There the question was whether evidence was admissible that the accused, prior to trial and over his protest, put on a blouse that fitted him. It was contended that compelling the accused to submit to the demand that he model the blouse violated the privilege. Mr. Justice Holmes, speaking for the Court, rejected the argument as "based upon an extravagant extension of the 5th Amendment," and went on to say: "[T]he prohibition of compelling a man in a criminal court to be witness against himself is a prohibition of the use of physical or moral compulsion to extort communications from him, not an exclusion of his body as evidence when it may be material. The objection in principle would forbid a jury to look at a prisoner and compare his features with a photograph in proof." 218 U.S., at 252–253, 31 S.Ct., at 6.

It is clear that the protection of the privilege reaches an accused's communications, whatever form they might take, and the compulsion of responses which are also communications, for example, compliance with a subpoena to produce one's papers. Boyd v. United States, 116 U.S. 616, 6 S.Ct. 524, 29 L.Ed. 746. On the other hand, both federal and state courts have usually held that it offers no protection against compulsion to submit to fingerprinting, photographing, or measurements, to write or speak for identification, to appear in court, to stand, to assume a stance, to walk, or to make a particular gesture. The distinction which has emerged, often expressed in different ways, is that the privilege is a bar against compelling "communications" or "testimony," but that compulsion which makes a suspect or accused the source of "real or physical evidence" does not violate it.

Although we agree that this distinction is a helpful framework for analysis, we are not to be understood to agree with past applications in all instances. There will be many cases in which such a distinction is not readily drawn. Some tests seemingly directed to obtain "physical evidence," for example, lie detector tests measuring changes in body function during interrogation, may actually be directed to eliciting responses which are essentially testimonial. To compel a person to submit to testing in which an effort will be made to determine his guilt or innocence on the basis of physiological responses, whether willed or not, is to evoke the spirit and history of the Fifth Amendment. Such situations call to mind the principle that the protection of the privilege "is as broad as the mischief against which it seeks to guard." Counselman v. Hitchcock, 142 U.S. 547, 562, 12 S.Ct. 195, 198.

In the present case, however, no such problem of application is presented. Not even a shadow of testimonial compulsion upon or enforced communication by the accused was involved either in the extraction or in the chemical analysis. Petitioner's testimonial capacities were in no way implicated; indeed, his participation, except as a donor, was irrelevant to the results of the test, which depend on chemical analysis and on that alone.[2]  Since the blood test evidence, although an incriminating product of compulsion, was neither petitioner's testimony nor evidence relating to some communicative act or writing by the petitioner, it was not inadmissible on privilege grounds.

\* \* \*

## IV.

### THE SEARCH AND SEIZURE CLAIM

In *Breithaupt*, as here, it was also contended that the chemical analysis should be excluded from evidence as the product of an unlawful search and seizure in violation of the Fourth and Fourteenth Amendments.  The Court did not decide whether the extraction of blood in that case was unlawful, but rejected the claim on the basis of Wolf v. People of State of Colorado, 338 U.S. 25, 69 S.Ct. 1359, 93 L.Ed. 1782.  That case had held that the Constitution did not require, in state prosecutions for state crimes, the exclusion of evidence obtained in violation of the Fourth Amendment's provisions.  We have since overruled *Wolf* in that respect, holding in Mapp v. Ohio, 367 U.S. 643, 81 S.Ct. 1684, 6 L.Ed.2d 1081, that the exclusionary rule adopted for federal prosecutions in Weeks v. United States, 232 U.S. 383, 34 S.Ct. 341, 58 L.Ed. 652, must also be applied in criminal prosecutions in state courts.  The question is squarely presented therefore, whether the chemical analysis introduced in evidence in this case should have been excluded as the product of an unconstitutional search and seizure.

The overriding function of the Fourth Amendment is to protect personal privacy and dignity against unwarranted intrusion by the State.  In *Wolf* we recognized "[t]he security of one's privacy against arbitrary intrusion by the police" as being "at the core of the Fourth Amendment" and "basic to a free society."  338 U.S., at 27, 69 S.Ct. at 1361.  We reaffirmed that broad view of the Amendment's purpose in applying the federal exclusionary rule to the States in *Mapp*.

The values protected by the Fourth Amendment thus substantially overlap those the Fifth Amendment helps to protect.  History and precedent have required that we today reject the claim that the Self-Incrimination Clause of the Fifth Amendment requires the human body in all circumstances to be held inviolate against state expeditions seeking evidence of crime.  But if compulsory administration of a blood test does not implicate the Fifth Amendment, it plainly involves the broadly conceived reach of a search and seizure under the Fourth Amendment.  That Amendment expressly provides that "[t]he right of

---

[2] This conclusion would not necessarily govern had the State tried to show that the accused had incriminated himself when told that he would have to be tested.  Such incriminating evidence may be an unavoidable by-product of the compulsion to take the test, especially for an individual who fears the extraction or opposes it on religious grounds.  If it wishes to compel persons to submit to such attempts to discover evidence, the State may have to forego the advantage of any *testimonial* products of administering the test—products which would fall within the privilege.  Indeed, there may be circumstances in which the pain, danger, or severity of an operation would almost inevitably cause a person to prefer confession to undergoing the "search," and nothing we say today should be taken as establishing the permissibility of compulsion in that case.  But no such situation is presented in this case. \* \* \*

the people to be secure in their *persons*, houses, papers, and effects, against unreasonable searches and seizures, shall not be violated * * * ." (Emphasis added.) It could not reasonably be argued, and indeed respondent does not argue, that the administration of the blood test in this case was free of the constraints of the Fourth Amendment. Such testing procedures plainly constitute searches of "persons," and depend antecedently upon seizures of "persons," within the meaning of that Amendment.

Because we are dealing with intrusions into the human body rather than with state interferences with property relationships or private papers—"houses, papers, and effects"—we write on a clean slate. Limitations on the kinds of property which may be seized under warrant, as distinct from the procedures for search and the permissible scope of search, are not instructive in this context. We begin with the assumption that once the privilege against self-incrimination has been found not to bar compelled intrusions into the body for blood to be analyzed for alcohol content, the Fourth Amendment's proper function is to constrain, not against all intrusions as such, but against intrusions which are not justified in the circumstances, or which are made in an improper manner. In other words, the questions we must decide in this case are whether the police were justified in requiring petitioner to submit to the blood test, and whether the means and procedures employed in taking his blood respected relevant Fourth Amendment standards of reasonableness.

In this case, as will often be true when charges of driving under the influence of alcohol are pressed, these questions arise in the context of an arrest made by an officer without a warrant. Here, there was plainly probable cause for the officer to arrest petitioner and charge him with driving an automobile while under the influence of intoxicating liquor. The police officer who arrived at the scene shortly after the accident smelled liquor on petitioner's breath, and testified that petitioner's eyes were "bloodshot, watery, sort of a glassy appearance." The officer saw petitioner again at the hospital, within two hours of the accident. There he noticed similar symptoms of drunkenness. He thereupon informed petitioner "that he was under arrest and that he was entitled to the services of an attorney, and that he could remain silent, and that anything that he told me would be used against him in evidence."

While early cases suggest that there is an unrestricted "right on the part of the government always recognized under English and American law, to search the person of the accused when legally arrested, to discover and seize the fruits or evidences of crime," Weeks v. United States, 232 U.S. 383, 392, 34 S.Ct. 341, 344, 58 L.Ed.2d 652; People v. Chiagles, 237 N.Y. 193, 142 N.E. 583 (1923) (Cardozo, J.), the mere fact of a lawful arrest does not end our inquiry. The suggestion of these cases apparently rests on two factors—first, there may be more immediate danger of concealed weapons or of destruction of evidence under the direct control of the accused, United States v. Rabinowitz, 339 U.S. 56, 72–73, 70 S.Ct. 430, 437, 438, 94 L.Ed. 653 (Frankfurter, J., dissenting); second, once a search of the arrested person for weapons is permitted, it would be both impractical and unnecessary to enforcement of the Fourth Amendment's purpose to attempt to confine the search to those objects alone. People v. Chiagles, 237 N.Y., at 197–198, 142 N.E., at 584. Whatever the validity of these considerations in general, they have little applicability with respect to searches involving intrusions beyond the body's surface. The interests in human dignity and privacy which the Fourth Amendment protects forbid any such intrusions on the mere chance that desired evidence might be obtained. In the absence of a clear indication that in fact such evidence will be found, these fundamental human interests require law officers to suffer the risk that such evidence may disappear unless there is an immediate search.

Although the facts which established probable cause to arrest in this case also suggested the required relevance and likely success of a test of petitioner's blood for alcohol, the question remains whether the arresting officer was permitted to draw these inferences himself, or was required instead to procure a warrant before proceeding with the test. Search warrants are ordinarily required for searches of dwellings, and absent an emergency, no less could be required where intrusions into the human body are concerned. The requirement that a warrant be obtained is a requirement that inferences to support the search "be drawn by a neutral and detached magistrate instead of being judged by the officer engaged in the often competitive enterprise of ferreting out crime." Johnson v. United States, 333 U.S. 10, 13–14, 68 S.Ct. 367, 369, 92 L.Ed. 436; see also Aguilar v. State of Texas, 378 U.S. 108, 110–111, 84 S.Ct. 1509, 1511, 1512, 12 L.Ed.2d 723. The importance of informed, detached and deliberate determinations of the issue whether or not to invade another's body in search of evidence of guilt is indisputable and great.

The officer in the present case, however, might reasonably have believed that he was confronted with an emergency, in which the delay necessary to obtain a warrant, under the circumstances, threatened "the destruction of evidence," Preston v. United States, 376 U.S. 364, 367, 84 S.Ct. 881, 883, 11 L.Ed.2d 777. We are told that the percentage of alcohol in the blood begins to diminish shortly after drinking stops, as the body functions to eliminate it from the system. Particularly in a case such as this, where time had to be taken to bring the accused to a hospital and to investigate the scene of the accident, there was no time to seek out a magistrate and secure a warrant. Given these special facts, we conclude that the attempt to secure evidence of blood-alcohol content in this case was an appropriate incident to petitioner's arrest.

Similarly, we are satisfied that the test chosen to measure petitioner's blood-alcohol level was a reasonable one. Extraction of blood samples for testing is a highly effective means of determining the degree to which a person is under the influence of alcohol. See Breithaupt v. Abram, 352 U.S., at 436, n. 3, 77 S.Ct. at 410, 1 L.Ed.2d 448. Such tests are a commonplace in these days of periodic physical examinations and experience with them teaches that the quantity of blood extracted is minimal, and that for most people the procedure involves virtually no risk, trauma, or pain. Petitioner is not one of the few who on grounds of fear, concern for health, or religious scruple might prefer some other means of testing, such as the "breathalyzer" test petitioner refused.   *   *   *   We need not decide whether such wishes would have to be respected.

Finally, the record shows that the test was performed in a reasonable manner.  Petitioner's blood was taken by a physician in a hospital environment according to accepted medical practices.  We are thus not presented with the serious questions which would arise if a search involving use of a medical technique, even of the most rudimentary sort, were made by other than medical personnel or in other than a medical environment—for example, if it were administered by police in the privacy of the stationhouse.  To tolerate searches under these conditions might be to invite an unjustified element of personal risk of infection and pain.

We thus conclude that the present record shows no violation of petitioner's right under the Fourth and Fourteenth Amendments to be free of unreasonable searches and seizures.  It bears repeating, however, that we reach this judgment only on the facts of the present record. The integrity of an individual's person is a cherished value of our society.  That we today hold that the Constitution does not forbid the States minor intrusions into an individual's body under stringently limited conditions in no way indicates that it permits more substantial intrusions, or intrusions under other conditions.

Affirmed.

### NOTES

1.  Applying the requirement that compelled conduct be "testimonial" has continued to be troublesome.  In United States v. Wade, 388 U.S. 218, 87 S.Ct. 1926, 18 L.Ed.2d 1149 (1967), the Court held that the Fifth Amendment was not invoked when Wade was required to wear strips of tape on his face similar to those worn by the perpetrator, to appear in a lineup, and to say the words uttered by the robber—"put the money in the bag."  Wade was required, the Court reasoned, only to use his voice to demonstrate its physical characteristics. 388 U.S. at 222–23, 87 S.Ct. at 1930, 18 L.Ed.2d at 1154–55.  See also, United States v. Dionisio, 410 U.S. 1, 93 S.Ct. 764, 35 L.Ed.2d 67 (1973) (Fifth Amendment not implicated by subponea directing suspect to appear at prosecutor's office and read into a recording device from a transcript); United States v. Mara, 410 U.S. 19, 93 S.Ct. 774, 35 L.Ed.2d 99 (1973) (Fifth Amendment not implicated by compulsion to prepare and provide exemplar of handwriting or printing).

In South Dakota v. Neville, 459 U.S. 553, 103 S.Ct. 916, 74 L.Ed.2d 748 (1983), the Court acknowledged that distinguishing communications from non-testimonial evidence sometimes presented difficulty.  It found "considerable force" in the argument that a suspect's refusal to give a blood or breath test is a physical act and not a testimonial communication, but did not resolve the issue. 459 U.S. at 561, 103 S.Ct. at 921–22, 74 L.Ed.2d at 757.

The Court discussed the Fifth Amendment requirement that a compelled act be "testimonial" and the rationale for this demand in Pennsylvania v. Muniz, ___ U.S. ___, 110 S.Ct. 2638, 110 L.Ed.2d 528 (1990), involving the processing—and videotaping—of a suspect arrested for driving while intoxicated.  Requiring the arrestee to speak to demonstrate the slurred nature of his speech, all justices agreed, did not involve compelled testimonial activity. "Requiring a suspect to reveal the physical manner in which he articulates words, like requiring him to reveal the physical properties of the sound produced by his voice \* \* \* does not, without more, compel him to provide a 'testimonial' response for purposes of the privilege." ___ U.S. at ___, 110 S.Ct. at 2645, 110 L.Ed.2d at 546. Having him perform sobriety tests (the "horizontal gaze nystagus" test, the "walk and turn" test and the "one leg stand" test), eight of the justices also held, did not implicate the Fifth Amendment. But asking him the date of his sixth birthday (apparently to determine if he could calculate that from his date of birth), a 5 to 4 majority concluded, did demand testimonial activity. It rejected the argument, accepted by the four dissenters, that this question simply sought a demonstration of the physiological functioning of the suspect's brain, and thus was no different from requiring him to demonstrate his ability to articulate words. Justice Brennan explained for the majority:

> We recently explained in Doe v. United States, 487 U.S. 201, 108 S.Ct. 2341, 101 L.Ed.2d 184 (1988), that "in order to be testimonial, an accused's communication must itself, explicitly or implicitly, relate a factual assertion or disclose information." Id., at 210. We reached this conclusion after addressing our reasoning in *Schmerber,* supra, and its progeny:
>
>> The Court accordingly held that the privilege was not implicated in [the line of cases beginning with *Schmerber*] because the suspect was not required "to disclose any knowledge he might have," or "to speak his guilt." *Wade,* 388 U.S., at 222–223, 87 S.Ct. at 1929–1930. It is the "extortion of information from the accused," the attempt to force him "to disclose the contents of his own mind," that implicates the Self–Incrimination Clause. . . . "Unless some attempt is made to secure a communication—written, oral or otherwise—upon which reliance is to be placed as involving (the accused's) consciousness of the facts and the operations of his mind in expressing it, the demand made upon him is not a testimonial one." 8 Wigmore § 2265, p. 386.
>
> 487 U.S., at 210–211, 108 S.Ct. at 2348.
>
> After canvassing the purposes of the privilege recognized in prior cases, we concluded that "[t]hese policies are served when the privilege is asserted to spare the accused from having to reveal, directly or indirectly, his knowledge of facts relating him to the offense or from having to share his thoughts and beliefs with the Government." Id., at 213, 108 S.Ct. at 2349.
>
> This definition of testimonial evidence reflects an awareness of the historical abuses against which the privilege against self-incrimination was aimed. "Historically, the privilege was intended to prevent the use of legal compulsion to extract from the accused a sworn communication of facts which would incriminate him. Such was the process of the ecclesiastical courts and the Star Chamber—the inquisitorial method of putting the accused upon his oath and compelling him to answer questions designed to uncover uncharged offenses, without evidence from another source. The major thrust of the policies undergirding the privilege is to prevent such compulsion." Id., at 212, 108 S.Ct. at 2348 (citations omitted). At its core, the privilege reflects our fierce "unwillingness to subject those suspected of crime to the cruel trilemma of self-accusation, perjury or contempt," that defined the operation of the Star Chamber, wherein suspects were forced to choose between revealing incriminating private thoughts and forsaking their oath by committing perjury. See United States v. Nobles, 422 U.S. 225, 233, 95 S.Ct. 2160, 2167, 45 L.Ed.2d 141 (1975) ("The Fifth Amendment

privilege against compulsory self-incrimination . . . protects 'a private inner sanctum of individual feeling and thought and proscribes state intrusion to extract self-condemnation' ").

We need not explore the outer boundaries of what is "testimonial" today, for our decision flows from the concept's core meaning. Because the privilege was designed primarily to prevent "a recurrence of the Inquisition and the Star Chamber, even if not in their stark brutality," it is evident that a suspect is "compelled . . . to be a witness against himself" at least whenever he must face the modern-day analog of the historic trilemma— either during a criminal trial where a sworn witness faces the identical three choices, or during custodial interrogation where ＊ ＊ ＊ the choices are analogous and hence raise similar concerns. Whatever else it may include, therefore, the definition of "testimonial" evidence ＊ ＊ ＊ must encompass all responses to questions that, if asked of a sworn suspect during a criminal trial, could place the suspect in the "cruel trilemma." This conclusion is consistent with our recognition in *Doe* that "[t]he vast majority of verbal statements thus will be testimonial" because "[t]here are very few instances in which a verbal statement, either oral or written, will not convey information or assert facts." 487 U.S., at 213, 108 S.Ct. at 2349. Whenever a suspect is asked for a response requiring him to communicate an express or implied assertion of fact or belief, the suspect confronts the "trilemma" of truth, falsity, or silence and hence the response (whether based on truth or falsity) contains a testimonial component.

—— U.S. at ——, 110 S.Ct. at 2646–48, 110 L.Ed.2d at 547–49.

Turning to the facts of the case, it continued:

When [the officer] asked Muniz if he knew the date of his sixth birthday and Muniz, for whatever reason, could not remember or calculate that date, he was confronted with the trilemma. By hypothesis the inherently coercive environment created by the custodial interrogation precluded the option of remaining silent. Muniz was left with the choice of incriminating himself by admitting that he did not then know the date of his sixth birthday, or answering untruthfully by reporting a date that he did not then believe to be accurate (an incorrect guess would be incriminating as well as untruthful). The content of his truthful answer supported an inference that his mental faculties were impaired, because his assertion (he did not know the date of his sixth birthday) was different from the assertion (he knew the date was (correct date)) that the trier of fact might reasonably have expected a lucid person to provide. Hence, the incriminating inference of impaired mental faculties stemmed, not just from the fact that Muniz slurred his response, but also from a testimonial aspect of that response.

—— U.S. at ——, 110 S.Ct. at 2649, 110 L.Ed.2d at 550. The Court did not reach whether asking Muniz to count out loud while performing the physical sobriety tests involved "testimonial" activity. During one test, he counted accurately and thus his responses were not incriminating. During another, he failed to count and did not argue that his silence had any "independent incriminating significance." —— U.S. at —— n. 17, 110 S.Ct. at 2651 n. 17, 110 L.Ed.2d at 553 n. 17.

2. The Fifth Amendment is violated only if compulsion to engage in testimonial and self-incriminating activity is impermissible. Many states provide under so-called "implied consent" statutes that under certain circumstances a person suspected of driving while intoxicated may be "requested" by an officer to provide a blood or breath sample but may not be forced to provide

the sample if he refuses. Such a refusal is itself often admissible against the suspect if he does not provide the requested sample. In South Dakota v. Neville, 459 U.S. 553, 103 S.Ct. 916, 74 L.Ed.2d 748 (1983), the Court held that whether or not such a refusal is "testimonial" (see note 1, supra), the Fifth Amendment does not bar use of such evidence because no "impermissible compulsion" is imposed upon the suspect. *Schmerber,* the Court observed, clearly permits a State under certain circumstances to force a person to submit to a blood test:

> Given * * * that the offer of taking a blood-alcohol test is clearly legitimate, the action becomes no *less* legitimate when the State offers a second option of refusing the test, with the attendant penalties of making that choice.

459 U.S. at 563, 103 S.Ct. at 923, 74 L.Ed.2d at 759 (emphasis in original).

3. State constitutional provisions might be construed so as to bar compulsion of even nontestimonial activity. In Hansen v. Owens, 619 P.2d 315 (Utah 1980), the Utah Supreme Court interpreted its constitutional provision (reprinted on page 61, supra) as barring the compulsion of a suspect to give examples of his handwriting. The court stressed that the state provision barred compulsion upon a person "to give evidence" and that this must have been intended to extend broader protection than the Fifth Amendment's prohibition against compelling a person "to be a witness against himself." 619 P.2d at 317. It also emphasized that the giving of a handwriting sample involves an "affirmative act." Id. Later the same year, however, it held that the state provision did not bar the taking of hair samples from a sexual assault suspect, reasoning that the taking of hair samples involved no "affirmative act" on the part of the suspect. State v. McCumber, 622 P.2d 353, 358 (Utah 1980).

But in American Fork City v. Crosgrove, 701 P.2d 1069 (Utah 1985), the Utah court considered the admissibility of evidence resulting from a breathalyzer test to which Crosgrove submitted only when told that his refusal could result in loss of his driver's license. Under *Hansen's* "affirmative act" construction of the state privilege, the court concluded, the evidence would have been obtained in violation of the privilege. It then proceeded to overrule *Hansen.* When the Utah constitution was adopted in 1895, about half the states recognizing the privilege against compelled self-incrimination in their constitutions did so with a bar to compelled giving of "evidence;" the others barred compelling a person to be a "witness" or protected citizens from "testifying" against themselves under coercion. "It was generally accepted at the time," the court observed, "that these differences in wording were insignificant." 701 P.2d at 1072. To the extent that the proceedings of the Utah Constitutional Convention provided any information, this suggested an intention to have the state privilege given the same scope as the common law privilege against self-incrimination. Id., at 1073. Turning to "underlying policy considerations that militate for or against an expansive construction" of the state privilege, the majority continued:

> The affirmative act standard * * * means that an accused may not be compelled to actively produce evidence against himself or to perform any affirmative act that will produce or create such evidence. Perhaps the best justification for the affirmative act standard is that it removes any incentive for the state to use cruelty in procuring evidence from the accused. As one commentator notes: "The whip would be just as effective in forcing the accused to place his foot in a shoe track [an affirmative act] as in forcing him to give up testimonial evidence." Note, The Georgia Right Against Self-Incrimination: Historical Anomaly or Vanguard of Justice? 15 Ga.L.Rev. 1104, 1115 (1981). However, the Utah Constitu-

tion's due process provision and its prohibition against unreasonable searches and seizures may be better suited than the self-incrimination clause for dealing with such governmental excesses.

The affirmative act standard also avoids the basic unfairness of forcing a witness to "choose among the three horns of the triceratops—harmful disclosure, contempt [and] perjury." 8 J. Wigmore [Evidence] § 2251, at 316 [ (McNaughton rev. 1961) ] (emphasis omitted). However, the standard is overinclusive in this regard. Not every affirmative act that the state might compel presents the accused with the temptation of perjury. Defendant Crosgrove, for example, could not have falsified his blood alcohol content.

Id., at 1074. Moreover, the court continued, the affirmative act approach requires distinctions to be drawn that are overly fine and that may not further significantly the policies of the privilege. It noted that under this approach, a suspect could not be compelled to place his foot in a footprint near the scene of a crime but an officer could forcibly remove the accused's shoe and place it in the track. Id., at 1074–74. On these grounds, it adopted a construction of article I, section 12 of the Utah constitution that limits its scope "to those situations where the state seeks evidence of a testimonial or communicative nature." Id., at 1075. Compelling Crosgrove to give a sample of his breath, then, did not violate the state provision.

4. The application of the privilege against compelled self-incrimination to subpoenas requiring the production of documents is considered in Chapter 9.

5. The Fifth Amendment prohibits compulsion upon a person to engage in testimonial activity only when that activity is "incriminating." In Minnesota v. Murphy, 465 U.S. 420, 104 S.Ct. 1136, 79 L.Ed.2d 409 (1984), the Supreme Court, in dicta, indicated that revocation of probation is not "incrimination" within the meaning of the privilege. Thus, probationers can apparently be compelled, without violation of the privilege, to answer questions that might result in revocation of probation but that pose "no realistic threat of incrimination in a separate criminal proceeding." 465 U.S. at 435 n. 7, 104 S.Ct. at 1147 n. 7, 79 L.Ed.2d at 425 n. 7.

Liability under the Illinois Sexually Dangerous Persons Act was held not to be "criminal" within the meaning of the Fifth Amendment privilege in Allen v. Illinois, 478 U.S. 364, 106 S.Ct. 2988, 92 L.Ed.2d 296 (1986). Specifically, the Fifth Amendment was held to impose no bar to Allen being compelled to provide information that might result in his being determined to be a sexually dangerous person, although that could result in commitment to "treatment" in a high security institution until he was no longer dangerous. No error was committed, therefore, in permitting testimony at his hearing on sexual dangerousness from psychiatrists who may have compelled him to provide information on which they based their testimony.

6. Fifth Amendment self-incrimination principles are examined more fully in the setting of police interrogation in Chapter 7.

## B.  THE FOURTH AMENDMENT'S PROHIBITION AGAINST UNREASONABLE SEARCHES AND SEIZURES

Perhaps in part because of the limited applicability of the Fifth Amendment, the Fourth Amendment's prohibition against unreasonable searches and seizures has become the major federal constitutional vehicle for regulating police conduct in the gathering of evidence.

Several threshold issues presented by efforts to invoke this prohibition are considered in this portion of the materials. The first two subsections consider when law enforcement conduct constitutes a "search" or a "seizure" so as to invoke the Fourth Amendment. The third subsection then addresses the effect of the requirement of standing and a narrow conception of what constitutes a "search." But first the limitation of the Fourth Amendment to official conduct is discussed.

## EDITORS' INTRODUCTION: PRIVATE PARTY SEARCHES

The Fourth Amendment's application is limited by the Supreme Court's position that it constrains only governmental action and does not apply to the conduct of a person acting purely in a private capacity. The leading case on private party searches is Burdeau v. McDowell, 256 U.S. 465, 41 S.Ct. 574, 65 L.Ed. 1048 (1921). The petitioner moved for return of private papers that had been wrongfully taken from his office and turned over to the government. The Court disposed of his Fourth Amendment claim with the following comments:

> The Fourth Amendment gives protection against unlawful searches and seizures, and * * * its protection applies to governmental actions. Its origin and history clearly show that it was intended as a restraint upon the activities of sovereign authority, and was not intended to be a limitation upon other than governmental agencies * * *.

> In the present case the record clearly shows that no official of the federal government had anything to do with the wrongful seizure of the petitioner's property, or any knowledge thereof until several months after the property had been taken from him and was in the possession of the Cities Service Company. It is manifest that there was no invasion of the security afforded by the Fourth Amendment against unreasonable searches and seizure, as whatever wrong was done was the act of individuals in taking the property of another. A portion of the property so taken and held was turned over to the prosecuting officers of the federal government. We assume that petitioner has an unquestionable right of redress against those who illegally and wrongfully took his private property under the circumstances here disclosed, but with such remedies we are not now concerned.

256 U.S. at 475, 41 S.Ct. at 576, 65 L.Ed. at 1051.

The Court has continued to apply this approach, although leaving open the possibility that in some cases the involvement of governmental officers in stimulating or conducting a search by a private person might render that search within the scope of the Fourth Amendment. See United States v. Jacobsen, 466 U.S. 109, 113, 104 S.Ct. 1652, 1657, 80 L.Ed.2d 85, 94 (1984); Walter v. United States, 447 U.S. 649, 100 S.Ct. 2395, 65 L.Ed.2d 410 (1980). In Coolidge v. New Hampshire, 403 U.S. 443, 91 S.Ct. 2022, 29 L.Ed.2d 564 (1971), the murder suspect's wife was interviewed at the couple's home while he was in custody. In response to the officers' inquiries concerning guns owned by her husband and the clothing he wore the day of the crime, she—apparently on her own initiative—obtained guns and clothing and offered them to the officers.  Rejecting Coolidge's argument that this was a "search" despite Burdeau v. McDowell, the Court explained:

> The question presented here is whether the conduct of the police officers at the Coolidge house was such as to make her actions their actions for purposes of the Fourth and Fourteenth Amendment and their attendant exclusionary rules.  The test * * * is whether Mrs. Coolidge, in light of all the circumstances of the case, must be regarded as having acted as an "instrument" or agent of the state when she produced her husband's belongings. * * * Mrs. Coolidge described her own motive as that of clearing her husband, and that she believed that she had nothing to hide. * * * The two officers who questioned her behaved, as her own testimony shows, with perfect courtesy.  There is not the slightest implication of an attempt of their part to coerce or dominate her, or, for that matter, to direct her actions by the more subtle techniques of suggestion that are available to officials in circumstances like these.

403 U.S. at 487–89, 91 S.Ct. at 2048–50, 29 L.Ed.2d at 595–96.

Another aspect of the Burdeau v. McDowell principle that has given rise to significant difficulties is the question of the extent to which law enforcement officers may duplicate or exceed wrongful actions by a private individual.  This is illustrated by Jacobsen v. United States, supra.  Federal Express employees inspecting a package that had been damaged by a forklift determined that it contained only crumpled newspaper and a silver tape tube.  Inside the tube were plastic bags containing a white powder.  The employees notified federal agents and replaced the bags (with the powder) in the tube and the tube and the newspaper in the box.  When the agents arrived, they removed the tube and the bags and visually inspected the powder.  Rejecting the argument that the agents' action was unreasonable, the Court concluded that a majority of its members had agreed in Walter v. United States, supra, that the legality of a governmental search that follows a private search must be determined by the scope of the antecedent private search.  In explanation, Justice Stevens stated for the Court:

> This standard follows from the analysis applicable when private parties reveal other kinds of private information to the authorities.  It is well-settled that when an individual reveals private information to another, he assumes the risk that his confidant will reveal that information to authorities, and if that occurs the Fourth Amendment does not prohibit governmental use of that information.  Once frustration of the original expectation of privacy occurs, the Fourth Amendment does not prohibit governmental use of the now-nonprivate information. * * * The Fourth Amendment is implicated only if the authorities use information with respect to which the expectation of privacy has not already been frustrated.  In such a case the authorities have not relied upon what is in effect a private search, and therefore presumptively violate the Fourth Amendment if they act without a warrant.

466 U.S. at 117–18, 104 S.Ct. at 1658–59, 80 L.Ed.2d at 96–97. Here, the federal agents were given information by the Federal Express employees that made clear that the box contained nothing of significance except the tube, the plastic bags, and the powder. Therefore, the agents' action in removing and inspecting the contents enabled them to learn nothing that had not previously been learned during the private search by the Federal Express employees and communicated to the agents. Further, the Court explained:

> The advantage the Government gained [by the agents' action in personally inspecting the contents of the package] was merely avoiding the risk of a flaw in the employees' recollection, rather than in further infringing respondents' privacy. Protecting the risk of misdescription hardly enhances any legitimate privacy interest, and is not protected by the Fourth Amendment. Respondents could have no privacy interest in the contents of the package, since it remained unsealed and since the Federal Express employees had just examined the package and had, of their own accord, invited the federal agents to their offices for the express purpose of viewing its contents.

466 U.S. at 119, 104 S.Ct. at 1659–60, 80 L.Ed.2d at 98.

In Walter v. United States, supra, private persons improperly opened a package and discovered film canisters displaying graphic and verbal descriptions of the contents as homosexual activities. The private persons opened several of the canisters and unsuccessfully attempted, without a projector, to determine the contents of the films. F.B.I. agents were called and took possession of the canisters and films. Later, and without a warrant, they viewed the films with a projector. A majority of the Court concluded that the viewing of the films by the agents was improper. Justice White, joined by Justice Brennan, expressed the view that the agents' could not have so viewed the films even if the private persons had, before calling the agents, themselves viewed the films with a projector. 447 U.S. at 662, 100 S.Ct. at 2404, 65 L.Ed.2d at 421 (White, J., concurring).

## 1.  POLICE ACTIVITY CONSTITUTING A "SEARCH"

### EDITORS' INTRODUCTION: THE *KATZ* STANDARD

Whether law enforcement conduct constitutes a "search" for purposes of the Fourth Amendment is generally determined by application of a standard derived from Katz v. United States, 389 U.S. 347, 88 S.Ct. 507, 19 L.Ed.2d 576 (1967). Prior to *Katz,* Fourth Amendment case law focused to some extent upon whether police had intruded in some physical sense into a protected area. In Silverman v. United States, 365 U.S. 505, 81 S.Ct. 679, 5 L.Ed.2d 734 (1961), for example, the Court held that officers engaged in a search when they used a "spike mike" to overhear conversations in an adjacent row house. The discussion suggested that this turned upon the showing that the microphone was inserted through the wall until it touched a heating duct in the suspects' house and thus the police conducted "an unauthorized physical penetration into the premises." 365 U.S. at 511, 81 S.Ct. at 682, 5 L.Ed.2d at 739.

In *Katz*, federal officers attached an electronic listening and recording device to the outside of a public telephone booth that they anticipated Katz would use. Katz did use the booth, and the officers were able to overhear his end of the conversation. Finding that the officers engaged in a "search," the Court stressed that this conclusion did not turn upon whether the phone booth was a protected area. Instead:

> What a person knowingly exposes to the public, even in his own home or office, is not a subject of Fourth Amendment protection. * * * But what he seeks to preserve as private, even in an area accessible to the public, may be constitutionally protected.

389 U.S. at 351, 88 S.Ct. at 511, 19 L.Ed.2d at 582. Later cases, however, have tended to cite and use language from a concurring opinion by Justice Harlan:

> My understanding of the rule [determining the protection provided by the Fourth Amendment] is that there is a twofold requirement, first that a person have exhibited an actual (subjective) expectation of privacy and, second, that the expectation be one that society is prepared to recognize as "reasonable."

389 U.S. at 361, 88 S.Ct. at 516, 19 L.Ed.2d at 587–88 (Harlan, J., concurring). Thus a search was conducted in *Katz* because when Katz used the telephone booth, he subjectively believed that his conversation was private between him and the other party and that belief was objectively reasonable.

Conduct constituting a search is often contrasted with what is characterized as officers' exercise of their right to engage in "plain view." In Colorado v. Bannister, 449 U.S. 1, 101 S.Ct. 42, 66 L.Ed.2d 1 (1980), for example, an officer standing next to a car noticed nuts and wrenches in the glove compartment and on the floor. Since the officer could observe these items from a location he "reasonably"—in Fourth Amendment terms—occupied, his observation of them was not a "search" but merely an exercise of his "right" to observe items left by Bannister in "plain view." This use of the term "plain view" must be distinguished from its use to characterize certain seizures as "plain view seizures." Such seizures are considered in the next subsection.

If, because of darkness, an officer cannot see what is in a parked car but shines his flashlight into the car and thus can observe incriminating items, has the officer "searched?" A plurality of the Court, with no disagreement from other justices, has indicted that "the use of artificial means to illuminate a darkened area," like the use of "a marine glass or a field glass," does not constitute a search. Texas v. Brown, 460 U.S. 730, 740, 103 S.Ct. 1535, 1541, 75 L.Ed.2d 502, 512 (1983) (opinion of Rehnquist, J., announcing the judgment of the Court).

*Katz* itself established that mechanical interception of spoken words is sometimes a "search," and thus gave rise to the law dealing with wiretapping and electronic surveillance considered in Chapter 6. But in Smith v. Maryland, 442 U.S. 735, 99 S.Ct. 2577, 61 L.Ed.2d 220

(1979), the Court considered the use of a pen register. Installed at the telephone company's main office, this device records the numbers dialed from a given telephone but does not permit the overhearing of conversations. Under *Katz,* this was not a search, the Court concluded, because telephone users cannot reasonably entertain an expectation of privacy in numbers dialed from telephones:

> All telephone users realize that they must "convey" phone numbers to the telephone company, since it is through telephone company switching equipment that their calls are completed. All subscribers realize, moreover, that the phone company has facilities for making permanent records of the numbers they dial, for they see a list of their long-distance (toll) calls on their monthly bills. * * * Although most people may be oblivious to a pen register's esoteric functions, they presumably have some awareness of one common use: to aid in the identification of persons making annoying or obscene calls.

442 U.S. at 742, 99 S.Ct. at 2581, 61 L.Ed.2d at 228.

The two principal cases in this subsection consider application of the *Katz* standard to two important areas: aerial surveillance and physical entry of private property. In each of these as in many other litigated cases, the police failed to obtain a warrant, so if their activity is found to be a search, that search will almost certainly be unreasonable and the evidence will be unavailable to the prosecution. But on a more general level, characterizing activity of the sort involved as a "search" does not mean that the Fourth Amendment prohibits police from engaging in that conduct. Rather, the conduct becomes subject to the requirements of Fourth Amendment reasonableness. Consider whether the Supreme Court is properly applying the Fourth Amendment so as to identify that law enforcement conduct which sufficiently intrudes upon privacy concerns that as a matter of sound Fourth Amendment policy the conduct should be regulated—although not necessarily prohibited—by application of the Fourth Amendment's requirement of reasonableness.

### OLIVER v. UNITED STATES

Supreme Court of the United States, 1984.
466 U.S. 170, 104 S.Ct. 1735, 80 L.Ed.2d 214.

JUSTICE POWELL delivered the opinion of the Court.

The "open fields" doctrine, first enunciated by this Court in Hester v. United States, 265 U.S. 57, 44 S.Ct. 445, 68 L.Ed. 898 (1924), permits police officers to enter and search a field without a warrant. We granted certiorari in these cases to clarify confusion that has arisen as to the continued vitality of the doctrine.

I

*No. 82–15.* Acting on reports that marijuana was being raised on the farm of petitioner Oliver, two narcotics agents of the Kentucky

State Police went to the farm to investigate.[3] Arriving at the farm, they drove past petitioner's house to a locked gate with a "No Trespassing" sign. A footpath led around one side of the gate. The agents walked around the gate and along the road for several hundred yards, passing a barn and a parked camper. At that point, someone standing in front of the camper shouted, "No hunting is allowed, come back here." The officers shouted back that they were Kentucky State Police officers, but found no one when they returned to the camper. The officers resumed their investigation of the farm and found a field of marijuana over a mile from petitioner's home.

Petitioner was arrested and indicted for "manufactur[ing]" a "controlled substance." 21 U.S.C. § 841(a)(1). After a pretrial hearing, the District Court suppressed evidence of the discovery of the marijuana fields. Applying Katz v. United States, 389 U.S. 347, 357, 88 S.Ct. 507, 514, 19 L.Ed.2d 576 (1967), the court found that petitioner had a reasonable expectation that the fields would remain private because petitioner "had done all that could be expected of him to assert his privacy in the area of farm that was searched." He had posted no trespassing signs at regular intervals and had locked the gate at the entrance to the center of the farm. Further, the court noted that the fields themselves are highly secluded: they are bounded on all sides by woods, fences and embankments and cannot be seen from any point of public access. The court concluded that this was not an "open" field that invited casual intrusion.

The Court of Appeals for the Sixth Circuit, sitting *en banc,* reversed the district court. United States v. Oliver, 686 F.2d 356 (CA6 1982). The court concluded that *Katz,* upon which the District Court relied, had not impaired the vitality of the open fields doctrine of *Hester.* Rather, the open fields doctrine was entirely compatible with *Katz's* emphasis on privacy. The court reasoned that the "human relations that create the need for privacy do not ordinarily take place" in open fields, and that the property owner's common law right to exclude trespassers is insufficiently linked to privacy to warrant the Fourth Amendment's protection. Id., at 360. We granted certiorari.

*No. 82–1273.* After receiving an anonymous tip that marijuana was being grown in the woods behind respondent Thornton's residence, two police officers entered the woods by a path between this residence and a neighboring house. They followed a footpath through the woods until they reached two marijuana patches fenced with chicken wire. Later, the officers determined that the patches were on the property of respondent, obtained a warrant to search the property and seized the marijuana. On the basis of this evidence, respondent was arrested and indicted.

The trial court granted respondent's motion to suppress the fruits of the second search. The warrant for this search was premised on information that the police had obtained during their previous warrant-

---

[3] It is conceded that the police did not have a warrant authorizing the search, that there was no probable cause for the search and that no exception to the warrant requirement is applicable.

less search, that the court found to be unreasonable. "No Trespassing" signs and the secluded location of the marijuana patches evinced a reasonable expectation of privacy. Therefore, the court held, the "open fields" doctrine did not apply.

The Maine Supreme Judicial Court affirmed. State v. Thornton, 453 A.2d 489 (Me.1982). It agreed with the trial court that the correct question was whether the search "is a violation of privacy on which the individual justifiably relied," id., at 493, and that the search violated respondent's privacy. The court also agreed that the "open fields" doctrine did not justify the search. That doctrine applies, according to the court, only when officers are lawfully present on property and observe "open and patent" activity. Id., at 495. In this case, the officers had trespassed upon defendant's property, and the respondent had made every effort to conceal his activity. We granted certiorari.

## II

The rule announced in Hester v. United States was founded upon the explicit language of the Fourth Amendment. That Amendment indicates with some precision the places and things encompassed by its protections. As Justice Holmes explained for the Court in his characteristically laconic style: "[T]he special protection accorded by the Fourth Amendment to the people in their 'persons, houses, papers, and effects,' is not extended to the open fields. The distinction between the latter and the house is as old as the common law." Hester v. United States, 265 U.S., at 59, 44 S.Ct., at 446.

Nor are the open fields "effects" within the meaning of the Fourth Amendment. In this respect, it is suggestive that James Madison's proposed draft of what became the Fourth Amendment preserves "[t]he rights of the people to be secured in their persons, their houses, their papers, and their other property, from all unreasonable searches and seizures. * * *" See N. Lasson, The History and Development of the Fourth Amendment to the United States Constitution 100, n. 77 (1937). Although Congress' revisions of Madison's proposal broadened the scope of the Amendment in some respects, id., at 100–103, the term "effects" is less inclusive than "property" and cannot be said to encompass open fields.[4] We conclude, as did the Court in deciding Hester v. United States, that the government's intrusion upon the open fields is not one of those "unreasonable searches" proscribed by the text of the Fourth Amendment.

## III

This interpretation of the Fourth Amendment's language is consistent with the understanding of the right to privacy expressed in our Fourth Amendment jurisprudence. Since Katz v. United States, 389 U.S. 347, 88 S.Ct. 507, 19 L.Ed.2d 576 (1967), the touchstone of Amendment analysis has been the question whether a person has a "constitu-

---

[4] The Framers would have understood the term "effects" to be limited to personal, rather than real, property. See gener-ally, Doe v. Dring, 2 M. & S. 448, 454 (1814) (discussing prior cases); 2 Blackstone, Commentaries 16, 384–385.

tionally protected reasonable expectation of privacy." 389 U.S., at 360, 88 S.Ct., at 516 (Harlan, J., concurring). The Amendment does not protect the merely subjective expectation of privacy, but only "those expectations that society is prepared to recognize as 'reasonable.'" Id., at 361, 88 S.Ct., at 516.

A

No single factor determines whether an individual legitimately may claim under the Fourth Amendment that a place should be free of government intrusion not authorized by warrant. See Rakas v. Illinois, 439 U.S. 128, 152–153, 99 S.Ct. 421, 435–436, 58 L.Ed.2d 387 (1978) (Powell, J., concurring). In assessing the degree to which a search infringes upon individual privacy, the Court has given weight to such factors as the intention of the Framers of the Fourth Amendment, e.g. United States v. Chadwick, 433 U.S. 1, 7–8, 97 S.Ct. 2476, 2481–2482, 53 L.Ed.2d 538 (1977), the uses to which the individual has put a location, e.g., Jones v. United States, 362 U.S. 257, 265, 80 S.Ct. 725, 733, 4 L.Ed. 2d 697 (1960), and our societal understanding that certain areas deserve the most scrupulous protection from government invasion, e.g., Payton v. New York, 445 U.S. 573, 100 S.Ct. 1371, 63 L.Ed.2d 639 (1980). These factors are equally relevant to determining whether the government's intrusion upon open fields without a warrant or probable cause violates reasonable expectations of privacy and is therefore a search proscribed by the Amendment.

In this light, the rule of Hester v. United States, supra, that we reaffirm today, may be understood as providing that an individual may not legitimately demand privacy for activities conducted out of doors in fields, except in the area immediately surrounding the home. This rule is true to the conception of the right to privacy embodied in the Fourth Amendment. The Amendment reflects the recognition of the Founders that certain enclaves should be free from arbitrary government interference. For example, the Court since the enactment of the Fourth Amendment has stressed "the overriding respect for the sanctity of the home that has been embedded in our traditions since the origins of the Republic." Payton v. New York, supra, 445 U.S., at 601, 100 S.Ct., at 1387.

In contrast, open fields do not provide the setting for those intimate activities that the Amendment is intended to shelter from government interference or surveillance. There is no societal interest in protecting the privacy of those activities, such as the cultivation of crops, that occur in open fields. Moreover, as a practical matter these lands usually are accessible to the public and the police in ways that a home, an office or commercial structure would not be. It is not generally true that fences or no trespassing signs effectively bar the public from viewing open fields in rural areas. And both petitioner Oliver and respondent Thornton concede that the public and police lawfully may survey lands from the air.[5] For these reasons, the asserted expectation

---

[5] In practical terms, petitioner Oliver's and respondent Thornton's analysis merely would require law enforcement officers, in most situations, to use aerial surveillance

of privacy in open fields is not an expectation that "society recognizes as reasonable." [6]

The historical underpinnings of the "open fields" doctrine also demonstrate that the doctrine is consistent with respect for "reasonable expectations of privacy." As Justice Holmes, writing for the Court, observed in *Hester,* 265 U.S., at 57, 44 S.Ct., at 446, the common law distinguished "open fields" from the "curtilage," the land immediately surrounding and associated with the home. See 4 Blackstone, Commentaries *225. The distinction implies that only the curtilage, not the neighboring open fields, warrants the Fourth Amendment protections that attach to the home. At common law, the curtilage is the area to which extends the intimate activity associated with the "sanctity of a man's home and the privacies of life," Boyd v. United States, 116 U.S. 616, 630, 6 S.Ct. 524, 532, 29 L.Ed. 746 (1886), and therefore has been considered part of home itself for Fourth Amendment purposes. Thus, courts have extended Fourth Amendment protection to the curtilage; and they have defined the curtilage, as did the common law, by reference to the factors that determine whether an individual reasonably may expect that an area immediately adjacent to the home will remain private. Conversely, the common law implies, as we reaffirm today, that no expectation of privacy legitimately attaches to open fields.[7]

We conclude, from the text of the Fourth Amendment and from the historical and contemporary understanding of its purposes, that an individual has no legitimate expectation that open fields will remain free from warrantless intrusion by government officers.

## B

Petitioner Oliver and respondent Thornton contend, to the contrary, that the circumstances of a search sometimes may indicate that

to gather the information necessary to obtain a warrant or to justify warrantless entry onto the property. It is not easy to see how such a requirement would advance legitimate privacy interests.

[6] The dissent conceives of open fields as bustling with private activity as diverse as lovers' trysts and worship services. But in most instances police will disturb no one when they enter upon open fields. These fields, by their very character as open and unoccupied, are unlikely to provide the setting for activities whose privacy is sought to be protected by the Fourth Amendment. One need think only of the vast expanse of some western ranches or of the undeveloped woods of the Northwest to see the unreality of the dissent's conception. Further, the Fourth Amendment provides ample protection to activities in the open fields that might implicate an individual's privacy. An individual who enters a place defined to be "public" for Fourth Amendment analysis does not lose all claims to

privacy or personal security. For example, the Fourth Amendment's protections against unreasonable arrest or unreasonable seizure of effects upon the person remain fully applicable.

[7] Neither petitioner Oliver nor respondent Thornton has contended that the property searched was within the curtilage. Nor is it necessary in this case to consider the scope of the curtilage exception to the open fields doctrine or the degree of Fourth Amendment protection afforded the curtilage, as opposed to the home itself. It is clear, however, that the term "open fields" may include any unoccupied or undeveloped area outside of the curtilage. An open field need be neither "open" nor a "field" as those terms are used in common speech. For example, contrary to respondent Thornton's suggestion, a thickly wooded area nonetheless may be an open field as that term is used in construing the Fourth Amendment.

reasonable expectations of privacy were violated; and that courts therefore should analyze these circumstances on a case-by-case basis. The language of the Fourth Amendment itself answers their contention.

Nor would a case-by-case approach provide a workable accommodation between the needs of law enforcement and the interests protected by the Fourth Amendment. Under this approach, police officers would have to guess before every search whether landowners had erected fences sufficiently high, posted a sufficient number of warning signs, or located contraband in an area sufficiently secluded to establish a right of privacy. The lawfulness of a search would turn on "[a] highly sophisticated set of rules, qualified by all sorts of ifs, ands, and buts and requiring the drawing of subtle nuances and hairline distinctions. * * *" New York v. Belton, 453 U.S. 454, 458, 101 S.Ct. 2860, 2863, 69 L.Ed.2d 768 (1981) (quoting LaFave, "Case-By-Case Adjudication" versus "Standardized Procedures": The Robinson Dilemma, 1974 S.Ct. Rev. 127, 142). This Court repeatedly has acknowledged the difficulties created for courts, police and citizens by an *ad hoc,* case-by-case definition of Fourth Amendment standards to be applied in differing factual circumstances. The *ad hoc* approach not only makes it difficult for the policeman to discern the scope of his authority; it also creates a danger that constitutional rights will be arbitrarily and inequitably enforced.[8]

### IV

In any event, while the factors that petitioner Oliver and respondent Thornton urge the courts to consider may be relevant to Fourth Amendment analysis in some contexts, these factors cannot be decisive on the question whether the search of an open field is subject to the Amendment. Initially, we reject the suggestion that steps taken to protect privacy establish that expectations of privacy in an open field are legitimate. It is true, of course, that petitioner Oliver and respondent Thornton, in order to conceal their criminal activities, planted the marijuana upon secluded land and erected fences and no trespassing signs around the property. And it may be that because of such precautions, few members of the public stumbled upon the marijuana crops seized by the police. Neither of these suppositions demonstrates, however, that the expectation of privacy was *legitimate* in the sense required by the Fourth Amendment. The test of legitimacy is not whether the individual chooses to conceal assertedly "private" activity. Rather, the correct inquiry is whether the government's intrusion infringes upon the personal and societal values protected by the Fourth

---

[8] The clarity of the open fields doctrine that we reaffirm today is not sacrificed, as the dissent suggests, by our recognition that the curtilage remains within the protections of the Fourth Amendment. Most of the many millions of acres that are "open fields" are not close to any structure and so not arguably within the curtilage. And, for most homes, the boundaries of the curtilage will be clearly marked; and the conception defining the curtilage—as the area around the home to which the activity of home life extends—is a familiar one easily understood from our daily experience. The occasional difficulties that courts might have in applying this, like other, legal concepts, do not argue for the unprecedented expansion of the Fourth Amendment advocated by the dissent.

Amendment. As we have explained, we find no basis for concluding that a police inspection of open fields accomplishes such an infringement.

Nor is the government's intrusion upon an open field a "search" in the constitutional sense because that intrusion is a trespass at common law. The existence of a property right is but one element in determining whether expectations of privacy are legitimate. " '[T]he premise that property interests control the right of the Government to search and seize has been discredited.' " *Katz*, 389 U.S., at 353, 88 S.Ct., at 512 (quoting Warden v. Hayden, 387 U.S. 294, 304, 87 S.Ct. 1642, 1648, 18 L.Ed.2d 782 (1967)). "[E]ven a property interest in premises may not be sufficient to establish a legitimate expectation of privacy with respect to particular items located on the premises or activity conducted thereon." Rakas v. Illinois, 439 U.S., at 144 n. 12, 99 S.Ct., at 431 n. 12.

The common law may guide consideration of what areas are protected by the Fourth Amendment search by defining areas whose invasion by others is wrongful. The law of trespass, however, forbids intrusions upon land that the Fourth Amendment would not proscribe. For trespass law extends to instances where the exercise of the right to exclude vindicates no legitimate privacy interest.[9] Thus, in the case of open fields, the general rights of property protected by the common law of trespass have little or no relevance to the applicability of the Fourth Amendment.

## V

We conclude that the open fields doctrine, as enunciated in *Hester*, is consistent with the plain language of the Fourth Amendment and its historical purposes. Moreover, Justice Holmes' interpretation of the Amendment in *Hester* accords with the "reasonable expectation of privacy" analysis developed in subsequent decisions of this Court. We therefore affirm Oliver v. United States; Maine v. Thornton is reversed and remanded for further proceedings not inconsistent with this opinion.

It is so ordered.

JUSTICE WHITE, concurring in part and in the judgment.

[9] The law of trespass recognizes the interest in possession and control of one's property and for that reason permits exclusion of unwanted intruders. But it does not follow that the right to exclude conferred by trespass law embodies a privacy interest also protected by the Fourth Amendment. To the contrary, the common law of trespass furthers a range of interests that have nothing to do with privacy and that would not be served by applying the strictures of trespass law to public officers. Criminal laws against trespass are prophylactic: they protect against intruders who poach, steal livestock and crops or vandalize property. And the civil action of trespass serves the important function of authorizing an owner to defeat claims of prescription by asserting his own title. In any event, unlicensed use of property by others is presumptively unjustified, as anyone who wishes to use the property is free to bargain for the right to do so with the property owner. For these reasons, the law of trespass confers protections from intrusion by others far broader than those required by Fourth Amendment interests.

I concur in the judgment and join Parts I and II of the Court's opinion. These parts dispose of the issue before us; there is no need to go further and deal with the expectation of privacy matter. However reasonable a landowner's expectations of privacy may be, those expectations cannot convert a field into a "house" or an "effect."

JUSTICE MARSHALL, with whom JUSTICE BRENNAN and JUSTICE STEVENS join, dissenting.

\* \* \*

## I

The first ground on which the Court rests its decision is that the Fourth Amendment "indicates with some precision the places and things encompassed by its protections," and that real property is not included in the list of protected spaces and possessions. This line of argument has several flaws. Most obviously, it is inconsistent with the results of many of our previous decisions, none of which the Court purports to overrule. For example, neither a public telephone booth nor a conversation conducted therein can fairly be described as a person, house, paper, or effect, yet we have held that the Fourth Amendment forbids the police without a warrant to eavesdrop on such a conversation. Katz v. United States, 389 U.S. 347, 88 S.Ct. 507, 19 L.Ed.2d 576 (1967). \* \* \*

## II

The second ground for the Court's decision is its contention that any interest a landowner might have in the privacy of his woods and fields is not one that "society is prepared to recognize as 'reasonable.'" The mode of analysis that underlies this assertion is certainly more consistent with our prior decisions than that discussed above. But the Court's conclusion cannot withstand scrutiny.

As the Court acknowledges, we have traditionally looked to a variety of factors in determining whether an expectation of privacy asserted in a physical space is "reasonable." Though those factors do not lend themselves to precise taxonomy, they may be roughly grouped into three categories. First, we consider whether the expectation at issue is rooted in entitlements defined by positive law. Second, we consider the nature of the uses to which spaces of the sort in question can be put. Third, we consider whether the person claiming a privacy interest manifested that interest to the public in a way that most people would understand and respect. When the expectations of privacy asserted by petitioner Oliver and respondent Thornton are examined through these lenses, it becomes clear that those expectations are entitled to constitutional protection.

## A

We have frequently acknowledged that privacy interests are not coterminous with property rights. However, because "property rights reflect society's explicit recognition of a person's authority to act as he wishes in certain areas, [they] should be considered in determining whether an individual's expectations of privacy are reasonable." Rakas v. Illinois, 439 U.S., at 153, 99 S.Ct., at 435 (Powell, J., concurring). * * *

It is undisputed that Oliver and Thornton each owned the land into which the police intruded. That fact alone provides considerable support for their assertion of legitimate privacy interests in their woods and fields. But even more telling is the nature of the sanctions that Oliver and Thornton could invoke, under local law, for violation of their property rights. In Kentucky, a knowing entry upon fenced or otherwise enclosed land, or upon unenclosed land conspicuously posted with signs excluding the public, constitutes criminal trespass. Ky.Rev.Stat. § 511.070(1), .080, .090(4) (1975 & 1982 Cum.Supp.). The law in Maine is similar. * * * Thus, positive law not only recognizes the legitimacy of Oliver's and Thornton's insistence that strangers keep off their land, but subjects those who refuse to respect their wishes to the most severe of penalties—criminal liability. Under these circumstances, it is hard to credit the Court's assertion that Oliver's and Thornton's expectations of privacy were not of a sort that society is prepared to recognize as reasonable.

## B

The uses to which a place is put are highly relevant to the assessment of a privacy interest asserted therein. If, in light of our shared sensibilities, those activities are of a kind in which people should be able to engage without fear of intrusion by private persons or government officials, we extend the protection of the Fourth Amendment to the space in question, even in the absence of any entitlement derived from positive law.

Privately-owned woods and fields that are not exposed to public view regularly are employed in a variety of ways that society acknowledges deserve privacy. Many landowners like to take solitary walks on their property, confident that they will not be confronted in their rambles by strangers or policemen. Others conduct agricultural businesses on their property. Some landowners use their secluded spaces to meet lovers, others to gather together with fellow worshippers, still others to engage in sustained creative endeavor. Private land is sometimes used as a refuge for wildlife, where flora and fauna are protected from human intervention of any kind. Our respect for the freedom of landowners to use their posted "open fields" in ways such as these partially explains the seriousness with which the positive law regards deliberate invasions of such spaces, and substantially reinforces the landowners' contention that their expectations of privacy are "reasonable."

## C

Whether a person "took normal precautions to maintain his privacy" in a given space affects whether his interest is one protected by the Fourth Amendment. Rawlings v. Kentucky, 448 U.S. 98, 105, 100 S.Ct. 2556, 2561, 65 L.Ed.2d 633 (1980). The reason why such precautions are relevant is that we do not insist that a person who has a right to exclude others exercise that right. A claim to privacy is therefore strengthened by the fact that the claimant somehow manifested to other people his desire that they keep their distance.

Certain spaces are so presumptively private that signals of this sort are unnecessary; a homeowner need not post a "do not enter" sign on his door in order to deny entrance to uninvited guests. Privacy interests in other spaces are more ambiguous, and the taking of precautions is consequently more important; placing a lock on one's footlocker strengthens one's claim that an examination of its contents is impermissible. Still other spaces are, by positive law and social convention, presumed accessible to members of the public *unless* the owner manifests his intention to exclude them.

Undeveloped land falls into the last-mentioned category. If a person has not marked the boundaries of his fields or woods in a way that informs passersby that they are not welcome, he cannot object if members of the public enter onto the property. There is no reason why he should have any greater rights as against government officials. Accordingly, we have held that an official may, without a warrant, enter private land from which the public is not excluded and make observations from that vantage point. Air Pollution Variance Board v. Western Alfalfa Corp., 416 U.S. 861, 865, 94 S.Ct. 2114, 2115, 40 L.Ed.2d 607 (1974). Fairly read, the case on which the majority so heavily relies, Hester v. United States, 265 U.S. 57, 44 S.Ct. 445, 68 L.Ed. 898 (1924), affirms little more than the foregoing unremarkable proposition. From aught that appears in the opinion in that case, the defendants, fleeing from revenue agents who had observed them committing a crime, abandoned incriminating evidence on private land from which the public had not been excluded. Under such circumstances, it is not surprising that the Court was unpersuaded by the defendants' argument that the entry onto their fields by the agents violated the Fourth Amendment.

A very different case is presented when the owner of undeveloped land has taken precautions to exclude the public. As indicated above, a deliberate entry by a private citizen onto private property marked with "no trespassing" signs will expose him to criminal liability. I see no reason why a government official should not be obliged to respect such unequivocal and universally understood manifestations of a landowner's desire for privacy.

In sum, examination of the three principal criteria we have traditionally used for assessing the reasonableness of a person's expectation that a given space would remain private indicates that interests of the sort asserted by Oliver and Thornton are entitled to constitutional protection. An owner's right to insist that others stay off his posted land is firmly grounded in positive law. Many of the uses to which such land may be put deserve privacy. And, by marking the boundaries of the land with warnings that the public should not intrude, the owner has dispelled any ambiguity as to his desires.

The police in these cases proffered no justification for their invasions of Oliver's and Thornton's privacy interests; in neither case was the entry legitimated by a warrant or by one of the established exceptions to the warrant requirement. I conclude, therefore, that the searches of their land violated the Fourth Amendment, and the evidence obtained in the course of those searches should have been suppressed.

## III

A clear, easily administrable rule emerges from the analysis set forth above: Private land marked in a fashion sufficient to render entry thereon a criminal trespass under the law of the state in which the land lies is protected by the Fourth Amendment's proscription of unreasonable searches and seizures. One of the advantages of the foregoing rule is that it draws upon a doctrine already familiar to both citizens and government officials. In each jurisdiction, a substantial body of statutory and case law defines the precautions a landowner must take in order to avail himself of the sanctions of the criminal law. The police know that body of law, because they are entrusted with responsibility for enforcing it against the public; it therefore would not be difficult for the police to abide by it themselves.

By contrast, the doctrine announced by the Court today is incapable of determinate application. Police officers, making warrantless entries upon private land, will be obliged in the future to make on-the-spot judgments as to how far the curtilage extends, and to stay outside that zone. In addition, we may expect to see a spate of litigation over the question of how much improvement is necessary to remove private land from the category of "unoccupied or undeveloped area" to which the "open fields exception" is now deemed applicable.

The Court's holding not only ill serves the need to make constitutional doctrine "workable for application by rank and file, trained police officers," Illinois v. Andreas, 463 U.S. 765, 772, 103 S.Ct. 3319, 3324, 77 L.Ed.2d 1003 (1983), it withdraws the shield of the Fourth Amendment from privacy interests that clearly deserve protection.

\* \* \*

I dissent.

## NOTES

1. The significance of the concept of "curtilage" as an aid in defining the scope of Fourth Amendment coverage was confirmed and that concept fleshed out in United States v. Dunn, 480 U.S. 294, 107 S.Ct. 1134, 94 L.Ed.2d 326 (1987). Federal officers, suspecting that Dunn was manufacturing controlled substances, went to his ranch on the evening of November 5, 1980. The ranch's 198 acres were completely encircled by a "perimeter fence" and contained a number of internal fenced areas. About a half-mile from a public road, an enclosure surrounded by a fence included the ranch house and a greenhouse. Approximately fifty yards from this fence were two barns. The larger of the two was enclosed by a wooden fence; locked waist-high gates prevented entry into the barn and a netting material was stretched from the ceiling of the barn to the top of the fence gates. The officers crossed over the perimeter fence,

climbed a barbed wire fence and the fence surrounding the large barn front and approached the barn. They walked under the overhang and up to the locked gates. By shining a flashlight through the netting, they were able to observe a drug laboratory. At no point did the officers physically enter the barn. Using the information obtained by looking into the barn, they obtained a search warrant and execution of the warrant resulted in the seizure of evidence of Dunn's manufacture of controlled substances. This was held inadmissible by the intermediate federal court, on the ground that this evidence was the product of a warrantless—and therefore unreasonable—search.

The Supreme Court reversed, concluding that under *Oliver* the officers did not engage in a "search." Whether the officers' approach to the barn constituted a search, Justice White explained for the Court, depended upon whether the barn was within the protected curtilage. Turning to the meaning of that term, they continued:

> [W]e believe that curtilage questions should be resolved with particular reference to four factors: the proximity of the area claimed to be curtilage to the home, whether the area is included within an enclosure surrounding the home, the nature of the uses to which the area is put, and the steps taken by the resident to protect the area from observation by people passing by. We do not suggest that combining these factors produces a finely tuned formula that, when mechanically applied, yields a "correct" answer to all extent-of-curtilage questions. Rather, these factors are useful analytical tools only to the degree that, in any given case, they bear upon the centrally relevant consideration—whether the area in question is so intimately tied to the home itself that it should be placed under the home's "umbrella" of Fourth Amendment protection.

480 U.S. at 301, 107 S.Ct. at 1139, 94 L.Ed.2d at 334–35. Applying this approach to the facts of *Dunn,* Justice White concluded, led the Court "with little difficulty" to the conclusion that the barn and the area immediately surrounding it lay outside the protected curtilage. First, the 50 yards separating the barn from the house—a "substantial distance"—rendered it "in isolation." Second, the fence surrounding the ranch house demarked "a specific area of land immediately adjacent to the house that is readily identifiable as part and parcel of the house", and the barn was not within it. Third, the officers had substantial information from surveillance and smells eminating from the barn indicating that it was being used for the manufacture of drugs and therefore also that "the use to which the barn was being put could not fairly be characterized as so associated with the activities and privacies of domestic life that the officers should have deemed the barn as part of [the] home." Finally, Dunn had done little to protect the barn area from observation by those "standing in the open fields." The fences were designed to corral livestock and did not tend to bar observations.

The majority also rejected Dunn's argument that, regardless of whether the barn was within the curtilage of the ranch house, the officers' actions intruded upon a protected privacy interest related to the barn and his use of it. Assuming that the barn was protected from entry by the Fourth Amendment, the Court stressed that it was situated on an "open field." The officers' progression up to the barn involved only entry onto "open fields" and did not constitute a "search," regardless of whether the objects they observed from this vantage point lay within an area that might be protected by the Fourth Amendment. 480 U.S. at 312, 107 S.Ct. at 1145, 94 L.Ed.2d at 337.

Justice Scalia concurred, expressing disagreement only with the Court's application of the third consideration in deciding whether the barn was within the curtilage:

What is significant is that the barn was not being [used for intimate activities of the home], whether or not the law enforcement activities knew it. The officers' perceptions might be relevant to whether intrusion upon curtilage was nevertheless reasonable, but they are no more relevant to whether the barn was curtilage than to whether the house was a house.

480 U.S. at 305, 107 S.Ct. at 1141, 94 L.Ed.2d at 337 (Scalia, J., concurring).

Justice Brennan, joined by Justice Marshall, dissented. Lower court decisions, he urged, consistently held that barns are within the curtilage of farmhouses and the Court provides "no justification for its indifference to the weight of state and federal precedent." The Court's result, he continued, shows the infirmities in the four-part test adopted by the majority and "reflects a fundamental misunderstanding of the typical role of the barn in rural domestic life." Whether or not the barn was within the curtilage of the ranch house, he urged, it and the area surrounding it were entitled to Fourth Amendment protection:

> A barn, like a factory, a plant, or a warehouse, is a business place not open to the general public. Like these other business establishments, the barn, and any area immediately surrounding or adjacent to it from which the public is excluded, should receive protection. A business operator is undisputably entitled to constitutional protection *within* the premises when steps have been taken to ensure privacy. It is equally clear that he or she is entitled to protection in those areas immediately surrounding the building when obvious efforts have been made to exclude the public.

480 U.S. at 319, 107 S.Ct. at 1148, 94 L.Ed.2d at 346 (Brennan, J., dissenting).

2. In United States v. Knotts, 460 U.S. 276, 103 S.Ct. 1081, 75 L.Ed.2d 55 (1983), the defendants were under suspicion because of reports that they were purchasing chemicals which could be used in the manufacture of illicit drugs. With the consent of the seller, federal agents placed a so-called "beeper" inside a five gallon container of chloroform that was to be sold to one of the defendants, Petschen. This beeper emitted radio signals that could be picked up by a radio receiver. Defendant Petschen, as he drove off with the container, was followed by means of both visual surveillance and a monitor which received signals from the beeper. The surveillance ended after Petschen took what were apparently evasive maneuvers. About one hour later, however, a monitoring device in a helicopter located the beeper at a cabin owned by defendant Knotts. On the basis of this and other information obtained during three days of intermittent visual surveillance of the cabin, a search warrant for the cabin was obtained. The resulting search disclosed a fully operable drug laboratory; the container of chloroform containing the beeper was found under a barrel outside the cabin. The Court held that the monitoring activities by the officers did not invade any legitimate expectation of privacy and therefore did not constitute a "search" under *Katz:*

> The governmental surveillance conducted by means of the beeper in this case amounted principally to the following of an automobile on public streets and highways. * * *

> A person travelling in an automobile on public thoroughfares has no reasonable expectation of privacy in his movements from one place to another. When Petschen travelled over the public street he voluntarily conveyed to anyone who wanted to look the fact that he was travelling over particular roads in a particular direction, the fact of whatever stops he made, and the fact of his final destination when he exited from public roads onto private property.

Respondent Knotts, as the owner of the cabin and surrounding premises to which Petschen drove, undoubtedly had the traditional expectation of privacy within a dwelling place insofar as the cabin was concerned * * *. But no such expectation of privacy extended to the visual observation of Petschen's automobile arriving on his premises after leaving a public highway, nor to movements of objects such as the drum of chloroform outside the cabin in the "open fields." Hester v. United States, 265 U.S. 57, 44 S.Ct. 445, 68 L.Ed. 898 (1924).

Visual surveillance from public places along Petschen's route or adjoining Knotts' premises would have sufficed to reveal all of these facts to the police. The fact that the officers in this case relied not only on visual surveillance, but on the use of the beeper to signal the presence of Petschen's automobile to the police receiver, does not alter the situation. Nothing in the Fourth Amendment prohibited the police from augmenting the sensory faculties bestowed upon them at birth with such enhancement as science and technology afforded them in this case.

460 U.S. at 282, 103 S.Ct. at 1085–86, 75 L.Ed.2d at 62–63. After noting that the visual surveillance had failed, the majority acknowledged that the use of the beeper enabled officers to ascertain the destination of the chloroform when they would not have been able to do this by reliance solely on their naked eyes. "But scientific enhancement of this sort raises no constitutional issues," the Court commented, "which visual surveillance would not also raise." 460 U.S. at 285, 103 S.Ct. at 1087, 75 L.Ed.2d at 64. It also noted that the record contained no indication that the beeper was used to reveal information concerning the movement of the drum inside the cabin or any other movement of it that would not have been visible to the naked eye outside the cabin. 460 U.S. at 285, 103 S.Ct. at 1087, 75 L.Ed.2d at 64. All members of the Court joined in the result.

The Court noted that the warrantless installation of the beeper had not been challenged and the propriety of this action by the officers was therefore not addressed. 460 U.S. at 279, 103 S.Ct. at 1084, 75 L.Ed.2d at 60 (unnumbered footnote). Justice Brennan, joined by Justice Marshall, commented that a challenge to the installation of the beeper would have made the case more difficult. 460 U.S. at 285, 103 S.Ct. at 1087, 75 L.Ed.2d at 65 (Brennan J., concurring in the judgment). Justice Blackmun, joined by Justices Brennan, Marshall and Stevens, objected to the Court's reference to the "open fields" doctrine on the ground that this doctrine was not concerned on the facts. 460 U.S. at 287, 103 S.Ct. at 1088, 75 L.Ed.2d at 66 (Blackmun, J., concurring in the judgment). Justice Stevens appeared to agree. 460 U.S. at 288, 103 S.Ct. at 1088–89, 75 L.Ed.2d at 66 (Stevens, J., concurring in the judgment). Justice Stevens, joined by Justices Brennan and Marshall, also commented:

[T]he Court suggests that the Fourth Amendment does not inhibit "the police from augmenting the sensory facilities bestowed upon them at birth with such enhancement as science and technology afforded them." But the Court held to the contrary in Katz v. United States, 389 U.S. 347, 88 S.Ct. 507, 19 L.Ed.2d 576 (1967). Although the augmentation in this case was unobjectionable, it by no means follows that the use of electronic detection techniques does not implicate especially sensitive concerns.

460 U.S. at 288, 103 S.Ct. at 1089, 75 L.Ed.2d at 66.

In United States v. Karo, 468 U.S. 705, 104 S.Ct. 3296, 82 L.Ed.2d 530 (1984), the Court returned to the "beeper" issues. A beeper was installed in a can of ether to be sold to the defendants; this beeper was then used to determine that the can was inside of a specific house. A majority of the Court held that no Fourth Amendment interest of the defendants was infringed by the installation of the beeper. At the time the device was placed in the can, the majority reasoned, the defendants had neither title to nor possession of the can. Therefore, installing the beeper in the can intruded upon no expectation of privacy.

But the Court found that the use of the beeper once installed constituted a search, because it enabled the officers to obtain information they could not have obtained by observation from outside the curtilage of the house:

> The beeper tells the agent that a particular article is actually located at a particular time in the private residence and is in the possession of the person or persons whose residence is being surveilled. Even if visual surveillance has revealed that the article to which the beeper is attached has entered the house, the later monitoring not only verifies the officers' observations but also establishes that the article remains on the premises.

468 U.S. at 715, 104 S.Ct. at 3303, 82 L.Ed.2d at 541. The *Karo* beeper, unlike the *Knotts'* beeper, revealed that the article to which it was attached was inside the house, a fact that could not have been determined by visual observation of the premises.

3. In United States v. Place, 462 U.S. 696, 103 S.Ct. 2637, 77 L.Ed.2d 110 (1983), the Court held that exposure of luggage, located in a public place, to "sniffing" by a drug detecting dog did not amount to a "search":

> A "canine sniff" by a well-trained dog * * * does not require opening the luggage. It does not expose noncontraband items that otherwise would remain hidden from public view, as does, for example, an officer's rummaging through the contents of the luggage. Thus, the manner in which information is obtained through this investigative technique is much less intrusive than a typical search. Moreover, the sniff discloses only the presence or absence of narcotics, a contraband item. Thus, despite the fact that the sniff tells the authorities something about the contents of the luggage, the information obtained is limited. This limited disclosure also ensures that the owner of the property is not subjected to the embarrassment and inconvenience entailed in less discriminate and more intrusive investigative methods.

462 U.S. at 707, 103 S.Ct. at 2644, 77 L.Ed.2d at 121. Justices Brennan, Marshall, and Blackmun indicated that they would not resolve the issue in the case before the Court. 462 U.S. at 710, 719, 103 S.Ct. at 2651, 2653, 77 L.Ed.2d at 129, 132 (Brennan, J., concurring in the result; Blackmun, J., concurring in the judgment).

4. Privacy interests in trash were considered in California v. Greenwood, 486 U.S. 35, 108 S.Ct. 1625, 100 L.Ed.2d 30 (1988). Suspicious that Greenwood might be involved in drug trafficking, a police officer asked the regular trash collector to pick up the plastic garbage bags from Greenwood's curb and turn them over to the officer rather than mixing them with other trash. Before going past Greenwood's curb, the garbage collector removed all previously-collected trash from his truck. He then collected the bags from Greenwood's curb, and gave them to the officer. The officer found in that trash items indicating that Greenwood used narcotics. The information was used to procure a search warrant for Greenwood's residence. Drugs were found during execution of that warrant. Greenwood and Dyanne Van Houten were arrested at the premises. After their release on bail, the process was repeated about a month later; inspection of the trash provided further indicators of drug use and a search pursuant to a warrant disclosed additional drugs. The state courts held that the officers' examinations of the trash constituted unreasonable

searches under the Fourth Amendment.  Reversing, a majority of the Supreme Court found no Fourth Amendment "search" in the officers' conduct:

> [Respondents] assert * * * that they had, and exhibited, an expectation of privacy with respect to the trash that was searched by the police: The trash, which was placed on the street for collection at a fixed time, was contained in opaque plastic bags, which the garbage collector was expected to pick up, mingle with the trash of others, and deposit at the garbage dump.  The trash was only temporarily on the street, and there was little likelihood that it would be inspected by anyone.

> It may well be that respondents did not expect that the contents of their garbage bags would become known to the police or any other members of the public.  An expectation of privacy does not give rise to Fourth Amendment protection, however, unless society is prepared to accept that expectation as objectively reasonable.

> Here, we conclude that respondents exposed their garbage to the public sufficiently to defeat their claim to Fourth Amendment protection.  It is common knowledge that plastic garbage bags left on or at the side of a public street are readily accessible to animals, children, scavengers, snoops, and other members of the public.  Moreover, respondents placed their refuse at the curb for the express purpose of conveying it to a third party, the trash collector, who might himself have sorted through respondents' trash or permitted others, such as the police, to do so.  Accordingly, having deposited their garbage "in an area particularly suited for public inspection, and, in a manner of speaking, public consumption, for the express purpose of having strangers take it," United States v. Reicherter, 647 F.2d 397, 399 (3rd Cir.1981), respondents could have had no reasonable expectation of privacy in the inculpatory items that they discarded.

486 U.S. at 39–40, 108 S.Ct. at 1628–29, 100 L.Ed.2d at 36–37.

California courts had held that the officers' conduct constituted an impermissible search under that state's constitution.  But a 1982 amendment to the state's constitution provided that the evidence was not to be excluded in criminal trials on this ground.  Greenwood argued, however, that since state constitutional law prohibited the officers from examining his trash, this automatically gave him a reasonable expectation of privacy in that trash which was consequently protected by the Fourth Amendment.  Rejecting this, the Supreme Court reasoned that the Fourth Amendment reasonableness of a search does not depend upon the law of the state in which the search occurs.  Specifically, it rejected Greenwood's suggestion that the privacy law of particular states determines the reach of the Fourth Amendment within that state.  486 U.S. at 42–44, 108 S.Ct. at 1630–31, 100 L.Ed.2d at 39.

Justice Kennedy did not participate in the case.  Justice Brennan, joined by Justice Marshall, dissented.  He argued that a trash bag, like other containers, is a repository of personal effects and therefore associated with privacy expectations.  Given the nature of trash and what it reveals about "sexual practices, health, and personal hygiene," a sealed trash bag often harbors evidence of private activities closely associated with the sanctity of the home and the privacies of life protected by the Fourth Amendment.  He continued:

> Had Greenwood flaunted his intimate activity by strewing his trash all over the curb for all to see, or had some nongovernmental intruder invaded his privacy and done the same, I could accept the Court's conclusion that an expectation of privacy would have been unreasonable.  Similarly, had police searching the city dump run across incriminating evidence that,

despite commingling with the trash of others, still retained its identity as Greenwood's, we would have a different case. * * *

The mere *possibility* that unwelcome meddlers *might* open and rummage through the containers does not negate the expectation of privacy in its contents any more than the possibility of a burglary negates an expectation of privacy in the home * * *.

Nor it is dispositive that "respondents placed their refuse at the curb * * *." In the first place, Greenwood can hardly be faulted for leaving trash on his curb when a county ordinance commanded him to do so * * *. More importantly, even the voluntary relinquishment of possession or control over an effect does not necessarily amount to a relinquishment of a privacy expectation in it. Were it otherwise, a letter or package would lose all Fourth Amendment protection when placed in a mail box * * *.

486 U.S. at 53–55, 108 S.Ct. at 1636–37, 100 L.Ed.2d at 45–46 (Brennan, J., dissenting).

## FLORIDA v. RILEY

Supreme Court of the United States, 1989.
488 U.S. 445, 109 S.Ct. 693, 102 L.Ed.2d 835.

JUSTICE WHITE announced the judgment of the Court and delivered an opinion, in which THE CHIEF JUSTICE, JUSTICE SCALIA and JUSTICE KENNEDY join.

On certification to it by a lower state court, the Florida Supreme Court addressed the following question: "Whether surveillance of the interior of a partially covered greenhouse in a residential backyard from the vantage point of a helicopter located 400 feet above the greenhouse constitutes a 'search' for which a warrant is required under the Fourth Amendment and Article I, Section 12 of the Florida Constitution." 511 So.2d 282 (1987). The court answered the question in the affirmative, and we granted the State's petition for certiorari challenging that conclusion.

Respondent Riley lived in a mobile home located on five acres of rural property. A greenhouse was located 10 to 20 feet behind the mobile home. Two sides of the greenhouse were enclosed. The other two sides were not enclosed but the contents of the greenhouse were obscured from view from surrounding property by trees, shrubs and the mobile home. The greenhouse was covered by corrugated roofing panels, some translucent and some opaque. At the time relevant to this case, two of the panels, amounting to approximately 10% of the roof area, were missing. A wire fence surrounded the mobile home and the greenhouse, and the property was posted with a "DO NOT ENTER" sign.

This case originated with an anonymous tip to the Pasco County Sheriff's office that marijuana was being grown on respondent's property. When an investigating officer discovered that he could not see the contents of the greenhouse from the road, he circled twice over respondent's property in a helicopter at the height of 400 feet. With his naked eye, he was able to see through the openings in the roof and one or more of the open sides of the greenhouse and to identify what he thought was marijuana growing in the structure. A warrant was obtained based on these observations, and the ensuing search revealed marijuana growing in the greenhouse. Respondent was charged with possession of marijuana under Florida law. The trial court granted his motion to suppress; the Florida Court of Appeals reversed but certified the case to the Florida Supreme Court, which quashed the decision of the Court of Appeals and reinstated the trial court's suppression order.

We agree with the State's submission that our decision in California v. Ciraolo, 476 U.S. 207, 106 S.Ct. 1809, 90 L.Ed.2d 210 (1986), controls this case. There, acting on a tip, the police inspected the back yard of a particular house while flying in a fixed-wing aircraft at 1,000 feet. With the naked eye the officers saw what they concluded was marijuana growing in the yard. A search warrant was obtained on the strength of this airborne inspection, and marijuana plants were found. The trial court refused to suppress this evidence, but a state appellate court held that the inspection violated the Fourth and Fourteenth Amendments of the United States Constitution and that the warrant was therefore invalid. We in turn reversed, holding that the inspection was not a search subject to the Fourth Amendment. We recognized that the yard was within the curtilage of the house, that a fence shielded the yard from observation from the street and that the occupant had a subjective expectation of privacy. We held, however, that such an expectation was not reasonable and not one "that society is prepared to honor." Id., at 214, 106 S.Ct., at 1813. Our reasoning was that the home and its curtilage are not necessarily protected from inspection that involves no physical invasion. " 'What a person knowingly exposes to the public, even in his own home or office, is not a subject of Fourth Amendment protection.' " Id., at 213, 106 S.Ct., at 1812, quoting Katz v. United States, 389 U.S. 347, 351, 88 S.Ct. 507, 511, 19 L.Ed.2d 576 (1967). As a general proposition, the police may see what may be seen "from a public vantage point where [they have] a right to be" 476 U.S., at 213, 106 S.Ct., at 1812. Thus the police, like the public, would have been free to inspect the backyard garden from the street if their view had been unobstructed. They were likewise, free to inspect the yard from the vantage point of an aircraft flying in the navigable airspace as this plane was. "In an age where private and commercial flight in the public airways is routine, it is unreasonable for respondent to expect that his marijuana plants were constitutionally protected from being observed with the naked eye from an altitude of 1,000 feet. The Fourth Amendment simply does not require the police traveling in the public airways at this altitude to obtain a warrant in order to observe what is visible to the naked eye." Id., at 215, 106 S.Ct., at 1813.

We arrive at the same conclusion in the present case. In this case, as in *Ciraolo,* the property surveyed was within the curtilage of respondent's home. Riley no doubt intended and expected that his greenhouse would not be open to public inspection, and the precautions he took protected against ground-level observation. Because the sides and roof of his greenhouse were left partially open, however, what was growing in the greenhouse was subject to viewing from the air. Under the holding in *Ciraolo,* Riley could not reasonably have expected the contents of his greenhouse to be immune from examination by an officer seated in a fixed-wing aircraft flying in navigable airspace at an altitude of 1,000 feet or, as the Florida Supreme Court seemed to recognize, at an altitude of 500 feet, the lower limit of the navigable airspace for such an aircraft. 511 So.2d, at 288. Here, the inspection was made from a helicopter, but as is the case with fixed-wing planes, "private and commercial flight [by helicopter] in the public airways is routine" in this country, *Ciraolo,* supra, 476 U.S., at 215, 106 S.Ct., at 1813, and there is no indication that such flights are unheard of in Pasco County, Florida. Riley could not reasonably have expected that his greenhouse was protected from public or official observation from a helicopter had it been flying within the navigable airspace for fixed-wing aircraft.

Nor on the facts before us, does it make a difference for Fourth Amendment purposes that the helicopter was flying at 400 feet when the officer saw what was growing in the greenhouse through the partially open roof and sides of the structure. We would have a different case if flying at that altitude had been contrary to law or regulation. But helicopters are not bound by the lower limits of the navigable airspace allowed to other aircraft.[10] Any member of the public could legally have been flying over Riley's property in a helicopter at the altitude of 400 feet and could have observed Riley's greenhouse. The police officer did no more. This is not to say that an inspection of the curtilage of a house from an aircraft will always pass muster under the Fourth Amendment simply because the plane is within the navigable airspace specified by law. But it is of obvious importance that the helicopter in this case was not violating the law, and there is nothing in the record or before us to suggest that helicopters flying at 400 feet are sufficiently rare in this country to lend substance to respondent's claim that he reasonably anticipated that his greenhouse would not be subject to observation from that altitude. Neither is there any intimation here that the helicopter interfered with respondent's normal use of the greenhouse or of other parts of the curtilage. As far as this record reveals, no intimate details connected with the use of the home or curtilage were observed, and there was no undue noise, no wind, dust, or threat of injury. In these circumstances, there was no violation of the Fourth Amendment.

The judgment of the Florida Supreme Court is accordingly reversed.

SO ORDERED.

JUSTICE O'CONNOR, concurring in the judgment.

I concur in the judgment reversing the Supreme Court of Florida because I agree that police observation of the greenhouse in Riley's

---

[10] While FAA regulations permit fixed wing aircraft to be operated at an altitude of 1,000 feet while flying over congested areas and at an altitude of 500 feet above the surface in other than congested areas, helicopters may be operated at less than the minimums for fixed wing aircraft "if the operation is conducted without hazard to persons or property on the surface. In addition, each person operating a helicopter shall comply with routes or altitudes specifically prescribed for helicopters by the [FAA] Administrator." 14 CFR § 91.79 (1988).

curtilage from a helicopter passing at an altitude of 400 feet did not violate an expectation of privacy "that society is prepared to recognize as 'reasonable.'" Katz v. United States, 389 U.S. 347, 361, 88 S.Ct. 507, 517, 19 L.Ed.2d 576 (1967) (Harlan, J., concurring). I write separately, however, to clarify the standard I believe follows from California v. Ciraolo, 476 U.S. 207, 106 S.Ct. 1809, 90 L.Ed.2d 210 (1986). In my view, the plurality's approach rests the scope of Fourth Amendment protection too heavily on compliance with FAA regulations whose purpose is to promote air safety not to protect "[t]he right of the people to be secure in their persons, houses, papers, and effects, against unreasonable searches and seizures." U.S. Const., Amdt. 4.

\* \* \*

Ciraolo's expectation of privacy was unreasonable not because the airplane was operating where it had a "right to be," but because public air travel at 1,000 feet is a sufficiently routine part of modern life that it is unreasonable for persons on the ground to expect that their curtilage will not be observed from the air at that altitude. \* \* \* Because the FAA has decided that helicopters can lawfully operate at virtually any altitude so long as they pose no safety hazard, it does not follow that the expectations of privacy "society is prepared to recognize as 'reasonable'" simply mirror the FAA's safety concerns.

\* \* \*

In determining whether Riley had a reasonable expectation of privacy from aerial observation, the relevant inquiry after *Ciraolo* is not whether the helicopter was where it had a right to be under FAA regulations. Rather, consistent with *Katz,* we must ask whether the helicopter was in the public airways at an altitude at which members of the public travel with sufficient regularity that Riley's expectation of privacy from aerial observation was not "one that society is prepared to recognize as 'reasonable.'" *Katz,* supra, 389 U.S., at 361, 88 S.Ct., at 516. \* \* \* [I]t is not conclusive to observe, as the plurality does, that "[a]ny member of the public could legally have been flying over Riley's property in a helicopter at the altitude of 400 feet and could have observed Riley's greenhouse." Nor is it conclusive that police helicopters may often fly at 400 feet. If the public rarely, if ever, travels overhead at such altitudes, the observation cannot be said to be from a vantage point generally used by the public and Riley cannot be said to have "knowingly expose[d]" his greenhouse to public view. However, if the public can generally be expected to travel over residential backyards at an altitude of 400 feet, Riley cannot reasonably expect his curtilage to be free from such aerial observation.

In my view, the defendant must bear the burden of proving that his expectation of privacy was a reasonable one, and thus that a "search" within the meaning of the Fourth Amendment even took place.

Because there is reason to believe that there is considerable public use of airspace at altitudes of 400 feet and above, and because Riley introduced no evidence to the contrary before the Florida courts, I conclude that Riley's expectation that his curtilage was protected from naked-eye aerial observation from that altitude was not a reasonable one. However, public use of altitudes lower than that—particularly public observations from helicopters circling over the curtilage of a home—may be sufficiently rare that police surveillance from such altitudes would violate reasonable expectations of privacy, despite compliance with FAA air safety regulations.

JUSTICE BRENNAN, with whom JUSTICE MARSHALL and JUSTICE STEVENS, join, dissenting.

* * *

The opinion for a plurality of the Court reads almost as if Katz v. United States, 389 U.S. 347, 88 S.Ct. 507, 19 L.Ed.2d 576 (1967), had never been decided. * * *

I agree, of course, that "[w]hat a person knowingly exposes to the public . . . is not a subject of Fourth Amendment protection." *Katz,* supra, at 351, 88 S.Ct., at 511. But I cannot agree that one "knowingly exposes [an area] to the public" solely because a helicopter may legally fly above it. Under the plurality's exceedingly grudging Fourth Amendment theory, the expectation of privacy is defeated if a single member of the public could conceivably position herself to see into the area in question without doing anything illegal. It is defeated whatever the difficulty a person would have in so positioning herself, and however infrequently anyone would in fact do so. In taking this view the plurality ignores the very essence of *Katz.* The reason why there is no reasonable expectation of privacy in an area that is exposed to the public is that little diminution in "the amount of privacy and freedom remaining to citizens" will result from police surveillance of something that any passerby readily sees. To pretend, as the plurality opinion does, that the same is true when the police use a helicopter to peer over high fences is, at best, disingenuous. * * *

* * * The question before us must be not whether the police were where they had a right to be, but whether public observation of Riley's curtilage was so commonplace that Riley's expectation of privacy in his backyard could not be considered reasonable. While, as we held in *Ciraolo,* air traffic at elevations of 1000 feet or more may be so common that whatever could be seen with the naked eye from that elevation is unprotected by the Fourth Amendment, it is a large step from there to say that the Amendment offers no protection against low-level helicopter surveillance of enclosed curtilage areas. To take this step is error enough. That the plurality does so with little analysis beyond its determination that the police complied with FAA regulations is particularly unfortunate.

* * *

Equally disconcerting is the lack of any meaningful limit to the plurality's holding. It is worth reiterating that the FAA regulations the plurality relies on as establishing that the officer was where he had a right to be set no minimum flight altitude for helicopters. It is difficult, therefore, to see what, if any, helicopter surveillance would run afoul of the plurality's rule that there exists no reasonable expectation of privacy as long as the helicopter is where it has a right to be.

* * *

Perhaps the most remarkable passage in the plurality opinion is its suggestion that the case might be a different one had any "intimate details connected with the use of the home or curtilage [been] observed." What, one wonders, is meant by "intimate details"? If the police had observed Riley embracing his wife in the backyard greenhouse, would we then say that his reasonable expectation of privacy had been infringed? Where in the Fourth Amendment or in our cases is there any warrant for imposing a requirement that the activity observed must be "intimate" in order to be protected by the Constitution?

It is difficult to avoid the conclusion that the plurality has allowed its analysis of Riley's expectation of privacy to be colored by its distaste for the activity in which he was engaged. It is indeed easy to forget, especially in view of current concern over drug trafficking, that the scope of the Fourth Amendment's protection does not turn on whether the activity disclosed by a search is illegal or innocuous. But we dismiss this as a "drug case" only at the peril of our own liberties.
\* \* \*

I find little to disagree with in the concurring opinion of Justice O'CONNOR, apart from its closing paragraphs. A majority of the Court thus agrees that the fundamental inquiry is not whether the police were where they had a right to be under FAA regulations, but rather whether Riley's expectation of privacy was rendered illusory by the extent of public observation of his backyard from aerial traffic at 400 feet.

What separates me from Justice O'CONNOR is essentially an empirical matter concerning the extent of public use of the airspace at that altitude, together with the question of how to resolve that issue. I do not think the constitutional claim should fail simply because "there is reason to believe" that there is "considerable" public flying this close to earth or because Riley "introduced no evidence to the contrary before the Florida courts." \* \* \* I think we could take judicial notice that, while there may be an occasional privately owned helicopter that flies over populated areas at an altitude of 400 feet, such flights are a rarity and are almost entirely limited to approaching or leaving airports or to reporting traffic congestion near major roadways.
\* \* \*

If, however, we are to resolve the issue by considering whether the appropriate party carried its burden of proof, I again think that Riley must prevail. Because the State has greater access to information concerning customary flight patterns and because the coercive power of the State ought not be brought to bear in cases in which it is unclear whether the prosecution is a product of an unconstitutional, warrantless search, the burden of proof properly rests with the State and not with the individual defendant. The State quite clearly has not carried this burden.

\* \* \*

    \* \* \* I respectfully dissent.

JUSTICE BLACKMUN, dissenting.

The question before the Court is whether the helicopter surveillance over Riley's property constituted a "search" within the meaning of the Fourth Amendment.  Like Justice Brennan, Justice Marshall, Justice Stevens, and Justice O'Connor, I believe that answering this question depends upon whether Riley has a "reasonable expectation of privacy" that no such surveillance would occur, and does not depend upon the fact that the helicopter was flying at a lawful altitude under FAA regulations.  A majority of this Court thus agrees to at least this much.

The inquiry then becomes how to determine whether Riley's expectation was a reasonable one.  Both Justice Brennan, and the two Justices who have joined him, and Justice O'Connor believe that the reasonableness of Riley's expectation depends, in large measure, on the frequency of nonpolice helicopter flights at an altitude of 400 feet. Again, I agree.

How is this factual issue to be decided?  Justice Brennan suggests that we may resolve it ourselves without any evidence in the record on this point.  I am wary of this approach.  While I, too, suspect that for most American communities it is a rare event when nonpolice helicopters fly over one's curtilage at an altitude of 400 feet, I am not convinced that we should establish a *per se* rule for the entire Nation based on judicial suspicion alone.  See Coffin, Judicial Balancing, 63 N.Y.U.L.Rev. 16, 37 (1988).

But we need not abandon our judicial intuition entirely.  *   *   * [I]t is appropriate for us to take into account our estimation of the frequency of nonpolice helicopter flights.  *   *   * [B]ecause I believe that private helicopters rarely fly over curtilages at an altitude of 400 feet, I would impose upon the prosecution the burden of proving contrary facts necessary to show that Riley lacked a reasonable expectation of privacy.  *   *   *

In this case, the prosecution did not meet this burden of proof, as Justice Brennan notes.  This failure should compel a finding that a Fourth Amendment search occurred.  But because our prior cases gave the parties little guidance on the burden of proof issue, I would remand this case to allow the prosecution an opportunity to meet this burden.

The order of this Court, however, is not to remand the case in this manner.  Rather, because Justice O'Connor would impose the burden of proof on Riley and because she would not allow Riley an opportunity to meet this burden, she joins the plurality's view that no Fourth Amendment search occurred.  The judgment of the Court, therefore, is to reverse outright on the Fourth Amendment issue.  Accordingly, for the reasons set forth above, I respectfully dissent.

### NOTE

In Dow Chemical Company v. United States, 476 U.S. 227, 106 S.Ct. 1819, 90 L.Ed.2d 226 (1986), investigators for the Environmental Protection Agency (EPA) used an airplane equipped with a precision aerial mapping camera to photograph Dow's Midland, Michigan plant from altitudes of 12,000, 3,000 and

1,200 feet. The plant was a 2,000 acre facility surrounded by a fence. Precautions were not taken to conceal all of the manufacturing equipment in the plant from aerial view. Nevertheless, its desire to protect trade secret information caused Dow to remain quite concerned about aerial photography. Low-flying planes were identified when possible and efforts were made to obtain possession of any photographs taken. A majority of the Court concluded that the EPA's actions did not constitute a "search" for Fourth Amendment purposes:

> Admittedly, Dow's enclosed plant complex, like the area in *Oliver,* does not fall precisely within the "open fields" doctrine. The area at issue here can perhaps be seen as falling somewhere between "open fields" and curtilage, but lacking some of the critical characteristics of both. Dow's inner manufacturing areas are elaborately secured to ensure they are not open or exposed to the public from the ground. Any actual physical entry by EPA into any enclosed area would raise significantly different questions * * *. The narrow issue raised by [Dow] * * * concerns aerial observation of a 2,000 acre outdoor manufacturing facility without physical entry.

* * *

> It may well be, as the Government concedes, that surveillance of private property by using highly sophisticated surveillance equipment not generally available to the public, such as satellite technology, might be constitutionally proscribed absent a warrant. But the photographs here are not so revealing of intimate details as to raise constitutional concerns. Although they undoubtedly give EPA more detailed information than naked-eye views, they remain limited to an outline of the facility's buildings and equipment. The mere fact that human vision is enhanced somewhat, at least to the degree here, does not give rise to constitutional problems.

476 U.S. at 236–38, 106 S.Ct. at 1825–27, 90 L.Ed.2d at 236–38.

Four members of the Court dissented in an opinion by Justice Powell:

> Since physical trespass no longer functions as a reliable proxy for intrusions upon privacy, it is necessary to determine if the surveillance, whatever its form, intruded on a reasonable expectation that a certain activity or area would remain private. * * * Dow has taken every feasible step to protect information claimed to constitute trade secrets from the public and particularly from its competitors. Accordingly, Dow has a reasonable expectation of privacy in its commercial facility in the sense required by the Fourth Amendment. EPA's conduct in this case intruded on that expectation because the aerial photography captured information that Dow had taken reasonable steps to preserve as private.

476 U.S. at 248–49, 106 S.Ct. at 1831–32, 90 L.Ed.2d at 244–45 (Powell, J., concurring and dissenting). Rejecting the majority's distinction among types of technology that might be used to secure information, he continued:

> *Katz* measures Fourth Amendment rights by reference to the privacy interests that a free society recognizes as reasonable, not by reference to the method of surveillance used in the particular case. If the Court's observations were to become the basis of a new Fourth Amendment standard that would replace the rule in *Katz,* privacy rights would be seriously at risk as technological advances become generally disseminated and available in our society.

476 U.S. at 251, 106 S.Ct. at 1833, 90 L.Ed.2d at 246.

## 2.  POLICE ACTIVITY CONSTITUTING A "SEIZURE"

The Fourth Amendment exclusionary rule is invoked if challenged evidence is tainted by an unreasonable "seizure" as well as if it is the product of an unreasonable "search."  Whether law enforcement activity constitutes a "seizure" is determined by criteria different from those that identify "searches," and the "reasonableness" of seizures is governed by Fourth Amendment requirements different from those applicable to searches.  A person as well as an item may, of course, be "seized," but seizures of persons are addressed in Chapter 4.

Fourth Amendment discussion, culminating in the principal case, has focused upon when, if ever, the Fourth Amendment requires judicial authorization for a seizure, in the form of a warrant or a specific provision in a warrant authorizing seizure of the property.  But several preliminary matters also deserve consideration.

*Definition of "Seizures."*  Whether police activity concerning places or items constitutes a "seizure" turns not upon whether that activity intrudes upon privacy interests but rather whether it constitutes a meaningful interference with the possessory interests of the suspect. United States v. Jacobsen, 466 U.S. 109, 113, 104 S.Ct. 1653, 1656, 80 L.Ed.2d 85, 94 (1984).  In United States v. Karo, 468 U.S. 705, 104 S.Ct. 3296, 82 L.Ed.2d 530 (1984), discussed at pages 94–95, supra, the defense urged that a "seizure" occurred when Karo took possession of a can of ether which, unknown to Karo, contained a "beeping" device placed there by federal officers.  Rejecting this, the Court explained:

> Although the can may have contained an unknown and unwanted foreign object, it cannot be said that anyone's possessory interest was interfered with in any meaningful way.  At most, there was a technical trespass on the space occupied by the beeper.  *  *  *

468 U.S. at 712, 104 S.Ct. at 3302, 82 L.Ed.2d at 540.

*Items Subject to Seizure.*  Officers are clearly entitled—if other requirements are met—to seize items which they reasonably believe are stolen property and other "fruits" of criminal conduct, instrumentalities used in the commission of crime, or contraband, i.e., items—such as drugs—the possession of which is prohibited by law.  But seizure of items of "mere evidence"—items which are of concern or value to public officers only because they constitute evidence of the commission of a crime or of someone's guilt of such a crime—was at one time barred by the Fourth Amendment.  Gouled v. United States, 255 U.S. 298, 311, 41 S.Ct. 261, 265, 65 L.Ed. 647, 653 (1921).  In Warden v. Hayden, 387 U.S. 294, 87 S.Ct. 1642, 18 L.Ed.2d 2d 782 (1967), the Supreme Court abandoned this rule and held that the Fourth Amendment did not absolutely bar seizure of "mere evidence."  No significant objective of the Amendment is served by the distinction, the Court noted, and citizens can be adequately protected from improper searches whether the object of those searches is to find and seize mere evidence or items subject to seizure under the traditional doctrines.  387 U.S. at 306–07, 87 S.Ct. at 1649–50, 18 L.Ed.2d at 971–92.

The traditional list of items subject to seizure—contraband, instrumentalities and fruits of crime, and evidence—may be incomplete. Law enforcement officers may sometimes have authority to assume possession of items that do not come within these categories. For example, an officer who arrests a suspect in or near the suspect's automobile may, under some circumstances, have authority to seize the automobile to protect the suspect's interest or to protect the officer from later claims that by his actions he subjected the automobile to increased risk of vandalism or other harm.

*Need for "Probable Cause."* Does a seizure require probable cause to believe that the item seized is one to which the officers are entitled to possession, i.e., probable cause to believe that the item is contraband, an instrument or fruit of a crime, or evidence? The plurality discussion in Coolidge v. New Hampshire, 403 U.S. 443, 91 S.Ct. 2022, 29 L.Ed.2d 564 (1971), discussed at length in the principal case, suggested that a "plain view" seizure requires that it be "immediately apparent" to the officer that the item is subject to seizure. Whether this means that probable cause is necessary was considered but not resolved in Texas v. Brown, 460 U.S. 730, 103 S.Ct. 1535, 75 L.Ed.2d 502 (1983). The Court returned to the question in Arizona v. Hicks, 480 U.S. 321, 107 S.Ct. 1149, 94 L.Ed. 2d 347 (1987), and addressed specifically whether probable cause was necessary for the "plain view" seizure of an item which officers came upon during a reasonable warrantless search of an apartment:

> We now hold that probable cause is required. To say otherwise would cut the "plain view" doctrine loose from its theoretical and practical moorings. The theory of that doctrine consists of extending to nonpublic places such as the home * * * the police's longstanding authority to make warrantless seizures in public places of such objects as weapons and contraband. And the practical justification for that extension is the desirability of sparing police, whose viewing of the object in the course of a lawful search is as legitimate as it would have been in a public place, the inconvenience and the risk—to themselves or to preservation of the evidence—of going to obtain a warrant. Dispensing with the need for a warrant is worlds apart from permitting a lesser standard of *cause* for the seizure than a warrant would require, i.e., the standard of probable cause. No reason is apparent why an object should routinely be seizable on lesser grounds, during an unrelated search and seizure, than would have been needed to obtain a warrant for the same object if it had been known to be on the premises.

480 U.S. at 326–27, 107 S.Ct. at 1153, 94 L.Ed.2d at 355.

## HORTON v. CALIFORNIA

Supreme Court of the United States, 1990.
____ U.S. ____, 110 S.Ct. 2301, 110 L.Ed.2d 112.

STEVENS, J.

In this case we revisit an issue that was considered, but not conclusively resolved, in Coolidge v. New Hampshire, 403 U.S. 443, 91

S.Ct. 2022, 29 L.Ed.2d 564 (1971): Whether the warrantless seizure of evidence of crime in plain view is prohibited by the Fourth Amendment if the discovery of the evidence was not inadvertent. We conclude that even though inadvertence is a characteristic of most legitimate "plain view" seizures, it is not a necessary condition.

## I

Petitioner was convicted of the armed robbery of Erwin Wallaker, the treasurer of the San Jose Coin Club. When Wallaker returned to his home after the Club's annual show, he entered his garage and was accosted by two masked men, one armed with a machine gun and the other with an electrical shocking device, sometimes referred to as a "stun gun." The two men shocked Wallaker, bound and handcuffed him, and robbed him of jewelry and cash. During the encounter sufficient conversation took place to enable Wallaker subsequently to identify petitioner's distinctive voice. His identification was partially corroborated by a witness who saw the robbers leaving the scene, and by evidence that petitioner had attended the coin show.

Sergeant LaRault, an experienced police officer, investigated the crime and determined that there was probable cause to search petitioner's home for the proceeds of the robbery and for the weapons used by the robbers. His affidavit for a search warrant referred to police reports that described the weapons as well as the proceeds, but the warrant issued by the Magistrate only authorized a search for the proceeds, including three specifically described rings.

Pursuant to the warrant, LaRault searched petitioner's residence, but he did not find the stolen property. During the course of the search, however, he discovered the weapons in plain view and seized them. Specifically, he seized an Uzi machine gun, a .38 caliber revolver, two stun guns, a handcuff key, a San Jose Coin Club advertising brochure, and a few items of clothing identified by the victim.[11] LaRault testified that while he was searching for the rings, he also was interested in finding other evidence connecting petitioner to the robbery. Thus, the seized evidence was not discovered "inadvertently."

The trial court refused to suppress the evidence found in petitioner's home and, after a jury trial, petitioner was found guilty and sentenced to prison. The California Court of Appeal affirmed. * * * The California Supreme Court denied petitioner's request for review.

* * *

## II

* * *

The right to security in person and property protected by the Fourth Amendment may be invaded in quite different ways by searches and seizures. A search compromises the individual interest in privacy;

---

[11] Although the officer viewed other handguns and rifles, he did not seize them because there was no probable cause to believe they were associated with criminal activity. App. 30; see Arizona v. Hicks, 480 U.S. 321, 327, 107 S.Ct. 1149, 1153, 94 L.Ed.2d 347 (1987).

a seizure deprives the individual of dominion over his or her person or property. The "plain view" doctrine is often considered an exception to the general rule that warrantless searches are presumptively unreasonable, but this characterization overlooks the important difference between searches and seizures.[12] If an article is already in plain view, neither its observation nor its seizure would involve any invasion of privacy. A seizure of the article, however, would obviously invade the owner's possessory interest. If "plain view" justifies an exception from an otherwise applicable warrant requirement, therefore, it must be an exception that is addressed to the concerns that are implicated by seizures rather than by searches.

The criteria that generally guide "plain view" seizures were set forth in Coolidge v. New Hampshire, 403 U.S. 443, 91 S.Ct. 2022, 29 L.Ed.2d 564 (1971). The Court held that the seizure of two automobiles parked in plain view on the defendant's driveway in the course of arresting the defendant violated the Fourth Amendment. Accordingly, particles of gun powder that had been subsequently found in vacuum sweepings from one of the cars could not be introduced in evidence against the defendant. The State endeavored to justify the seizure of the automobiles, and their subsequent search at the police station, on four different grounds, including the "plain view" doctrine. The scope of that doctrine as it had developed in earlier cases was fairly summarized in these three paragraphs from Justice Stewart's opinion:

> It is well established that under certain circumstances the police may seize evidence in plain view without a warrant. But it is important to keep in mind that, in the vast majority of cases, ANY evidence seized by the police will be in plain view, at least at the moment of seizure. The problem with the "plain view" doctrine has been to identify the circumstances in which plain view has legal significance rather than being simply the normal concomitant of any search, legal or illegal.

> An example of the applicability of the "plain view" doctrine is the situation in which the police have a warrant to search a given area for specified objects, and in the course of the search come across some other article of incriminating character. Where the initial intrusion that brings the police within plain view of such an article is supported, not by a warrant, but by one of the recognized exceptions to the warrant requirement, the seizure is also legitimate. Thus the police may inadvertently come across evidence while in "hot pursuit" of a fleeing suspect. And an object that comes into view during a search incident to arrest that is appropriately limited in scope under existing law may be seized without a warrant. Finally, the "plain view" doctrine has been applied where a police officer is not searching for evidence against the

---

[12] It is important to distinguish "plain view," as used in *Coolidge* to justify seizure of an object, from an officer's mere observation of an item left in plain view. Whereas the latter generally involves no Fourth Amendment search, the former generally does implicate the Amendment's limitations upon seizures of personal property.

accused, but nonetheless inadvertently comes across an incriminating object.

What the "plain view" cases have in common is that the police officer in each of them had a prior justification for an intrusion in the course of which he came inadvertently across a piece of evidence incriminating the accused. The doctrine serves to supplement the prior justification—whether it be a warrant for another object, hot pursuit, search incident to lawful arrest, or some other legitimate reason for being present unconnected with a search directed against the accused—and permits the warrantless seizure. Of course, the extension of the original justification is legitimate only where it is immediately apparent to the police that they have evidence before them; the "plain view" doctrine may not be used to extend a general exploratory search from one object to another until something incriminating at last emerges. Id., at 465–466, 91 S.Ct., at 2037–2038 (footnote omitted).

Justice Stewart then described the two limitations on the doctrine that he found implicit in its rationale: First, "that plain view ALONE is never enough to justify the warrantless seizure of evidence,"; and second, "that the discovery of evidence in plain view must be inadvertent."

Justice Stewart's analysis of the "plain view" doctrine did not command a majority and a plurality of the Court has since made clear that the discussion is "not a binding precedent." Texas v. Brown, [460 U.S. 730, 737, 103 S.Ct. 1535, 1541, 75 L.Ed.2d 502 (1983)] (opinion of REHNQUIST, J.). Justice Harlan, who concurred in the Court's judgment and in its response to the dissenting opinions, did not join the plurality's discussion of the "plain view" doctrine. The decision nonetheless is a binding precedent. Before discussing the second limitation, which is implicated in this case, it is therefore necessary to explain why the first adequately supports the Court's judgment.

It is, of course, an essential predicate to any valid warrantless seizure of incriminating evidence that the officer did not violate the Fourth Amendment in arriving at the place from which the evidence could be plainly viewed. There are, moreover, two additional conditions that must be satisfied to justify the warrantless seizure. First, not only must the item be in plain view, its incriminating character must also be "immediately apparent." Thus, in *Coolidge,* the cars were obviously in plain view, but their probative value remained uncertain until after the interiors were swept and examined microscopically. Second, not only must the officer be lawfully located in a place from which the object can be plainly seen, but he or she must also have a lawful right of access to the object itself. As the Solicitor General has suggested, Justice Harlan's vote in *Coolidge* may have rested on the fact that the seizure of the cars was accomplished by means of a warrantless trespass on the defendant's property.

In all events, we are satisfied that the absence of inadvertence was not essential to the Court's rejection of the State's "plain view" argument in *Coolidge.*

### III

Justice Stewart concluded that the inadvertence requirement was necessary to avoid a violation of the express constitutional requirement that a valid warrant must particularly describe the things to be seized. He explained:

> The rationale of the exception to the warrant requirement, as just stated, is that a plain-view seizure will not turn an initially valid (and therefore limited) search into a "general" one, while the inconvenience of procuring a warrant to cover an inadvertent discovery is great. But where the discovery is anticipated, where the police know in advance the location of the evidence and intend to seize it, the situation is altogether different. The requirement of a warrant to seize imposes no inconvenience whatever, or at least none which is constitutionally cognizable in a legal system that regards warrantless searches as "per se unreasonable" in the absence of "exigent circumstances."

> If the initial intrusion is bottomed upon a warrant that fails to mention a particular object, though the police know its location and intend to seize it, then there is a violation of the express constitutional requirement of "Warrants . . . particularly describing . . . [the] things to be seized." 403 U.S., at 469–471, 91 S.Ct., at 2040–2041.

We find two flaws in this reasoning. First, evenhanded law enforcement is best achieved by the application of objective standards of conduct, rather than standards that depend upon the subjective state of mind of the officer. The fact that an officer is interested in an item of evidence and fully expects to find it in the course of a search should not invalidate its seizure if the search is confined in area and duration by the terms of a warrant or a valid exception to the warrant requirement. If the officer has knowledge approaching certainty that the item will be found, we see no reason why he or she would deliberately omit a particular description of the item to be seized from the application for a search warrant. Specification of the additional item could only permit the officer to expand the scope of the search. On the other hand, if he or she has a valid warrant to search for one item and merely a suspicion concerning the second, whether or not it amounts to probable cause, we fail to see why that suspicion should immunize the second item from seizure if it is found during a lawful search for the first.

\* \* \*

Second, the suggestion that the inadvertence requirement is necessary to prevent the police from conducting general searches, or from converting specific warrants into general warrants, is not persuasive because that interest is already served by the requirements that no warrant issue unless it "particularly describ[es] the place to be searched and the persons or things to be seized," and that a warrantless search be circumscribed by the exigencies which justify its initiation. Scrupulous adherence to these requirements serves the interests in limiting the area and duration of the search that the inadvertence requirement inadequately protects. Once those commands have been satisfied and the officer has a lawful right of access, however, no additional Fourth Amendment interest is furthered by requiring that the discovery of evidence be inadvertent. If the scope of the search exceeds that permitted by the terms of a validly issued warrant or the character of the relevant exception from the warrant requirement, the subsequent seizure is unconstitutional without more. * * *

In this case, the scope of the search was not enlarged in the slightest by the omission of any reference to the weapons in the warrant. Indeed, if the three rings and other items named in the warrant had been found at the outset—or if petitioner had them in his possession and had responded to the warrant by producing them immediately—no search for weapons could have taken place. * * * JUSTICE WHITE's dissenting opinion in *Coolidge* is instructive:

> Police with a warrant for a rifle may search only places where rifles might be and must terminate the search once the rifle is found; the inadvertence rule will in no way reduce the number of places into which they may lawfully look. 403 U.S., at 517, 91 S.Ct., at 2063.

As we have already suggested, by hypothesis the seizure of an object in plain view does not involve an intrusion on privacy.[13] If the interest in privacy has been invaded, the violation must have occurred before the object came into plain view and there is no need for an inadvertence limitation on seizures to condemn it. The prohibition against general searches and general warrants serves primarily as a protection against unjustified intrusions on privacy. But reliance on privacy concerns that support that prohibition is misplaced when the inquiry concerns the scope of an exception that merely authorizes an officer with a lawful right of access to an item to seize it without a warrant.

In this case the items seized from petitioner's home were discovered during a lawful search authorized by a valid warrant. When they were discovered, it was immediately apparent to the officer that they constituted incriminating evidence. He had probable cause, not only to obtain a warrant to search for the stolen property, but also to believe that the weapons and handguns had been used in the crime he was investigating. The search was authorized by the warrant, the seizure was authorized by the "plain view" doctrine. The judgment is affirmed.

It is so ordered.

JUSTICE BRENNAN, with whom JUSTICE MARSHALL joins, dissenting.

* * *

The Fourth Amendment * * * protects two distinct interests. The prohibition against unreasonable searches and the requirement

---

[13] Even if the item is a container, its seizure does not compromise the interest in preserving the privacy of its contents because it may only be opened pursuant to either a search warrant, see * * * United States v. Chadwick, 433 U.S. 1, 97 S.Ct. 2476, 53 L.Ed.2d 538 (1977) * * *, or one of the well-delineated exceptions to the warrant requirement.

that a warrant "particularly describ[e] the place to be searched" protect an interest in privacy. The prohibition against unreasonable seizures and the requirement that a warrant "particularly describ[e] . . . the . . . things to be seized" protect a possessory interest in property. The Fourth Amendment, by its terms, declares the privacy and possessory interests to be equally important. As this Court recently stated, "Although the interest protected by the Fourth Amendment injunction against unreasonable searches is quite different from that protected by its injunction against unreasonable seizures, neither the one nor the other is of inferior worth or necessarily requires only lesser protection." Arizona v. Hicks, 480 U.S. 321, 328, 107 S.Ct. 1149, 1154, 94 L.Ed.2d 347 (1987) (citation omitted).

The Amendment protects these equally important interests in precisely the same manner: by requiring a neutral and detached magistrate to evaluate, before the search or seizure, the government's showing of probable cause and its particular description of the place to be searched and the items to be seized. Accordingly, just as a warrantless search is per se unreasonable absent exigent circumstances, so too a seizure of personal property is "per se unreasonable within the meaning of the Fourth Amendment unless it is accomplished pursuant to a judicial warrant issued upon probable cause and particularly describing the items to be seized." * * *

The plain view doctrine is an exception to the general rule that a seizure of personal property must be authorized by a warrant. As Justice Stewart explained in *Coolidge,* we accept a warrantless seizure when an officer is lawfully in a location and inadvertently sees evidence of a crime because of "the inconvenience of procuring a warrant" to seize this newly discovered piece of evidence. But "where the discovery is anticipated, where the police know in advance the location of the evidence and intend to seize it," the argument that procuring a warrant would be "inconvenient" loses much, if not all, of its force. Barring an exigency, there is no reason why the police officers could not have obtained a warrant to seize this evidence before entering the premises. The rationale behind the inadvertent discovery requirement is simply that we will not excuse officers from the general requirement of a warrant to seize if the officers know the location of evidence, have probable cause to seize it, intend to seize it, and yet do not bother to obtain a warrant particularly describing that evidence. To do so would violate "the express constitutional requirement of 'Warrants . . . particularly describing . . . [the] things to be seized,' and would 'fly in the face of the basic rule that no amount of probable cause can justify a warrantless seizure.' "

* * *

The Court posits two "flaws" in Justice Stewart's reasoning that it believes demonstrate the inappropriateness of the inadvertent discovery requirement. But these flaws are illusory. First, the majority explains that it can see no reason why an officer who "has knowledge approaching certainty" that an item will be found in a particular location "would deliberately omit a particular description of the item to be seized from the application for a search warrant." * * * [T]here are[, however,] a number of instances in which a law enforcement officer might deliberately choose to omit certain items from a warrant application even though he has probable cause to seize them, knows they are on the premises, and intends to seize them when they are discovered in plain view. For example, the warrant application process can often be time-consuming, especially when the police attempt to seize a large number of items. An officer interested in conducting a search as soon as possible might decide to save time by listing only one or two hard-to-find items, such as the stolen rings in this case, confident that he will find in plain view all of the other evidence he is looking for before he discovers the listed items. Because rings could be located almost anywhere inside or outside a house, it is unlikely that a warrant to search for and seize the rings would restrict the scope of the search. An officer might rationally find the risk of immediately discovering the items listed in the warrant—thereby forcing him to conclude the search immediately—outweighed by the time saved in the application process.

The majority also contends that, once an officer is lawfully in a house and the scope of his search is adequately circumscribed by a warrant, "no additional Fourth Amendment interest is furthered by requiring that the discovery of evidence be inadvertent." * * * The majority is correct, but it has asked the wrong question. It is true that the inadvertent discovery requirement furthers no privacy interests. The requirement in no way reduces the scope of a search or the number of places into which officers may look. But it does protect possessory interests. The inadvertent discovery requirement is essential if we are to take seriously the Fourth Amendment's protection of possessory interests as well as privacy interests. The Court today eliminates a rule designed to further possessory interests on the ground that it fails to further privacy interests. I cannot countenance such constitutional legerdemain.

* * *

* * * I respectfully dissent.

### NOTES

1. In United States v. Jacobsen, 466 U.S. 109, 104 S.Ct. 1652, 80 L.Ed.2d 85 (1984), federal Drug Enforcement Administration (DEA) officers properly intercepted plastic bags containing a white powder. Before permitting the powder to be delivered to Jacobsen, the agents—without a warrant—conducted two field tests on it to determine whether it was cocaine. These tests involved taking very small amounts of the substance and placing them sequentially in three test tubes containing specific liquids. If the liquids turn certain colors, this indicates that the substance is cocaine. No evidence was introduced that the tests could reveal anything about the substance tested other than whether it was cocaine. In addressing whether the agents' conduct amounted to an unreasonable search or seizure, the Court considered two aspects of it. First, did the determination of whether the substance was cocaine or not intrude upon a reasonable expectation of privacy? Answering this in the negative, the Court relied heavily upon *Place,* discussed in note 3 on page 95, supra. It stressed that Congress had decided to criminalize even private possession of cocaine; "thus governmental conduct that can reveal whether a substance is

cocaine, and no other arguably 'private' fact, compromises no legitimate privacy interest."   466 U.S. at 123, 104 S.Ct. at 1662, 80 L.Ed.2d at 101.

Second, the test resulted in destruction of a quantity of the powder.  Did this permanent deprivation of the suspects' possessory (and other) interests in the destroyed powder render the otherwise valid seizure of the powder unreasonable?  To answer this, the Court balanced the nature and quality of the intrusion against the importance of the governmental interests:

> [W]e conclude that the destruction of the powder during the course of the field test was reasonable.  The law enforcement interests justifying the procedure were substantial; the suspicious nature of the material made it virtually certain that the substance tested was in fact contraband.  Conversely, because only a trace amount of material was involved, the loss of which appears to have gone unnoticed by respondents, and since the property had already been lawfully detained, the "seizure" could, at most, have only a *de minimis* impact on any protected property interest.  *  *  *  Under these circumstances, the safeguards of a warrant would only minimally advance Fourth Amendment interests.  This warrantless "seizure" was reasonable.

466 U.S. at 125, 104 S.Ct. at 1663, 80 L.Ed.2d at 102.

2.  If officers "secure" premises, as for example pending application for a search warrant, by preventing the owner or residents from entering, have they "seized" those premises?  The Court has not resolved this.  See Segura v. United States, 468 U.S. 796, 104 S.Ct. 3380, 82 L.Ed.2d 599 (1984).

3.  The difficulty of distinguishing between, and properly relating, "searches" and "seizures" was illustrated by Arizona v. Hicks, 480 U.S. 321, 107 S.Ct. 1149, 94 L.Ed.2d 347 (1987).  Officers responded to a complaint that someone had fired a bullet through the floor of Hicks' apartment, injuring a man in the apartment below.  The officers entered the apartment to search for the shooter and found (and seized) several weapons.  One policeman—Officer Nelson— noticed some expensive stereo equipment, which he believed was "out of place" in the "squalid" apartment.  He moved several pieces slightly so as to be able to determine their serial numbers.  When a check with headquarters revealed that one of the items had been taken in an armed robbery, he seized it.  Later, information was developed that the other stereo items had also been taken in the robbery and a warrant was obtained and executed for those items.  At Hicks' trial for the robbery, however, all of the items were suppressed.  The Supreme Court, in an opinion written by Justice Scalia, affirmed.

First, the Court agreed that recording the serial numbers of the stereo equipment did not constitute a "seizure," as it involved no meaningful interference with Hicks' possessory interests.  But Officer Nelson's moving of the stereo equipment so as to ascertain the numbers was a "search" "separate and apart" from the search of the apartment for the shooter, victims and weapons.  Although the search for the shooter and related items was reasonable because of the exigencies of the situation, those exigencies did not justify the warrantless search of the stereo equipment.  Nor was there any other Fourth Amendment justification for the warrantless search.  Under the "plain view" doctrine, Justice Scalia explained, the search would have been reasonable if Officer Nelson could have "seized" the equipment.  But such a seizure required probable cause, see the discussion supra at page 106, and Nelson lacked this.

Returning to the significance of Officer Nelson having "searched" the equipment rather than "seizing" it, the Court concluded that the same considerations precluded a holding that searches—as contrasted with seizures—of items in plain view can be sustained on less than probable cause:

[W]hether legal authority to move the equipment could be found only as an inevitable concomitant of the authority to seize it, or also as a consequence of some independent power to search certain objects in plain view, probable cause to believe the equipment was stolen was required.

480 U.S. at 328, 107 S.Ct. at 1154, 94 L.Ed.2d at 356.

But, the Court emphasized, the fact that the officers' actions with regard to the stereo equipment was unrelated to the justification for their entry into the apartment did not render that action *ipso facto* unreasonable. Where the plain view doctrine does apply, the seizure (or search) need not be related to the justification for the initial intrusion. 480 U.S. at 323, 107 S.Ct. at 1151, 94 L.Ed.2d at 354. With regard to whether Officer Nelson had the probable cause necessary for his examination of the stereo equipment, the majority noted that the State had conceded that only "reasonable suspicion" existed. This, it reasoned, precluded the Court from considering the question on the merits and required it to assume that probable cause was lacking. 480 U.S. at 323, 107 S.Ct. at 1151, 94 L.Ed.2d at 355.

Justice O'Connor, joined by the Chief Justice and Justice Powell, dissented. Officer Nelson's action, she argued, was not a "full-blown search" but rather a "cursory inspection of an item in view" that should be reasonable upon the "reasonable suspicion" that Nelson had. If—but only if—officers wish to go beyond such cursory inspections should they be required to have probable cause:

[T]he balance of the governmental and privacy interests strongly supports a reasonable suspicion standard for the cursory examination of items in plain view. The additional intrusion caused by an inspection of an item in plain view for its serial number is minuscule. * * *

Weighed against this * * * are rather major gains in law enforcement. The use of identification numbers in tracing stolen property is a powerful law enforcement tool. Serial numbers are far more helpful and accurate in detecting stolen property than simple police recollection of the evidence. Given the prevalence of mass produced goods in our national economy, a serial number is often the only sure method of detecting stolen property.

480 U.S. at 338–89, 107 S.Ct. at 1159–60 94 L.Ed.2d at 355 (O'Connor, J., dissenting). Justice Scalia's opinion, however, rejected this:

[A] truly cursory inspection—one that involves merely looking at what is already exposed to view, without disturbing it—is not a "search" for Fourth Amendment purposes, and therefore does not even require reasonable suspicion. We are unwilling to send police and judges into a new thicket of Fourth Amendment law, to seek a creature of uncertain description that is neither a plain-view inspection nor yet a "full-blown search."

480 U.S. at 328, 107 S.Ct. at 1154, 94 L.Ed.2d at 356. Justice Powell also authored a dissent, joined by the Chief Justice and Justice O'Connor, emphasizing his view that the majority unreasonably distinguished between "looking" at a suspicious item and " 'moving' it even a few inches." This distinction, he offered, "trivializes the Fourth Amendment," causes uncertainty, could deter conscientious officers from lawfully obtaining evidence, and "may handicap law enforcement without enhancing privacy interests." 480 U.S. at 333, 107 S.Ct. at 1157, 94 L.Ed.2d at 359 (Powell, J., dissenting).

4. If an item is "seized" under the Fourth Amendment and that seizure is "reasonable," what additional is necessary before officers may "search" that item? In United States v. Chadwick, 433 U.S. 1, 97 S.Ct. 2476, 53 L.Ed.2d 538

(1977), cited in footnote 13 of the principal case, officers observed two Amtrak rail passengers arrive in Boston, and suspected that the large footlocker they brought contained contraband. A trained dog released near the footlocker signaled that it contained a controlled substance. Chadwick met the two passengers and the footlocker was placed in the trunk of Chadwick's car, parked outside the rail station. While the trunk of the car was still open, officers arrested all three and seized the footlocker. The footlocker was taken to the federal building in Boston. An hour and a half after the arrests, the footlocker was opened and searched. It was locked with a padlock and a regular trunk lock; how the officers opened it was not established. Marijuana was found inside. Assuming that the officers had validly seized the footlocker, the Court nevertheless held that their search of it was unreasonable because no warrant had been obtained:

> Once law enforcement authorities have reduced luggage or other personal property not immediately associated with the person of [an] arrestee to their exclusive control, and there is no longer any danger that the arrestee might gain access to the property to seize a weapon or destroy evidence, a search of that property is no longer an incident of the arrest.
>
> Here the search was conducted more than an hour after federal agents had gained exclusive control of the footlocker and long after [the arrestees] were securely in custody; the search therefore cannot be viewed as incidental to the arrest or as justified by any other exigency. Even though on this record the issuance of a warrant by a judicial officer was reasonably predictable, a line must be drawn. In our view, where no exigency is shown to support the need for an immediate search, the Warrant Clause places the line at the point where the property to be searched comes under the exclusive dominion of police authority.

433 U.S. at 15, 97 S.Ct. at 2485–86, 53 L.Ed.2d at 551.

*Chadwick* has given rise to significant later difficulties, especially with regard to "containers" found in automobiles. These issues are considered in Chapters 4 and 5, infra.

## 3.  APPLYING THE "STANDING" REQUIREMENT IN SEARCH AND SEIZURE

As *Wong Sun* and the material in Part B of Chapter 1 makes clear, the Supreme Court has traditionally limited defendants to claims that evidence was obtained in violation of their own federal constitutional rights. Application of this requirement has presented the greatest difficulty in search and seizure cases. Once it is determined that the officers' activity did constitute a "search," a "seizure," or both, it is often a further and sometimes difficult task to determine whose Fourth Amendment interests were infringed by those searches and seizures that occurred. This task is the subject of the principal case in this subsection.

### RAKAS v. ILLINOIS

Supreme Court of the United States, 1978.
439 U.S. 128, 99 S.Ct. 421, 58 L.Ed.2d 387.

MR. JUSTICE REHNQUIST delivered the opinion of the Court.

Petitioners were convicted of armed robbery in the Circuit Court of Kankakee County, Ill., and their convictions were affirmed on appeal.

At their trial, the prosecution offered into evidence a sawed-off rifle and rifle shells that had been seized by police during a search of an automobile in which petitioners had been passengers. Neither petitioner is the owner of the automobile and neither has ever asserted that he owned the rifle or shells seized. The Illinois Appellate Court held that petitioners lacked standing to object to the allegedly unlawful search and seizure and denied their motion to suppress the evidence. We granted certiorari in light of the obvious importance of the issues raised to the administration of criminal justice, 435 U.S. 922, 98 S.Ct. 1483, 55 L.Ed.2d 515 (1978), and now affirm.

## I.

Because we are not here concerned with the issue of probable cause, a brief description of the events leading to the search of the automobile will suffice. A police officer on a routine patrol received a radio call notifying him of a robbery of a clothing store in Bourbonnais, Ill., and describing the getaway car. Shortly thereafter, the officer spotted an automobile which he thought might be the getaway car. After following the car for some time and after the arrival of assistance, he and several other officers stopped the vehicle. The occupants of the automobile, petitioners and two female companions, were ordered out of the car and after the occupants had left the car, two officers searched the interior of the vehicle. They discovered a box of rifle shells in the glove compartment, which had been locked, and a sawed-off rifle under the front passenger seat. After discovering the rifle and the shells, the officer took petitioners to the station and placed them under arrest.

Before trial petitioners moved to suppress the rifle and shells seized from the car on the ground that the search violated the Fourth and Fourteenth Amendments. They conceded that they did not own the automobile and were simply passengers; the owner of the car had been the driver of the vehicle at the time of the search. Nor did they assert that they owned the rifle or the shells seized. The prosecutor challenged petitioners' standing to object to the lawfulness of the search of the car because neither the car, the shells nor the rifle belonged to them. The trial court agreed that petitioners lacked standing and denied the motion to suppress the evidence. In view of this holding, the court did not determine whether there was probable cause for the search and seizure. On appeal after petitioners' conviction, the Appellate Court of Illinois, Third Judicial District, affirmed the trial court's denial of petitioners' motion to suppress because it held that "without a proprietary or other similar interest in an automobile, a mere passenger therein lacks standing to challenge the legality of the search of the vehicle." 46 Ill.App.3d 569, 571, 4 Ill.Dec. 877, 878, 360 N.E.2d 1252, 1253 (1977). * * * The Illinois Supreme Court denied petitioners leave to appeal.

## II.

* * *

[The Court's rejection of petitioners' argument that the traditional standing requirement should be relaxed or broadened is discussed at page 35, supra. After adhering to its traditional position, the Court further commented, see page 95, supra, that "the type of standing requirement * * * reaffirmed today is more properly subsumed under substantive Fourth Amendment doctrine." Editors.]

Analyzed in these terms, the question is whether the challenged search or seizure violated the Fourth Amendment rights of a criminal defendant who seeks to exclude the evidence obtained during it. That inquiry in turn requires a determination of whether the disputed search and seizure has infringed an interest of the defendant which the Fourth Amendment was designed to protect. We are under no illusion that by dispensing with the rubric of standing * * * we have rendered any simpler the determination of whether the proponent of a motion to suppress is entitled to contest the legality of a search and seizure. But by frankly recognizing that this aspect of the analysis belongs more properly under the heading of substantive Fourth Amendment doctrine than under the heading of standing, we think the decision of this issue will rest on sounder logical footing.

C.

Here petitioners, who were passengers occupying a car which they neither owned nor leased, seek to analogize their position to that of the defendant in Jones v. United States, 362 U.S. 257, 80 S.Ct. 725, 4 L.Ed.2d 697 (1960). In *Jones*, petitioner was present at the time of the search of an apartment which was owned by a friend. The friend had given Jones permission to use the apartment and a key to it, with which Jones had admitted himself on the day of the search. He had a suit and shirt at the apartment and had slept there "maybe a night," but his home was elsewhere. At the time of the search, Jones was the only occupant of the apartment because the lessee was away for a period of several days. Id., at 259, 80 S.Ct., at 730. Under these circumstances, this Court stated that while one wrongfully on the premises could not move to suppress evidence obtained as a result of searching them, "anyone legitimately on premises where a search occurs may challenge its legality." 362 U.S., at 267, 80 S.Ct., at 734. Petitioners argue that their occupancy of the automobile in question was comparable to that of Jones in the apartment and that they therefore have standing to contest the legality of the search—or as we have rephrased the inquiry, that they, like Jones, had their Fourth Amendment rights violated by the search.

We do not question the conclusion in *Jones* that the defendant in that case suffered a violation of his personal Fourth Amendment rights if the search in question was unlawful. Nonetheless, we believe that the phrase "legitimately on premises" coined in *Jones* creates too broad a gauge for measurement of Fourth Amendment rights. For example, applied literally, this statement would permit a casual visitor who has never seen, or been permitted to visit the basement of another's house to object to a search of the basement if the visitor happened to be in the kitchen of the house at the time of the search.  Likewise, a casual visitor who walks into a house one minute before a search of the house commences and leaves one minute after the search ends would be able to contest the legality of the search.  The first visitor would have absolutely no interest or legitimate expectation of privacy in the basement, the second would have none in the house, and it advances no purpose served by the Fourth Amendment to permit either of them to object to the lawfulness of the search.

We think that *Jones* on its facts merely stands for the unremarkable proposition that a person can have a legally sufficient interest in a place other than his own home so that the Fourth Amendment protects him from unreasonable governmental intrusion into that place.  In defining the scope of that interest, we adhere to the view expressed in *Jones* and echoed in later cases that arcane distinctions developed in property and tort law between guests, licensees, invitees, and the like, ought not to control.  Id., at 266, 80 S.Ct., at 733; see Mancusi v. DeForte, 392 U.S. 364, 88 S.Ct. 2120, 20 L.Ed.2d 1154 (1968).  But the *Jones* statement that a person need only be "legitimately on premises" in order to challenge the validity of the search of a dwelling place cannot be taken in its full sweep beyond the facts of that case.

\* \* \*

Our Brother White in dissent expresses the view that by rejecting the phrase "legitimately on [the] premises" as the appropriate measure of Fourth Amendment rights, we are abandoning a thoroughly workable, "bright line" test in favor of a less certain analysis of whether the facts of a particular case give rise to a legitimate expectation of privacy. If "legitimately on premises" were the successful litmus test of Fourth Amendment rights that he assumes it is, his approach would have at least the merit of easy application, whatever it lacked in fidelity to the history and purposes of the Fourth Amendment.  But a reading of lower court cases that have applied the phrase "legitimately on premises," and of the dissent itself, reveals that this expression is not a shorthand summary for a bright line rule which somehow encapsulates the "core" of the Fourth Amendment's protections.

The dissent itself shows that the facile consistency it is striving for is illusory.  The dissenters concede that "there comes a point when use of an area is shared with so many that one simply cannot reasonably expect seclusion."  But surely the "point" referred to is not one demarcating a line which is black on one side and white on another; it is inevitably a point which separates one shade of gray from another. We are likewise told by the dissent that a person "legitimately on *private* premises  \*  \*  \*, though his privacy is *not absolute*, is entitled to expect that he is sharing it only with those persons and that governmental officials will intrude only with *consent* or by complying with the Fourth Amendment." (emphasis added).  This single sentence describing the contours of the supposedly easily applied rule virtually abounds with unanswered questions: What are "private" premises? Indeed, what are the "premises?"  It may be easy to describe the "premises" when one is confronted with a one-room apartment, but what of the case of a 10-room house, or of a house with an attached garage that is searched? Also, if one's privacy is not absolute, how is it bounded? If he risks governmental intrusion "with consent," who may give that consent?

Again, we are told by the dissent that the Fourth Amendment assures that "*some* expectations of privacy are justified and will be protected from official intrusion." (emphasis added). But we are not told which of many possible expectations of privacy are embraced within this sentence. And our dissenting Brethren concede that "perhaps the Constitution provides some degree less protection for the personal freedom from unreasonable governmental intrusion when one does not have a possessory interest in the invaded private place." But how much "less" protection is available when one does not have such a possessory interest?

*   *   *

D.

Judged by the foregoing analysis, petitioners' claims must fail. They asserted neither a property nor a possessory interest in the automobile, nor an interest in the property seized. And as we have previously indicated, the fact that they were "legitimately on [the] premises" in the sense that they were in the car with the permission of its owner is not determinative of whether they had a legitimate expectation of privacy in the particular areas of the automobile searched. It is unnecessary for us to decide here whether the same expectations of privacy are warranted in a car as would be justified in a dwelling place in analogous circumstances. We have on numerous occasions pointed out that cars are not to be treated identically with houses or apartments for Fourth Amendment purposes. But here petitioners' claim is one which would fail even in an analogous situation in a dwelling place since they made no showing that they had any legitimate expectation of privacy in the glove compartment or area under the seat of the car in which they were merely passengers. Like the trunk of an automobile, these are areas in which a passenger *qua* passenger simply would not normally have a legitimate expectation of privacy.

Jones v. United States, 362 U.S. 257, 80 S.Ct. 725, 4 L.Ed.2d 697 (1960), involved significantly different factual circumstances. Jones not only had permission to use the apartment of his friend, but had a key to the apartment with which he admitted himself on the day of the search and kept possessions in the apartment. Except with respect to his friend, Jones had complete dominion and control over the apartment and could exclude others from it. *   *   *

IV.

The Illinois courts were therefore correct in concluding that it was unnecessary to decide whether the search of the car might have violated the rights secured to someone else by the Fourth and Fourteenth Amendments to the United States Constitution. Since it did not violate any rights of these petitioners, their judgment of conviction is

Affirmed.

* * *

MR. JUSTICE WHITE, with whom MR. JUSTICE BRENNAN, MR. JUSTICE MARSHALL, and MR. JUSTICE STEVENS, join, dissenting.

The Court today holds that the Fourth Amendment protects property, not people, and specifically that a legitimate occupant of an automobile may not invoke the exclusionary rule and challenge a search of that vehicle unless he happens to own or have a possessory interest in it. * * * If the Court is troubled by the practical impact of the exclusionary rule, it should face the issue of that rule's continued validity squarely instead of distorting other doctrines in an attempt to reach what are perceived as the correct results in specific cases.

* * *

Though we had reserved the very issue over 50 years ago, see Carroll v. United States, 267 U.S. 132, 162, 45 S.Ct. 280, 288, 69 L.Ed. 543 (1925), and never expressly dealt with it again until today, many of our opinions have assumed that a mere passenger in an automobile is entitled to protection against unreasonable searches occurring in his presence. In decisions upholding the validity of automobile searches, we have gone directly to the merits even though some of the petitioners did not own or possess the vehicles in question. * * * The Court's silence on this issue in light of its actions can only mean that, until now, we, like most lower courts, had assumed that Jones foreclosed the answer now supplied by the majority. That assumption was perfectly understandable, since all private premises would seem to be the same for the purposes of the analysis set out in Jones.

* * * My Brethren in the majority assertedly do not deny that automobiles warrant at least some protection from official interference with privacy. Thus, the next step is to decide who is entitled, vis à vis the State, to enjoy that privacy. The answer to that question must be found by determining "whether petitioner had an interest in connection with the searched premises that gave rise to 'a reasonable expectation [on his part] of freedom from governmental intrusion' upon those premises." Combs v. United States, 408 U.S. 224, 227, 92 S.Ct. 2284, 2286, 33 L.Ed.2d 308 (1972), quoting Mancusi v. DeForte, 392 U.S. 364, 368, 88 S.Ct. 2120, 2123, 20 L.Ed.2d 1154 (1968) (bracketed material in original).

Not only does Combs supply the relevant inquiry, it also directs us to the proper answer. We recognized there that Jones had held that one of those protected interests is created by legitimate presence on the searched premises, even absent any possessory interest. This makes unquestionable sense. We have concluded on numerous occasions that the entitlement to an expectation of privacy does not hinge on ownership * * *.

* * *

[O]ne consistent theme in our decisions under the Fourth Amendment has been, until now, that "the Amendment does not shield only those who have title to the searched premises." Mancusi v. DeForte, 392 U.S. 364, 367, 88 S.Ct. 2120, 2123, 20 L.Ed.2d 1154 (1968). Though there comes a point when use of an area is shared with so many that one simply cannot reasonably expect seclusion, short of that limit a person legitimately on private premises knows the others allowed there and, though his privacy is not absolute, is entitled to expect that he is sharing it only with those persons and that governmental officials will intrude only with consent or by complying with the Fourth Amendment.

It is true that the Court asserts that it is not limiting the Fourth Amendment bar against unreasonable searches to the protection of property rights, but in reality it is doing exactly that.[14] Petitioners were in a private place with the permission of the owner, but the Court states that that is not sufficient to establish entitlement to a legitimate expectation of privacy. But if that is not sufficient, what would be? We are not told, and it is hard to imagine anything short of a property interest that would satisfy the majority. Insofar as the Court's rationale is concerned, no passenger in an automobile, without an ownership or possessory interest and regardless of his relationship to the owner, may claim Fourth Amendment protection against illegal stops and searches of the automobile in which he is rightfully present. The Court approves the result in *Jones*, but it fails to give any explanation why the facts in *Jones* differ, in a fashion material to the Fourth Amendment, from the facts here.[15] More importantly, how is the Court able to avoid answering the question why presence in a private place with the owner's permission is insufficient?　*　*　*

*　*　*

*　*　* If the owner of the car had not only invited petitioners to join her but had said to them, "I give you a temporary possessory interest in my vehicle so that you will share the right to privacy that the Supreme Court says that I own," then apparently the majority would reverse. But people seldom say such things, though they may mean their invitation to encompass them if only they had thought of the problem. If the nonowner were the spouse or child of the owner, would the Court recognize a sufficient interest? If so, would distant relatives somehow have more of an expectation of privacy than close

[14] The Court's reliance on property law concepts is additionally shown by its suggestion that visitors could "contest the lawfulness of the seizure of evidence or the search if their own property were seized during the search." What difference should that property interest make to constitutional protection against unreasonable searches, which is concerned with privacy? Contrary to the Court's suggestion, a legitimate passenger in a car expects to enjoy the privacy of the vehicle whether or not he happens to carry some item along for the ride. We have never before limited our concern for a person's privacy to those situations in which he is in possession of personal property. Even a person living in a barren room without possessions is entitled to expect that the police will not intrude without cause.

[15] Jones had permission to use the apartment, had slept in it one night, had a key, had left a suit and a shirt there, and was the only occupant at the time of the search. Petitioners here had permission to be in the car and were occupying it at the time of the search. Thus the only distinguishing fact is that Jones could exclude others from the apartment by using his friend's key. But petitioners and their friend the owner had excluded others by entering the automobile and shutting the doors. Petitioners did not need a key because the owner was present. *　*　*

friends? What if the nonowner were driving with the owner's permission? Would nonowning drivers have more of an expectation of privacy than mere passengers? What about a passenger in a taxicab?　*　*　*

* * * The *Jones* rule is relatively easily applied by police and courts; the rule announced today will not provide law enforcement officials with a bright line between the protected and the unprotected. Only rarely will police know whether one private party has or has not been granted a sufficient possessory or other interest by another private party. Surely in this case the officers had no such knowledge. The Court's rule will ensnare defendants and police in needless litigation over factors that should not be determinative of Fourth Amendment rights.

More importantly, the ruling today undercuts the force of the exclusionary rule in the one area in which its use is most certainly justified—the deterrence of bad-faith violations of the Fourth Amendment. This decision invites police to engage in patently unreasonable searches every time an automobile contains more than one occupant. Should something be found, only the owner of the vehicle, or of the item, will have standing to seek suppression, and the evidence will presumably be usable against the other occupants. The danger of such bad faith is especially high in cases such as this one where the officers are only after the passengers and can usually infer accurately that the driver is the owner. The suppression remedy for those owners in whose vehicles something is found and who are charged with crime is small consolation for all those owners *and* occupants whose privacy will be needlessly invaded by officers following mistaken hunches not rising to the level of probable cause but operated on in the knowledge that someone in a crowded car will probably be unprotected if contraband or incriminating evidence happens to be found. After this decision, police will have little to lose by unreasonably searching vehicles occupied by more than one person.

*　*　*

NOTES

1. Under what circumstances does a passenger in an automobile have "standing" to challenge a search of that vehicle? If, for example, the automobile in which Rakas had been riding had been a taxi which he had "hired," would he have had standing?

2. In Minnesota v. Olson, ___ U.S. ___, 110 S.Ct. 1684, 109 L.Ed.2d 85 (1990), defendant Olson was arrested in a duplex unit used as a residence by Luanne and Julie Bergstrom. Olson, with permission of the Bergstroms, had spent the previous night in the duplex (sleeping on the floor) and had a change of clothes with him. At issue was whether Olson could contest the reasonableness of police entry of the duplex unit. The Supreme Court held that he could: "Olson's status as an overnight guest is alone enough to show that he had an expectation of privacy in the home that society is prepared to recognize as reasonable." ___ U.S. at ___, 110 S.Ct. at 1688, 109 L.Ed.2d at 93. Jones v. United States, distinguished in *Rakas,* was controlling, Justice White explained, despite the State's argument that Olson, unlike Jones, was never left alone in the unit and was never given a key to it.

That the guest has a host who has ultimate control of the house is not inconsistent with the guest having a legitimate expectation of privacy. * * * [H]osts will more likely than not respect the privacy interests of their guests, who are entitled to a legitimate expectation of privacy despite the fact that they have no legal interest in the premises and do not have the legal authority to determine who may or may not enter the household.

___ U.S. at ___, 110 S.Ct. at 1689, 109 L.Ed.2d at 95.  Chief Justice Rehnquist and Justice Blackmun dissented without opinion.

# Chapter 3

# ISSUANCE AND EXECUTION OF ARREST AND SEARCH WARRANTS

*Analysis*

A warrant is a court order authorizing a law enforcement officer to arrest an identified person or to search a specified place for and to seize specific items, or for both arrest and search. It also typically commands the officer executing the warrant to bring the person or items seized to the issuing court. For obvious reasons, a warrant is issued by a judge, or sometimes a clerk, *ex parte*, that is, without notice to the person whose arrest is sought or whose property is to be searched. The warrant is issued upon presentation of information believed to justify arrest or search. When an arrest warrant is sought, that information is presented in a document called various names, but which is usually called a complaint. When it is a search warrant that is desired, the document of application is ordinarily called simply an affidavit. The warrant may be executed by any law enforcement officer in the jurisdiction of the issuing judge; the executing officers are not necessarily the same persons who supplied the information upon which issuance was based.

Warrants play an important role in the theory of Fourth Amendment law. The Fourth Amendment itself concludes with the admonition that "no Warrants shall issue, but upon probable cause supported by Oath or affirmation, and particularly describing the place to be searched, and the persons or things to be seized." It is clear in theory that it is highly desirable to encourage resort by law enforcement to arrest and search warrants whenever possible. This is to be preferred to authorizing action without warrants because the warrant process interposes a decision by an official—called a magistrate when performing warrant issuance functions—between the desires of the police to apprehend violators and the privacy and liberty of citizens. This point was made by Justice Jackson in language that has been repeated numerous times in Supreme Court opinions:

> The point of the Fourth Amendment, which often is not grasped by zealous officers, is not that it denies law enforcement the support of the usual inferences which reasonable men draw from evidence. Its protection consists in requiring that those inferences be drawn by a neutral and detached magistrate instead of being judged by the officer engaged in the often competitive enterprise of ferreting out crime.

Johnson v. United States, 333 U.S. 10, 13–14, 68 S.Ct. 367, 369, 92 L.Ed. 436, 440 (1948). Presumably, by involving the judiciary in the investigative process before action is taken by law enforcement that touches upon Fourth Amendment interests in a certain number of instances violations of constitutional rights will be prevented from occurring. Furthermore, in those situations, the legal system has avoided altogether the difficult problem of litigating after-the-fact whether a violation occurred and of selecting an appropriate remedy if a violation is found. Finally, when an arrest or search warrant has been issued, it gives specific instructions to law enforcement officers as to what they may and may not do in execution of the warrant. It also subjects further investigative effort to supervision of the judiciary by requiring a report of action taken under the warrant in the form of a return (and inventory of items seized) on a search warrant or bringing the arrestee before the court with respect to an arrest warrant.

The extent to which the warrant process actually functions in the manner intended by Fourth Amendment theory has been the subject of much speculation. An extensive empirical study of search warrant practices was recently conducted by the National Center for State Courts. The results are reported in Van Duizend, Sutton and Cater, The Search Warrant Process: Preconceptions, Perceptions, and Practices (National Center for State Courts, undated). Probably the most important part of the study consisted of examining 844 search warrant cases and resulting prosecutions in seven different cities. In addition, interviews with police, judges, prosecutors and defense lawyers were conducted in these seven cities and direct observations of the warrant issuing process were undertaken in one location.

The study confirmed that search warrants are sought in relatively few investigations and that the vast majority of searches are conducted without a warrant. Id., at 20–21. In regard to those search warrants issued, an average (or "mean") of 38% involved drug offenses and 29% concerned property crimes. But an average of 21% were used in investigations of violent offenses. Id., at 33. An average of 40% of the warrants were issued in part upon the basis of information received from a confidential informant, that is, an informant not identified. Id., at 40.

Many of the judges who issued warrants perceived themselves as performing a role independent of that of law enforcement, but a few saw their role as "assisting the police." Id., at 64. Often, officers were able, by "judge shopping," to avoid submitting a request for a warrant to a judge known to be particularly demanding. Because of difficulty in locating applications that had been rejected, the study was unable to address how often warrant applications were rejected. But the authors suggested that the rate of "outright rejection" was probably "extremely low." Id., at 32. On the other hand, warrant applications were often reviewed and screened by a superior police official or a prosecutor. While this apparently led to few "screening outs," the process sometimes resulted in the officer being requested to add further information to the application. Id., at 24–25. Similarly, judicial officers who did not reject applications with some frequency required additional information from the applying officers. The judge's review seldom was lengthy. Of the warrant proceedings directly observed, 65% lasted 2.5 minutes or less. Only 11% lasted longer than five minutes. Id., at 31.

In all of the cities studied, searches conducted pursuant to those warrants actually served resulted in the discovery of something which the officers thought worth seizing in at least 90% of the cases. Id., at 52. In an average of over one third of the cases, the things seized included items not specifically identified in the warrant. Id.

Motions to suppress evidence were filed in a significant number of the prosecutions arising out of the searches. But they were seldom granted. Of 347 warrant-related prosecutions studied, motions to suppress evidence were granted in only 17. In at least 12 of these 17, convictions were nevertheless obtained. Id., at 56.

Police officers interviewed often complained of the delay involved in applying for and getting a search warrant and of the loss of "good cases" that resulted. But the study found little relationship between the delay and the actual loss of cases. Id., at 96.

In regard to "bottom lines," the study concluded that the search warrant requirement has several beneficial effects. First, it requires officers to "at least contemplate" the requirement of probable cause before a search, and this reflection induces a higher standard of care than would otherwise be used. Second, it appears to produce "a multi-layered review that reduces the likelihood that a search will occur in the absence of probable cause." Finally, it provides a clear and tangible record that permits a more objective later evaluation of the search. Id., at 148. On the other hand, the study concluded that "it was clear in many cases that the review process was largely perfunctory," id., and that there was "infrequent but significant" evidence of efforts that undermined "and sometimes entirely defeated" the integrity of the review process. Id., at 148–49. But "the most striking and significant—and perhaps the most troubling—discovery," the report concluded, was the infrequency with which the search warrant process is invoked. It is perceived as "burdensome, time-consuming, intimidating, frustrating, and confusing." Many easier methods of obtaining incriminating evidence or of developing a case against a suspect exist. "It is not surprising \* \* \*," the report concluded, "that many officers tend to regard the warrant option as a last resort." Id., at 149.

Does the study suggest reason to rethink the central role of warrants in the theory of Fourth Amendment law? Or, to the extent that there are deficiencies in warrant practice, should efforts be focused upon making practice more closely correspond with theory?

This Chapter addresses separately the three major aspects of Fourth Amendment "warrant law." First, it considers the requirement that the warrant be issued by a person meeting certain minimal requirements. Second, it turns to the requirement of probable cause and several related issues. Finally, attention is devoted to the execution of the warrant and to the role in this process of the terms of the warrant itself.

## A. THE "NEUTRAL AND DETACHED" MAGISTRATE

The review that the Fourth Amendment assumes will occur in the warrant process depends, of course, upon the issuing person being both able and inclined to scrutinize the sufficiency of the information offered by the officers in support of their request for authority to search, seize, or arrest. A number of the Fourth Amendment requirements imposed by the Supreme Court's case law are designed to assure that these prerequisites for such review will exist in each case. One of these requirements, addressed in this section, concerns the person authorized to issue the warrant and, of course, to conduct the review.

The objective of assuring that effective review occurs in each case also raises significant questions concerning the extent to which defendants must or should be permitted to attach the process by which a warrant was issued. Permitting such attacks, of course, may tend to assure that the warrant process is a meaningful one. But there are countervailing considerations as well. Resolving these attacks on a case-by-case basis may require substantial time and effort and may interfere with the processing of many cases. There may also be legitimate "comity" concerns; inquiry into whether a state official in fact performed his or her function, for example, may constitute a significant insult to the dignity to which state legal processes and those who participate in them are entitled.

### SHADWICK v. TAMPA
Supreme Court of the United States, 1972.
407 U.S. 345, 92 S.Ct. 2119, 32 L.Ed.2d 783.

MR. JUSTICE POWELL delivered the opinion of the Court.

The charter of Tampa, Florida, authorizes the issuance of certain arrest warrants by clerks of the Tampa Municipal Court. The sole question in this case is whether these clerks qualify as neutral and detached magistrates for purposes of the Fourth Amendment. We hold that they do.

Appellant was arrested for impaired driving on a warrant issued by a clerk of the municipal court. He moved the court to quash the warrant on the ground that it was issued by a nonjudicial officer in violation of the Fourth and Fourteenth Amendments. When the motion was denied, he initiated proceedings in the Florida courts by means of that State's writ of common-law certiorari. The state proceedings culminated in the holding of the Florida Supreme Court that "[t]he clerk and deputy clerks of the municipal court of the City of Tampa are neutral and detached 'magistrates' * * * for the purpose of issuing arrest warrants within the requirements of the United States Constitution * * *" 250 So.2d 4, 5 (1971). We noted probable jurisdiction, 404 U.S. 1014, 92 S.Ct. 697, 30 L.Ed.2d 660 (1972).

I

A clerk of the municipal court is appointed by the city clerk from a classified list of civil servants and assigned to work in the municipal court. The statute does not specify the qualifications necessary for this job, but no law degree or special legal training is required. The clerk's duties are to receive traffic fines, prepare the court's dockets and records, fill out commitment papers and perform other routine clerical tasks. Apparently he may issue subpoenas. He may not, however, sit as a judge, and he may not issue a search warrant or even a felony or misdemeanor arrest warrant for violations of state laws. The only warrants he may issue are for the arrest of those charged with having breached municipal ordinances of the city of Tampa.

Appellant, contending that the Fourth Amendment requires that warrants be issued by "judicial officers," argues that even this limited warrant authority is constitutionally invalid. He reasons that warrant applications of whatever nature cannot be assured the discerning, independent review compelled by the Fourth Amendment when the review is performed by less than a judicial officer. It is less than clear, however, as to who would qualify as a "judicial officer" under appellant's theory. There is some suggestion in appellant's brief that a judicial officer must be a lawyer or the municipal court judge himself. A more complete portrayal of appellant's position would be that the Tampa clerks are disqualified as judicial officers not merely because they are not lawyers or judges, but because they lack the institutional independence associated with the judiciary in that they are members of the civil service, appointed by the city clerk, "an executive official," and enjoy no statutorily specified tenure in office.

II

Past decisions of the Court have mentioned review by a "judicial officer" prior to issuance of a warrant. In some cases the term "judicial officer" appears to have been used interchangeably with that of "magistrate." * * * The substance of the Constitution's warrant requirements does not turn on the labeling of the issuing party. The warrant traditionally has represented an independent assurance that a search and arrest will not proceed without probable cause to believe that a crime has been committed and that the person or place named in the warrant is involved in the crime. Thus, an issuing magistrate must meet two tests. He must be neutral and detached, and he must be capable of determining whether probable cause exists for the requested arrest or search. This Court long has insisted that inferences of probable cause be drawn by "a neutral and detached magistrate instead of being judged by the officer engaged in the often competitive enterprise of ferreting out crime." In Coolidge v. New Hampshire [403 U.S. 443, 91 S.Ct. 2022, 29 L.Ed.2d 564 (1971)], the Court last Term voided a search warrant issued by the state attorney general "who was actively in charge of the investigation and later was to be chief prosecutor at trial." Id., at 450 of 403 U.S., at 2029 of 91 S.Ct. If, on the other hand, detachment and capacity do conjoin, the magistrate has satisfied the Fourth Amendment's purpose.

## III

The requisite detachment is present in the case at hand. Whatever else neutrality and detachment might entail, it is clear that they require severance and disengagement from activities of law enforcement. There has been no showing whatever here of partiality, or affiliation of these clerks with prosecutors or police. The record shows no connection with any law enforcement activity or authority which would distort the independent judgment the Fourth Amendment requires. Appellant himself expressly refused to allege anything to that effect. The municipal court clerk is assigned not to the police or prosecutor but to the municipal court judge for whom he does much of his work. In this sense, he may well be termed a "judicial officer." While a statutorily specified term of office and appointment by someone other than "an executive authority" might be desirable, the absence of such features is hardly disqualifying. Judges themselves take office under differing circumstances. Some are appointed, but many are elected by legislative bodies or by the people. Many enjoy but limited terms and are subject to re-appointment or re-election. Most depend for their salary level upon the legislative branch. We will not elevate requirements for the independence of a municipal clerk to a level higher than that prevailing with respect to many judges. The clerk's neutrality has not been impeached: he is removed from prosecutor or police and works within the judicial branch subject to the supervision of the municipal court judge.

Appellant likewise has failed to demonstrate that these clerks lack capacity to determine probable cause. The clerk's authority extends only to the issuance of arrest warrants for breach of municipal ordinances. We presume from the nature of the clerk's position that he would be able to deduce from the facts on an affidavit before him whether there was probable cause to believe a citizen guilty of impaired driving, breach of peace, drunkenness, trespass, or the multiple other common offenses covered by a municipal code. There has been no showing that this is too difficult a task for a clerk to accomplish. Our legal system has long entrusted nonlawyers to evaluate more complex and significant factual data than that in the case at hand. Grand juries daily determine probable cause prior to rendering indictments, and trial juries assess whether guilt is proved beyond a reasonable doubt. The significance and responsibility of these lay judgments betray any belief that the Tampa clerks could not determine probable cause for arrest.

\* \* \*

[We need not today] determine whether a State may lodge warrant authority in someone entirely outside the sphere of the judicial branch. Many persons may not qualify as the kind of "public civil officers" we have come to associate with the term "magistrate." Had the Tampa clerk been entirely divorced from a judicial position, this case would have presented different considerations. Here, however, the clerk is an employee of the judicial branch of the city of Tampa, disassociated from the role of law enforcement. On the record in this case, the independent status of the clerk cannot be questioned.

What we do reject today is any *per se* invalidation of a state or local warrant system on the ground that the issuing magistrate is not a lawyer or judge. Communities may have sound reasons for delegating the responsibility of issuing warrants to competent personnel other than judges or lawyers. Many municipal courts face stiff and unrelenting caseloads. A judge pressured with the docket before him may give warrant applications more brisk and summary treatment than would a clerk. All this is not to imply that a judge or lawyer would not normally provide the most desirable review of warrant requests. But our federal system warns of converting desirable practice into constitutional commandment. It recognizes in plural and diverse state activities one key to national innovation and vitality. States are entitled to some flexibility and leeway in their designation of magistrates, so long as all are neutral and detached and capable of the probable-cause determination required of them.

We affirm the judgment of the Florida Supreme Court.

Affirmed.

### NOTES

1. In Connally v. Georgia, 429 U.S. 245, 97 S.Ct. 546, 50 L.Ed.2d 444 (1977) (per curiam), a state statute provided that justices of the peace were empowered to issue search warrants. Further, they were to be paid a fee of $5.00 for each warrant issued but nothing for warrant applications that were refused. Finding that this subjected suspects to "judicial action by an officer of a court who has 'a direct, personal, substantial, pecuniary interest' in his conclusion to issue or to deny the warrant," 429 U.S. at 250, 97 S.Ct. at 548, 50 L.Ed.2d at 448, the Court held that issuance of a search warrant by such a justice violated the suspect's Fourth Amendment rights.

2. In Lo-Ji Sales, Inc. v. New York, 442 U.S. 319, 99 S.Ct. 2319, 60 L.Ed.2d 920 (1979), upon a showing that two obscene films had been purchased by a police officer at a bookstore, a Town Justice issued a search warrant for other copies of the films. In addition, the warrant authorized the officers to seize the "following" items "that the Court independently [on examination] has deter-

mined to be" obscene. No items were listed. But the Justice accompanied the officers to the bookstore and there examined numerous items. Those he found obscene were listed on the warrant by an officer. The Court held that this violated the Fourth Amendment:

> The Town Justice did not manifest that neutrality and detachment demanded of a judicial officer when presented with a warrant application for a search and seizure. We need not question the subjective belief of the Town Justice in the propriety of his actions, but the objective facts of record manifest an erosion of whatever neutral and detached posture existed at the outset. He allowed himself to become a member, if not the leader, of the search party which was essentially a police operation.

442 U.S. at 326–27, 99 S.Ct. at 2324, 60 L.Ed.2d at 928–29. It continued:

> We do not suggest, of course, that a "neutral and detached magistrate" loses his character as such merely because he leaves his regular office in order to make himself readily available to law enforcement officers who may wish to seek the issuance of warrants by him. * * * But * * * [in] this case * * * the Town Justice undertook not merely to issue a warrant, but to participate with the police and prosecutors in its execution.

442 U.S. at 328 n. 6, 99 S.Ct. 2325 n. 6, 60 L.Ed.2d at 930 n. 6.

3. Should a defendant be able to attack a warrant on the ground that the person who issued it did not actually read the affidavit submitted with the application? on the ground that the issuing person did not have the background necessary to determine, under the case law, whether affidavits of this sort showed probable cause?

## B.  THE SHOWING OF PROBABLE CAUSE

The essence of the warrant process is the judicial scrutiny of the information submitted as justification for issuance of the warrant. Effective scrutiny requires, of course, that the information presented be sufficient and adequately detailed to permit this. The information required to support issuance of a warrant is considered in the first subsection. A defendant's later ability to challenge the accuracy of this information is addressed in the next subsection. Information on which warrants issue often includes "tips" from informants who are not identified in the process of applying for the warrant. The last subsection addresses a defendant's ability in later litigation to secure disclosure of an informant's identity. Such disclosure, of course, may be a necessary prerequisite to determining whether the information submitted in support of a warrant application accurately represented the information given by the informant to law enforcement personnel. Disclosure may have ramifications for other issues in criminal litigation. But because of the extensive reliance upon informants in warrant cases, it is useful to consider it here.

### 1.  THE INITIAL SHOWING BEFORE THE MAGISTRATE

### EDITORS' INTRODUCTION: THE "PROBABLE CAUSE" SHOWING

The specific terms of the Fourth Amendment prohibit the issuance of a warrant except "upon probable cause supported by Oath or affirmation." A warrant application often is accompanied by a written and sworn affidavit setting out the facts which the applying officers believe constitute the required probable cause. In many cases, then, the issuing magistrate's function consists largely of reviewing the affidavit to determine if the alleged information rises to this level.

There appears to be no federal constitutional requirement that all or even any of the information submitted to the magistrate be written. Statutes and court rules sometimes authorize issuance of a warrant in whole or in part upon oral information. Rule 41(c)(1) of the Federal Rules of Criminal Procedure requires, as a general rule, that a search warrant issue on the basis of a sworn affidavit. But it further provides:

> Before ruling on a request for a warrant the federal magistrate
> * * * may require the affiant to appear personally and may
> examine under oath the affiant and any witnesses he may produce,
> provided that such proceedings shall be taken down by a court
> reporter or recording equipment and made part of the affidavit.

If a magistrate requires such additional information beyond the affidavit, it is quite likely, of course, that any warrant ultimately issued will be based in part upon that additional and oral information. Generally, however, this is not done. Therefore, the magistrate's task is usually one of reviewing the affidavit "on its face"—probably assuming the correctness of the facts alleged—to determine if those facts establish probable cause. Insofar as this is the process, no critical consideration of whether the facts alleged are correct occurs until and if the defendant later challenges the accuracy of the "face" of the affidavit. Defendants' ability to make such challenges is considered in the next subsection.

Rule 41(c)(2) authorizes the issuance of a warrant "upon sworn oral testimony communicated by telephone or other appropriate means" if "circumstances make it reasonable to dispense with a written affidavit." Where application for a warrant is made by telephone, the applicant is to prepare a "duplicate original" warrant and read it to the magistrate. The magistrate may then sign the original warrant (which is before the magistrate) and authorize the applicant to sign the magistrate's name to the duplicate original. If a voice recording device is available, the magistrate is to record the telephone call, have the recording transcribed, certify the accuracy of the recording, and file a copy with the court. If no such device is available, a stenographic or longhand verbatim record is to be made, and a copy signed by the magistrate is to be filed. Fed.R.Crim.P. 41(D). Interestingly, the rule provides that absent a "finding of bad faith," evidence obtained pursuant to a warrant is not subject to a motion to suppress on the ground that the circumstances were not such as to make it reasonable to dispense with a written affidavit. Fed.R.Crim.P. 41(G).

The Supreme Court decisions addressing the sufficiency of warrant affidavits involve situations in which the information submitted for a warrant consists in part of information from persons other than the affiant. The leading—or at least the seminal—case is Aguilar v. Texas, 378 U.S. 108, 84 S.Ct. 1509, 12 L.Ed.2d 723 (1964). Two police officers had submitted to a Justice of the Peace an application for a search warrant for Aguilar's home. In support, they provided an affidavit which stated:

> Affiants have received reliable information from a credible person and do believe that heroin, marijuana, barbiturates and other narcotics and narcotics paraphernalia are being kept at the above described premises for the purpose of sale and use contrary to the provisions of the law.

The warrant was issued and drugs were found. These drugs were admitted into evidence at Aguilar's trial. Finding constitutional error, the Supreme Court reasoned that the guiding principles must be that the magistrate must decide for himself whether probable cause exists and not accept without question the officers' "mere conclusion" and that this requires an affidavit permitting the magistrate to do this. Further:

> Although an affidavit may be based on hearsay information and need not reflect the direct personal observations of the affiant, the magistrate must be informed of some of the underlying circumstances from which the informant concluded that the narcotics were where he claimed they were, and some of the underlying circumstances from which the officer concluded that the informant, whose identity need not be disclosed, was "credible" or his information "reliable." Otherwise, "the inferences from the facts which lead to the complaint" will be drawn not "by a neutral and detached magistrate," as the Constitution requires, but instead, by a police officer * * *, or, as in this case, by an unidentified informant.

378 U.S. at 114–15, 84 S.Ct. at 1514, 12 L.Ed.2d at 729.

> This approach was developed further in Spinelli v. United States, 393 U.S. 410, 89 S.Ct. 584, 21 L.Ed.2d 637 (1969). Evidence of gambling activities had been obtained in a search pursuant to a warrant of an apartment located in St. Louis. The affidavit on which the warrant was issued recited in part:

> > The Federal Bureau of Investigation has been informed by a confidential reliable informant that William Spinelli is operating a handbook and accepting wagers and disseminating wagering information by means of the telephones which have been assigned the numbers WYdown 4–0029 and WYdown 4–0136.

In addition, the affidavit recited that telephone company records disclosed that the phones to which those numbers were assigned were located in a specific apartment under the name of Grace B. Hagen. Further, the affidavit stated that federal agents conducting surveillance had observed Spinelli enter the apartment once and on several other occasions had observed him in the parking lot of the apartment building or in its vicinity. Holding the warrant invalid, a majority of the Court noted that the tip met neither prong of *Aguilar*. It then suggested that a tip that was not sufficient under *Aguilar* might nevertheless establish probable cause for either of two reasons. First, the tip might describe the suspect's criminal activity in sufficient detail that a magistrate could infer from this detail that the informant had gained the information in a reliable way. 393 U.S. at 416–17, 89 S.Ct. at 589, 21 L.Ed.2d at 643–44. Second, other reliable information might sufficiently corroborate parts of the information in the tip to justify a magistrate in concluding that the tip should be relied upon. 393 U.S. at 417–18, 89 S.Ct. at 589–90, 21 L.Ed.2d at 644. Neither method "cured" the *Spinelli* affidavit, however. The detailed information in the tip concerning the telephones was a "meager report" that "could easily have been obtained from an offhand remark heard at a neighborhood bar." 393 U.S. at 419, 89 S.Ct. at 589, 21 L.Ed.2d at 644. The corroborating evidence gathered by the federal agents "at most ∗ ∗ ∗ indicated that Spinelli could have used the telephones specified by the informant for some purpose." Id.

As the principal case in this subsection makes clear, the *Aguilar-Spinelli* approach has not survived further consideration.

## ILLINOIS v. GATES

Supreme Court of the United States, 1983,
462 U.S. 213, 103 S.Ct. 2317, 76 L.Ed.2d 527.

JUSTICE REHNQUIST delivered the opinion of the Court.

Respondents Lance and Susan Gates were indicted for violation of state drug laws after police officers, executing a search warrant, discovered marijuana and other contraband in their automobile and home. Prior to trial the Gates moved to suppress evidence seized during this search. The Illinois Supreme Court affirmed the decisions of lower state courts granting the motion. It held that the affidavit submitted in support of the State's application for a warrant to search the Gates' property was inadequate under this Court's decisions in Aguilar v. Texas, 378 U.S. 108, 84 S.Ct. 1509, 12 L.Ed.2d 723 (1964) and Spinelli v. United States, 393 U.S. 410, 89 S.Ct. 584, 21 L.Ed.2d 637 (1969).

∗ ∗ ∗

## II

We now turn to ∗ ∗ ∗ whether respondents' rights under the Fourth and Fourteenth Amendments were violated by the search of their car and house. A chronological statement of events usefully introduces the issues at stake. Bloomingdale, Ill., is a suburb of Chicago located in DuPage County. On May 3, 1978, the Bloomingdale Police Department received by mail an anonymous handwritten letter which read as follows:

"This letter is to inform you that you have a couple in your town who strictly make their living on selling drugs. They are Sue and Lance Gates, they live on Greenway, off Bloomingdale Rd. in the condominiums. Most of their buys are done in Florida. Sue his wife drives their car to Florida, where she leaves it to be loaded up with drugs, then Lance flys down and drives it back. Sue flys back after she drops the car off in Florida. May 3 she is driving down there again and Lance will be flying down in a few days to drive it back. At the time Lance drives the car back he has the trunk loaded with over $100,000.00 in drugs.  Presently they have over $100,000.00 worth of drugs in their basement.

They brag about the fact they never have to work, and make their entire living on pushers.

I guarantee if you watch them carefully you will make a big catch.  They are friends with some big drugs dealers, who visit their house often.

Lance & Susan Gates
Greenway
in Condominiums"

The letter was referred by the Chief of Police of the Bloomingdale Police Department to Detective Mader, who decided to pursue the tip. Mader learned, from the office of the Illinois Secretary of State, that an Illinois driver's license had been issued to one Lance Gates, residing at a stated address in Bloomingdale.  He contacted a confidential informant, whose examination of certain financial records revealed a more recent address for the Gates, and he also learned from a police officer assigned to O'Hare Airport that "L. Gates" had made a reservation on Eastern Airlines flight 245 to West Palm Beach, Fla., scheduled to depart from Chicago on May 5 at 4:15 p.m.

Mader then made arrangements with an agent of the Drug Enforcement Administration for surveillance of the May 5 Eastern Airlines flight.  The agent later reported to Mader that Gates had boarded the flight, and that federal agents in Florida had observed him arrive in West Palm Beach and take a taxi to the nearby Holiday Inn.  They also reported that Gates went to a room registered to one Susan Gates and that, at 7:00 a.m. the next morning, Gates and an unidentified woman left the motel in a Mercury bearing Illinois license plates and drove northbound on an interstate frequently used by travelers to the Chicago area.  In addition, the DEA agent informed Mader that the license plate number on the Mercury registered to a Hornet station wagon owned by Gates.  The agent also advised Mader that the driving time between West Palm Beach and Bloomingdale was approximately 22 to 24 hours.

Mader signed an affidavit setting forth the foregoing facts, and submitted it to a judge of the Circuit Court of DuPage County, together with a copy of the anonymous letter.  The judge of that court thereupon issued a search warrant for the Gates' residence and for their automobile.  The judge, in deciding to issue the warrant, could have determined that the *modus operandi* of the Gates had been substantially corroborated.  As the anonymous letter predicted, Lance Gates had flown from Chicago to West Palm Beach late in the afternoon of May 5th, had checked into a hotel room registered in the name of his wife, and, at 7:00 a.m. the following morning, had headed north, accompanied by an unidentified woman, out of West Palm Beach on an interstate highway used by travelers from South Florida to Chicago in an automobile bearing a license plate issued to him.

At 5:15 a.m. on May 7th, only 36 hours after he had flown out of Chicago, Lance Gates, and his wife, returned to their home in Bloomingdale, driving the car in which they had left West Palm Beach some 22 hours earlier. The Bloomingdale police were awaiting them, searched the trunk of the Mercury, and uncovered approximately 350 pounds of marijuana. A search of the Gates' home revealed marijuana, weapons, and other contraband. The Illinois Circuit Court ordered suppression of all these items, on the ground that the affidavit submitted to the Circuit Judge failed to support the necessary determination of probable cause to believe that the Gates' automobile and home contained the contraband in question. This decision was affirmed in turn by the Illinois Appellate Court and by a divided vote of the Supreme Court of Illinois.

The Illinois Supreme Court concluded—and we are inclined to agree—that, standing alone, the anonymous letter sent to the Bloomingdale Police Department would not provide the basis for a magistrate's determination that there was probable cause to believe contraband would be found in the Gates' car and home. The letter provides virtually nothing from which one might conclude that its author is either honest or his information reliable; likewise, the letter gives absolutely no indication of the basis for the writer's predictions regarding the Gates' criminal activities. Something more was required, then, before a magistrate could conclude that there was probable cause to believe that contraband would be found in the Gates' home and car.

The Illinois Supreme Court also properly recognized that Detective Mader's affidavit might be capable of supplementing the anonymous letter with information sufficient to permit a determination of probable cause. In holding that the affidavit in fact did not contain sufficient additional information to sustain a determination of probable cause, the Illinois court applied a "two-pronged test," derived from our decision in Spinelli v. United States, 393 U.S. 410, 89 S.Ct. 584, 21 L.Ed.2d 637 (1969). The Illinois Supreme Court, like some others, apparently understood *Spinelli* as requiring that the anonymous letter satisfy each of two independent requirements before it could be relied on. According to this view, the letter, as supplemented by Mader's affidavit, first had to adequately reveal the "basis of knowledge" of the letter writer—the particular means by which he came by the information given in his report. Second, it had to provide facts sufficiently establishing either the "veracity" of the affiant's informant, or, alternatively, the "reliability" of the informant's report in this particular case.

The Illinois court, alluding to an elaborate set of legal rules that have developed among various lower courts to enforce the "two-pronged test," found that the test had not been satisfied. First, the "veracity" prong was not satisfied because, "there was simply no basis [for] * * * conclud[ing] that the anonymous person [who wrote the letter to the Bloomingdale Police Department] was credible." The court indicated that corroboration by police of details contained in the letter might never satisfy the "veracity" prong, and in any event, could not do so if, as in the present case, only "innocent" details are corroborated. In addition, the letter gave no indication of the basis of its writer's knowledge of the Gates' activities. The Illinois court understood *Spinelli* as permitting the detail contained in a tip to be used to infer that the informant had a reliable basis for his statements, but it thought that the anonymous letter failed to provide sufficient detail to permit such an inference. Thus, it concluded that no showing of probable cause had been made.

We agree with the Illinois Supreme Court that an informant's "veracity," "reliability" and "basis of knowledge" are all highly relevant in determining the value of his report. We do not agree, however, that these elements should be understood as entirely separate and independent requirements to be rigidly exacted in every case, which the opinion of the Supreme Court of Illinois would imply. Rather, as detailed below, they should be understood simply as closely intertwined issues that may usefully illuminate the common-sense, practical question whether there is "probable cause" to believe that contraband or evidence is located in a particular place.

## III

This totality of the circumstances approach is far more consistent with our prior treatment of probable cause than is any rigid demand that specific "tests" be satisfied by every informant's tip. Perhaps the central teaching of our decisions bearing on the probable cause standard is that it is a "practical, nontechnical conception." Brinegar v. United States, 338 U.S. 160, 176, 69 S.Ct. 1302, 1311, 93 L.Ed.2d 1879 (1949). * * * [P]robable cause is a fluid concept—turning on the assessment of probabilities in particular factual contexts—not readily, or even usefully, reduced to a neat set of legal rules. Informants' tips doubtless come in many shapes and sizes from many different types of persons. * * * Rigid legal rules are ill-suited to an area of such diversity. * * *

Moreover, the "two-pronged test" directs analysis into two largely independent channels—the informant's "veracity" or "reliability" and his "basis of knowledge." There are persuasive arguments against according these two elements such independent status. Instead, they are better understood as relevant considerations in the totality of circumstances analysis that traditionally has guided probable cause determinations: a deficiency in one may be compensated for, in determining the overall reliability of a tip, by a strong showing as to the other, or by some other indicia of reliability. * * * Unlike a totality of circumstances analysis, which permits a balanced assessment of the relative weights of all the various indicia of reliability (and unreliability) attending an informant's tip, the "two-pronged test" has encouraged an excessively technical dissection of informants' tips, with undue attention being focused on isolated issues that cannot sensibly be divorced from the other facts presented to the magistrate.

* * *

We * * * have recognized that affidavits "are normally drafted by nonlawyers in the midst and haste of a criminal investigation. Technical requirements of elaborate specificity once exacted under common law pleading have no proper place in this area." Likewise, search and arrest warrants long have been issued by persons who are neither lawyers nor judges, and who certainly do not remain abreast of each judicial refinement of the nature of "probable cause." The rigorous inquiry into the *Spinelli* prongs and the complex superstructure of evidentiary and analytical rules that some have seen implicit in our *Spinelli* decision, cannot be reconciled with the fact that many warrants are—quite properly—issued on the basis of nontechnical, common-sense judgments of laymen applying a standard less demanding than those used in more formal legal proceedings. Likewise, given the informal, often hurried context in which it must be applied, the "built-in subtleties," of the "two-pronged test" are particularly unlikely to assist magistrates in determining probable cause.

Similarly, we have repeatedly said that after-the-fact scrutiny by courts of the sufficiency of an affidavit should not take the form of *de novo* review. A magistrate's "determination of probable cause should be paid great deference by reviewing courts." *Spinelli,* supra, 393 U.S., at 419, 89 S.Ct., at 590 \* \* \*.

If the affidavits submitted by police officers are subjected to the type of scrutiny some courts have deemed appropriate, police might well resort to warrantless searches, with the hope of relying on consent or some other exception to the warrant clause that might develop at the time of the search. \* \* \* Reflecting this preference for the warrant process, the traditional standard for review of an issuing magistrate's probable cause determination has been that so long as the magistrate had a "substantial basis for \* \* \* conclud[ing]" that a search would uncover evidence of wrongdoing, the Fourth Amendment requires no more. Jones v. United States, 362 U.S. 257, 271, 80 S.Ct. 725, 736, 4 L.Ed.2d 697 (1960). We think reaffirmation of this standard better serves the purpose of encouraging recourse to the warrant procedure and is more consistent with our traditional deference to the probable cause determinations of magistrates than is the "two-pronged test."

Finally, the direction taken by decisions following *Spinelli* poorly serves "the most basic function of any government": "to provide for the security of the individual and of his property." The strictures that inevitably accompany the "two-pronged test" cannot avoid seriously impeding the task of law enforcement. If, as the Illinois Supreme Court apparently thought, that test must be rigorously applied in every case, anonymous tips seldom would be of greatly diminished value in police work. Ordinary citizens, like ordinary witnesses, generally do not provide extensive recitations of the basis of their everyday observations. Likewise, as the Illinois Supreme Court observed in this case, the veracity of persons supplying anonymous tips is by hypothesis largely unknown, and unknowable. As a result, anonymous tips seldom could survive a rigorous application of either of the *Spinelli* prongs. Yet, such tips, particularly when supplemented by independent police investigation, frequently contribute to the solution of otherwise "perfect crimes." While a conscientious assessment of the basis for crediting such tips is required by the Fourth Amendment, a standard that leaves virtually no place for anonymous citizen informants is not.

For all these reasons, we conclude that it is wiser to abandon the "two-pronged test" established by our decisions in *Aguilar* and *Spinelli*.[1] In its place we reaffirm the totality of the circumstances analysis that traditionally has informed probable cause determinations. See Jones v. United States, supra * * *. The task of the issuing magistrate is simply to make a practical, common-sense decision whether, given all the circumstances set forth in the affidavit before him, including the "veracity" and "basis of knowledge" of persons supplying hearsay information, there is a fair probability that contraband or evidence of a crime will be found in a particular place. And the duty of a reviewing court is simply to ensure that the magistrate had a "substantial basis for * * * conclud[ing]" that probable cause existed. Jones v. United States, supra, 362 U.S., at 271, 80 S.Ct., at 736. We are convinced that this flexible, easily applied standard will better achieve the accommodation of public and private interests that the Fourth Amendment requires than does the approach that has developed from *Aguilar* and *Spinelli*.

Our earlier cases illustrate the limits beyond which a magistrate may not venture in issuing a warrant. A sworn statement of an affiant that "he has cause to suspect and does believe that" liquor illegally brought into the United States is located on certain premises will not do. Nathanson v. United States, 290 U.S. 41, 54 S.Ct. 11, 78 L.Ed. 159 (1933). An affidavit must provide the magistrate with a substantial basis for determining the existence of probable cause, and the wholly conclusory statement at issue in *Nathanson* failed to meet this requirement. An officer's statement that "affiants have received reliable information from a credible person and believe" that heroin is stored in a home, is likewise inadequate. Aguilar v. Texas, 378 U.S. 108, 84 S.Ct. 1509, 12 L.Ed.2d 723 (1964). As in *Nathanson,* this is a mere conclusory statement that gives the magistrate virtually no basis at all for making a judgment regarding probable cause. Sufficient information must be presented to the magistrate to allow that official to determine probable cause; his action cannot be a mere ratification of the bare conclusions of others. In order to ensure that such an abdication of the magistrate's duty does not occur, courts must continue to conscientiously review the sufficiency of affidavits on which warrants are issued. But when we move beyond the "bare bones" affidavits present in cases such as *Nathanson* and *Aguilar,* this area simply does not lend itself to a prescribed set of rules, like that which had developed from *Spinelli.* Instead, the flexible, common-sense standard * * * better serves the purposes of the Fourth Amendment's probable cause requirement.

* * *

[1] * * *

Whether the allegations submitted to the magistrate in *Spinelli* would, under the view we now take, have supported a finding of probable cause, we think it would not be profitable to decide. There are so many variables in the probable cause equation that one determination will seldom be a useful "precedent" for another. Suffice it to say that while we in no way abandon *Spinelli's* concern for the trustworthiness of informers and for the principle that it is the magistrate who must ultimately make a finding of probable cause, we reject the rigid categorization suggested by some of its language.

IV

Our decisions applying the totality of circumstances analysis outlined above have consistently recognized the value of corroboration of details of an informant's tip by independent police work.  \*  \*  \*

Our decision in Draper v. United States, 358 U.S. 307, 79 S.Ct. 329, 3 L.Ed.2d 327 (1959), however, is the classic case on the value of corroborative efforts of police officials.  There, an informant named Hereford reported that Draper would arrive in Denver on a train from Chicago on one of two days, and that he would be carrying a quantity of heroin.  The informant also supplied a fairly detailed physical description of Draper, and predicted that he would be wearing a light colored raincoat, brown slacks and black shoes, and would be walking "real fast."  Hereford gave no indication of the basis for his information.

On one of the stated dates police officers observed a man matching this description exit a train arriving from Chicago; his attire and luggage matched Hereford's report and he was walking rapidly.  We explained in *Draper* that, by this point in his investigation, the arresting officer "had personally verified every facet of the information given him by Hereford except whether petitioner had accomplished his mission and had the three ounces of heroin on his person or in his bag. And surely, with every other bit of Hereford's information being thus personally verified, [the officer] had 'reasonable grounds' to believe that the remaining unverified bit of Hereford's information—that Draper would have the heroin with him—was likewise true," id., at 313, 79 S.Ct., at 333.

The showing of probable cause in the present case was fully as compelling as that in *Draper*.  Even standing alone, the facts obtained through the independent investigation of Mader and the DEA at least suggested that the Gates were involved in drug trafficking.  In addition to being a popular vacation site, Florida is well-known as a source of narcotics and other illegal drugs.  Lance Gates' flight to Palm Beach, his brief, overnight stay in a motel, and apparent immediate return north to Chicago in the family car, conveniently awaiting him in West Palm Beach, is as suggestive of a pre-arranged drug run, as it is of an ordinary vacation trip.

In addition, the magistrate could rely on the anonymous letter, which had been corroborated in major part by Mader's efforts—just as had occurred in *Draper*.  The Supreme Court of Illinois reasoned that *Draper* involved an informant who had given reliable information on previous occasions, while the honesty and reliability of the anonymous informant in this case were unknown to the Bloomingdale police. While this distinction might be an apt one at the time the police department received the anonymous letter, it became far less significant after Mader's independent investigative work occurred.  The corroboration of the letter's predictions that the Gates' car would be in Florida, that Lance Gates would fly to Florida in the next day or so, and that he would drive the car north toward Bloomingdale all indicated, albeit not with certainty, that the informant's other assertions also were true. "Because an informant is right about some things, he is more probably right about other facts," *Spinelli,* supra, 393 U.S., at 427, 89 S.Ct., at 594 (White, J., concurring)—including the claim regarding the Gates' illegal activity. This may well not be the type of "reliability" or "veracity" necessary to satisfy some views of the "veracity prong" of *Spinelli,* but we think it suffices for the practical, common-sense judgment called for in making a probable cause determination. It is enough, for purposes of assessing probable cause, that "corroboration through other sources of information reduced the chances of a reckless or prevaricating tale," thus providing "a substantial basis for crediting the hearsay." Jones v. United States, supra, 362 U.S., at 269, 271, 80 S.Ct., at 735, 736.

Finally, the anonymous letter contained a range of details relating not just to easily obtained facts and conditions existing at the time of the tip, but to future actions of third parties ordinarily not easily predicted. The letter writer's accurate information as to the travel plans of each of the Gates was of a character likely obtained only from the Gates themselves, or from someone familiar with their not entirely ordinary travel plans. If the informant had access to accurate information of this type a magistrate could properly conclude that it was not unlikely that he also had access to reliable information of the Gates' alleged illegal activities.[2] Of course, the Gates' travel plans might have been learned from a talkative neighbor or travel agent; under the "two-pronged test" developed from *Spinelli,* the character of the details in the anonymous letter might well not permit a sufficiently clear inference regarding the letter writer's "basis of knowledge." But, as discussed previously, probable cause does not demand the certainty we associate with formal trials. It is enough that there was a fair probability that the writer of the anonymous letter had obtained his entire story either from the Gates or someone they trusted. And

[2] The dissent seizes on one inaccuracy in the anonymous informant's letter—its statement that Sue Gates would fly from Florida to Illinois, when in fact she drove—and argues that the probative value of the entire tip was undermined by this allegedly "material mistake." We have never required that informants used by the police be infallible, and can see no reason to impose such a requirement in this case. Probable cause, particularly when police have obtained a warrant, simply does not require the perfection the dissent finds necessary.

Likewise, there is no force to the dissent's argument that the Gates' action in leaving their home unguarded undercut the informant's claim that drugs were hidden there. Indeed, the line-by-line scrutiny that the dissent applies to the anonymous letter is akin to that we find inappropriate in reviewing magistrate's decisions. The dissent apparently attributes to the magistrate who issued the warrant in this case the rather implausible notion that persons dealing in drugs always stay at home, apparently out of fear that to leave might risk intrusion by criminals. If accurate, one could not help sympathizing with the self-imposed isolation of people so situated. In reality, however, it is scarcely likely that the magistrate ever thought that the anonymous tip "kept one spouse" at home, much less that he relied on the theory advanced by the dissent. The letter simply says that Sue would fly from Florida to Illinois, without indicating whether the Gates made the bitter choice of leaving the drugs in their house, or those in their car, unguarded. The magistrate's determination that there might be drugs or evidence of criminal activity in the Gates' home was well-supported by the less speculative theory, noted in text, that if the informant could predict with considerable accuracy the somewhat unusual travel plans of the Gates, he probably also had a reliable basis for his statements that the Gates kept a large quantity of drugs in their home and frequently were visited by other drug traffickers there.

corroboration of major portions of the letter's predictions provides just this probability. It is apparent, therefore, that the judge issuing the warrant had a "substantial basis for * * * conclud[ing]" that probable cause to search the Gates' home and car existed. The judgment of the Supreme Court of Illinois therefore must be

Reversed.

JUSTICE WHITE, concurring in the judgment.

* * * Although I agree that the warrant should be upheld, I reach this conclusion in accordance with the *Aguilar-Spinelli* framework.

## A

* * *

In the present case, it is undisputed that the anonymous tip, by itself, did not furnish probable cause. The question is whether those portions of the affidavit describing the results of the police investigation of the respondents, when considered in light of the tip, "would permit the suspicions engendered by the informant's report to ripen into a judgment that a crime was probably being committed." *Spinelli*, supra, at 418, 89 S.Ct., at 590. * * *

In my view, the lower court's characterization of the Gates' activity here as totally "innocent" is dubious. In fact, the behavior was quite suspicious. I agree with the Court, that Lance Gates' flight to Palm Beach, an area known to be a source of narcotics, the brief overnight stay in a motel, and apparent immediate return North, suggest a pattern that trained law-enforcement officers have recognized as indicative of illicit drug-dealing activity.

Even, however, had the corroboration related only to completely innocuous activities, this fact alone would not preclude the issuance of a valid warrant. The critical issue is not whether the activities observed by the police are innocent or suspicious. Instead, the proper focus should be on whether the actions of the suspects, whatever their nature, give rise to an inference that the informant is credible and that he obtained his information in a reliable manner.

* * *

As in *Draper*, the police investigation in the present case satisfactorily demonstrated that the informant's tip was as trustworthy as one that would alone satisfy the *Aguilar* tests. The tip predicted that Sue Gates would drive to Florida, that Lance Gates would fly there a few days after May 3, and that Lance would then drive the car back. After the police corroborated these facts, the magistrate could reasonably have inferred, as he apparently did, that the informant, who had specific knowledge of these unusual travel plans, did not make up his story and that he obtained his information in a reliable way. * * *

## B

The Court agrees that the warrant was valid, but, in the process of reaching this conclusion, it overrules the *Aguilar-Spinelli* tests and replaces them with a "totality of the circumstances" standard. As shown above, it is not at all necessary to overrule *Aguilar-Spinelli* in order to reverse the judgment below. Therefore, because I am inclined to believe that, when applied properly, the *Aguilar-Spinelli* rules play an appropriate role in probable cause determinations, and because the Court's holding may foretell an evisceration of the probable cause standard, I do not join the Court's holding.

\*    \*    \*

JUSTICE BRENNAN, with whom JUSTICE MARSHALL joins, dissenting.

Although I join Justice Stevens' dissenting opinion and agree with him that the warrant is invalid even under the Court's newly announced "totality of the circumstances" test, I write separately to dissent from the Court's unjustified and ill-advised rejection of the two-prong test for evaluating the validity of a warrant based on hearsay announced in Aguilar v. Texas, 378 U.S. 108, 84 S.Ct. 1509, 12 L.Ed.2d 723 (1964), and refined in Spinelli v. United States, 393 U.S. 410, 89 S.Ct. 584, 21 L.Ed.2d 637 (1969).

I

\*    \*    \*

Although the rules drawn from the [*Aguilar-Spinelli* line of cases] are cast in procedural terms, they advance an important underlying substantive value: Findings of probable cause, and attendant intrusions, should not be authorized unless there is some assurance that the information on which they are based has been obtained in a reliable way by an honest or credible person. As applied to police officers, the rules focus on the way in which the information was acquired. As applied to informants, the rules focus both on the honesty or credibility of the informant and on the reliability of the way in which the information was acquired. Insofar as it is more complicated, an evaluation of affidavits based on hearsay involves a more difficult inquiry. This suggests a need to structure the inquiry in an effort to insure greater accuracy. The standards announced in *Aguilar,* as refined by *Spinelli,* fulfill that need. The standards inform the police of what information they have to provide and magistrates of what information they should demand. The standards also inform magistrates of the subsidiary findings they must make in order to arrive at an ultimate finding of probable cause. *Spinelli,* properly understood, directs the magistrate's attention to the possibility that the presence of self-verifying detail might satisfy *Aguilar's* basis of knowledge prong and that corroboration of the details of a tip might satisfy *Aguilar's* veracity prong. By requiring police to provide certain crucial information to magistrates and by structuring magistrates' probable cause inquiries, *Aguilar* and *Spinelli* assure the magistrate's role as an independent arbiter of probable cause, insure greater accuracy in probable cause determinations, and advance the substantive value identified above.

\*    \*    \*

II

\*    \*    \*

At the heart of the Court's decision to abandon *Aguilar* and *Spinelli* appears to be its belief that "the direction taken by decisions following *Spinelli* poorly serves 'the most basic function of any government: to provide for the security of the individual and of his property.' " This conclusion rests on the judgment that *Aguilar* and *Spinelli* "seriously imped[e] the task of law enforcement," and render anonymous tips valueless in police work. Surely, the Court overstates its case. But of particular concern to all Americans must be that the Court gives virtually no consideration to the value of insuring that findings of probable cause are based on information that a magistrate can reasonably say has been obtained in a reliable way by an honest or credible person.  *  *  *

JUSTICE STEVENS, with whom JUSTICE BRENNAN joins, dissenting.

The fact that Lance and Sue Gates made a 22-hour nonstop drive from West Palm Beach, Florida, to Bloomingdale, Illinois, only a few hours after Lance had flown to Florida provided persuasive evidence that they were engaged in illicit activity. That fact, however, was not known to the magistrate when he issued the warrant to search their home.

What the magistrate did know at that time was that the anonymous informant had not been completely accurate in his or her predictions. The informant had indicated that "Sue drives their car to Florida *where she leaves it to be loaded up with drugs * * *. Sue flies back after she drops the car off in Florida.*" (emphasis added). Yet Detective Mader's affidavit reported that she "left the West Palm Beach area driving the Mercury northbound."

The discrepancy between the informant's predictions and the facts known to Detective Mader is significant for three reasons. First, it cast doubt on the informant's hypothesis that the Gates already had "over $100,000 worth of drugs in their basement." The informant had predicted an itinerary that always kept one spouse in Bloomingdale, suggesting that the Gates did not want to leave their home unguarded because something valuable was hidden within. That inference obviously could not be drawn when it was known that the pair was actually together over a thousand miles from home.

Second, the discrepancy made the Gates' conduct seem substantially less unusual than the informant had predicted it would be. It would have been odd if, as predicted, Sue had driven down to Florida on Wednesday, left the car, and flown right back to Illinois. But the mere facts that Sue was in West Palm Beach with the car, that she was joined by her husband at the Holiday Inn on Friday, and that the couple drove north together the next morning are neither unusual nor probative of criminal activity.

Third, the fact that the anonymous letter contained a material mistake undermines the reasonableness of relying on it as a basis for making a forcible entry into a private home.

Of course, the activities in this case did not stop when the magistrate issued the warrant. The Gates drove all night to Bloomingdale, the officers searched the car and found 400 pounds of marijuana, and then they searched the house. However, none of these subsequent events may be considered in evaluating the warrant, and the search of the house was legal only if the warrant was valid. I cannot accept the Court's casual conclusion that, *before the Gates arrived in Bloomingdale,* there was probable cause to justify a valid entry and search of a private home. No one knows who the informant in this case was, or what motivated him or her to write the note. Given that the note's predictions were faulty in one significant respect, and were corroborated by nothing except ordinary innocent activity, I must surmise that the Court's evaluation of the warrant's validity has been colored by subsequent events.[3]

Although the foregoing analysis is determinative as to the house search, the car search raises additional issues because "there is a constitutional difference between houses and cars." Chambers v. Maroney, 399 U.S. 42, 52, 90 S.Ct. 1975, 1981, 26 L.Ed.2d 419 (1970). An officer who has probable cause to suspect that a highly movable automobile contains contraband does not need a valid warrant in order to search it. This point was developed in our opinion in United States v. Ross, 456 U.S. 798, 102 S.Ct. 2157, 72 L.Ed.2d 572 (1982), which was not decided until after the Illinois Supreme Court rendered its decision in this case. Under *Ross,* the car search may have been valid if the officers had probable cause *after* the Gates arrived.

\* \* \* [T]he Court \* \* \* attaches no weight to the conclusions of the Circuit Judge of DuPage County, Illinois, of the three judges of the Second District of the Illinois Appellate Court, or of the five justices of the Illinois Supreme Court, all of whom concluded that the warrant was not based on probable cause. In a fact-bound inquiry of this sort, the judgment of three levels of state courts, all of whom are better able to evaluate the probable reliability of anonymous informants in Bloomingdale, Illinois, than we are, should be entitled to at least a presumption of accuracy.[4] I would simply vacate the judgment of the Illinois Supreme Court and remand the case for reconsideration in the light of our intervening decision in United States v. Ross.

## NOTES

1. *Gates* was further developed in Massachusetts v. Upton, 466 U.S. 727, 104 S.Ct. 2085, 80 L.Ed.2d 721 (1984) (per curiam). On September 11, 1980, one Lt. Beland, a police officer, participated in the search of a motel room reserved

[3] Draper v. United States, 358 U.S. 307, 79 S.Ct. 329, 3 L.Ed.2d 327 (1959), affords no support for today's holding. That case did not involve an anonymous informant. On the contrary, as the Court twice noted, Mr. Hereford was "employed for that purpose and [his] information had always been found accurate and reliable." Id., at 313, 79 S.Ct., at 333; see id., at 309, 79 S.Ct., at 331. In this case, the police had no prior experience with the informant, and some of his or her information in this case was unreliable and inaccurate.

[4] The Court holds that what were heretofore considered two independent "prongs"—"veracity" and "basis of knowledge"—are now to be considered together as circumstances whose totality must be appraised. "A deficiency in one may be compensated for, in determining the overall reliability of a tip, by a strong showing as to the other, or by some other indicia of reliability." Yet in this case, the lower courts found *neither* factor present. And the supposed "other indicia" in the affidavit take the form of activity that is not particularly remarkable. I do not understand how the Court can find that the "totality" so far exceeds the sum of its "circumstances."

by Richard Kelleher. Credit cards and other items of identification belonging to the victims of two recent burglaries were seized, but the property taken during the burglaries—including jewelry, silver and gold—was not found. Later the same day, Lt. Beland received a telephone call from a woman who refused to identify herself. She told him that there was a "motor home full of stolen stuff," including jewelry, silver and gold, parked behind the home of George Upton and his mother, that she had seen the items, that Upton had purchased these items from Ricky Kelleher, and that Upton was going to move the motor home "any time now" because Kelleher's motel room had been raided. Although the woman refused to identify herself because of fear that Upton would kill her, Beland told her that he knew she was Upton's girlfriend, Lynn Alberico. She then represented that she was Alberico but that she had broken up with Upton and wanted to "burn" him. The woman refused to provide Beland with her address or phone number, but stated that she would contact Beland "if need be." Beland went to Upton's house and verified that a motor home was parked on the property. He then put all the accumulated information in an affidavit, attached the police reports on the two burglaries, and applied for a warrant authorizing a search of the motor home. The warrant was issued and the search resulted in the seizure of items taken during the burglaries and other incriminating evidence.

The state appellate court held the warrant invalid under *Gates*, which it read as merely indicating that substantial corroboration may save a warrant issued on the basis of an affidavit failing the "two pronged" test. Holding the affidavit insufficient, it stressed that the caller had not represented specifically seeing the stolen items in the motor home, that she was not a mere citizen informant and had not been firmly identified as Alberico, and that the corroborating information was insufficient. The Supreme Court reversed, holding that the state tribunal had erred in several ways. First, it had misread *Gates*, which explicitly rejected the "two pronged test." Second, it failed to grant deference to the decision of the magistrate who originally issued the warrant. When evaluated pursuant to a correct reading of *Gates*, the affidavit was sufficient; it provided a substantial basis for the issuance of the warrant and supported the issuing magistrate's determination that "a fair probability" existed that the stolen items would be found in the motor home:

> The informant claimed to have seen the stolen goods and gave a description of them which tallied with the items taken in recent burglaries. She knew of the raid on the motel room—which produced evidence connected to those burglaries—and that the room had been reserved by Kelleher. She explained the connection between Kelleher's motel room and the stolen goods in Upton's motor home. And she provided a motive both for her attempt at anonymity—fear of Upton's retaliation—and for furnishing the information—her recent breakup with Upton and here desire "to burn him."

466 U.S. at 733–34, 104 S.Ct. at 2088, 80 L.Ed.2d at 727–28.

2. Despite *Gates*, the *Aguilar-Spinelli* test may have continued vitality in the jurisprudence of some states. In State v. Jackson, 102 Wn.2d 432, 688 P.2d 136 (1984), for example, the Washington Supreme Court held that Article 1, Section 7 of the state's constitution (reprinted at page 14, supra) required a search warrant affidavit to meet the requirements developed in *Spinelli*. In part, the Washington court reasoned, the substantial differences in wording between the state and federal provisions mandates that the state provision be construed so as to provide suspects with greater protection. 102 Wn.2d at 442, 688 P.2d at 141. In addition, however, the court simply rejected on the merits the *Gates'* majority conclusion that the *Aguilar-Spinelli* analysis provided

insufficient additional protection for citizens to warrant its rigidity.  See 102 Wn.2d at 443, 688 P.2d at 141–43.

3.  In *Spinelli*, the affidavit recited, among other things, that the suspect "is known to this affiant and to federal law enforcement agents and local law enforcement agents as a bookmaker, an associate of bookmakers, a gambler, and an associate of gamblers."  In considering whether the affidavit supported the magistrate's determination that probable cause existed, the Court commented that his allegation "is but a bald and unilluminating assertion of suspicion that is entitled to no weight in appraising the magistrate's decision."  393 U.S. at 414, 89 S.Ct. at 588, 21 L.Ed.2d at 643.  In United States v. Harris, 403 U.S. 573, 91 S.Ct. 2075, 29 L.Ed.2d 723 (1971), the affidavit recited that the suspect "has had a reputation with me for over four years as being a trafficker of nontaxpaid distilled spirits * * *."  There was no opinion of the Court; the judgment of the Court was announced in an opinion by the Chief Justice.  In a portion of that opinion joined by two other members of the Court, he considered the significance of this allegation in the warrant affidavit:

> We cannot conclude that a policeman's knowledge of a suspect's reputation—something that policemen frequently know * * *—is not a "practical consideration of everyday life" upon which an officer (or a magistrate) may properly rely in assessing the reliability of an informant's tip.  To the extent that *Spinelli* prohibits the use of such probative information, it has no support in our prior cases, logic, or experience and we decline to apply it to preclude a magistrate from relying on a law enforcement officer's knowledge of a suspect's reputation.

403 U.S. at 583, 91 S.Ct. at 2081–82, 29 L.Ed.2d at 733 (opinion of Burger, C.J., announcing the judgment of the Court).

## 2.  CHALLENGING FACTUAL STATEMENTS IN THE AFFIDAVIT

Prior to the principal case in this subsection, many courts took the position that whether there was probable cause for issuance of an arrest or search warrant could be determined only from the face of the affidavit or complaint.  The facts alleged were to be accepted as true and the sole question for debate was whether they established probable cause.  To some extent, this position—that barred defendants from attacking the "face" of a warrant affidavit—was based on the perception that the appropriate inquiry was whether the magistrate had probable cause to issue the warrant.  If so, it was reasoned, no significance attached to the fact that the officer who applied for the warrant may not have had probable cause justifying a request for a warrant.

The principal case in this subsection requires that defendants, to some extent, be permitted to challenge the accuracy of the facts in a warrant affidavit.  Consider separately (although not necessarily in this order) what facts a defendant must establish to prevail on a challenge of this sort and what a defendant must do in order to have a factual hearing at which he has an opportunity to establish those facts.

### FRANKS v. DELAWARE
Supreme Court of the United States, 1978.
438 U.S. 154, 98 S.Ct. 2674, 57 L.Ed.2d 667.

MR. JUSTICE BLACKMUN delivered the opinion of the Court.

This case presents an important and longstanding issue of Fourth Amendment law. Does a defendant in a criminal proceeding ever have the right, under the Fourth and Fourteenth Amendments, subsequent to the *ex parte* issuance of a search warrant, to challenge the truthfulness of factual statements made in an affidavit supporting the warrant?

In the present case the Supreme Court of Delaware held, as a matter of first impression for it, that a defendant under *no* circumstances may so challenge the veracity of a sworn statement used by police to procure a search warrant. We reverse, and we hold that, where the defendant makes a substantial preliminary showing that a false statement knowingly and intentionally, or with reckless disregard for the truth, was included by the affiant in the warrant affidavit, and if the allegedly false statement is necessary to the finding of probable cause, the Fourth Amendment requires that a hearing be held at the defendant's request. In the event that at that hearing the allegation of perjury or reckless disregard is established by the defendant by a preponderance of the evidence, and, with the affidavit's false material set to one side, the affidavit's remaining content is insufficient to establish probable cause, the search warrant must be voided and the fruits of the search excluded to the same extent as if probable cause was lacking on the face of the affidavit.

I.

The controversy over the veracity of the search warrant affidavit in this case arose in connection with petitioner Jerome Franks' state conviction for rape, kidnapping, and burglary. On Friday, March 5, 1976, Mrs. Cynthia Bailey told police in Dover, Delaware, that she had been confronted in her home earlier that morning by a man with a knife, and that he had sexually assaulted her. She described her assailant's age, race, height, build, and facial hair, and gave a detailed description of his clothing as consisting of a white thermal undershirt, black pants with a silver or gold buckle, a brown leather three-quarter length coat, and a dark knit cap that he wore pulled down around his eyes.

That same day, petitioner Franks coincidentally was taken into custody for an assault involving a 15-year-old girl, Brenda B. _____, six days earlier. After his formal arrest, and while awaiting a bail hearing in Family Court, petitioner allegedly stated to Robert McClements, the youth officer accompanying him, that he was surprised the bail hearing was "about Brenda B. _____. I know her. I thought you said Bailey. I don't know her." At the time of this statement, the police allegedly had not yet recited to petitioner his rights under Miranda v. Arizona, 384 U.S. 436, 86 S.Ct. 1602, 16 L.Ed.2d 694 (1966).

On the following Monday, March 8, officer McClements happened to mention the courthouse incident to a detective, Ronald R. Brooks, who was working on the Bailey case. On March 9, detective Brooks and detective Larry D. Gray submitted a sworn affidavit to a justice of the peace in Dover, in support of a warrant to search petitioner's apartment.[5] In paragraph 8 of the affidavit's "probable cause page" mention was made of petitioner's statement to McClements. In paragraph 10, it was noted that the description of the assailant given to the police by Mrs. Bailey included the above-mentioned clothing. Finally, the affidavit also described the attempt made by police to confirm that petitioner's typical outfit matched that of the assailant. Paragraph 15 recited: "On Tuesday, 3/9/76, your affiant contacted Mr. James Williams and Mr. Wesley Lucas of the Delaware Youth Center where Jerome Franks is employed and did have personal conversation with both these people." Paragraphs 16 and 17 respectively stated: "Mr. James Williams revealed to your affiant that the normal dress of Jerome Franks does consist of a white knit thermal undershirt and a brown leather jacket," and "Mr. Wesley Lucas revealed to your affiant that in addition to the thermal undershirt and jacket, Jerome Franks often wears a large green knit hat."

The warrant was issued on the basis of this affidavit. Pursuant to the warrant, police searched petitioner's apartment and found a white thermal undershirt, a knit hat, dark pants, and a leather jacket, and, on petitioner's kitchen table, a single-blade knife. All these ultimately were introduced in evidence at trial.

Prior to the trial, however, petitioner's counsel filed a written motion to suppress the clothing and the knife found in the search; this motion alleged that the warrant on its face did not show probable cause and that the search and seizure were in violation of the Fourth and Fourteenth Amendments. At the hearing on the motion to suppress, defense counsel orally amended the challenge to include an attack on the veracity of the warrant affidavit; he also specifically requested the right to call as witnesses detective Brooks, Wesley Lucas of the Youth Center, and James D. Morrison, formerly of the Youth Center.[6] Counsel asserted that Lucas and Morrison would testify that neither had been personally interviewed by the warrant affiants, and that, although they might have talked to another police officer, any information given by them to that officer was "somewhat different" from what was recited in the affidavit. Defense counsel charged that the misstatements were included in the affidavit not inadvertently, but in "bad faith." Counsel also sought permission to call officer McClements and petitioner as witnesses, to seek to establish that petitioner's courthouse statement to police had been obtained in violation of petitioner's *Miranda* rights, and that the search warrant was thereby tainted as the fruit of an illegally obtained confession.

[5] The affidavit is reproduced as Appendix A of this opinion.

[6] The references in paragraphs 15 and 16 of the warrant affidavit's probable cause page to "James Williams" appear to have been intended as references to James D. Morrison, who was petitioner's supervisor at the Youth Center. This misapprehension on the part of the State continued until shortly before trial. Eleven days prior to trial, the prosecution requested the clerk of the Kent County Superior Court to summon "James Williams, Delaware Youth Center," for petitioner's trial. In his return on the summons, Record Document No. 15, the Kent County sheriff stated that he "[s]erved the within summons upon * * * James Williams (Morrison)." The summons actually delivered was made out in the name of James Morrison.

In rebuttal, the State's attorney argued in detail (a) that Del.Code Ann., Tit. 11, §§ 2306 and 2307 (1974), contemplated that any challenge to a search warrant was to be limited to questions of sufficiency based on the face of the affidavit; (b) that, purportedly, a majority of the States whose practice was not dictated by statute observed such a rule; and (c) that federal cases on the issue were to be distinguished because of Fed. Rule Crim.Proc. 41(e). * * * The State objected to petitioner's "going behind [the warrant affidavit] in any way," and argued that the court must decide petitioner's motion "on the four corners" of the affidavit.

The trial court sustained the State's objection to petitioner's proposed evidence. The motion to suppress was denied, and the clothing and knife were admitted as evidence at the ensuing trial. Petitioner was convicted. In a written Motion for Judgment of Acquittal and/or New Trial, petitioner repeated his objection to the admission of the evidence, stating that he "should have been allowed to impeach the Affidavit used in the Search Warrant to show purposeful misrepresentation of information contained therein." The motion was denied, and petitioner was sentenced to two consecutive terms of 25 years each and an additional consecutive life sentence.

On appeal, the Supreme Court of Delaware affirmed. 373 A.2d 578 (1977). It agreed with what it deemed to be the "majority rule" that no attack upon the veracity of a warrant affidavit could be made:

"We agree with the majority rule for two reasons. First, it is the function of the issuing magistrate to determine the reliability of information and credibility of affiants in deciding whether the requirement of probable cause has been met. There has been no need demonstrated for interfering with this function. Second, neither the probable cause nor suppression hearings are adjudications of guilt or innocence; the matters asserted by defendant are more properly considered in a trial on the merits." Id., at 580.

Because of this resolution, the Delaware Supreme Court noted that there was no need to consider petitioner's "other contentions, relating to the evidence that would have been introduced for impeachment purposes." Ibid.

Franks' petition for certiorari presented only the issue whether the trial court had erred in refusing to consider his allegation of misrepresentation in the warrant affidavit.[7] Because of the importance of the question, and because of the conflict among both state and federal courts, we granted certiorari. 434 U.S. 889, 98 S.Ct. 261, 54 L.Ed.2d 174 (1977).

## II.

* * *

Respondent * * * suggests that any error here was harmless. Assuming, *arguendo*, respondent says, that petitioner's Fourth Amend-

[7] Franks did not raise in his petition the issue of his Miranda challenge to the courthouse statement given to police and the use of that statement in the warrant affidavit. The propriety of the trial court's refusal to hear testimony on that subject is therefore not before us. It also appears that Franks did not take that issue to the Supreme Court of Delaware.

ment claim was valid, and that the warrant should have been tested for veracity and the evidence excluded, it is still clear beyond a reasonable doubt that the evidence complained of did not contribute to petitioner's conviction. Chambers v. Maroney, 399 U.S. 42, 52–53, 90 S.Ct. 1975, 1981–1982, 26 L.Ed.2d 419 (1970). This contention falls of its own weight. The sole issue at trial was that of consent. Petitioner admitted that he had engaged in sexual relations with Mrs. Bailey on the day in question. She testified that she had not consented to this, and that petitioner, upon first encountering her in the house, had threatened her with a knife to force her to submit. Petitioner claimed that she had given full consent and that no knife had been present. To corroborate its contention that consent was lacking, the State introduced in evidence a stainless steel wooden-handled kitchen knife found by the detectives on the kitchen table in petitioner's apartment four days after the alleged rape. Defense counsel objected to its admission, arguing that Mrs. Bailey had not given any detailed description of the knife alleged to be involved in the incident and had claimed to have seen the knife only in "pitch blackness." The State obtained its admission, however, as a knife that matched the description contained in the search warrant, and Mrs. Bailey testified that the knife allegedly used was, like the knife in evidence, single-edged and not a pocket knife, and that the knife in evidence was the same length and thickness as the knife used in the crime. The State carefully elicited from detective Brooks the fact that this was the only knife found in petitioner's apartment. Although respondent argues that the knife was presented to the jury as "merely exemplary of the generic class of weapon testimonially described by the victim," Brief for Respondent 15–16, the State at trial clearly meant to suggest that this was the knife that had been used against Mrs. Bailey. Had the warrant been quashed, and the knife excluded from the trial as evidence, we cannot say with any assurance that the jury would have reached the same decision on the issue of consent, particularly since there was other countervailing evidence on that issue.

*   *   *

III.

Whether the Fourth and Fourteenth Amendments, and the derivative exclusionary rule made applicable to the States under Mapp v. Ohio, 367 U.S. 643, 81 S.Ct. 1684, 6 L.Ed.2d 1081 (1961), ever mandate that a defendant be permitted to attack the veracity of a warrant affidavit after the warrant has been issued and executed, is a question that encounters conflicting values. The bulwark of Fourth Amendment protection, of course, is the Warrant Clause, requiring that, absent certain exceptions, police obtain a warrant from a neutral and disinterested magistrate before embarking upon a search. In deciding today, that, in certain circumstances, a challenge to a warrant's veracity must be permitted, we derive our ground from language of the Warrant Clause itself, which surely takes the affiant's good faith as its premise: "[N]o warrants shall issue, but upon probable cause, supported by Oath or affirmation * * *." Judge Frankel, in United

States v. Halsey, 257 F.Supp. 1002, 1005 (S.D.N.Y.1966), aff'd, Docket No. 31369 (CA2, June 12, 1967) (unreported), put the matter simply: "[W]hen the Fourth Amendment demands a factual showing sufficient to comprise 'probable cause,' the obvious assumption is that there will be a *truthful* showing" (emphasis in original). This does not mean "truthful" in the sense that every fact recited in the warrant affidavit is necessarily correct, for probable cause may be founded upon hearsay and upon information received from informants, as well as upon information within the affiant's own knowledge that sometimes must be garnered hastily. But surely it is to be "truthful" in the sense that the information put forth is believed or appropriately accepted by the affiant as true. It is established law that a warrant affidavit must set forth particular facts and circumstances underlying the existence of probable cause, so as to allow the magistrate to make an independent evaluation of the matter. If an informant's tip is the source of information, the affidavit must recite "some of the underlying circumstances from which the informant concluded" that relevant evidence might be discovered, and "some of the underlying circumstances from which the officer concluded that the informant, whose identity need not be disclosed, * * * was 'credible' or his information 'reliable.'" Id., at 114, 84 S.Ct., at 1514. Because it is the magistrate who must determine independently whether there is probable cause; it would be an unthinkable imposition upon his authority if a warrant affidavit, revealed after the fact to contain a deliberately or recklessly false statement, were to stand beyond impeachment.

In saying this, however, one must give cognizance to competing values that lead us to impose limitations. They perhaps can best be addressed by noting the arguments of respondent and others against allowing veracity challenges. The arguments are several:

First, respondent argues that the exclusionary rule, created in Weeks v. United States, 232 U.S. 383, 34 S.Ct. 341, 58 L.Ed. 652 (1914), is not a personal constitutional right, but only a judicially created remedy extended where its benefit as a deterrent promises to outweigh the societal cost of its use * * *. Respondent argues that applying the exclusionary rule to another situation—the deterrence of deliberate or reckless untruthfulness in a warrant affidavit—is not justified * * * [because] interfering with a criminal conviction in order to deter official misconduct is a burden too great to impose on society.

Second, respondent argues that a citizen's privacy interests are adequately protected by a requirement that applicants for a warrant submit a sworn affidavit and by the magistrate's independent determination of sufficiency based on the face of the affidavit. Applying the exclusionary rule to attacks upon veracity would weed out a minimal number of perjurious government statements, says respondent, but would overlap unnecessarily with existing penalties against perjury, including criminal prosecutions, departmental discipline for misconduct, contempt of court, and civil actions.

Third, it is argued that the magistrate already is equipped to conduct a fairly vigorous inquiry into the accuracy of the factual affidavit supporting a warrant application. He may question the affiant, or summon other persons to give testimony at the warrant proceeding. The incremental gain from a post-search adversary proceeding, it is said, would not be great.

Fourth, it is argued that it would unwisely diminish the solemnity and moment of the magistrate's proceeding to make his inquiry into probable cause reviewable in regard to veracity. The less final, and less deference paid to, the magistrate's determination of veracity, the less initiative will he use in that task. Denigration of the magistrate's function would be imprudent insofar as his scrutiny is the last bulwark preventing any particular invasion of privacy before it happens.

Fifth, it is argued that permitting a post-search evidentiary hearing on issues of veracity would confuse the pressing issue of guilt or innocence with the collateral question as to whether there had been official misconduct in the drafting of the affidavit. The weight of criminal dockets, and the need to prevent diversion of attention from the main issue of guilt or innocence, militate against such an added burden on the trial courts. And if such hearings were conducted routinely, it is said, they would be misused by defendants as a convenient source of discovery. Defendants might even use the hearings in an attempt to force revelation of the identity of informants.

Sixth and finally, it is argued that a post-search veracity challenge is inappropriate because the accuracy of an affidavit in large part is beyond the control of the affiant. An affidavit may properly be based on hearsay, on fleeting observations, and on tips received from unnamed informants whose identity often will be properly protected from revelation under McCray v. Illinois, 386 U.S. 300, 87 S.Ct. 1056, 18 L.Ed.2d 62 (1967).

None of these considerations is trivial. Indeed, because of them, the rule announced today has a limited scope, both in regard to when exclusion of the seized evidence is mandated, and when a hearing on allegations of misstatements must be accorded. But neither do the considerations cited by respondent and others have a fully controlling weight; we conclude that they are insufficient to justify an *absolute* ban on post-search impeachment of veracity. On this side of the balance, also, there are pressing considerations:

First, a flat ban on impeachment of veracity could denude the probable cause requirement of all real meaning. The requirement that a warrant not issue "but upon probable cause, supported by Oath or affirmation," would be reduced to a nullity if a police officer was able to use deliberately falsified allegations to demonstrate probable cause, and, having misled the magistrate, then was able to remain confident that the ploy was worthwhile. It is this spector of intentional falsification that, we think, has evoked such widespread opposition to the flat nonimpeachment rule from the commentators, from the American Law Institute in its Model Code of Pre-Arraignment Procedure, § SS290.3(1), from the federal courts of appeals, and from state courts. On occasion, of course, an instance of deliberate falsity will be exposed and confirmed without a special inquiry either at trial, or at a hearing on the sufficiency of the affidavit. A flat nonimpeachment rule would bar re-examination of the warrant even in these cases.

Second, the hearing before the magistrate not always will suffice to discourage lawless or reckless misconduct. The pre-search proceeding is necessarily *ex parte*, since the subject of the search cannot be tipped off to the application for a warrant lest he destroy or remove evidence. The usual reliance of our legal system on adversary proceedings itself should be an indication that an *ex parte* inquiry is likely to be less vigorous. The magistrate has no acquaintance with the information that may contradict the good faith and reasonable basis of the affiant's allegations. The pre-search proceeding will frequently be marked by haste, because of the understandable desire to act before the evidence disappears; this urgency will not always permit the magistrate to make an extended independent examination of the affiant or other witnesses.

Third, the alternative sanctions of a perjury prosecution, administrative discipline, contempt, or a civil suit are not likely to fill the gap. Mapp v. Ohio, supra, implicitly rejected the adequacy of these alternatives. * * *

Fourth, allowing an evidentiary hearing, after a suitable preliminary proffer of material falsity, would not diminish the importance and solemnity of the warrant-issuing process. It is the *ex parte* nature of the initial hearing, rather than the magistrate's capacity, that is the reason for the review. A magistrate's determination is presently subject to review before trial as to *sufficiency* without any undue interference with the dignity of the magistrate's function. Our reluctance today to extend the rule of exclusion beyond instances of deliberate misstatements, and those of reckless disregard, leaves a broad field where the magistrate is the sole protection of a citizen's Fourth Amendment rights, namely, in instances where police have been merely negligent in checking or recording the facts relevant to a probable cause determination.

Fifth, the claim that a post-search hearing will confuse the issue of the defendant's guilt with the issue of the State's possible misbehavior is footless. The hearing will not be in the presence of the jury. An issue extraneous to guilt already is examined in any probable cause determination or review of probable cause. Nor, if a sensible threshold showing is required and sensible substantive requirements for suppression are maintained, need there be any new large-scale commitment of judicial resources; many claims will wash out at an early stage, and the more substantial ones in any event would require judicial resources for vindication if the suggested alternative sanctions were truly to be effective. The requirement of a substantial preliminary showing should suffice to prevent the misuse of a veracity hearing for purposes of discovery or obstruction. And because we are faced today with only the question of the integrity of the affiant's representations as to his own activities, we need not decide, and we in no way predetermine, the difficult question whether a reviewing court must ever require the revelation of the identity of an informant once a substantial preliminary showing of falsity has been made. McCray v. Illinois, 386 U.S. 300,

87 S.Ct. 1056, 18 L.Ed.2d 62 (1967), the Court's earlier disquisition in this area, concluded only that the Due Process Clause of the Fourteenth Amendment did not require the State to expose an informant's identity routinely, upon a defendant's mere demand, when there was ample evidence in the probable cause hearing to show that the informant was reliable and his information credible.

Sixth and finally, as to the argument that the exclusionary rule should not be extended to a "new" area, we cannot regard any such extension really to be at issue here. Despite the deep skepticism of Members of this Court as to the wisdom of extending the exclusionary rule to collateral areas, such as civil or grand jury proceedings, the Court has not questioned, in the absence of a more efficacious sanction, the continued application of the rule to suppress evidence from the State's case where a Fourth Amendment violation has been substantial and deliberate. We see no principled basis for distinguishing between the question of the sufficiency of an affidavit, which also is subject to a post-search re-examination, and the question of its integrity.

## IV.

In sum, and to repeat with some embellishment what we stated at the beginning of this opinion: There is, of course, a presumption of validity with respect to the affidavit supporting the search warrant. To mandate an evidentiary hearing, the challenger's attack must be more than conclusory and must be supported by more than a mere desire to cross-examine. There must be allegations of deliberate falsehood or of reckless disregard for the truth, and those allegations must be accompanied by an offer of proof. They should point out specifically the portion of the warrant affidavit that is claimed to be false; and they should be accompanied by a statement of supporting reasons. Affidavits or sworn or otherwise reliable statements of witnesses should be furnished, or their absence satisfactorily explained. Allegations of negligence or innocent mistake are insufficient. The deliberate falsity or reckless disregard whose impeachment is permitted today is only that of the affiant, not of any nongovernmental informant. Finally, if these requirements are met, and if, when material that is the subject of the alleged falsity or reckless disregard is set to one side, there remains sufficient content in the warrant affidavit to support a finding of probable cause, no hearing is required.[8] On the other hand, if the remaining content is insufficient, the defendant is entitled, under the Fourth Amendment, to his hearing. Whether he will prevail at that hearing is, of course, another issue.

Because of Delaware's absolute rule, its courts did not have occasion to consider the proffer put forward by petitioner Franks. Since the framing of suitable rules to govern proffers is a matter properly left to the States, we decline ourselves to pass on petitioner's proffer. The

---

[8] Petitioner conceded that if what is left is sufficient to sustain probable cause, the inaccuracies are irrelevant. Petitioner also conceded that if the warrant affiant had no reason to believe the information was false, there was no violation of the Fourth Amendment.

judgment of the Supreme Court of Delaware is reversed, and the case is remanded for further proceedings not inconsistent with this opinion.

It is so ordered.

## APPENDIX A

J.P.Court # 7

In the matter of: Jerome Franks, B/M, DOB: 10/9/54 and 222 S. Governors Ave., Apt. # 3, Dover, Delaware. A two room apartment located on the South side, second floor, of a white block building on the west side of S. Governors Avenue, between Loockerman Street and North Street, in the City of Dover. The ground floor of this building houses Wayman's Barber Shop.

STATE OF DELAWARE  
COUNTY OF KENT          ss:

Be it remembered that on this 9th day of March A.D. 1976 before me John Green, personally appeared Det. Ronald R. Brooks and Det. Larry Gray of the Dover Police Department who being by me duly sworn depose and say:

That they have reason to believe and do believe that in the 222 S. Governors Avenue, Apartment # 3, Dover, Delaware. A two room apartment located on the South side second floor of a white block building on the west side of S. Governors Avenue between Loockerman Street and North Street in the City of Dover. The ground floor of this building houses Wayman's Barber Shop the occupant of which is Jerome Franks. There has been and/or there is now located and/or concealed certain property in said house, place, conveyance and/or on the person or persons of the occupants thereof, consisting of property, papers, articles, or things which are the instruments of criminal offense, and/or obtained in the commission of a crime, and/or designated to be used in the commission of a crime, and not reasonably calculated to be used for any other purpose and/or the possession of which is unlawful, papers, articles, or things which are of an evidentiary nature pertaining to the commission of a crime or crimes specified therein and in particular, a white knit thermal undershirt; a brown ¾ length leather jacket with a tie-belt; a pair of black mens pants; a dark colored knit hat; a long thin bladed knife or other instruments or items relating to the crime.

Articles, or things were, are, or will be possessed and/or used in violation of Title 11, Sub-Chapter D, Section 763, Delaware Code in that [See attached probable cause page].

Wherefore, affiants pray that a search warrant may be issued authorizing a search of the aforesaid 222 S. Governors Avenue, Apartment # 3, Dover, Delaware. A two room apartment located on the south side second floor of a white block building on the west side of S. Governors Avenue between Loockerman St. and North Street, in the City of Dover in the manner provided by law.

/s/   Det. Ronald R. Brooks

    Affiant

/s/   Det. Larry D. Gray

    Affiant

Sworn to (or affirmed) and subscribed before me this 9th day of March A.D. 1976.

/s/   John [illegible] Green

    Judge Ct 7

The facts tending to establish probable cause for the issuance of this search warrant are:

    1.   On Saturday, 2/28/76, Brenda L. B. _____, W/F/15, reported to the Dover Police Department that she had been kidnapped and raped.

    2.   An investigation of this complaint was conducted by Det. Boyce Failing of the Dover Police Department.

    3.   Investigation of the aforementioned complaint revealed that Brenda B. _____, while under the influence of drugs, was taken to 222 S. Governors Avenue, Apartment 3, Dover, Delaware.

    4.   Investigation of the aforementioned complaint revealed that 222 S. Governors Avenue, Apartment # 3, Dover, Delaware, is the residence of Jerome Franks, B/M DOB: 10/9/54.

    5.   Investigation of the aforementioned complaint revealed that on Saturday, 2/29/76, Jerome Franks did have sexual contact with Brenda B. _____ without her consent.

    6.   On Thursday, 3/4/76 at the Dover Police Department, Brenda B. _____, revealed to Det. Boyce Failing that Jerome Franks was the person who committed the Sexual Assault against her.

    7.   On Friday, 3/5/76, Jerome Franks was placed under arrest by Cpl. Robert McClements of the Dover Police Department, and charged with Sexual Misconduct.

    8.   On 3/5/76 at Family Court in Dover, Delaware, Jerome Franks did, after being arrested on the charge of Sexual Misconduct, make a statement of Cpl. Robert McClements, that he thought the charge was concerning Cynthia Bailey not Brenda B. _____.

    9.   On Friday, 3/5/76, Cynthia C. Bailey, W/F/21 of 132 North Street, Dover, Delaware, did report to Dover Police Department that she had been raped at her residence during the night.

    10.   Investigation conducted by your affiant on Friday, 3/5/76, revealed the perpetrator of the crime to be an unknown black male, approximately 57, 150 lbs., dark complexion, wearing white thermal undershirt, black pants with a belt having a silver or gold buckle, a brown leather ¾ length coat with a tie belt in the front, and a dark knit cap pulled around the eyes.

    11.   Your affiant can state, that during the commission of this crime, Cynthia Bailey was forced at knife point and with the threat

of death to engage in sexual intercourse with the perpetrator of the crime.

12. Your affiant can state that entry was gained to the residence of Cynthia Bailey through a window located on the east side of the residence.

13. Your affiant can state that the residence of Jerome Franks is within a very short distance and direct sight of the residence of Cynthia Bailey.

14. Your affiant can state that the description given by Cynthia Bailey of the unknown black male does coincide with the description of Jerome Franks.

15. On Tuesday, 3/9/76, your affiant contacted Mr. James Williams and Mr. Wesley Lucas of the Delaware Youth Center where Jerome Franks is employed and did have personal conversation with both these people.

16. On Tuesday, 3/9/76, Mr. James Williams revealed to your affiant that the normal dress of Jerome Franks does consist of a white knit thermal undershirt and a brown leather jacket.

17. On Tuesday, 3/9/76, Mr. Wesley Lucas revealed to your affiant that in addition to the thermal undershirt and jacket, Jerome Franks often wears a dark green knit hat.

18. Your affiant can state that a check of official records reveals that in 1971 Jerome Franks was arrested for the crime of rape and subsequently convicted with Assault with intent to Rape.

* * *

[The dissenting opinion of Justice Rehnquist, joined by the Chief Justice, is omitted.]

### NOTES

1. Suppose on remand a hearing was held and Franks proved that neither Morrison nor Lucas had talked with either Brooks or Gray. Suppose further that the defense proved that the misrepresentation concerning this in the affidavit was made with the requisite intent. But in addition suppose that the prosecution proved that both Lucas and Morrison had spoken with another Dover police officer and had told that officer essentially what the affidavit represents was told to "your affiant." How should the judge go about determining the materiality of the error? Should paragraphs 15 through 17 be struck from the affidavit and the remainder evaluated to determine whether probable cause existed? Should any references in those paragraphs as to how the affiants came about the information as to what Morrison and Lucas said be struck but the remainder left and considered? Or should the paragraphs be considered as "amended" by what the affiants would have said if they had been accurate, i.e., that this information was provided to another officer who then communicated it to the affiants?

2. On remand in *Franks*, the Delaware Supreme Court held that even if paragraphs 15 through 17 were set aside in their entirety, the remaining allegations were sufficient to establish probable cause. Consequently, Franks' proffer of evidence to contradict the facts alleged in the affidavit was insufficient and the trial judge did err in failing to hold an evidentiary hearing. The

conviction was, therefore, again upheld by that court.  Franks v. State, 398 A.2d 783 (Del.1979).

## 3.  DISCLOSURE OF INFORMANTS' IDENTITY

Where informants have been involved in the preparation of the prosecution's case, the identity of those informants is often sought by the defense.  Under local privilege law, a governmental unit is generally privileged to withhold the identity of persons providing that unit with information.  See McCormick on Evidence § 111 (3rd ed., E. Cleary ed., 1984).

In some circumstances, federal constitutional considerations require disclosure whatever local privilege may exist.  The leading case is Roviaro v. United States, 353 U.S. 53, 77 S.Ct. 623, 1 L.Ed.2d 639 (1957), a prosecution for sale of drugs.  According to the government's evidence, the informant—identified as "John Doe"—met Roviaro in Doe's car (which had been previously searched and found to contain no drugs) and purchased drugs from him.  An officer concealed in the car trunk overheard the transaction;  further, other officers observed Roviaro enter Doe's car and leave it and then recovered an illicit drug from the car.  But no officer actually observed the sale.  Doe did not testify at trial.  Despite defense counsel's request, the trial judge refused to require the government to identify the informant.  The Supreme Court found error.  "[F]undamental requirements of fairness," it reasoned, require disclosure when the informant's identity or the contents of the informant's communication "is relevant and helpful to the defense of an accused, or is essential to a fair determination of a cause * * *." 353 U.S. at 60–61, 77 S.Ct. at 628, 1 L.Ed.2d at 645.  *Roviaro* is discussed further in the principal case in this subsection.

Among the information which defense counsel might hope to obtain from an informant, of course, is information on which to mount an attack upon the admissibility of some or all of the prosecution's evidence.  Does it—and should it—make any difference that disclosure is sought for this purpose rather than to raise some affirmative assertion tending to show that the defendant is innocent of the offense charged?

### McCRAY v. ILLINOIS
Supreme Court of the United States, 1967.
386 U.S. 300, 87 S.Ct. 1056, 18 L.Ed.2d 62.

MR. JUSTICE STEWART delivered the opinion of the Court.

\* \* \*

The petitioner was arrested in Chicago, Illinois, on the morning of January 16, 1964, for possession of narcotics.  The Chicago police officers who made the arrest found a package containing heroin on his person and he was indicted for its unlawful possession.  Prior to trial he filed a motion to suppress the heroin * * *. After a hearing, the court denied the motion, and the petitioner was subsequently convicted upon the evidence of the heroin the arresting officers had found in his possession.  The judgment of conviction was affirmed by the Supreme Court of Illinois, and we granted certiorari to consider the petitioner's claim that the hearing on his motion to suppress was constitutionally defective.

The petitioner's arrest occurred near the intersection of 49th Street and Calumet Avenue at about seven in the morning. At the hearing on the motion to suppress, * * * Officer Jackson stated that he and two fellow officers had had a conversation with an informant [who] * * * told them that the petitioner, with whom Jackson was acquainted, "was selling narcotics and had narcotics on his person and that he could be found in the vicinity of 47th and Calumet at this particular time." Jackson said that he and his fellow officers drove to that vicinity in the [unmarked] police car and that when they spotted the petitioner, the informant pointed him out and then departed on foot. Jackson stated that the officers observed the petitioner walking with a woman, then separating from her and meeting briefly with a man, then proceeding alone, and finally, after seeing the police car, "hurriedly walk[ing] between two buildings." "At this point," Jackson testified, "my partner and myself got out of the car and informed him we had information he had narcotics on his person, placed him in the police vehicle at this point." Jackson stated that the officers then searched the petitioner and found the heroin in a cigarette package.

Jackson testified that he had been acquainted with the informant for approximately a year, that during this period the informant had supplied him with information about narcotics activities "fifteen, sixteen times at least," that the information had proved to be accurate and had resulted in numerous arrests and convictions. On cross-examination, Jackson was even more specific as to the informant's previous reliability, giving the names of people who had been convicted of narcotics violations as the result of information the informant had supplied. When Jackson was asked for the informant's name and address, counsel for the State objected, and the objection was sustained by the court.

* * *

[The precise federal constitutional grounds on which petitioner relied are unclear. Apparently, however, he urged that his Fourth and Fourteenth Amendments right to be free from improper searches and seizures included the right to access to that information bearing upon the reasonableness of his arrest and search. Unless disclosure is required, in other words, defendants arrested without actual probable cause will be unable to establish that fact and therefore their right to be free from such arrests will be rendered illusory. In his brief petitioner argued:

> Where an arrest is purportedly predicated solely upon an alleged communication from a purported but unidentified "Reliable Informer", the arresting officer becomes the sole judge of the validity of his own arrest. No post-arrest judicial check is afforded and the [courts] * * * are completely precluded from ever determining the actual existence of an informer; in short, whether, in fact, there was probable cause for the arrest. Only by requiring disclosure and giving the defendant an opportunity to present contrary

evidence as to the truth of the officer's testimony and the reasonableness of his reliance on the supposed informer, can the courts make a fair determination of the issue.

Brief for Petitioner, at ii.   Editors.]

There can be no doubt, upon the basis of the circumstances related by Officers Jackson and Arnold, that there was probable cause to sustain the arrest and incidental search in this case.   Draper v. United States, 358 U.S. 307, 79 S.Ct. 329, 3 L.Ed.2d 327.   Unlike the situation in Beck v. State of Ohio, 379 U.S. 89, 85 S.Ct. 223, 13 L.Ed.2d 142, each of the officers in this case described with specificity "what the informer actually said, and why the officer thought the information was credible."   379 U.S. at 97, 85 S.Ct. at 229.   The testimony of each of the officers informed the court of the "underlying circumstances from which the informant concluded that the narcotics were where he claimed they were, and some of the underlying circumstances from which the officer concluded that the informant  *  *  *  was 'credible' or his information 'reliable.'"   Aguilar v. State of Texas, 378 U.S. 108, 114, 84 S.Ct. 1509, 1514, 12 L.Ed.2d 723.  *  *  *  Upon the basis of those circumstances, along with the officers' personal observations of the petitioner, the court was fully justified in holding that at the time the officers made the arrest "the facts and circumstances within their knowledge and of which they had reasonably trustworthy information were sufficient to warrant a prudent man in believing that the petitioner had committed or was committing an offense.   Brinegar v. United States, 338 U.S. 160, 175–176, 69 S.Ct. 1302, 1310–1311, 93 L.Ed. 1879; Henry v. United States, 361 U.S. 98, 102, 80 S.Ct. 168, 171, 4 L.Ed.2d 134," Beck v. State of Ohio, supra, 379 U.S. at 91, 85 S.Ct. at 225.   It is the petitioner's claim, however, that even though the officers' sworn testimony fully supported a finding of probable cause for the arrest and search, the state court nonetheless violated the Constitution when it sustained objections to the petitioner's questions as to the identity of the informant.   We cannot agree.

In permitting the officers to withhold the informant's identity, the court was following well-settled Illinois law.   When the issue is not guilt or innocence, but, as here, the question of probable cause for an arrest or search, the Illinois Supreme Court has held that police officers need not invariably be required to disclose an informant's identity if the trial judge is convinced, by evidence submitted in open court and subject to cross-examination, that the officers did rely in good faith upon credible information supplied by a reliable informant.   This Illinois evidentiary rule is consistent with the law of many other States.

*  *  *  Professor Wigmore, not known as an enthusiastic advocate of testimonial privileges generally has described that privilege in these words:

"A genuine privilege, on  *  *  *  fundamental principle  *  *  *, must be recognized for the *identity of persons supplying the government with information concerning the commission of crimes.*   Communications of this kind ought to receive encouragement.   They are discouraged if the informer's identity is disclosed.   Whether an informer is motivated by good citizenship, promise of leniency or prospect of pecuniary reward, he will usually condition his cooperation on an assurance of anonymity—to protect himself and his family from harm, to preclude adverse social reactions and to avoid the risk of defamation or malicious prosecution actions against him.  The government also has an interest in nondisclosure of the identity of its informers.  Law enforcement officers often depend upon professional informers to furnish them with a flow of information about criminal activities.  Revelation of the dual role played by such persons ends their usefulness to the government and discourages others from entering into a like relationship.

* * *

This Court, * * * has the ultimate task of defining the scope to be accorded to the various common law evidentiary privileges in the trial of federal criminal cases. * * * This is a task which is quite different, of course, from the responsibility of constitutional adjudication.  In the exercise of this supervisory jurisdiction the Court had occasion 10 years ago, in Roviaro v. United States, 353 U.S. 53, 77 S.Ct. 623, 1 L.Ed.2d 639, to give thorough consideration to one aspect of the informer's privilege, the privilege itself having long been recognized in the federal judicial system.

* * *

This Court held that where, in an actual trial of a federal criminal case,

"the disclosure of an informer's identity * * * is relevant and helpful to the defense of an accused, or is essential to a fair determination of a cause, the privilege must give way.  In these situations the trial court may require disclosure and, if the Government withholds the information, dismiss the action. * * *

* * *

"We believe that no fixed rule with respect to disclosure is justifiable.  The problem is one that calls for balancing the public interest in protecting the flow of information against the individual's right to prepare his defense.  Whether a proper balance renders nondisclosure erroneous must depend on the particular circumstances of each case, taking into consideration the crime charged, the possible defenses, the possible significance of the informer's testimony, and other relevant factors."  353 U.S., at 60–61, 62, 77 S.Ct., at 628.  (Footnotes omitted.)

The Court's opinion then carefully reviewed the particular circumstances of Roviaro's trial, pointing out that the informer's "possible testimony was highly relevant * * *," that he "might have disclosed an entrapment * * *," "might have thrown doubt upon petitioner's identity or on the identity of the package * * *," "might have testified to petitioner's possible lack of knowledge of the contents of the package that he 'transported' * * *," and that the "informer was the sole participant, other than the accused, in the transaction charged."  353 U.S., at 63–64, 77 S.Ct., at 629–630.  The Court concluded "that, under these circumstances, the trial court committed prejudicial error in permitting the Government to withhold the identity of its undercover employee in the face of repeated demands by the accused for his disclosure." 353 U.S., at 65, 77 S.Ct., at 630.

What *Roviaro* thus makes clear is that this Court was unwilling to impose any absolute rule requiring disclosure of an informer's identity even in formulating evidentiary rules for federal criminal trials. Much less has the Court ever approached the formulation of a federal evidentiary rule of compulsory disclosure where the issue is the preliminary one of probable cause, and guilt or innocence is not at stake. Indeed, we have repeatedly made clear that federal officers need *not* disclose an informer's identity in applying for an arrest or search warrant. * * * And just this Term we have taken occasion to point out that a rule virtually prohibiting the use of informers would "severely hamper the Government" in enforcement of the narcotics laws. Lewis v. United States, 385 U.S. 206, 210, 87 S.Ct. 424, 427, 17 L.Ed.2d 312.

In sum, the Court in the exercise of its power to formulate evidentiary rules for federal criminal cases has consistently declined to hold that an informer's identity need always be disclosed in a federal criminal trial, let alone in a preliminary hearing to determine probable cause for an arrest or search.

\* \* \*

The arresting officers in this case testified, in open court, fully and in precise detail as to what the informer told them and as to why they had reason to believe his information was trustworthy. Each officer was under oath. Each was subjected to searching cross-examination. The judge was obviously satisfied that each was telling the truth, and for that reason he exercised the discretion conferred upon him by the established law of Illinois to respect the informer's privilege.

Nothing in the Due Process Clause of the Fourteenth Amendment requires a state court judge in every such hearing to assume the arresting officers are committing perjury. "To take such a step would be quite beyond the pale of this Court's proper function in our federal system. It would be a wholly unjustifiable encroachment by this Court upon the constitutional power of States to promulgate their own rules of evidence * * * in their own state courts * * *." Spencer v. State of Texas, 385 U.S. 554, 568–569, 87 S.Ct. 648, 656, 17 L.Ed.2d 606.

\* \* \*

Affirmed.

MR. JUSTICE DOUGLAS, with whom THE CHIEF JUSTICE, MR. JUSTICE BRENNAN and MR. JUSTICE FORTAS concur, dissenting.

\* \* \*

Only through the informer's testimony can anyone other than the arresting officers determine "the persuasiveness of the facts relied on * * * to show probable cause." Aguilar v. State of Texas, 378 U.S. 108, 113, 84 S.Ct. 1509, 1513, 12 L.Ed.2d 723. Without that disclosure neither we nor the lower courts can ever know whether there was "probable cause" for the arrest. * * *

NOTES

1. Is the result in *McCray* based upon the fact that the issue arose in a "preliminary hearing to determine probable cause for [the] arrest" or upon the proposition that the only possible significance to the defense of the informant's identity was to challenge the admissibility of the evidence? Is it conceivable that the informant might have had information suggesting that the drugs had been "planted" on McCray? If so, why was disclosure not required under the rationale of *Roviaro*?

2. The Model Code of Pre-arraignment Procedure would require disclosure of the identity of an informant where the information relied upon to establish probable cause includes a report of information from that informant unless the judge finds "that the issue of [probable] cause can be fairly determined without such disclosure." Model Code of Pre-arraignment Procedure § 290.4 (Official Draft, 1975). Disclosure would not be required, however, if (a) the evidence at issue had been seized under a search warrant; or (b) the prosecution produced "substantial corroboration of the informant's existence and reliability" consisting of testimony of someone other than the person to whom the informant gave his information. For purposes of deciding whether a "fair" determination can be made without disclosure, the judge is authorized to require the prosecution, *in camera*, to disclose the informant's identity or to produce the informant for questioning by the judge. Id. Is this approach inconsistent with *Roviaro* and *McCray*? Perhaps *McCray* can be read a case in which the trial judge implicitly found on the facts before him that a "fair" determination of whether the officers had probable cause could be made without requiring disclosure.

3. *McCray* was decided before Franks v. Delaware. Is it possible that *Franks* requires or suggests an expansion of defendants' right to disclosure beyond what was required by *McCray*? Perhaps the right to attack the accuracy of affidavits, recognized in *Franks*, cannot be implemented in the context of warrants based upon informant's tips, unless the defense has access to the informants.

## C. THE REQUIREMENT OF PARTICULARITY AND EXECUTION OF WARRANTS

The Fourth Amendment reasonableness of a search or arrest pursuant to a warrant may be affected by the manner in which it is carried out as well as by the procedure followed in issuing the warrant. Some, although not all, Fourth Amendment requirements affecting the execution of warrants flow from limits imposed by the terms of the warrants themselves; this is particularly true with regard to search warrants. It is therefore useful to consider together the Fourth Amendment requirements governing what the warrant itself must specify and the often-related requirements applicable to the manner in which officers execute warrants.

In connection with the material in this section, reconsider Horton v. California, ___ U.S. ___, 110 S.Ct. 2301, 110 L.Ed.2d 112 (1990), reprinted at page 106, supra, concerning the right of officers executing a search warrant to seize undescribed items found in "plain view" during the course of the search.

## EDITORS' INTRODUCTION: PARTICULARITY AND ITS EFFECT ON EXECUTION OF THE WARRANT

The terms of the Fourth Amendment provide in part that "no Warrants shall issue, but \* \* \* particularly describing the place to be searched, and the persons or things to be seized." Compared to the probable cause requirement for warrant issuance, however, the mandate of particularity in the warrant itself has received relatively little attention from the Supreme Court. It is clear, however, that the particularity requirement is related to the execution of the warrant and is designed to limit the officers' activity under the warrant. Without a warrant describing with precision the place to be searched and the things to be seized, the Court has observed, "officers are free to determine for themselves the extent of their search and the precise objects to be seized." Trupiano v. United States, 334 U.S. 699, 710, 68 S.Ct. 1229, 1235, 92 L.Ed. 1663, 1672 (1948).

*The Place to Be Searched.* Until the case reprinted in this section, the Supreme Court had seldom addressed the requirement that the place to be searched be described with precision. In United States v. Karo, 468 U.S. 705, 104 S.Ct. 3296, 82 L.Ed.2d 530 (1984), however, the Court did indirectly consider the scope of this Fourth Amendment demand. The discussion makes clear that the Court regards the precision requirements as having sufficient flexibility to accommodate use of warrants for law enforcement activity other than traditional searches of premises that can generally be described quite easily.

Karo contended that the Government's concealment of an electronic beeping device in a can of chemicals to be transferred to Karo and the Government's use of that device to trace Karo's activity with the car was a search. The Government urged that if this was a search, no valid warrant could be obtained for it because the Government would not be able to describe the "place to be searched" with adequate precision. In fact, it suggested, the very purpose of the use of the beeper was to determine the place to be searched, i.e., the place to which the can of chemicals would be taken. The Court rejected the Government's argument:

> [I]t will still be possible to describe the object into which the beeper is to be placed, the circumstances that led agents to wish to install the beeper, and the length of time for which beeper surveillance is requested. In our view, this information will suffice to permit issuance of a warrant authorizing beeper installation and surveillance.

468 U.S. at 718, 104 S.Ct. at 3305, 82 L.Ed.2d at 543. How should a warrant for such activity be phrased?

*Things to Be Seized.* As to the purpose of the mandate that "things to be seized" be described with precision, the Court has offered:

> The requirement \* \* \* makes general searches under [warrants] impossible and prevents the seizure of one thing under a warrant describing another. As to what is to be taken, nothing is left to the discretion of the officer executing the warrant.

Marron v. United States, 275 U.S. 192, 196, 48 S.Ct. 74, 76, 72 L.Ed. 231, 237 (1927). To some extent, this seems incorrect. Under the "plain view seizure rule" (see page 106, supra), officers may sometimes seize items not described in the search warrant if they have probable cause to believe the items are subject to seizure and they come upon the items while searching within the terms of the warrant.

But the description of "things" may limit the officers' authority to search within the described premises. This is illustrated by Stanley v. Georgia, 394 U.S. 557, 89 S.Ct. 1243, 22 L.Ed.2d 542 (1969). Officers searched Stanley's residence under a warrant that authorized them to search the premises for, and to seize, numerous categories of items related to bookmaking. While searching the drawers of a desk in a bedroom, they discovered three reels of eight millimeter film. Using Stanley's projector and screen, they viewed the films. This screening convinced the officers—apparently with good cause—that the films were obscene and they seized them. At Stanley's trial for possession of the films, the films were admitted into evidence over his objection. A majority of the Supreme Court reversed Stanley's conviction on other grounds and did not reach the propriety of the officers' actions. Justice Stewart, however, concurred on the ground that the films had been improperly seized:

> To condone what happened here is to invite a governmental official to use a seemingly precise and legal warrant only as a ticket to get into a man's home, and, once inside, to launch forth upon unconfined searches and indiscriminate seizures as if armed with all the unbridled and illegal power of a general warrant.

394 U.S. at 572, 89 S.Ct. at 1251–52, 22 L.Ed.2d at 553. Under this approach, when did the officers' conduct become improper? Did the warrant authorize them to look into closed desk drawers? Almost certainly so, since the bookmaking items might well have been located there. But did it authorize them to examine the film in such a manner as was necessary to determine its contents? to screen the film as they did? Perhaps this turns upon whether the officers could reasonably have anticipated that this action—examining the film—would enable them to locate and seize those items which the warrant specified.

If the specificity of description of the things to be searched for and seized in a search warrant limits the officers' right to search the premises, this may explain the requirement of specificity. Only a specific warrant can limit the officers to a search of no greater scope or intensity than is necessary to locate the items which the officers have reason to believe are in the premises.

The Court has addressed the required specificity in regard to "things." In Stanford v. Texas, 379 U.S. 476, 85 S.Ct. 506, 13 L.Ed.2d 431 (1965), a search warrant was issued that listed various materials believed to be related to the operation of the Communist Party in Texas. The Court invalidated the resulting conviction on the ground that the warrant on its face offended the requirement of particularity:

> We need not decide in the present case whether the description of the things to be seized would have been too generalized to pass

constitutional muster, had the things been weapons, narcotics or "cases of whiskey." \* \* \* The point is that it was not any contraband of that kind which was ordered to be seized, but literary material—"books, records, pamphlets, cards, receipts, lists, memoranda, pictures, recordings and other written instruments concerning the Communist Party of Texas and the operation of the Communist Party in Texas." The indiscriminate sweep of that language is constitutionally intolerable. To hold otherwise would be false to the terms of the Fourth Amendment, false to its meaning, and false to its history.

379 U.S. at 486, 85 S.Ct. at 512, 13 L.Ed.2d at 437–38.

In Andresen v. Maryland, 427 U.S. 463, 96 S.Ct. 2737, 49 L.Ed.2d 627 (1976), on the other hand, the warrant listed numerous documents believed related to the fraudulent transfer of a specifically described piece of realty. It concluded with authorization to seize "other fruits, instrumentalities and evidence of crime at this [time] unknown." The Court construed this as limited to other evidence relating to the crime committed by transfer of the identified lot. As so construed, it concluded, the warrant did not authorize the officers to conduct a search for evidence of other crimes and therefore was sufficiently precise. 427 U.S. at 481–82, 96 S.Ct. at 2749, 49 L.Ed.2d at 643. Andresen apparently did not argue that it was constitutionally necessary for the warrant to describe the evidence of the crime more specifically. But he did argue that the list of the specified documents constituted a prohibited "general warrant." The Court responded:

> We disagree. Under investigation was a complex real estate scheme whose existence could be proved only by piecing together many bits of evidence. \* \* \* The complexity of an illegal scheme may not be used as a shield to avoid detection when the State has demonstrated probable cause to believe that a crime has been committed and probable cause to believe that evidence of this crime is in the suspect's possession. \* \* \*

427 U.S. at 480 n. 10, 96 S.Ct. at 2748–49 n. 10, 49 L.Ed.2d at 642–43 n. 10. Does this mean that the complexity of the crime and the resulting difficulty of knowing in advance of a search what documents would constitute evidence of its commission justifies some relaxation of the specificity requirement? The things sought in *Stanford* (or the things that might have been seized under the warrant in that case) were more likely to be protected by the First Amendment than the items sought in *Andresen*. Does this explain the demand for greater specificity on the facts of *Stanford*?

*Persons to Be Seized.* The terms of the Fourth Amendment also require that at least certain warrants describe the "persons \* \* \* to be seized" with particularity. Presumably, this requirement applies to arrest warrants. When is a person described with sufficient particularity? Is a name sufficient? A name and a date of birth? A physical description without a name? In Visor v. State, 660 S.W.2d 816 (Tex. Crim.App.1983), the arrest warrant described the person to be arrested as an "unknown black female." Holding that this aspect of the warrant was ineffective, the court observed that to uphold it "would be to approve a general warrant prohibited by the federal constitution."

\* \* \*

The principal case in this section addresses the criterion for determining whether a warrant is sufficiently precise for Fourth Amendment purposes. In addition, however, it considers the demands upon officers who in the process of executing a warrant discover that the warrant is not as precise—at least "as applied"—as they previously thought. Is the Court's approach to the second question the appropriate one?

## MARYLAND v. GARRISON

Supreme Court of the United States, 1987.
480 U.S. 79, 107 S.Ct. 1013, 94 L.Ed.2d 72.

JUSTICE STEVENS delivered the opinion of the Court.

Baltimore police officers obtained and executed a warrant to search the person of Lawrence McWebb and "the premises known as 2036 Park Avenue third floor apartment." When the police applied for the warrant and when they conducted the search pursuant to the warrant, they reasonably believed that there was only one apartment on the premises described in the warrant. In fact, the third floor was divided into two apartments, one occupied by McWebb and one by respondent. Before the officers executing the warrant became aware that they were in a separate apartment occupied by respondent, they had discovered the contraband that provided the basis for respondent's conviction for violating Maryland's Controlled Substances Act. The question presented is whether the seizure of that contraband was prohibited by the Fourth Amendment.

The trial court denied respondent's motion to suppress the evidence seized from his apartment, and the Maryland Special Court of Appeals affirmed. The Court of Appeals of Maryland reversed and remanded with instructions to remand the case for a new trial.

There is no question that the warrant was valid and was supported by probable cause. The trial court found, and the two appellate courts did not dispute, that after making a reasonable investigation, including a verification of information obtained from a reliable informant, an exterior examination of the three-story building at 2036 Park Avenue, and an inquiry of the utility company, the officer who obtained the warrant reasonably concluded that there was only one apartment on the third floor and that it was occupied by McWebb. When six Baltimore police officers executed the warrant, they fortuitously encountered McWebb in front of the building and used his key to gain admittance to the first floor hallway and to the locked door at the top of the stairs to the third floor. As they entered the vestibule on the third floor, they encountered respondent, who was standing in the hallway area. The police could see into the interior of both McWebb's apartment to the left and respondent's to the right, for the doors to both were open. Only after respondent's apartment had been entered and heroin, cash, and drug paraphernalia had been found did any of the officers realize that the third floor contained two apartments. As soon as they became aware of that fact, the search was discontinued. All of the officers reasonably believed that they were searching McWebb's apartment.[9] No further search of respondent's apartment was made.

The matter on which there is a difference of opinion concerns the proper interpretation of the warrant. A literal reading of its plain language, as well as the language used in the application for the warrant, indicates that it was intended to authorize a search of the entire third floor.[10] [T]he Court of Appeals[, however,] concluded that the warrant [authorized a search of McWebb's apartment only and thus] did not authorize the search of respondent's apartment and the police had no justification for making a warrantless entry into his premises.

\* \* \*

In our view, the case presents two separate constitutional issues, one concerning the validity of the warrant and the other concerning the reasonableness of the manner in which it was executed. We shall discuss the questions separately.

I

The Warrant Clause of the Fourth Amendment categorically prohibits the issuance of any warrant except one "particularly describing the place to be searched and the persons or things to be seized." The manifest purpose of this particularity requirement was to prevent general searches. By limiting the authorization to search to the specific areas and things for which there is probable cause to search, the requirement ensures that the search will be carefully tailored to its justifications, and will not take on the character of the wide-ranging exploratory searches the Framers intended to prohibit. Thus, the scope of a lawful search is "defined by the object of the search and the places in which there is probable cause to believe that it may be found. Just as probable cause to believe that a stolen lawnmower may be found in a garage will not support a warrant to search an upstairs bedroom, probable cause to believe that undocumented aliens are being transported in a van will not justify a warrantless search of a suitcase."

In this case there is no claim that the "persons or things to be seized" were inadequately described or that there was no probable cause to believe that those things might be found in "the place to be

---

[9] While the search was in progress, an officer in respondent's apartment answered the telephone. The caller asked for "Red Cross"; that was the name by which McWebb was known to the confidential informant. Neither respondent nor McWebb indicated to the police during the search that there were two apartments.

[10] The warrant states:

"Affidavit having been made before me by Detective Albert Marcus, Baltimore Police Department, Narcotic Unit, that he has reason to believe that on the person of Lawrence Meril McWebb . . . (and) that on the premises known as 2036 Park Avenue third floor apartment, described as a three story brick dwelling with the numerals 2-0-3-6 affixed to the front of same in the City of Baltimore, there is now being concealed certain property. . . .

You are therefor commanded, with the necessary and proper assistants, to search forthwith the person/premises hereinabove described for the property specified, executing this warrant and making the search. . . ."

searched" as it was described in the warrant. With the benefit of hindsight, however, we now know that the description of that place was broader than appropriate because it was based on the mistaken belief that there was only one apartment on the third floor of the building at 2036 Park Avenue. The question is whether that factual mistake invalidated a warrant that undoubtedly would have been valid if it had reflected a completely accurate understanding of the building's floor plan. Plainly, if the officers had known, or even if they should have known, that there were two separate dwelling units on the third floor of 2036 Park Avenue, they would have been obligated to exclude respondent's apartment from the scope of the requested warrant. But we must judge the constitutionality of their conduct in light of the information available to them at the time they acted. Those items of evidence that emerge after the warrant is issued have no bearing on whether or not a warrant was validly issued. Just as the discovery of contraband cannot validate a warrant invalid when issued, so is it equally clear that the discovery of facts demonstrating that a valid warrant was unnecessarily broad does not retroactively invalidate the warrant. The validity of the warrant must be assessed on the basis of the information that the officers disclosed, or had a duty to discover and to disclose, to the issuing magistrate.[11] On the basis of that information, we agree with the conclusion of all three Maryland courts that the warrant, insofar as it authorized a search that turned out to be ambiguous in scope, was valid when it issued.

## II

The question whether the execution of the warrant violated respondent's constitutional right to be secure in his home is somewhat less clear. We have no difficulty concluding that the officers' entry into the third-floor common area was legal; they carried a warrant for those premises, and they were accompanied by McWebb, who provided the key that they used to open the door giving access to the third-floor common area. If the officers had known, or should have known, that the third floor contained two apartments before they entered the living

---

[11] Arguments can certainly be made that the police in this case should have been able to ascertain that there was more than one apartment on the third floor of this building. It contained seven separate dwelling units and it was surely possible that two of them might be on the third floor. But the record also establishes that Officer Marcus made specific inquiries to determine the identity of the occupants of the third floor premises. The officer went to 2036 Park Avenue and found that it matched the description given by the informant: a three-story brick dwelling with the numerals 2–0–3–6 affixed to the front of the premises. The officer "made a check with the Baltimore Gas and Electric Company and discovered that the premises of 2036 Park Ave. third floor was in the name of Lawrence McWebb." Officer Mar-

cus testified at the suppression hearing that he inquired of the Baltimore Gas and Electric Company in whose name the third floor apartment was listed: "I asked if there is a front or rear or middle room. They told me, one third floor was only listed to Lawrence McWebb." The officer also discovered from a check with the Baltimore police department that the police records of Lawrence McWebb matched the address and physical description given by the informant. The Maryland courts that are presumptively familiar with local conditions were unanimous in concluding that the officer reasonably believed McWebb was the only tenant on that floor. Because the evidence supports their conclusion, we accept that conclusion for the purpose of our decision.

quarters on the third floor, and thus had been aware of the error in the warrant, they would have been obligated to limit their search to McWebb's apartment. Moreover, as the officers recognized, they were required to discontinue the search of respondent's apartment as soon as they discovered that there were two separate units on the third floor and therefore were put on notice of the risk that they might be in a unit erroneously included within the terms of the warrant. The officers' conduct and the limits of the search were based on the information available as the search proceeded. While the purposes justifying a police search strictly limit the permissible extent of the search, the Court has also recognized the need to allow some latitude for honest mistakes that are made by officers in the dangerous and difficult process of making arrests and executing search warrants.

In Hill v. California, 401 U.S. 797, 91 S.Ct. 1106, 28 L.Ed.2d 484 (1971), we considered the validity of the arrest of a man named Miller based on the mistaken belief that he was Hill. The police had probable cause to arrest Hill and they in good faith believed that Miller was Hill when they found him in Hill's apartment. As we explained:

> "The upshot was that the officers in good faith believed Miller was Hill and arrested him. They were quite wrong as it turned out, and subjective good-faith belief would not in itself justify either the arrest or the subsequent search. But sufficient probability, not certainty, is the touchstone of reasonableness under the Fourth Amendment and on the record before us the officers' mistake was understandable and the arrest a reasonable response to the situation facing them at the time." Id., at 803–804, 91 S.Ct., at 1110–1111.

While *Hill* involved an arrest without a warrant, its underlying rationale that an officer's reasonable misidentification of a person does not invalidate a valid arrest is equally applicable to an officer's reasonable failure to appreciate that a valid warrant describes too broadly the premises to be searched. Under the reasoning in *Hill*, the validity of the search of respondent's apartment pursuant to a warrant authorizing the search of the entire third floor depends on whether the officers' failure to realize the overbreadth of the warrant was objectively understandable and reasonable. Here it unquestionably was. The objective facts available to the officers at the time suggested no distinction between McWebb's apartment and the third-floor premises.[12]

For that reason, the officers properly responded to the command contained in a valid warrant even if the warrant is interpreted as authorizing a search limited to McWebb's apartment rather than the entire third floor. Prior to the officers' discovery of the factual mistake, they perceived McWebb's apartment and the third-floor premises

[12] Nothing McWebb did or said after he was detained outside 2036 Park Avenue would have suggested to the police that there were two apartments on the third floor. McWebb provided the key that opened the doors on the first floor and on the third floor. The police could reasonably have believed that McWebb was admitting them to an undivided apartment on the third floor. When the officers entered the foyer on the third floor, neither McWebb nor Garrison informed them that they lived in separate apartments.

as one and the same; therefore their execution of the warrant reasonably included the entire third floor.[13]  Under either interpretation of the warrant, the officers' conduct was consistent with a reasonable effort to ascertain and identify the place intended to be searched within the meaning of the Fourth Amendment.[14]

The judgment of the Court of Appeals is reversed, and the case is remanded for further proceedings not inconsistent with this opinion.

It is so ordered.

JUSTICE BLACKMUN, with whom JUSTICE BRENNAN and JUSTICE MARSHALL join, dissenting.

\*   \*   \*

## I

\*   \*   \*

\*   \*   \* The words of the warrant were plain and distinctive: the warrant directed the officers to seize marijuana and drug paraphernalia on the person of McWebb and in McWebb's apartment, i.e., "on the premises known as 2036 Park Avenue third floor apartment." As the Court of Appeals observed, this warrant specifically authorized a search only of McWebb's—not respondent's—residence. In its interpretation of the warrant, the majority suggests that the language of this document, as well as that in the supporting affidavit, permitted a search of the entire third floor. It escapes me why the language in question, "third floor apartment," when used with reference to a single unit in a multiple-occupancy building and in the context of one person's residence, plainly has the meaning the majority discerns, rather than its apparent and, indeed, obvious signification—one apartment located on the third floor. Accordingly, if, as appears to be the case, the warrant was limited in its description to the third floor apartment of McWebb, then the search of an additional apartment—respondent's—was warrantless and is presumed unreasonable "in the absence of some one of a number of well defined 'exigent circumstances.'"  Because the State has not advanced any such exception to the warrant requirement, the evidence obtained as a result of this search should have been excluded.[15]

[13] We expressly distinguish the facts of this case from a situation in which the police know there are two apartments on a certain floor of a building, and have probable cause to believe that drugs are being sold out of that floor, but do not know in which of the two apartments the illegal transactions are taking place.  A search pursuant to a warrant authorizing a search of the entire floor under those circumstances would present quite different issues from the ones before us in this case.

[14] \*   \*   \* Respondent proposes that the police conduct a preliminary survey of the premises whenever they search a building in which there are multiple dwelling units, in order to determine the extent of the premises to be searched.  We find no per-suasive reason to impose such a burden over and above the bedrock requirement that, with the exceptions we have traced in our cases, the police may conduct searches only pursuant to a reasonably detailed warrant.

[15] If the officers were confused about the residence of respondent when they encountered him in the third floor vestibule \*   \*   \*, they might have been justified in detaining him temporarily as an occupant of McWebb's apartment.  The officers asserted that, upon entering the vestibule, they observed marijuana lying upon a dresser in respondent's bedroom, the door to respondent's apartment being open.  Although it is not entirely clear that the drug could have been seized immediately under

## II

Because the Court cannot justify the officers' search under the "exceptional circumstances" rubric, it analyzes the police conduct here in terms of "mistake." According to the Court, hindsight makes it clear that the officers were mistaken, first, in not describing McWebb's apartment with greater specificity in the warrant, and, second, in including respondent's apartment within the scope of the execution of the warrant. The Court's inquiry focuses on what the officers knew or should have known at these particular junctures. The Court reasons that if, in light of the officers' actual or imputed knowledge, their behavior was reasonable, then their mistakes did not constitute an infringement on respondent's Fourth Amendment rights. In this case, the Court finds no Fourth Amendment violation because the officers could not reasonably have drawn the warrant with any greater particularity and because, until the moment when the officers realized that they were in fact searching two different apartments, they had no reason to believe that McWebb's residence did not cover the entire third floor.

\* \* \* It may make some sense to excuse a reasonable mistake by police that produces evidence against the intended target of an investigation or warrant if the officers had probable cause for arresting that individual or searching his residence. Similar reasoning does not apply with respect to one whom probable cause has not singled out and who is the victim of the officers' error.

Even if one accepts the majority's view that there is no Fourth Amendment violation where the officers' mistake is reasonable, it is questionable whether that standard was met in this case. The "place" at issue here is a small multiple-occupancy building. Such forms of habitation are now common in this country, particularly in neighborhoods with changing populations and of declining affluence. Accordingly, any analysis of the "reasonableness" of the officers' behavior here must be done with this context in mind.

The efforts of Detective Marcus, the officer who procured the search warrant, do not meet a standard of reasonableness, particularly considering that the detective knew the search concerned a unit in a multiple-occupancy building. Upon learning from his informant that McWebb was selling marijuana in his third floor apartment, Marcus inspected the outside of the building. He did not approach it, however, to gather information about the configuration of the apartments. Had he done so, he would have discovered, as did another officer on the day of executing the warrant, that there were seven separate mailboxes and bells on the porch outside the main entrance to the house. Although there is some dispute over whether names were affixed near these

the "plain view" exception to the warrant requirement, for this would depend upon whether the officers' "access to the object has some prior Fourth Amendment justification," the officers probably would have had probable cause to obtain a search warrant and conceivably could have impounded respondent's apartment while seeking the warrant. Nothing, however, justified the full-scale search of respondent's apartment in which the officers engaged.

boxes and bells, their existence alone puts a reasonable observer on notice that the three-story structure (with, possibly, a basement) had seven individual units. The detective, therefore, should have been aware that further investigation was necessary to eliminate the possibility of more than one unit's being located on the third floor. Moreover, when Detective Marcus' informant told him that he had purchased drugs in McWebb's apartment, it appears that the detective never thought to ask the informant whether McWebb's apartment was the only one on the third floor. These efforts, which would have placed a slight burden upon the detective, are necessary in order to render reasonable the officer's behavior in seeking the warrant.

Moreover, even if one believed that Marcus' efforts in providing information for issuance of the warrant were reasonable, I doubt whether the officers' execution of the warrant could meet such a standard. In the Court's view, the "objective facts" did not put the officers on notice that they were dealing with two separate apartments on the third floor until the moment, considerably into the search after they had rummaged through a dresser and a closet in respondent's apartment and had discovered evidence incriminating him, when they realized their "mistake." The Court appears to base its conclusion that the officers' error here was reasonable on the fact that neither McWebb nor respondent ever told the officers during the search that they lived in separate apartments.

In my view, however, the "objective facts" should have made the officers aware that there were two different apartments on the third floor well before they discovered the incriminating evidence in respondent's apartment. Before McWebb happened to drive up while the search party was preparing to execute the warrant, one of the officers, Detective Shea, somewhat disguised as a construction worker, was already on the porch of the row house and was seeking to gain access to the locked first-floor door that permitted entrance into the building. From this vantage point he had time to observe the seven mailboxes and bells; indeed, he rang all seven bells, apparently in an effort to summon some resident to open the front door to the search party. A reasonable officer in Detective Shea's position, already aware that this was a multiunit building and now armed with further knowledge of the number of units in the structure, would have conducted at that time more investigation to specify the exact location of McWebb's apartment before proceeding further. For example, he might have questioned another resident of the building.

It is surprising, moreover, that the Court places so much emphasis on the failure of McWebb to volunteer information about the exact location of his apartment. When McWebb drove up, one of the police vehicles blocked his car and the officers surrounded him and his passenger as they got out. Although the officers had no arrest warrant for McWebb, but only a search warrant for his person and apartment, and although they testified that they did not arrest him at that time, it was clear that neither McWebb nor his passenger was free to leave. In such circumstances, which strongly suggest that McWebb was already in custody, it was proper for the officers to administer to him warnings pursuant to Miranda v. Arizona, 384 U.S. 436, 86 S.Ct. 1602, 16 L.Ed.2d 694 (1966). It would then have been reasonable for the officers, aware of the problem, from Detective Shea's discovery, in the specificity of their warrant, to ask McWebb whether his apartment was the only one on the third floor. As it is, the officers made several requests of and questioned McWebb, without giving him *Miranda* warnings, and yet failed to ask him the question, obvious in the circumstances, concerning the exact location of his apartment.

Moreover, a reasonable officer would have realized the mistake in the warrant during the moments following the officers' entrance to the third floor. The officers gained access to the vestibule separating McWebb's and respondent's apartments through a locked door for which McWebb supplied the key. There, in the open doorway to his apartment, they encountered respondent, clad in pajamas and wearing a half-body cast as a result of a recent spinal operation. Although the facts concerning what next occurred are somewhat in dispute, it appears that respondent, together with McWebb and the passenger from McWebb's car, were shepherded into McWebb's apartment across the vestibule from his own. Once again, the officers were curiously silent. The informant had not led the officers to believe that anyone other than McWebb lived in the third-floor apartment; the search party had McWebb, the person targeted by the search warrant, in custody when it gained access to the vestibule; yet when they met respondent on the third floor, they simply asked him who he was but never where he lived. Had they done so, it is likely that they would have discovered the mistake in the warrant before they began their search.

Finally and most importantly, even if the officers had learned nothing from respondent, they should have realized the error in the warrant from their initial security sweep. Once on the third floor, the officers first fanned out through the rooms to conduct a preliminary check for other occupants who might pose a danger to them. \* \* \* [T]he two apartments were almost a mirror image of each other—each had a bathroom, a kitchen, a living room, and a bedroom. Given the somewhat symmetrical layout of the apartments, it is difficult to imagine that, in the initial security sweep, a reasonable officer would not have discerned that two apartments were on the third floor, realized his mistake, and then confined the ensuing search to McWebb's residence.

Accordingly, even if a reasonable error on the part of police officers prevents a Fourth Amendment violation, the mistakes here, both with respect to obtaining and executing the warrant, are not reasonable and could easily have been avoided.

I respectfully dissent.

### NOTES

1. The extent to which a search warrant does and can authorize officers to search persons on the premises to be searched pursuant to a warrant was addressed in Ybarra v. Illinois, 444 U.S. 85, 100 S.Ct. 338, 62 L.Ed.2d 238 (1979). In support of the warrant application, officers recounted a tip from an inform-

ant that he had observed tin-foil packets on the person of "Greg," bartender at the Aurora Tap Tavern, and behind the bar. He had also previously observed such packets in the same places. The informant knew from experience that such tin-foil packets are a common method of packaging heroin. In addition, Greg told the informant that Greg would have heroin for sale on March 1. A warrant was obtained authorizing the search of "the Aurora Tap Tavern" and "the person of 'Greg,' the bartender," for controlled substances. An Illinois statute purported to authorize officers executing a search warrant to detain and search "any person in the place at the time" either to protect themselves from attack or to prevent disposal or concealment of items described in the warrant. Ill.Rev.Stat., ch. 38, section 108–9. When, on March 1, the warrant was executed, Ybarra was one of about a dozen persons in the bar. He was first "frisked" and then more thoroughly searched. Drugs were found. Addressing the officers' right under the warrant to search Ybarra, the Court first indicated that the warrant did not authorize such a search given the specific authorization to search the person of "Greg:"

> Had the issuing judge intended that the warrant would or could authorize a search of every person found within the tavern, he would hardly have specifically authorized the search of "Greg" alone. "Greg" was an employee of the tavern, and the complaint upon which the search warrant was issued gave every indication that he would be present at the tavern on March 1.

444 U.S. at 90 n. 2, 100 S.Ct. at 342 n. 2, 62 L.Ed.2d at 245 n. 2. It then suggested that the warrant could not constitutionally be read as authorizing such a search. The officers' probable cause, the Court stressed, did not extend to Ybarra and others like him. 444 U.S. at 90–91, 100 S.Ct. at 342, 62 L.Ed.2d at 245. Moreover:

> The Fourth Amendment directs that "no Warrants shall issue, but upon probable cause . . . and particularly describing the place to be searched, and the persons or things to be seized." Thus, "open-ended" or "general" warrants are constitutionally prohibited. It follows that a warrant to search a place cannot normally be construed to authorize a search of each individual in that place. The warrant for the Aurora Tap Tavern provided no basis for departing from this general rule. Consequently, we need not consider situations where the warrant itself authorizes the search of unnamed persons in a place and is supported by probable cause to believe that persons who will be in the place at the time of the search will be in possession of illegal drugs.

444 U.S. at 92 n. 4, 100 S.Ct. at 342 n. 4, 62 L.Ed.2d at 246 n. 4.

> Finally, the prosecution asked that the Court recognize a "new" exception to the warrant requirement

> to permit evidence searches of persons who, at the commencement of the search, are on "compact" premises subject to a search warrant, at least where the police have a "reasonable belief" that such persons "are connected with" drug tafficking and "may be concealing or carrying away the contraband."

Rejecting this, the Court simply explained that the "long-prevailing" standard of probable cause embodies the appropriate compromise between citizens' interests and law enforcement, and the Court was unprepared to deviate from that standard in this situation. 444 U.S. at 95–96, 100 S.Ct. at 344, 62 L.Ed.2d at 248.

Three members of the Court, after noting that the Court has had very few opportunities to consider the acceptable scope of searches under warrants, concluded that the warrant gave the officers authority to search Ybarra:

> [T]he police had obtained a warrant to search for precisely the item that Officer Johnson [, the searching officer,] suspected was present in Ybarra's pocket. Whether Officer Johnson's level of certainty could be labeled "probable cause," "reasonable suspicion," or some indeterminate, intermediate level of cognition, the limited pursuit of his suspicions by extracting the items from Ybarra's pocket was reasonable. The justification for the intrusion was linked closely to the terms of the search warrant; the intrusion itself was carefully tailored to conform to its justification.

444 U.S. at 109, 100 S.Ct. at 351–52, 62 L.Ed.2d at 257 (Rehnquist, J., dissenting).

The State also defended the first frisk of Ybarra as a permissible weapons search under Terry v. Ohio, 392 U.S. 1, 88 S.Ct. 1868, 20 L.Ed.2d 990 (1968). This aspect of the case is discussed in Chapter 4 at pages 231–32, infra.

2. Should the limitations on searching persons present when a search warrant is being executed apply to the occupants of a private residence being searched? In Michigan v. Summers, 452 U.S. 692, 101 S.Ct. 2587, 69 L.Ed.2d 340 (1981) law officers were approaching respondent's home to execute a search warrant for contraband when they observed him leave the residence. They detained him while the home was searched. When the search revealed narcotics, they arrested respondent, whom they knew to be the owner of the premises and searched his person, finding still more narcotics. He was prosecuted for possession of the drugs found on his person. The state argued that the authority to search premises granted by the warrant implicitly included the authority to search persons on those premises, just as that authority included an authorization to search furniture and containers in which the particular things described might be concealed. But the Court, in an opinion authored by Justice Stevens, did not rule on that contention because it found that the search warrant implicitly authorized the temporary detention of respondent while the search was conducted and that the discovery of the contraband in respondent's home gave the police authority to arrest him for possession of contraband. The search of his person was justified as a search incident to his lawful arrest. Justices Stewart, Brennan and Marshall dissented.

3. What actions, if any, should officers executing a search warrant in circumstances such as those presented by *Ybarra* be permitted to take in self-protection? Should they be permitted: (1) to require patrons to move to a designated portion of the room; (2) to require patrons to leave certain places, such as rest rooms; (3) to require patrons to stand with their hands exposed to the view of the officers; (4) to require patrons to "spread-eagle" with their hands on a wall and their feet apart? Should the police be authorized to require the patrons immediately to leave the tavern or to be subjected to a pat-down if they choose to remain?

4. Are there situations in which a magistrate would be justified under the Fourth Amendment in authorizing a search of described premises and of persons who may be present when the warrant is executed?

5. Statutes or rules of court typically require that a search warrant be executed promptly after it is issued by the magistrate. Rule 41(c)(1) of the Federal Rules of Criminal Procedure, for example, requires that the warrant "command the officer to search, within a specified period of time not to exceed 10 days" the person or place named in the warrant. What are the reasons for such requirements? How, if at all, are they related to the policies of the Fourth

Amendment.  What remedy, if any, should be provided if a prompt execution provision in a warrant, statute or rule of court is violated?

6.  Statutes or rules of court typically require law enforcement officers to announce their authority and purpose before forcibly entering a residence to execute a search warrant, or an arrest warrant.  For example, 18 U.S.C.A. § 3109 provides:

> The officer may break open any outer or inner door or window of a house, or any part of a house, or anything therein, to execute a search warrant, if, after notice of his authority and purpose, he is refused admittance or when necessary to liberate himself or a person aiding him in the execution of the warrant.

The Supreme Court has held that if entry is made without complying with Section 3109 any evidence discovered in the residence must be suppressed. Sabbath v. United States, 391 U.S. 585, 88 S.Ct. 1755, 20 L.Ed.2d 828 (1968); Miller v. United States, 357 U.S. 301, 78 S.Ct. 1190, 2 L.Ed.2d 1332 (1958).

The Supreme Court has never definitively addressed the extent to which, if any, prior announcement is required by the Fourth Amendment.  Ker v. California, 374 U.S. 23, 83 S.Ct. 1623, 10 L.Ed.2d 726 (1963) (discussed at page 190, infra), however, is widely regarded as suggesting a Fourth Amendment requirement and the lower courts have generally assumed that such a demand exists.  E.g., State v. Cleveland, 118 Wis.2d 615, 623, 348 N.W.2d 512, 517 (1984).  In *Cleveland*, the court observed:

> The rule serves three important purposes: (1) protecting the individual's privacy in the home; (2) decreasing the potential for violence by alerting the resident that the officer is legitimately on the premises; and (3) preventing the physical destruction of property by giving the resident the opportunity to admit the officer voluntarily.

118 Wis.2d at 623, 348 N.W.2d at 517.  As the *Cleveland* court further noted, however, there is general agreement that announcement is not necessary—that so-called "no-knock" entries may be made—where the officers reasonably believe that announcement would endanger the safety of the officers or others or that unannounced entry is necessary to prevent the destruction of the items to be seized.  Id.  Perhaps the most controversial question is the type of showing necessary to justify a "no-knock" entry under the second situation.

In *Cleveland*, the search warrant affidavit recited that an informant had told the affiant that he had observed the occupants of a cabin in possession of PCP, a controlled substance, that the occupants had sold PCP, and that the occupants would soon be leaving.  The affiant, a sheriff's investigator, further alleged that his ten years experience in drug investigations had taught him that drugs and evidence of sale of drugs are readily disposed of or concealed when officers enter a location.  A search warrant issued for the cabin.  The officers executing it found the door unlocked, opened the door and walked in. Only when the male defendant was located in the bedroom with a female companion did the officers identify themselves and announce their purpose. The Wisconsin court held that a prohibited no-knock entry had occurred and that the search was therefore unreasonable.  Explaining, the Court rejected a blanket rule that because drugs are generally capable of rapid destruction warrants for drugs require no prior announcement.  It further rejected the State's argument that the evidence of sale made a no-knock entry permissible:

> It may be true that some drug dealers have made preparations to destroy their contraband in the event of a search.  On the other hand, drug dealers are probably more likely than drug users to possess a sufficiently large quantity of drugs that rapid destruction would be difficult if not impossible.

Thus, without further particular information such as, e.g., the quantity of drugs expected to be discovered and that this amount is readily destroyed if announcement is made, or the preparations that have been made to facilitate the destruction of the drugs, or the defendant's destruction of drugs during a previous attempt to search the premises, an allegation that drugs have been sold on the premises is an inadequate reason to believe that the evidence will be destroyed if the police announce their presence prior to the search.

118 Wis.2d at 629–30, 348 N.W.2d at 520.  Nor, the court concluded, did the officers encounter additional circumstances as they executed the warrant that justified no-knock entry:

They did not, for example, observe that the defendant was aware of their approach.  They heard no cries of alarm or scurrying feet.  They did not see or hear anything that would lead them to reasonably believe that an attempt was being or would be made to destroy the evidence.

118 Wis.2d at 631, 348 N.W.2d at 521.

7.  Statutes sometimes restrict the execution of search warrants to the daytime unless special circumstances justify nighttime searches.  Under some provisions, nighttime execution of warrants requires specific authorization by the issuing magistrate based upon a showing beyond the general requirement of probable cause.  For example, Rule 41(c)(1) of the Federal Rules of Criminal Procedure provides that "the warrant shall be served in the daytime, unless the issuing authority, by appropriate provision in the warrant, and for reasonable cause shown, authorizes its execution at times other than daytime."  Prior to 1972, the Rule had simply directed that search warrants were to be served in the daytime unless "the affidavits are positive that the property is on the person or in the place to be searched."

Are Fourth Amendment interests implicated by whether law enforcement officers choose to execute a search warrant by searching a residence in the nighttime rather than during the day?  In Gooding v. United States, 416 U.S. 430, 94 S.Ct. 1780, 40 L.Ed.2d 250 (1974), a warrant had been issued to search Gooding's apartment for drugs.  The warrant specifically stated that the search could be made "at any time in the day or night."  In fact, the warrant was executed at 9:30 p.m.  The Court rejected Gooding's argument that the evidence seized had to be excluded because of the timing of the search.  After considering a variety of statutes which might govern the warrant at issue, a majority determined that the situation was controlled by 21 U.S.C.A. § 879(a):

A search warrant relating to offenses involving controlled substances may be served at any time of the day or night if the judge or United States magistrate issuing the warrant is satisfied that there is probable cause to believe that grounds exist for the warrant and for its service at this time.

Relying upon the legislative history of this provision, a majority rejected the argument that the statute required some special showing before nighttime execution of a search warrant could be authorized.  All that is necessary is

a showing that the contraband is likely to be on the property or person to be searched at that time.  We believe that the showing was met in this case.  The affidavit * * * suggested that there was a continuing traffic of drugs from [Gooding's] apartment, and an informer had confirmed that drugs were available.  This was sufficient.

416 U.S. at 458, 94 S.Ct. at 1794–95, 40 L.Ed.2d at 269.  Justice Marshall, dissenting, accused the majority of being "totally oblivious" to Fourth Amendment concerns:

Taking [these concerns] into account, I find that the only acceptable interpretation of the statute is one which requires some additional justification for authorizing a nighttime search over and above the ordinary showing of probable cause to believe that a crime has been committed and that evidence of the crime will be found upon the search.

Fundamentally at issue in this case is the extent of the protection which we will enjoy from police intrusion into the privacy of our homes during the middle of the night. The Fourth Amendment was intended to protect our reasonable expectations of privacy from unjustified governmental intrusion. * * * In my view, there is no expectation of privacy more reasonable and more demanding of constitutional protection than our right to expect that we will be let alone in the privacy of our homes during the night. The idea of the police unnecessarily forcing their way into the homes in the middle of the night * * * [,] rousing the residents out of their beds, and forcing them to stand by in indignity in their night clothes while the police rummage through their belonging does indeed smack of a " 'police state' lacking in the respect for * * * the right of privacy dictated by the U.S. Constitution."

416 U.S. at 462, 94 S.Ct. at 1796, 40 L.Ed.2d at 271.

8. When, if ever, would it be appropriate to exclude the fruits of a residential search because the initial entry was lawful but the officers executing the warrant committed extensive and perhaps unnecessary property damage during the course of the search or used unnecessary or perhaps otherwise excessive force upon persons on the premises? See State v. Sierra, 338 So.2d 609 (La.1976), refusing to find a Fourth Amendment violation in such circumstances. Is this affected by the Supreme Court's recent holdings—see page 193, infra—that under certain circumstances the Fourth Amendment prohibits the use of excessive force to make an arrest?

9. Statutes or rules of court sometimes require that a copy of the search warrant be served upon the person whose premises are searched or the person present when the officers arrive to make the search. Minn.Stat.Ann. § 626.16 ("When the officer conducts the search he must give a copy of the warrant * * * to the person in whose possession the premises * * * were found * * * .). They also commonly provide for some judicial supervision of the execution process by requiring the officers to make a "return" on the warrant to the issuing magistrate. See Fed.R.Crim.P. 41(c)–(d) (warrant is to be "promptly" returned to federal magistrate). Officers are often also directed to compile an inventory of items seized during the search and to file the inventory with the return. Fed.R.Crim.P. 41(d). What if any Fourth Amendment implications are there in such requirements? Are there circumstances in which failure to observe these requirements means that the Fourth Amendment demands the exclusion of evidence obtained in the search? In Cady v. Dombrowski, 413 U.S. 433, 93 S.Ct. 2523, 37 L.Ed.2d 706 (1973), the officers failed to list all items seized on the inventory filed with the court that had issued the search warrant. The Court rejected the argument that this required the exclusion of the unlisted items:

As these items were constitutionally seized, we do not deem it constitutionally significant that they were not listed in the return of the warrant. The ramification of that "defect," if such it was, is purely a question of state law.

93 U.S. at 449, 93 S.Ct. at 2532, 37 L.Ed.2d at 719. As a matter of "state law," should the items be excluded?

# Chapter 4

## DETENTIONS OF PERSONS AND RELATED SEARCHES

### Analysis

---

## EDITORS' INTRODUCTION: DETENTIONS AND THEIR CHARACTERIZATION

This Chapter deals with law enforcement detentions of persons suspected of crime—seizures of the person in the language of the Fourth Amendment—and related searches. An lawful detention may, in theory at least, create civil or possibly even criminal liability on the part of the officer effecting it. In most circumstances, however, the legality of an arrest or other detention is of practical significance only if it is accompanied by or leads to a search that yields incriminating evidence. Should such evidence be offered against the suspect at later trial and be challenged, its admissibility will often be affected by the validity of the detention.

At one time, all detentions were regarded as indistinguishable and characterized as arrests. This is no longer the case. Case law, much of it involving the Fourth Amendment requirement that "seizures" of the person be "reasonable," has distinguished a variety of detentions. Given the different requirements that have developed for different detentions and the variation in the searches that can be made in relation to different types of detentions, how a detention is characterized is often an important question. See generally, LaFave, "Seizure" Typology: Classifying Detentions of the Person To Resolve Warrant, Grounds, and Search Issues, 17 U.Mich.J.L.Reform 417 (1984).

The Supreme Court's case law has distinguished arrests from detentions which the Court has characterized as "investigatory stops," e.g., United States v. Hensley, 469 U.S. 221, 226, 105 S.Ct. 675, 679, 83 L.Ed.2d 604, 610 (1985), and "traffic stops," Berkemer v. McCarty, 468 U.S. 420, 104 S.Ct. 3138, 3142, 82 L.Ed.2d 317, 327 (1984). There may be others as well. Further, in United States v. Robinson, 414 U.S. 218, 235, 94 S.Ct. 467, 477, 38 L.Ed.2d 427, 440 (1973), the Court began to speak of "custodial arrests" as if such detentions were somehow different from other detentions that might be called arrests. Precisely how detentions are to be placed in these sorts of schemes is not entirely clear.

This chapter begins with detentions or seizures constituting "arrests," which are the benchmark of Fourth Amendment analysis in this area. It then turns to field detentions—so-called *"Terry"* stops—and the right to make weapon searches where no arrest has occurred. Next, certain non-arrest detentions of persons in automobiles are considered. Finally, attention is turned to the "pretext" issue—whether an otherwise proper arrest or detention is invalidated if the officer's "intention" is to circumvent certain legal requirements.

## A.  ARRESTS AND ASSOCIATED SEARCHES

### EDITORS' INTRODUCTION: ARRESTS AND THEIR VALIDITY

The right to search that arises by virtue of the effectuation of certain "arrests" is quite broad, or at least broader than the right to search that arises when other detentions are made. It is important, therefore, to be able to identify those detentions that constitute an arrest and—within this category—to identify those arrests that create the broadest rights to search. It is clear that a prerequisite to a search incident to an arrest is—generally speaking, at least—the occurrence of a valid arrest. Before considering the scope of the permitted search, then, it is also necessary to address the validity of arrests themselves.

*Definition of "Arrest."* The increased complexity of the law relating to detentions has made the definition of arrest more difficult. In part, this is because the definition may be called into play to distinguish arrests from other detentions of the person. One court—with these considerations in mind—recently offered:

> The classic definition of arrest consists of " ' * * * the apprehending or restraining of one's person, in order to be forthcoming to answer an alleged or suspected crime.' " E. Fisher, *Laws of Arrest* 7 (1967) (quoting 4 W. Blackstone, *Commentaries* * * * 288, 289). The necessary first step in determining whether there

has been an arrest is to ask whether the individual was free to leave the presence of the police.

A second element of arrest is the likelihood that the present confinement will be accompanied by future interference with the individual's freedom of movement. This element reflects the common law notion that an arrest is more than a present confinement. To be an arrest, confinement should simply be the initial action in criminal prosecution.

State v. Rupe, 101 Wn.2d 664, 683–84, 683 P.2d 571, 584 (1984). Does this definition suggest that an arrest requires a certain intention on the part of the officer? Discussions of arrest sometimes speak of a necessity of an intent to effect an arrest. E.g., United States v. Chaffen, 587 F.2d 920, 923 (8th Cir.1978). If this is required, what is "an intent to effect an arrest?" Some discussions suggest that it means that the officers must have the purpose of requiring the defendant to "answer" for the commission of a suspected crime. State v. Boone, 220 Kan. 758, 764, 556 P.2d 864, 870 (1976).

*"Custodial" and Other "Arrests."* As the cases discussed in this section and elsewhere in these materials make clear, the Supreme Court's case law sometimes speaks in terms of "custodial" arrests. Precisely what is meant by this has never been developed by the Court. Perhaps, however, the Court intends to distinguish those arrests that will result in the release of the suspect in the field from those that will result in the suspect's being removed to some other location—a stationhouse or courtroom—for further "processing."

In a number of jurisdictions, police officers are specifically authorized to release a suspect upon providing the suspect with a directive to appear in court, usually at a specified time or place. Such directives are often referred to in common usage as "citations" or—especially in the context of a traffic offense—as "tickets." When a suspect may be released with a directive of this sort and what label is attached to the detention culminating in such release differ among jurisdictions. Some jurisdictions regard the detention necessary for providing such directives as an arrest. A Michigan statute, for example, provides that an officer who has arrested a person for a minor offense may, instead of taking the person before a magistrate and filing a complaint, "issue to and serve upon the person an appearance ticket * * *." Mich.Code Crim.Pro. § 764.9c. A "minor offense" is a misdemeanor or ordinance violation punishable by imprisonment for not more than 92 days and a mine not exceeding $500. Id., at § 761.1(k). See also, Vernon's Ann. Tex.Civ.Stat. art. 6701d, § 148, authorizing a similar procedure for violations of traffic laws punishable as a misdemeanor.

Other jurisdictions characterize the detentions as other than arrests. The relevant New York statute, for example, provides that an officer authorized to arrest a person without a warrant for an offense other than a felony may, instead, "issue to and serve upon such person an appearance ticket." N.Y.—McKinney's Crim.Proc.L. § 150.20. See also, Ill.Rev.Stat.1977, ch. 38, § 107–12 (authorizing officer to issue "notice to appear" whenever the officer is authorized to arrest a person without a warrant).

In Berkemer v. McCarty, 468 U.S. 420, 104 S.Ct. 3138, 82 L.Ed.2d 317 (1984), reprinted at page 460, infra, the Court discussed—in the context of determining whether a person is "in custody" so as to bring into play the requirements of Miranda v. Arizona, 384 U.S. 436, 86 S.Ct. 1602, 16 L.Ed.2d 694 (1966)—"arrests," "formal arrests," and "traffic stops." In this regard, the Court commented:

> [D]etention of a motorist pursuant to a traffic stop is presumptively temporary and brief. The vast majority of roadside detentions last only a few minutes. A motorist's expectations, when he sees a policeman's light flashing behind him, are that he will be obliged to spend a short period of time answering questions and waiting while the officer checks his license and registration, that he may then be given a citation, but that in the end he most likely will be allowed to continue on his way.

468 U.S. at 437, 104 S.Ct. at 3149, 82 L.Ed.2d at 333.

*"Formal" Arrests.* The Supreme Court's cases also refer to "formal" arrests. Berkemer v. McCarty, 468 U.S. 420, 441, 104 S.Ct. 3138, 3151, 82 L.Ed.2d 317, 336 (1984); Rawlings v. Kentucky, 448 U.S. 98, 111, 100 S.Ct. 2556, 2564, 65 L.Ed.2d 633, 645 (1980). Again, however, the Court has not defined this term. It seems likely, however, that the Court regards a "formal" arrest as a detention accompanied by the officer's expressed announcement to the detained person that an arrest has been made. Some jurisdictions impose a requirement of announcements of this sort. In a number of jurisdictions, for example, an officer is directed to inform the person of the officer's authority and the reason or cause for the arrest. Exceptions are commonly provided for situations in which the suspect's flight or resistance make such action by the officer impractical. E.g., Mich.Code Crim.Pro. § 764.19; N.Y.—McKinney's Crim.Pro.L. § 140.15(2). Nevertheless, the lower courts have held that compliance with provisions such as these is not necessary to the making of a valid arrest under state law. E.g., Williams v. State, 278 Ark. 9, 12, 642 S.W.2d 887, 889 (1982). The Supreme Court has never indicated that the Fourth Amendment requires such an announcement even when the arrest is made by an officer of a state in which state law imposes such a requirement. Nor has an announcement of this sort been required by the lower courts as a matter of federal constitutional law. As one federal court recently stated, "the determination of whether an arrest has occurred for Fourth Amendment purposes does not depend upon whether the officers announced that they were placing the suspects under arrest." United States v. Rose, 731 F.2d 1337, 1342 (8th Cir.1984).

*Warrant Requirements—Arrests.* Arrests may be made pursuant to arrest warrants, issued by judicial officers on the basis of information found by those officers to constitute probable cause to believe the persons guilty of offenses. See, for example, Rule 4 of the Federal Rules of Criminal Procedure, authorizing the issuance of an arrest warrant.

In United States v. Watson, 423 U.S. 411, 96 S.Ct. 820, 46 L.Ed.2d 598 (1976), the Supreme Court considered whether the Fourth Amendment requires—in the absence of exigent circumstances—that an arrest warrant be procured for an arrest in a public place.   The Court noted long and widespread acceptance of the common law rule that a warrantless arrest for a felony was permissible, even if the felony was not committed in the presence of the officer, if the officer had probable cause to believe the suspect guilty.   Congressional enactments authorizing such arrests reflected the understanding of that body that the Fourth Amendment did not require more.   Thus, the Court concluded:

> Law enforcement officers may find it wise to seek arrest warrants where practicable to do so, and their judgments about probable cause may be more readily accepted where backed by a warrant issued by a magistrate.   But we decline to transform this judicial preference into a constitutional rule when the judgment of the Nation and Congress has for so long been to authorize warrantless public arrests on probable cause rather than to encumber criminal prosecutions with endless litigation with respect to the existence of exigent circumstances, whether it was practicable to get a warrant, whether the suspect was about to flee, and the like.

423 U.S. at 423–24, 96 S.Ct. at 827–28, 46 L.Ed.2d at 609.

In regard to misdemeanors, the law is less clear.   At common law, a warrantless arrest was permitted for a misdemeanor only if the offense was a breach of the peace and it was committed in the presence of the officer.   See Commonwealth v. Reeves, 223 Pa.Super. 51, 52–53, 297 A.2d 142, 143 (1972).   In many American jurisdictions, however, this has been broadened.   Warrantless arrests are often permitted for any misdemeanor committed in the presence of the officer.   Brown v. State, 442 N.E.2d 1109, 1115 (Ind.1982);  State v. Luna, 93 N.M. 773, 606 P.2d 183 (1980).   Sometimes state statutory authority or case law is broader.   See State v. Martin, 275 S.C. 141, 268 S.E.2d 105 (1980), construing the South Carolina statutes as permitting an officer to make a warrantless arrest for a misdemeanor when the facts and circumstances observed by the officer give the officer probable cause to believe that a misdemeanor has been "freshly committed."

If a misdemeanor arrest is invalid *under state law* because an arrest warrant was necessary but not obtained, does the Fourth Amendment as construed in Mapp v. Ohio (see page 18, supra) require suppression of evidence obtained in a search incident to that arrest?   If not, does state law?   Some courts—without much consideration—conclude that evidence of this sort cannot be used.   See Commonwealth v. Trefry, 249 Pa.Super. 117, 375 A.2d 786 (1977);  Commonwealth v. Reeves, supra.

Does the Fourth Amendment impose some version of the traditional requirement of an arrest warrant for certain arrests?   *Watson* relied heavily upon acceptance of the common law rule that felony arrests did not require warrants.   Perhaps the widespread acceptance of the common law notion that at least some misdemeanor arrests demand warrants means that a warrant requirement for such arrests is incorporated into the Fourth Amendment.  The Supreme Court has never addressed the issue.

*Warrant Requirements—Search for Person to be Arrested.*  When an arrest requires entry into premises to find the suspect and to effectuate the arrest, it is clear that the Fourth Amendment's warrant requirement comes into play.  In Payton v. New York, 445 U.S. 573, 100 S.Ct. 1371, 63 L.Ed.2d 639 (1980), officers entered the suspects' own residences seeking them for purposes of arrest.  Such activity, the Court reasoned, breaches the entrance of an individual's home just as does a search for evidence.  "Absent exigent circumstance," it concluded, "that threshold may not reasonably be crossed without a warrant." 445 U.S. at 590, 100 S.Ct. at 1382, 63 L.Ed.2d at 653.  It then continued:

> [W]e note the State's suggestion that only a search warrant based on probable cause to believe the suspect is at home at a given time can adequately protect the privacy interests at stake, and since such a warrant requirement is manifestly impractical, there need be no warrant of any kind.  We find this ingenious argument unpersuasive.  It is true that an arrest warrant requirement may afford less protection than a search warrant requirement, but it will suffice to interpose the magistrate's determination of probable cause between the zealous officer and the citizen.  If there is sufficient evidence of a citizen's participation in a felony to persuade a judicial officer that his arrest is justified, it is constitutionally reasonable to require him to open his doors to the officers of the law.  Thus, for Fourth Amendment purposes, an arrest warrant founded on probable cause implicitly carries with it the limited authority to enter a dwelling in which the suspect lives when there is reason to believe the suspect is within.

445 U.S. at 602–03, 100 S.Ct. at 1388, 63 L.Ed.2d at 660–61.

But when the premises entered are not those of the suspect, a different situation is presented.  In Steagald v. United States, 451 U.S. 204, 101 S.Ct. 1642, 68 L.Ed.2d 38 (1981), federal drug Enforcement Administration agents had a warrant for the arrest of Lyons.  Two days after receiving a tip from an informant that Lyons could be found at a particular residence, they searched that residence.  They did not find Lyons but did discover a substantial quantity of cocaine and this was admitted at Steagald's trial for possession of that substance.  Finding constitutional error, the Supreme Court held that the absence of a valid search warrant rendered the search unreasonable:

> [W]hile the [arrest] warrant * * * may have protected Lyons from an unreasonable seizure, it did absolutely nothing to protect [Steagald's] privacy interest in being free from an unreasonable invasion and search of his home.  Instead, [Steagald's] only protection from an illegal entry and search was the agent's personal determination of probable cause.  In the absence of exigent circumstances, we have consistently held that such judicially untested determinations are not reliable enough to justify an entry into a person's home to arrest him without a warrant, or a search of a home for objects in the absence of a search warrant.  We see no

reason to depart from this settled course when the search of a home is for a person rather than an object.

451 U.S. at 213–14, 101 S.Ct. at 1648, 68 L.Ed.2d at 46. In *Steagald,* Steagald and one Gaultney were apprehended standing outside of the house; Gaultney's wife was inside when it was searched. Before the Supreme Court, the Government urged that Steagald had failed to demonstrate that he had an expectation of privacy in the house. The Court, however, concluded that the Government had effectively conceded in the lower courts that Steagald had a privacy interest in the premises and that it could therefore not challenge the matter before the Court. 451 U.S. at 208–11, 101 S.Ct. at 1646–47, 68 L.Ed.2d at 43–45. In future cases where a suspect is found during a search of a third party's premises, will the suspect be able to show a sufficient privacy interest in those premises to enable him to challenge the absence of the search warrant required by *Steagald?*

The warrant requirement here, just as the general search warrant requirement (see Chapter 5, Section A, infra), is subject to an emergency exception. The matter was addressed in Welsh v. Wisconsin, 466 U.S. 740, 104 S.Ct. 2091, 80 L.Ed.2d 732 (1984). Information from a witness led police officers to believe that Welsh had, while intoxicated, driven his automobile off the highway into a field, abandoned it, and gone to his nearby residence. Police went to his residence, entered, and—upon finding Welsh lying naked in bed—placed him under arrest for driving a motor vehicle under the influence of an intoxicant. He was taken to the station, where he refused to submit to a breathalyzer test. Subsequently, proceedings to revoke his driver's license were begun, based upon his refusal to submit to the breathalyzer test. Under Wisconsin law, if his arrest had been unlawful his refusal to submit to the breathalyzer test would have been reasonable and that refusal could not serve as the basis for revocation. The state courts ultimately rejected Welsh's argument that his arrest violated the Fourth Amendment; the lack of a warrant was not controlling in view of the officers' "hot pursuit," the risk of harm to the public and Welsh himself, and the need for an immediate arrest and breath test before the alcohol in Welsh's blood disappeared from his system.

The Supreme Court reversed. Justice Brennan, writing for the Court, acknowledged that some "emergency conditions" would sometimes justify warrantless home arrests. But, he continued:

> [A]n important factor to be considered when determining whether any exigency exists is the gravity of the underlying offense for which the arrest is being made. * * * [A]pplication of the exigent-circumstances exception in the context of a home entry should rarely be sanctioned where there is probable cause to believe that only a minor offense, such as the kind at issue in this case, has been committed.

466 U.S. at 753, 104 S.Ct. at 2099, 80 L.Ed.2d at 745. Under Wisconsin law, first offense driving while intoxicated is a noncriminal civil forfeiture offense for which the maximum penalty was, at the time, a $200 fine. Turning to the facts of the case, the Court continued:

[T]he claim of hot pursuit is unconvincing because there was no immediate or continuous pursuit of the petitioner from the scene of a crime. Moreover, because the petitioner had already arrived home and had abandoned his car at the scene of the accident, there was little remaining threat to the public safety. Hence, the only potential emergency claimed by the State was the need to ascertain the petitioner's blood-alcohol level.

Even assuming, however, that the underlying facts would support a finding of this exigent circumstance, mere similarity to other cases involving the imminent destruction of evidence is not sufficient. [Wisconsin's classification of driving while intoxicated as a civil offense for which no imprisonment is possible] * * * is the best indication of the state's interest in precipitating an arrest, and is one that can easily be identified both by the courts and by officers faced with a decision to arrest. Given this expression of the state's interest, a warrantless home arrest cannot be upheld simply because evidence of the petitioner's blood-alcohol level might have dissipated while the police obtained a warrant.

466 U.S. at 753–54, 104 S.Ct. at 2099–3000, 80 L.Ed.2d at 745–46.

In view of this conclusion, the Court found "no occasion to consider whether the Fourth Amendment might impose an absolute ban on warrantless home arrests for certain minor offenses." 466 U.S. at 749 n. 11, 104 S.Ct. at 2097 n. 11, 80 L.Ed.2d at 743 n. 11. Whether valid consent to enter was obtained by the officers had not been addressed by the lower courts and the Supreme Court assumed no valid consent existed. "On remand," it commented, "the state courts may consider whether the petitioner's arrest was justified because the police had validly obtained consent to enter his home." 466 U.S. at 755 n. 15, 104 S.Ct. at 2100 n. 15, 80 L.Ed.2d at 746 n. 15.

Justice White observed that the Court did not adopt a possible "bright-line distinction" between felonies and misdemeanors. Such a line would be untenable, he suggested, because the modern category of misdemeanor contains certain serious offenses for which warrantless home arrests might be justifiable under exigent circumstances. But as a result, he continued, "[t]he Court's approach will necessitate a case-by-case evaluation of the seriousness of particular crimes, a difficult task for which officers and courts are poorly equipped." 466 U.S. at 761–62, 104 S.Ct. at 2104, 80 L.Ed.2d at 751 (White, J., dissenting).

There also is a "hot pursuit" sort of exception to the warrant requirement in this context. In United States v. Santana, 427 U.S. 38, 96 S.Ct. 2406, 49 L.Ed.2d 300 (1976), officers in an automobile pulled up in front of Santana's residence. She was standing in the door. When the officers shouted, "Police," displayed their badges and advanced, she "retreated" into the vestibule of her house. The officers—without a warrant—followed her into the vestibule and arrested her. No constitutional defect was found in the officers' actions. While she was in her doorway, the Court reasoned, Santana was in a "public place" and, under *Watson,* no warrant was required. Where the police follow in "true 'hot pursuit,' " a suspect may not, by retreating into a house,

"defeat an arrest which has been set in motion in a public place
\* \* \*." 427 U.S. at 43, 96 S.Ct. at 2410, 49 L.Ed.2d at 306.

*Entry to Arrest—Announcement Requirement.* Where officers rely
upon a search warrant as authority to enter premises and search those
premises for a suspect they seek to arrest, the propriety of the officers'
actions in gaining entry is probably governed by the rules relating to
entry to execute a search warrant; see Chapter 3 at pages 179–80,
supra. In other situations, however, must officers make some sort of
preliminary announcements—as, for example, as to their purpose—and
perhaps also a request to be admitted before entering? In Miller v.
United States, 357 U.S. 301, 78 S.Ct. 1190, 2 L.Ed.2d 1332 (1958), the
Government conceded that the validity of an entry to make an arrest
without a warrant was to be tested by criteria identical to those which
18 U.S.C.A. § 3109 [set out at page 179, supra] imposes upon entry to
execute a search warrant. Since the officers in *Miller* failed to give
notice of their authority and purpose before breaking to enter to locate
and arrest Miller, the entry, Miller's arrest, and the search incident to
the arrest were held invalid and the evidence obtained in the search
was inadmissible. In Sabbath v. United States, 391 U.S. 585, 88 S.Ct.
1755, 20 L.Ed.2d 828 (1968), the officers had gone to Sabbath's apartment door, knocked, waited a "few seconds," opened the unlocked but
closed door, and entered. They came upon Sabbath and placed him
under arrest; a search incident to that arrest resulted in discovery of
cocaine. The Court rejected the argument that the officers did not
"break open" the door within the meaning of 18 U.S.C.A. § 3109:

> An unannounced intrusion into a dwelling—what § 3109 basically
> proscribes—is no less an unannounced intrusion whether officers
> break down a door, force open a chain lock on a partially open door,
> open a locked door by use of a passkey, or, as here, open a closed
> but unlocked door.

391 U.S. at 590, 88 S.Ct. at 1758, 20 L.Ed.2d at 834. Since the officers
did "break open" the door and failed to comply with the statute, the
cocaine was inadmissible.

The Court has never specifically held that the Fourth Amendment
requires notice before entry to make an arrest. In Ker v. California,
374 U.S. 23, 83 S.Ct. 1623, 10 L.Ed.2d 726 (1963), eight members of the
Court considered whether an unannounced entry by California officers
to make an arrest violated the "reasonableness" requirement of the
Fourth Amendment. Four indicated that a Fourth Amendment requirement existed and was violated on the facts of the case. 374 U.S. at
47, 60–64, 83 S.Ct. at 1635, 1643–45, 10 L.Ed.2d at 746, 753–55 (Brennan, J., dissenting). The view of the four-justice "plurality" appears to
have been that the facts before the Court brought the entry at issue
within an exception to any such Fourth Amendment requirement as
might exist and therefore it was unnecessary to consider whether such
a requirement was in fact imposed by the Amendment. 374 U.S. at 37–
41, 83 S.Ct. at 1632–34, 10 L.Ed.2d at 740–42 (opinion of Clark, J.).
Justice Harlan maintained that the only issue that should be addressed
was whether the state search violated flexible due process notions of

"fundamental fairness." He concluded that it did not. 374 U.S. at 44–46, 83 S.Ct. at 1645–46, 10 L.Ed.2d at 744–45 (Harlan, J., concurring in the result). The Court has, however, suggested that there may be exceptions to any such constitutional requirement as may exist. Sabbath v. United States, supra, 391 U.S. at 591 n. 8, 88 S.Ct. at 1759 n. 8, 20 L.Ed.2d at 834 n. 8.

State law often imposes a notice requirement and frequently provides for exceptions. Under New York statutory law, for example, an officer must, before entering to effect an arrest, give "or make reasonable effort to give" notice of "his authority and purpose." This is not required if the officer has reasonable cause to believe that giving of notice will result in the suspect escaping (or attempting to escape), the life or safety of anyone being endangered, or the destruction, damaging or secretion of material evidence. N.Y.—McKinney's Crim.Proc.L. §§ 120.80(4) (arrests under arrest warrants), 140.15(4) (warrantless arrests). See also, West's Ann.Cal.Penal Code § 844 (officer may "break open the door or window" to make an arrest "after having demanded admittance and explained the purpose for which admittance is desired").

*Probable Cause Requirement—In General.* Although the warrant requirement has relatively little application to the reasonableness of an arrest, the Fourth Amendment's requirement of probable cause does have substantial significance:

> Whether [an] arrest was constitutionally valid depends ∗  ∗  ∗ upon whether, at the moment the arrest was made, the officers had probable cause to make it—whether at that moment the facts and circumstances within their knowledge and of which they had reasonably trustworthy information were sufficient to warrant a prudent man in believing that the [suspect] had committed or was committing an offense.

Beck v. Ohio, 379 U.S. 89, 91, 85 S.Ct. 223, 225, 13 L.Ed.2d 142, 145 (1964).

A subaspect of the probable cause issue is the effect of an arrest under a law later determined to be invalid. In Michigan v. DeFillippo, 443 U.S. 31, 99 S.Ct. 2627, 61 L.Ed.2d 343 (1979), DeFillippo was arrested under a Detroit ordinance. A search incident to that arrest resulted in discovery of controlled substances and DeFillippo was prosecuted for possession of those substances. The state courts held that the ordinance under which he was arrested was unconstitutionally vague and therefore the arrest and the incidental search were invalid. The Supreme Court reversed, holding that the information indicating that DeFillippo had violated the ordinance rendered the arrest constitutionally permissible. As to the unconstitutionality of the ordinance, the Court continued:

> Police are charged to enforce laws until and unless they are declared unconstitutional. The enactment of a law forecloses speculation by enforcement officers concerning its constitutionality— with the possible exception of a law so grossly and flagrantly unconstitutional that any person of reasonable prudence would be

bound to see its flaws. Society would be ill-served if its police officers took upon themselves to determine which laws are and which are not constitutionally entitled to enforcement.

443 U.S. at 38, 99 S.Ct. at 2632, 61 L.Ed.2d at 350.

*Probable Cause—Cooperative Action and "Collective" Information.* Given the complexity of many criminal offenses and the mobility of many suspects, investigations often involve several different jurisdictions. Action by law enforcement officers of one jurisdiction may be taken upon request of officers of another jurisdiction. When an arrest is made by one officer or agency upon the request of another officer or police agency, what information is to be considered in determining whether probable cause exists? In Whiteley v. Warden, 401 U.S. 560, 91 S.Ct. 1031, 28 L.Ed.2d 306 (1971), a Carbon County, Wyoming sheriff issued a message through a statewide law enforcement radio network describing a suspect and stating that an arrest warrant had been issued for the suspect. The information submitted in support of the warrant request was not set out in the message. In response to the message, officers in another Wyoming locality—Laramie—arrested and searched the suspect. During the suspect's later prosecution, items found in the search were admitted into evidence over his objection. The State urged that with regard to the Laramie officers the radio request constituted probable cause on which they could act regardless of the validity of the warrant on which the request was based. After concluding that the warrant was invalid because it was issued without information amounting to probable cause, the Court continued:

> We do not * * * question that the Laramie police were entitled to act on the strength of the radio bulletin. Certainly police officers called upon to aid other officers in executing arrest warrants are entitled to assume that the officers requesting aid offered the magistrate the information requisite to support an independent judicial assessment of probable cause. Where, however, the contrary turns out to be true, an otherwise illegal arrest cannot be insulated from challenge by the decision of the instigating officer to rely on fellow officers to make the arrest.

401 U.S. at 568, 91 S.Ct. at 1037, 28 L.Ed.2d at 313.

In United States v. Hensley, 469 U.S. 221, 105 S.Ct. 675, 83 L.Ed.2d 604 (1985), the Court developed the implications of this holding:

> *Whiteley* supports the proposition that, when evidence is uncovered during a search incident to an arrest in reliance merely on a flyer or bulletin, its admissibility turns on whether the officers who *issued* the flyer possessed probable cause to make the arrest. It does not turn on whether those relying on the flyer were themselves aware of the specific facts which led their colleagues to seek their assistance. In an era when criminal suspects are increasingly mobile and increasingly likely to flee across jurisdictional boundaries, this rule is a matter of common sense: it minimizes the volume of information concerning suspects that must be transmitted to other jurisdictions and enables police in one jurisdiction to act promptly in reliance on information from another jurisdiction.

469 U.S. at 231, 105 S.Ct. at 681, 83 L.Ed.2d at 613–14.

*Excessive Force.* Traditionally, the amount of force that could be used to effect an arrest has been a matter of nonconstitutional law. In Tennessee v. Garner, 471 U.S. 1, 105 S.Ct. 1694, 85 L.Ed.2d 1 (1985), however, the Supreme Court held that excessive deadly force in making an otherwise proper arrest renders that arrest "unreasonable" under the Fourth Amendment. Such "reasonableness," the Court explained, depends not simply upon whether there are grounds for an arrest—that is, probable cause—"but also on how [the arrest] is carried out." 471 U.S. at 8, 105 S.Ct. 1699, 85 L.Ed.2d at 7–8. In Graham v. Connor, 490 U.S. 386, 109 S.Ct. 1865, 104 L.Ed.2d 443 (1989), it held that nondeadly but excessive force could have the same effect. *Garner* further defined acceptable force for purposes of the Fourth Amendment rule as narrower than the traditional rule, which permitted officers to use deadly force whenever they reasonably believed that necessary to make the arrest of a person reasonably believed to have committed a felony. Use of deadly force, the Court concluded, is unreasonable if used against a nondangerous suspect. Putting the holding affirmatively, it explained:

> Where the officer has probable cause to believe that the suspect poses a threat of serious physical harm, either to the officer or to others, it is not constitutionally unreasonable to prevent escape by using deadly force. Thus, if the suspect threatens the officer with a weapon or there is probable cause to believe that he has committed a crime involving the infliction or threatened infliction of serious physical harm, deadly force may be used if necessary to prevent escape, and if, where feasible, some warning has been given.

471 U.S. at 11–12, 105 S.Ct. at 1701, 85 L.Ed.2d at 10. On the facts of *Garner,* the Court held that the officer's reasonable belief that the suspect had committed nighttime burglary was not sufficient to justify the use of the fatal gunfire there at issue to stop the suspect.

In *Graham,* the Court explained that whether nondeadly force was excessive

> requires careful attention to the facts and circumstances of each particular case, including the severity of the crime at issue, whether the suspect poses an immediate threat to the safety of officers or others, and whether he is actively resisting arrest or attempting to evade arrest by flight.

490 U.S. at ___, 109 S.Ct. at 1871–72, 104 L.Ed.2d at 454–55. Courts must consider the evidence "from the perspective of a reasonable officer on the scene," rather than with "the 20–20 vision of hindsight," and make allowances for officers' need to make split-second judgments in situations that are tense, uncertain, and rapidly evolving.

Both *Garner* and *Graham* were civil cases in which damages were sought under 42 U.S.C.A. § 1983 on the theory that the officers' use of force had made the arrests unreasonable. When, if ever, will force that is excessive under these cases render evidence inadmissible? Suppose, for example, that in *Garner* the officer's gunfire had not killed Garner but had disabled him and thus enabled the officer to arrest him.

Suppose further than in a search incident to this arrest, items taken from the burglarized premises were found on Garner's person. Would these items be inadmissible because of the excessive force? Reconsider New York v. Harris, ___ U.S. ___, 110 S.Ct. 1640, 109 L.Ed.2d 13 (1990), discussed on page 38, supra, emphasizing that evidence must be excluded only if it was obtained by "exploiting" the illegality. Several courts have reasoned in excessive force situations that challenged evidence was not obtained by "exploitation" of the excessive force and thus is admissible. City of St. Louis Park v. Berg, 433 N.W.2d 87 (Minn.1988); State v. Chamberlain, 109 N.M. 173, 783 P.2d 483 (App.1989), cert. denied 109 N.M. 154, 782 P.2d 1351 (1989).

## 1. SEARCHES INCIDENT TO ARRESTS

The occurrence of a valid arrest itself brings into play a right to make certain searches. This right to search because of an arrest is the subject of the present subsection.

### CHIMEL v. CALIFORNIA

Supreme Court of the United States, 1969.
395 U.S. 752, 89 S.Ct. 2034, 23 L.Ed.2d 685.

MR. JUSTICE STEWART delivered the opinion of the Court.

This case raises basic questions concerning the permissible scope under the Fourth Amendment of a search incident to a lawful arrest.

The relevant facts are essentially undisputed. Late in the afternoon of September 13, 1965, three police officers arrived at the Santa Ana, California, home of the petitioner with a warrant authorizing his arrest for the burglary of a coin shop. The officers knocked on the door, identified themselves to the petitioner's wife, and asked if they might come inside. She ushered them into the house, where they waited 10 or 15 minutes until the petitioner returned home from work. When the petitioner entered the house, one of the officers handed him the arrest warrant and asked for permission to "look around." The petitioner objected, but was advised that "on the basis of the lawful arrest," the officers would nonetheless conduct a search. No search warrant had been issued.

Accompanied by the petitioner's wife, the officers then looked through the entire three-bedroom house, including the attic, the garage, and a small workshop. In some rooms the search was relatively cursory. In the master bedroom and sewing room, however, the officers directed the petitioner's wife to open drawers and "to physically move contents of the drawers from side to side so that [they] might view any items that would have come from [the] burglary." After completing the search, they seized numerous items—primarily coins, but also several medals, tokens, and a few other objects. The entire search took between 45 minutes and an hour.

At the petitioner's subsequent state trial on two charges of burglary, the items taken from his house were admitted into evidence against him, over his objection that they had been unconstitutionally seized.

He was convicted, and the judgments of conviction were affirmed by both the California Court of Appeal, 61 Cal.Rptr. 714, and the California Supreme Court, 68 Cal.2d 436, 67 Cal.Rptr. 421, 439 P.2d 333.  Both courts accepted the petitioner's contention that the arrest warrant was invalid because the supporting affidavit was set out in conclusory terms, but held that since the arresting officers had procured the warrant "in good faith," and since in any event they had had sufficient information to constitute probable cause for the petitioner's arrest, that arrest had been lawful.  From this conclusion the appellate courts went on to hold that the search of the petitioner's home had been justified, despite the absence of a search warrant, on the ground that it had been incident to a valid arrest.    *    *    *

Without deciding the question, we proceed on the hypothesis that the California courts were correct in holding that the arrest of the petitioner was valid under the Constitution.  This brings us directly to the question whether the warrantless search of the petitioner's entire house can be constitutionally justified as incident to that arrest.  The decisions of this Court bearing upon that question have been far from consistent, as even the most cursory review makes evident.

Approval of a warrantless search incident to a lawful arrest seems first to have been articulated by the Court in 1914 as dictum in Weeks v. United States, 232 U.S. 383, 34 S.Ct. 341, 58 L.Ed. 652.    *    *    *

That statement made no reference to any right to search the *place* where an arrest occurs, but was limited to a right to search the "person."    *    *    *

In 1950, *    *    * came United States v. Rabinowitz, 339 U.S. 56, 70 S.Ct. 430, 94 L.Ed. 653, the decision upon which California primarily relies in the case now before us.  In *Rabinowitz*, federal authorities had been informed that the defendant was dealing in stamps bearing forged overprints.  On the basis of that information they secured a warrant for his arrest, which they executed at his one-room business office.  At the time of the arrest, the officers "searched the desk, safe, and file cabinets in the office for about an hour and a half," id. at 59, 70 S.Ct., at 432, and seized 573 stamps with forged overprints.  The stamps were admitted into evidence at the defendant's trial, and this Court affirmed his conviction, rejecting the contention that the warrantless search had been unlawful.  The Court held that the search in its entirety fell within the principle giving law enforcement authorities "[t]he right 'to search the place where the arrest is made in order to find and seize things connected with the crime    *    *    *.'"  Id., at 61, 70 S.Ct., at 433.  *    *    *  The opinion rejected the rule *    *    * that "in seizing goods and articles, law enforcement agents must secure and use search warrants wherever reasonably practicable."  The test, said the Court, "is not whether it is reasonable to procure a search warrant, but whether the search was reasonable."  Id., at 66, 70 S.Ct., at 435.

*Rabinowitz* has come to stand for the proposition, *inter alia*, that a warrantless search "incident to a lawful arrest" may generally extend to the area that is considered to be in the "possession" or under the "control" of the person arrested. And it was on the basis of that proposition that the California courts upheld the search of the petitioner's entire house in this case. That doctrine, however, at least in the broad sense in which it was applied by the California courts in this case, can withstand neither historical nor rational analysis.

Even limited to its own facts, the *Rabinowitz* decision was \* \* \* hardly founded on an unimpeachable line of authority. \* \* \* Nor is the rationale by which the State seeks here to sustain the search of the petitioner's house supported by a reasoned view of the background and purpose of the Fourth Amendment.

\* \* \*

Only last Term in Terry v. Ohio, 392 U.S. 1, 88 S.Ct. 1868, 20 L.Ed. 2d 889, we emphasized that "the police must, whenever practicable, obtain advance judicial approval of searches and seizures through the warrant procedure," id., at 20, 88 S.Ct., at 1879, and that "[t]he scope of [a] search must be 'strictly tied to and justified by' the circumstances which rendered its initiation permissible." Id., at 19, 88 S.Ct., at 1878.

\* \* \*

A similar analysis underlies the "search incident to arrest" principle, and marks its proper extent. When an arrest is made, it is reasonable for the arresting officer to search the person arrested in order to remove any weapons that the latter might seek to use in order to resist arrest or effect his escape. Otherwise, the officer's safety might well be endangered, and the arrest itself frustrated. In addition, it is entirely reasonable for the arresting officer to search for and seize any evidence on the arrestee's person in order to prevent its concealment or destruction. And the area into which an arrestee might reach in order to grab a weapon or evidentiary items must, of course, be governed by a like rule. A gun on a table or in a drawer in front of one who is arrested can be as dangerous to the arresting officer as one concealed in the clothing of the person arrested. There is ample justification, therefore, for a search of the arrestee's person and the area "within his immediate control"—construing that phrase to mean the area from within which he might gain possession of a weapon or destructible evidence.

There is no comparable justification, however, for routinely searching any room other than that in which an arrest occurs—or, for that matter, for searching through all the desk drawers or other closed or concealed areas in that room itself. Such searches, in the absence of well-recognized exceptions, may be made only under the authority of a search warrant. The "adherence to judicial processes" mandated by the Fourth Amendment requires no less.

\* \* \*

It is argued in the present case that it is "reasonable" to search a man's house when he is arrested in it. Under such an unconfined analysis, Fourth Amendment protection in this area would approach the evaporation point. It is not easy to explain why, for instance, it is less subjectively "reasonable" to search a man's house when he is arrested on his front lawn—or just down the street—than it is when he happens to be in the house at the time of arrest.

No consideration relevant to the Fourth Amendment suggests any point of rational limitation, once the search is allowed to go beyond the area from which the person arrested might obtain weapons or evidentiary items. The only reasoned distinction is one between a search of the person arrested and the area within his reach on the one hand and more extensive searches on the other.[1]

The petitioner correctly points out that one result of decisions such as *Rabinowitz* * * * is to give law enforcement officials the opportunity to engage in searches not justified by probable cause, by the simple expedient of arranging to arrest suspects at home rather than elsewhere. We do not suggest that the petitioner is necessarily correct in his assertion that such a strategy was utilized here but the fact remains that had he been arrested earlier in the day, at his place of employment rather than at home, no search of his house could have been made without a search warrant.

* * *

*Rabinowitz* * * * [has] been the subject of critical commentary for many years, and [has] been relied upon less and less in our own decisions. It is time, for the reasons we have stated, to hold that * * * [it is] no longer to be followed.

Application of sound Fourth Amendment principles to the facts of this case produces a clear result. The search here went far beyond the petitioner's person and the area from within which he might have obtained either a weapon or something that could have been used as evidence against him. There was no constitutional justification, in the absence of a search warrant, for extending the search beyond that area. The scope of the search was, therefore, "unreasonable" under the Fourth and Fourteenth Amendments and the petitioner's conviction cannot stand.

Reversed.

[1] It is argued in dissent that so long as there is probable cause to search the place where an arrest occurs, a search of that place should be permitted even though no search warrant has been obtained. This position seems to be based principally on two premises: first, that once an arrest has been made, the additional invasion of privacy stemming from the accompanying search is "relatively minor"; and second, that the victim of the search may "shortly thereafter" obtain a judicial determination of whether the search was justified by probable cause. With respect to the second premise, one may initially question whether all of the States in fact provide the speedy suppression procedures the dissent assumes. More fundamentally, however, we cannot accept the view that Fourth Amendment interests are vindicated so long as "the rights of the criminal" are "protect[ed] * * * against introduction of evidence seized without probable cause." The Amendment is designed to prevent, not simply to redress, unlawful police action. In any event, we cannot join in characterizing the invasion of privacy that results from a top-to-bottom search of a man's house as "minor." And we can see no reason why, simply because some interference with an individual's privacy and freedom of movement has lawfully taken place, further intrusions should automatically be allowed despite the absence of a warrant that the Fourth Amendment would otherwise require.

MR. JUSTICE WHITE, with whom MR. JUSTICE BLACK joins, dissenting.

\*   \*   \*

The Amendment does not proscribe "warrantless searches" but instead it proscribes "unreasonable searches" and this Court has never held nor does the majority today assert that warrantless searches are necessarily unreasonable.

Applying this reasonableness test to the area of searches incident to arrests, one thing is clear at the outset. Search of an arrested man and of the items within his immediate reach must in almost every case be reasonable.

\*   \*   \*

The justifications which make such a search reasonable obviously do not apply to the search of areas to which the accused does not have ready physical access. This is not enough, however, to prove such searches unconstitutional. The Court has always held, and does not today deny, that when there is probable cause to search and it is "impracticable" for one reason or another to get a search warrant, then a warrantless search may be reasonable.

\*   \*   \*

This is the case whether an arrest was made at the time of the search or not.

This is not to say that a search can be reasonable without regard to the probable cause to believe that seizable items are on the premises. But when there are exigent circumstances, and probable cause, then the search may be made without a warrant, reasonably. An arrest itself may often create an emergency situation making it impracticable to obtain a warrant before embarking on a related search. Again assuming that there is probable cause to search premises at the spot where a suspect is arrested, it seems to me unreasonable to require the police to leave the scene in order to obtain a search warrant when they are already legally there to make a valid arrest, and when there must almost always be a strong possibility that confederates of the arrested man will in the meanwhile remove the items for which the police have probable cause to search. This must so often be the case that it seems to me as unreasonable to require a warrant for a search of the premises as to require a warrant for search of the person and his very immediate surroundings.

This case provides a good illustration of my point that it is unreasonable to require police to leave the scene of an arrest in order to obtain a search warrant when they already have probable cause to search and there is a clear danger that the items for which they may reasonably search will be removed before they return with a warrant.

\*   \*   \*   Had the police simply arrested petitioner, taken him off to the station house, and later returned with a warrant,[2] it seems very

---

[2] There were three officers at the scene of the arrest, one from the city where the coin burglary had occurred, and two from the city where the arrest was made. Assuming that one policeman from each city would be needed to bring the petitioner in and obtain a search warrant, one policeman could have been left to guard the house. However, if he not only could have remained in the house against petitioner's wife's will, but followed her about to assure that no evidence was being tampered with,

likely that petitioner's wife, who in view of petitioner's generally garrulous nature must have known of the robbery, would have removed the coins. For the police to search the house while the evidence they had probable cause to search out and seize was still there cannot be considered unreasonable.

*    *    *

If circumstances so often require the warrantless arrest that the law generally permits it, the typical situation will find the arresting officers lawfully on the premises without arrest or search warrant. Like the majority, I would permit the police to search the person of a suspect and the area under his immediate control either to assure the safety of the officers or to prevent the destruction of evidence. And like the majority, I see nothing in the arrest alone furnishing probable cause for a search of any broader scope. However, where as here the existence of probable cause is independently established and would justify a warrant for a broader search for evidence, I would follow past cases and permit such a search to be carried out without a warrant, since the fact of arrest supplies an exigent circumstance justifying police action before the evidence can be removed, and also alerts the suspect to the fact of the search so that he can immediately seek judicial determination of probable cause in an adversary proceeding, and appropriate redress.

*    *    *

## NOTES

1.  Is it important when the formal arrest occurs? In Rawlings v. Kentucky, 448 U.S. 98, 100 S.Ct. 2556, 65 L.Ed.2d 633 (1980), Rawlings was present when officers searched the purse of a companion; they found 1,800 tablets of LSD and a variety of other controlled substances. When the companion told Rawlings to "take what was his," he claimed ownership of all of the substances. One of the officers searched Rawlings and found $4,500 in a shirt pocket and a knife in a sheath at his side. Rawlings was then placed under "formal arrest." Challenging the admissibility of the money and the knife, Rawlings argued that the search could not be justified as "incident to" his arrest since the arrest did not occur until after the search. A majority of the Court experienced "no difficulty" in rejecting this claim:

> Once [Rawlings] admitted ownership of the sizable quantity of drugs found in [the] purse, the police clearly had probable cause to place [him] under arrest. Where the formal arrest followed quickly on the heels of the challenged search of [Rawlings'] person, we do not believe it particularly important that the search preceded the arrest rather than vice versa.

448 U.S. at 111, 100 S.Ct. at 2564, 65 L.Ed.2d at 645–46.

2.  In United States v. Robinson, 414 U.S. 218, 94 S.Ct. 467, 38 L.Ed.2d 427 (1973), District of Columbia police officer Jenks stopped respondent Robinson's automobile to arrest him for driving after revocation of his motor vehicle operator's license. Previous investigation had given the officer reason to believe that respondent's license had been revoked. Metropolitan Police Department regulations required that the officer make a full-custody arrest (take

the invasion of her privacy would be almost as great as that accompanying an actual search. Moreover, had the wife summoned an accomplice, one officer could not have watched them both.

the person to the station) for the offense of driving after revocation. Jenks informed respondent that he was under arrest for operating a motor vehicle after revocation.

In accordance with procedures prescribed in Police Department instructions, Jenks then began to search respondent. He explained at a subsequent hearing that he was "face to face" with the respondent, and "placed [his] hands on [the respondent], my right hand to his left breast like this (demonstrating) and proceeded to pat him down thus (with the right hand)." During this patdown, Jenks felt an object in the left breast pocket of the heavy coat respondent was wearing, but testified that he "couldn't tell what it was" and also that he "couldn't actually tell the size of it." Jenks then reached into the pocket and pulled out the object, which turned out to be a "crumpled up cigarette package." Jenks testified that at this point he still did not know what was in the package:

"As I felt the package I could feel objects in the package but I couldn't tell what they were  *  *  *.  I knew they weren't cigarettes."

The officer then opened the cigarette pack and found 14 gelatin capsules of white powder which he thought to be, and which later analysis proved to be, heroin. Jenks then continued his search of respondent to completion, feeling around his waist and trouser legs, and examining the remaining pockets. The heroin seized from the respondent was admitted into evidence at the trial which resulted in his conviction in the District Court.

414 U.S. at 221–23, 94 S.Ct. at 470–71, 38 L.Ed.2d at 433–34.

The Court of Appeals reversed respondent's conviction on the ground that when an officer makes an arrest for an offense such as that involved in this case, the officer may not conduct a full field search but may conduct only a limited frisk for weapons and that Officer Jenks' actions in this case exceeded his frisking privilege. The Supreme Court, in an opinion authored by Justice Rehnquist, reversed the Court of Appeals. The Court rejected the Court of Appeals' view that the only justification for a full search incident to arrest is to discover evidence of crime: "The justification or reason for the authority to search incident to a lawful arrest rests quite as much on the need to disarm the suspect in order to take him into custody as it does on the need to preserve evidence on his person for later use at trial.  *  *  *  It is scarcely open to doubt that the danger to an officer is far greater in the case of the extended exposure which follows the taking of a suspect into custody and transporting him to the police station than in the case of the relatively fleeting contact resulting from the typical [temporary field detention, during which only a limited frisk for weapons is authorized]. This is an adequate basis for treating all custodial arrests alike for purposes of search justification." 414 U.S. at 234–35, 94 S.Ct. at 476, 38 L.Ed.2d at 439–40. The Court then addressed the need to provide law enforcement officers with clear guidance as to their authority to search when arresting:

[O]ur more fundamental disagreement with the Court of Appeals arises from its suggestion that there must be litigated in each case the issue of whether or not there was present one of the reasons supporting the authority for a search of the person incident to a lawful arrest. We do not think the long line of authorities of this Court dating back to *Weeks*, nor what we can glean from the history of practice in this country and in England, requires such a case by case adjudication. A police officer's determination as to how and where to search the person of a suspect whom he has arrested is necessarily a quick *ad hoc* judgment which the Fourth

Amendment does not require to be broken down in each instance into an analysis of each step in the search. The authority to search the person incident to a lawful custodial arrest, while based upon the need to disarm and to discover evidence, does not depend on what a court may later decide was the probability in a particular arrest situation that weapons or evidence would in fact be found upon the person of the suspect. A custodial arrest of a suspect based on probable cause is a reasonable intrusion under the Fourth Amendment; that intrusion being lawful, a search incident to the arrest requires no additional justification. It is the fact of the lawful arrest which establishes the authority to search, and we hold that in the case of a lawful custodial arrest a full search of the person is not only an exception to the warrant requirement of the Fourth Amendment, but is also a "reasonable" search under that Amendment.

414 U.S. at 235, 94 S.Ct. at 477, 38 L.Ed.2d at 440–41. Justices Marshall, Douglas and Brennan dissented.

3. Gustafson v. Florida, 414 U.S. 260, 94 S.Ct. 488, 38 L.Ed.2d 456 (1973) was a companion case to *Robinson*. Gustafson was stopped by a police officer when the car he was driving was observed to weave back and forth on the road several times. The officer asked Gustafson to produce a driver's license and Gustafson responded that he had a valid license at his place of residence. Gustafson was placed under arrest for driving without a valid license in his possession. The officer then conducted a field search of Gustafson, quite thorough, and discovered several marijuana cigarettes in a Benson and Hedges cigarette box. He then placed Gustafson under arrest for possession of marijuana. Under Florida law and applicable police department regulations, the officer had discretion to issue a traffic citation to Gustafson for driving without a license or to arrest him and transport him to the police station. The officer testified that about three or four out of every ten persons he stopped for that offense were taken to the police station. The Court upheld the search and refused to distinguish *Robinson* on the ground that departmental regulations required the officer to take the suspect into custody in *Robinson* while in *Gustafson* the officer had discretion: "It is sufficient that the officer had probable cause to arrest the petitioner and that he lawfully effectuated the arrest, and placed the petitioner in custody. In addition, as our decision in *Robinson* makes clear, the arguable absence of 'evidentiary' purpose for a search incident to a lawful arrest is not controlling." 414 U.S. at 265, 94 S.Ct. at 491–92, 38 L.Ed.2d at 461.

In his concurring opinion in *Gustafson*, Justice Stewart commented that petitioner had conceded the constitutional validity of his custodial arrest and challenged only the incidental search. He also noted that "a persuasive claim might have been made in this case that the custodial arrest of the petitioner for a minor traffic offense violated his rights under the Fourth and Fourteenth Amendments." 414 U.S. at 266–67, 94 S.Ct. at 492, 38 L.Ed.2d at 464 (Stewart, J., concurring).

4. May an officer who has arrested a suspect in a public place accompany the suspect into his dwelling as an incident of the arrest? In Washington v. Chrisman, 455 U.S. 1, 102 S.Ct. 812, 70 L.Ed.2d 778 (1982), a campus police officer observed a student exit a dormitory carrying a half-gallon bottle of gin. The student appeared to the officer to be underage. The officer stopped him and asked for identification. The student, Overdahl, responded that his identification was in his dormitory room and asked whether the officer could wait until he retrieved it. The officer replied that he would have to accompany Overdahl to his room, to which Overdahl responded, "O.K." Overdahl's roommate, Chrisman, was in the room when the officer and Overdahl reached

it. The officer remained at the doorway while Overdahl entered the room to look for identification. While at the doorway, the officer observed what he believed to be marijuana seeds and a pipe on a desk about 8 to 10 feet away. He entered the room and confirmed that they were what they appeared to be. He placed the roommates under arrest and obtained their consent to a search of the room. Further drugs were found. Chrisman was prosecuted for possession of controlled substances. His conviction was overturned by the Washington Supreme Court on the ground that although the officer could have accompanied Overdahl into the room after arresting him, he was not permitted under the Fourth Amendment to enter the room to seize evidence of crime without a warrant or exigent circumstances.

The Supreme Court, in an opinion authored by the Chief Justice, reversed. The majority reasoned that every arrest, no matter how routine, involves a risk of escape, destruction of evidence, or injury to the officer. The Fourth Amendment permits the officer "to remain literally at [the arrestee's] elbow at all times":

> [I]t is not "unreasonable" under the Fourth Amendment for a police officer, as a matter of routine, to monitor the movements of an arrested person, as his judgment dictates, following the arrest. The officer's need to ensure his own safety—as well as the integrity of the arrest—is compelling. Such surveillance is not an impermissible invasion of the privacy or personal liberty of an individual who has been arrested.

455 U.S. at 7, 102 S.Ct. at 817, 70 L.Ed.2d at 785. The majority also concluded that since the officer could have accompanied Overdahl into the dormitory room, the fact that he remained in the doorway did not make his entry into the room after seeing contraband in plain view a Fourth Amendment violation. The majority also believed that the circumstances of this case were distinguishable from ones in which an officer, "who happens to pass by chance an open doorway to a residence, observes what he believes to be contraband inside" and enters the residence to seize it without a warrant or exigent circumstances. Justice White, joined by Justices Brennan and Marshall, dissented on the ground that although the officer had consent from Overdahl to enter the room, he chose not to do so and could not later enter the room to seize evidence of crime without a warrant or exigent circumstances.

5. What action may officers take at the scene of an arrest to protect themselves from persons other than the individual arrested? In Maryland v. Buie, ___ U.S. ___, ___, 110 S.Ct. 1093, 1098, 108 L.Ed.2d 276, 286 (1990), the Court commented that officers making an arrest in a private residence could, "as an incident to the arrest * * *, as a precautionary matter and without probable cause or reasonable suspicion, look in closets and other spaces immediately adjoining the place of arrest from which an attack could be immediately launched." But to conduct a more intensive and extensive "protective sweep" of the premises, officers had to have some basis for their concern; this is discussed at pages 274–75, infra.

6. The right to search a suspect incident to the arrest must be distinguished from what may be done later. In Illinois v. LaFayette, 462 U.S. 640, 103 S.Ct. 2605, 77 L.Ed.2d 65 (1983), LaFayette had been arrested and handcuffed at a theater for disturbing the peace. He carried a "purse-type shoulder bag" with him to the police station. Upon arrival at the station, LaFayette was taken to the "booking room" and the contents of the bag were examined; amphetamines were found. These were admitted into evidence at LaFayette's prosecution for possession of a controlled substance. The Supreme Court found no constitutional error, reasoning that "it is not 'unreasonable' for police, as part of the routine procedure incident to incarcerating an arrested person, to

search any container or article in his possession, in accordance with established inventory procedures." 462 U.S. at 648, 103 S.Ct. at 2611, 77 L.Ed.2d at 73. Characterizing an inventory search as "not an independent legal consent but rather an incidental administrative step following arrest and preceding incarceration," the majority explained its holding:

> At the stationhouse, it is entirely proper for police to remove and list or inventory property found on the person or in the possession of an arrested person who is to be jailed. A range of governmental interests support such an inventory process. It is not unheard of for persons employed in police activities to steal property taken from arrested persons; similarly, arrested persons have been known to make false claims regarding what was taken from their possession at the stationhouse. A standardized procedure for making a list or inventory as soon as reasonable after reaching the stationhouse not only deters false claims but also inhibits theft or careless handling of articles taken from the arrested person. Arrested persons have also been known to injure themselves—or others— with belts, knives, drugs or other items on their persons while being detained. Dangerous instrumentalities—such as razor blades, bombs, or weapons—can be concealed in innocent-looking articles taken from the arrestee's possession. The bare recital of these mundane realities justifies reasonable measures by police to limit these risks—either while the items are in police possession or at the time they are returned to the arrestee upon his release. Examining all the items removed from the arrestee's person or possession and listing or inventorying them is an entirely reasonable administrative procedure. It is immaterial whether the police actually fear any particular package or container; the need to protect against such risks arises independent of a particular officer's subjective concerns. Finally, inspection of an arrestee's personal property may assist the police in ascertaining or verifying his identity.

462 U.S. at 646, 105 S.Ct. at 2609–10, 77 L.Ed.2d at 71. These interests, the Court noted, may sometimes be greater than those supporting a search immediately after arrest:

> Consequently, the scope of a stationhouse search will often vary from that made at the time of arrest. Police conduct that would be impractical or unreasonable—or embarrassingly intrusive—on the street can more readily—and privately—be performed at the station. For example, the interest supporting a search incident to arrest would hardly justify disrobing an arrestee on the street, but the practical necessities of routine jail administration may even justify taking a prisoner's clothing from him before confining him, although that step would be rare.

462 U.S. at 645, 103 S.Ct. at 2609, 77 L.Ed.2d at 70–71. The majority noted that it was not addressing the circumstances in which a strip search of an arrestee "may or may not be appropriate." 462 U.S. at 646 n. 2, 103 S.Ct. at 2609 n. 2, 77 L.Ed.2d at 71 n. 2.

The Illinois court had held the search of LaFayette's shoulder bag unreasonable because the State's interests could be served by less intrusive methods, such as placing the bag in a secured locker or sealing it in a plastic bag. Granting that this might have been so, a majority of the Supreme Court rejected the position that the Fourth Amendment required the Illinois police to use such less intrusive methods:

> The reasonableness of any particular governmental activity does not necessarily or invariably turn on the existence of alternative "less intrusive" means. * * * We are hardly in a position to second-guess police

departments as to what practical administrative method will best deter theft by and false claims against its employees and preserve the security of the stationhouse. * * *

Even if less intrusive means existed of protecting some particular types of property, it would be unreasonable to expect police officers in the everyday course of business to make fine and subtle distinctions in deciding which containers or items may be searched and which must be sealed as a unit.

462 U.S. at 647–48, 103 S.Ct. at 2610, 77 L.Ed.2d at 72. But the Court apparently intended to limit inventory inspections to situations in which the suspect would be more than "booked." It noted uncertainty in the record as to whether LaFayette was to be incarcerated after being booked for disturbing the peace. "That," it offered, "is an appropriate inquiry on remand." 462 U.S. at 648 n. 3, 103 S.Ct. at 2611 n. 3, 77 L.Ed.2d at 73 n. 3.

## 2. "Incidental" Searches of Automobiles

Searches of automobiles have given rise to particularly difficult problems. The Supreme Court's approach to these problems has been colored by—among other matters—its perception that persons have a less significant privacy interest in their vehicles than in their residences. This is developed further in Part D of Chapter 5, considering the so-called "automobile exception" to the requirement of a warrant; this exception permits warrantless searches of certain automobiles *if* if the officers have probable cause to believe that the vehicles contain items they are entitled to seize. As the principal case in this subsection makes clear, however, officers may often search vehicles incident to the arrest of person in and perhaps around those vehicles, regardless of whether those searches would be "reasonable" under the "automobile exception."

Consider whether in the principal case the Supreme Court is being "true" to the rationale and spirit of *Chimel.*

### NEW YORK v. BELTON

Supreme Court of the United States, 1981.
453 U.S. 454, 101 S.Ct. 2860, 69 L.Ed.2d 768.

JUSTICE STEWART delivered the opinion of the Court.

When the occupant of an automobile is subject to a lawful custodial arrest, does the constitutionally permissible scope of a search incident to his arrest include the passenger compartment of the automobile in which he was riding? That is the question at issue in the present case.

I.

On April 9, 1978, Trooper Douglas Nicot, a New York State policeman driving an unmarked car on the New York Thruway, was passed by another automobile travelling at an excessive rate of speed. Nicot gave chase, overtook the speeding vehicle, and ordered its driver to pull it over to the side of the road and stop. There were four men in the car, one of whom was Roger Belton, the respondent in this case. The policeman asked to see the driver's license and automobile registration, and discovered that none of the men owned the vehicle or was related to its owner.   Meanwhile, the policeman had smelled burnt marihuana and had seen on the floor of the car an envelope marked "Supergold" that he associated with marihuana.   He therefore directed the men to get out of the car, and placed them under arrest for the unlawful possession of marihuana.   He patted down each of the men and "split them up into four separate areas of the Thruway at this time so they would not be in physical touching area of each other."   He then picked up the envelope marked "Supergold" and found that it contained marihuana.   After giving the arrestees the warnings required by Miranda v. Arizona, 384 U.S. 436, 86 S.Ct. 1602, 16 L.Ed.2d 694, the state policeman searched each one of them.   He then searched the passenger compartment of the car.   On the back seat he found a black leather jacket belonging to Belton.   He unzipped one of the pockets of the jacket and discovered cocaine.   Placing the jacket in his automobile, he drove the four arrestees to a nearby police station.

Belton was subsequently indicted for criminal possession of a controlled substance.   In the trial court he moved that the cocaine the trooper had seized from the jacket pocket be suppressed.   The court denied the motion.   Belton then pleaded guilty to a lesser included offense, but preserved his claim that the cocaine had been seized in violation of the Fourth and Fourteenth Amendments.   See Lefkowitz v. Newsome, 420 U.S. 283, 95 S.Ct. 886, 43 L.Ed.2d 196.   The Appellate Division of the New York Supreme Court upheld the constitutionality of the search and seizure, reasoning that "[o]nce defendant was validly arrested for possession of marihuana, the officer was justified in searching the immediate area for other contraband."   68 A.D.2d 198, 201, 416 N.Y.S.2d 922.

The New York Court of Appeals reversed, holding that "[a] warrantless search of the zippered pockets of an unaccessible jacket may not be upheld as a search incident to a lawful arrest where there is no longer any danger that the arrestee or a confederate might gain access to the article."   50 N.Y.2d 447, 449, 429 N.Y.S.2d 574, 575, 407 N.E.2d 420, 421.   Two judges dissented.   They pointed out that the "search was conducted by a lone peace officer who was in the process of arresting four unknown individuals whom he had stopped in a speeding car owned by none of them and apparently containing an uncertain quantity of a controlled substance.   The suspects were standing by the side of the car as the officer gave it a quick check to confirm his suspicions before attempting to transport them to police headquarters ∗   ∗   ∗ "   Id., at 454, 429, N.Y.S.2d 574, 578, 407 N.E.2d 420, 424.   We granted certiorari to consider the constitutionally permissible scope of a search in circumstances such as these.   449 U.S. 1109, 101 S.Ct. 917, 66 L.Ed. 2d 838.

## II.

It is a first principle of Fourth Amendment jurisprudence that the police may not conduct a search unless they first convince a neutral magistrate that there is probable cause to do so.   This Court has recognized, however, that "the exigencies of the situation" may sometimes make exemption from the warrant requirement "imperative." McDonald v. United States, 335 U.S. 451, 456, 69 S.Ct. 191, 193, 93 L.Ed. 153. Specifically, the Court held in Chimel v. California, 395 U.S. 752, 89 S.Ct. 2034, 23 L.Ed.2d 685, that a lawful custodial arrest creates a situation which justifies the contemporaneous search without a warrant of the person arrested and of the immediately surrounding area. Such searches have long been considered valid because of the need "to remove any weapons that [the arrestee] might seek to use in order to resist arrest or effect his escape" and the need to prevent the concealment or destruction of evidence. Id., at 763, 89 S.Ct., at 2040.

The Court's opinion in *Chimel* emphasized the principle that, as the Court had said in Terry v. Ohio, 392 U.S. 1, 19, 88 S.Ct. 1868, 1878, 20 L.Ed.2d 889, "The scope of [a] search must be 'strictly tied to and justified by' the circumstances which rendered its initiation permissible." Quoted in Chimel v. California, supra, at 762, 89 S.Ct., at 2039. Thus while the Court in *Chimel* found "ample justification" for a search of "the area from within which [an arrestee] might gain possession of a weapon or destructible evidence," the Court found "no comparable justification * * * for routinely searching any room other than that in which an arrest occurs—or, for that matter, for searching through all the desk drawers or other closed or concealed areas in that room itself." Id., at 763, 89 S.Ct., at 2040.

Although the principle that limits a search incident to a lawful custodial arrest may be stated clearly enough, courts have discovered the principle difficult to apply in specific cases. Yet, as one commentator has pointed out, the protection of the Fourth and Fourteenth Amendments "can only be realized if the police are acting under a set of rules which, in most instances, makes it possible to reach a correct determination beforehand as to whether an invasion of privacy is justified in the interest of law enforcement." LaFave, "Case-by-Case Adjudication" versus "Standardized Procedures": The Robinson Dilemma, 1974 Sup.Ct.Rev. 127, 142. This is because

"Fourth Amendment doctrine, given force and effect by the exclusionary rule, is primarily intended to regulate the police in their day-to-day activities and thus ought to be expressed in terms that are readily applicable by the police in the context of the law enforcement activities in which they are necessarily engaged. A highly sophisticated set of rules, qualified by all sorts of ifs, ands, and buts and requiring the drawing of subtle nuances and hairline distinctions, may be the sort of heady stuff upon which the facile minds of lawyers and judges eagerly feed, but they may be 'literally impossible of application by the officer in the field.'" Id., at 141.

In short, "A single, familiar standard is essential to guide police officers, who have only limited time and expertise to reflect on and balance the social and individual interests involved in the specific circumstances they confront." Dunaway v. New York, 442 U.S. 200, 213–214, 99 S.Ct. 2248, 60 L.Ed.2d 824.

So it was that, in United States v. Robinson, 414 U.S. 218, 94 S.Ct. 467, 38 L.Ed.2d 427, the Court hewed to a straightforward rule, easily applied, and predictably enforced: "[I]n the case of a lawful custodial arrest a full search of the person is not only an exception to the warrant requirement, but it is also a 'reasonable' search under that amendment." In so holding, the Court rejected the suggestion "that there must be litigated in each case the issue of whether or not there was present one of the reasons supporting the authority for a search of the person incident to a lawful arrest." 414 U.S. at 235, 94 S.Ct., at 476.

But no straightforward rule has emerged from the litigated cases respecting the question involved here—the question of the proper scope of a search of the interior of an automobile incident to a lawful custodial arrest of its occupants. * * *

When a person cannot know how a court will apply a settled principle to a recurring factual situation, that person cannot know the scope of his constitutional protection, nor can a policeman know the scope of his authority. While the *Chimel* case established that a search incident to an arrest may not stray beyond the area within the immediate control of the arrestee, courts have found no workable definition of "the area within the immediate control of the arrestee" when that area arguably includes the interior of an automobile and the arrestee is its recent occupant. Our reading of the cases suggests the generalization that articles inside the relatively narrow compass of the passenger compartment of an automobile are in fact generally, even if not inevitably, within "the area into which an arrestee might reach in order to grab a weapon or evidentiary item." *Chimel*, supra, at 763, 89 S.Ct., at 2040. In order to establish the workable rule this category of cases requires, we read *Chimel's* definition of the limits of the area that may be searched in light of that generalization. Accordingly, we hold that when a policeman has made a lawful custodial arrest of the occupant of an automobile, he may, as a contemporaneous incident of that arrest, search the passenger compartment of that automobile.[3]

It follows from this conclusion that the police may also examine the contents of any containers found within the passenger compartment, for if the passenger compartment is within reach of the arrestee, so also will containers in it be within his reach.[4] United States v. Robinson, supra; Draper v. United States, 358 U.S. 307, 79 S.Ct. 329, 3 L.Ed.2d 327. Such a container may, of course, be searched whether it is open or closed, since the justification for the search is not that the arrestee has no privacy interest in the container, but that the lawful custodial arrest justifies the infringement of any privacy interest the arrestee may

---

[3] Our holding today does no more than determine the meaning of *Chimel's* principles in this particular and problematic content. It in no way alters the fundamental principles established in the *Chimel* case regarding the basic scope of searches incident to lawful custodial arrests.

[4] "Container" here denotes any object capable of holding another object. It thus includes closed or open glove compartments, consoles, or other receptacles located anywhere within the passenger compartment, as well as luggage, boxes, bags, clothing, and the like. Our holding encompasses only the interior of the passenger compartment of an automobile and does not encompass the trunk.

have.  Thus, while the Court in *Chimel* held that the police could not search all the drawers in an arrestee's house simply because the police had arrested him at home, the Court noted that drawers within an arrestee's reach could be searched because of the danger their contents might pose to the police.  Chimel v. California, supra, at 763, 89 S.Ct., at 2040.

It is true, of course, that these containers will sometimes be such that they could hold neither a weapon nor evidence of the criminal conduct for which the suspect was arrested.  However, in United States v. Robinson, supra, the Court rejected the argument that such a container—there a "crumpled up cigarette package"—located during a search of Robinson incident to his arrest could not be searched: "The authority to search the person incident to a lawful custodial arrest, while based upon the need to disarm and to discover evidence, does not depend on what a court may later decide was the probability in a particular arrest situation that weapons or evidence would in fact be found upon the person of the suspect.  A custodial arrest of a suspect based on probable cause is a reasonable intrusion under the Fourth Amendment; that intrusion being lawful, a search incident to the arrest requires no additional justification."  Id., at 235, 94 S.Ct., at 476.

The New York Court of Appeals relied upon United States v. Chadwick, 433 U.S. 1, 97 S.Ct. 2476, 53 L.Ed.2d 538, and Arkansas v. Sanders, 442 U.S. 753, 99 S.Ct. 2586, 61 L.Ed.2d 235, in concluding that the search and seizure in the present case were constitutionally invalid.[5]  But neither of those cases involved an arguably valid search incident to a lawful custodial arrest.  *  *  *

### III.

It is not questioned that the respondent was the subject of a lawful custodial arrest on a charge of possessing marihuana.  The search of the respondent's jacket followed immediately upon that arrest.  The jacket was located inside the passenger compartment of the car in which the respondent had been a passenger just before he was arrested.  The jacket was thus within the area which we have concluded was "within the arrestee's immediate control" within the meaning of the *Chimel* case.[6]  The search of the jacket, therefore, was a search incident to a lawful custodial arrest, and it did not violate the Fourth and Fourteenth Amendments.  Accordingly, the judgment is reversed.

It is so ordered.

[5] It seems to have been the theory of the Court of Appeals that the search and seizure in the present case could not have been incident to the respondent's arrest, because Trooper Nicot, by the very act of searching the respondent's jacket and seizing the contents of its pocket, had gained "exclusive control" of them. 50 N.Y.2d, at 451, 429 N.Y.S.2d 574, 407 N.E.2d 420. But under this fallacious theory no search or seizure incident to a lawful custodial arrest would ever be valid; by seizing an article even on the arrestee's person an officer may be said to have reduced that article to his "exclusive control."

[6] Because of this disposition of the case, there is no need here to consider whether the search and seizure were permissible under the so-called "automobile exception."

[The opinion of Justice Stevens, concurring in the judgment, is omitted.]

JUSTICE BRENNAN, with whom JUSTICE MARSHALL joins, dissenting.

\* \* \*

The Court seeks to justify its departure from the principles underlying *Chimel* by proclaiming the need for a new bright line rule to guide the officer in the field. As we pointed out in Mincey v. Arizona, 437 U.S. [385, 393, 98 S.Ct. 2408, 2413, 57 L.Ed.2d 290], however, "the mere fact that law enforcement may be made more efficient can never by itself justify disregard of the Fourth Amendment." Moreover, the Court's attempt to forge a "bright line" rule fails on its own terms. While the "interior/trunk" distinction may provide a workable guide in certain routine cases—for example, where the officer arrests the driver of a car and then immediately searches the seats and floor—in the long run, I suspect it will create far more problems than it solves. The Court's new approach leaves open too many questions and, more important, it provides the police and the courts with too few tools with which to find the answers.

Thus, although the Court concludes that a warrantless search of a car may take place even though the suspect was arrested outside the car, it does not indicate how long after the suspect's arrest that search may validly be conducted. Would a warrantless search incident to arrest be valid if conducted five minutes after the suspect left his car? Thirty minutes? Three hours? Does it matter whether the suspect is standing in close proximity to the car when the search is conducted? Does it matter whether the police formed probable cause to arrest before or after the suspect left his car? And *why* is the rule announced today necessarily limited to searches of cars? What if a suspect is seen walking out of a house where the police, peering in from outside, had formed probable cause to believe a crime was being committed? Could the police then arrest that suspect and enter the house to conduct a search incident to arrest? Even assuming today's rule is limited to searches of the "interior" of cars—an assumption not demanded by logic—what is meant by "interior"? Does it include locked glove compartments, the interior of door panels, or the area under the floorboards? Are special rules necessary for station wagons and hatchbacks, where the luggage compartment may be reached through the interior, or taxicabs, where a glass panel might separate the driver's compartment from the rest of the car? Are the only containers that may be searched those that are large enough to be "capable of holding another object"? Or does the new rule apply to any container, even if it "could hold neither a weapon nor evidence of the criminal conduct for which the suspect was arrested"?

[The dissenting opinion of Justice White, joined by Justice Marshall, is omitted.]

## B. FIELD DETENTIONS AND RELATED SEARCHES

### EDITORS' INTRODUCTION: NONARREST DETENTIONS

Law enforcement practice distinguished among various detentions before these differences were accommodated or even recognized by legal doctrines. In large part, this was probably because of doubt that the Fourth Amendment permitted any detentions other than "arrests" based upon information amounting to "probable cause." The Supreme Court first addressed the Fourth Amendment issues presented by nonarrest detentions in a trilogy of cases decided in 1968—Terry v. Ohio, 392 U.S. 1, 88 S.Ct. 1868, 20 L.Ed.2d 889 (1968), and two companion cases, Sibron v. New York and Peters v. New York, 392 U.S. 40, 88 S.Ct. 1889, 20 L.Ed.2d 917 (1968). As the materials in this section make clear, the Court has decided a number of such cases since 1968. Nevertheless, significant Fourth Amendment issues relating to nonarrest detentions and related searches remain.

It remains unclear how many different types of nonarrest detentions might usefully or perhaps must be distinguished for Fourth Amendment purposes. Those detentions of major concern are what is often called "investigatory stops," "investigatory detentions," "field stops," or—memorializing Terry v. Ohio, supra—"*Terry* stops." They are widely assumed to be detentions made in the field for the purpose of gathering further information upon which to base a decision as to whether or not to arrest the suspect. It is similarly assumed that they are and should be effected in situations presenting inadequate grounds for arrest and that they cannot involve either prolonged detention of the suspect or substantial movement of the suspect during the detention.

The existence of different categories of detentions greatly complicates the process of analyzing law enforcement conduct. As a preliminary matter, of course, it is necessary to determine whether there was a detention (or, in Fourth Amendment terms, a "seizure") at all. If there was a detention, however, should it be analyzed as an arrest or as a nonarrest detention? Perhaps in some situations, a detention can only be upheld as an arrest. Consider these questions in connection with the cases reprinted or discussed in this section.

Investigatory stops may be an important part of what is sometimes referred to as "aggressive patrol strategy." This involves having patrol officers "maximiz[e] the number of interventions in and observations of the community." Wilson and Boland, The Effect of the Police on Crime, 12 Law & Society Rev. 367, 370 (1978). Specifically, officers employing such an approach frequently question suspicious persons, stop cars to issue citations for moving violations and to check for stolen vehicles and wanted fugitives, and employ "decoy" or stake-out procedures. Id. How effective is aggressive patrol in general, and investigatory stops in particular, in serving law enforcement purposes? Insofar as these techniques are effective, *how* do they achieve this impact?

A careful study was conducted in San Diego during 1973–74. Field interrogations were halted in a test area during a seven month experimental period.  The rate of reported crimes was then considered for the experimental area—before, during, and after the suspension of field interrogations—and this was compared to a control area in which field interrogations had continued.  A statistically significant increase in the crime rate occurred in the experimental area during the period when field interrogations were not used; after the interrogations were resumed, there was a significant decrease in the rate of reported offenses.  The monthly mean number of reported offenses in the experimental area before the experiment was 74.7.  During the suspension of field interrogations, this rose to 103.9, but after field interrogations were resumed the rate dropped to 81.2.  No similar fluctuation occurred in the control area.  J. Boydstun, San Diego Field Interrogation Final Report 30 (Police Foundation, 1975).

A more recent study examined the effect of various aspects of aggressive patrol on victimization rates in sixty residential neighborhoods in three metropolitan areas.  "Suspicion stops" were found to have a strong negative effect on robbery and a greater but not stable effect on auto theft and vandalism.  The rate at which officers conducted residence security checks had a much smaller effect on victimization rates.  Almost no effect was found to flow from "officer initiated investigative activity" (warrantless searches, crime scene inspections, and questioning of potential witnesses not at the immediate crime scene) and "order maintenance intervention" (officer initiated encounters with drunks, loiterers and others "not otherwise 'suspicious'").  Whitaker, Phillips, Haas and Worder, Aggressive Policing and the Deterrence of Crime, 7 Law and Policy 395 (1985).

To the extent that field stops affect the crime rate, how do they accomplish this?  The San Diego study included analysis of 21,179 field interrogations; less than two percent resulted in arrests.  Boydstun, supra, at 45.  The Whitaker et al., study reported that only 1.9 percent of the stops considered there resulted in arrest.  Whitaker, et al., supra, at 401.  This suggests that the effect of field interrogations is "direct," in the sense that field interrogations "emphasize to potential offenders that the police are aware of their specific identity, presence, and activity in the community" and thereby discourage them from engaging in criminal activity.  Boydstun, supra, at 7.  To put the matter another way, this evidence suggests that stops do not usually lead to arrests which in turn influence the crime rate.

Many of the issues concerning nonarrest detentions raised by the material in this section are discussed in Dix, Nonarrest Investigatory Detentions in Search and Seizure Law, 1985 Duke L.J. 849.

Questioning of suspects during a nonarrest detention raises special issues concerning the suspects' right to be free from compelled self-incrimination and related matters.  These are considered in Chapter 7.

## TERRY v. OHIO

Supreme Court of the United States, 1968.
392 U.S. 1, 88 S.Ct. 1868, 20 L.Ed.2d 889.

MR. CHIEF JUSTICE WARREN delivered the opinion of the Court.

This case presents serious questions concerning the role of the Fourth Amendment in the confrontation on the street between the citizen and the policeman investigating suspicious circumstances.

Petitioner Terry was convicted of carrying a concealed weapon and sentenced to the statutorily prescribed term of one to three years in the penitentiary. Following the denial of a pretrial motion to suppress, the prosecution introduced in evidence two revolvers and a number of bullets seized from Terry and a codefendant, Richard Chilton, by Cleveland Police Detective Martin McFadden. At the hearing on the motion to suppress this evidence, Officer McFadden testified that while he was patrolling in plain clothes in downtown Cleveland at approximately 2:30 in the afternoon of October 31, 1963, his attention was attracted by two men, Chilton and Terry, standing on the corner of Huron Road and Euclid Avenue. He had never seen the two men before, and he was unable to say precisely what first drew his eye to them. However, he testified that he had been a policeman for 39 years and a detective for 35 and that he had been assigned to patrol this vicinity of downtown Cleveland for shoplifters and pickpockets for 30 years. He explained that he had developed routine habits of observation over the years and that he would "stand and watch people or walk and watch people at many intervals of the day." He added: "Now, in this case when I looked over they didn't look right to me at the time."

His interest aroused, Officer McFadden took up a post of observation in the entrance to a store 300 to 400 feet away from the two men. "I get more purpose to watch them when I seen their movements," he testified. He saw one of the men leave the other one and walk southwest on Huron Road, past some stores. The man paused for a moment and looked in a store window, then walked on a short distance, turned around and walked back toward the corner, pausing once again to look in the same store window. He rejoined his companion at the corner, and the two conferred briefly. Then the second man went through the same series of motions, strolling down Huron Road, looking in the same window, walking on a short distance, turning back, peering in the store window again, and returning to confer with the first man at the corner. The two men repeated this ritual alternately between five and six times apiece—in all, roughly a dozen trips. At one point, while the two were standing together on the corner, a third man approached them and engaged them briefly in conversation. This man then left the two others and walked west on Euclid Avenue. Chilton and Terry resumed their measured pacing, peering and conferring. After this had gone on for 10 to 12 minutes, the two men walked off together, heading west on Euclid Avenue, following the path taken earlier by the third man.

By this time Officer McFadden had become thoroughly suspicious. He testified that after observing their elaborately casual and oft-repeated reconnaissance of the store window on Huron Road, he suspected the two men of "casing a job, a stick-up," and that he considered it his duty as a police officer to investigate further. He added that he feared "they may have a gun." Thus, Officer McFadden followed Chilton and Terry and saw them stop in front of Zucker's store to talk to the same man who had conferred with them earlier on the street corner. Deciding that the situation was ripe for direct action, Officer McFadden approached the three men, identified himself as a police officer and asked for their names. At this point his knowledge was confined to what he had observed. He was not acquainted with any of the three men by name or by sight, and he had received no information concerning them from any other source. When the men "mumbled something" in response to his inquiries, Officer McFadden grabbed petitioner Terry, spun him around so that they were facing the other two, with Terry between McFadden and the others, and patted down the outside of his clothing. In the left breast pocket of Terry's overcoat Officer McFadden felt a pistol. He reached inside the overcoat pocket, but was unable to remove the gun. At this point, keeping Terry between himself and the others, the officer ordered all three men to enter Zucker's store. As they went in, he removed Terry's overcoat completely, removed a .38 caliber revolver from the pocket and ordered all three men to face the wall with their hands raised. Officer McFadden proceeded to pat down the outer clothing of Chilton and the third man, Katz. He discovered another revolver in the outer pocket of Chilton's overcoat, but no weapons were found on Katz. The officer testified that he only patted the men down to see whether they had weapons, and that he did not put his hands beneath the outer garments of either Terry or Chilton until he felt their guns. So far as appears from the record, he never placed his hands beneath Katz' outer garments. Officer McFadden seized Chilton's gun, asked the proprietor of the store to call a police wagon, and took all three men to the station, where Chilton and Terry were formally charged with carrying concealed weapons.

On the motion to suppress the guns the prosecution took the position that they had been seized following a search incident to a lawful arrest. The trial court rejected this theory, stating that it "would be stretching the facts beyond reasonable comprehension" to find that Officer McFadden had had probable cause to arrest the men before he patted them down for weapons. However, the court denied the defendants' motion on the ground that Officer McFadden, on the basis of his experience, "had reasonable cause to believe  *  *  *  that the defendants were conducting themselves suspiciously, and some interrogation should be made of their action." Purely for his own protection, the court held, the officer had the right to pat down the outer clothing of these men, who he had reasonable cause to believe might be armed. The court distinguished between an investigatory "stop" and an arrest, and between a "frisk" of the outer clothing for weapons and a full-blown search for evidence of crime. The frisk, it held, was essential to the proper performance of the officer's investigatory duties, for without it "the answer to the police officer may be a bullet, and a loaded pistol discovered during the frisk is admissible."

After the court denied their motion to suppress, Chilton and Terry waived jury trial and pleaded not guilty. The court adjudged them guilty, and the Court of Appeals for the Eighth Judicial District, Cuyahoga County, affirmed. State v. Terry, 5 Ohio App.2d 122, 214

N.E.2d 114 (1966). The Supreme Court of Ohio dismissed their appeal on the ground that no "substantial constitutional question" was involved. We granted certiorari, 387 U.S. 929, 87 S.Ct. 2050, 18 L.Ed.2d 989 (1967), to determine whether the admission of the revolvers in evidence violated petitioner's rights under the Fourth Amendment, made applicable to the States by the Fourteenth. Mapp v. Ohio, 367 U.S. 643, 81 S.Ct. 1684, 6 L.Ed.2d 1081 (1961). We affirm the conviction.

I.

\* \* \*

We would be less than candid if we did not acknowledge that [the] question [in this case] thrusts to the fore difficult and troublesome issues regarding a sensitive area of police activity—issues which have never before been squarely presented to this Court. Reflective of the tensions involved are the practical and constitutional arguments pressed with great vigor on both sides of the public debate over the power of the police to "stop and frisk"—as it is sometimes euphemistically termed—suspicious persons.

On the one hand, it is frequently argued that in dealing with the rapidly unfolding and often dangerous situations on city streets the police are in need of an escalating set of flexible responses, graduated in relation to the amount of information they possess. For this purpose it is urged that distinctions should be made between a "stop" and an "arrest" (or a "seizure" of a person), and between a "frisk" and a "search." Thus, it is argued, the police should be allowed to "stop" a person and detain him briefly for questioning upon suspicion that he may be connected with criminal activity. Upon suspicion that the person may be armed, the police should have the power to "frisk" him for weapons. If the "stop" and the "frisk" give rise to probable cause to believe that the suspect has committed a crime, then the police should be empowered to make a formal "arrest," and a full incident "search" of the person. This scheme is justified in part upon the notion that a "stop" and a "frisk" amount to a mere "minor inconvenience and petty indignity," which can properly be imposed upon the citizen in the interest of effective law enforcement on the basis of a police officer's suspicion.

On the other side the argument is made that the authority of the police must be strictly circumscribed by the law of arrest and search as it has developed to date in the traditional jurisprudence of the Fourth Amendment. It is contended with some force that there is not—and cannot be—a variety of police activity which does not depend solely upon the voluntary cooperation of the citizen and yet which stops short of an arrest based upon probable cause to make such an arrest. The heart of the Fourth Amendment, the argument runs, is a severe requirement of specific justification for any intrusion upon protected personal security, coupled with a highly developed system of judicial controls to enforce upon the agents of the State the commands of the Constitution. Acquiescence by the courts in the compulsion inherent in the field interrogation practices at issue here, it is urged, would constitute an abdication of judicial control over, and indeed an encouragement of, substantial interference with liberty and personal security by police officers whose judgment is necessarily colored by their primary involvement in "the often competitive enterprise of ferreting out crime." Johnson v. United States, 333 U.S. 10, 14, 68 S.Ct. 367, 369, 92 L.Ed. 436 (1948). This, it is argued, can only serve to exacerbate police-community tensions in the crowded centers of our Nation's cities.

In this context we approach the issues in this case mindful of the limitations of the judicial function in controlling the myriad daily situations in which policemen and citizens confront each other on the street. The State has characterized the issue here as "the right of a police officer * * * to make an on-the-street stop, interrogate and pat down for weapons (known in street vernacular as 'stop and frisk')." But this is only partly accurate. For the issue is not the abstract propriety of the police conduct, but the admissibility against petitioner of the evidence uncovered by the search and seizure. Ever since its inception, the rule excluding evidence seized in violation of the Fourth Amendment has been recognized as a principal mode of discouraging lawless police conduct. * * *

The exclusionary rule has its limitations, however, as a tool of judicial control. It cannot properly be invoked to exclude the products of legitimate police investigative techniques on the ground that much conduct which is closely similar involves unwarranted intrusions upon constitutional protections. Moreover, in some contexts the rule is ineffective as a deterrent. Street encounters between citizens and police officers are incredibly rich in diversity. They range from wholly friendly exchanges of pleasantries or mutually useful information to hostile confrontations of armed men involving arrests, or injuries, or loss of life. Moreover, hostile confrontations are not all of a piece. Some of them begin in a friendly enough manner only to take a different turn upon the injection of some unexpected element into the conversation. Encounters are initiated by the police for a wide variety of purposes, some of which are wholly unrelated to a desire to prosecute for crime.[7] Doubtless some police "field interrogation" conduct violates the Fourth Amendment. But a stern refusal by this Court to condone such activity does not necessarily render it responsive to the exclusionary rule. Regardless of how effective the rule may be where obtaining convictions is an important objective of the police, it is powerless to deter invasions of constitutionally guaranteed rights where the police either have no interest in prosecuting or are willing to forgo successful prosecution in the interest of serving some other goal.

[7] See L. Tiffany, D. McIntyre & D. Rotenberg, Detection of Crime: Stopping and Questioning, Search and Seizure, Encouragement and Entrapment 18–56 (1967). This sort of police conduct may, for example, be designed simply to help an intoxicated person find his way home, with no intention of arresting him unless he becomes obstreperous. Or the police may be seeking to mediate a domestic quarrel which threatens to erupt into violence. They may accost a woman in an area known for prostitution as part of a harassment campaign designed to drive prostitutes away without the considerable difficulty involved in prosecuting them. Or they may be conducting a dragnet search of all teenagers in a particular section of the city for weapons because they have heard rumors of an impending gang fight.

Proper adjudication of cases in which the exclusionary rule is invoked demands a constant awareness of these limitations. The wholesale harassment by certain elements of the police community, of which minority groups, particularly Negroes, frequently complain [8] will not be stopped by the exclusion of any evidence from any criminal trial. Yet a rigid and unthinking application of the exclusionary rule, in futile protest against practices which it can never be used effectively to control, may exact a high toll in human injury and frustration of efforts to prevent crime. No judicial opinion can comprehend the protean variety of the street encounter, and we can only judge the facts of the case before us. Nothing we say today is to be taken as indicating approval of police conduct outside the legitimate investigative sphere. Under our decision, courts still retain their traditional responsibility to guard against police conduct which is overbearing or harassing, or which trenches upon personal security without the objective evidentiary justification which the Constitution requires. When such conduct is identified, it must be condemned by the judiciary and its fruits must be excluded from evidence in criminal trials. And, of course, our approval of legitimate and restrained investigative conduct undertaken on the basis of ample factual justification should in no way discourage the employment of other remedies than the exclusionary rule to curtail abuses for which that sanction may prove inappropriate.

Having thus roughly sketched the perimeters of the constitutional debate over the limits on police investigative conduct in general and the background against which this case presents itself, we turn our attention to the quite narrow question posed by the facts before us: whether it is always unreasonable for a policeman to seize a person and subject him to a limited search for weapons unless there is probable cause for an arrest. Given the narrowness of this question, we have no occasion to canvass in detail the constitutional limitations upon the scope of a policeman's power when he confronts a citizen without probable cause to arrest him.

## II.

Our first task is to establish at what point in this encounter the Fourth Amendment becomes relevant. That is, we must decide wheth-

---

[8] The President's Commission on Law Enforcement and Administration of Justice found that "[i]n many communities, field interrogations are a major source of friction between the police and minority groups." President's Commission on Law Enforcement and Administration of Justice, Task Force Report: The Police 183 (1967). It was reported that the friction caused by "[m]isuse of field interrogations" increases "as more police departments adopt 'aggressive patrol' in which officers are encouraged routinely to stop and question persons on the street who are unknown to them, who are suspicious, or whose purpose for being abroad is not readily evident." Id., at 184. While the fre- quency with which "frisking" forms a part of field interrogation practice varies tremendously with the locale, the objective of the interrogation, and the particular officer, see Tiffany, McIntyre & Rotenberg, supra, * * * at 47–48, it cannot help but be a severely exacerbating factor in police-community tensions. This is particularly true in situations where the "stop and frisk" of youths or minority group members is "motivated by the officers' perceived need to maintain the power image of the beat officer, an aim sometimes accomplished by humiliating anyone who attempts to undermine police control of the streets." Ibid.

er and when Officer McFadden "seized" Terry and whether and when he conducted a "search."   There is some suggestion in the use of such terms as "stop" and "frisk" that such police conduct is outside the purview of the Fourth Amendment because neither action rises to the level of a "search" or "seizure" within the meaning of the Constitution. We emphatically reject this notion.   It is quite plain that the Fourth Amendment governs "seizures" of the person which do not eventuate in a trip to the station house and prosecution for crime—"arrests" in traditional terminology.   It must be recognized that whenever a police officer accosts an individual and restrains his freedom to walk away, he has "seized" that person.   And it is nothing less than sheer torture of the English language to suggest that a careful exploration of the outer surfaces of a person's clothing all over his or her body in an attempt to find weapons is not a "search."   Moreover, it is simply fantastic to urge that such a procedure performed in public by a policeman while the citizen stands helpless, perhaps facing a wall with his hands raised, is a "petty indignity."[9]   It is a serious intrusion upon the sanctity of the person, which may inflict great indignity and arouse strong resentment, and it is not to be undertaken lightly.[10]

The danger in the logic which proceeds upon distinctions between a "stop" and an "arrest," or "seizure" of the person, and between a "frisk" and a "search" is twofold.   It seeks to isolate from constitutional scrutiny the initial stages of the contact between the policeman and the citizen.   And by suggesting a rigid all-or-nothing model of justification and regulation under the Amendment, it obscures the utility of limitations upon the scope, as well as the initiation, of police action as a means of constitutional regulation.   This Court has held in the past that a search which is reasonable at its inception may violate the Fourth Amendment by virtue of its intolerable intensity and scope. Kremen v. United States, 353 U.S. 346, 77 S.Ct. 828, 1 L.Ed.2d 876 (1957); * * *   The scope of the search must be "strictly tied to and justified by" the circumstances which rendered its initiation permissible.   Warden v. Hayden, 387 U.S. 294, 310, 87 S.Ct. 1642, 1652 (1967) (Mr. Justice Fortas, concurring); * * *.

The distinctions of classical "stop-and-frisk" theory thus serve to divert attention from the central inquiry under the Fourth Amendment—the reasonableness in all the circumstances of the particular governmental invasion of a citizen's personal security.   "Search" and

---

[9] Consider the following apt description:

"[T]he officer must feel with sensitive fingers every portion of the prisoner's body.   A thorough search must be made of the prisoner's arms and armpits, waistline and back, the groin and area about the testicles, and entire surface of the legs down to the feet."   Priar & Martin, Searching and Disarming Criminals, 45 J.Crim.L.C. & P.S. 481 (1954).

[10] * * *

We have noted that the abusive practices which play a major, though by no means exclusive, role in creating this friction are not susceptible of control by means of the exclusionary rule, and cannot properly dictate our decision with respect to the powers of the police in genuine investigative and preventive situations.   However, the degree of community resentment aroused by particular practices is clearly relevant to an assessment of the quality of the intrusion upon reasonable expectations of personal security caused by those practices.

"seizure" are not talismans. We therefore reject the notions that the Fourth Amendment does not come into play at all as a limitation upon police conduct if the officers stop short of something called a "technical arrest" or a "full-blown search."

In this case there can be no question, then, that Officer McFadden "seized" petitioner and subjected him to a "search" when he took hold of him and patted down the outer surfaces of his clothing. We must decide whether at that point it was reasonable for Officer McFadden to have interfered with petitioner's personal security as he did.[11] And in determining whether the seizure and search were "unreasonable" our inquiry is a dual one—whether the officer's action was justified at its inception, and whether it was reasonably related in scope to the circumstances which justified the interference in the first place.

### III.

If this case involved police conduct subject to the Warrant Clause of the Fourth Amendment, we would have to ascertain whether "probable cause" existed to justify the search and seizure which took place. However, that is not the case. We do not retreat from our holdings that the police must, whenever practicable, obtain advance judicial approval of searches and seizures through the warrant procedure, see e.g., Beck v. State of Ohio, 379 U.S. 89, 96, 85 S.Ct. 223, 228, 13 L.Ed.2d 142 (1964), or that in most instances failure to comply with the warrant requirement can only be excused by exigent circumstances. But we deal here with an entire rubric of police conduct—necessarily swift action predicated upon the on-the-spot observations of the officer on the beat—which historically has not been, and as a practical matter could not be, subjected to the warrant procedure. Instead, the conduct involved in this case must be tested by the Fourth Amendment's general proscription against unreasonable searches and seizures.

Nonetheless, the notions which underlie both the warrant procedure and the requirement of probable cause remain fully relevant in this context. In order to assess the reasonableness of Officer McFadden's conduct as a general proposition, it is necessary "first to focus upon the governmental interest which allegedly justifies official intrusion upon the constitutionally protected interests of the private citizen," for there is "no ready test for determining reasonableness other than by balancing the need to search [or seize] against the invasion which the search [or seizure] entails." Camara v. Municipal Court, 387 U.S. 523, 534–535, 536–537, 87 S.Ct. 1727, 1735, 18 L.Ed.2d 930 (1967). And in justifying the particular intrusion the police officer must be able

---

[11] We thus decide nothing today concerning the constitutional propriety of an investigative "seizure" upon less than probable cause for purposes of "detention" and/ or interrogation. Obviously, not all personal intercourse between policemen and citizens involves "seizures" of persons. Only when the officer, by means of physical force or show of authority, has in some way restrained the liberty of a citizen may we conclude that a "seizure" has occurred. We cannot tell with any certainty upon this record whether any such "seizure" took place here prior to Officer McFadden's initiation of physical contact for purposes of searching Terry for weapons, and we thus may assume that up to that point no intrusion upon constitutionally protected rights had occurred.

to point to specific and articulable facts which, taken together with rational inferences from those facts, reasonably warrant that intrusion. The scheme of the Fourth Amendment becomes meaningful only when it is assured that at some point the conduct of those charged with enforcing the laws can be subjected to the more detached, neutral scrutiny of a judge who must evaluate the reasonableness of a particular search or seizure in light of the particular circumstances. And in making that assessment it is imperative that the facts be judged against an objective standard: would the facts available to the officer at the moment of the seizure or the search "warrant a man of reasonable caution in the belief" that the action taken was appropriate?  *  *  * Anything less would invite intrusions upon constitutionally guaranteed rights based on nothing more substantial than inarticulate hunches, a result this Court has consistently refused to sanction.  *  *  *  And simple " 'good faith on the part of the arresting officer is not enough.' *  *  *  If subjective good faith alone were the test, the protections of the Fourth Amendment would evaporate, and the people would be 'secure in their persons, houses, papers and effects,' only in the discretion of the police."   Beck v. Ohio, supra, at 97, 85 S.Ct. at 229.

Applying these principles to this case, we consider first the nature and extent of the governmental interests involved.  One general interest is of course that of effective crime prevention and detection; it is this interest which underlies the recognition that a police officer may in appropriate circumstances and in an appropriate manner approach a person for purposes of investigating possibly criminal behavior even though there is no probable cause to make an arrest.  It was this legitimate investigative function Officer McFadden was discharging when he decided to approach petitioner and his companions.  He had observed Terry, Chilton, and Katz go through a series of acts, each of them perhaps innocent in itself, but which taken together warranted further investigation.  There is nothing unusual in two men standing together on a street corner, perhaps waiting for someone.  Nor is there anything suspicious about people in such circumstances strolling up and down the street, singly or in pairs.  Store windows, moreover, are made to be looked in.  But the story is quite different where, as here, two men hover about a street corner for an extended period of time, at the end of which it becomes apparent that they are not waiting for anyone or anything; where these men pace alternately along an identical route, pausing to stare in the same store window roughly 24 times; where each completion of this route is followed immediately by a conference between the two men on the corner; where they are joined in one of these conferences by a third man who leaves swiftly; and where the two men finally follow the third and rejoin him a couple of blocks away.  It would have been poor police work indeed for an officer of 30 years' experience in the detection of thievery from stores in this same neighborhood to have failed to investigate this behavior further.

The crux of this case, however, is not the propriety of Officer McFadden's taking steps to investigate petitioner's suspicious behavior, but rather, whether there was justification for McFadden's invasion of Terry's personal security by searching him for weapons in the course of that investigation. We are now concerned with more than the governmental interest in investigating crime; in addition, there is the more immediate interest of the police officer in taking steps to assure himself that the person with whom he is dealing is not armed with a weapon that could unexpectedly and fatally be used against him. Certainly it would be unreasonable to require that police officers take unnecessary risks in the performance of their duties. American criminals have a long tradition of armed violence, and every year in this country many law enforcement officers are killed in the line of duty, and thousands more are wounded. Virtually all of these deaths and a substantial portion of the injuries are inflicted with guns and knives.

In view of these facts, we cannot blind ourselves to the need for law enforcement officers to protect themselves and other prospective victims of violence in situations where they may lack probable cause for an arrest. When an officer is justified in believing that the individual whose suspicious behavior he is investigating at close range is armed and presently dangerous to the officer or to others, it would appear to be clearly unreasonable to deny the officer the power to take necessary measures to determine whether the person is in fact carrying a weapon and to neutralize the threat of physical harm.

We must still consider, however, the nature and quality of the intrusion on individual rights which must be accepted if police officers are to be conceded the right to search for weapons in situations where probable cause to arrest for crime is lacking. Even a limited search of the outer clothing for weapons constitutes a severe, though brief, intrusion upon cherished personal security, and it must surely be an annoying, frightening, and perhaps humiliating experience. Petitioner contends that such an intrusion is permissible only incident to a lawful arrest, either for a crime involving the possession of weapons or for a crime the commission of which led the officer to investigate in the first place. However, this argument must be closely examined.

Petitioner does not argue that a police officer should refrain from making any investigation of suspicious circumstances until such time as he has probable cause to make an arrest; nor does he deny that police officers in properly discharging their investigative function may find themselves confronting persons who might well be armed and dangerous. Moreover, he does not say that an officer is always unjustified in searching a suspect to discover weapons. Rather, he says it is unreasonable for the policeman to take that step until such time as the situation evolves to a point where there is probable cause to make an arrest. When that point has been reached, petitioner would concede the officer's right to conduct a search of the suspect for weapons, fruits or instrumentalities of the crime, or "mere" evidence, incident to the arrest.

There are two weaknesses in this line of reasoning however. First, it fails to take account of traditional limitations upon the scope of searches, and thus recognizes no distinction in purpose, character, and extent between a search incident to an arrest and a limited search for weapons. The former, although justified in part by the acknowledged necessity to protect the arresting officer from assault with a concealed weapon, is also justified on other grounds, ibid., and can therefore involve a relatively extensive exploration of the person. A search for weapons in the absence of probable cause to arrest, however, must, like any other search, be strictly circumscribed by the exigencies which justify its initiation. Thus it must be limited to that which is necessary for the discovery of weapons which might be used to harm the officer or others nearby, and may realistically be characterized as something less than a "full" search, even though it remains a serious intrusion.

A second, and related, objection to petitioner's argument is that it assumes that the law of arrest has already worked out the balance between the particular interests involved here—the neutralization of danger to the policeman in the investigative circumstance and the sanctity of the individual. But this is not so. An arrest is a wholly different kind of intrusion upon individual freedom from a limited search for weapons, and the interests each is designed to serve are likewise quite different. An arrest is the initial stage of a criminal prosecution. It is intended to vindicate society's interest in having its laws obeyed, and it is inevitably accompanied by future interference with the individual's freedom of movement, whether or not trial or conviction ultimately follows. The protective search for weapons, on the other hand, constitutes a brief, though far from inconsiderable, intrusion upon the sanctity of the person. It does not follow that because an officer may lawfully arrest a person only when he is apprised of facts sufficient to warrant a belief that the person has committed or is committing a crime, the officer is equally unjustified, absent that kind of evidence, in making any intrusions short of an arrest. Moreover, a perfectly reasonable apprehension of danger may arise long before the officer is possessed of adequate information to justify taking a person into custody for the purpose of prosecuting him for a crime. Petitioner's reliance on cases which have worked out standards of reasonableness with regard to "seizures" constituting arrests and searches incident thereto is thus misplaced. It assumes that the interests sought to be vindicated and the invasions of personal security may be equated in the two cases, and thereby ignores a vital aspect of the analysis of the reasonableness of particular types of conduct under the Fourth Amendment.

Our evaluation of the proper balance that has to be struck in this type of case leads us to conclude that there must be a narrowly drawn authority to permit a reasonable search for weapons for the protection of the police officer, where he has reason to believe that he is dealing with an armed and dangerous individual, regardless of whether he has probable cause to arrest the individual for a crime. The officer need not be absolutely certain that the individual is armed; the issue is whether a reasonably prudent man in the circumstances would be warranted in the belief that his safety or that of others was in danger. * * * And in determining whether the officer acted reasonably in such circumstances, due weight must be given, not to his inchoate and unparticularized suspicion or "hunch," but to the specific reasonable inferences which he is entitled to draw from the facts in light of his experience.

## IV.

We must now examine the conduct of Officer McFadden in this case to determine whether his search and seizure of petitioner were reasonable, both at their inception and as conducted. He had observed Terry, together with Chilton and another man, acting in a manner he took to be preface to a "stick-up." We think on the facts and circumstances Officer McFadden detailed before the trial judge a reasonably prudent man would have been warranted in believing petitioner was armed and thus presented a threat to the officer's safety while he was investigating his suspicious behavior. The actions of Terry and Chilton were consistent with McFadden's hypothesis that these men were contemplating a daylight robbery—which, it is reasonable to assume, would be likely to involve the use of weapons—and nothing in their conduct from the time he first noticed them until the time he confronted them and identified himself as a police officer gave him sufficient reason to negate that hypothesis. Although the trio had departed the original scene, there was nothing to indicate abandonment of an intent to commit a robbery at some point. Thus, when Officer McFadden approached the three men gathered before the display window at Zucker's store he had observed enough to make it quite reasonable to fear that they were armed; and nothing in their response to his hailing them, identifying himself as a police officer, and asking their names served to dispel that reasonable belief. We cannot say his decision at that point to seize Terry and pat his clothing for weapons was the product of a volatile or inventive imagination, or was undertaken simply as an act of harassment; the record evidences the tempered act of a policeman who in the course of an investigation had to make a quick decision as to how to protect himself and others from possible danger, and took limited steps to do so.

The manner in which the seizure and search were conducted is, of course, as vital a part of the inquiry as whether they were warranted at all. The Fourth Amendment proceeds as much by limitations upon the scope of governmental action as by imposing preconditions upon its initiation. The entire deterrent purpose of the rule excluding evidence seized in violation of the Fourth Amendment rests on the assumption that "limitations upon the fruit to be gathered tend to limit the quest itself." * * *. Thus, evidence may not be introduced if it was discovered by means of a seizure and search which were not reasonably related in scope to the justification for their initiation.

We need not develop at length in this case, however, the limitations which the Fourth Amendment places upon a protective seizure and search for weapons. These limitations will have to be developed in the concrete factual circumstances of individual cases. Suffice it to note that such a search, unlike a search without a warrant incident to a lawful arrest, is not justified by any need to prevent the disappearance or destruction of evidence of crime. The sole justification of the search in the present situation is the protection of the police officer and others nearby, and it must therefore be confined in scope to an intrusion reasonably designed to discover guns, knives, clubs, or other hidden instruments for the assault of the police officer.

The scope of the search in this case presents no serious problem in light of these standards. Officer McFadden patted down the outer clothing of petitioner and his two companions. He did not place his hands in their pockets or under the outer surface of their garments until he had felt weapons, and then he merely reached for and removed the guns. He never did invade Katz' person beyond the outer surfaces of his clothes, since he discovered nothing in his patdown which might have been a weapon. Officer McFadden confined his search strictly to what was minimally necessary to learn whether the men were armed and to disarm them once he discovered the weapons. He did not conduct a general exploratory search for what ever evidence of criminal activity he might find.

V.

We conclude that the revolver seized from Terry was properly admitted in evidence against him. At the time he seized petitioner and searched him for weapons, Officer McFadden had reasonable grounds to believe that petitioner was armed and dangerous, and it was necessary for the protection of himself and others to take swift measures to discover the true facts and neutralize the threat of harm if it materialized. The policeman carefully restricted his search to what was appropriate to the discovery of the particular items which he sought. Each case of this sort will, of course, have to be decided on its own facts. We merely hold today that where a police officer observes unusual conduct which leads him reasonably to conclude in light of his experience that criminal activity may be afoot and that the persons with whom he is dealing may be armed and presently dangerous, where in the course of investigating this behavior he identifies himself as a policeman and makes reasonable inquiries, and where nothing in the initial stages of the encounter serves to dispel his reasonable fear for his own or others' safety, he is entitled for the protection of himself and others in the area to conduct a carefully limited search of the outer clothing of such persons in an attempt to discover weapons which might be used to assault him.

Such a search is a reasonable search under the Fourth Amendment, and any weapons seized may properly be introduced in evidence against the person from whom they were taken.

Affirmed.

MR. JUSTICE BLACK concurs in the judgment and the opinion except where the opinion quotes from and relies upon this Court's opinion in Katz v. United States and the concurring opinion in Warden v. Hayden.

MR. JUSTICE HARLAN, concurring.

While I unreservedly agree with the Court's ultimate holding in this case, I am constrained to fill in a few gaps, as I see them, in its opinion.  *  *  *

 *  *  * [I]f [a] frisk is justified in order to protect the officer during an encounter with a citizen, the officer must first have constitutional grounds to insist on an encounter, to make a *forcible* stop. Any person, including a policeman, is at liberty to avoid a person he considers dangerous. If and when a policeman has a right instead to disarm such a person for his own protection, he must first have a right not to avoid him but to be in his presence. That right must be more than the liberty (again, possessed by every citizen) to address questions to other persons, for ordinarily the person addressed has an equal right to ignore his interrogator and walk away; he certainly need not submit to a frisk for the questioner's protection. I would make it perfectly clear that the right to frisk in this case depends upon the reasonableness of a forcible stop to investigate a suspected crime.

*   *   *

Upon the foregoing premises, I join the opinion of the Court.

NOTES

1.   Sibron v. New York and Peters v. New York, 392 U.S. 40, 88 S.Ct. 1889, 20 L.Ed.2d 917 (1968), were companion cases to *Terry*. In each, the parties sought an adjudication of the constitutionality of a New York "stop-and-frisk" statute, which provided:

> 1.   A police officer may stop any person abroad in a public place whom he reasonably suspects is committing, has committed or is about to commit a felony or any of the offenses specified in section five hundred fifty-two of this chapter, and may demand of him his name, address and an explanation of his actions.

> 2.   When a police officer has stopped a person for questioning pursuant to this section and reasonably suspects that he is in danger of life or limb, he may search such person for a dangerous weapon. If the police officer finds such a weapon or any other thing the possession of which may constitute a crime, he may take and keep it until the completion of the questioning, at which time he shall either return it, if lawfully possessed, or arrest such person.

The Court refused to rule upon the constitutionality of the statute, commenting:

> The operative categories of [the New York statute] are not the categories of the Fourth Amendment, and they are susceptible of a wide variety of interpretations. New York is, of course, free to develop its own law of search and seizure to meet the needs of local law enforcement  *  *  * and in the process it may call the standards it employs by any names it may choose. It may not, however, authorize police conduct which trenches upon Fourth Amendment rights, regardless of the labels which it attaches to such conduct. The question in this Court upon review of a state-approved search or seizure "is not whether the search [or seizure] was authorized by state law. The question is rather whether the search was reasonable under the Fourth Amendment. Just as a search authorized by state law may be an unreasonable one under that amendment, so may a search not expressly authorized by state law be justified as a constitutional-

ly reasonable one." Cooper v. State of California, 386 U.S. 58, 61, 87 S.Ct. 788, 790, 17 L.Ed.2d 730 (1967).

392 U.S. at 60–61, 88 S.Ct. at 1901–02, 20 L.Ed.2d at 933–34.

A number of other jurisdictions have enacted legislation addressing the authority to make nonarrest detentions. Consider the Montana provisions, which read in part as follows:

> 46–5–401. *Stop and frisk—when authorized.* (1) A peace officer may stop any person he observes in circumstances that give him reasonable cause to suspect that the person has committed, is committing, or is about to commit an offense involving the use or attempted use of force against a person or theft, damage, or destruction of property if the stop is reasonably necessary to obtain or verify an account of the person's presence or conduct or to determine whether to arrest the person.

* * *

> 46–5–402. *Stop and frisk—procedure.* (1) A peace officer who has lawfully stopped a person * * * may:

> (a) frisk the person and take other reasonably necessary steps for protection if he has reasonable cause to suspect that the person is armed and presently dangerous to him or another person present; and

> (b) take possession of any object that he discovers during the course of the frisk if he has probable cause to believe the object is a deadly weapon.

> (2) A peace officer who has lawfully stopped a person * * * may demand of the person his name and his present or last address.

> (3) A peace officer who has lawfully stopped a person * * * shall inform the person, as promptly as possible under the circumstances and in any case before questioning the person, that he is a peace officer, that the stop is not an arrest but rather a temporary detention for an investigation, and that upon completion of the investigation the person will be released unless he is arrested.

> (4) After the authorized purpose of the stop has been accomplished or 30 minutes have elapsed, whichever occurs first, the peace officer shall allow the person to go unless he has arrested the person.

2. The Court stated the facts in *Sibron* as follows:

> Sibron, the appellant in No. 63, was convicted of the unlawful possession of heroin. He moved before trial to suppress the heroin seized from his person by the arresting officer, Brooklyn Patrolman Anthony Martin. After the trial court denied his motion, Sibron pleaded guilty to the charge, preserving his right to appeal the evidentiary ruling. At the hearing on the motion to suppress, Officer Martin testified that while he was patrolling his beat in uniform on March 9, 1965, he observed Sibron "continually from the hours of 4:00 P.M. to 12:00, midnight * * * in the vicinity of 742 Broadway." He stated that during this period of time he saw Sibron in conversation with six or eight persons whom he (Patrolman Martin) knew from past experience to be narcotics addicts. The officer testified that he did not overhear any of these conversations, and that he did not see anything pass between Sibron and any of the others. Late in the evening Sibron entered a restaurant. Patrolman Martin saw Sibron speak with three more known addicts inside the restaurant. Once again, nothing was overheard and nothing was seen to pass between Sibron and the addicts. Sibron sat down and ordered pie and coffee, and, as he was eating Patrolman Martin approached him and told him to come outside. Once outside, the officer said to Sibron, "You know what I am after." According

to the officer, Sibron "mumbled something and reached into his pocket." Simultaneously, Patrolman Martin thrust his hand into the same pocket, discovering several glassine envelopes, which, it turned out, contained heroin.

The State has had some difficulty in settling upon a theory for the admissibility of these envelopes of heroin. In his sworn complaint Patrolman Martin stated:

> "As the officer approached the defendant, the latter being in the direction of the officer and seeing him, he did put his hand in his left jacket pocket and pulled out a tinfoil envelope and did attempt to throw same to the ground. The officer never losing sight of the said envelope seized it from the def[endan]t's left hand, examined it and found it to contain ten glascine [sic] envelopes with a white substance alleged to be Heroin."

This version of the encounter, however, bears very little resemblance to Patrolman Martin's testimony at the hearing on the motion to suppress. In fact, he discarded the abandonment theory at the hearing. Nor did the officer ever seriously suggest that he was in fear of bodily harm and that he searched Sibron in self-protection to find weapons.

392 U.S. at 44–46, 88 S.Ct. at 1893–94, 20 L.Ed.2d at 924–25. The Court concluded that Officer Martin lacked probable cause to arrest until after the heroin was seized. It then turned to the question whether the officer's conduct could be upheld under *Terry*. As to whether the officer was entitled under *Terry* to frisk Sibron, the Court observed:

> The suspect's mere act of talking with a number of known addicts over an eight-hour period no more gives rise to reasonable fear of life or limb on the part of the police officer than it justifies an arrest for committing a crime. Nor did Patrolman Martin urge that when Sibron put his hand in his pocket, he feared that he was going for a weapon and acted in self-defense. His opening statement to Sibron—"You know what I am after"—made it abundantly clear that he sought narcotics, and his testimony at the hearing left no doubt that he thought there were narcotics in Sibron's pocket.

392 U.S. at 64, 88 S.Ct. at 1903, 20 L.Ed.2d at 935. Finally, the Court concluded that even if the officer had been authorized to frisk Sibron, what the officer did went beyond a self-protective search and constituted a search for evidence: "[W]ith no attempt at an initial limited exploration for arms, Patrolman Martin thrust his hand into Sibron's pocket and took from him envelopes of heroin. His testimony shows that he was looking for narcotics, and he found them. The search was not reasonably limited in scope to the accomplishment of the only goal which might conceivably have justified its inception—the protection of the officer by disarming a potentially dangerous man." 392 U.S. at 65, 88 S.Ct. at 1904, 20 L.Ed.2d at 936.

In *Peters,* the Court found that the officer "arrested" Peters and thus the Court had no reason to consider the effect of the "stop-and-frisk" statute on the case.

3. Whether or not the Court in the *Terry* trilogy successfully avoided deciding the validity of field detentions for investigation, it soon assumed them to be valid at least in situations where the officer has "reasonable suspicion" or "some objective manifestation" that the suspect is at the time actually involved in criminal activity. See Adams v. Williams, 407 U.S. 143, 92 S.Ct. 1921, 32 L.Ed.2d 612 (1972), in which the officer reasonably suspected the person to be in criminal possession of drugs. It also assumed without discussion that a nonarrest detention of this sort could be made of a suspect driving an automobile;

such a detention, of course, necessarily involves stopping the automobile. United States v. Cortez, 449 U.S. 411, 101 S.Ct. 690, 66 L.Ed.2d 621 (1981). Not until United States v. Hensley, 469 U.S. 221, 105 S.Ct. 675, 83 L.Ed.2d 604 (1985), however, did the Court squarely confront whether a stop was permissible where the suspected crime had clearly been completed. Hensley was stopped in connection with the investigation of a robbery committed twelve days before. Upholding the detention, the Court noted that Fourth Amendment reasonableness requires that it balance the intrusion on personal security against the importance of the governmental interests offered to justify that intrusion:

> The factors in the balance may be somewhat different when a stop to investigate past criminal activity is involved rather than a stop to investigate ongoing criminal conduct.  *  *  * [O]ne general interest present in the context of ongoing or imminent criminal activity is "that of effective crime prevention and detention." A stop to investigate an already completed crime does not necessarily promote the interest of crime prevention as directly as a stop to investigate suspected ongoing criminal activity. Similarly, the exigent circumstances which require a police officer to step in before a crime is committed or completed are not necessarily as pressing long afterwards. Public safety may be less threatened by a suspect in a past crime who now appears to be going about his lawful business than it is by a suspect who is currently in the process of violating the law. Finally, officers making a stop to investigate past crimes may have a wider range of opportunity to choose the time and circumstances of the stop.

469 U.S. at 228–29, 105 S.Ct. at 680, 83 L.Ed.2d at 612. Nevertheless, the Court concluded that the law enforcement interests involved in stops for completed crimes—solving such crimes, convicting the perpetrators, and removing them from the community as soon as possible—outweighed the intrusions upon personal security. Id.

But if stops for past and current criminal conduct are permissible, does it follow that stops upon suspicion that the person will engage in criminal conduct in the future are "reasonable" as well? How "imminent" must an officer suspect that a person's criminal conduct is to justify such a stop? Specifically, in *Terry,* could the officer have made a stop of Terry and his companions as they walked *away* from the store which the officer suspected they planned to rob?

4.   Are there any limits on the offenses for which field stops may be made? In Adams v. Williams, 407 U.S. 143, 92 S.Ct. 1921, 32 L.Ed.2d 612 (1972), the officer's suspicion concerned the suspect's possible commission of crimes consisting of possessing items—possession of drugs and possession of a prohibited weapon. One of the judges in the Court of Appeals had urged that stops not be permitted for such "possessory" crimes:

> There is too much danger that, instead of the stop being the object and the protective frisk an incident thereto, the reverse will be true.

Williams v. Adams, 436 F.2d 30, 38 (2d Cir.1970) (Friendly, J., dissenting), reversed 441 F.2d 394 (2d Cir. 1971) (en banc) (per curiam). This was adopted by Justice Brennan. 407 U.S. at 151–53, 92 S.Ct. at 1926–27, 32 L.Ed.2d at 620 (Brennan, J., dissenting). The opinion of the Court, written by Justice Rehnquist, did not address the matter.

In United States v. Hensley, supra, the Court was careful to limit its statements to investigatory stops involving past *serious* offenses:

> We need not and do not decide today whether *Terry* stops to investigate all past crimes, however serious, are permitted. It is enough to say that, if police have a reasonable suspicion, grounded in specific and articulable

facts, that a person they encounter was involved in or is wanted in connection with a completed felony, then a *Terry* stop may be made to investigate that suspicion.

469 U.S. at 229, 105 S.Ct. at 680, 83 L.Ed.2d at 612.

5. What amounts to grounds for a valid nonarrest field detention is obviously a difficult question. Several cases, however, have addressed the matter. Adams v. Williams, 407 U.S. 143, 92 S.Ct. 1921, 32 L.Ed.2d 612 (1972), involved an informant who approached a police cruiser and informed the officer that a person seated in a nearby vehicle was carrying narcotics and had a gun at his waist. The informant was known to the officer and had provided information to the officer in the past. On the other hand, this information appeared to have involved claims of homosexual activity in a local railroad station and the followup investigation resulted in neither confirmation nor arrests. The officer located the person described by the informant and detained him. Upholding the detention, the Supreme Court rejected the proposition that the necessary "reasonable cause" must be based upon the officer's personal observation. While the "tip" may not have amounted to probable cause justifying an arrest, it did support the action taken:

> This is a stronger case than obtains in the case of an anonymous telephone tip. The informant here came forward personally to give information that was immediately verifiable at the scene. Indeed, * * * the informant might have been subject to immediate arrest for making a false complaint had [the] investigation proved the tip incorrect.

407 U.S. at 146–47, 92 S.Ct. at 1923, 32 L.Ed.2d at 617.

An anonymous tip was at issue in Alabama v. White, ___ U.S. ___, 110 S.Ct. 2412, 110 L.Ed.2d 301 (1990). The facts were as follows:

> On April 22, 1987, at approximately 3 p.m., Corporal B.H. Davis of the Montgomery Police Department received a telephone call from an anonymous person, stating that Vanessa White would be leaving 235–C Lynwood Terrace Apartments at a particular time in a brown Plymouth station wagon with the right taillight lens broken, that she would be going to Dobey's Motel, and that she would be in possession of about an ounce of cocaine inside a brown attache case. Corporal Davis and his partner, Corporal P.A. Reynolds, proceeded to the Lynwood Terrace Apartments. The officers saw a brown Plymouth station wagon with a broken right taillight in the parking lot in front of the 235 building. The officers observed [White] leave the 235 building, carrying nothing in her hands, and enter the station wagon. They followed the vehicle as it drove the most direct route to Dobey's Motel. When the vehicle reached the Mobile Highway, on which Dobey's Motel is located, Corporal Reynolds requested a patrol unit to stop the vehicle. The vehicle was stopped at approximately 4:18 p.m., just short of Dobey's Motel. Corporal Davis asked [White] to step to the rear of her car, where he informed her that she had been stopped because she was suspected of carrying cocaine in the vehicle. He asked if they could look for cocaine and [White] said they could look. The officers found a locked brown attache case in the car and, upon request, [White] provided the combination to the lock. The officers found marijuana in the attache case and placed [White] under arrest. During processing at the station, the officers found three milligrams of cocaine in [White's] purse.

___ U.S. at ___, 110 S.Ct. at 2414–15, 110 L.Ed.2d at 306–07. Relying heavily upon Illinois v. Gates, reprinted at page 135, supra, the Court held that Gates' totality of the circumstances approach should be taken in the context before it, with appropriate accommodation for the less demanding standard applicable in field stop situations.  Refusing to conclude that an anonymous caller's tip alone could never provide reasonable suspicion, the Court nevertheless held that the tip in *White* lacked sufficient indicia of reliability to itself constitute reasonable suspicion.  It did, however, stress the range of detailed assertions in the tip. Considering this, the majority acknowledged that the case was a close one but ultimately concluded that when the officers stopped White the tip had been sufficiently corroborated to furnish reasonable suspicion that White was engaged in criminal activity:

> What was important was the caller's ability to predict [White's] *future behavior,* because it demonstrated inside information—a special familiarity with [White's] affairs.  The general public would have no way of knowing that [White] would shortly leave the building, get in the described car, and drive the most direct route to Dobey's Motel.  Because only a small number of people are generally privy to an individual's itinerary, it is reasonable for police to believe that a person with access to such information is likely to also have access to reliable information about that individual's illegal activities.  When significant aspects of the caller's predictions were verified, there was reason to believe not only that the caller was honest but also that he was well informed, at least well enough to justify the stop.

___ U.S. at ___, 110 S.Ct. at 2417, 110 L.Ed.2d at 310.

Justice Stevens, joined by Justices Brennan and Marshall, dissented.

In Brown v. Texas, 443 U.S. 47, 99 S.Ct. 2637, 61 L.Ed.2d 357 (1979), the facts were described as follows:

> At 12:45 on the afternoon of December 9, 1977, officers Venegas and Soleto of the El Paso Police Department were cruising in a patrol car. They observed [Brown] and another man walking in opposite directions away from one another in an alley.  Although the two men were a few feet apart when they were first seen, officer Venegas later testified that both officers believed the two had been together or were about to meet until the patrol car appeared.

The area had a high incidence of drug traffic.  Brown was stopped because, as one officer testified, the situation "looked suspicious" and the officers had never seen Brown in the area before.  The Supreme Court held the stop unreasonable:

> Officer Venegas testified at [Brown's] trial that the situation in the alley "looked suspicious," but he was unable to point to any facts supporting that conclusion.  There is no indication in the record that it was unusual for people to be in the alley.  The fact that [Brown] was in a neighborhood frequented by drug users, standing alone, is not a basis for concluding that [Brown] himself was engaged in criminal conduct.  *  *  * When pressed, Officer Venegas acknowledged that the only reason he stopped [Brown] was to ascertain his identity.  The record suggests an understandable desire to assert a police presence; however that purpose does not negate Fourth Amendment guarantees.

443 U.S. at 52, 99 S.Ct. at 2641, 61 L.Ed.2d at 362–63.

In United States v. Hensley, 469 U.S. 221, 105 S.Ct. 675, 83 L.Ed.2d 604 (1985), a St. Bernard, Ohio police officer was told by an informant that Hensley had driven the getaway car in a recent tavern robbery.  A "wanted flyer" was issued to other police departments in the area, describing the robbery and stating that Hensley was "wanted for investigation" of that robbery.  The other departments were asked to pick up Hensley and hold him for the St. Bernard department, if he was located.  Officers of the Covington, Kentucky police department, recalling the flyer, detained Hensley when he was located in their city. A lower federal court held that the detention was unreasonable because the Covington officers could not rely on the flyer, apparently because it failed to set out the facts on which the issuing department's suspicions were based. The Supreme Court noted that an arrest made in reliance upon a flyer reporting that an arrest warrant exists is apparently reasonable as long as a valid warrant has in fact been issued; see page 192, supra. It then rejected the proposition that police reliance on reports that an arrest warrant has been issued is significantly different than reliance upon a report that another agency has grounds for an investigatory stop:

> The law enforcement interests promoted by allowing one department to make investigatory stops based upon another department's bulletins or flyers are considerable, while the intrusion on personal privacy is minimal.
>
> \* \* \*
>
> We conclude that, if a flyer or bulletin has been issued on the basis of articulable facts supporting a reasonable suspicion that the wanted person has committed an offense, then reliance on that flyer or bulletin justifies a stop to check identification, to pose questions to the person, or to detain the person briefly while attempting to obtain further information. \* \* \* If the flyer has been issued in the absence of a reasonable suspicion, then a stop in the objective reliance upon it violates the Fourth Amendment. \* \* \* [T]he evidence uncovered in the course of the stop is admissible if the police who *issued* the flyer or bulletin possessed a reasonable suspicion justifying a stop, and if the stop that in fact occurred was not significantly more intrusive than would have been permitted the issuing department.

469 U.S. at 232–33, 105 S.Ct. at 682–83, 83 L.Ed.2d at 614–15 (emphasis in original). Turning to the facts of the case, the Court concluded that the St. Bernard police had reasonable suspicion; the informant provided "a wealth of detail" concerning the robbery and admitted to "tangential participation" in it. The flyer itself met Fourth Amendment requirements: "An objective reading of the entire flyer would lead an experienced officer to conclude that Thomas Hensley was at least wanted for questioning and investigation in St. Bernard." 469 U.S. at 234, 105 S.Ct. at 684, 83 L.Ed.2d at 616. Consequently, the detention made by the Covington officers was proper.

6. Investigatory stops at airports have given rise to particular difficulties. Barebones testimony that a passenger meets a "drug carrier profile" does not constitute reasonable suspicion. Reid v. Georgia, 448 U.S. 438, 100 S.Ct. 2752, 65 L.Ed.2d 890 (1980) (per curiam). But evasive and objectively suspicious behavior by the passengers may meet the standard. Florida v. Rodriguez, 469 U.S. 1, 105 S.Ct. 308, 83 L.Ed.2d 165 (1984). Airport stops were recently addressed again in United States v. Sokolow, 490 U.S. 1, 109 S.Ct. 1581, 104 L.Ed.2d 1 (1989). In July of 1984, Andrew Sokolow and a female companion flew from Honolulu to Miami, a 20 hour flight. When they returned after a 48 hour stay in Miami, Sokolow was stopped for investigative purposes by DEA officers. The officers had the following information: Sokolow was about 25 years old. He paid $2,100 for the tickets with cash from a roll of $20 bills that appeared to contain about $4,000. He was wearing a black jumpsuit and gold jewelry and appeared nervous. His destination was Miami, a "source city for drugs." Neither Sokolow nor his companion checked their luggage. Sokolow gave the ticket agent a home telephone number. Although he gave his name to the agent as "Andrew Kray," the number was found to be listed to one "Karl Herman." The agent, however, identified the voice on the answering machine tape at the number as that of the man who had purchased the tickets. (Herman, it was later discovered, was Sokolow's roommate.) The majority acknowledged that Sokolow's activity was itself "lawful" but held that it

established reasonable suspicion. It stressed the evidence that Sokolow was traveling under an alias, that he conducted a large-scale purchase in cash, and that his trip to a source city was surprisingly short for the expense involved. After concluding that reasonable suspicion had been shown, the majority noted that one of the agents had testified that Sokolow's behavior "had all the classic aspects of a drug courier." It continued:

> We do not agree with [Sokolow] that our analysis is somehow changed by the agents' belief that his behavior was consistent with one of the DEA's "drug courier profiles." A court sitting to determine the existence of reasonable suspicion must require the agent to articulate the factors leading to that conclusion, but the fact that these factors may be set forth in a "profile" does not somehow detract from their evidentiary significance as seen by a trained agent.

490 U.S. at ___, 109 S.Ct. at 1587, 104 L.Ed.2d at 12. Justice Marshall, joined by Justice Brennan, dissented.

7. *Terry* itself makes clear that during police-citizen encounters not amounting to custodial arrests officers may make some sort of "weapons search" despite the absence of traditional probable cause to believe the citizen is in possession of a weapon. When can such searches be conducted and what, if any, limits are there upon the manner in which they must be made? *Sibron* strongly suggested that the weapons search must consist initially of a patdown or "frisk." In Adams v. Williams, supra, the officer—Sgt. Connolly—had been told that the suspect was carrying drugs and had a gun at his waist. It was 2:15 a.m. when the officer approached the suspect as the suspect was seated in a car; the area was known to the officer as a high crime rate area. He tapped on the car window and asked the suspect to open the door. The suspect instead rolled down the window. At that point, the officer reached into the car and "removed" a loaded revolver from the suspect's waistband. The Court upheld the action, explaining:

> Sgt. Connolly had ample reason to fear for his safety. When Williams rolled down his window, rather than complying with the policeman's request to step out of the car so that his movements could more easily be seen, the revolver allegedly at Williams' waist became an even greater threat. Under these circumstances the policeman's action in reaching to the spot where the gun was thought to be hidden constituted a limited intrusion designed to insure his safety, and we conclude that it was reasonable.

407 U.S. at 147–48, 92 S.Ct. at 1924, 32 L.Ed.2d at 618.

In Pennsylvania v. Mimms, 434 U.S. 106, 98 S.Ct. 330, 54 L.Ed.2d 331 (1977) (per curiam), an officer had stopped a car driven by Mimms to issue him a traffic citation for having an expired license plate. When Mimms stepped out of the car, the officer observed a large bulge under Mimms' sports jacket. Under *Terry*, the Court held, the bulge permitted the officer to conclude that Mimms posed a serious and present danger to the officer's safety. Thus, the officer properly conducted a pat down of Mimms. The pat down revealed that Mimms was in fact armed. 434 U.S. at 112, 98 S.Ct. at 334, 54 L.Ed.2d at 337–38.

The required basis for a weapons frisk or search was again considered in Ybarra v. Illinois, 444 U.S. 85, 100 S.Ct. 338, 62 L.Ed.2d 238 (1979) (discussed at page 176, supra). Officers obtained a valid search warrant authorizing the search of the Aurora Tap Tavern and Greg, the bartender. When the officers entered the tavern in late afternoon, between 9 and 13 customers—including Ybarra—were present. All were "frisked" and the officer felt "a cigarette pack with objects in it" in Ybarra's pocket; he did not at that time remove it. Several minutes later, Ybarra was searched again, this time more thoroughly. Drugs were found in the cigarette package. The State argued that the first patdown frisk was permissible under *Terry* and since this revealed probable cause to believe Ybarra was in possession of drugs, the second and thorough search was permissible as an exigent circumstances search made on probable cause. Without addressing whether the frisk gave rise to probable cause, a majority of the Court held the frisk invalid:

> The initial frisk of Ybarra was simply not supported by a reasonable belief that he was armed and presently dangerous, a belief which this Court has invariably held must form the predicate to a patdown of a person for weapons. When the police entered the Aurora Tap Tavern on March 1, 1976, the lighting was sufficient for them to observe the customers. Upon seeing Ybarra, they neither recognized him as a person with a criminal history nor had any particular reason to believe that he might be inclined to assault them. Moreover, as Police Agent Johnson later testified, Ybarra, whose hands were empty, gave no indication of possessing a weapon, made no gestures or other actions indicative of an intent to commit an assault, and acted generally in a manner that was not threatening. At the suppression hearing, the most Agent Johnson could point to was that Ybarra was wearing a ¾-length lumber jacket, clothing which the State admits could be expected on almost any tavern patron in Illinois in early March. In short, the State is unable to articulate any specific fact that would have justified a police officer at the scene in even suspecting that Ybarra was armed and dangerous.
>
> The *Terry* case created an exception to the requirement of probable cause, an exception whose "narrow scope" this Court "has been careful to maintain." Under that doctrine a law enforcement officer, for his own protection and safety, may conduct a patdown to find weapons that he reasonably believes or suspects are then in the possession of the person he has accosted. Nothing in *Terry* can be understood to allow a generalized "cursory search for weapons" or, indeed, any search whatever for anything but weapons. The "narrow scope" of the *Terry* exception does not permit a frisk for weapons on less than reasonable belief or suspicion directed at the person to be frisked, even though that person happens to be on premises where an authorized narcotics search is taking place.

444 U.S. at 92–94, 100 S.Ct. at 343, 62 L.Ed.2d at 246–47. Chief Justice Burger, joined by Justices Blackmun and Rehnquist, dissented on this issue:

> The Court would require a particularized and individualized suspicion that a person is armed and dangerous as a condition to a *Terry* search. This goes beyond the rationale of *Terry* and overlooks the practicalities of a situation which no doubt often confronts officers executing a valid search warrant. * * * I would hold that when police execute a search warrant for narcotics in a place of known narcotics activity they may protect themselves by conducting a *Terry* search. * * *

444 U.S. at 97, 100 S.Ct. at 345, 62 L.Ed.2d at 249–50 (Burger, C.J., dissenting).

8. Some seizures of items as well as persons may be made upon less than probable cause. In United States v. Place, 462 U.S. 696, 103 S.Ct. 2637, 77 L.Ed.2d 110 (1983), Drug Enforcement Administration officers approached Place at New York's LaGuardia airport after he had aroused suspicion while departing from Miami and upon arrival in New York. Discrepancies were noted concerning the addresses placed on his two pieces of luggage. At both Miami and New York, he volunteered to officers who approached him that he

had recognized them as police officers. At New York, he had falsely claimed that his baggage had been searched in Miami. He refused to consent to a search of the luggage at the New York airport. One of the agents then informed him that the luggage was to be taken before a federal judge for purposes of applying for a search warrant and that Place was free to accompany the officers (and the luggage). Place declined the invitation, but obtained a number at which the officers indicated they could be reached. The officers took the bags to another airport where, one hour and thirty minutes later, a trained narcotics detention dog reacted positively to the smaller bag but "ambiguously" to the larger one. As it was late on Friday, the agents retained the bags until Monday and at that time obtained a search warrant. The smaller bag was found to contain cocaine. Applying the principles of *Terry,* the Supreme Court concluded that certain seizures of personal luggage on the basis of "reasonable, articulable suspicion, premised on objective facts," would be reasonable under the Fourth Amendment. Balancing the relevant interests, the Court observed that the governmental interest in a brief seizure of luggage believed to contain drugs is substantial. On the other hand, at least some brief seizures of luggage intrude only minimally upon the owner's Fourth Amendment protected interests:

> In sum, we conclude that when an officer's observations lead him reasonably to believe that a traveler is carrying luggage that contains narcotics, the principles of *Terry* and its progeny would permit the officer to detain the luggage briefly to investigate the circumstances that aroused his suspicion, provided that the investigative detention is properly limited in scope.

462 U.S. at 706, 103 S.Ct. at 2644, 77 L.Ed.2d at 120. But the Court further concluded that the length of the detention before it exceeded what was permissible on less than probable cause; see note 3 at page 241, infra. Justice Brennan, joined by Justice Marshall, acknowledged that nonarrest detentions of a person necessarily involve seizures of the personal effects which the individual has in his possession at the time and that this is permitted under the *Terry* line of cases. But, he urged, seizures of property such as luggage independent of any seizure of the person significantly and unjustifiably expand what may be done on reasonable suspicion. Such seizures, in his view, should be permitted only on the basis of probable cause. 462 U.S. at 716–18, 103 S.Ct. at 2649–50, 77 L.Ed.2d at 127–28 (Brennan, J., dissenting).

## FLORIDA v. ROYER

Supreme Court of the United States, 1983.
460 U.S. 491, 103 S.Ct. 1319, 75 L.Ed.2d 229.

JUSTICE WHITE announced the judgment of the Court and delivered an opinion in which JUSTICES MARSHALL, POWELL and STEVENS joined.

\* \* \*

### I

On January 3, 1978, Royer was observed at Miami International Airport by two plain-clothes detectives of the Dade County, Florida, Public Safety Department assigned to the County's Organized Crime Bureau, Narcotics Investigation Section. Detectives Johnson and Magdalena believed that Royer's appearance, mannerisms, luggage, and actions fit the so-called "drug courier profile." Royer, apparently unaware of the attention he had attracted, purchased a one-way ticket to New York City and checked his two suitcases, placing on each suitcase an identification tag bearing the name "Holt" and the destination, "LaGuardia". As Royer made his way to the concourse which led to the airline boarding area, the two detectives approached him, identified themselves as policemen working out of the sheriff's office, and asked if Royer had a "moment" to speak with them; Royer said "Yes."

Upon request, but without oral consent, Royer produced for the detectives his airline ticket and his driver's license. The airline ticket, like the baggage identification tags, bore the name "Holt," while the driver's license carried respondent's correct name, "Royer." When the detectives asked about the discrepancy, Royer explained that a friend had made the reservation in the name of "Holt." Royer became noticeably more nervous during this conversation, whereupon the detectives informed Royer that they were in fact narcotics investigators and that they had reason to suspect him of transporting narcotics.

The detectives did not return his airline ticket and identification but asked Royer to accompany them to a room, approximately forty feet away, adjacent to the concourse. Royer said nothing in response but went with the officers as he had been asked to do. The room was later described by Detective Johnson as a "large storage closet," located in the stewardesses' lounge and containing a small desk and two chairs. Without Royer's consent or agreement, Detective Johnson, using Royer's baggage check stubs, retrieved the "Holt" luggage from the airline and brought it to the room where respondent and Detective Magdalena were waiting. Royer was asked if he would consent to a search of the suitcases. Without orally responding to this request, Royer produced a key and unlocked one of the suitcases, which the detective then opened without seeking further assent from Royer. Drugs were found in that suitcase. According to Detective Johnson, Royer stated that he did not know the combination to the lock on the second suitcase. When asked if he objected to the detective opening the second suitcase, Royer said "no, go ahead," and did not object when the detective explained that the suitcase might have to be broken open. The suitcase was pried open by the officers and more marihuana was found. Royer was then told that he was under arrest. Approximately fifteen minutes had elapsed from the time the detectives initially approached respondent until his arrest upon the discovery of the contraband.

Prior to his trial for felony possession of marihuana, Royer made a motion to suppress the evidence obtained in the search of the suitcases. The trial court found that Royer's consent to the search was "freely and voluntarily given," and that, regardless of the consent, the warrantless search was reasonable because "the officer doesn't have the time to run out and get a search warrant because the plane is going to take off." Following the denial of the motion to suppress, Royer changed his plea from "not guilty" to "nolo contendere," specifically reserving the right to appeal the denial of the motion to suppress. Royer was convicted.

The District Court of Appeal, sitting en banc, reversed Royer's conviction. * * * We granted the State's petition for certiorari, and now affirm.

## II

* * * The Florida Court of Appeal * * * concluded * * *
that Royer had been seized when he gave his consent to search his
luggage [and] also that the bounds of an investigative stop had been
exceeded.  In its view the "confinement" in this case went beyond the
limited restraint of a *Terry* investigative stop, and Royer's consent was
thus tainted by the illegality, a conclusion that required reversal in the
absence of probable cause to arrest.  The question before us is whether
the record warrants that conclusion.  We think that it does.

## III

The State proffers three reasons for holding that when Royer
consented to the search of his luggage, he was not being illegally
detained.  First, it is submitted that the entire encounter was consensual and hence Royer was not being held against his will at all.  We find
this submission untenable.  Asking for and examining Royer's ticket
and his driver's license were no doubt permissible in themselves, but
when the officers identified themselves as narcotics agents, told Royer
that he was suspected of transporting narcotics, and asked him to
accompany them to the police room, while retaining his ticket and
driver's license and without indicating in any way that he was free to
depart, Royer was effectively seized for the purposes of the Fourth
Amendment.  These circumstances surely amount to a show of official
authority such that "a reasonable person would have believed he was
not free to leave."  United States v. Mendenhall, 446 U.S. 544, 554, 100
S.Ct. 1870, 1877, 64 L.Ed.2d 497 (Opinion of Stewart, J.).

Second, the State submits that if Royer was seized, there existed
reasonable, articulable suspicion to justify a temporary detention and
that the limits of a *Terry*-type stop were never exceeded.  We agree
with the State that when the officers discovered that Royer was
travelling under an assumed name, this fact, and the facts already
known to the officers—paying cash for a one-way ticket, the mode of
checking the two bags, and Royer's appearance and conduct in general—were adequate grounds for suspecting Royer of carrying drugs and
for temporarily detaining him and his luggage while they attempted to
verify or dispel their suspicions in a manner that did not exceed the
limits of an investigative detention.  We also agree that had Royer
voluntarily consented to the search of his luggage while he was justifiably being detained on reasonable suspicion, the products of the search
would be admissible against him.  We have concluded, however, that at
the time Royer produced the key to his suitcase, the detention to which
he was then subjected was a more serious intrusion on his personal
liberty than is allowable on mere suspicion of criminal activity.

By the time Royer was informed that the officers wished to examine his luggage, he had identified himself when approached by the
officers and had attempted to explain the discrepancy between the
name shown on his identification and the name under which he had
purchased his ticket and identified his luggage.  The officers were not

satisfied, for they informed him they were narcotics agents and had reason to believe that he was carrying illegal drugs. They requested him to accompany them to the police room. Royer went with them. He found himself in a small room—a large closet—equipped with a desk and two chairs. He was alone with two police officers who again told him that they thought he was carrying narcotics. He also found that the officers, without his consent, had retrieved his checked luggage from the airlines. What had begun as a consensual inquiry in a public place had escalated into an investigatory procedure in a police interrogation room, where the police, unsatisfied with previous explanations, sought to confirm their suspicions. The officers had Royer's ticket, they had his identification, and they had seized his luggage. Royer was never informed that he was free to board his plane if he so chose, and he reasonably believed that he was being detained. At least as of that moment, any consensual aspects of the encounter had evaporated, and we cannot fault the Florida Court of Appeal for concluding that Terry v. Ohio and the cases following it did not justify the restraint to which Royer was then subjected. As a practical matter, Royer was under arrest. Consistent with this conclusion, the State conceded in the Florida courts that Royer would not have been free to leave the interrogation room had he asked to do so. Furthermore, the state's brief in this Court interprets the testimony of the officers at the suppression hearing as indicating that had Royer refused to consent to a search of his luggage, the officers would have held the luggage and sought a warrant to authorize the search.

We also think that the officers' conduct was more intrusive than necessary to effectuate an investigative detention otherwise authorized by the *Terry* line of cases. First, by returning his ticket and driver's license, and informing him that he was free to go if he so desired, the officers may have obviated any claim that the encounter was anything but a consensual matter from start to finish. Second, there are undoubtedly reasons of safety and security that would justify moving a suspect from one location to another during an investigatory detention, such as from an airport concourse to a more private area. There is no indication in this case that such reasons prompted the officers to transfer the site of the encounter from the concourse to the interrogation room. It appears, rather, that the primary interest of the officers was not in having an extended conversation with Royer but in the contents of his luggage, a matter which the officers did not pursue orally with Royer until after the encounter was relocated to the police room. The record does not reflect any facts which would support a finding that the legitimate law enforcement purposes which justified the detention in the first instance were furthered by removing Royer to the police room prior to the officer's attempt to gain his consent to a search of his luggage. As we have noted, had Royer consented to a search on the spot, the search could have been conducted with Royer present in the area where the bags were retrieved by Officer Johnson and any evidence recovered would have been admissible against him. If the search proved negative, Royer would have been free to go much earlier and with less likelihood of missing his flight, which in itself can be a very serious matter in a variety of circumstances.

Third, the State has not touched on the question whether it would have been feasible to investigate the contents of Royer's bags in a more expeditious way. The courts are not strangers to the use of trained dogs to detect the presence of controlled substances in luggage. There is no indication here that this means was not feasible and available. If it had been used, Royer and his luggage could have been momentarily detained while this investigative procedure was carried out. Indeed, it may be that no detention at all would have been necessary. A negative result would have freed Royer in short order; a positive result would have resulted in his justifiable arrest on probable cause.

We do not suggest that there is a litmus-paper test for distinguishing a consensual encounter from a seizure or for determining when a seizure exceeds the bounds of an investigative stop. Even in the discrete category of airport encounters, there will be endless variations in the facts and circumstances, so much variation that it is unlikely that the courts can reduce to a sentence or a paragraph a rule that will provide unarguable answers to the question whether there has been an unreasonable search or seizure in violation of the Fourth Amendment. Nevertheless, we must render judgment, and we think that the Florida Court of Appeal cannot be faulted in concluding that the limits of a *Terry*-stop had been exceeded.

## IV

The State's third and final argument is that Royer was not being illegally held when he gave his consent because there was probable cause to arrest him at that time. Officer Johnson testified at the suppression hearing and the Florida Court of Appeal held that there was no probable cause to arrest until Royer's bags were opened, but the fact that the officers did not believe there was probable cause and proceeded on a consensual or *Terry*-stop rationale would not foreclose the State from justifying Royer's custody by proving probable cause and hence removing any barrier to relying on Royer's consent to search. We agree with the Florida Court of Appeal, however, that probable cause to arrest Royer did not exist at the time he consented to the search of his luggage. The facts are that a nervous young man with two American Tourister bags paid cash for an airline ticket to a "target city." These facts led to inquiry, which in turn revealed that the ticket had been bought under an assumed name. The proffered explanation did not satisfy the officers. We cannot agree with the State, if this is its position, that every nervous young man paying cash for a ticket to New York City under an assumed name and carrying two heavy American Tourister bags may be arrested and held to answer for a serious felony charge.

## V

Because we affirm the Florida Court of Appeal's conclusion that Royer was being illegally detained when he consented to the search of his luggage, we agree that the consent was tainted by the illegality and was ineffective to justify the search. The judgment of the Florida Court of Appeal is accordingly

Affirmed.

[The concurring opinion of JUSTICE POWELL and the dissenting opinion of JUSTICE BLACKMUN are omitted.]

JUSTICE BRENNAN, concurring in the result.

\* \* \*

To the extent that the plurality endorses the legality of the officers' initial stop of Royer, it was wholly unnecessary to reach that question. For even assuming the legality of the initial stop, the plurality correctly holds, and I agree, that the officers' subsequent actions clearly exceeded the permissible bounds of a *Terry* "investigative" stop. \* \* \* [9]

In any event, I dissent from the plurality's view that the initial stop of Royer was legal. For plainly Royer was "seized" \* \* \*. [The] facts clearly are not sufficient to provide the reasonable suspicion of criminal activity necessary to justify the \* \* \* seizure \* \* \*.

JUSTICE REHNQUIST, with whom THE CHIEF JUSTICE and JUSTICE O'CONNOR join, dissenting.

\* \* \*

I think the articulable suspicion which concededly focused upon Royer [after the officers' initial conversation with him] justified the length and nature of his detention.

The reasonableness of the officers' activity in this case did not depend upon Royer's consent to the investigation. Nevertheless, the presence of consent further justifies the action taken. \* \* \* [I]f Royer was legally approached in the first instance and consented to accompany the detectives to the room, it does not follow that his consent went up in smoke and he was "arrested" upon entering the room. \* \* \* [L]ogical analysis would focus on whether the environment in the room rendered the subsequent consent to a search of the luggage involuntary.

\* \* \* [T]here is nothing in the record which would indicate that Royer's resistance was overborne by anything \* \* \*.

[9] I interpret the plurality's requirement that the investigative methods employed pursuant to a *Terry* stop be "the least intrusive means reasonably available to verify or dispel the officer's suspicion in a short period of time," to mean that the availability of a less intrusive means may make an otherwise reasonable stop unreasonable. I do not interpret it to mean that the absence of a less intrusive means can make an otherwise unreasonable stop reasonable.

In addition, contrary to the plurality's apparent suggestion, I am not at all certain that the use of trained narcotics dogs constitutes a less intrusive means of conducting a lawful *Terry* investigative stop. Such a suggestion finds no support in our cases and any question concerning the use of trained dogs to detect the presence of controlled substances in luggage is clearly not before us.

In any event, the relevance of a least intrusive means requirement within the context of a *Terry* investigative stop is not clear to me. As I have discussed, a lawful stop must be so strictly limited that it is difficult to conceive of a less intrusive means that would be effective to accomplish the purpose of the stop.

## NOTES

1. At what point during the confrontation was Royer "seized" so as to require that the officers had reasonable suspicion? In 1984, the Court indicated that "police questioning, by itself" is unlikely to result in a seizure. An officer "detains" a person by approaching him and posing questions only if "the circumstances of the encounter are so intimidating as to demonstrate that a reasonable person would have believed he was not free to leave if he [did not respond]." Immigration and Naturalization Service v. Delgado, 466 U.S. 210, 216, 104 S.Ct. 1758, 1762, 80 L.Ed.2d 247, 255 (1984). The standard was applied in Michigan v. Chesternut, 486 U.S. 567, 108 S.Ct. 1975, 100 L.Ed.2d 565 (1988). Four Detroit officers were engaged in routine patrol in a marked police cruiser. As the cruiser came to an intersection, one officer saw a car pull over to the curb and an occupant alight. This person approached Chesternut, who was standing alone on the corner. Chesternut saw the cruiser as it approached; he immediately turned and ran. The cruiser caught up with him and drove alongside Chesternut for a short distance. During this time, the officers observed Chesternut pull several packets from his pocket and discard them. Chesternut then stopped and one officer examined the discarded packets. Concluding that the packets contained codeine, the officers placed Chesternut under arrest. A search revealed other drugs, including heroin. After Chesternut was charged with drug offenses, a magistrate held that he had been unlawfully seized during the events before he discarded the codeine. This was affirmed on appeal in reliance upon state court holdings that any police pursuit was a "seizure." Since the officers did not have reasonable suspicion when their pursuit of Chesternut began, the state courts reasoned, their seizure of him was unreasonable.

A unanimous Supreme Court reversed. Justice Blackmun, writing for the Court, rejected both the position that any pursuit is a "seizure" and the view that no seizure can occur until and if the officer actually apprehends the person. Instead, he indicated, the Court will continue to apply its traditional "contextual approach." Under this approach, "the police can be said to have seized an individual 'only if, in view of all of the circumstances surrounding the incident, a reasonable person would have believed that he was not free to leave.'" Applying this standard, the Court found that no seizure occurred before Chesternut discarded the packets:

> [T]he police conduct involved here would not have communicated to the reasonable person an attempt to capture or otherwise intrude upon [the person's] freedom of movement. The record does not reflect that the police activated a siren or flashers; or that they commanded [Chesternut] to halt, or displayed any weapons; or that they operated the car in an aggressive manner to block [Chesternut's] course or otherwise control the direction or speed of his movement. While the very presence of a police car driving parallel to a running pedestrian could be somewhat intimidating, this kind of police presence does not, standing alone, constitute a seizure.

486 U.S. at 575, 108 S.Ct. at 1980, 100 L.Ed.2d at 573. Consequently, reasonable and particularized suspicion need not have existed prior to Chesternut's discarding of the packets.

2. How much movement of the suspect under what conditions is permissible during a nonarrest investigatory detention? In Dunaway v. New York, 442 U.S. 200, 99 S.Ct. 2248, 60 L.Ed.2d 824 (1979), officers with information—but less than probable cause—connecting Dunaway with a robbery-murder had Dunaway "picked up" at a neighbor's home. He was driven to police headquar-

ters, placed in an interrogation room, warned of his rights, and questioned. Finding that Dunaway's detention was "in important respects indistinguishable from an arrest," the Court held that the lack of probable cause rendered the detention invalid.   442 U.S. at 212, 99 S.Ct. at 2256, 60 L.Ed.2d at 835–36.

The suggestion that movement to the stationhouse is prohibited was confirmed in Hayes v. Florida, 470 U.S. 811, 105 S.Ct. 1643, 84 L.Ed.2d 705 (1985).  Hayes was a suspect in a series of burglary-rapes.  Fingerprints were found at the scene of one of the offenses and officers believed they belonged to the perpetrator.  Several officers came to Hayes' home and spoke to him on his front porch.  When he expressed reluctance to accompany them to the station for fingerprints, they explained that they would then arrest him.  He agreed to go to the stationhouse and did so.  Fingerprints obtained from him at the stationhouse matched those at the scene.  At Hayes' trial for burglary and sexual battery, fingerprint evidence was admitted over his objection that it was the fruit of his illegal detention.  The Supreme Court reversed his conviction:

> There is no doubt that at some point in the investigative process, police procedures can qualitatively and quantitatively be so intrusive with respect to a suspect's freedom of movement and privacy interests as to trigger the full protection of the Fourth and Fourteenth Amendments.  And our view continues to be that the line is crossed when the police, without probable cause or a warrant, forcibly remove a person from his home or other place in which he is entitled to be and transport him to the police station, where he is detained, although briefly, for investigative purposes.  We adhere to the view that such seizures, at least where not under judicial supervision, are sufficiently like arrests to invoke the traditional rule that arrests may constitutionally be made only on probable cause.

470 U.S. at 815–16, 105 S.Ct. at 1646–47, 84 L.Ed.2d at 710.  Justice Brennan, joined by Justice Marshall, concurred in the judgment.  He expressed concern, however, regarding the Court's suggestion that fingerprinting during an investigatory stop would be permissible.  Especially if undertaken in view of passersby, this might be quite intrusive.  Moreover, it raises further and difficult questions such as the officers' right to further detain the suspect, as while the fingerprints taken are compared with those of the perpetrator.  Given these uncertainties, he indicated he would withhold comment on such practices until a case involving them was before the Court.  470 U.S. at 818–20, 105 S.Ct. at 1648–49, 84 L.Ed.2d at 712–13 (Brennan, J., concurring in the judgment).

In Davis v. Mississippi, 394 U.S. 721, 89 S.Ct. 1394, 22 L.Ed.2d 676 (1969), however, the Court had indicated in dicta that stationhouse detentions for fingerprinting might be permissible upon less than probable cause:

> It is arguable * * * that, because of the unique nature of the fingerprinting process, * * * detentions [for fingerprinting] might, under narrowly defined circumstances, be found to comply with the Fourth Amendment even though there is no probable cause in the traditional sense.  Detention for fingerprinting may constitute a much less serious intrusion upon personal security than other types of police searches and detentions. Fingerprinting involves none of the probing into an individual's private life and thoughts that mark an interrogation or search.  Nor can fingerprint detention be employed repeatedly to harass any individual, since the police need only one set of each person's prints.  Furthermore, fingerprinting is an inherently more reliable and effective crime-stopping tool than eyewitness identification or confessions and is not subject to such abuses as the improper lineup and the "third degree."  Finally, because there is no danger of destruction of fingerprints, the limited detention need not come unexpectedly or at an inconvenient time.  For this same reason, the

general requirement that the authorization of a judicial officer be obtained in advance of detention would seem not to admit of any exception in the fingerprinting context.

394 U.S. at 727–28, 89 S.Ct. at 1397–98, 22 L.Ed.2d at 681. In *Hayes*, the majority indicated that it was not abandoning the "suggestion" in *Davis* and noted that a number of jurisdictions, in reliance on that suggestion, had enacted provisions for judicial authorizations for fingerprinting detentions. 470 U.S. at 817, 105 S.Ct. at 1647, 84 L.Ed.2d at 711.

3. How long may a non-arrest investigatory detention last? The American Law Institute's proposal would limit such detentions to a "period as is reasonably necessary for the accomplishment of the purposes authorized * * * but in no case for more than twenty minutes * * *. Model Code of Pre-arraignment Procedure § 110.2(1) (Official Draft 1975). In United States v. Place, 462 U.S. 696, 103 S.Ct. 2637, 77 L.Ed.2d 110 (1983), dealing with detention of luggage (see note 8 at page 232, supra), the Court noted the Institute's proposal but declined "to adopt any outside time limitation for a permissible *Terry* stop:"

> We understand the desirability of providing law enforcement authorities with a clear rule to guide their conduct. Nevertheless, we question the wisdom of a rigid time limitation. Such a limit would undermine the equally important need to allow authorities to graduate their responses to the demands of any particular situation.

462 U.S. at 709 n. 10, 103 S.Ct. at 2646 n. 10, 77 L.Ed.2d at 122 n. 10. But it then continued:

> The length of the detention of [Place's] luggage alone precludes the conclusion that the seizure was reasonable in the absence of probable cause. Although we have recognized the reasonableness of seizures longer than the momentary ones in *Terry* [and] *Adams* * * *, the brevity of the invasion of the individual's Fourth Amendment interests is an important factor in determining whether the seizure is so minimally intrusive as to be justifiable on reasonable suspicion. Moreover, in assessing the effect of the length of the detention, we take into account whether the police diligently pursue their investigation. We note that here the New York agents knew the time of Place's scheduled arrival at LaGuardia [Airport], had ample time to arrange for their additional investigation at that location, and thereby could have minimized the intrusion on [Place's] Fourth Amendment interests. * * * [W]e have never approved a seizure of the person for the prolonged 90-minute period involved here and cannot do so on the facts presented by this case.

462 U.S. at 709–10, 103 S.Ct. at 2645–46, 77 L.Ed.2d at 122.

The permissible length of investigatory detentions was again addressed in United States v. Sharpe, 470 U.S. 675, 105 S.Ct. 1568, 84 L.Ed.2d 605 (1985). Drug Enforcement Administration agent Cooke was patrolling a costal road in North Carolina and observed a pickup truck (driven by Savage) and a Pontiac (driven by Sharpe) traveling "in tandem." After observing that the pickup truck appeared to be heavily loaded, Cooke called for assistance. Highway patrol officer Thrasher, driving a marked patrol car, responded. Within a minute or so of Thrasher's joining the "procession," the truck and the Pontiac turned off the highway onto a campground road and—despite the 35 mph speed limit—progressed at 55 to 60 mph until the road looped back onto the highway. A decision was made to stop the vehicles and Thrasher pulled aside the Pontiac (which was in the lead), turned on his flashing light, and motioned for the driver to pull over. As the Pontiac pulled over, the pickup truck "cut" between the Pontiac and the patrol car and continued down the highway. Thrasher pursued the truck and Cooke pulled over behind the Pontiac. Cooke obtained identification from Sharpe, the driver of the Pontiac. When he was unable to make radio contact with Thrasher, he called local police, directed them to "maintain the situation," and joined Thrasher.

Thrasher had secured identification from the driver of the truck, Savage. Savage explained that the truck belonged to a friend (and produced a bill of sale) and that he was taking the truck to have its shock absorbers repaired. Thrasher told Savage that the two would await the arrival of a DEA agent. Savage became nervous and asked for his identification; Thrasher told him that he was not free to leave. Cooke arrived at the scene about 15 minutes after the truck had been stopped. When Cooke stated that he believed the truck contained marihuana and twice asked for permission to search it, Savage twice refused. Cooke stepped on the rear of the truck, noting that it did not sink. He then put his nose against the rear window, reported that he could smell marihuana, and searched the vehicle. Bales of marihuana were found and Savage was placed under arrest. Cooke then returned to the Pontiac and arrested Sharpe; this was about 30 to 40 minutes from the time the Pontiac was stopped. At the trial of Sharpe and Savage for possession of the marihuana, the marihuana was admitted into evidence. On appeal, the Court of Appeals reversed, reasoning that the detentions of Sharpe and Savage were too long to be supported on less than probable cause and that these detentions tainted the discovery and seizure of the marihuana.

The Supreme Court reversed. Writing for the Court, Chief Justice Burger reaffirmed that the Fourth Amendment imposes no "hard-and-fast" time limit upon the duration of a *Terry* stop:

> In assessing whether a detention is too long in duration to be justified as an investigative stop, we consider it appropriate to examine whether the police diligently pursued a means of investigation that was likely to confirm or dispel their suspicions quickly, during which time it was necessary to detain the defendant. A court making this assessment should take care to consider whether the police are acting in a swiftly developing situation, and in such cases the court should not indulge in unrealistic second-guessing. * * * The question is not simply whether some other alternative was available, but whether the police acted unreasonably in failing to recognize or pursue it.

470 U.S. at 686–87, 105 S.Ct. at 1575–76, 84 L.Ed.2d at 615–16. On the facts before it, the Court concluded, Cooke pursued the investigation with regard to Savage in a diligent and reasonable manner. Most of the delay was attributable to Savage's actions in maneuvering around the Pontiac and Thrasher's patrol car, which required separate stops of the two vehicles. The Court assumed that this was an conscious effort by Savage to elude the officers, but commented that Savage's actions would also justify the delay even if they were "innocent." To affirm the decision of the lower court with regard to Savage's 20 minute detention, the majority concluded, would be to "effectively establish a *per se* rule that a 20-minute detention is too long to be justified under the *Terry* doctrine." This the Court was unwilling to do. In regard to Sharpe's detention, the Court found no reason to consider the validity of its 30 to 40 minute duration. The challenged evidence was obtained by searching the truck and could not be said to be "fruit" of any improper detention of Sharpe as may have taken place.

Justice Marshall concurred in the judgment, on the ground that the Court's opinion, although arriving at the correct result, "understates the importance of *Terry's* brevity requirement to the constitutionality of *Terry* stops." 470 U.S. at

689, 105 S.Ct. at 1577, 84 L.Ed.2d at 617 (Marshall, J., concurring in the judgment).   Any detention beyond the few minutes necessary to stop the suspect, ask questions, or check identification, he urged, should be presumptively a *de facto* arrest:

> That presumption can be overcome by showing that a lengthier detention was not unduly *intrusive* for some reason;  as in this case, for example, the suspects, rather than the police, may have prolonged the stop.   It cannot, however, be overcome simply by showing that police needs required a more intrusive stop.

470 U.S. at 697, 105 S.Ct. at 1581, 84 L.Ed.2d at 623 (emphasis in original). Justice Brennan dissented, in part upon the ground that the Court of Appeals correctly held that the detentions violated "*Terry's* threshold brevity requirement."   470 U.S. at 711, 105 S.Ct. at 1589, 84 L.Ed.2d at 631–32 (1985) (Brennan, J., dissenting).   He emphasized that Savage's actions were not shown to be an intentional evasion of Thrasher's efforts to stop the vehicles.   In addition, he urged that the officers failed to comply with what he read as the *Royer* requirement that the investigation be conducted in the most expeditious way.   The officers could have stopped both vehicles together.   Cooke could have followed the truck and hence expedited the inquiry into its contents.   Thrasher, a trained patrol officer, could have carried out the limited investigation permitted into the contents of the truck.   To the extent that a DEA agent was needed to conduct the investigation of the truck, Justice Brennan read the record as showing that the unavailability of such agents (and hence the need to rely on Thrasher) was due to poor communications between Cooke and other agents.   470 U.S. at 713–16, 105 S.Ct. at 1589–91, 84 L.Ed.2d at 632–33.

4.   What, if any, limits does or should the Fourth Amendment place upon the use of force to make an investigatory stop.   In light of the limits on the use of force to make an arrest, see page 193, supra, should deadly force ever be "reasonable" in the absence of probable cause?

5.   What is or should be the significance of the officer's intention at the time a suspect is initially seized?   In United States v. Hensley, 469 U.S. 221, 105 S.Ct. 675, 83 L.Ed.2d 604 (1985), Covington, Kentucky officers stopped Hensley on the basis of a flyer from the St. Bernard, Ohio police that asked any police agency locating Hensley to pick up and hold him in connection with a robbery investigation by the St. Bernard department.   Hensley was driving a car when stopped.   Upon observing a revolver protruding from underneath the passenger's seat, the officers arrested Hensley's passenger and searched the car. When several additional firearms were located, Hensley was arrested, apparently for violation of Kentucky handgun possession laws.   The flyer, concluded the Supreme Court, authorized the Covington officers to briefly detain Hensley to conduct an investigation.   At the time of the stop, the Court assumed, the Covington officers intended to comply with the flyer's request that Hensley be "held" for the St. Bernard department.   "[S]uch a detention," the Court commented, "might well be so lengthy or intrusive as to exceed the permissible limits of a *Terry* stop."   469 U.S. at 235, 105 S.Ct. at 683, 83 L.Ed.2d at 616. But since grounds for arrest on the weapons charge developed soon after the detention began, the Covington officers detained Hensley on the basis of the flyer only until their arrest provided an independent basis for his continued custody.   Rejecting the argument that the detention was invalid from its onset because of the officers' intention, the Court explained:

> It is irrelevant whether the Covington officers intended to detain Hensley only long enough to confirm the existence of a warrant, or for some longer period;  what matters is that the stop and detention that occurred were in

fact no more intrusive than would have been permitted an experienced officer on an objective reading of the flyer.

469 U.S. at 234–35, 105 S.Ct. at 683, 83 L.Ed.2d at 616.

## C. TRAFFIC "STOPS," SOBRIETY CHECKPOINTS, AND RELATED DETENTIONS

When law enforcement officers stop a car being driven on public roadways, there is obviously some sort of "seizure" of at least the driver and perhaps also of any passengers in the car. These seizures, however, present difficult Fourth Amendment questions, including ones of necessary and useful classification. A person in an automobile may be the subject of a field stop or *"Terry"* stop, and presumably this requires the same sort of reasonable or objective suspicion that would be necessary if the person was on foot. See United States v. Hensley, 469 U.S. 221, 105 S.Ct. 675, 83 L.Ed.2d 604 (1985). But detentions of motorists may also be for reasons that require the application of different Fourth Amendment standards.

### EDITORS' INTRODUCTION: "TRAFFIC STOPS" AND RELATED MATTERS

Despite the frequency with which courts discuss detentions labeled "traffic stops," there is some uncertainty as to how these are to be defined and distinguished from other detentions, most significantly arrests. There is also uncertainty as to what rights officers have to search "incident to" detentions that are only "traffic stops."

*"Routine Traffic Stops."* The Supreme Court has discussed "routine traffic stops" on the assumption that they are distinguishable from arrests. United States v. Robinson, 414 U.S. 218, 236 n. 6, 94 S.Ct. 467, 477 n. 6, 38 L.Ed.2d 427, 441 n. 6 (1973) ("full-custody arrest" distinguished from what the lower court "characterized as 'a routine traffic stop,' i.e., where the officer would simply issue a notice of violation and allow the offender to proceed"). In Berkemer v. McCarty, 468 U.S. 420, 104 S.Ct. 3138, 82 L.Ed.2d 317 (1984), the Court discussed "a routine traffic stop," which it apparently defined as a relatively short detention during which a driver "answer[s] questions and wait[s] while the officer checks his license and registration." The driver "may then be given a citation" but "he most likely will be allowed to continue on his way," that is, without being incarcerated in a detention facility or being taken before a judicial officer. 468 U.S. at 435–37, 104 S.Ct. 3147–49, 82 L.Ed. 2d at 331–33. For purposes of determining whether a person was "in custody" and therefore whether *Miranda* requirements applied, the Court distinguished such stops from "arrests" for the same traffic offenses. 468 U.S. at 429–35, 104 S.Ct. at 3145–47, 82 L.Ed.2d at 328–31. It has not discussed what the Fourth Amendment requires for such detentions. Most likely, an "arrest"—even for a traffic offense—requires "probable cause" to believe the suspect committed the traffic offense. Whether "a routine traffic stop," to issue a ticket or citation, is permissible on less—such as reasonable suspicion—is not as clear.

What right do officers have to search the motorist and his vehicle during "a routine traffic stop"? When, in United States v. Robinson, discussed at page 199, supra, the Court held that a "custodial" arrest creates an automatic right to search the arrested person, it carefully noted that it was not reaching officers' authority during routine traffic stops. 414 U.S. at 236 n. 6, 94 S.Ct. at 477 n. 6, 38 L.Ed.2d at 441 n. 6. Lower courts, however, have generally assumed that such routine traffic stops are not sufficient to invoke the *Chimel–Robinson* right to search. E.g., Johnson v. State, 537 So.2d 117, 119 (Fla.App.1988) ("The routine stopping of an automobile for a traffic citation does not give rise to any reason or authorization for a search."); People v. Penny, 188 Ill. App.3d 499, 136 Ill.Dec. 240, 544 N.E.2d 1015, 1017 (1989) ("Stopping a vehicle for a minor traffic violation does not, by itself, justify a search of the detainee's person or vehicle."). As a Massachusettes court explained:

> Detentions for frisking, questioning, routine traffic stops, and the like, where the detainee is released after the police business is transacted, are treated as " 'seizures' of the person," subject to Fourth Amendment scrutiny, but are differentiated from "formal", or "custodial", arrests, the custodial aspect of which serves as the theoretical justification for the incident[al] search.

Commonwealth v. Skea, 18 Mass.App.Ct. 685, 690, 470 N.E.2d 385, 390–91 (1984). Where an officer has authority to either issue a citation or make a custodial arrest for the traffic offense at issue, there is authority for the proposition that the right to make an "incidental" search depends upon whether in the particular case the officer made an arrest or rather merely a traffic stop to issue a citation. See People v. Meredith, 763 P.2d 562 (Colo.1988).

If—but only if, perhaps—the officer reasonably fears for his safety, he may make a limited *Terry* search for weapons. Moreover, under certain circumstances at least the right to so frisk extends beyond the person of the suspect and includes at least some parts of an automobile. In Michigan v. Long, 463 U.S. 1032, 103 S.Ct. 3469, 77 L.Ed.2d 1201 (1983), two Michigan sheriff's deputies, Howell and Lewis, were on routine patrol in a rural area. Shortly after midnight, they observed a car being driven erratically and at excessive speeds. When it swerved into a ditch, they stopped to investigate. Long, the only occupant of the vehicle, met the officers at the rear of the car which protruded from the ditch onto the road. Howell asked Long to produce his operator's license; Long did not respond until the request was repeated. When asked to produce the registration for the vehicle, Long again failed to respond. When this request was repeated, Long turned and began walking towards the front open door on the driver's side of the vehicle. The officers followed Long and observed a large hunting knife on the floorboard of the vehicle. They then stopped Long and conducted a patdown; no weapons were found. Shining a flashlight into the car, one deputy noticed "something" protruding from under the armrest on the front seat. He entered the car, knelt, and lifted the armrest. This revealed an open leather pouch on the seat; the officer then "determined" that the pouch contained marihuana. At issue before the

Supreme Court was the propriety of the officers' action that led to the discovery of the marihuana as a *Terry*-type weapons search conducted on less than probable cause.

Neither *Terry's* language nor its rationale, Justice O'Connor concluded for the Court, required that the right to search for weapons during a nonarrest detention be restricted to the person of the detained suspect. To the contrary, suspects confronted while in automobiles present special dangers to officers' safety because of their access to weapons that might be in the vehicles. Consequently, during a nonarrest detention of a suspect:

> the search of the passenger compartment of an automobile, limited to those areas in which a weapon might be placed or hidden, is permissible if the police officer possessed a reasonable belief based on "specific and articulable facts which, taken together with the rational inferences from those facts, reasonably warrant" the officers in believing that the suspect is dangerous and the suspect may gain immediate control of weapons. \* \* \* If, while conducting a legitimate *Terry* search of the interior of the automobile, the officer should \* \* \* discover contraband other than weapons, he clearly cannot be required to ignore the contraband, and the Fourth Amendment does not require its suppression in such circumstances.

463 U.S. at 1049–50, 103 S.Ct. at 3480–81, 77 L.Ed.2d at 1220. Turning to the facts before it, the Court held that the deputies entertained the requisite reasonable fear for their safety. The rural nature of the area and the late time of the stop were relevant. Further, the officers had reason to believe Long was intoxicated and their pre-search observations disclosed a knife in the car. Although Long was, in some sense, under the "control" of the officers, he might still have been able to obtain and use weapons located in the car. If released after the detention, he would in any event have had access to any such weapons. Even if methods other than the search were available to the officers to assure their safety, in contexts such as this in which quick decisions must be made, the Court has "not required that officers adopt alternative means to ensure their safety in order to avoid the intrusion involved in a *Terry* encounter." 463 U.S. at 1053, 103 S.Ct. at 3482, 77 L.Ed.2d at 1222. Once begun, the search was properly limited. It was restricted to "those areas to which Long would generally have immediate control, and that could contain a weapon." Examining the contents of the pouch was permissible; the trial court had determined that the pouch "could have contained a weapon." 463 U.S. at 1050–51, 103 S.Ct. at 3481, 77 L.Ed.2d at 1221.

Justice Brennan, joined by Justice Marshall, dissented. A search of a suspect's car and containers therein, he urged, constitutes a privacy intrusion more serious in degree and kind than a *Terry* frisk. It should not be regarded as "reasonable" absent probable cause. The majority's requirement of reasonable suspicion that a suspect is armed and dangerous, as applied, is of little significance, Justice Brennan continued. Possession of the knife observed by the officers was not unlawful and many items likely to be in a car might serve as weapons. Other factors stressed by the majority did tend to indicate that Long was intoxicated, he agreed.   But

> [a] drunk driver is indeed dangerous while driving, but not while stopped on the roadside by the police.   Even when an intoxicated person lawfully has in his car an object that could be used as a weapon, it requires imagination to conclude that he is presently dangerous.

463 U.S. at 1061–62, 103 S.Ct. at 3487, 77 L.Ed.2d at 1228 (Brennan, J., dissenting).   Justice Stevens also dissented, but on the basis that the state court holding under review rested upon an independent state ground and therefore the Supreme Court lacked jurisdiction.   463 U.S. at 1065–66, 103 S.Ct. at 3489, 77 L.Ed.2d at 1231 (Stevens, J., dissenting).

Some protective action by officers during at least a traffic stop does not require even the justification demanded by the Court for the search in *Long.*   In Pennsylvania v. Mimms, 434 U.S. 106, 98 S.Ct. 330, 54 L.Ed.2d 331 (1977) (per curiam), an officer stopped Mimms for driving an automobile with an expired license plate, intending to issue a traffic citation.   The officer asked Mimms to step out of the car and produce his owner's card and operator's license.   When Mimms complied, the officer noticed a large bulge under Mimms' sports jacket.   A frisk of Mimms resulted in discovery of a revolver.   The state court held that ordering Mimms out of his car was unreasonable because the officer lacked any reason to believe criminal activity was afoot or that the officer was in danger; the State conceded that the officer had no reason to fear Mimms particularly.   Reversing, the Supreme Court held the officers' action permissible.   Conversing with a driver while standing exposed to traffic, it emphasized, creates a risk of injury to the officer. On the other hand, given the fact that the motorist has already been stopped, the additional intrusion involved in requiring the motorist to get out of the car "can only be described as *de minimis.*"   434 U.S. at 111, 98 S.Ct. at 333, 54 L.Ed.2d at 337.   Once the officer observed the bulge in Mimms' jacket, the Court continued, *Terry* justified the officer's further action:

> The bulge in the jacket permitted the officer to conclude that Mimms was armed and thus posed a serious and present danger to the safety of the officer.   In these circumstances, any man of "reasonable caution" would likely have conducted the "pat-down."

434 U.S. at 112, 98 S.Ct. at 334, 54 L.Ed.2d at 338.

In New York v. Class, 475 U.S. 106, 106 S.Ct. 960, 89 L.Ed.2d 81 (1986), the Court indicated that a demand that the officer be permitted to see the "vehicle identification number" (the "VIN") "is within the scope of police authority pursuant to a traffic stop."   If the VIN is visible from outside the automobile, this does not permit any entry of the vehicle.   If it is not, however, the officers have considerable discretion as to how to determine the VIN.   In *Class,* Class had been stopped for two traffic violations and during the stop he "voluntarily" got out of the car.   An officer opened the door to determine if the VIN was on the door jamb and, when he found it was not, he reached into the car to move papers on the dashboard obscuring the portion of the dashboard on which the VIN is often located. While doing this, he observed a gun. Rejecting Class's argument that the officers were required to ask Class to return to his car and himself move the papers on the dash, the Court stressed the officers' right under *Mimms* to detain him briefly outside the car once he got out, the minimal intrusion involved in reaching into the car, and the officers' earlier observation of Class committing two traffic offenses. 475 U.S. at 111–19, 106 S.Ct. at 964–69, 89 L.Ed.2d at 88–94.

*License Check Stops.* In Delaware v. Prouse, 440 U.S. 648, 99 S.Ct. 1391, 59 L.Ed.2d 660 (1979), the Court considered the Fourth Amendment requirements for the stop of a motorist to determine whether he was in possession of a valid driver's license and registration for the vehicle being driven. Delaware argued that the need to assure public safety on the highways permitted the states to authorize officers to make such stops at random and at their discretion, i.e., without even the "reasonable suspicion" required for field stops. Rejecting this, the Court explained:

> We agree that the States have a vital interest in ensuring that only those qualified to do so are permitted to operate motor vehicles, that these vehicles are fit for safe operation, and hence that licensing, registration, and vehicle inspection requirements are being observed. * * *

> The question remains, however, whether in the service of these important ends the discretionary spot check is a sufficiently productive mechanism to justify the intrusion upon Fourth Amendment interests which such stops entail. On the record before us, that question must be answered in the negative. Given the alternative mechanisms available, both those in use and those that might be adopted, we are unconvinced that the incremental contribution to highway safety of the random spot check justifies the practice under the Fourth Amendment.

> The foremost method of enforcing traffic and vehicle safety regulations, it must be recalled, is acting upon observed violations. Vehicle stops for traffic violations occur countless times each day; and on these occasions, licenses and registration papers are subject to inspection and drivers without them will be ascertained. Furthermore, drivers without licenses are presumably the less safe drivers whose propensities may well exhibit themselves. Absent some empirical data to the contrary, it must be assumed that finding an unlicensed driver among those who commit traffic violations is a much more likely event than finding an unlicensed driver by choosing randomly from the entire universe of drivers. If this were not so, licensing of drivers would hardly be an effective means of promoting roadway safety. It seems common sense that the percentage of all drivers on the road who are driving without a license is very small and that the number of licensed drivers who will be stopped in order to find one unlicensed operator will be

large indeed.  The contribution to highway safety made by discretionary stops selected from among drivers generally will therefore be marginal at best.  Furthermore, and again absent something more than mere assertion to the contrary, we find it difficult to believe that the unlicensed driver would not be deterred by the possibility of being involved in a traffic violation or having some other experience calling for proof of his entitlement to drive but that he would be deterred by the possibility that he would be one of those chosen for a spot check.  In terms of actually discovering unlicensed drivers or deterring them from driving, the spot check does not appear sufficiently productive to qualify as a reasonable law-enforcement practice under the Fourth Amendment.

Much the same can be said about the safety aspects of automobiles as distinguished from drivers.  *  *  *

The marginal contribution to roadway safety possibly resulting from a system of spot checks cannot justify subjecting every occupant of every vehicle on the roads to a seizure—limited in magnitude compared to other intrusions but nonetheless constitutionally cognizable—at the unbridled discretion of law-enforcement officials.  *  *  * This kind of standardless and unconstrained discretion is the evil the Court has discerned when in previous cases it has insisted that the discretion of the official in the field be circumscribed, at least to some extent.  *  *  *

The "grave danger" of abuse of discretion does not disappear simply because the automobile is subject to state regulation resulting in numerous instances of police-citizen contact *  *  *.

An individual operating or travelling in an automobile does not lose all reasonable expectation of privacy simply because the automobile and its use are subject to government regulation.  Automobile travel is a basic, pervasive, and often necessary mode of transportation to and from one's home, workplace, and leisure activities.  Many people spend more hours each day travelling in cars than walking on the streets.  Undoubtedly, many find a greater sense of security and privacy in travelling in an automobile than they do in exposing themselves by pedestrian or other modes of travel.  Were the individual subject to unfettered governmental intrusion every time he entered an automobile, the security guaranteed by the Fourth Amendment would be seriously circumscribed.  *  *  *

Accordingly, we hold that except in those situations in which there is at least articulable and reasonable suspicion that a motorist is unlicensed or that an automobile is not registered, or that either the vehicle or an occupant is otherwise subject to seizure for violation of law, stopping an automobile and detaining the driver in order to check his driver's license and the registration of the automobile are unreasonable under the Fourth Amendment.  This holding does not preclude the State of Delaware or other States from developing methods for spot checks that involve less intrusion or that do not involve the unconstrained exercise of discretion.

Questioning of all oncoming traffic at roadblock-type stops is one possible alternative. We hold only that persons in automobiles on public roadways may not for that reason alone have their travel and privacy interfered with at the unbridled discretion of police officers.

440 U.S. at 658–63, 99 S.Ct. at 1398–1401, 59 L.Ed.2d at 670–74. Justices Blackmun and Powell concurred and specifically expressed their approval of the use of a roadblock to check for operator's licenses as well as other methods, such as stopping every 10th car to pass a given point, that are non-random but less intrusive than a roadblock. 440 U.S. at 664–65, 99 S.Ct. at 1401, 59 L.Ed.2d at 674. Justice Rehnquist dissented, noting that the majority's statement concerning roadblocks "elevates the adage 'misery loves company' to a novel role in Fourth Amendment jurisprudence." 440 U.S. at 664, 99 S.Ct. at 1402, 59 L.Ed.2d at 674.

\* \* \*

Detentions of these sorts might be distinguished from brief stops at checkpoints designed to permit law enforcement officers to make limited observations of vehicles and drivers and query the latter. The principal case in this subsection concerns checkpoints to determine whether motorists may be driving while intoxicated. Such checkpoints have stimulated a substantial amount of litigation. The Court's discussion as well as that of the dissent draws upon its prior decisions concerning border-related activity; these are presented in section E of Chapter 5.

## MICHIGAN v. SITZ

Supreme Court of the United States, 1990.
—— U.S. ——, 110 S.Ct. 2481, 110 L.Ed.2d 412.

CHIEF JUSTICE REHNQUIST delivered the opinion of the Court.

This case poses the question whether a State's use of highway sobriety checkpoints violates the Fourth and Fourteenth Amendments to the United States Constitution. We hold that it does not and therefore reverse the contrary holding of the Court of Appeals of Michigan.

Petitioners, the Michigan Department of State Police and its Director, established a sobriety checkpoint pilot program in early 1986. The Director appointed a Sobriety Checkpoint Advisory Committee comprising representatives of the State Police force, local police forces, state prosecutors, and the University of Michigan Transportation Research Institute. Pursuant to its charge, the Advisory Committee created guidelines setting forth procedures governing checkpoint operations, site selection, and publicity.

Under the guidelines, checkpoints would be set up at selected sites along state roads. All vehicles passing through a checkpoint would be stopped and their drivers briefly examined for signs of intoxication. In cases where a checkpoint officer detected signs of intoxication, the motorist would be directed to a location out of the traffic flow where an officer would check the motorist's driver's license and car registration and, if warranted, conduct further sobriety tests. Should the field tests and the officer's observations suggest that the driver was intoxicated, an arrest would be made. All other drivers would be permitted to resume their journey immediately.

The first—and to date the only—sobriety checkpoint operated under the program was conducted in Saginaw County with the assistance of the Saginaw County Sheriff's Department. During the hour-and-fifteen-minute duration of the checkpoint's operation, 126 vehicles passed through the checkpoint. The average delay for each vehicle was approximately 25 seconds. Two drivers were detained for field sobriety testing, and one of the two was arrested for driving under the influence of alcohol. A third driver who drove through without stopping was pulled over by an officer in an observation vehicle and arrested for driving under the influence.

On the day before the operation of the Saginaw County checkpoint, respondents filed a complaint in the Circuit Court of Wayne County seeking declaratory and injunctive relief from potential subjection to the checkpoints. * * * During pretrial proceedings, petitioners agreed to delay further implementation of the checkpoint program pending the outcome of this litigation.

After the trial, at which the court heard extensive testimony concerning, inter alia, the "effectiveness" of highway sobriety checkpoint programs, the court ruled that the Michigan program violated the Fourth Amendment and Art. 1, § 11, of the Michigan Constitution. On appeal, the Michigan Court of Appeals affirmed the holding that the program violated the Fourth Amendment and, for that reason, did not consider whether the program violated the Michigan Constitution. After the Michigan Supreme Court denied petitioners' application for leave to appeal, we granted certiorari.

To decide this case the [lower courts] performed a balancing test derived from our opinion in Brown v. Texas, 443 U.S. 47, 99 S.Ct. 2637, 61 L.Ed.2d 357 (1979) [which involved] "balancing the state's interest in preventing accidents caused by drunk drivers, the effectiveness of sobriety checkpoints in achieving that goal, and the level of intrusion on an individual's privacy caused by the checkpoints." * * *

As characterized by the Court of Appeals, the trial court's findings with respect to the balancing factors were that the State has "a grave and legitimate" interest in curbing drunken driving; that sobriety checkpoint programs are generally "ineffective" and, therefore, do not significantly further that interest; and that the checkpoints' "subjective intrusion" on individual liberties is substantial. According to the court, the record disclosed no basis for disturbing the trial court's findings, which were made within the context of an analytical framework prescribed by this Court for determining the constitutionality of seizures less intrusive than traditional arrests. * * *

[United States v.] Martinez–Fuerte, [428 U.S. 543, 96 S.Ct. 3074, 49 L.Ed.2d 1116 (1976)], which utilized a balancing analysis in approving highway checkpoints for detecting illegal aliens, and Brown v. Texas, supra, are the relevant authorities here.

Petitioners concede, correctly in our view, that a Fourth Amendment "seizure" occurs when a vehicle is stopped at a checkpoint. The question thus becomes whether such seizures are "reasonable" under the Fourth Amendment.

It is important to recognize what our inquiry is NOT about. No allegations are before us of unreasonable treatment of any person after an actual detention at a particular checkpoint. See *Martinez–Fuerte,* 428 U.S., at 559, 96 S.Ct. at 3083 ("claim that a particular exercise of discretion in locating or operating a checkpoint is unreasonable is subject to post-stop judicial review"). As pursued in the lower courts, the instant action challenges only the use of sobriety checkpoints generally. We address only the initial stop of each motorist passing through a checkpoint and the associated preliminary questioning and observation by checkpoint officers. Detention of particular motorists for more extensive field sobriety testing may require satisfaction of an individualized suspicion standard. Id., at 567, 96 S.Ct. at 3087.

No one can seriously dispute the magnitude of the drunken driving problem or the States' interest in eradicating it. \* \* \*

Conversely, the weight bearing on the other scale—the measure of the intrusion on motorists stopped briefly at sobriety checkpoints—is slight. We reached a similar conclusion as to the intrusion on motorists subjected to a brief stop at a highway checkpoint for detecting illegal aliens. See *Martinez–Fuerte,* supra, at 558, 96 S.Ct. at 3083. We see virtually no difference between the levels of intrusion on law-abiding motorists from the brief stops necessary to the effectuation of these two types of checkpoints, which to the average motorist would seem identical save for the nature of the questions the checkpoint officers might ask. The trial court and the Court of Appeals, thus, accurately gauged the "objective" intrusion, measured by the duration of the seizure and the intensity of the investigation, as minimal.

With respect to what it perceived to be the "subjective" intrusion on motorists, however, the Court of Appeals found such intrusion substantial. The court first affirmed the trial court's finding that the guidelines governing checkpoint operation minimize the discretion of the officers on the scene. But the court also agreed with the trial court's conclusion that the checkpoints have the potential to generate fear and surprise in motorists. This was so because the record failed to demonstrate that approaching motorists would be aware of their option to make U-turns or turnoffs to avoid the checkpoints. On that basis, the court deemed the subjective intrusion from the checkpoints unreasonable.

We believe the Michigan courts misread our cases concerning the degree of "subjective intrusion" and the potential for generating fear and surprise. The "fear and surprise" to be considered are not the natural fear of one who has been drinking over the prospect of being stopped at a sobriety checkpoint but, rather, the fear and surprise engendered in law abiding motorists by the nature of the stop. \* \* \* Here, checkpoints are selected pursuant to the guidelines, and uniformed police officers stop every approaching vehicle. The intrusion resulting from the brief stop at the sobriety checkpoint is for constitutional purposes indistinguishable from the checkpoint stops we upheld in *Martinez–Fuerte.*

The Court of Appeals went on to consider as part of the balancing analysis the "effectiveness" of the proposed checkpoint program. Based on extensive testimony in the trial record, the court concluded that the checkpoint program failed the "effectiveness" part of the test, and that this failure materially discounted petitioners' strong interest in implementing the program. We think the Court of Appeals was wrong on this point as well.

The actual language from Brown v. Texas, upon which the Michigan courts based their evaluation of "effectiveness," describes the balancing factor as "the degree to which the seizure advances the public interest." 443 U.S., at 51, 99 S.Ct. at 2640. This passage from *Brown* was not meant to transfer from politically accountable officials to the courts the decision as to which among reasonable alternative law enforcement techniques should be employed to deal with a serious public danger. Experts in police science might disagree over which of several methods of apprehending drunken drivers is preferable as an ideal. But for purposes of Fourth Amendment analysis, the choice among such reasonable alternatives remains with the governmental officials who have a unique understanding of, and a responsibility for, limited public resources, including a finite number of police officers.

\*   \*   \*

In Delaware v. Prouse, [440 U.S. 648, 99 S.Ct. 1391, 59 L.Ed.2d 660 (1979)], we disapproved random stops made by Delaware Highway Patrol officers in an effort to apprehend unlicensed drivers and unsafe vehicles. We observed that NO empirical evidence indicated that such stops would be an effective means of promoting roadway safety and said that "[i]t seems common sense that the percentage of all drivers on the road who are driving without a license is very small and that the number of licensed drivers who will be stopped in order to find one unlicensed operator will be large indeed." 440 U.S., at 659–660, 99 S.Ct. at 1399. We observed that the random stops involved the "kind of standardless and unconstrained discretion [which] is the evil the Court has discerned when in previous cases it has insisted that the discretion of the official in the field be circumscribed, at least to some extent." Id., at 661, 99 S.Ct. at 1400. We went on to state that our holding did not "cast doubt on the permissibility of roadside truck weigh-stations and inspection checkpoints, at which some vehicles may be subject to further detention for safety and regulatory inspection than are others." Id., at 663, n. 26, 99 S.Ct. at 1401, n. 26.

Unlike *Prouse,* this case involves neither a complete absence of empirical data nor a challenge to random highway stops. During the operation of the Saginaw County checkpoint, the detention of each of the 126 vehicles that entered the checkpoint resulted in the arrest of two drunken drivers. Stated as a percentage, approximately 1.5 percent of the drivers passing through the checkpoint were arrested for alcohol impairment. In addition, an expert witness testified at the trial that experience in other States demonstrated that, on the whole, sobriety checkpoints resulted in drunken driving arrests of around 1 percent of all motorists stopped. By way of comparison, the record from one of the consolidated cases in *Martinez–Fuerte,* showed that in the associated checkpoint, illegal aliens were found in only 0.12 percent of the vehicles passing through the checkpoint. The ratio of illegal aliens detected to vehicles stopped (considering that on occasion two or more illegal aliens were found in a single vehicle) was approximately 0.5 percent. We concluded that this "record . . . provides a rather complete picture of the effectiveness of the San Clemente checkpoint", and we sustained its constitutionality. We see no justification for a different conclusion here.

In sum, the balance of the State's interest in preventing drunken driving, the extent to which this system can reasonably be said to advance that interest, and the degree of intrusion upon individual motorists who are briefly stopped, weighs in favor of the state program. We therefore hold that it is consistent with the Fourth Amendment. The judgment of the Michigan Court of Appeals is accordingly reversed, and the cause is remanded for further proceedings not inconsistent with this opinion.

Reversed.

[The opinions of Justice Blackmun, concurring in the judgment, and of Justice Brennan, joined by Justice Marshall, dissenting, are omitted.]

JUSTICE STEVENS, with whom JUSTICE BRENNAN and JUSTICE MAR-SHALL join as to Parts I and II, dissenting.

A sobriety checkpoint is usually operated at night at an unannounced location. Surprise is crucial to its method. The test operation conducted by the Michigan State Police and the Saginaw County Sheriff's Department began shortly after midnight and lasted until about 1 a.m. During that period, the 19 officers participating in the operation made two arrests and stopped and questioned 125 other unsuspecting and innocent drivers. It is, of course, not known how many arrests would have been made during that period if those officers had been engaged in normal patrol activities. However, the findings of the trial court, based on an extensive record and affirmed by the Michigan Court of Appeals, indicate that the net effect of sobriety checkpoints on traffic safety is infinitesimal and possibly negative.

Indeed, the record in this case makes clear that a decision holding these suspicionless seizures unconstitutional would not impede the law enforcement community's remarkable progress in reducing the death toll on our highways. Because the Michigan program was patterned after an older program in Maryland, the trial judge gave special attention to that State's experience. Over a period of several years, Maryland operated 125 checkpoints; of the 41,000 motorists passing through those checkpoints, only 143 persons (0.3%) were arrested. The number of man-hours devoted to these operations is not in the record, but it seems inconceivable that a higher arrest rate could not have been achieved by more conventional means. Yet, even if the 143 checkpoint arrests were assumed to involve a net increase in the number of drunk driving arrests per year, the figure would still be insignificant by comparison to the 71,000 such arrests made by Michigan State Police without checkpoints in 1984 alone.

Any relationship between sobriety checkpoints and an actual reduction in highway fatalities is even less substantial than the minimal impact on arrest rates. As the Michigan Court of Appeals pointed out, "Maryland had conducted a study comparing traffic statistics between a county using checkpoints and a control county. The results of the study showed that alcohol-related accidents in the checkpoint county decreased by ten percent, whereas the control county saw an eleven percent decrease; and while fatal accidents in the control county fell from sixteen to three, fatal accidents in the checkpoint county actually doubled from the prior year."

In light of these considerations, it seems evident that the Court today misapplies the balancing test announced in Brown v. Texas, 443 U.S. 47, 50–51, 99 S.Ct. 2637, 2640, 61 L.Ed.2d 357 (1979). The Court overvalues the law enforcement interest in using sobriety checkpoints, undervalues the citizen's interest in freedom from random, unannounced investigatory seizures, and mistakenly assumes that there is "virtually no difference" between a routine stop at a permanent, fixed checkpoint and a surprise stop at a sobriety checkpoint. I believe this case is controlled by our several precedents condemning suspicionless random stops of motorists for investigatory purposes. Delaware v. Prouse, 440 U.S. 648, 99 S.Ct. 1391, 59 L.Ed.2d 660 (1979); United States v. Brignoni–Ponce, 422 U.S. 873, 95 S.Ct. 2574, 45 L.Ed.2d 607 (1975); United States v. Ortiz, 422 U.S. 891, 95 S.Ct. 2585, 45 L.Ed.2d 623 (1975); Almeida–Sanchez v. United States, 413 U.S. 266, 93 S.Ct. 2535, 37 L.Ed.2d 596 (1973).

## I

There is a critical difference between a seizure that is preceded by fair notice and one that is effected by surprise. That is one reason why a border search, or indeed any search at a permanent and fixed checkpoint, is much less intrusive than a random stop. A motorist with advance notice of the location of a permanent checkpoint has an opportunity to avoid the search entirely, or at least to prepare for, and limit, the intrusion on her privacy.

No such opportunity is available in the case of a random stop or a temporary checkpoint, which both depend for their effectiveness on the element of surprise. A driver who discovers an unexpected checkpoint on a familiar local road will be startled and distressed. She may infer, correctly, that the checkpoint is not simply "business as usual," and may likewise infer, again correctly, that the police have made a discretionary decision to focus their law enforcement efforts upon her and others who pass the chosen point.

This element of surprise is the most obvious distinction between the sobriety checkpoints permitted by today's majority and the interior border checkpoints approved by this Court in *Martinez–Fuerte*. The distinction casts immediate doubt upon the majority's argument, for *Martinez–Fuerte* is the only case in which we have upheld suspicionless seizures of motorists. But the difference between notice and surprise is only one of the important reasons for distinguishing between permanent and mobile checkpoints. With respect to the former, there is no room for discretion in either the timing or the location of the stop—it is a permanent part of the landscape. In the latter case, however, although the checkpoint is most frequently employed during the hours of darkness on weekends (because that is when drivers with alcohol in their blood are most apt to be found on the road), the police have extremely broad discretion in determining the exact timing and placement of the roadblock.

There is also a significant difference between the kind of discretion that the officer exercises after the stop is made. A check for a driver's license, or for identification papers at an immigration checkpoint, is far more easily standardized than is a search for evidence of intoxication. A Michigan officer who questions a motorist at a sobriety checkpoint has virtually unlimited discretion to detain the driver on the basis of the slightest suspicion. A ruddy complexion, an unbuttoned shirt, bloodshot eyes or a speech impediment may suffice to prolong the detention. Any driver who had just consumed a glass of beer, or even a sip of wine, would almost certainly have the burden of demonstrating to the officer that her driving ability was not impaired.

Finally, it is significant that many of the stops at permanent checkpoints occur during daylight hours, whereas the sobriety checkpoints are almost invariably operated at night. A seizure followed by interrogation and even a cursory search at night is surely more offensive than a daytime stop that is almost as routine as going through a toll gate. Thus we thought it important to point out that the random stops at issue in *Ortiz* frequently occurred at night.

These fears are not, as the Court would have it, solely the lot of the guilty. To be law abiding is not necessarily to be spotless, and even the most virtuous can be unlucky. Unwanted attention from the local police need not be less discomforting simply because one's secrets are not the stuff of criminal prosecutions. Moreover, those who have found—by reason of prejudice or misfortune—that encounters with the police may become adversarial or unpleasant without good cause will have grounds for worrying at any stop designed to elicit signs of suspicious behavior. Being stopped by the police is distressing even when it should not be terrifying, and what begins mildly may by happenstance turn severe.

For all these reasons, I do not believe that this case is analogous to *Martinez–Fuerte*. In my opinion, the sobriety checkpoints are instead similar to—and in some respects more intrusive than—the random investigative stops that the Court held unconstitutional in *Brignoni–Ponce* and *Prouse*. *   *   *

## II

The Court, unable to draw any persuasive analogy to *Martinez–Fuerte,* rests its decision today on application of a more general balancing test taken from Brown v. Texas, 443 U.S. 47, 99 S.Ct. 2637, 61 L.Ed. 2d 357 (1979).   *   *   *

The gravity of the public concern with highway safety that is implicated by this case is, of course, undisputed.   Yet, that same grave concern was implicated in Delaware v. Prouse.   Moreover, I do not understand the Court to have placed any lesser value on the importance of the drug problem implicated in Texas v. Brown, or on the need to control the illegal border crossings that were at stake in *Almeida–Sanchez* and its progeny.   A different result in this case must be justified by the other two factors in the *Brown* formulation.

As I have already explained, I believe the Court is quite wrong in blithely asserting that a sobriety checkpoint is no more intrusive than a permanent checkpoint.   In my opinion, unannounced investigatory seizures are, particularly when they take place at night, the hallmark of regimes far different from ours; the surprise intrusion upon individual liberty is not minimal.   On that issue, my difference with the Court may amount to nothing less than a difference in our respective evaluations of the importance of individual liberty, a serious albeit inevitable source of constitutional disagreement.   On the degree to which the sobriety checkpoint seizures advance the public interest, however, the Court's position is wholly indefensible.

The Court's analysis of this issue resembles a business decision that measures profits by counting gross receipts and ignoring expenses.   The evidence in this case indicates that sobriety checkpoints result in the arrest of a fraction of one percent of the drivers who are stopped, but there is absolutely no evidence that this figure represents an increase over the number of arrests that would have been made by using the same law enforcement resources in conventional patrols.   Thus, although the GROSS number of arrests is more than zero, there is a complete failure of proof on the question whether the wholesale seizures have produced any NET advance in the public interest in arresting intoxicated drivers.

*   *   *

## III

The most disturbing aspect of the Court's decision today is that it appears to give no weight to the citizen's interest in freedom from suspicionless unannounced investigatory seizures.   Perhaps this *   *   * can be explained by the Court's obvious concern about the slaughter on our highways, and a resultant tolerance for policies designed to alleviate the problem by "setting an example" of a few motorists.   This possibility prompts two observations.

First, my objections to random seizures or temporary checkpoints do not apply to a host of other investigatory procedures that do not depend upon surprise and are unquestionably permissible.   These procedures have been used to address other threats to human life no less pressing than the threat posed by drunken drivers. It is, for example, common practice to require every prospective airline passenger, or every visitor to a public building, to pass through a metal detector that will reveal the presence of a firearm or an explosive. Permanent, nondiscretionary checkpoints could be used to control serious dangers at other publicly operated facilities. Because concealed weapons obviously represent one such substantial threat to public safety, I would suppose that all subway passengers could be required to pass through metal detectors, so long as the detectors were permanent and every passenger was subjected to the same search. Likewise, I would suppose that a State could condition access to its toll roads upon not only paying the toll but also taking a uniformly administered breathalizer test. That requirement might well keep all drunken drivers off the highways that serve the fastest and most dangerous traffic. This procedure would not be subject to the constitutional objections that control this case: the checkpoints would be permanently fixed, the stopping procedure would apply to all users of the toll road in precisely the same way, and police officers would not be free to make arbitrary choices about which neighborhoods should be targeted or about which individuals should be more thoroughly searched. * * *

Second, sobriety checkpoints are elaborate, and disquieting, publicity stunts. The possibility that anybody, no matter how innocent, may be stopped for police inspection is nothing if not attention-getting. The shock value of the checkpoint program may be its most effective feature * * *.

This is a case that is driven by nothing more than symbolic state action—an insufficient justification for an otherwise unreasonable program of random seizures. Unfortunately, the Court is transfixed by the wrong symbol—the illusory prospect of punishing countless intoxicated motorists—when it should keep its eyes on the road plainly marked by the Constitution.

I respectfully dissent.

## D. "PRETEXT" DETENTIONS AND THEIR VALIDITY

American courts disagree on whether law enforcement activity that is objectively within legal limits can be successfully challenged on the basis that the motive of the officers rendered it a "pretext" and hence invalid. Arrests and other detentions are probably attacked on this basis more frequently than other types of law enforcement activity. As the principal case below demonstrates, the Supreme Court has not addressed the extent to which the Fourth Amendment provides a basis for this sort of attack.

There is considerable inconsistency in the terminology used, but this may simply reflect underlying conceptual confusion. Lower courts differ on precisely what constitutes a "pretext arrest," for example, as well as on whether a criminal defendant gains any advantage by convincing a court that his arrest was such a "pretext arrest." Moreover, there is confusion regarding the need to, or wisdom of, inquiring whether an arrest was made "on" various possible grounds and—to the extent such inquiries are undertaken—how to determine whether a particular arrest was made "on" a particular ground.

In connection with the pretext issue, consider the Supreme Court's willingness in other contexts to tie the validity of law enforcement action to the officers' subjective state of mind. Reconsider, for example, the argument that an investigatory stop is invalid if the officer intended to detain the suspect longer than Fourth Amendment law permits; see the discussion on pages 243–44, supra. Do the Supreme Court's holdings on such issues have implications for the pretext arrest issue?

## STATE v. BLAIR

Supreme Court of Missouri, En Banc, 1985.
691 S.W.2d 259.

HIGGINS, JUDGE.

Zola Blair, charged with murder, moved to suppress certain evidence, including her palm prints and statements made to the police, and to quash an arrest warrant. The trial court, after evidentiary hearing, sustained her motion. The State of Missouri filed an interlocutory appeal * * *. The question is whether, in the circumstances of this case, defendant's initial arrest was pretextual and rendered her subsequent detention unlawful and evidence obtained incident thereto inadmissible. * * *

Police discovered a murder on November 24, 1981; the only evidence found was a palm print. On January 22, 1982, an informer implicated Zola Blair and her family in the murder. Comparison of the palm prints of other family members with the print found at the scene of the crime failed to produce a match; defendant's print was not in the police file. On January 23, Detective Lauffer requested that defendant be picked up for homicide but did not ask for a homicide arrest or search warrant because he believed there was not enough evidence to support a warrant. The police then learned that she was the subject of an outstanding city warrant for a traffic violation. On February 5, 1982, police arrested defendant at her home, took her to the homicide unit, booked her on a charge of homicide, and took her palm and finger prints. Later that day, she was questioned about the homicide. After the interrogation, the officer requested that her palm print be compared with that taken from the crime scene. She was detained for homicide overnight and released at 10:45 a.m. the next day. Fourteen minutes later she was booked on the municipal court parking warrant. At 12:55 p.m., she posted bond on the traffic violation and was released.

On February 8, 1982, upon learning that defendant's print matched the print found at the scene of the crime, police sought and received an arrest warrant on the homicide. She was arrested at 5:30 p.m. on that day and booked shortly thereafter. During an interrogation that began at 6:15 p.m., officers confronted her with evidence of the matching prints and obtained inculpatory statements.

For reversal the State contends that once a legal basis for an arrest exists—in this case the outstanding traffic warrant—the subjective motives of the police become irrelevant; therefore, defendant was in lawful custody pursuant to the parking violation warrant when fingerprinted, and the prints obtained then, as well as the statements that followed, are admissible. Respondent argues that the trial court correctly found that she was not in lawful custody because the arrest was but a pretext for a search; and that the palm print and statements obtained on February 5, 1982, are inadmissible as products of an illegal detention, and the February 8th statements are also inadmissible as the "fruit" of the illegally seized palm print. * * *

In this case it is undisputed that the police lacked probable cause to arrest defendant on the homicide charge; to establish the legality of the warrantless search and seizure here, then, the State must show that one of the exceptions to the warrant requirement applies.

Appellant seeks to bring the challenged fingerprinting within the search incident to a lawful arrest exception to the warrant requirement. A valid custodial arrest of a suspect authorizes, without more, a search incident to the arrest. It is also true that a suspect in lawful custody is subject to fingerprinting as part of routine identification procedure. Prerequisites to application of the foregoing are a lawful arrest, and lawful custody.

The evidence conflicts on whether the officers arrested defendant on the outstanding parking violation warrant. Officer Stewart testified that he "arrested her for an outstanding city warrant and also asked her to accompany (them) with regards to a pickup order issued by the crimes against persons unit." He also testified that he went to her residence to take her into custody on the homicide pickup order and he did not have an arrest warrant. He advised defendant of her constitutional rights in compliance with *Miranda* although such warnings are not given on arrests for parking violations that do not involve criminal activity. Officer Stewart's partner, Officer Thomas, filed the report of the arrest under the homicide charge number as "investigation arrest— criminal homicide"; and the officers followed the procedure used for arresting and booking an individual on a homicide charge rather than that used for a traffic violation. Defendant was taken to the homicide unit at the police department's downtown station and booked there on a state charge for homicide, not for the parking violation at the district station on 63rd street. Under the normal procedure for booking a person on a municipal court parking violation, the police obtain one fingerprint of the person and allow the person to remain at the district station for four hours in order to post bond. In this case, the suspect was taken to the homicide unit where a complete set of defendant's palm and finger prints was taken, she underwent interrogation regarding the homicide, and was detained overnight. It was after all this that the police booked her on the parking violation.

The conflicts thus raised by the evidence were for the trial court to resolve. The trial court resolved them in favor of defendant, and this

Court defers to the trial court's determination because it is supported in the evidence.  *  *  *

Assuming an arrest for the parking violation, the arrest, in the circumstances of this case, was at best a pretext employed to gather evidence on an unrelated homicide, and this Court cannot say, on this record, that the trial court erred in suppressing the evidence so seized. A well established limitation on the search incident to a valid arrest exception is the rule that an arrest may not be used as a pretext to search for evidence.  *  *  *

The rule rendering evidence procured by means of a pretextual arrest inadmissible is oft stated. None of the cases cited by the parties or found by the Court's research, however, involves precisely the circumstances of the instant case.  *  *  * The State  *  *  * cites cases from other jurisdictions for the proposition that where the police have a valid reason to arrest for a traffic violation and conduct a search reasonably related to the arrest, evidence seized is admissible regardless of the motives of the arresting officer. Each of the cases cited is readily distinguishable as presenting a situation where the defendant commits an offense in the presence of the officers, who then immediately arrest and search incident thereto. Underlying these cases is appreciation for the far reaching consequences of allowing the common offense of a traffic violation to serve as justification for an otherwise unconstitutional search.

The record in this case supports the ruling of the trial court. The execution of the parking violation warrant was but a subterfuge or pretext, not pursued, to gather evidence of the unrelated crime of homicide. The palm and finger prints and statements obtained on February 5, 1982, were properly suppressed because they resulted from an unlawful arrest and search. Because the illegally seized evidence provided the sole basis for the arrest warrant for homicide of February 8, 1982, and led directly to respondent's statements on that day, the warrant and statement are also inadmissible as "fruits of the poisonous tree." The contention that the challenged evidence falls within the ultimate or inevitable discovery exception to the exclusionary rule is without merit.  *  *  * Nix v. Williams, 467 U.S. 431, 104 S.Ct. 2501, 81 L.Ed.2d 377 (1984), requires  *  *  * that the prosecution establish "by a preponderance of the evidence that the information ultimately or inevitably would have been discovered by lawful means. . . ." The State has not done so. Nor does the good faith exception to the fourth amendment exclusionary rule articulated in the recent cases of United States v. Leon, 468 U.S. 897, 104 S.Ct. 3405, 82 L.Ed.2d 677 (1984), and Massachusetts v. Sheppard, 468 U.S. 981, 104 S.Ct. 3424, 82 L.Ed.2d 737 (1984), serve to salvage the pretextual "seizure" of evidence in this case. Indeed, suppression of the evidence on this record is consistent with the Supreme Court's focus on deterrence in applying the exclusionary rule. The State asks the Court to ignore the motives of the arresting officers because of the existence of the parking warrant, yet if the recent pronouncements of the United States Supreme Court have any applicability to the instant appeal, it is in their acknowledgment that courts can and will consider the question of good faith, or lack thereof, on the part of the police.

The order of the trial court sustaining the motion to suppress is affirmed, and the case is remanded for further proceedings.

BILLINGS, DONNELLY and WELLIVER, JJ., concur.

BLACKMAR, J., dissents in separate opinion filed.

RENDLEN, C.J., and GUNN, J., dissent and concur in separate dissenting opinion of BLACKMAR, J.

BLACKMAR, JUDGE, dissenting.

\* \* \*

I submit that the police had not only the right but even the positive duty to obtain the defendant's fingerprints by any lawful means. The defendant could be lawfully arrested on the traffic warrant, and, having been arrested, was subject to search just as any other arrestee would be. If the search disclosed evidence of other crimes, this evidence could be used for prosecution. The search could include the taking of fingerprints for routine identification purposes. Because of the outstanding traffic warrant the defendant had no privilege of withholding her fingerprints.

The defendant's excellent briefs set forth her essential contention in the following language:

> It is an abuse of police power and authority to lawfully arrest an individual for a parking warrant so that, as an incident to that arrest, they may search for and seize evidence on an exploratory basis while investigating a totally unrelated offense . . .

This proposition is unsound, and is supported by no controlling authority. If the defendant is lawfully arrested the police have the right to exercise the power incident to lawful arrest. The defendant has no standing to complain simply because she was specially selected from among those subject to arrest on traffic warrants. Nor may she complain that her palm print was taken, while only one fingerprint is customarily taken from other traffic arrestees. The extent of the fingerprint identification taken is a matter for police discretion.

\* \* \*

The cases cited by the majority for the proposition that an arrest may not be used as a pretext for a search are distinguishable, and not helpful in solving the problem before us. \* \* \*

The common theme of the pretext cases is that the police arrested people without reason. The police had a valid pre-existing warrant for Zola Blair's arrest. Any procedural irregularities which occurred afterward should not invalidate the arrest. \* \* \*

The order of suppression should be reversed and the case remanded for further proceedings.

## EDITORS' NOTE: FURTHER PROCEEDINGS
## IN MISSOURI v. BLAIR

The prosecution sought review of the Missouri Supreme Court's decision by the United States Supreme Court. It urged that the case presented the following question:

> Does the fact that a police department has an ulterior motive in making an arrest on a valid municipal warrant make the arrest pretexual so as to invalidate the arrest, the fingerprinting of the arrestee and a confession to a felony subsequently made by the arrestee-suspect as a matter of law?

Missour v. Blair, Petition for Writ of Certiorari, at I (No. 85–303). The Supreme Court granted review. Missouri v. Blair, 474 U.S. 1049, 106 S.Ct. 784, 88 L.Ed.2d 762 (1986).

At oral argument, the Justices expressed concern regarding how to classify the situation as well as the criterion to determine the reasonableness of the law enforcement action. Counsel for the petitioner, Albert A. Riederer, was questioned, for example, on what needed to be shown for law enforcement officers to rely upon a traffic warrant:

> QUESTION: Is it enough for the arresting officers to merely know of the warrant, or must they rely on it in making the arrest?

Pressed, Mr. Riederer took the position that it would be enough if they knew about it. He was asked whether the State's position would be the same if the arresting officers in *Blair* had not learned of the traffic warrant until after Blair had been taken into custody. He responded, "Well, I don't know that our position would be the same. . . ." Missouri v. Blair, supra, Transcript of Oral Argument, page 8.

One justice quizzed Mr. Riederer regarding the significance of the booking:

> QUESTION: What does it mean, booked for homicide? Does that mean that she's charged with it?
>
> MR. RIEDERER: It does not mean that she's charged with it. I think the booking is simply an internal bookkeeping procedure for the police department * * *. I think it indicates that the officers * * * were in fact not only interested in her because of the parking warrant, they were interested in talking to her about this homicide.

Id. at 18.

Counsel for Blair, Jospeh Locascio, was pressed by one member of the Court as to whether the Missouri Supreme Court had concluded that there had been no arrest whatsoever on the parking ticket or, alternatively, that there was an arrest on the parking ticket but that the police "were really doing it * * * to get her on the homicide." Id. at 30–31. Mr. Locascio suggested that the Missouri court had concluded first and primarily that the arrest was for homicide and not the parking offense and was invalid because probable cause was lacking. It had secondarily, and apparently alternatively, concluded, he argued, that *if* there was an arrest on the parking warrant it was invalid as a pretext arrest.  Id. at 32.  He was queried at length concerning the criterion for catagorizing the arrest:

> QUESTION: How do you decide whether a person was arrested [, quote,] on, close quote, a particular warrant?  * * * What's the legal test?  * * *

Id. at 36.  He did not offer a specific response.

Turning to the pretext argument, one Justice pressed Mr. Locascio regarding the ramifications of his proposed construction of the Fourth Amendment:

> QUESTION:  * * * We'd endlessly be inquiring into what the real motive of the [police] officer was.  For example, the Coast Guard is allowed to board ships to examine the ship's papers. Now, do we have to entertain an argument in every case where they board the ship that their real reason for going on was not to look at the papers, but rather to see if there was any marijuana on board, if there was * * * a drug party going on, or something like that?

> MR. LOCASCIO: I think under your example that you do have to look at the purpose.  But [this] doesn't necessarily mean that you would have to look at the subjective intent.

> You could just look at what the objective factors tell you to have been the purpose of * * * the boarding of the ship.  * * *

> QUESTION: I don't know what you mean, the objective factor[s].  * * *

> MR. LOCASCIO:  * * * [N]ot even getting into subjective intent [in the case before the Court], the objective facts alone tell us that [the officers'] primary motive was to investigate homicide.

> * * *

> So you don't * * * have to get into delving [into subjective intent].  [I]f you go into the subjective minds of the police, you're really getting into an area that may be a waste of judicial time.

> Because it's very difficult to determine what subjectively is going on in the mind of the police.  However, in this case, you don't even have to do that.  Because if you just consider the objective facts involved, the objective facts will tell you * * * that the primary purpose of picking her up * * * was for homicide.

Id. at 47–50.

When Mr. Riederer resumed his argument, he was asked what the State had "to support the proposition that the arrest was at least facially on the parking ticket."  He emphasized: (a) Officer Stewart testified several times that he had arrested Blair on the outstanding parking warrant; (b) the booking record referred to the warrant "as being a reason for her detention;" and (c) Officer Thomas' police report, written the day of the arrest, referred to the parking warrant by number.  Id. at 59–60.  He acknowledged that the Supreme Court of Missouri "apparently did not agree" that the arrest was on the parking warrant.  In reaction, one member of the Court commented:

QUESTION: So that even if we agree with you on the pretextual point, the most we could do is remand to the Supreme Court of Missouri to have them make clear how they come out on the other part.

Or do you want us to make the judgment?

Mr. Riederer indicated he thought the United States Supreme Court should make the judgment. Id. at 59–60.

The Court, after oral argument, dismissed the writ of certiorari as improvidently granted. 480 U.S. 698, 107 S.Ct. 1596, 94 L.Ed.2d 678 (1987).

## NOTE

The pretext question continues to trouble the courts. In United States v. Causey, 818 F.2d 354 (5th Cir.1987), 834 F.2d 1179 (en banc) (5th Cir.1987), an anonymous tipster identified Causey as the robber of a bank. Believing they lacked probable cause, police discovered an arrest warrant for nonappearance on a petty theft charge issued several years earlier. They executed it and while Causey was in custody they interrogated him and persuaded him to confess to the robbery. One officer testified that the only reason for executing the warrant was to take Causey "downtown" for investigation of the robbery. A panel of the Fifth Circuit held that the officers' motive rendered the arrest pretextual and invalid and this tainted the confession. By a vote of 8–6, the en banc court reversed. The majority overruled a line of cases appearing to hold that police activity could be attacked on the basis of motive:

Again and again * * * the [Supreme] Court has told us that where police officers are objectively doing what they are legally authorized to do—as in arresting Causey pursuant to the valid warrant outstanding against him and interrogating him without coercion after reading him repeated *Miranda* warnings—the results of their investigations are not to be called in question on the basis of any subjective intent with which they acted.

834 F.2d at 1184. The dissented responded:

An arrest is arbitrary, hence unconstitutional, if it is made in accordance with a potentially discriminatory plan, even when the same action, undertaken in accordance with neutral principles, would be permissible. * * * [I]t would be reasonable, not abitrary, hence unobjectionable, if a police department decided to work through its backlog of old warrants by executing them according to some nondiscriminatory scheme, even if, after such a warrant was executed, they interrogated the arrested person about other matters, but it is impermissible for a police department to decide which warrants to execute by looking for people they want to question but do no have sufficient grounds to arrest.

Id. at 1188 (Rubin, J., dissenting).

# Chapter 5

# "WARRANTLESS" SEARCHES

*Analysis*

---

If law enforcement or other official conduct constitutes a "search," the material in Chapters 2 and 3 made clear that—as a general rule—certain "benchmark" Fourth Amendment requirements apply. Information amounting to "probable cause" to believe that the intrusion is justified must be present. In addition, a judicial determination that probable cause exists must be obtained before the intrusion through the search warrant process.

But the Fourth Amendment requirement of "reasonableness" has significant flexibility and it is clear that in some situations either or both of these benchmark requirements of probable cause and a search warrant may be modified or abandoned. This has been explored to some extent in Chapter 4, which considered officers' right to conduct certain searches as incidents to arrests or because of nonarrest police-citizen contacts. Other situations in which the Fourth Amendment's demands may deviate from the benchmark requirements are the subject of the present chapter.

Most of these situations involve law enforcement activity designed to determine whether a criminal offense has been committed and, if so, the identity of the offender. But this is not always the case. The so-called "administrative" searches considered in Section B, for example, may be conducted by inspectors who are not law enforcement officers and who may be seeking to end violation of legal but noncriminal requirements by means other than criminal prosecution of those found in noncompliance with the law's demands. Whether a noncriminal objective justifies relaxation of Fourth Amendment requirements, of course, is among the issues raised by such inspections.

Each situation discussed in this Chapter presents two major categories of issues. The first concerns the requirement of a search warrant. In many situations, the issue is whether this requirement should be abandoned entirely and so-called "warrantless" searches regarded as reasonable. In other situations, however, the question may be whether the warrant requirement should be retained but relaxed somewhat in order to accommodate the special needs presented by the situation. And in others, the issue is whether Fourth Amendment reasonableness should be retained and modified so as to impose *more* stringent requirements than are involved in the traditional warrant process considered in Chapter 3.

Although these situations are often discussed as if the only question is whether—and when—"warrantless" searches are reasonable, many also present issues in a second category. These concern possible changes in the traditional requirement of probable cause. If a decision is made to dispense with the requirement of a warrant, of course, Fourth Amendment reasonableness might still be construed as requiring that an officer have information amounting to probable cause before beginning the search. But in some situations persuasive arguments can be made for demanding information meeting a less stringent standard or for dispensing entirely with any requirement that the officer have information indicating that a search is justified. Even if a warrant or court order is determined to be necessary, the standard for deciding whether that order or warrant can issue might be stated so as to demand less than traditional probable cause. But in some situations, the unusually intrusive nature of the search or other considerations may suggest that a warrant issue or that a warrantless search be permitted only under a *more* stringent standard than the traditional probable cause requirement.

The significance of these issues often results from the application of the "plain view seizure" rule, considered in Section B(2) of Chapter 2. If law enforcement officers or other public officials are engaged in a proper, i.e., "reasonable," search and in the course of that search come upon items in "plain view," they may seize those items as long as they have probable cause to believe the items are contraband, evidence, or something else which the officers are entitled to take into their possession. Whether the search that placed the items in the officers' "plain view" was proper may, in many cases, determine whether the seizure was permissible. If the officers came upon the items in the course of an unreasonable search, the discovery and seizure of the items is quite likely to constitute tainted "fruit" of the improper search.

The case law presented in this Chapter consists entirely of United States Supreme Court decisions construing the Fourth Amendment requirement of reasonableness. It is important to keep in mind, however, that state constitutional, statutory or case law may impose more stringent requirements upon the official activity than is mandated by the federal constitutional provision.

Several subsequent chapters address other areas of official conduct that raise issues similar to those raised by the situations considered in this Chapter. Electronic surveillance, for example, is considered in Chapter 6 and use of grand jury subpoenas is discussed in Chapter 9. Among the issues raised in Chapter 8 is the extent to which, if any, undercover law enforcement activity intrudes upon privacy in such a manner as to justify subjecting such activity to Fourth Amendment reasonableness requirements. If this activity were to be subjected to the Fourth Amendment, it would be necessary to address the extent and nature of the regulation which Fourth Amendment reasonableness would impose.

## A. THE EMERGENCY DOCTRINE

The Supreme Court has upheld certain searches without warrants upon a demonstration that the officer reasonably believed that the delay necessary to apply for a search warrant would result in destruction of the evidence or contraband sought. See Schmerber v. California, 384 U.S. 757, 86 S.Ct. 1826, 16 L.Ed.2d 908 (1966) (reprinted at page 65, supra), upholding a warrantless taking of a blood sample where the officer feared that delaying the process would result in the suspect's body eliminating alcohol from his system. But it remains somewhat unclear how great a risk the officer must perceive before a warrantless search becomes permissible.

If exigent circumstances—or an "emergency"—exist, it is generally assumed that this dispenses only with the need for a warrant. The officer must still have probable cause to believe the evidence or contraband will be found by the search. Perhaps, however, the standards for determining when probable cause exists are relaxed somewhat when the officer was required to evaluate the facts under the pressure of emergency situations.

In a sense, the emergency exception is a benchmark for analysis of other situations that may dispense with the need for a warrant and perhaps with the need for probable cause as well. In regard to the warrant requirement, many of the other exceptions—such as that for certain automobiles—involve situations in which a claim might be made that an emergency exists. Fitting a case within one of the other exceptions, however, dispenses with the need for the prosecution to show that *on the facts of the particular case* delay to apply for a warrant created a sufficient risk of loss of the evidence or contraband. In considering the wisdom of various other exceptions and perhaps the scope of those exceptions, this might usefully be kept in mind. If a case falls without any other exception, the prosecution always has the opportunity to demonstrate that on the facts of the particular situation the emergency exception to the requirement of a warrant applied.

## VALE v. LOUISIANA

Supreme Court of the United States, 1970.
399 U.S. 30, 90 S.Ct. 1969, 26 L.Ed.2d 409.

MR. JUSTICE STEWART delivered the opinion of the Court.

The appellant, Donald Vale, was convicted in a Louisiana court on a charge of possessing heroin and was sentenced as a multiple offender to 15 years' imprisonment at hard labor. The Louisiana Supreme Court affirmed the conviction, rejecting the claim that evidence introduced at the trial was the product of an unlawful search and seizure. 252 La. 1056, 215 So.2d 811. * * *

The evidence adduced at the pretrial hearing on a motion to suppress showed that on April 24, 1967, officers possessing two warrants for Vale's arrest and having information that he was residing at a specified address proceeded there in an unmarked car and set up a surveillance of the house. The evidence of what then took place was summarized by the Louisiana Supreme Court as follows:

"After approximately 15 minutes the officers observed a green 1958 Chevrolet drive up and sound the horn and after backing into a parking place, again blew the horn. At this juncture Donald Vale, who was well known to Officer Brady having arrested him twice in the previous month, was seen coming out of the house and walk up to the passenger side of the Chevrolet where he had a close brief conversation with the driver; and after looking up and down the street returned inside of the house. Within a few minutes he reappeared on the porch, and again cautiously looked up and down the street before proceeding to the passenger side of the Chevrolet, leaning through the window. From this the officers were convinced a narcotics sale had taken place. They returned to their car and immediately drove toward Donald Vale, and as they reached within approximately three car lengths from the accused, (Donald Vale) he looked up and, obviously recognizing the officers, turned around, walking quickly toward the house. At the same time the driver of the Chevrolet started to make his get away when the car was blocked by the police vehicle. The three officers promptly alighted from the car, whereupon Officers Soule and Laumann called to Donald Vale to stop as he reached the front steps of the house, telling him he was under arrest. Officer Brady at the same time, seeing the driver of the Chevrolet, Arizzio Saucier, whom the officers knew to be a narcotic addict, place something hurriedly in his mouth, immediately placed him under arrest and joined his co-officers. Because of the transaction they had just observed they, informed Donald Vale they were going to search the house, and thereupon advised him of his constitutional rights. After they all entered the front room, Officer Laumann made a cursory inspection of the house to ascertain if anyone else was present and within about three minutes Mrs. Vale and James Vale, mother and brother of Donald Vale, returned home carrying groceries and were informed of the arrest and impending search." 252 La., at 1067–1068, 215 So.2d, at 815. (Footnote omitted.)

The search of a rear bedroom revealed a quantity of narcotics.

\* \* \*

The Louisiana Supreme Court thought the search \* \* \* supportable because it involved narcotics, which are easily removed, hidden, or destroyed. It would be unreasonable, the Louisiana court concluded, "to require the officers under the facts of the case to first secure a search warrant before searching the premises, as time is of the essence inasmuch as the officers never know whether there is anyone on the premises to be searched who could very easily destroy the evidence." 252 La., at 1070, 215 So.2d, at 816. Such a rationale could not apply to the present case, since by their own account the arresting officers satisfied themselves that no one else was in the house when they first entered the premises. But entirely apart from that point, our past decisions make clear that only in "a few specifically established and well-delineated" situations, Katz v. United States, 389 U.S. 347, 357, 88 S.Ct. 507, 19 L.Ed.2d 576, may a warrantless search of a dwelling withstand constitutional scrutiny, even though the authorities have probable cause to conduct it. The burden rests on the State to show the existence of such an exceptional situation. And the record before us discloses none.

There is no suggestion that anyone consented to the search. The officers were not responding to an emergency. They were not in hot pursuit of a fleeing felon. Warden v. Hayden, 387 U.S. 294, 298–299, 87 S.Ct. 1642, 1645–1646, 18 L.Ed.2d 782. The goods ultimately seized were not in the process of destruction. Schmerber v. California, 384 U.S. 757, 770–771, 86 S.Ct. 1826, 1835–1836, 16 L.Ed.2d 908. Nor were they about to be removed from the jurisdiction.

The officers were able to procure two warrants for Vale's arrest. They also had information that he was residing at the address where they found him. There is thus no reason, so far as anything before us appears, to suppose that it was impracticable for them to obtain a search warrant as well. \* \* \* We decline to hold that an arrest on the street can provide its own "exigent circumstance" so as to justify a warrantless search of the arrestee's house.

\* \* \*

Reversed and remanded.

MR. JUSTICE BLACKMUN took no part in the consideration or decision of this case.

MR. JUSTICE BLACK, with whom THE CHIEF JUSTICE joins, dissenting.

\* \* \*

\* \* \* [T]he police had probable cause to believe that Vale was engaged in a narcotics transfer, and that a supply of narcotics would be found in the house, to which Vale had returned after his first conversation, from which he had emerged furtively bearing what the police could readily deduce was a supply of narcotics, and toward which he hurried after seeing the police. But the police did not know then who else might be in the house. Vale's arrest took place near the house, and anyone observing from inside would surely have been alerted to destroy the stocks of contraband which the police believed Vale had left there. The police had already seen Saucier, the narcotics addict, apparently swallow what Vale had given him. Believing that some evidence had already been destroyed and that other evidence might well be, the police were faced with the choice of risking the immediate destruction of evidence or entering the house and conducting a search. I cannot say that their decision to search was unreasonable. Delay in order to obtain a warrant would have given an accomplice just the time he needed.

\* \* \*

\* \* \* [T]he circumstances here were sufficiently exceptional to justify a search, \* \* \*. The Court recognizes that searches to prevent the destruction or removal of evidence have long been held reasonable by the Court. \* \* \* It is only necessary to find that, given Vale's arrest in a spot readily visible to anyone in the house and the probable existence of narcotics inside, it was reasonable for the police to conduct an immediate search of the premises.

The Court, however, finds the search here unreasonable. First, the Court suggests that the contraband was not "in the process of destruction." None of the cases cited by the Court supports the proposition that "exceptional circumstances" exist only when the process of destruction has already begun. On the contrary we implied that those circumstances did exist when "evidence or contraband was *threatened* with removal or destruction." Johnson v. United States, [333 U.S. 10, 15, 68 S.Ct. 367, 369, 92 L.Ed. 436 (1948)] (emphasis added).

Second, the Court seems to argue that the search was unreasonable because the police officers had time to obtain a warrant. I agree that the opportunity to obtain a warrant is one of the factors to be weighed in determining reasonableness. But the record conclusively shows that there was no such opportunity here. As I noted above, once the officers had observed Vale's conduct in front of the house they had probable cause to believe that a felony had been committed and that immediate action was necessary. At no time after the events in front of Mrs. Vale's house would it have been prudent for the officers to leave the house in order to secure a warrant.

The Court asserts, however, that because the police obtained two warrants for Vale's arrest there is "no reason \* \* \* to suppose that it was impracticable for them to obtain a search warrant as well." The difficulty is that the two arrest warrants on which the Court seems to rely so heavily were not issued because of any present misconduct of Vale's; they were issued because the bond had been increased for an earlier narcotics charge then pending against Vale. When the police came to arrest Vale, they knew only that his bond had been increased. There is nothing in the record to indicate that, absent the increased bond, there would have been probable cause for an arrest, much less a search. Probable cause for the search arose for the first time when the police observed the activity of Vale and Saucier in and around the house.

I do not suggest that all arrests necessarily provide the basis for a search of the arrestee's house. In this case there is far more than a mere street arrest. The police also observed Vale's use of the house as a base of operations for his commercial business, his attempt to return hurriedly to the house on seeing the officers, and the apparent destruction of evidence by the man with whom Vale was dealing. Furthermore the police arrival and Vale's arrest were plainly visible to anyone within the house, and the police had every reason to believe that someone in the house was likely to destroy the contraband if the search were postponed.

This case raises most graphically the question how does a policeman protect evidence necessary to the State if he must leave the premises to get a warrant, allowing the evidence he seeks to be destroyed. The Court's answer to that question makes unnecessarily difficult the conviction of those who prey upon society.

## NOTES

1. In Minnesota v. Olson, ___ U.S. ___, 110 S.Ct. 1684, 109 L.Ed.2d 85 (1990), officers investigating a robbery-murder that occurred about 6 a.m. on July 18, 1987 developed probable cause to believe that Olson was the driver of the getaway car. On July 19, they determined that Olson had been staying in a duplex unit occupied by Louanne and Julie Bergstrom. The occupant of the other duplex unit promised to call when Olson returned; officers were directed to stay away from the duplex in the interim. At 2:45 p.m., the neighbor called and told police Olson had returned. Officers surrounded the unit and telephoned Julie Bergstrom to tell her that Olson should come out. The telephoning detective heard a male voice say, "[T]ell them I left." Julie said that "Rob" had left. At 3 p.m., police entered and found Olson hiding in a closet. The Minnesota Supreme Court found that this warrantless entry of the duplex was not justified by exigent circumstances. In the absence of hot pursuit, it reasoned, officers must have probable cause to believe that the situation involved a risk of imminent destruction of evidence, escape of the suspect, or danger to police or persons inside or outside the dwelling. In assessing these risks, it also concluded, the gravity of the crime and the likelihood that the suspect is armed are to be considered. Applying this standard, the state court held that the entry was not justified. A majority of the Supreme Court held that the state tribunal "applied essentially the correct standard in determining whether exigent circumstances existed." ___ U.S. at ___, 110 S.Ct. at 1690, 109 L.Ed.2d at 95. Moreover, it declined to disagree with the state court's "fact-specific application" of the standard:

> The [state] court pointed out that although a grave crime was involved, [Olson] "was known not to be the murderer but thought to be the driver of

the getaway car," and that the police had already recovered the murder weapon. "The police knew that Louanne and Julie were with the suspect in the upstairs duplex with no suggestion of danger to them. Three or four Minneapolis police squads surrounded the house. The time was 3 p.m., Sunday. . . . It was evident the suspect was going nowhere. If he came out of the house he would have been promptly apprehended." We do not disturb the state court's judgment that these facts do not add up to exigent circumstances.

___ U.S. at ___, 110 S.Ct. at 1690, 109 L.Ed.2d at 96. Justice Kennedy joined with the "understanding" that the Court's discussion was not an endorsement of the state court's application of the standard. ___ U.S. at ___, 110 S.Ct. at 1691, 109 L.Ed.2d at 97 (Kennedy, J., concurring). Chief Justice Rehnquist and Justice Blackmun dissented without opinion.

2. In Warden v. Hayden, 387 U.S. 294, 87 S.Ct. 1642, 18 L.Ed.2d 782 (1967), two cab drivers followed the armed robber of the cab company to a residence. A description of the robber and the drivers' information was relayed to police, who arrived at the residence within minutes. They knocked on the door and told the woman who answered that they had reason to believe a robber had entered the house. The officers asked to search and the woman offered no objection. Hayden was found in an upstairs bedroom feigning sleep, and was arrested when no other male was found in the house. One officer was attracted to a bathroom adjoining that in which Hayden was found; in the flush tank of a toilet he found a shotgun and pistol. Another officer who was searching the cellar for the gun or the money looked in a washing machine and found a jacket and trousers of the type the fleeing robber had worn. Under the mattress of Hayden's bed the officers found ammunition for the pistol and a cap. Additional ammunition was found in the drawer of a bureau in the room. Upholding the admission of these items into evidence, the Supreme Court held that the entry of the premises and the search for the robber and his weapons without a warrant was reasonable, because delay might have endangered the officers or others. "[O]nly a thorough search of the house for persons or weapons could have insured that Hayden was the only man present and that the police had control of all weapons which could be used against them or to effect an escape." 387 U.S. at 299, 87 S.Ct. at 1646, 18 L.Ed.2d at 787. *Hayden* is sometimes—as in the principal case—cited as a "hot pursuit" case. Was it?

3. If the officers in *Vale* could not conduct a warrantless search of the premises, could they have prevented Vale's mother and brother from entering the premises until the officers had time to apply for a search warrant? When—and even whether—officers may "secure" a residence pending application for and arrival of a search warrant remains uncertain. See Rawlings v. Kentucky, 448 U.S. 98, 106, 100 S.Ct. 2556, 2562, 65 L.Ed. 2d 633, 643 (1980), assuming that officers who detained the occupants of a house for about an hour pending application for a warrant did so improperly. See also, Segura v. United States, 468 U.S. 796, 104 S.Ct. 3380, 82 L.Ed.2d 599 (1984).

If officers may secure premises pending application for a warrant, does this mean that there are two levels of emergency? Perhaps one authorizes a warrantless search while the other permits only the securing of the premises pending application for a warrant.

4. In Mincey v. Arizona, 437 U.S. 385, 98 S.Ct. 2408, 57 L.Ed.2d 290 (1978), the Supreme Court rejected the proposition that emergency considerations justify a broad exception to the warrant requirement for the scenes of even serious offenses such as homicides. Police officers entered Mincey's apartment to arrest him for possession of drugs. A police officer was shot and killed and Mincey was wounded. Officers secured the apartment and arrested Mincey

and the other occupants. There then ensued four days of searching the apartment for evidence related to the homicide; two or three hundred items were seized and inventoried. No warrant was obtained. Mincey was convicted of murder and other offenses after a trial in which some of the seized items were introduced. The Arizona Supreme Court affirmed in part, holding that the search was permissible without a warrant because the place searched was a "murder scene." The Supreme Court reversed:

> We do not question the right of the police to respond to emergency situations. Numerous state and federal cases have recognized that the Fourth Amendment does not bar police officers from making warrantless entries and searches when they reasonably believe that a person within is in need of immediate aid. Similarly, when the police come upon the scene of a homicide they may make a prompt warrantless search of the area to see if there are other victims or if a killer is still on the premises.

437 U.S. at 392, 98 S.Ct. at 2413, 57 L.Ed.2d at 300. But the search conducted in *Mincey* exceeded what emergency justification the case presented:

> All the persons in Mincey's apartment had been located before the investigating homicide officers arrived there and began their search. And a four-day search that included opening dresser drawers and ripping up carpets can hardly be rationalized in terms of the legitimate concerns that justify an emergency search.

437 U.S. at 393, 98 S.Ct. at 2414, 57 L.Ed.2d at 300. See also, Thompson v. Louisiana, 469 U.S. 17, 105 S.Ct. 409, 83 L.Ed.2d 246 (1984) (per curiam).

5. At issue in Maryland v. Buie, ___ U.S. ___, 110 S.Ct. 1093, 108 L.Ed.2d 276 (1990) was a "protective sweep," described by the Court as "a quick and limited search of a premises, incident to an arrest and conducted to protect the safety of officers or others." Officers obtained an arrest warrant for Buie, based on probable cause to believe he and an accomplice had committed an armed robbery. One of the robbers had worn a red running suit. Six or seven officers proceeded to Buie's home to execute the warrant. After entering, they fanned out through the two floors. Officer Rozar announced he would "freeze" the basement so no one would come up and surprise the officers. With his pistol drawn, he shouted down that anyone there should come up. A voice responded. At Rozar's direction, the person showed his hand and emerged. It was Buie and he was arrested. Detective Frolich then went into the basement, as he later explained, "in case there was someone else" down there. While in the basement, he noticed a red running suit lying in "plain view" and seized it. The Maryland Court of Appeals held Frolich's entry into the basement unreasonable, reasoning that even a protective sweep requires probable cause to believe that a serious and demonstrable potentiality for danger exists.

The Supreme Court, after addressing Fourth Amendment demands in these situations, reversed and remanded the case for further consideration by the state court in light of those demands. *Terry v. Ohio* (reprinted supra, at page 211) and *Michigan v. Long* (discussed supra, at page 245, it reasoned, provided the basis for analysis:

> [A] warrant was not required. * * * [A]s an incident to the arrest the officers could, as a precautionary matter and without probable cause or reasonable suspicion, look in closets and other spaces immediately adjoining the place of arrest from which an attack could be immediately launched. Beyond that, however, we hold that there must be articulable facts which, taken together with the rational inferences from those facts, would warrant a reasonably prudent officer in believing that the area to be

swept harbors an individual posing a danger to those on the arrest scene. This is no more and no less than was required in *Terry* and *Long* * * *.

We should emphasize that such a protective sweep, aimed at protecting the arresting officers, if justified by the circumstances, is nevertheless not a full search of the premises, but may extend only to a cursory inspection of those spaces where a person may be found. The sweep lasts no longer than is necessary to dispel the reasonable suspicion of danger and in any event no longer than it takes to complete the arrest and depart the premises.

___ U.S. at ___, 110 S.Ct. at 1098–99, 108 L.Ed.2d at 286–87.

Justice Stevens concurred to offer his view that "[t]he State may * * * face a formidable task on remand." It must show a reasonable basis for believing someone in the basement might attack the officers. Buie's surrender without resistance, he suggested, from the basement makes this difficult. The State must also show "that it would be safer to go down the stairs instead of simply guarding them from above until [Buie] had been removed from the house." ___ U.S. at ___, 110 S.Ct. at 1100, 108 L.Ed.2d at 288 (Stevens, J., concurring). Justice Kennedy also concurred, disagreeing with Justice Stevens' "gratuitous observation." The record, he concluded, indicates that the officers acted appropriately. ___ U.S. at ___, 110 S.Ct. at 1101, 108 L.Ed.2d at 289 (Kennedy, J., concurring). Justice Brennan, joined by Justice Marshall, dissented, arguing that the Fourth Amendment demands that officers conducting a sweep have probable cause to fear that their safety is threatened by a confederate of the arrestee. ___ U.S. at ___, 110 S.Ct. at 1103, 108 L.Ed.2d at 292 (Brennan, J., concurring).

## B. ADMINISTRATIVE INSPECTIONS AND SEARCHES OF LICENSED PREMISES

The Fourth Amendment by its terms is not limited to traditional criminal investigation but is potentially applicable to any governmental activity that meets the threshold requirements of a "search" or a "seizure." Supreme Court case law, however, has tended to dilute the requirements of the Amendment when the governmental activity has a purpose other than the location of evidence to use in a criminal prosecution.

This was clearly evidenced in Frank v. Maryland, 359 U.S. 360, 78 S.Ct. 804, 3 L.Ed.2d 877 (1959). The Health Code of the City of Baltimore required that all dwellings be kept clean and free from rodent infestation. Health inspectors having "cause to suspect" a violation were authorized to demand entry to premises for purposes of inspecting them. Frank was convicted and fined $20 for refusing to permit an inspector to enter his premises to look for rats. Finding no federal constitutional defect in this conviction, a majority of the Supreme Court explained:

> The attempted inspection of appellant's home is merely to determine whether conditions exist which the Baltimore Health Code proscribes. If they do appellant is notified to remedy the infringing condition. No evidence for criminal prosecution is sought to be seized. * * * The power of inspection granted by the Baltimore City Code is strictly limited * * *. Valid grounds for suspicion of the existence of a nuisance must exist. * * * The inspection

must be made in the day time. * * * Moreover, the inspector has no power to force entry * * *. A fine is imposed for resistance, but officials are not authorized to break past the unwilling occupant.

> Thus, not only does the inspection touch at most upon the periphery of the important interests safeguarded by the Fourteenth Amendment's protection against official intrusion, but it is hedged about with safeguards designed to make the least possible demand on the individual occupant, and to cause only the slightest restriction on his claims of privacy.

359 U.S. at 366–67, 79 S.Ct. at 808–09, 3 L.Ed. at 882. Against this, the Court continued, must be weighed the interests served by inspections:

> Time and experience have forcefully taught that the power to inspect dwelling places, either as a matter of systematic area-by-area search or * * * to treat a specific problem, is of indispensable importance to the maintenance of community health; a power that would be greatly hobbled by the blanket requirement of the safeguards necessary for a search of evidence for criminal acts.

359 U.S. at 372, 79 S.Ct. at 811, 3 L.Ed.2d at 885. In light of this, a five justice majority of the Court upheld Frank's conviction.

As the cases in this section make clear, post-*Frank* decisions of the Supreme Court have refined and to some extent changed this initial position.

## 1. ADMINISTRATIVE INSPECTIONS

In the principal cases in this subsection, the Supreme Court reexamined the considerations which led the *Frank* court to its holding that the Fourth Amendment's warrant clause does not apply to certain inspections conducted for purposes other than collecting evidence to use in a criminal prosecution.

### CAMARA v. MUNICIPAL COURT

Supreme Court of the United States, 1967.
387 U.S. 523, 87 S.Ct. 1727, 18 L.Ed.2d 930.

MR. JUSTICE WHITE delivered the opinion of the Court.

\* \* \*

On November 6, 1963, an inspector of the Division of Housing Inspection of the San Francisco Department of Public Health entered an apartment building to make a routine annual inspection for possible violations of the city's Housing Code. The building's manager informed the inspector that appellant, lessee of the ground floor, was using the rear of his leasehold as a personal residence. Claiming that the building's occupancy permit did not allow residential use of the ground floor, the inspector confronted appellant and demanded that he permit an inspection of the premises. Appellant refused to allow the inspection because the inspector lacked a search warrant.

The inspector returned on November 8, again without a warrant, and appellant again refused to allow an inspection. A citation was then mailed ordering appellant to appear at the district attorney's office. When appellant failed to appear, two inspectors returned to his apartment on November 22. They informed appellant that he was required by law to permit an inspection under § 503 of the Housing Code:

> "Sec. 503 Right to Enter Building. Authorized employees of the City departments or City agencies, so far as may be necessary for the performance of their duties, shall, upon presentation of proper credentials, have the right to enter, at reasonable times, any building, structure, or premises in the City to perform any duty imposed upon them by the Municipal Code."

Appellant nevertheless refused the inspectors access to his apartment without a search warrant. Thereafter, a complaint was filed charging him with refusing to permit a lawful inspection in violation of § 507 of the Code. Appellant was arrested on December 2 and released on bail. When his demurrer to the criminal complaint was denied, appellant filed this petition for a writ of prohibition.

\* \* \* [W]e hold that administrative searches of the kind at issue here are significant intrusions upon the interests protected by the Fourth Amendment, that such searches when authorized and conducted without a warrant procedure lack the traditional safeguards which the Fourth Amendment guarantees to the individual. \* \* \* [A]ppellant argues not only that code enforcement inspection programs must be circumscribed by a warrant procedure, but also that warrants should issue only when the inspector possesses probable cause to believe that a particular dwelling contains violations of the minimum standards prescribed by the code being enforced. We disagree.

\* \* \*

Unlike the search pursuant to a criminal investigation, the inspection programs at issue here are aimed at securing city-wide compliance with minimum physical standards for private property. The primary governmental interest at stake is to prevent even the unintentional development of conditions which are hazardous to public health and safety. \* \* \* In determining whether a particular inspection is reasonable—and thus in determining whether there is probable cause to issue a warrant for that inspection—the need for the inspection must be weighed in terms of these reasonable goals of code enforcement.

There is unanimous agreement among those most familiar with this field that the only effective way to seek universal compliance with the minimum standards required by municipal codes is through routine periodic inspections of all structures. It is here that the probable cause debate is focused, for the agency's decision to conduct an area inspection is unavoidably based on its appraisal of conditions in the area as a whole, not on its knowledge of conditions in each particular building. Appellee contends that, if the probable cause standard urged by appellant is adopted, the area inspection will be eliminated as a means of seeking compliance with code standards and the reasonable goals of code enforcement will be dealt a crushing blow.

In meeting this contention, appellant argues first, that his probable cause standard would not jeopardize area inspection programs because only a minute portion of the population will refuse to consent to such inspections, and second, that individual privacy in any event should be given preference to the public interest in conducting such inspections. The first argument, even if true, is irrelevant to the question whether the area inspection is reasonable within the meaning of the Fourth Amendment. The second argument is in effect an assertion that the area inspection is an unreasonable search. Unfortunately, there can be no ready test for determining reasonableness other than by balancing the need to search against the invasion which the search entails. But we think that a number of persuasive factors combine to support the reasonableness of area code-enforcement inspections. First, such programs have a long history of judicial and public acceptance.  *  *  * Second, the public interest demands that all dangerous conditions be prevented or abated, yet it is doubtful that any other canvassing technique would achieve acceptable results.

*  *  *

Finally,  *  *  * the inspections are neither personal in nature nor aimed at the discovery of evidence of crime, they involve a relatively limited invasion of the urban citizen's privacy.  *  *  * Having concluded that the area inspection is a "reasonable" search of private property within the meaning of the Fourth Amendment, it is obvious that "probable cause" to issue a warrant to inspect must exist if reasonable legislative or administrative standards for conducting an area inspection are satisfied with respect to a particular dwelling. Such standards, which will vary with the municipal program being enforced, may be based upon the passage of time, the nature of the building (e.g., a multi-family apartment house), or the condition of the entire area, but they will not necessarily depend upon specific knowledge of the condition of the particular dwelling. It has been suggested that to so vary the probable cause test from the standard applied in criminal cases would be to authorize a "synthetic search warrant" and thereby to lessen the overall protections of the Fourth Amendment.

*  *  *

But we do not agree. The warrant procedure is designed to guarantee that a decision to search private property is justified by a reasonable governmental interest. But reasonableness is still the ultimate standard. If a valid public interest justifies the intrusion contemplated, then there is probable cause to issue a suitably restricted search warrant.  *  *  * Such an approach neither endangers time-honored doctrines applicable to criminal investigations nor makes a nullity of the probable cause requirement in this area. It merely gives full recognition to the competing public and private interests here at stake and, in so doing, best fulfills the historic purpose behind the constitutional right to be free from unreasonable government invasions of privacy.  *  *  *

Since our holding emphasizes the controlling standard of reasonableness, nothing we say today is intended to foreclose prompt inspections, even without a warrant, that the law has traditionally upheld in emergency situations. See North American Cold Storage Co. v. City of Chicago, 211 U.S. 306, 29 S.Ct. 101, 53 L.Ed. 195 (seizure of unwholesome food); Jacobson v. Commonwealth of Massachusetts, 197 U.S. 11, 25 S.Ct. 358, 49 L.Ed. 643 (compulsory smallpox vaccination); Compagnie Francaise de Navigation à Vapeur v. Louisiana State Board of Health, 186 U.S. 380, 22 S.Ct. 811, 46 L.Ed. 1209 (health quarantine); Kroplin v. Truax, 119 Ohio St. 610, 165 N.E. 498 (summary destruction of tubercular cattle). On the other hand, in the case of most routine area inspections, there is no compelling urgency to inspect at a particular time or on a particular day. Moreover, most citizens allow inspections of their property without a warrant. Thus, as a practical matter and in light of the Fourth Amendment's requirement that a warrant specify the property to be searched, it seems likely that warrants should normally be sought only after entry is refused unless there has been a citizen complaint or there is other satisfactory reason for securing immediate entry. Similarly, the requirement of a warrant procedure does not suggest any change in what seems to be the prevailing local policy, in most situations, of authorizing entry, but not entry by force, to inspect.

\* \* \*

[For the dissenting opinion of Mr. Justice Clark, see See v. City of Seattle, immediately below.]

### SEE v. CITY OF SEATTLE

Supreme Court of the United States, 1967.
387 U.S. 541, 87 S.Ct. 1737, 18 L.Ed.2d 943.

MR. JUSTICE WHITE delivered the opinion of the Court.

\* \* \*

In *Camara*, we held that the Fourth Amendment bars prosecution of a person who has refused to permit a warrantless code-enforcement inspection of his personal residence. The only question which this case presents is whether *Camara* applies to similar inspections of commercial structures which are not used as private residences.

\* \* \* As we explained in *Camara*, a search of private houses is presumptively unreasonable if conducted without a warrant. The businessman, like the occupant of a residence, has a constitutional right to go about his business free from unreasonable official entries upon his private commercial property. The businessman, too, has that right placed in jeopardy if the decision to enter and inspect for violation of regulatory laws can be made and enforced by the inspector in the field without official authority evidenced by warrant.

\* \* \*

It is now settled that, when an administrative agency subpoenas corporate books or records, the Fourth Amendment requires that the subpoena be sufficiently limited in scope, relevant in purpose, and specific in directive so that compliance will not be unreasonably burdensome. \* \* \* It is these rather minimal limitations on administrative action which we think are constitutionally required in the case of investigative entry upon commercial establishments. The agency's particular demand for access will of course be measured, in terms of probable cause to issue a warrant, against a flexible standard of reasonableness that takes into account the public need for effective enforcement of the particular regulation involved. But the decision to enter and inspect will not be the product of the unreviewed discretion of the enforcement officer in the field.[1]  *  *  *

We therefore conclude that administrative entry, without consent, upon the portions of commercial premises which are not open to the public may only be compelled through prosecution or physical force within the framework of a warrant procedure. We do not in any way imply that business premises may not reasonably be inspected in many more situations than private homes, nor do we question such accepted regulatory techniques as licensing programs which require inspections prior to operating a business or marketing a product. Any constitutional challenge to such programs can only be resolved, as many have been in the past, on a case-by-case basis under the general Fourth Amendment standard of reasonableness. We hold only that the basic component of a reasonable search under the Fourth Amendment—that it not be enforced without a suitable warrant procedure—is applicable in this context, as in others, to business as well as to residential premises. Therefore, appellant may not be prosecuted for exercising his constitutional right to insist that the fire inspector obtain a warrant authorizing entry upon appellant's locked warehouse.

Reversed.

*  *  *

MR. JUSTICE CLARK, with whom MR. JUSTICE HARLAN and MR. JUSTICE STEWART join, dissenting.

*  *  *

Today the Court  *  *  * prostitutes the command of the Fourth Amendment that "no Warrants shall issue, but upon probable cause" and sets up in the health and safety codes area inspection a newfangled "warrant" system that is entirely foreign to Fourth Amendment standards. It is regrettable that the Court wipes out such a long and widely accepted practice and creates in its place such enormous confusion in all of our towns and metropolitan cities in one fell swoop.

*  *  *

The majority  *  *  * would permit the issuance of paper warrants, in area inspection programs, with probable cause based on area inspection standards as set out in municipal codes, and with warrants issued by the rubber stamp of a willing magistrate.[2] In my view, this degrades the Fourth Amendment.

---

[1] We do not decide whether warrants to inspect business premises may be issued only after access is refused; since surprise may often be a crucial aspect of routine inspections of business establishments, the reasonableness of warrants issued in advance of inspection will necessarily vary with the nature of the regulation involved and may differ from standards applicable to private homes.

[2] Under the probable-cause standard laid down by the Court, it appears to me that the issuance of warrants could more appropriately be the function of the agency involved than that of the magistrate. This would also relieve magistrates of an intolerable burden. It is therefore unfortunate that the Court fails to pass on the validity of the use of administrative warrants.

I submit that under the carefully circumscribed requirements of health and safety codes, as well as the facts and circumstances of these particular inspections, there is nothing unreasonable about the ones undertaken here.

The majority say, however, that under the present system the occupant has no way of knowing the necessity for the inspection, the limits of the inspector's power, or whether the inspector is himself authorized to perform the search.

\* \* \*

[A]ll of these doubts raised by the Court could be resolved very quickly. Indeed, the inspectors all have identification cards which they show the occupant and the latter could easily resolve the remaining questions by a call to the inspector's superior or, upon demand, receive a written answer thereto. The record here shows these challenges could have been easily interposed. \* \* \* To say, therefore, that the inspection is left to the discretion of the officer in the field is to reach a conclusion not authorized by this record or the ordinances involved here.

\* \* \*

The majority propose two answers to this admittedly pressing problem of need for constant inspection of premises for fire, health, and safety infractions of municipal codes. First, they say that there will be few refusals of entry to inspect. Unlike the attitude of householders as to codes requiring entry for inspection, we have few empirical statistics on attitudes where consent must be obtained. It is true that in the required entry-to-inspect situations most occupants welcome the periodic visits of municipal inspectors. In my view this will not be true when consent is necessary. The City of Portland, Oregon, has a voluntary home inspection program. The 1966 record shows that out of 16,171 calls where the occupant was at home, entry was refused in 2,540 cases—approximately one out of six. This is a large percentage and would place an intolerable burden on the inspection service when required to secure warrants. What is more important is that out of the houses inspected 4,515 hazardous conditions were found! Hence, on the same percentage, there would be approximately 840 hazardous situations in the 2,540 in which inspection was refused in Portland.

Human nature being what it is, we must face up to the fact that thousands of inspections are going to be denied. The economics of the situation alone will force this result. Homeowners generally try to minimize maintenance costs, and some landlords make needed repairs only when required to do so. Immediate prospects for costly repairs to correct possible defects are going to keep many a door closed to the inspector. \* \* \* The majority seem to hold that warrants may be obtained after a refusal of initial entry; I can find no such constitutional distinction or command. These boxcar warrants will be identical as to every dwelling in the area, save the street number itself. I daresay they will be printed up in pads of a thousand or more—with space for the street number to be inserted—and issued by magistrates in broadcast fashion as a matter of course.

I ask: Why go through such an exercise, such a pretense? As the same essentials are being followed under the present procedures, I ask: Why the ceremony, the delay, the expense, the abuse of the search warrant? In my view this will not only destroy its integrity but will degrade the magistrate issuing them and soon bring disrepute not only upon the practice but upon the judicial process. It will be very costly to the city in paperwork incident to the issuance of the paper warrants, in loss of time of inspectors and waste of the time of magistrates and will result in more annoyance to the public. It will also be more burdensome to the occupant of the premises to be inspected. Under a search warrant the inspector can enter any time he chooses. Under the existing procedures he can enter only at reasonable times and invariably the convenience of the occupant is considered. I submit that the identical grounds for action elaborated today give more support—both legal and practical—to the present practice.

### NOTES

1. The Supreme Court has explored the relationship among emergency searches, "administrative" warrant searches, and traditional searches for criminal evidence in the context of arson investigations. In Michigan v. Tyler, 436 U.S. 499, 98 S.Ct. 1942, 56 L.Ed.2d 486 (1978), firemen arrived at a furniture store ablaze at midnight and extinguished the fire by 4 a.m. Two plastic containers containing a flammable liquid were discovered during the course of extinguishing the fire. It was not possible to conduct a thorough investigation of the scene when the fire was extinguished because of the darkness and the smoke. The fire chief returned at 9 a.m. the next morning and discovered some suspicious burn marks in the carpeting. Samples of the carpet were seized. Three weeks later a state fire inspector entered the premises several times and seized several additional items. No warrant had been obtained. Tyler was subsequently tried for arson of the store. The items seized in both inspections and evidence derived from them was admitted over defense objection and Tyler was convicted.

The Supreme Court held that this was constitutional error. Firefighters do not need a warrant to enter a burning building and extinguish the fire, Justice Stewart's opinion for the Court explained. Moreover:

> Prompt determination of the fire's origin may be necessary to prevent its recurrence, as through the detection of continuing dangers such as faulty wiring or a defective furnace. Immediate investigation may also be necessary to preserve evidence from intentional or accidental destruction.
> * * * For these reasons, officials need no warrant to remain in a building for a reasonable time to investigate the cause of a blaze after it has been extinguished.

436 U.S. at 510, 98 S.Ct. at 1950, 56 L.Ed.2d at 498–99. But other entries require a warrant. Despite the fire, citizens' privacy interests may still be involved. In some situations, premises are still used for living or business purposes after a fire; in others, private effects are often left at the scene of a fire. A traditional search warrant is not necessarily required, however. In some situations, an administrative warrant will suffice. Rejecting the argument that an administrative warrant would serve no purpose, Justice Stewart stated:

> To secure a warrant to investigate the cause of a fire, an official must show more than the bare fact that a fire has occurred. The magistrate's duty is

to assure that the proposed search will be reasonable, a determination that requires inquiry into the need for the intrusion on the one hand, and the threat of disruption of the occupant on the other. * * * Even though a fire victim's privacy must normally yield to the vital social objective of ascertaining the cause of the fire, the magistrate can perform the important function of preventing harassment by keeping that invasion to a minimum.

In addition, * * * [another] major function of the warrant is to provide the property owner with sufficient information to reassure him of the entry's legality.

436 U.S. at 507–08, 98 L.Ed.2d at 1949, 57 L.Ed.2d at 497. But, Justice Stewart continued for the Court:

[I]f the investigating officials find probable cause to believe that arson has occurred and require further access to gather evidence for a possible prosecution, they may obtain a warrant only upon a traditional showing of probable cause applicable to searches for evidence of crime.

436 U.S. at 512, 98 S.Ct. at 1951, 57 L.Ed.2d at 500. On the facts of the case, the Court concluded that the entry on the morning after the fire was "no more than an actual continuation" of the firefighters' entry the previous night to extinguish the fire and to conduct an immediate investigation into its origin; no warrant was, therefore, needed. But the later entries required a warrant. Since none had been secured, the evidence obtained from those entries should not have been used against Tyler.

The issue was placed before the Court again in Michigan v. Clifford, 464 U.S. 287, 104 S.Ct. 641, 78 L.Ed.2d 477 (1984). In *Clifford,* a majority of the Court's members appeared to reject *Tyler's* analysis. Justice Rehnquist, joined by the Chief Justice and Justices Blackmun and O'Connor, took the position that no warrant whatsoever is necessary for a post-fire investigation conducted within a reasonable time of a fire. Since the right to enter is contingent upon the happening of an event—a fire—over which the authorities have no control, application of the warrant requirement is not necessary to protect citizens from being subjected to the power to initiate searches. Property owners could be adequately assured of the legality of an inspection by providing inspectors with identification or efforts to notify the owners before the inspection. 464 U.S. at 309, 104 S.Ct. at 655, 78 L.Ed.2d at 494–95 (Rehnquist, J., dissenting). Justice Stevens construed the Fourth Amendment as requiring a traditional search warrant for an unannounced entry. But an entry without any warrant would be reasonable, he concluded, if the inspector had either given the owner sufficient advance notice to enable him or an agent to be present at the inspection or had made a reasonable effort to provide such notice. 464 U.S. at 303, 104 S.Ct. at 652, 78 L.Ed.2d at 490 (Stevens, J., concurring in the judgment).

2. Administrative-like considerations were held to justify considerable flexibility in the Fourth Amendment as it applies to searches of probationers in Griffin v. Wisconsin, 483 U.S. 868, 107 S.Ct. 3164, 97 L.Ed.2d 709 (1987). Application of Fourth Amendment standards to searches by a public employer of employee workplaces split the Court in O'Connor v. Ortega, 480 U.S. 709, 107 S.Ct. 1492, 94 L.Ed.2d 714 (1987).

## 2. "PERVASIVELY REGULATED" BUSINESSES

Fourth Amendment standards are even more significantly relaxed for inspections of premises used for certain highly regulated commercial purposes. The principal case in this subsection is the culmination of a series of decisions addressing, first, which premises are subject to only these more relaxed standards and, second, the content of those standards.

## NEW YORK v. BURGER

Supreme Court of the United States, 1987.
482 U.S. 691, 107 S.Ct. 2636, 96 L.Ed.2d 601.

JUSTICE BLACKMUN delivered the opinion of the Court.

This case presents the question whether the warrantless search of an automobile junkyard, conducted pursuant to a statute authorizing such a search, falls within the exception to the warrant requirement for administrative inspections of pervasively regulated industries. The case also presents the question whether an otherwise proper administrative inspection is unconstitutional because the ultimate purpose of the regulatory statute pursuant to which the search is done—the deterrence of criminal behavior—is the same as that of penal laws, with the result that the inspection may disclose violations not only of the regulatory statute but also of the penal statutes.

### I

Respondent Joseph Burger is the owner of a junkyard in Brooklyn, N.Y. His business consists, in part, of the dismantling of automobiles and the selling of their parts. His junkyard is an open lot with no buildings. A high metal fence surrounds it, wherein are located, among other things, vehicles and parts of vehicles. At approximately noon on November 17, 1982, Officer Joseph Vega and four other plainclothes officers, all members of the Auto Crimes Division of the New York City Police Department, entered respondent's junkyard to conduct an inspection pursuant to N.Y.Veh. & Traf.Law § 415–a5 (McKinney 1986). On any given day, the Division conducts from 5 to 10 inspections of vehicle dismantlers, automobile junkyards, and related businesses.

Upon entering the junkyard, the officers asked to see Burger's license [3] and his "police book"—the record of the automobiles and vehicle parts in his possession. Burger replied that he had neither a license nor a police book. The officers then announced their intention to conduct a § 415–a inspection. Burger did not object. In accordance with their practice, the officers copied down the Vehicle Inspection Numbers (VINs) of several vehicles and parts of vehicles that were in the junkyard. After checking these numbers against a police computer, the officers determined that respondent was in possession of stolen

---

[3] An individual operating a vehicle-dismantling business in New York is required to have a license:

"Definition and registration of vehicle dismantlers. A vehicle dismantler is any person who is engaged in the business of acquiring motor vehicles or trailers for the purpose of dismantling the same for parts or reselling such vehicles as scrap. No person shall engage in the business of or operate as a vehicle dismantler unless there shall have been issued to him a registration in accordance with the provisions of this section. A violation of this subdivision shall be a class E felony." N.Y.Veh. & Traf.Laws 415–a1 (McKinney 1986).

vehicles and parts. Accordingly, Burger was arrested and charged with five counts of possession of stolen property and one count of unregistered operation as a vehicle dismantler, in violation of § 415–a1.

In the Kings County Supreme Court, Burger moved to suppress the evidence obtained as a result of the inspection, primarily on the ground that § 415–a5 was unconstitutional. After a hearing, the court denied the motion. * * *

The New York Court of Appeals, however, reversed. 67 N.Y.2d 338, 502 N.Y.S.2d 702, 493 N.E.2d 926 (1986). In its view, § 415–a5 violated the Fourth Amendment's prohibition of unreasonable searches and seizures. According to the Court of Appeals, "[t]he fundamental defect [of § 415–a5] . . . is that [it] authorize[s] searches undertaken solely to uncover evidence of criminality and not to enforce a comprehensive regulatory scheme. The asserted 'administrative schem[e]' here [is], in reality, designed simply to give the police an expedient means of enforcing penal sanctions for possession of stolen property." 67 N.Y.2d, at 344, 502 N.Y.S.2d, at 705, 493 N.E.2d, at 929. * * * [W]e granted certiorari.

## II

## A

The Court long has recognized that the Fourth Amendment's prohibition on unreasonable searches and seizures is applicable to commercial premises, as well as to private homes. An owner or operator of a business thus has an expectation of privacy in commercial property, which society is prepared to consider to be reasonable. This expectation exists not only with respect to traditional police searches conducted for the gathering of criminal evidence but also with respect to administrative inspections designed to enforce regulatory statutes. See Marshall v. Barlow's, Inc., 436 U.S. 307, 312–313, 98 S.Ct. 1816, 1820–1821, 56 L.Ed.2d 305 (1978). An expectation of privacy in commercial premises, however, is different from, and indeed less than, a similar expectation in an individual's home. See Donovan v. Dewey, 452 U.S. 594, 598–599, 101 S.Ct. 2534, 2537–2538, 69 L.Ed.2d 262 (1981). This expectation is particularly attenuated in commercial property employed in "closely regulated" industries. The Court observed in Marshall v. Barlow's, Inc.: "Certain industries have such a history of government oversight that no reasonable expectation of privacy, see Katz v. United States, 389 U.S. 347, 351–352, 88 S.Ct. 507, 511–512, 19 L.Ed.2d 576 (1967), could exist for a proprietor over the stock of such an enterprise." 436 U.S., at 313, 98 S.Ct., at 1821.

The Court first examined the "unique" problem of inspections of "closely regulated" businesses in two enterprises that had "a long tradition of close government supervision." In Colonnade Corp. v. United States, 397 U.S. 72, 90 S.Ct. 774, 25 L.Ed.2d 60 (1970), it considered a warrantless search of a catering business pursuant to several federal revenue statutes authorizing the inspection of the premises of liquor dealers. Although the Court disapproved the search because the statute provided that a sanction be imposed when entry was refused, and because it did not authorize entry without a warrant as an alternative in this situation, it recognized that "the liquor industry [was] long subject to close supervision and inspection."

We returned to this issue in United States v. Biswell, 406 U.S. 311, 92 S.Ct. 1593, 32 L.Ed.2d 87 (1972), which involved a warrantless inspection of the premises of a pawn shop operator, who was federally licensed to sell sporting weapons pursuant to the Gun Control Act of 1968, 82 Stat. 1213, 18 U.S.C. § 921 et seq. While noting that "[f]ederal regulation of the interstate traffic in firearms is not as deeply rooted in history as is governmental control of the liquor industry," we nonetheless concluded that the warrantless inspections authorized by the Gun Control Act would "pose only limited threats to the dealer's justifiable expectations of privacy." Id., at 316, 92 S.Ct., at 1596. We observed: "When a dealer chooses to engage in this pervasively regulated business and to accept a federal license, he does so with the knowledge that his business records, firearms, and ammunition will be subject to effective inspection." Ibid.

The "*Colonnade–Biswell*" doctrine, stating the reduced expectation of privacy by an owner of commercial premises in a "closely regulated" industry, has received renewed emphasis in more recent decisions. In *Marshall v. Barlow's, Inc.*, we noted its continued vitality but declined to find that warrantless inspections, made pursuant to the Occupational Safety and Health Act of 1970, 84 Stat. 1598, 29 U.S.C. §§ 657(a), of all businesses engaged in interstate commerce fell within the narrow focus of this doctrine. However, we found warrantless inspections made pursuant to the Federal Mine Safety and Health Act of 1977, 91 Stat. 1290, 30 U.S.C. § 801 et seq., proper because they were of a "closely regulated" industry. *Donovan v. Dewey*, supra.

Indeed, in Donovan v. Dewey, we declined to limit our consideration to the length of time during which the business in question—stone quarries—had been subject to federal regulation. We pointed out that the doctrine is essentially defined by "the pervasiveness and regularity of the federal regulation" and the effect of such regulation upon an owner's expectation of privacy. We observed, however, that "the duration of a particular regulatory scheme" would remain an "important factor" in deciding whether a warrantless inspection pursuant to the scheme is permissible.

### B

Because the owner or operator of commercial premises in a "closely regulated" industry has a reduced expectation of privacy, the warrant and probable cause requirements, which fulfill the traditional Fourth Amendment standard of reasonableness for a government search, have lessened application in this context. Rather, we conclude that, as in other situations of "special need," where the privacy interests of the owner are weakened and the government interests in regulating particular businesses are concomitantly heightened, a warrantless inspection of commercial premises may well be reasonable within the meaning of the Fourth Amendment.

This warrantless inspection, however, even in the context of a pervasively regulated business, will be deemed to be reasonable only so long as three criteria are met. First, there must be a "substantial" government interest that informs the regulatory scheme pursuant to which the inspection is made. See Donovan v. Dewey, 452 U.S., at 602, 101 S.Ct., at 2540 ("substantial federal interest in improving the health and safety conditions in the Nation's underground and surface mines"); United States v. Biswell, 406 U.S., at 315, 92 S.Ct., at 1596 (regulation of firearms is "of central importance to federal efforts to prevent violent crime and to assist the States in regulating the firearms traffic within their borders"); Colonnade Corp. v. United States, 397 U.S., at 75, 90 S.Ct., at 776 (federal interest "in protecting the revenue against various types of fraud").

Second, the warrantless inspections must be "necessary to further [the] regulatory scheme." Donovan v. Dewey, 452 U.S., at 600, 101 S.Ct., at 2539. For example, in *Dewey* we recognized that forcing mine inspectors to obtain a warrant before every inspection might alert mine owners or operators to the impending inspection, thereby frustrating the purposes of the Mine Safety and Health Act—to detect and thus to deter safety and health violations.

Finally, "the statute's inspection program, in terms of the certainty and regularity of its application, [must] provid[e] a constitutionally adequate substitute for a warrant." In other words, the regulatory statute must perform the two basic functions of a warrant: it must advise the owner of the commercial premises that the search is being made pursuant to the law and has a properly defined scope, and it must limit the discretion of the inspecting officers. To perform this first function, the statute must be "sufficiently comprehensive and defined that the owner of commercial property cannot help but be aware that his property will be subject to periodic inspections undertaken for specific purposes." Donovan v. Dewey, 452 U.S., at 600, 101 S.Ct., at 2539. In addition, in defining how a statute limits the discretion of the inspectors, we have observed that it must be "carefully limited in time, place, and scope." United States v. Biswell, 406 U.S., at 315, 92 S.Ct., at 1596.

### III

### A

Searches made pursuant to § 415–a, in our view, clearly fall within this established exception to the warrant requirement for administrative inspections in "closely regulated" businesses. First, the nature of the regulatory statute reveals that the operation of a junkyard, part of which is devoted to vehicle dismantling, is a "closely regulated" business in the State of New York. The provisions regulating the activity of vehicle dismantling are extensive. An operator cannot engage in this industry without first obtaining a license, which means that he must meet the registration requirements and must pay a fee. Under § 415–a5(a), the operator must maintain a police book recording the acquisition and disposition of motor vehicles and vehicle parts, and make such records and inventory available for inspection by the police or any agent of the Department of Motor Vehicles. The operator also must display his registration number prominently at his place of business, on business documentation, and on vehicles and parts that pass through his business. Moreover, the person engaged in this activity is subject to criminal penalties, as well as to loss of license or civil fines, for failure to comply with these provisions. That other States besides New York have imposed similarly extensive regulations on automobile junkyards further supports the "closely regulated" status of this industry.

In determining whether vehicle dismantlers constitute a "closely regulated" industry, the "duration of [this] particular regulatory scheme," Donovan v. Dewey, 452 U.S., at 606, 101 S.Ct., at 2542, has some relevancy. Section 415–a could be said to be of fairly recent vintage, and the inspection provision of § 415–a5 was added only in 1979. But because the automobile is a relatively new phenomenon in our society and because its widespread use is even newer, automobile junkyards and vehicle dismantlers have not been in existence very long and thus do not have an ancient history of government oversight.

\* \* \*

The automobile junkyard business \* \* \* is simply a new branch of an industry that has existed, and has been closely regulated, for many years. The automobile junkyard is closely akin to the second-hand shop or the general junkyard. Both share the purpose of recycling salvageable articles and components of items no longer usable in their original form. As such, vehicle dismantlers represent a modern, specialized version of a traditional activity.

In New York, general junkyards and secondhand shops long have been subject to regulation. \* \* \* The history of government regulation of junk-related activities argues strongly in favor of the "closely regulated" status of the automobile junkyard.

Accordingly, in light of the regulatory framework governing his business and the history of regulation of related industries, an operator of a junkyard engaging in vehicle dismantling has a reduced expectation of privacy in this "closely regulated" business.

### B

The New York regulatory scheme satisfies the three criteria necessary to make reasonable warrantless inspections pursuant to § 415–a5. First, the State has a substantial interest in regulating the vehicle-dismantling and automobile-junkyard industry because motor vehicle theft has increased in the State and because the problem of theft is associated with this industry. In this day, automobile theft has become a significant social problem, placing enormous economic and personal burdens upon the citizens of different States. \* \* \* Because contemporary automobiles are made from standardized parts, the nationwide extent of vehicle theft and concern about it are understandable.

Second, regulation of the vehicle-dismantling industry reasonably serves the State's substantial interest in eradicating automobile theft.

It is well established that the theft problem can be addressed effectively by controlling the receiver of, or market in, stolen property. Automobile junkyards and vehicle dismantlers provide the major market for stolen vehicles and vehicle parts. Thus, the State rationally may believe that it will reduce car theft by regulations that prevent automobile junkyards from becoming markets for stolen vehicles and that help trace the origin and destination of vehicle parts.

Moreover, the warrantless administrative inspections pursuant to § 415–a5 "are necessary to further [the] regulatory scheme." In this respect, we see no difference between these inspections and those approved by the Court in United States v. Biswell and Donovan v. Dewey. We explained in *Biswell:*

> "[I]f inspection is to be effective and serve as a credible deterrent, unannounced, even frequent, inspections are essential. In this context, the prerequisite of a warrant could easily frustrate inspection; and if the necessary flexibility as to time, scope, and frequency is to be preserved, the protections afforded by a warrant would be negligible." 406 U.S., at 316, 92 S.Ct., at 1596.

Similarly, in the present case, a warrant requirement would interfere with the statute's purpose of deterring automobile theft accomplished by identifying vehicles and parts as stolen and shutting down the market in such items. Because stolen cars and parts often pass quickly through an automobile junkyard, "frequent" and "unannounced" inspections are necessary in order to detect them. In sum, surprise is crucial if the regulatory scheme aimed at remedying this major social problem is to function at all.

Third, § 415–a5 provides a "constitutionally adequate substitute for a warrant." The statute informs the operator of a vehicle dismantling business that inspections will be made on a regular basis. Thus, the vehicle dismantler knows that the inspections to which he is subject do not constitute discretionary acts by a government official but are conducted pursuant to statute. Section 415–a5 also sets forth the scope of the inspection and, accordingly, places the operator on notice as to how to comply with the statute. In addition, it notifies the operator as to who is authorized to conduct an inspection.

Finally, the "time, place, and scope" of the inspection is limited, to place appropriate restraints upon the discretion of the inspecting officers. The officers are allowed to conduct an inspection only "during [the] regular and usual business hours." [4] The inspections can be made only of vehicle-dismantling and related industries. And the permissible scope of these searches is narrowly defined: the inspectors may examine the records, as well as "any vehicles or parts of vehicles which are subject to the record keeping requirements of this section and which are on the premises."

---

[4] Respondent contends that § 415–a5 is unconstitutional because it fails to limit the number of searches that may be conducted of a particular business during any given period. While such limitations, or the absence thereof, are a factor in an analysis of the adequacy of a particular statute, they are not determinative of the result so long as the statute, as a whole, places adequate limits upon the discretion of the inspecting officers. * * *

IV

A search conducted pursuant to § 415–a5, therefore, clearly falls within the well-established exception to the warrant requirement for administrative inspections of "closely regulated" businesses. The Court of Appeals, nevertheless, struck down the statute as violative of the Fourth Amendment because, in its view, the statute had no truly administrative purpose but was "designed simply to give the police an expedient means of enforcing penal sanctions for possession of stolen property." The court rested its conclusion that the administrative goal of the statute was pretextual and that § 415–a5 really "authorize[d] searches undertaken solely to uncover evidence of criminality" particularly on the fact that, even if an operator failed to produce his police book, the inspecting officers could continue their inspection for stolen vehicles and parts. The court also suggested that the identity of the inspectors—police officers—was significant in revealing the true nature of the statutory scheme.

In arriving at this conclusion, the Court of Appeals failed to recognize that a State can address a major social problem both by way of an administrative scheme and through penal sanctions. Administrative statutes and penal laws may have the same ultimate purpose of remedying the social problem, but they have different subsidiary purposes and prescribe different methods of addressing the problem. An administrative statute establishes how a particular business in a "closely regulated" industry should be operated, setting forth rules to guide an operator's conduct of the business and allowing government officials to ensure that those rules are followed. Such a regulatory approach contrasts with that of the penal laws, a major emphasis of which is the punishment of individuals for specific acts of behavior.

\* \* \*

Accordingly, to state that § 415–a5 is "really" designed to gather evidence to enable convictions under the penal laws is to ignore the plain administrative purposes of § 415–a, in general, and § 415–a5, in particular. If the administrative goals of § 415–a5 are recognized, the difficulty the Court of Appeals perceives in allowing inspecting officers to examine vehicles and vehicle parts even in the absence of records evaporates. The regulatory purposes of § 415–a5 certainly are served by having the inspecting officers compare the records of a particular vehicle dismantler with vehicles and vehicle parts in the junkyard. The purposes of maintaining junkyards in the hands of legitimate-business persons and of tracing vehicles that pass through these businesses, however, also are served by having the officers examine the operator's inventory even when the operator, for whatever reason, fails to produce the police book. Forbidding inspecting officers from examining the inventory in this situation would permit an illegitimate vehicle dismantler to thwart the purposes of the administrative scheme and would have the absurd result of subjecting his counterpart who maintained records to a more extensive search.

Nor do we think that this administrative scheme is unconstitutional simply because, in the course of enforcing it, an inspecting officer may discover evidence of crimes, besides violations of the scheme itself. The discovery of evidence of crimes in the course of an otherwise proper administrative inspection does not render that search illegal or the administrative scheme suspect.

Finally, we fail to see any constitutional significance in the fact that police officers, rather than "administrative" agents, are permitted to conduct the § 415–a5 inspection. The significance respondent alleges lies in the role of police officers as enforcers of the penal laws and in the officers' power to arrest for offenses other than violations of the administrative scheme. It is, however, important to note that state police officers, like those in New York, have numerous duties in addition to those associated with traditional police work. As a practical matter, many States do not have the resources to assign the enforcement of a particular administrative scheme to a specialized agency. So long as a regulatory scheme is properly administrative, it is not rendered illegal by the fact that the inspecting officer has the power to arrest individuals for violations other than those created by the scheme itself. In sum, we decline to impose upon the States the burden of requiring the enforcement of their regulatory statutes to be carried out by specialized agents.

## V

Accordingly, the judgment of the New York Court of Appeals is reversed and the case is remanded to that court for further proceedings not inconsistent with this opinion.

It is so ordered.

JUSTICE BRENNAN, with whom JUSTICE MARSHALL joins, and with whom JUSTICE O'CONNOR joins as to all but Part III, dissenting.

Warrantless inspections of pervasively regulated businesses are valid if necessary to further an urgent state interest, and if authorized by a statute that carefully limits their time, place, and scope. I have no objection to this general rule. Today, however, the Court finds pervasive regulation in the barest of administrative schemes. Burger's vehicle-dismantling business is not closely regulated (unless most New York City businesses are), and an administrative warrant therefore was required to search it. The Court also perceives careful guidance and control of police discretion in a statute that is patently insufficient to eliminate the need for a warrant. Finally, the Court characterizes as administrative a search for evidence of only criminal wrongdoing. As a result, the Court renders virtually meaningless the general rule that a warrant is required for administrative searches of commercial property.

## I

In See v. City of Seattle, 387 U.S. 541, 543, 87 S.Ct. 1737, 1739, 18 L.Ed.2d 943 (1967), we held that an administrative search of commercial property generally must be supported by a warrant. We make an exception to this rule, and dispense with the warrant requirement, in cases involving "closely regulated" industries, where we believe that the commercial operator's privacy interest is adequately protected by detailed regulatory schemes authorizing warrantless inspections. See Donovan v. Dewey, 452 U.S. 594, 599, 101 S.Ct. 2534, 2538, 69 L.Ed.2d 262 (1981).[5] * * *

* * * In *Dewey* * * * we clarified that, although historical supervision may help to demonstrate that close regulation exists, it is "the pervasiveness and regularity of . . . regulation that ultimately determines whether a warrant is necessary to render an inspection program reasonable under the Fourth Amendment." 452 U.S., at 606, 101 S.Ct., at 2542.

The provisions governing vehicle dismantling in New York simply are not extensive. A vehicle dismantler must register and pay a fee, display the registration in various circumstances, maintain a police book, and allow inspections. See N.Y.Veh. & Traf.Law § 415–a(1–6) (McKinney 1986). Of course, the inspections themselves cannot be cited as proof of pervasive regulation justifying elimination of the warrant requirement; that would be obvious bootstrapping. Nor can registration and recordkeeping requirements be characterized as close regulation. New York City, like many States and municipalities, imposes similar, and often more stringent licensing, recordkeeping, and other regulatory requirements on a myriad of trades and businesses. Few substantive qualifications are required of an aspiring vehicle dismantler; no regulation governs the condition of the premises, the method of operation, the hours of operation, the equipment utilized, etc. This scheme stands in marked contrast to, e.g., the mine safety regulations relevant in *Dewey,* supra.

In sum, if New York City's administrative scheme renders the vehicle-dismantling business closely regulated, few businesses will escape such a finding. Under these circumstances, the warrant requirement is the exception not the rule, and *See* has been constructively overruled.[6]

## II

Even if vehicle dismantling were a closely regulated industry, I would nonetheless conclude that this search violated the Fourth Amendment. The warrant requirement protects the owner of a business from the "unbridled discretion [of] executive and administrative officers," by ensuring that "reasonable legislative or administrative standards for conducting an . . . inspection are satisfied with respect to a particular [business]." In order to serve as the equivalent of a

[5] In only three industries have we invoked this exception. See Colonnade Catering Corp. v. United States, 397 U.S. 72, 90 S.Ct. 774, 25 L.Ed.2d 60 (1970) (liquor industry), United States v. Biswell, 406 U.S. 311, 92 S.Ct. 1593, 32 L.Ed.2d 87 (1972) (firearm and ammunitions sales), Donovan v. Dewey, 452 U.S. 594, 101 S.Ct. 2534, 69 L.Ed.2d 262 (1981) (coal mining).

[6] The Court further weakens limitations on the closely regulated industries category when it allows the government to proceed without a warrant upon a showing of a substantial state interest. The Court should require a warrant for inspections in closely regulated industries unless the inspection scheme furthers an urgent governmental interest.

warrant, an administrative statute must create "a predictable and guided (governmental) presence," *Dewey,* 452 U.S., at 604, 101 S.Ct., at 2541. Section 415–a5 does not approach the level of "certainty and regularity of . . . application" necessary to provide "a constitutionally adequate substitute for a warrant." [7]

The statute does not inform the operator of a vehicle-dismantling business that inspections will be made on a regular basis; in fact, there is no assurance that any inspections at all will occur. There is neither an upper nor a lower limit on the number of searches that may be conducted at any given operator's establishment in any given time period. Neither the statute, nor any regulations, nor any regulatory body, provide limits or guidance on the selection of vehicle dismantlers for inspection. In fact, the State could not explain why Burger's operation was selected for inspection. This is precisely what was objectionable about the inspection scheme invalidated in *Marshall*: It failed to "provide any standards to guide inspectors either in their selection of establishments to be searched or in the exercise of their authority to search." *Dewey,* supra, 452 U.S., at 601, 101 S.Ct., at 2539.

The Court also maintains that this statute effectively limits the scope of the search. We have previously found significant that "the standards with which a [business] operator is required to comply are all specifically set forth," 452 U.S., at 604, 101 S.Ct., at 2541, reasoning that a clear and complete definition of potential administrative violations constitutes an implied limitation on the scope of any inspection. Plainly, a statute authorizing a search which can uncover no administrative violations is not sufficiently limited in scope to avoid the warrant requirement. This statute fails to tailor the scope of administrative inspection to the particular concerns posed by the regulated business. I conclude that "the frequency and purpose of the inspections [are left] to the unchecked discretion of Government officers." Ibid. The conduct of the police in this case underscores this point. The police removed identification numbers from a walker and a wheelchair, neither of which fell within the statutory scope of a permissible administrative search.

The Court also finds significant that an operator is on notice as to who is authorized to search the premises; I do not find the statutory limitation—to "any police officer" or "agent of the commissioner"— significant. The sole limitation I see on a police search of the premises of a vehicle dismantler is that it must occur during business hours; otherwise it is open season. The unguided discretion afforded police in this scheme precludes its substitution for a warrant.

### III

The fundamental defect in § 415–a5 is that it authorizes searches intended solely to uncover evidence of criminal acts. The New York

---

[7] I also dispute the contention that warrantless searches are necessary to further the regulatory scheme, because of the need for unexpected and/or frequent searches. If surprise is essential (as it usually is in a criminal case), a warrant may be obtained ex parte. If the State seeks to conduct frequent inspections, then the statute (or some regulatory authority) should somewhere inform the industry of that fact.

Court of Appeals correctly found that § 415–a5 authorized a search of Burger's business "solely to discover whether defendant was storing stolen property on his premises." In the law of administrative searches, one principle emerges with unusual clarity and unanimous acceptance: the government may not use an administrative inspection scheme to search for criminal violations. \* \* \*

Here the State has used an administrative scheme as a pretext to search without probable cause for evidence of criminal violations. It thus circumvented the requirements of the Fourth Amendment by altering the label placed on the search. This crucial point is most clearly illustrated by the fact that the police copied the serial numbers from a wheelchair and a handicapped person's walker that were found on the premises, and determined that these items had been stolen. Obviously, these objects are not vehicles or parts of vehicles, and were in no way relevant to the State's enforcement of its administrative scheme. The scope of the search alone reveals that it was undertaken solely to uncover evidence of criminal wrongdoing.[8]

Moreover, it is factually impossible that the search was intended to discover wrongdoing subject to administrative sanction. Burger stated that he was not registered to dismantle vehicles as required by § 415–a1, and that he did not have a police book, as required by § 415–a5(a). At that point he had violated every requirement of the administrative scheme. There is no administrative provision forbidding possession of stolen automobiles or automobile parts. The inspection became a search for evidence of criminal acts when all possible administrative violations had been uncovered.

The Court \* \* \* implicitly holds that if an administrative scheme has certain goals and if the search serves those goals, it may be upheld even if no concrete administrative consequences could follow from a particular search. This is a dangerous suggestion, for the goals of administrative schemes often overlap with the goals of the criminal law. Thus, on the Court's reasoning, administrative inspections would evade the requirements of the Fourth Amendment so long as they served an abstract administrative goal, such as the prevention of automobile theft. A legislature cannot abrogate constitutional protections simply by saying that the purpose of an administrative search scheme is to prevent a certain type of crime. If the Fourth Amendment is to retain meaning in the commercial context, it must be applied to searches for evidence of criminal acts even if those searches would also serve an administrative purpose, unless that administrative purpose takes the concrete form of seeking an administrative violation.

## IV

The implications of the Court's opinion, if realized, will virtually eliminate Fourth Amendment protection of commercial entities in the

---

[8] Thus, I respectfully disagree with the Court's conclusion that there is "no reason to believe that the instant inspection was actually a 'pretext' for obtaining evidence of respondent's violation of the penal laws." Inspection of the serial numbers on the wheelchair and walker demonstrate that the search went beyond any conceivable administrative purpose. \* \* \*

context of administrative searches. No State may require, as a condition of doing business, a blanket submission to warrantless searches for any purpose. I respectfully dissent.

## C. CONSENT SEARCHES

Evidence obtained by a search need not be excluded if the search was conducted pursuant to an effective consent given by a person with authority to provide it. See Katz v. United States, 389 U.S. 347, 358 n. 22, 88 S.Ct. 507, 515 n. 22, 19 L.Ed.2d 576, 586 n. 22 (1967). This means that the absence of a warrant will not render the evidence inadmissible, even if under general Fourth Amendment requirements a warrant is usually required for searches of the sort at issue. In addition, the officers need not have had information rising to the level of "probable cause."

Consent searches present two major categories of issues. First are those issues related to the legal "effectiveness" of words that on their face appear to constitute consent to search; these are addressed in the first subsection. Second are those issues related to the authority of the consenting person to consent to the particular search at issue; these are addressed in the second subsection.

### 1. THE EFFECTIVENESS OF CONSENT

The Supreme Court has long recognized that not all words or actions of consent will be effective. In Amos v. United States, 255 U.S. 313, 41 S.Ct. 266, 65 L.Ed. 654 (1921), for example, the officers testified that they went to Amos' residence and told the only person there, who represented that she was Amos' wife, that they had come to search the premises. She opened the nearby store and the officers entered and searched. The Court held:

> The contention that the constitutional rights of defendant were waived when his wife admitted to his home the governmental officers * * * cannot be entertained. * * * [I]t is perfectly clear that, under the implied coercion here presented, no such waiver was intended or effected.

255 U.S. at 317, 41 S.Ct. at 268, 65 L.Ed. at 656. But under what circumstances will words of consent have their full effect? In developing this, is it necessary or permissible to conceptualize consent as a "waiver" of the right to be free from searches in the absence of compliance with certain requirements, such as a search warrant based on probable cause? To the extent that consent operates as a waiver, perhaps it must meet standards developed in other contexts for determining the effectiveness of a waiver of federal constitutional rights. These issues are addressed in the following case.

## SCHNECKLOTH v. BUSTAMONTE

Supreme Court of the United States, 1973.
412 U.S. 218, 93 S.Ct. 2041, 36 L.Ed.2d 854.

Mr. Justice Stewart delivered the opinion of the Court.

\* \* \*

### I.

The respondent was brought to trial in a California court upon a charge of possessing a check with intent to defraud. He moved to suppress the introduction of certain material as evidence against him on the ground that the material had been acquired through an unconstitutional search and seizure. In response to the motion, the trial judge conducted an evidentiary hearing where it was established that the material in question had been acquired by the State under the following circumstances:

While on routine patrol in Sunnyvale, California, at approximately 2:40 in the morning, Police Officer James Rand stopped an automobile when he observed that one headlight and its license plate light were burned out. Six men were in the vehicle. Joe Alcala and the respondent, Robert Bustamonte, were in the front seat with Joe Gonzales, the driver. Three older men were seated in the rear. When, in response to the policeman's question, Gonzales could not produce a driver's license, Officer Rand asked if any of the other five had any evidence of identification. Only Alcala produced a license, and he explained that the car was his brother's. After the six occupants had stepped out of the car at the officer's request and after two additional policemen had arrived, Officer Rand asked Alcala if he could search the car. Alcala replied, "Sure, go ahead." Prior to the search no one was threatened with arrest and, according to Officer Rand's uncontradicted testimony, it "was all very congenial at this time." Gonzales testified that Alcala actually helped in the search of the car, by opening the trunk and glove compartment. In Gonzales' words: " \* \* \* the police officer asked Joe [Alcala], he goes, 'Does the trunk open?' And Joe said, 'Yes.' He went to the car and got the keys and opened up the trunk." Wadded up under the left rear seat, the police officers found three checks that had previously been stolen from a car wash.

[Bustamonte, by means never explained, had come into possession of a checkwriting machine previously stolen from a car wash. He, Alcala, and Gonzales had cashed at least one check from the machine. On the day prior to the stop in Sunnydale, the three had gone to San Jose to find other people willing to use false identification to cash checks written on the machine. The three passengers in the rear seat of the car at the time of the stop had joined the trio for this purpose. By the time Alcala gave his consent to the search, there were four police cars and an undetermined number of officers at the scene. The facts do not suggest that the officers connected the car and its occupants with the theft of the checkwriting machine or the passing of the checks before the search. Two of the older men seated in the rear seat had given inconsistent stories concerning the situation. One officer stated that permission to search the car was sought because things "just didn't fit in right." The search was quite intensive; the officers removed the rear seat from the car. After discovery of the checks, Gonzales "cooperated" with the officers and provided information that linked Bustamonte and the others to the checkwriting machine and the scheme to cash the forged checks. Editors.]

The trial judge denied the motion to suppress, and the checks in question were admitted in evidence at Bustamonte's trial. On the basis of this and other evidence he was convicted, and the California Court of Appeals for the First Appellate District affirmed the conviction. 270 Cal.App.2d 648, 76 Cal.Rptr. 17. In agreeing that the search and seizure were constitutionally valid, the appellate court applied the standard earlier formulated by the Supreme Court of California in an opinion by then Justice Traynor: "Whether in a particular case an apparent consent was in fact voluntarily given or was in submission to an express or implied assertion of authority, is a question of fact to be determined in the light of all the circumstances." People v. Michael, 45 Cal.2d 751, 753, 290 P.2d 852, 854. The appellate court found that "[i]n the instant case the prosecution met the necessary burden of showing consent  *  *  * since there were clearly circumstances from which the trial court could ascertain that consent had been freely given without coercion or submission to authority. Not only officer Rand, but Gonzales, the driver of the automobile, testified that Alcala's assent to the search of his brother's automobile was freely, even casually given. At the time of the request to search the automobile the atmosphere, according to Rand, was 'congenial' and there had been no discussion of any crime. As noted, Gonzales said Alcala even attempted to aid in the search." 270 Cal.App.2d, at 652, 76 Cal.Rptr., at 20. The California Supreme Court denied review.

Thereafter, the respondent sought a writ of habeas corpus in a federal district court. It was denied. On appeal, the Court of Appeals for the Ninth Circuit * * * set aside the District Court's order. 448 F.2d 699. The appellate court reasoned that a consent was a waiver of a person's Fourth and Fourteenth Amendment rights, and that the State was under an obligation to demonstrate not only that the consent had been uncoerced, but that it had been given with an understanding that it could be freely and effectively withheld. Consent could not be found, the court held, solely from the absence of coercion and a verbal expression of assent. Since the District Court had not determined that Alcala had *known* that his consent could be withheld and that he could have refused to have his vehicle searched, the Court of Appeals vacated the order denying the writ and remanded the case for further proceedings. We granted the State's petition for certiorari to determine whether the Fourth and Fourteenth Amendments require the showing thought necessary by the Court of Appeals. 405 U.S. 953, 92 S.Ct. 1168, 31 L.Ed.2d 230.

II.

It is important to make it clear at the outset what is not involved in this case. The respondent concedes that a search conducted pursuant to a valid consent is constitutionally permissible. * * * And similarly the State concedes that "[w]hen a prosecutor seeks to rely upon consent to justify the lawfulness of a search he has the burden of proving that the consent was, in fact, freely and voluntarily given." Bumper v. North Carolina, 391 U.S. 543, 548, 88 S.Ct. 1788, 1792, 20 L.Ed.2d 797.

The precise question in this case, then, is what must the state prove to demonstrate that a consent was "voluntarily" given. * * *

A.

The most extensive judicial exposition of the meaning of "voluntariness" has been developed in those cases in which the Court has had to determine the "voluntariness" of a defendant's confession for purposes of the Fourteenth Amendment. * * * It is to that body of case law to which we turn for initial guidance on the meaning of "voluntariness" in the present context.

Those cases yield no talismanic definition of "voluntariness," mechanically applicable to the host of situations where the question has arisen. "The notion of 'voluntariness,'" Mr. Justice Frankfurter once wrote, "is itself an amphibian." Culombe v. Connecticut, 367 U.S. 568, 604–605, 81 S.Ct. 1860, 1880–1881, 6 L.Ed.2d 1037. It cannot be taken literally to mean a "knowing" choice. "Except where a person is unconscious or drugged or otherwise lacks capacity for conscious choice, all incriminating statements—even those made under brutal treatment—are 'voluntary' in the sense of representing a choice of alternatives. On the other hand, if 'voluntariness' incorporates notions of 'but-for' cause, the question should be whether the statement would have been made even absent inquiry or other official action. Under such a test, virtually no statement would be voluntary because very few people give incriminating statements in the absence of official action of some kind." It is thus evident that neither linguistics nor epistemology will provide a ready definition of the meaning of "voluntariness."

Rather, "voluntariness" has reflected an accommodation of the complex of values implicated in police questioning of a suspect. At one end of the spectrum is the acknowledged need for police questioning as a tool for the effective enforcement of criminal laws. Without such investigation, those who were innocent might be falsely accused, those who were guilty might wholly escape prosecution, and many crimes would go unsolved. In short, the security of all would be diminished. At the other end of the spectrum, is the set of values reflecting society's deeply felt belief that the criminal law cannot be used as an instrument of unfairness, and that the possibility of unfair and even brutal police tactics poses a real and serious threat to civilized notions of justice. "[I]n cases involving involuntary confessions, this Court enforces the strongly felt attitude of our society that important human values are sacrificed where an agency of the government, in the course of securing a conviction, wrings a confession out of an accused against his will."

This Court's decisions reflect a frank recognition that the Constitution requires the sacrifice of neither security nor liberty. The Due Process Clause does not mandate that the police forego all questioning, nor that they be given carte blanche to extract what they can from a suspect. "The ultimate test remains that which has been the only clearly established test in Anglo-American courts for two hundred years: the test of voluntariness. Is the confession the product of an essentially free and unconstrained choice by its maker? If it is, if he has willed to confess, it may be used against him. If it is not, if his will has been overborne and his capacity for self-determination critically impaired, the use of his confession offends due process." Culombe v. Connecticut, supra, 367 U.S., at 602, 81 S.Ct., at 1879.

In determining whether a defendant's will was overborne in a particular case, the Court has assessed the totality of all the surrounding circumstances—both the characteristics of the accused and the details of the interrogation. Some of the factors taken into account have included the youth of the accused, his lack of education, or his low intelligence, the lack of any advice to the accused of his constitutional rights, the length of detention, the repeated and prolonged nature of the questioning, and the use of physical punishment such as the deprivation of food or sleep. In all of these cases, the Court determined the factual circumstances surrounding the confession, assessed the psychological impact on the accused, and evaluated the legal significance of how the accused reacted.

The significant fact about all of these decisions is that none of them turned on the presence or absence of a single controlling criterion; each reflected a careful scrutiny of all the surrounding circumstances. In none of them did the Court rule that the Due Process Clause required the prosecution to prove as part of its initial burden that the defendant knew he had a right to refuse to answer the questions that were put. While the state of the accused's mind, and the failure of the police to advise the accused of his rights, were certainly factors to be evaluated in assessing the "voluntariness" of an accused's responses, they were not in and of themselves determinative.

## B.

Similar considerations lead us to agree with the courts of California that the question whether a consent to a search was in fact "voluntary" or was the product of duress or coercion, express or implied, is a question of fact to be determined from the totality of all the circumstances. While knowledge of the right to refuse consent is one factor to be taken into account, the government need not establish such knowledge as the *sine qua non* of an effective consent. As with police questioning, two competing concerns must be accommodated in determining the meaning of a "voluntary" consent—the legitimate need for such searches and the equally important requirement of assuring the absence of coercion.

In situations where the police have some evidence of illicit activity, but lack probable cause to arrest or search, a search authorized by a valid consent may be the only means of obtaining important and reliable evidence. In the present case for example, while the police had reason to stop the car for traffic violations, the State does not contend that there was probable cause to search the vehicle or that the search was incident to a valid arrest of any of the occupants. Yet, the search yielded tangible evidence that served as a basis for a prosecution, and provided some assurance that others, wholly innocent of the crime, were not mistakenly brought to trial. And in those cases where there is probable cause to arrest or search, but where the police lack a warrant, a consent search may still be valuable. If the search is conducted and proves fruitless, that in itself may convince the police that an arrest with its possible stigma and embarrassment is unnecessary, or that a far more extensive search pursuant to a warrant is not justified. In short, a search pursuant to consent may result in considerably less inconvenience for the subject of the search, and, properly conducted, is a constitutionally permissible and wholly legitimate aspect of effective police activity.

But the Fourth and Fourteenth Amendments require that a consent not be coerced, by explicit or implicit means, by implied threat or covert force. For, no matter how subtly the coercion were applied, the resulting "consent" would be no more than a pretext for the unjustified police intrusion against which the Fourth Amendment is directed.

\*   \*   \*

The problem of reconciling the recognized legitimacy of consent searches with the requirement that they be free from any aspect of official coercion cannot be resolved by any infallible touchstone. To approve such searches without the most careful scrutiny would sanction the possibility of official coercion; to place artificial restrictions upon such searches would jeopardize their basic validity. Just as was true with confessions, the requirement of a "voluntary" consent reflects a fair accommodation of the constitutional requirements involved. In examining all the surrounding circumstances to determine if in fact the consent to search was coerced, account must be taken of subtly coercive police questions, as well as the possibly vulnerable subjective state of the person who consents. Those searches that are the product of police coercion can thus be filtered out without undermining the continuing validity of consent searches. In sum, there is no reason for us to depart in the area of consent searches, from the traditional definition of "voluntariness."

The approach of the Court of Appeals for the Ninth Circuit finds no support in any of our decisions that have attempted to define the meaning of "voluntariness." Its ruling, that the State must affirmatively prove that the subject of the search knew that he had a right to refuse consent, would, in practice, create serious doubt whether consent searches could continue to be conducted. There might be rare cases where it could be proved from the record that a person in fact affirmatively knew of his right to refuse—such as a case where he announced to the police that if he didn't sign the consent form, "you [police] are going to get a search warrant;" or a case where by prior experience and training a person had clearly and convincingly demonstrated such knowledge. But more commonly where there was no evidence of any coercion, explicit or implicit, the prosecution would nevertheless be unable to demonstrate that the subject of the search in fact had known of his right to refuse consent.

The very object of the inquiry—the nature of a person's subjective understanding—underlines the difficulty of the prosecution's burden under the rule applied by the Court of Appeals in this case. Any defendant who was the subject of a search authorized solely by his consent could effectively frustrate the introduction into evidence of the fruits of that search by simply failing to testify that he in fact knew he could refuse to consent. And the near impossibility of meeting this prosecutorial burden suggests why this Court has never accepted any such litmus-paper test of voluntariness. * * *

One alternative that would go far towards proving that the subject of a search did know he had a right to refuse consent would be to advise him of that right before eliciting his consent. That, however, is a suggestion that has been almost universally repudiated by both federal and state courts, and, we think, rightly so. For it would be thoroughly impractical to impose on the normal consent search the detailed requirements of an effective warning. Consent searches are part of the standard investigatory techniques of law enforcement agencies. They normally occur on the highway, or in a person's home or office, and under informal and unstructured conditions. The circumstances that prompt the initial request to search may develop quickly or be a logical extension of investigative police questioning. The police may seek to investigate further suspicious circumstances or to follow up leads developed in questioning persons at the scene of a crime. These situations are a far cry from the structured atmosphere of a trial where, assisted by counsel if he chooses, a defendant is informed of his trial rights. Cf. Boykin v. Alabama, 395 U.S. 238, 243, 89 S.Ct. 1709, 1712, 23 L.Ed.2d 274. And, while surely a closer question, these situations are still immeasurably, far removed from "custodial interrogation" where * * * we found that the Constitution required certain now familiar warnings as a prerequisite to police interrogation. * * *

Consequently, we cannot accept the position of the Court of Appeals in this case that proof of knowledge of the right to refuse consent is a necessary prerequisite to demonstrating a "voluntary" consent. Rather it is only by analyzing all the circumstances of an individual consent that it can be ascertained whether in fact it was voluntary or coerced. It is this careful sifting of the unique facts and circumstances of each case that is evidenced in our prior decisions involving consent searches.

* * *

[I]f under all the circumstances it has appeared that the consent was not given voluntarily—that it was coerced by threats or force, or granted only in submission to a claim of lawful authority—then we have found the consent invalid and the search unreasonable. See, e.g.,

Bumper v. North Carolina, supra, 391 U.S., at 548–549, 88 S.Ct. at 1791–1792, 20 L.Ed.2d 797. In *Bumper*, a 66-year-old Negro widow, who lived in a house located in a rural area at the end of an isolated mile-long dirt road, allowed four white law enforcement officials to search her home after they asserted they had a warrant to search the house. We held the alleged consent to be invalid, noting that "[w]hen a law enforcement officer claims authority to search a home under a warrant, he announces in effect that the occupant has no right to resist the search. The situation is instinct with coercion—albeit colorably lawful coercion. Where there is coercion there cannot be consent." Id., 391 U.S., at 550, 88 S.Ct., at 1792.

Implicit in all of these cases is the recognition that knowledge of a right to refuse is not a prerequisite of a voluntary consent. If the prosecution were required to demonstrate such knowledge, \* \* \* [the] opinions would surely have focused upon the subjective mental state of the person who consented. Yet they did not.

In short, neither this Court's prior cases, nor the traditional definition of "voluntariness" requires proof of knowledge of a right to refuse as the *sine qua non* of an effective consent to a search.

### C.

It is said, however, that a "consent" is a "waiver" of a person's rights under the Fourth and Fourteenth Amendments. The argument is that by allowing the police to conduct a search, a person "waives" whatever right he had to prevent the police from searching. It is argued that under the doctrine of Johnson v. Zerbst, 304 U.S. 458, 464, 58 S.Ct. 1019, 1023, 82 L.Ed. 1461, to establish such a "waiver" the state must demonstrate "an intentional relinquishment or abandonment of a known right or privilege."

But these standards were enunciated in *Johnson* in the context of the safeguards of a fair criminal trial. Our cases do not reflect an uncritical demand for a knowing and intelligent waiver in every situation where a person has failed to invoke a constitutional protection. As Mr. Justice Black once observed for the Court: " 'Waiver' is a vague term used for a great variety of purposes, good and bad, in the law." Green v. United States, 355 U.S. 184, 191, 78 S.Ct. 221, 226, 2 L.Ed.2d 199. \* \* \*

The requirement of a "knowing" and "intelligent" waiver was articulated in a case involving the validity of a defendant's decision to forego a right constitutionally guaranteed to protect a fair trial and the reliability of the truth-determining process. Johnson v. Zerbst, supra, dealt with the denial of counsel in a federal criminal trial. There the Court held that under the Sixth Amendment a criminal defendant is entitled to the assistance of counsel, and that if he lacks sufficient funds to retain counsel, it is the Government's obligation to furnish him with a lawyer. \* \* \* To preserve the fairness of the trial process the Court established an appropriately heavy burden on the government before waiver could be found—"an intentional relinquishment or abandonment of a known right or privilege." Id., at 464, 58 S.Ct., at 1023.

Almost without exception the requirement of a knowing and intelligent waiver has been applied only to those rights which the Constitution guarantees to a criminal defendant in order to preserve a fair trial. Hence, and hardly surprisingly in view of the facts of *Johnson* itself, the standard of a knowing and intelligent waiver has most often been applied to test the validity of a waiver of counsel, either at trial, or upon a guilty plea. And the Court has also applied the *Johnson* criteria to assess the effectiveness of a waiver of other trial rights such as the right to confrontation, to a jury trial and to a speedy trial, and the right to be free from twice being placed in jeopardy. Guilty pleas have been carefully scrutinized to determine whether the accused knew and understood all the rights to which he would be entitled at trial, and that he had intentionally chosen to forego them. And the Court has evaluated the knowing and intelligent nature of the waiver of trial rights in trial-type situations, such as the waiver of the privilege against compulsory self-incrimination before an administrative agency or a congressional committee or the waiver of counsel in a juvenile proceeding.

The guarantees afforded a criminal defendant at trial also protect him at certain stages before the actual trial, and any alleged waiver must meet the strict standard of an intentional relinquishment of a "known" right. But the "trial" guarantees that have been applied to the "pretrial" stage of the criminal process are similarly designed to protect the fairness of the trial itself.

\*    \*    \*

There is a vast difference between those rights that protect a fair criminal trial and the rights guaranteed under the Fourth Amendment. Nothing, either in the purposes behind requiring a "knowing" and "intelligent" waiver of trial rights, or in the practical application of such a requirement suggests that it ought to be extended to the constitutional guarantee against unreasonable searches and seizures.

A strict standard of waiver has been applied to those rights guaranteed to a criminal defendant to insure that he will be accorded the greatest possible opportunity to utilize every facet of the constitutional model of a fair criminal trial. Any trial conducted in derogation of that model leaves open the possibility that the trial reached an unfair result precisely because all the protections specified in the Constitution were not provided. A prime example is the right to counsel. For without that right, a wholly innocent accused faces the real and substantial danger that simply because of his lack of legal expertise he may be convicted. \* \* \* The Constitution requires that every effort be made to see to it that a defendant in a criminal case has not unknowingly relinquished the basic protections that the Framers thought indispensible to a fair trial.

The protections of the Fourth Amendment are of a wholly different order, and have nothing whatever to do with promoting the fair ascertainment of truth at a criminal trial. Rather, as Mr. Justice Frankfurter's opinion for the Court put it in Wolf v. Colorado, 338 U.S. 25, 27, 69 S.Ct. 1359, 1361, 93 L.Ed. 1782, the Fourth Amendment protects the "security of one's privacy against arbitrary intrusion by the police.　＊　＊　＊"　＊ ＊ ＊　The Fourth Amendment "is not an adjunct to the ascertainment of truth." The guarantees of the Fourth Amendment stand "as a protection of quite different constitutional values—values reflecting the concern of our society for the right of each individual to be let alone. To recognize this is no more than to accord those values undiluted respect." Tehan v. United States ex rel. Shott, 382 U.S. 406, 416, 86 S.Ct. 459, 465, 15 L.Ed.2d 453.

Nor can it even be said that a search, as opposed to an eventual trial, is somehow "unfair" if a person consents to a search. While the Fourth and Fourteenth Amendments limit the circumstances under which the police can conduct a search, there is nothing constitutionally suspect in a person voluntarily allowing a search. The actual conduct of the search may be precisely the same as if the police had obtained a warrant. And, unlike those constitutional guarantees that protect a defendant at trial, it cannot be said every reasonable presumption ought to be indulged against voluntary relinquishment. We have only recently stated: "[I]t is no part of the policy underlying the Fourth and Fourteenth Amendments to discourage citizens from aiding to the utmost of their ability in the apprehension of criminals." Coolidge v. New Hampshire, 403 U.S. 443, 448, 91 S.Ct. 2022, 2049, 29 L.Ed.2d 564. Rather the community has a real interest in encouraging consent, for the resulting search may yield necessary evidence for the solution and prosecution of crime, evidence that may insure that a wholly innocent person is not wrongly charged with a criminal offense.

Those cases that have dealt with the application of the Johnson v. Zerbst rule make clear that it would be next to impossible to apply to a consent search the standard of "an intentional relinquishment or abandonment of a known right or privilege." To be true to *Johnson* and its progeny, there must be examination into the knowing and understanding nature of the waiver, an examination that was designed for a trial judge in the structured atmosphere of a courtroom.　＊　＊　＊

It would be unrealistic to expect that in the informal, unstructured context of a consent search a policeman, upon pain of tainting the evidence obtained, could make the detailed type of examination demanded by *Johnson*. And, if for this reason a diluted form of "waiver" were found acceptable, that would itself be ample recognition of the fact that there is no universal standard that must be applied in every situation where a person forgoes a constitutional right.

Similarly, a "waiver" approach to consent searches would be thoroughly inconsistent with our decisions that have approved "third party consents."　＊ ＊ ＊　[I]t is inconceivable that the Constitution could countenance the waiver of a defendant's right to counsel by a third party, or that a waiver could be found because a trial judge reasonably though mistakenly believed a defendant had waived his right to plead not guilty.

In short, there is nothing in the purposes or application of the waiver requirements of Johnson v. Zerbst that justifies, much less compels, the easy equation of a knowing waiver with a consent search.

To make such an equation is to generalize from the broad rhetoric of some of our decisions, and to ignore the substance of the differing constitutional guarantees. We decline to follow what one judicial scholar has termed "the domino method of constitutional adjudication * * * wherein every explanatory statement in a previous opinion is made the basis for extension to a wholly different situation."

## D.

Much of what has already been said disposes of the argument that the Court's decision in the *Miranda* case requires the conclusion that knowledge of a right to refuse is an indispensable element of a valid consent. The considerations that informed the Court's holding in *Miranda* are simply inapplicable in the present case. In *Miranda* the Court found that the techniques of police questioning and the nature of custodial surroundings produce an inherently coercive situation. * * *

In this case there is no evidence of any inherently coercive tactics—either from the nature of the police questioning or the environment in which it took place. Indeed, since consent searches will normally occur on a person's own familiar territory, the spectre of incommunicado police interrogation in some remote station house is simply inapposite. There is no reason to believe, under circumstances such as are present here, that the response to a policeman's question is presumptively coerced; and there is, therefore, no reason to reject the traditional test for determining the voluntariness of a person's response. *Miranda*, of course, did not reach investigative questioning of a person not in custody, which is most directly analogous to the situation of a consent search, and it assuredly did not indicate that such questioning ought to be deemed inherently coercive. * * *

It is also argued that the failure to require the Government to establish knowledge as a prerequisite to a valid consent, will relegate the Fourth Amendment to the special province of "the sophisticated, the knowledgeable, and the privileged." We cannot agree. The traditional definition of voluntariness we accept today has always taken into account evidence of minimal schooling, low intelligence, and the lack of any effective warnings to a person of his rights; and the voluntariness of any statement taken under those conditions has been carefully scrutinized to determine whether it was in fact voluntarily given.

## E.

Our decision today is a narrow one. We hold only that when the subject of a search is not in custody and the State attempts to justify a search on the basis of his consent, the Fourth and Fourteenth Amendments require that it demonstrate that the consent was in fact voluntarily given, and not the result of duress or coercion, express or implied. Voluntariness is a question of fact to be determined from all the circumstances, and while the subject's knowledge of a right to refuse is a factor to be taken into account, the prosecution is not required to demonstrate such knowledge as a prerequisite to establishing a voluntary consent. Because the California courts followed these principles in affirming the respondent's conviction, and because the Court of Appeals for the Ninth Circuit in remanding for an evidentiary hearing required more, its judgment must be reversed.

It is so ordered.

MR. JUSTICE MARSHALL, dissenting.

Several years ago, Mr. Justice Stewart reminded us that "[t]he Constitution guarantees  *  *  *  a society of free choice.  Such a society presupposes the capacity of its members to choose."  Ginsberg v. New York, 390 U.S. 629, 649, 88 S.Ct. 1274, 1285, 20 L.Ed.2d 195 (1968) (concurring opinion).  I would have thought that the capacity to choose necessarily depends upon knowledge that there is a choice to be made. But today the Court reaches the curious result that one can choose to relinquish a constitutional right—the right to be free of unreasonable searches—without knowing that he has the alternative of refusing to accede to a police request to search.  I cannot agree, and therefore dissent.

[The dissenting opinions of Mr. Justice Douglas and Mr. Justice Brennan are omitted.]

NOTES

1.  Despite the limitations placed by the Court upon its holding in the principal case, the same analysis was soon applied to a consent given by a person who had been arrested.  United States v. Watson, 423 U.S. 411, 96 S.Ct. 820, 46 L.Ed.2d 598 (1976).

2.  In United States v. Mendenhall, 446 U.S. 544, 100 S.Ct. 1870, 64 L.Ed. 2d 497 (1980), Ms. Mendenhall had been approached by two Drug Enforcement Administration agents after she disembarked at the Detroit Metropolitan Airport from a Los Angeles flight.  Mendenhall was black; the agents were white.  The agents' inquiries disclosed that she had been in Los Angeles only two days and that her ticket was issued in a name other than her own. Mendenhall agreed to accompany the agents to a nearby office "for further questions."  In this office, one agent asked if she would consent to a search of her person and handbag and told her she had a right to decline the search if she desired.  Mendenhall responded, "Go ahead," and handed her purse to one of the agents.  A female officer arrived and Mendenhall accompanied this officer into a private room.  The officer asked her if she consented to the search, and she responded that she did.  When told that the search would require her to remove her clothing, Mendenhall stated that she had a plane to catch.  The officer, however, assured her that if she were carrying no drugs "there would be no problem."  After beginning to disrobe, Mendenhall took two small packages from her undergarments and handed them to the officer.  One contained heroin and Mendenhall was subsequently convicted for possession of this heroin.  Her motion to suppress the heroin was denied.

The Supreme Court affirmed.  The majority disagreed on whether the pre-search situation constituted a detention of Mendenhall.  Justices Stewart and Rehnquist found no detention; Justice Powell, joined by the Chief Justice and Justice Blackmun, found a detention justified by reasonable suspicion.  All five agreed, however, that the record supported the District Court's finding that the consent to the search given by Mendenhall was voluntary.  Justice Stewart's opinion reasoned:

> First, we note that [Mendenhall], who was 22 years old and had an 11th grade education, was plainly capable of a knowing consent. Second, it is especially significant that [she] was twice expressly told that she was free to decline to consent to the search, and only thereafter explicitly consented to it. Although the Constitution does not require "proof of knowledge of a right to refuse as the *sine qua non* of an effective consent to a search" * * * such knowledge was highly relevant to the determination that there had been consent. And, perhaps more important for present purposes, the fact that the officers themselves informed [her] that she was free to withhold her consent substantially lessened the probability that their conduct could reasonably have appeared to her to be coercive.

446 U.S. at 558–59, 100 S.Ct. at 1879, 64 L.Ed.2d at 512. Rejecting the argument that Mendenhall's statement that she had a plane to catch was "resistance" to the search, Justice Stewart reasoned that the trial judge was entitled to regard this as merely an expression of concern that the search be conducted quickly. He emphasized that after being told there would be no problem if the search turned up nothing incriminating, Mendenhall began to undress without further comment. Nor—in view of the fact that her presence in the office was voluntary—could the surroundings in which the consent was obtained be regarded as "inherently coercive." Finally, he rejected the assertion that Mendenhall would not have voluntarily consented to a search that was likely to disclose the incriminating narcotics she carried. "[T]he question," he responded, "is not whether [she] acted in her ultimate self-interest, but whether she acted voluntarily." Nevertheless, he noted the possibility that Mendenhall may have thought she was acting in her self-interest by voluntarily cooperating with the officers in a manner which she perceived would result in more lenient treatment later. 446 U.S. at 559–60, 100 S.Ct. at 1880, 64 L.Ed.2d at 512–13.

Justice White, joined by Justices Brennan, Marshall, and Stevens, concluded that Mendenhall had been detained and that the detention was unreasonable under Fourth Amendment standards. Consequently, "her suppression motion should have been granted in the absence of evidence to dissipate the taint."

## 2. AUTHORITY TO CONSENT: "THIRD PARTY" CONSENTS

In a substantial number of cases, law enforcement officers rely upon consent provided by persons other than those against whom the discovered evidence is eventually offered at trial. The sufficiency of such consents was addressed in United States v. Matlock, 415 U.S. 164, 94 S.Ct. 988, 39 L.Ed.2d 242 (1974):

> This Court left open in Amos v. United States, 255 U.S. 313, 317, 41 S.Ct. 266, 267, 65 L.Ed. 654 (1921), the question whether a wife's permission to search the residence in which she lived with her husband could "waive his constitutional rights," but more recent authority here clearly indicates that the consent of one who possesses common authority over premises or effects is valid as against the absent, nonconsenting person with whom that authority is shared. In Frazier v. Cupp, 394 U.S. 731, 740, 89 S.Ct. 1420, 1425, 22 L.Ed.2d 684 (1969), the Court "dismissed rather quickly" the contention that the consent of the petitioner's cousin to the search of a duffel bag, which was being used jointly by both men and had

been left in the cousin's home, would not justify the seizure of petitioner's clothing found inside; joint use of the bag rendered the cousin's authority to consent to the search clear. Indeed, the Court was unwilling to engage in the "metaphysical subtleties" raised by Frazier's claim that his cousin only had permission to use one compartment within the bag. By allowing the cousin the use of the bag, and by leaving it in his house, Frazier was held to have assumed the risk that his cousin would allow someone else to look inside. Ibid. * * * [W]hen the prosecution seeks to justify a warrantless search by proof of voluntary consent, it is not limited to proof that consent was given by the defendant, but may show that permission to search was obtained from a third party who possessed common authority over or other sufficient relationship to the premises or effect sought to be inspected.

415 U.S. at 170–71, 94 S.Ct. at 993, 39 L.Ed.2d at 249–50. The Court elaborated further:

Common authority is * * * not to be implied from the mere property interest a third party has in the premises. The authority which justifies the third-party consent does not rest upon the law of property, with its attendant historical and legal refinements, see Chapman v. United States, 365 U.S. 610, 81 S.Ct. 776, 5 L.Ed.2d 828 (1961) (landlord could not validly consent to the search of a house he had rented to another), Stoner v. California, 376 U.S. 483, 84 S.Ct. 889, 11 L.Ed.2d 856 (1964) (night hotel clerk could not validly consent to search of customer's room) but rests rather on mutual use of the property by persons generally having joint access or control for most purposes, so that it is reasonable to recognize that any of the cohabitants has the right to permit the inspection in his own right and that the others have assumed the risk that one of their number might permit the common area to be searched.

415 U.S. at 171 n. 7, 94 S.Ct. at 993 n. 7, 39 L.Ed.2d at 250 n. 7.

In *Matlock,* the search was of a room in a house leased by Mr. and Mrs. Marshall and occupied by Mrs. Marshall, several of her children including Gayle Graff, Graff's three-year old son, and Matlock. Matlock was arrested in the yard of the house. Several officers, without consulting Matlock, went to the door, met Mrs. Graff, and—after telling her they were looking for money and a gun—asked Graff if they could search the house. She consented. While going through an upstairs bedroom occupied by Matlock and Graff, officers found $4,995 in cash concealed in a diaper bag in the only closet in the room. At issue in the case was the admissibility at the hearing on the motion to suppress of Graff's out-of-court statements concerning her joint occupancy of the bedroom and similar statements by both Graff and Matlock representing themselves as husband and wife. After finding that the statements were admissible, the Court concluded that the Government's evidence was sufficient to prove that Graff's consent was "legally sufficient." But since the Court preferred that the trial court first pass on the sufficiency of that evidence in light of the *Matlock* opinion, it remanded the case for such reconsideration. 415 U.S. at 177–78, 94 S.Ct. at 996, 39 L.Ed.2d at 253.

## ILLINOIS v. RODRIGUEZ

Supreme Court of the United States, 1990.
___ U.S. ___, 110 S.Ct. 2793, 111 L.Ed.2d 148.

JUSTICE SCALIA delivered the opinion of the Court.

In United States v. Matlock, 415 U.S. 164, 94 S.Ct. 988, 39 L.Ed.2d 242 (1974), this Court reaffirmed that a warrantless entry and search by law enforcement officers does not violate the Fourth Amendment's proscription of "unreasonable searches and seizures" if the officers have obtained the consent of a third party who possesses common authority over the premises. The present case presents an issue we expressly reserved in Matlock, see id., at 177, n. 14, 94 S.Ct., at 996: whether a warrantless entry is valid when based upon the consent of a third party whom the police, at the time of the entry, reasonably believe to possess common authority over the premises, but who in fact does not do so.

### I

Respondent Edward Rodriguez was arrested in his apartment by law enforcement officers and charged with possession of illegal drugs. The police gained entry to the apartment with the consent and assistance of Gail Fischer, who had lived there with respondent for several months. The relevant facts leading to the arrest are as follows.

On July 26, 1985, police were summoned to the residence of Dorothy Jackson on South Wolcott in Chicago. They were met by Ms. Jackson's daughter, Gail Fischer, who showed signs of a severe beating. She told the officers that she had been assaulted by respondent Edward Rodriguez earlier that day in an apartment on South California. Fischer stated that Rodriguez was then asleep in the apartment, and she consented to travel there with the police in order to unlock the door with her key so that the officers could enter and arrest him. During this conversation, Fischer several times referred to the apartment on South California as "our" apartment, and said that she had clothes and furniture there. It is unclear whether she indicated that she currently lived at the apartment, or only that she used to live there.

The police officers drove to the apartment on South California, accompanied by Fischer. They did not obtain an arrest warrant for Rodriguez, nor did they seek a search warrant for the apartment. At the apartment, Fischer unlocked the door with her key and gave the officers permission to enter. They moved through the door into the living room, where they observed in plain view drug paraphernalia and containers filled with white powder that they believed (correctly, as later analysis showed) to be cocaine. They proceeded to the bedroom, where they found Rodriguez asleep and discovered additional containers of white powder in two open attache cases. The officers arrested Rodriguez and seized the drugs and related paraphernalia.

Rodriguez was charged with possession of a controlled substance with intent to deliver. He moved to suppress all evidence seized at the time of his arrest, claiming that Fischer had vacated the apartment several weeks earlier and had no authority to consent to the entry. The Cook County Circuit Court granted the motion, holding that at the time she consented to the entry Fischer did not have common authority over the apartment. The Court concluded that Fischer was not a "usual resident" but rather an "infrequent visitor" at the apartment on South California, based upon its findings that Fischer's name was not on the lease, that she did not contribute to the rent, that she was not allowed to invite others to the apartment on her own, that she did not have access to the apartment when respondent was away, and that she had moved some of her possessions from the apartment. The Circuit Court also rejected the State's contention that, even if Fischer did not possess common authority over the premises, there was no Fourth Amendment violation if the police reasonably believed at the time of their entry that Fischer possessed the authority to consent.

The Appellate Court of Illinois affirmed the Circuit Court in all respects. The Illinois Supreme Court denied the State's Petition for Leave to Appeal, and we granted certiorari.

## II

The Fourth Amendment generally prohibits the warrantless entry of a person's home, whether to make an arrest or to search for specific objects. Payton v. New York, 445 U.S. 573, 100 S.Ct. 1371, 63 L.Ed.2d 639 (1980); Johnson v. United States, 333 U.S. 10, 68 S.Ct. 367, 92 L.Ed. 436 (1948). The prohibition does not apply, however, to situations in which voluntary consent has been obtained, either from the individual whose property is searched, see Schneckloth v. Bustamonte, 412 U.S. 218, 93 S.Ct. 2041, 36 L.Ed.2d 854 (1973), or from a third party who possesses common authority over the premises, see United States v. Matlock, supra, 415 U.S., at 171, 94 S.Ct., at 993. The State of Illinois contends that that exception applies in the present case.

As we stated in *Matlock,* 415 U.S., at 171, n. 7, 94 S.Ct., at 993, n. 7, "[c]ommon authority" rests "on mutual use of the property by persons generally having joint access or control for most purposes. . . ." The burden of establishing that common authority rests upon the State. On the basis of this record, it is clear that burden was not sustained. The evidence showed that although Fischer, with her two small children, had lived with Rodriguez beginning in December 1984, she had moved out on July 1, 1985, almost a month before the search at issue here, and had gone to live with her mother. She took her and her children's clothing with her, though leaving behind some furniture and household effects. During the period after July 1 she sometimes spent the night at Rodriguez's apartment, but never invited her friends there, and never went there herself when he was not home. Her name was not on the lease nor did she contribute to the rent. She had a key to the apartment, which she said at trial she had taken without Rodriguez's knowledge (though she testified at the preliminary hearing that Rodriguez had given her the key). On these facts the State has not established that, with respect to the South California apartment, Fischer had "joint access or control for most purposes." To the contrary, the Appellate Court's determination of no common authority over the apartment was obviously correct.

### III

### A

The State contends that, even if Fischer did not in fact have authority to give consent, it suffices to validate the entry that the law enforcement officers reasonably believed she did. * * *

### B

* * * [R]espondent asserts that permitting a reasonable belief of common authority to validate an entry would cause a defendant's Fourth Amendment rights to be "vicariously waived." Brief for Respondent 32. We disagree. We have been unyielding in our insistence that a defendant's waiver of his trial rights cannot be given effect unless it is "knowing" and "intelligent." Colorado v. Spring, 479 U.S. 564, 574–575, 107 S.Ct. 851, 857–858, 93 L.Ed.2d 954 (1987); Johnson v. Zerbst, 304 U.S. 458, 58 S.Ct. 1019, 82 L.Ed. 1461 (1938). We would assuredly not permit, therefore, evidence seized in violation of the Fourth Amendment to be introduced on the basis of a trial court's mere "reasonable belief"—derived from statements by unauthorized persons—that the defendant has waived his objection. But one must make a distinction between, on the one hand, trial rights that derive from the violation of constitutional guarantees and, on the other hand, the nature of those constitutional guarantees themselves. As we said in *Schneckloth*:

> "There is a vast difference between those rights that protect a fair criminal trial and the rights guaranteed under the Fourth Amendment. Nothing, either in the purposes behind requiring a 'knowing' and 'intelligent' waiver of trial rights, or in the practical application of such a requirement suggests that it ought to be extended to the constitutional guarantee against unreasonable searches and seizures." 412 U.S., at 241, 93 S.Ct., at 2055.

What Rodriguez is assured by the trial right of the exclusionary rule, where it applies, is that no evidence seized in violation of the Fourth Amendment will be introduced at his trial unless he consents. What he is assured by the Fourth Amendment itself, however, is not that no government search of his house will occur unless he consents; but that no such search will occur that is "unreasonable." U.S. Const., Amdt. 4. There are various elements, of course, that can make a search of a person's house "reasonable"—one of which is the consent of the person or his cotenant. The essence of respondent's argument is that we should impose upon this element a requirement that we have not imposed upon other elements that regularly compel government officers to exercise judgment regarding the facts: namely, the requirement that their judgment be not only responsible but correct.

The fundamental objective that alone validates all unconsented government searches is, of course, the seizure of persons who have committed or are about to commit crimes, or of evidence related to crimes. But "reasonableness," with respect to this necessary element, does not demand that the government be factually correct in its assessment that that is what a search will produce. Warrants need only be supported by "probable cause," which demands no more than a proper "assessment of probabilities in particular factual contexts. . . ." Illinois v. Gates, 462 U.S. 213, 232, 103 S.Ct. 2317, 2329, 76 L.Ed.2d 527 (1983). If a magistrate, based upon seemingly reliable but factually inaccurate information, issues a warrant for the search of a house in which the sought-after felon is not present, has never been present, and was never likely to have been present, the owner of that house suffers one of the inconveniences we all expose ourselves to as the cost of living in a safe society; he does not suffer a violation of the Fourth Amendment.

Another element often, though not invariably, required in order to render an unconsented search "reasonable" is, of course, that the officer be authorized by a valid warrant. Here also we have not held that "reasonableness" precludes error with respect to those factual judgments that law enforcement officials are expected to make. In Maryland v. Garrison, 480 U.S. 79, 107 S.Ct. 1013, 94 L.Ed.2d 72 (1987), a warrant supported by probable cause with respect to one apartment was erroneously issued for an entire floor that was divided (though not clearly) into two apartments. We upheld the search of the apartment not properly covered by the warrant. We said:

> "[T]he validity of the search of respondent's apartment pursuant to a warrant authorizing the search of the entire third floor depends on whether the officers' failure to realize the overbreadth of the warrant was objectively understandable and reasonable. Here it unquestionably was. The objective facts available to the officers at the time suggested no distinction between [the suspect's] apartment and the third-floor premises." Id., at 88, 107 S.Ct., at 1019.

The ordinary requirement of a warrant is sometimes supplanted by other elements that render the unconsented search "reasonable." Here also we have not held that the Fourth Amendment requires factual accuracy. A warrant is not needed, for example, where the search is incident to an arrest. In Hill v. California, 401 U.S. 797, 91 S.Ct. 1106, 28 L.Ed.2d 484 (1971), we upheld a search incident to an arrest, even though the arrest was made of the wrong person. We said:

> "The upshot was that the officers in good faith believed Miller was Hill and arrested him. They were quite wrong as it turned out, and subjective good-faith belief would not in itself justify either the arrest or the subsequent search. But sufficient probability, not certainty, is the touchstone of reasonableness under the Fourth Amendment and on the record before us the officers' mistake was

understandable and the arrest a reasonable response to the situation facing them at the time." Id., at 803–804, 91 S.Ct., at 1110–1111.

It would be superfluous to multiply these examples. It is apparent that in order to satisfy the "reasonableness" requirement of the Fourth Amendment, what is generally demanded of the many factual determinations that must regularly be made by agents of the government—whether the magistrate issuing a warrant, the police officer executing a warrant, or the police officer conducting a search or seizure under one of the exceptions to the warrant requirement—is not that they always be correct, but that they always be reasonable. As we put it in Brinegar v. United States, 338 U.S. 160, 176, 69 S.Ct. 1302, 1311, 93 L.Ed. 1879 (1949):

> "Because many situations which confront officers in the course of executing their duties are more or less ambiguous, room must be allowed for some mistakes on their part. But the mistakes must be those of reasonable men, acting on facts leading sensibly to their conclusions of probability."

We see no reason to depart from this general rule with respect to facts bearing upon the authority to consent to a search. Whether the basis for such authority exists is the sort of recurring factual question to which law enforcement officials must be expected to apply their judgment; and all the Fourth Amendment requires is that they answer it reasonably. The Constitution is no more violated when officers enter without a warrant because they reasonably (though erroneously) believe that the person who has consented to their entry is a resident of the premises, than it is violated when they enter without a warrant because they reasonably (though erroneously) believe they are in pursuit of a violent felon who is about to escape.[9]

\* \* \*

\* \* \* [W]hat we hold today does not suggest that law enforcement officers may always accept a person's invitation to enter premises. Even when the invitation is accompanied by an explicit assertion that the person lives there, the surrounding circumstances could conceivably be such that a reasonable person would doubt its truth and not act upon it without further inquiry. As with other factual determinations bearing upon search and seizure, determination of consent to enter must "be judged against an objective standard: would the facts available to the officer at the moment . . . 'warrant a man of reasonable

---

[9] Justice Marshall's dissent rests upon a rejection of the proposition that searches pursuant to valid third-party consent are "generally reasonable." Only a warrant or exigent circumstances, he contends, can produce "reasonableness"; consent validates the search only because the object of the search thereby "limit[s] his expectation of privacy," so that the search becomes not really a search at all. We see no basis for making such an artificial distinction. To describe a consented search as a non-invasion of privacy and thus a non-search is strange in the extreme. And while it must be admitted that this ingenious device can explain why consented searches are lawful, it cannot explain why seemingly consented searches are "unreasonable," which is all that the Constitution forbids. The only basis for contending that the constitutional standard could not possibly have been met here is the argument that reasonableness must be judged by the facts as they were, rather than by the facts as they were known. As we have discussed in text, that argument has long since been rejected.

caution in the belief' " that the consenting party had authority over the premises? Terry v. Ohio, 392 U.S. 1, 21–22, 88 S.Ct. 1868, 1880, 20 L.Ed.2d 889 (1968). If not, then warrantless entry without further inquiry is unlawful unless authority actually exists. But if so, the search is valid.

\* \* \*

In the present case, the Appellate Court found it unnecessary to determine whether the officers reasonably believed that Fischer had the authority to consent, because it ruled as a matter of law that a reasonable belief could not validate the entry. Since we find that ruling to be in error, we remand for consideration of that question. The judgment of the Illinois Appellate Court is reversed and remanded for further proceedings not inconsistent with this opinion.

So ordered.

JUSTICE MARSHALL, with whom JUSTICE BRENNAN and JUSTICE STEVENS join, dissenting.

\* \* \*

The majority [concludes] that Fischer did not have authority to consent to the officers' entry of Rodriguez's apartment. The Court holds that the warrantless entry into Rodriguez's home was nonetheless valid if the officers reasonably believed that Fischer had authority to consent. The majority's defense of this position rests on a misconception of the basis for third-party consent searches. That such searches do not give rise to claims of constitutional violations rests not on the premise that they are "reasonable" under the Fourth Amendment, but on the premise that a person may voluntarily limit his expectation of privacy by allowing others to exercise authority over his possessions. Cf. Katz v. United States, 389 U.S. 347, 351, 88 S.Ct. 507, 511, 19 L.Ed. 2d 576 (1967) ("What a person knowingly exposes to the public, even in his home or office, is not a subject of Fourth Amendment protection"). Thus, an individual's decision to permit another "joint access [to] or control [over the property] for most purposes," United States v. Matlock, 415 U.S. 164, 171, n. 7, 94 S.Ct. 988, 993, n. 7, 39 L.Ed.2d 242 (1974), limits that individual's reasonable expectation of privacy and to that extent limits his Fourth Amendment protections. If an individual has not so limited his expectation of privacy, the police may not dispense with the safeguards established by the Fourth Amendment.

\* \* \*

I

The Fourth Amendment provides that "[t]he right of the people to be secure in their . . . houses . . . shall not be violated." We have recognized that the "physical entry of the home is the chief evil against which the wording of the Fourth Amendment is directed." United States v. United States District Court, 407 U.S. 297, 313, 92 S.Ct. 2125, 2134, 32 L.Ed.2d 752 (1972). We have further held that "a search or seizure carried out on a suspect's premises without a warrant is per se unreasonable, unless the police can show that it falls within one of a carefully defined set of exceptions." Coolidge v. New Hampshire, 403 U.S. 443, 474, 91 S.Ct. 2022, 2042, 29 L.Ed.2d 564 (1971). * * *

The Court has tolerated departures from the warrant requirement only when an exigency makes a warrantless search imperative to the safety of the police and of the community. The Court has often heard, and steadfastly rejected, the invitation to carve out further exceptions to the warrant requirement for searches of the home because of the burdens on police investigation and prosecution of crime. Our rejection of such claims is not due to a lack of appreciation of the difficulty and importance of effective law enforcement, but rather to our firm commitment to "the view of those who wrote the Bill of Rights that the privacy of a person's home and property may not be totally sacrificed in the name of maximum simplicity in enforcement of the criminal law." Mincey [v. Arizona, 437 U.S. 385, 393, 98 S.Ct. 2408, 2414, 57 L.Ed.2d 290 (1978) ], (citing United States v. Chadwick, 433 U.S. 1, 6–11, 97 S.Ct. 2476, 2480–2483, 53 L.Ed.2d 538 (1977)).

In the absence of an exigency, then, warrantless home searches and seizures are unreasonable under the Fourth Amendment. The weighty constitutional interest in preventing unauthorized intrusions into the home overrides any law enforcement interest in relying on the reasonable but potentially mistaken belief that a third party has authority to consent to such a search or seizure. Indeed, as the present case illustrates, only the minimal interest in avoiding the inconvenience of obtaining a warrant weighs in on the law enforcement side.

* * *

Unlike searches conducted pursuant to the recognized exceptions to the warrant requirement, third-party consent searches are not based on an exigency and therefore serve no compelling social goal. Police officers, when faced with the choice of relying on consent by a third party or securing a warrant, should secure a warrant, and must therefore accept the risk of error should they instead choose to rely on consent.

## II

Our prior cases discussing searches based on third-party consent have never suggested that such searches are "reasonable." * * * As the Court's assumption-of-risk analysis makes clear, third-party consent limits a person's ability to challenge the reasonableness of the search only because that person voluntarily has relinquished some of his expectation of privacy by sharing access or control over his property with another person.

A search conducted pursuant to an officer's reasonable but mistaken belief that a third party had authority to consent is thus on an entirely different constitutional footing from one based on the consent of a third party who in fact has such authority. Even if the officers reasonably believed that Fischer had authority to consent, she did not, and Rodriguez's expectation of privacy was therefore undiminished.

Rodriguez accordingly can challenge the warrantless intrusion into his home as a violation of the Fourth Amendment.

\*   \*   \*

## III

Acknowledging that the third party in this case lacked authority to consent, the majority seeks to rely on cases suggesting that reasonable but mistaken factual judgments by police will not invalidate otherwise reasonable searches. The majority reads these cases as establishing a "general rule" that "what is generally demanded of the many factual determinations that must regularly be made by agents of the government—whether the magistrate issuing a warrant, the police officer executing a warrant, or the police officer conducting a search or seizure under one of the exceptions to the warrant requirement—is not that they always be correct, but that they always be reasonable."

The majority's assertion, however, is premised on the erroneous assumption that third-party consent searches are generally reasonable. The cases the majority cites thus provide no support for its holding. \*   \*   \* Because reasonable factual errors by law enforcement officers will not validate unreasonable searches, the reasonableness of the officer's mistaken belief that the third party had authority to consent is irrelevant.

\*   \*   \*

## IV

Our cases demonstrate that third-party consent searches are free from constitutional challenge only to the extent that they rest on consent by a party empowered to do so. The majority's conclusion to the contrary ignores the legitimate expectations of privacy on which individuals are entitled to rely. That a person who allows another joint access over his property thereby limits his expectation of privacy does not justify trampling the rights of a person who has not similarly relinquished any of his privacy expectation.

Instead of judging the validity of consent searches, as we have in the past, based on whether a defendant has in fact limited his expectation of privacy, the Court today carves out an additional exception to the warrant requirement for third-party consent searches without pausing to consider whether " 'the exigencies of the situation' make the needs of law enforcement so compelling that the warrantless search is objectively reasonable under the Fourth Amendment," *Mincey,* 437 U.S., at 394, 98 S.Ct., at 2414 (citations omitted). Where this free-floating creation of "reasonable" exceptions to the warrant requirement will end, now that the Court has departed from the balancing approach that has long been part of our Fourth Amendment jurisprudence, is unclear. But by allowing a person to be subjected to a warrantless search in his home without his consent and without exigency, the majority has taken away some of the liberty that the Fourth Amendment was designed to protect.

## D.  AUTOMOBILE SEARCHES AND SEIZURES

Searches and seizures of automobiles have probably given rise to more difficulties than any other single category of searches.  Common to much automobile search or seizure case law is the assumption that citizens' privacy interests in automobiles and their contents is or at least should be less than the privacy citizens expect in homes and some other places:

> One has a lesser expectation of privacy in a motor vehicle because its function is transportation and it seldom serves as one's residence or as the repository of personal effects.  A car has little capacity for escaping public scrutiny.  It travels public thoroughfares where both its occupants and its contents are in plain view.

Cardwell v. Lewis, 417 U.S. 583, 590, 94 S.Ct. 2464, 2469, 41 L.Ed.2d 325, 335 (1974) (opinion of Blackmun, J., announcing the judgment of the Court).

Searches of automobiles may be permissible under any of a number of doctrines.  The right to search a car "incident to" the arrest of a person in the car was considered in Chapter 4, as was the right to make a weapons search of some cars during non-arrest confrontations between officers and citizens.  This section presents the traditional "automobile exception" to the requirement of a search warrant;  the second subsection considers officers' ability to search containers found in automobiles being searched under this doctrine.

If an automobile has itself been seized, a search of the vehicle may be rendered reasonable by the right to inventory seized vehicles.  The Fourth Amendment law dealing with inventory searches and related matters is considered first in the introductory note.

### EDITORS' INTRODUCTION:  AUTOMOBILES, IMPOUNDMENTS AND INVENTORIES

Two related but distinguishable issues are raised by the frequent law enforcement "inventory" of vehicles which officers seize.  First is the question of when and how officers may conduct such a search of a properly-seized vehicle.  Second is when and how officers may seize or "impound" a vehicle.

*Inventory Inspections of Seized Automobiles.*  Just as officers may conduct an inventory inspection of the personal possessions of a person who is to be incarcerated after arrest (see Chapter 4, at page 202, supra), the Supreme Court had held that the Fourth Amendment permits some inventory inspections of seized automobiles.  The leading case is South Dakota v. Opperman, 428 U.S. 364, 96 S.Ct. 3092, 49 L.Ed. 2d 1000 (1976).  At 3 A.M., a Vermillion, South Dakota police officer noted Opperman's car parked in a downtown area in violation of an ordinance prohibiting parking in such areas between 2 a.m. and 6 a.m. He issued a citation and placed it on the windshield.  After another officer issued a second citation at 10 a.m., the vehicle was "inspected" and towed to the city impound lot.  At the lot, an officer noted a watch on the dashboard and other items of personal property on the back seat and back floorboard. The locked car doors were opened and "using a standard inventory form, pursuant to police procedures, the officer inventoried the contents of the car * * *." The glove compartment was not locked; upon opening it, the officer discovered marihuana in a plastic bag. All items found in the car were removed to the police department for safekeeping. Opperman was prosecuted for possession of the marihuana. His objection to the admissibility of the marihuana was overruled and he was convicted. Finding the police activity reasonable, a majority of the Supreme Court explained:

> When vehicles are impounded, local police departments generally follow a routine practice of securing and inventorying the automobiles' contents. These procedures developed in response to three distinct needs: the protection of the owner's property while it remains in police custody; the protection of the police against claims or disputes over lost or stolen property; and the protection of the police from potential danger. The practice has been viewed as essential to respond to incidents of theft or vandalism. In addition, police frequently attempt to determine whether a vehicle has been stolen and thereafter abandoned. * * *

> The decisions of this Court point unmistakably to the conclusion * * * that inventories pursuant to standard police procedures are reasonable.

> The Vermillion police were indisputably engaged in a caretaking search of a lawfully impounded automobile. The inventory was conducted only after the car had been impounded for multiple parking violations. The owner, having left his car illegally parked for an extended period, and thus subject to impoundment, was not present to make other arrangements for the safekeeping of his belongings. The inventory itself was prompted by the presence in plain view of a number of valuables inside the car. * * * [T]here is no suggestion whatever that this standard procedure * * * was a pretext concealing an investigatory motive.

428 U.S. at 369, 372, 375–76, 96 S.Ct. at 3097–99, 3100, 49 L.Ed.2d at 1005, 1007, 1009. Nor, the majority continued, was the inventory unlawful in scope because it extended to items not in plain view from outside the car:

> [O]nce the policeman was lawfully inside the car to secure the personal property in plain view, it was not unreasonable to open the unlocked glove compartment, to which vandals would have had ready and unobstructed access once inside the car.

428 U.S. at 376 n. 10, 96 S.Ct. at 3100 n. 10, 49 L.Ed.2d at 1009 n. 10.

The intensity of a permissible inventory inspection, and specifically officials' right to examine the content of "containers," was addressed in Colorado v. Bertine, 479 U.S. 367, 107 S.Ct. 738, 93 L.Ed.2d 739 (1987). Bertine was arrested in Boulder, Colorado for driving under the influence of alcohol and the van in which he was driving at the time was impounded; the impoundment is discussed later in this note. While waiting for the arrival of a towtruck, the officer examined the van's contents. He found a backpack directly behind the front seat. In an outside zippered pouch of the backsack, the officer observed a sealed envelope and inside the backpack he found a nylon bag containing mental cannisters. Upon examining the contents of these, he determined that the envelope contained $210 in cash and the cannisters contained cocaine, methaqualone tablets, cocaine paraphernalia and $700 in cash. In the trial court, Bertine successfully challenged the admissibility of these items in his prosecution for various drug offenses. Finding that the suppression of the items was not required by the Fourth Amendment, the Supreme Court addressed the propriety— assuming the validity of the impoundment—of the "inventory inspection" of the contents of the containers found in the van. Under *Opperman* and Illinois v. Lafayette (discussed supra, at page 202), the majority concluded, the officers acted permissibly. They were following "standardized procedures" and no showing was made that they acted "in bad faith or for the sole purpose of investigation." United States v. Chadwick, discussed supra, at page 115 was not controlling, because in that case the officers were searching "solely for purposes of investigating criminal conduct," and therefore the validity of the searches was "dependent on the application of the probable cause and warrant requirements of the Fourth Amendment." Where the search is an inventory search "reasonable" despite the absence of probable cause, the warrant requirement does not apply. 479 U.S. at 371, 107 S.Ct. at 741, 93 L.Ed.2d at 745. The examination of the contents of the containers was not unreasonable because the van had been towed to a secure facility or because Bertine himself could have been offered the opportunity to make other arrangements for the safekeeping of his property. Nor did the Fourth Amendment require that the police weigh the strength of Bertine's privacy interest in the containers against the risk that they might contain dangerous or valuable items; given the limited time and expertise of the officers, the Fourth Amendment does not require less instrusive methods even if, in hindsight, those would seem to have been sufficient.

Justice Marshall, joined by Justice Brennan, dissented. *Opperman* and *Lafayette* should not govern, he urged, because the government's interest in *Bertine* was far less than in those cases. Since the van was in a secure facility, no protection from claims of theft was needed by the police. No need for protection would justify the inventory; a sane person does not search for bombs by opening a container suspected of harboring a bomb. Other options were available to safeguard Bertine's interest in his property's safety. Moreover, the greater intensity of the examination meant that the suspect's interests were of greater weight in *Bertine* than in *Opperman* and *Lafayette*. 479 U.S. at 381–87, 107 S.Ct. at 746–49, 93 L.Ed.2d at 754–55 (Marshall, J., dissenting).

*Bertine's* emphasis upon the need for "standardized procedures" was developed in Florida v. Wells, ___ U.S. ___, 110 S.Ct. 1632, 109 L.Ed.2d 1 (1990). Officers had examined the contents of a suitcase found in an impounded car. The state court had held the search improper, because no evidence had been produced that the police agency had any policy concerning the opening of closed containers found during inventory searches. The Supreme Court affirmed, reasoning that "absent [a policy with respect to the opening of closed containers encountered during an inventory search], the instant search was not sufficiently regulated to satisfy the Fourth Amendment * * *." ___ U.S. at ___, 110 S.Ct. at 1635, 109 L.Ed.2d at 7. Chief Justice Rehnquist, writing for the majority, explained:

> Our view that standardized criteria or established routine must regulate the opening of containers found during inventory searches is based on the principle that an inventory search must not be a ruse for a general rummaging in order to discover incriminating evidence. The policy or practice governing inventory searches should be designed to produce an inventory. The individual police officer must not be allowed so much latitude that inventory inspections are turned into "a purposeful and general means of discovering evidence of crime," *Bertine,* supra, 479 U.S., at 376, 107 S.Ct., at 744 (Blackmun, J., concurring).

___ U.S. at ___, 110 S.Ct. at 1635, 109 L.Ed.2d at 6. He expressed disagreement, however, with the state court's comment that under *Bertine* the policy must mandate either that all or no containers be opened:

> A police officer may be allowed sufficient latitude whether a particular container should or should not be opened in light of the nature of the search and characteristics of the container itself. Thus, while policies of opening all containers or of opening no containers are unquestionably permissible, it would be equally permissible, for example, to allow the opening of closed containers whose contents officers determine they are unable to ascertain from examining the containers' exteriors. The allowance of the exercise of judgment based on concerns relevant to the purposes of an inventory search does not violate the Fourth Amendment.

___ U.S. at ___, 110 S.Ct. at 1635, 109 L.Ed.2d at 6–7.

Justice Brennan, joined by Justice Marshall, disagreed that the majority's dicta was consistent with *Bertine,* which he read as the Florida court had. ___ U.S. at ___, 110 S.Ct. at 1638, 109 L.Ed.2d at 9 (Brennan, J, dissenting). Justice Blackmun agreed that the Florida court was wrong in reading *Bertine* as requiring that all or no containers be opened but complained that the majority's dicta permitted too much flexibility:

> A State * * * probably could adopt a policy which requires the opening of all containers that are not locked, or a policy which requires the opening of all containers over or under a certain size, even though these policies do not call for the opening of all or no containers. In other words, a State has the discretion to choose a scheme that lies somewhere between the extremes identified by the Florida Supreme Court.
>
> It is an entirely different matter, however, to say, as this majority does, that an individual policeman may be afforded discretion in conducting an inventory search The exercise of discretion by an individual officer, especially when it cannot be measured

against objective, standard criteria, creates the potential for abuse of Fourth Amendment rights our earlier inventory search cases were designed to guard against.

\_\_\_ U.S. at \_\_\_, 110 S.Ct. at 1639, 109 L.Ed.2d at 11 (Blackmun, J., concurring in the judgment). Justice Stevens agreed. \_\_\_ U.S. at \_\_\_, 110 S.Ct. at 1639, 109 L.Ed.2d at 11 (Stevens, J., concurring in the judgment).

*Seizures or Impoundments of Automobiles.* Whether an automobile has been permissibly seized or impounded may be important for a variety of reasons, including compliance with any requirement of a reasonable seizure that *Opperman* may impose for a valid inventory inspection. Despite the frequency with which police agencies assume control over automobiles, the extent of officers' authority to impound vehicles has not been well developed in the case law. Several situations, however, seem quite settled. In *Opperman* itself, the Court commented that "The authority of police to seize and remove from the streets vehicles impeding traffic or threatening public safety and convenience is beyond challenge." 428 U.S. at 369, 96 S.Ct. at 3097, 49 L.Ed. 2d at 1005. Statutes in many jurisdictions authorize judicial proceedings for the forfeiture of vehicles used in certain illegal ways, such as in the commission of particular criminal offenses. When officers have probable cause to believe that a vehicle is subject to forfeiture under such provisions, it appears clear that they may seize the vehicle and hold it pending the completion of judicial forfeiture proceedings. Cf. Cooper v. California, 386 U.S. 58, 87 S.Ct. 788, 17 L.Ed.2d 730 (1967).

It has also been suggested that grounds for impoundment exist when—or at least when officers have reason to believe—the automobile has been abandoned or stolen, the automobile constitutes evidence of the commission of a crime or of someone's guilt of a crime, or the driver (as by reason of injury, intoxication or mental incapacitation) is unable to attend to the car. See State v. Singleton, 9 Wn.App. 327, 332–33, 511 P.2d 1396, 1399–1400 (1973).

Most controversy has involved situations in which an automobile was impounded after the driver was arrested. Unfortunately, judicial discussions often do not clearly distinguish between questions concerning the validity of the initial impoundment in contrast to those concerning the validity of an inventory inspection of a vehicle properly in official custody.

Impoundment issues were somewhat addressed in *Bertine*. Under a Boulder ordinance, an officer was authorized to impound a vehicle when the driver was taken into custody. A Boulder police department directive provided that in such a situation an officer had three options with regard to the arrestee's vehicle. First, he could turn it over to a third person. Second, he could take it to the nearest public parking facility, lock it, and take the keys. Third, he could impound the vehicle. Under the first option, he was not authorized to make any search of the vehicle. Under the second option, he could search the vehicle but this search could not include examining the contents of containers that gave no indication of containing either weapons or valuables. If he took the third option, a thorough search of the vehicle—including examination of all containers in the vehicle—was permitted. The officer took the third alternative with regard to the van Bertine was driving at the time of his arrest.

Bertine did not specifically argue that the impoundment of his van was independently improper, but the Court addressed separately whether officers' discretion concerning impoundments rendered the impoundment/inventory unreasonable. The Boulder police department directive setting out the officer's options provided some criteria for exercising this discretion; the "park and lock" option, for example, was not be be used where reasonable risk of damage or vandalism to the vehicle existed or where the approval of the arrested person for this course of action could not be obtained. Rejecting Bertine's argument, the majority explained:

> Nothing * * * prohibits the exercise of police discretion so long as that discretion is exercised according to standard criteria and on the basis of something other than suspicion of criminal activity. Here, the discretion afforded the Boulder police was exercised in light of standardized criteria, related to the feasibility and appropriateness of parking and locking a vehicle rather than impounding it. There was no showing that the police chose to impound Bertine's van in order to investigate suspected criminal activity.

479 U.S. at 375, 107 S.Ct. at 743, 93 L.Ed.2d at 748.

Justice Marshall, joined by Justice Brennan, dissented, urging that the criteria in the police department directive were not, as a practical matter, sufficient to limit officers' discretion. The officer who conducted the inventory testified at the suppression hearing, Justice Marshall pointed out, that the decision not to "park and lock" the van was his "own individual discretionary decision." Moreover, the dissent argued, adequate criteria—if they had existed—would have directed the officers not to impound Bertine's van:

> Since there was ample public parking adjacent to the intersection where [Bertine] was stopped, consideration of "feasibility" would certainly have militated in favor of the "park and lock" option, not against it. * * * [This] option would seem particularly appropriate in this case, where [Bertine] was stopped for a traffic offense and was not likely to be in custody for a significant length of time. * * * [Bertine] was never advised of [the park and lock] option and had no opportunity to consent. At the suppression hearing, he indicated that he would have consented to such a procedure.

479 U.S. at 378, 380 n. 5, 107 S.Ct. at 745, 746 n. 5, 93 L.Ed.2d at 750, 751 n. 5.

Does *Bertine* bear upon when the Fourth Amendment prohibits the impoundment of an arrested person's car? A few lower court cases have found impoundments improper after drivers' arrest for traffic violations. In State v. Stortroen, 53 Wn.App. 654, 769 P.2d 321 (1989), for example, the defendant had been "pulled over" onto the shoulder of an interstate highway that the officer testified was "[a]s safe as any."

The car did not impede traffic; the officer, however, testified he thought it might distract drivers. Stortroen was not offered the opportunity to sign a "standard form release" absolving the state from liability for loss caused by leaving the vehicle at the location. The prosecution conceded that the impoundment was improper and the court agreed. Where a "reliable" friend is on the scene and is capable of removing the vehicle which an arrested defendant was driving, some courts have held, impoundment of the vehicle is improper and the later inventory unreasonable. E.g., State v. King, 191 Ga.App. 706, 382 S.E.2d 613 (1989). See also, State v. Barajas, 57 Wash.App. 556, 789 P.2d 321 (1990), review denied, 115 Wash.2d 1006, 795 P.2d 1157 (1990) (impoundment improper where arrested driver had apparently valid identification, car was not traffic hazard, and officer did not discuss with driver his desire to contact owner of car or other alternatives to impoundment). And in Fenton v. State, 785 S.W.2d 443 (Tex.App.1990), the defendant pulled into a public parking lot, where he was arrested for speeding and driving with a suspended license. He was taken into custody to give an appearance bond and he had sufficient cash to make that bond. Holding the impoundment unlawful, the court explained:

> There is * * * no evidence that his vehicle was illegally parked in the public parking lot or that it impeded traffic, that he was injured or incapacitated, that the vehicle was stolen or had been used in committing another crime, *or that a necessity existed for protecting Fenton's property because his detention would be more than temporary as he was booked and made bond.*

785 S.W.2d at 445 (emphasis by the court).

Are these analyses and results required by the Fourth Amendment? In *Bertine*, the Supreme Court disapproved the state court's "view" that "the search was unreasonable because * * * Bertine himself could have been offered the opportunity to make other arrangements for the safekeeping of his property." Although this "would undoubtedly have been possible," the Court concluded, Fourth Amendment reasonableness does not necessarily or inevitably turn on the absence of less intrusive means. "[R]easonable police regulations relating to inventory procedures administered in good faith satisfy the Fourth Amendment," it explained, "even though courts might as a matter of hindsight be able to devise equally reasonable rules requiring a different procedure." 479 U.S. at 374, 107 S.Ct. at 742, 93 L.Ed.2d at 747. Does this establish that with regard to the impoundment of a car, in contrast with a search of an impounded vehicle, the Fourth Amendment *never* requires that alternatives to impoundment be taken or at least explored? Some courts seem to read *Bertine* as so holding. See Folly v. State, 28 Ark.App. 98, 771 S.W.2d 306, 310–11 (1989). In People v. Wells, supra, the Florida Supreme Court observed that under *Bertine* police are not constitutionally compelled to provide an alternative to impoundment. State v. Wells, 539 So.2d 464, 469 (Fla.1989). See Green v. State, 550 So.2d 535, 536 (Fla.App.1989). The Supreme Court's opinion in *Wells* did not address this aspect of the state court's discussion.

## 1.  THE "AUTOMOBILE" EXCEPTION

In two early cases, the Supreme Court recognized a right on the part of law enforcement officers to conduct warrantless searches of automobiles independent of the officers' right to arrest the occupants. In Carroll v. United States, 267 U.S. 132, 45 S.Ct. 280, 69 L.Ed. 543 (1925), officers observed a car coming from the direction of Detroit, which they knew to be a location at which much illicit liquor entered the United States.  Several months earlier the officers, acting in an undercover capacity, had met with two men who agreed to sell the officers illicit liquor; the men had come to the meeting in the same automobile.  The officers stopped the car and searched it; 68 bottles of illicit liquor were found concealed under the seat upholstery.  Finding the search reasonable, the Supreme Court noted that there is

> a necessary difference between a search of a store, dwelling house or other structure in respect of which a proper official warrant readily may be obtained, and a search of a ship, motor boat, wagon or automobile for contraband goods, where it is not practicable to secure a warrant because the vehicle can be quickly moved out of the locality or jurisdiction in which the warrant must be sought.

267 U.S. at 153, 45 S.Ct. at 285, 69 L.Ed. at 551.  The right of those using the public highways to free passage without interruption or search, it continued, is adequately protected by the prohibition against search of vehicles "unless there is known to a competent official authorized to search, probable cause for believing that their vehicles are carrying contraband or illegal merchandise."  267 U.S. at 154, 45 S.Ct. at 285, 69 L.Ed. at 552.  Transporting the liquor was in violation of the National Prohibition Act.  Those transporting it were guilty of a criminal offense; the first two offenses were misdemeanors but a third conviction constituted a felony.  Carroll urged that federal law permitted a warrantless arrest for a misdemeanor only if the offense was committed in the officers' presence and consequently that the officers lacked authority to make a warrantless arrest of him.  It followed, he argued, that the officers should not be permitted to make a warrantless search related to a crime for which no warrantless arrest was permissible.  The Court responded:

> The argument of defendants is based on the theory that the seizure in this case can only be \* \* \* justified [on the ground that it was incident to a lawful arrest].  If their theory were sound, their conclusion would be.  The validity of the seizure would turn wholly on the validity of the arrest without a seizure.  But the theory is unsound.  The right to search and the validity of the seizure are not dependent on the right to arrest.  They are dependent on the reasonable cause the seizing officers has for belief that the contents of the automobile offend against the law.  The seizure in such a proceeding comes before the arrest \* \* \*.  The character of the offense for which, after the contraband liquor is found and seized, the driver can be prosecuted does not affect the validity of the seizure.

267 U.S. at 158–59, 45 S.Ct. at 287, 69 L.Ed. at 553–54. The *Carroll* approach was reaffirmed in the second leading case, Brinegar v. United States, 338 U.S. 160, 69 S.Ct. 1302, 93 L.Ed. 1879 (1949), involving quite similar facts.

Chief Justice Burger's opinion for the Court in California v. Carney, 471 U.S. 386, 105 S.Ct. 2066, 85 L.Ed.2d 406 (1985) traced the evolution of the rationale for the exception as follows:

> [A]lthough ready mobility alone was perhaps the original justification for the vehicle exception, our later cases have made clear that ready mobility is not the only basis for the exception. The reasons for the vehicle exception, we have said, are twofold. "Besides the element of mobility, less rigorous warrant requirements govern because the expectation of privacy with respect to one's automobile is significantly less than that relating to one's home or office." [South Dakota v. Opperman, 428 U.S. 364, 367, 96 S.Ct. 3092, 49 L.Ed.2d 1000 (1976)].

> \* \* \*

> These reduced expectations of privacy derive not from the fact that the area to be searched is in plain view, but from the pervasive regulation of vehicles capable of traveling on the public roadway. As we explained in South Dakota v. Opperman \* \* \*:

> > "Automobiles, unlike homes, are subjected to pervasive and continuing governmental regulations and controls, including periodic inspection and licensing requirements. As an everyday occurrence, police stop and examine vehicles when license plates or inspection stickers have expired, or if other violations, such as exhaust fumes or excessive noise, are noted, or if headlights or other safety equipment are not in proper working order." 428 U.S., at 368, 96 S.Ct. at 3096.

> The public is fully aware that it is accorded less privacy in its automobiles because of this compelling governmental need for regulation. Historically, "individuals always [have] been on notice that movable vessels may be stopped and searched on facts giving rise to probable cause that the vehicle contains contraband, without the protection afforded by a magistrate's prior evaluation of those facts." [United States v.] Ross, [456 U.S. 798, 806 n. 8, 102 S.Ct. 2157, 2163 n. 8, 72 L.Ed.2d 572, 582 n. 8 (1982)].

471 U.S. at 391–92, 105 S.Ct. at 2069–70, 85 L.Ed.2d at 413–14.

### CHAMBERS v. MARONEY

Supreme Court of the United States, 1970.
399 U.S. 42, 90 S.Ct. 1975, 26 L.Ed.2d 419.

MR. JUSTICE WHITE delivered the opinion of the Court.

The principal question in this case concerns the admissibility of evidence seized from an automobile, in which petitioner was riding at the time of his arrest, after the automobile was taken to a police station and was there thoroughly searched without a warrant.

\* \* \*

## I

During the night of May 20, 1963, a Gulf service station in North Braddock, Pennsylvania, was robbed by two men, each of whom carried and displayed a gun. The robbers took the currency from the cash register; the service station attendant, one Stephen Kovacich, was directed to place the coins in his right-hand glove, which was then taken by the robbers. Two teen-agers, who had earlier noticed a blue compact station wagon circling the block in the vicinity of the Gulf station, then saw the station wagon speed away from a parking lot close to the Gulf station. About the same time, they learned that the Gulf station had been robbed. They reported to police, who arrived immediately, that four men were in the station wagon and one was wearing a green sweater. Kovacich told the police that one of the men who robbed him was wearing a green sweater and the other was wearing a trench coat. A description of the car and the two robbers was broadcast over the police radio. Within an hour, a light blue compact station wagon answering the description and carrying four men was stopped by the police about two miles from the Gulf station. Petitioner was one of the men in the station wagon. He was wearing a green sweater and there was a trench coat in the car. The occupants were arrested and the car was driven to the police station. In the course of a thorough search of the car at the station, the police found concealed in a compartment under the dashboard two .38-caliber revolvers (one loaded with dumdum bullets), a right-hand glove containing small change, and certain cards bearing the name of Raymond Havicon, the attendant at a Boron service station in McKeesport, Pennsylvania, who had been robbed at gunpoint on May 13, 1963. * * *

Petitioner was indicted for both robberies. * * * The materials taken from the station wagon were introduced into evidence, Kovacich identifying his glove and Havicon the cards taken in the May 13 robbery. Petitioner was sentenced to a term of four to eight years' imprisonment for the May 13 robbery and to a term of two to seven years' imprisonment for the May 20 robbery, the sentences to run consecutively. Petitioner did not take a direct appeal from these convictions. In 1965, petitioner sought a writ of habeas corpus in the state court, which denied the writ after a brief evidentiary hearing; the denial of the writ was affirmed on appeal in the Pennsylvania appellate courts. Habeas corpus proceedings were then commenced in the United States District Court for the Western District of Pennsylvania. An order to show cause was issued. Based on the State's response and the state court record, the petition for habeas corpus was denied without a hearing. The Court of Appeals for the Third Circuit affirmed and we granted certiorari.

## II

We pass quickly the claim that the search of the automobile was the fruit of an unlawful arrest. Both the courts below thought the arresting officers had probable cause to make the arrest. We agree.

Having talked to the teen-age observers and to the victim Kovacich, the police had ample cause to stop a light blue compact station wagon carrying four men and to arrest the occupants, one of whom was wearing a green sweater and one of whom had a trench coat with him in the car.

Even so, the search that produced the incriminating evidence was made at the police station some time after the arrest and cannot be justified as a search incident to an arrest: "Once an accused is under arrest and in custody, then a search made at another place, without a warrant, is simply not incident to the arrest." Preston v. United States, 376 U.S. 364, 367, 84 S.Ct. 881, 883, 11 L.Ed.2d 777 (1964).

There are, however alternative grounds arguably justifying the search of the car in this case.  *  *  *  Here  *  *  *  the police had probable cause to believe that the robbers, carrying guns and the fruits of the crime, had fled the scene in a light blue compact station wagon which would be carrying four men, one wearing a green sweater and another wearing a trench coat.  As the state courts correctly held, there was probable cause to arrest the occupants of the station wagon that the officers stopped; just as obviously was there probable cause to search the car for guns and stolen money.

In terms of the circumstances justifying a warrantless search, the Court has long distinguished between an automobile and a home or office.  In Carroll v. United States, 267 U.S. 132, 45 S.Ct. 280, 69 L.Ed. 453 (1925), the issue was the admissibility in evidence of contraband liquor seized in a warrantless search of a car on the highway.  After surveying the law from the time of the adoption of the Fourth Amendment onward, the Court held that automobiles and other conveyances may be searched without a warrant in circumstances that would not justify the search without a warrant of a house or an office, provided that there is probable cause to believe that the car contains articles that the officers are entitled to seize.  *  *  *  Finding that there was probable cause for the search and seizure at issue before it, the Court affirmed the convictions.

*  *  *

Neither *Carroll,* supra, nor other cases in this Court require or suggest that in every conceivable circumstance the search of an auto even with probable cause may be made without the extra protection for privacy that a warrant affords.  But the circumstances that furnish probable cause to search a particular auto for particular articles are most often unforeseeable; moreover, the opportunity to search is fleeting since a car is readily movable.  Where this is true, as in *Carroll* and the case before us now, if an effective search is to be made at any time, either the search must be made immediately without a warrant or the car itself must be seized and held without a warrant for whatever period is necessary to obtain a warrant for the search.

In enforcing the Fourth Amendment's prohibition against unreasonable searches and seizures, the Court has insisted upon probable cause as a minimum requirement for a reasonable search permitted by the Constitution.  As a general rule, it has also required the judgment of a magistrate on the probable-cause issue and the issuance of a warrant before a search is made. Only in exigent circumstances will the judgment of the police as to probable cause serve as a sufficient authorization for a search. *Carroll*, supra, holds a search warrant unnecessary where there is probable cause to search an automobile stopped on the highway; the car is movable, the occupants are alerted, and the car's contents may never be found again if a warrant must be obtained. Hence an immediate search is constitutionally permissible. * * * 10

\* \* \*

Arguably, because of the preference for a magistrate's judgment, only the immobilization of the car should be permitted until a search warrant is obtained; arguably, only the "lesser" intrusion is permissible until the magistrate authorizes the "greater." But which is the "greater" and which the "lesser" intrusion is itself a debatable question and the answer may depend on a variety of circumstances. For constitutional purposes, we see no difference between on the one hand seizing and holding a car before presenting the probable cause issue to a magistrate and on the other hand carrying out an immediate search without a warrant. Given probable cause to search, either course is reasonable under the Fourth Amendment.

On the facts before us, the blue station wagon could have been searched on the spot when it was stopped since there was probable cause to search and it was a fleeting target for a search. The probable cause factor still obtained at the station house and so did the mobility of the car unless the Fourth Amendment permits a warrantless seizure of the car and the denial of its use to anyone until a warrant is secured. In that event there is little to choose in terms of practical consequences between an immediate search without a warrant and the car's immobilization until a warrant is obtained.[11] The same consequences may not follow where there is unforeseeable cause to search a house. Compare Vale v. Louisiana, 399 U.S. 30, 90 S.Ct. 1969. But as *Carroll*, supra, held, for the purposes of the Fourth Amendment there is a constitutional difference between houses and cars.

\* \* \*

Affirmed.

Mr. Justice Harlan, concurring in part and dissenting in part.

\* \* \*

In sustaining the search of the automobile I believe the Court ignores the framework of our past decisions circumscribing the scope of permissible search without a warrant. * * * The "general require-

[10] Following the car until a warrant can be obtained seems an impractical alternative since, among other things, the car may be taken out of the jurisdiction. Tracing the car and searching it hours or days later would of course permit instruments or fruits of crime to be removed from the car before the search.

[11] It was not unreasonable in this case to take the car to the station house. All occupants in the car were arrested in a dark parking lot in the middle of the night. A careful search at that point was impractical and perhaps not safe for the officers, and it would serve the owner's convenience and the safety of his car to have the vehicle and the keys together at the station house.

ment that a warrant be obtained" is basic to the [Fourth] Amendment's protection of privacy, and "the burden is on those seeking [an] exemption * * * to show the need for it."

\* \* \*

Fidelity to this established principle requires that, where exceptions are made to accommodate the exigencies of particular situations, those exceptions be no broader than necessitated by the circumstances presented.

\* \* \*

Where officers have probable cause to search a vehicle on a public way, a * * * limited exception to the warrant requirement is reasonable * * *. I agree with the Court that they should be permitted to take the steps necessary to preserve evidence and to make a search possible.[12] Cf. A.L.I., Model Code of Pre-Arraignment Procedure § 6.03 (Tent.Dr. No. 3, 1970) The Court holds that those steps include making a warrantless search of the entire vehicle on the highway—a conclusion reached by the Court in *Carroll* without discussion—and indeed appears to go further and to condone the removal of the car to the police station for a warrantless search there at the convenience of the police.[13] I cannot agree that this result is consistent with our insistence in other areas that departures from the warrant requirement strictly conform to the exigency presented.

The Court concedes that the police could prevent removal of the evidence by temporarily seizing the car for the time necessary to obtain a warrant. It does not dispute that such a course would fully protect the interests of effective law enforcement; rather it states that whether temporary seizure is a "lesser" intrusion than warrantless search "is itself a debatable question and the answer may depend on a variety of circumstances." [14] * * * I believe it clear that a warrantless search involves the greater sacrifice of Fourth Amendment values.

The Fourth Amendment proscribes, to be sure, unreasonable "seizures" as well as "searches." However, in the circumstances in which this problem is likely to occur the lesser intrusion will almost always be the simple seizure of the car for the period—perhaps a day—

[12] Where a suspect is lawfully arrested in the automobile, the officers may, of course, perform a search within the limits prescribed by *Chimel* [v. California, 395 U.S. 752, 89 S.Ct. 2034, 23 L.Ed.2d 685 (1969)] as an incident to the lawful arrest. However, as the Court recognizes, the search here exceeded those limits. Nor was the search here within the limits imposed by pre-*Chimel* law for searches incident to arrest; therefore, the retroactivity of *Chimel* is not drawn in question in this case. * * *

[13] The Court disregards the fact that *Carroll* and each of this Court's decisions upholding a warrantless vehicle search on its authority, involved a search for contraband. * * * Although subsequent dicta have omitted this limitation, * * * the *Carroll* decision has not until today been held to authorize a general search of a vehicle for evidence of crime, without a warrant, in every case where probable cause exists.

[14] The Court, unable to decide whether search or temporary seizure is the "lesser" intrusion, in this case authorizes both. The Court concludes that it was reasonable for the police to take the car to the station, where they searched it once to no avail. The searching officers then entered the station, interrogated petitioner and the car's owner, and returned later for another search of the car—this one successful. At all times the car and its contents were secure against removal or destruction. Nevertheless the Court approves the searches without even an inquiry into the officers' ability promptly to take their case before a magistrate.

necessary to enable the officers to obtain a search warrant. In the first place, as this case shows, the very facts establishing probable cause to search will often also justify arrest of the occupants of the vehicle. Since the occupants themselves are to be taken into custody, they will suffer minimal further inconvenience from the temporary immobilization of their vehicle. Even where no arrests are made, persons who wish to avoid a search—either to protect their privacy or to conceal incriminating evidence—will almost certainly prefer a brief loss of the use of the vehicle in exchange for the opportunity to have a magistrate pass upon the justification for the search. To be sure, one can conceive of instances in which the occupant, having nothing to hide and lacking concern for the privacy of the automobile, would be more deeply offended by a temporary immobilization of his vehicle than by a prompt search of it. However, such a person always remains free to consent to an immediate search, thus avoiding any delay. Where consent is not forthcoming, the occupants of the car have an interest in privacy that is protected by the Fourth Amendment even where the circumstances justify a temporary seizure. * * * The Court's endorsement of a warrantless invasion of that privacy where another course would suffice is simply inconsistent with our repeated stress on the Fourth Amendment's mandate of "adherence to judicial processes." [15]

\* \* \*

## NOTES

1. Is there a requirement that a search of an automobile in the field be impractical to justify searching it at the station without a warrant under *Chambers*? In Texas v. White, 423 U.S. 67, 96 S.Ct. 304, 46 L.Ed.2d 209 (1975), the Court reversed the Texas Court of Criminal Appeals, which had invalidated the search of the automobile on the ground that in *White*, unlike in *Chambers*, there was no reason why officers could not have conducted a thorough search of the car at the scene of the arrest. White had been arrested at 1:30 p. m. at the drive-in window of a bank for attempting to pass fraudulent checks. An officer drove White's car from its spot in the bank parking lot to the police station and searched it there without a warrant. The Court, in per curiam reversal, said: "In Chambers v. Maroney we held that police officers with probable cause to search an automobile on the scene where it was stopped could constitutionally do so later at the station house without first obtaining a warrant. There, as here, '[t]he probable cause factor' that developed on the scene 'still obtained at the station house.'" 423 U.S. at 68, 96 S.Ct. at 305, 46 L.Ed.2d at 211.

2. What vehicles are within the "automobile exception?" In California v. Carney, 471 U.S. 386, 105 S.Ct. 2066, 85 L.Ed.2d 406 (1985), DEA agents had received uncorroborated information that Carney's Dodge Mini Motor Home was being used by someone else for purposes of exchanging marihuana for sex. An agent observed Carney approach a youth in downtown San Diego; the two went to Carney's motor home, which was parked in a nearby lot. The shades of the motor home were drawn and the youth remained in it for about one and

---

[15] Circumstances might arise in which it would be impracticable to immobilize the car for the time required to obtain a warrant—for example, where a single police officer must take arrested suspects to the station, and has no way of protecting the suspects' car during his absence. In such situations it might be wholly reasonable to perform an on-the-spot search based on probable cause. However, where nothing in the situation makes impracticable the obtaining of a warrant, I cannot join the Court in shunting aside that vital Fourth Amendment safeguard.

one-quarter hours. After the youth left, the agents stopped him and elicited from him that he had received marihuana in return for allowing Carney sexual contacts. At the agent's request, the youth knocked on the motor home door. Carney came out. An agent immediately entered and observed marihuana and related items. The Supreme Court, in an opinion by Chief Justice Burger, held that the motor home was within the automobile exception:

> While it is true that [Carney's] vehicle possessed some, if not many of the attributes of a home, it is equally clear that the vehicle falls clearly within the scope of the exception * * *. Like the automobile in *Carroll*, [Carney's] motor home was readily mobile. Absent the prompt search and seizure, it could readily have been moved beyond the reach of the police. Furthermore, the vehicle was licensed to "operate on public streets; [was] serviced in public places; * * * and [was] subject to extensive regulation and inspection." Rakas v. Illinois, 439 U.S. 128, 154, n. 2, 99 S.Ct. 421, 436, n. 2, 58 L.Ed.2d 387 (1978) (Powell, J., concurring). And the vehicle was so situated that an objective observer would conclude that it was being used not as a residence, but as a vehicle. * * *

> Our application of the vehicle exception has never turned on the other uses to which a vehicle might be put. * * *

471 U.S. at 393–94, 105 S.Ct. at 2070, 85 L.Ed.2d at 414–15. The Court added:

> We need not pass on the application of the vehicle exception to a motor home that is situated in a way or place that objectively indicates that it is being used as a residence. Among the factors that might be relevant in determining whether a warrant would be required in such a circumstance is its location, whether the vehicle is readily mobile or instead, for instance, elevated on blocks, whether the vehicle is licensed, whether it is connected to utilities, and whether it has convenient access to a public road.

471 U.S. at 394 n. 3, 105 S.Ct. at 2071 n. 3, 85 L.Ed.2d at 415 n. 3. The information available to the agents, the Court also concluded, gave them "abundant probable cause" to enter and search the vehicle for evidence of a crime. As a result, the search was "reasonable" for Fourth Amendment purposes.

> Justice Stevens, joined by Justices Brennan and Marshall, dissented:

> Our prior cases teach us that inherent mobility is not a sufficient justification for the fashioning of an exception to the warrant requirement, especially in the face of heightened expectations of privacy in the location searched. Motor homes, by their common use and construction, afford their owners a substantial and legitimate expectation of privacy when they dwell within. When a motor home is parked in a location that is removed from the public highway, I believe that society is prepared to recognize that the expectations of privacy within it are not unlike the expectations one has in a fixed dwelling. As a general rule, such places may only be searched with a warrant based upon probable cause. Warrantless searches of motor homes are only reasonable when the motor home is traveling on the public streets or highways, or when exigent circumstances otherwise require an immediate search without the expenditure of time necessary to obtain a warrant.

471 U.S. at 402, 105 S.Ct. at 2075, 85 L.Ed.2d at 420 (Stevens, J., dissenting).

3. Does *Carney* also signal another expansion of the exception? Carney's motor home had not been stopped by the officer but instead was come upon while parked in an off-the-street lot. The Court's opinion appears to equate "a

vehicle * * * being used on the highways"—like those in *Carroll* and *Chambers*—with one—like Carney's motor home—"readily capable of such use and * * * found stationary in a place not regularly used for residential purposes." 471 U.S. at 392, 105 S.Ct. at 2070, 85 L.Ed.2d at 414.   Justice Stevens commented:

> Until today, * * * the Court has never decided whether the practical justifications that apply to a vehicle stopped in transit on a public way apply with the same force to a vehicle parked in a lot near a court house where it could easily be detained while a warrant is issued.

471 U.S. at 403, 105 S.Ct. at 2075, 85 L.Ed.2d at 421 (Stevens, J., dissenting).

## 2.   SEARCHES OF CONTAINERS

In United States v. Chadwick, 433 U.S. 1, 97 S.Ct. 2476, 53 L.Ed.2d 538 (1977), discussed in Chapter 2 at pages 115–16, supra, the Supreme Court held that in some circumstances officers may seize a "container" but may not search it until and if they obtain a valid search warrant. Applying *Chadwick* has presented special problems with regard to containers found in automobiles.   Several issues of this sort have been considered already.   Officers' right to search containers found in a car that is being searched incident to a valid custodial arrest was considered in New York v. Belton, reprinted at page 204, supra.   Containers found in impounded automobiles being inventoried were considered in the introductory note at pages 318–21, supra.   This subsection focuses upon containers in vehicles being searched pursuant to the doctrine developed in Chambers v. Maroney.

The Supreme Court's struggle to properly develop *Chadwick* as it applies to this context, culminating in the principal case in this subsection, involved two major cases decided between *Chadwick* and the principal case.

In Arkansas v. Sanders, 442 U.S. 753, 99 S.Ct. 2586, 61 L.Ed.2d 235 (1979), an informant of demonstrated reliability told a Little Rock officer that Sanders—who was known to both the informant and the officer—would arrive at a specific gate at the Municipal Airport that afternoon and would be carrying a green suitcase containing marihuana.   During surveillance, the officers observed Sanders' arrival at the designated gate and followed him while he met another man and obtained a green suitcase from the airline baggage.   Sanders and the other man hailed a taxi, placed the green suitcase in the trunk, and entered the taxi.   Several blocks from the airport, the officers stopped the taxi, retrieved the green suitcase from the trunk, and searched the suitcase.   Marihuana was found.   The Supreme Court concluded that the officers had probable cause to believe the suitcase contained marihuana and that they acted properly in seizing the suitcase.   But, it continued, the search of the suitcase without a warrant offended the Fourth Amendment:

> A closed suitcase in the trunk of an automobile may be as mobile as the automobile in which it rides.   But * * * the exigencies of mobility must be assessed at the point immediately before the search—after the police have seized the object to be searched and

have it securely within their control. Once police have seized a suitcase, as they did here, the extent of its mobility is in no way affected by the place from which it was taken. Accordingly as a general rule there is no greater need for warrantless searches of luggage taken from automobiles than of luggage taken from other places.

442 U.S. at 763–64, 99 S.Ct. at 2593, 61 L.Ed.2d at 244–45.

In Robbins v. California, 453 U.S. 420, 101 S.Ct. 2841, 69 L.Ed.2d 744 (1981), an officer had stopped Robbins' station wagon for a traffic violation. During the stop, the officer smelled marihuana and found some in the vehicle's passenger compartment. He then opened a recessed luggage compartment in the rear of the vehicle and observed two packages wrapped in green opaque plastic. The packages were unwrapped and marihuana was found inside. Evidence found as a result of unwrapping the packages was admitted at Robbins' trial for possession of marihuana. The Supreme Court granted certiorari and reversed. No opinion of the Court was issued. A plurality opinion authored by Justice Stewart took the position that closed opaque containers such as the plastic-covered ones at issue cannot be opened by police without a warrant, even if found in the course of a lawful search of a car. 453 U.S. at 428–29, 101 S.Ct. at 2847, 69 L.Ed.2d at 752 (Stewart, J., announcing the judgment of the Court). The Chief Justice concurred in the result without an opinion. Justice Powell concurred in the result as justified by *Sanders,* but refused to join the plurality's "mechanical requirement for a warrant before police may search any closed container." 453 U.S. at 433, 101 S.Ct. at 2849, 69 L.Ed.2d at 755 (Powell, J., concurring in the judgment).

*Robbins* was decided on July 1, 1981; on July 2, the Court adjourned for its summer recess. The 1981 term began on October 5, 1981. On October 13, the Court granted review in the case reprinted in this subsection and directed the parties to address whether the Court should reconsider *Robbins.* 454 U.S. 891, 102 S.Ct. 386, 70 L.Ed.2d 205 (1981).

## UNITED STATES v. ROSS

Supreme Court of the United States, 1982.
456 U.S. 798, 102 S.Ct. 2157, 72 L.Ed.2d 572.

JUSTICE STEVENS delivered the opinion of the Court.

In Carroll v. United States, 267 U.S. 132, 45 S.Ct. 280, 69 L.Ed. 543, the Court held that a warrantless search of an automobile stopped by police officers who had probable cause to believe the vehicle contained contraband was not unreasonable within the meaning of the Fourth Amendment. The Court in *Carroll* did not explicitly address the scope of the search that is permissible. In this case, we consider the extent to which police officers—who have legitimately stopped an automobile and who have probable cause to believe that contraband is concealed somewhere within it—may conduct a probing search of compartments and containers within the vehicle whose contents are not in plain view. We hold that they may conduct a search of the vehicle that is as thorough as a magistrate could authorize in a warrant "particularly describing the place to be searched."

I

In the evening of November 27, 1978, an informant who had previously proved to be reliable telephoned Detective Marcum of the District of Columbia Police Department and told him that an individual known as "Bandit" was selling narcotics kept in the trunk of a car parked at 439 Ridge Street. The informant stated that he had just observed "Bandit" complete a sale and that "Bandit" had told him that additional narcotics were in the trunk. The informant gave Marcum a detailed description of "Bandit" and stated that the car was a "purplish maroon" Chevrolet Malibu with District of Columbia license plates.

Accompanied by Detective Cassidy and Sergeant Gonzales, Marcum immediately drove to the area and found a maroon Malibu parked in front of 439 Ridge Street. A license check disclosed that the car was registered to Albert Ross; a computer check on Ross revealed that he fit the informant's description and used the alias "Bandit." In two passes through the neighborhood the officers did not observe anyone matching the informant's description. To avoid alerting persons on the street, they left the area.

The officers returned five minutes later and observed the maroon Malibu turning off Ridge Street onto Fourth Street. They pulled alongside the Malibu, noticed that the driver matched the informant's description, and stopped the car. Marcum and Cassidy told the driver—later identified as Albert Ross, the respondent in this action—to get out of the vehicle. While they searched Ross, Sergeant Gonzales discovered a bullet on the car's front seat. He searched the interior of the car and found a pistol in the glove compartment. Ross then was arrested and handcuffed. Detective Cassidy took Ross' keys and opened the trunk, where he found a closed brown paper bag. He opened the bag and discovered a number of glassine bags containing a white powder. Cassidy replaced the bag, closed the trunk, and drove the car to Headquarters.

At the police station Cassidy thoroughly searched the car. In addition to the "lunch-type" brown paper bag, Cassidy found in the trunk a zippered red leather pouch. He unzipped the pouch and discovered $3,200 in cash. The police laboratory later determined that the powder in the paper bag was heroin. No warrant was obtained.

Ross was charged with possession of heroin with intent to distribute, in violation of 21 U.S.C. § 841(a). Prior to trial, he moved to suppress the heroin found in the paper bag and the currency found in the leather pouch. After an evidentiary hearing, the District Court denied the motion to suppress. The heroin and currency were introduced in evidence at trial and Ross was convicted.

A three-judge panel of the Court of Appeals reversed the conviction. It held that the police had probable cause to stop and search Ross' car and that, under Carroll v. United States, supra, and Chambers v. Maroney, 399 U.S. 42, 90 S.Ct. 1975, 26 L.Ed.2d 419, the officers lawfully could search the automobile—including its trunk—without a warrant. The court considered separately, however, the warrantless search of the two containers found in the trunk. On the basis of Arkansas v. Sanders, 442 U.S. 753, 99 S.Ct. 2586, 61 L.Ed.2d 235, the court concluded that the constitutionality of a warrantless search of a container found in an automobile depends on whether the owner possesses a reasonable expectation of privacy in its contents. Applying that test, the court held that the warrantless search of the paper bag was valid but the search of the leather pouch was not. The court remanded for a new trial at which the items taken from the paper bag, but not those from the leather pouch, could be admitted.[16]

The entire Court of Appeals then voted to rehear the case en banc. A majority of the court rejected the panel's conclusion that a distinction of constitutional significance existed between the two containers found in respondent's trunk; it held that the police should not have opened either container without first obtaining a warrant. The court reasoned:

"No specific, well-delineated exception called to our attention permits the police to dispense with a warrant to open and search 'unworthy' containers. Moreover, we believe that a rule under which the validity of a warrantless search would turn on judgments about the durability of a container would impose an unreasonable and unmanageable burden on police and courts. For these reasons, and because the Fourth Amendment protects all persons, not just those with the resources or fastidiousness to place their effects in containers that decision-makers would rank in the luggage line, we hold that the Fourth Amendment warrant requirement forbids the warrantless opening of a closed, opaque paper bag to the same extent that it forbids the warrantless opening of a small unlocked suitcase or a zippered leather pouch." 655 F.2d 1159, 1161 (CADC 1981) (footnote omitted).

The en banc Court of Appeals considered, and rejected, the argument that it was reasonable for the police to open both the paper bag and the leather pouch because they were entitled to conduct a warrantless search of the entire vehicle in which the two containers were found. The majority concluded that this argument was foreclosed by Sanders.

\* \* \*

There is \* \* \* no dispute among judges about the importance of striving for clarification in this area of the law. For countless vehicles are stopped on highways and public streets every day and our cases demonstrate that it is not uncommon for police officers to have probable cause to believe that contraband may be found in a stopped vehicle. In every such case a conflict is presented between the individual's constitutionally protected interest in privacy and the public interest in effective law enforcement. No single rule of law can resolve every conflict, but our conviction that clarification is feasible led us to grant the Government's petition for certiorari in this case and to invite the

[16] The court rejected the Government's argument that the warrantless search of the leather pouch was justified as incident to respondent's arrest. The Government has not challenged this holding.

parties to address the question whether the decision in *Robbins* should be reconsidered.   454 U.S. 891, 102 S.Ct. 386, 70 L.Ed.2d 205.

\* \* \*

[The Court's extensive review of its prior "automobile search" cases is omitted.  Editors.]  Unlike *Chadwick* and *Sanders*, in this case police officers had probable cause to search respondent's entire vehicle.  Unlike *Robbins*, in this case the parties have squarely addressed the question whether, in the course of a legitimate warrantless search of an automobile, police are entitled to open containers found within the vehicle.  We now address that question.  Its answer is determined by the scope of the search that is authorized by the exception to the warrant requirement set forth in *Carroll*.

### IV

In *Carroll* itself, the whiskey that the prohibition agents seized was not in plain view.  It was discovered only after an officer opened the rumble seat and tore open the upholstery of the lazyback.  The Court did not find the scope of the search unreasonable.  Having stopped Carroll and Kiro on a public road and subjected them to the indignity of a vehicle search—which the Court found to be a reasonable intrusion on their privacy because it was based on probable cause that their vehicle was transporting contraband—prohibition agents were entitled to tear open a portion of the roadster itself.  The scope of the search was no greater than a magistrate could have authorized by issuing a warrant based on the probable cause that justified the search.  Since such a warrant could have authorized the agents to open the rear portion of the roadster and to rip the upholstery in their search for concealed whiskey, the search was constitutionally permissible.

In Chambers v. Maroney the police found weapons and stolen property "concealed in a compartment under the dashboard."  399 U.S., at 44, 90 S.Ct., at 1977.  No suggestion was made that the scope of the search was impermissible.  It would be illogical to assume that the outcome of *Chambers*—or the outcome of *Carroll* itself—would have been different if the police had found the secreted contraband enclosed within a secondary container and had opened that container without a warrant.  If it was reasonable for prohibition agents to rip open the upholstery in *Carroll*, it certainly would have been reasonable for them to look into a burlap sack stashed inside;  if it was reasonable to open the concealed compartment in *Chambers*, it would have been equally reasonable to open a paper bag crumpled within it.  A contrary rule could produce absurd results inconsistent with the decision in *Carroll* itself.

In its application of *Carroll*, this Court in fact has sustained warrantless searches of containers found during a lawful search of an automobile.  In Husty v. United States, 282 U.S. 694, 51 S.Ct. 240, 75 L.Ed. 629, the Court upheld a warrantless seizure of whiskey found during a search of an automobile, some of which was discovered in "whiskey bags" that could have contained other goods.  In Scher v. United States, 305 U.S. 251, 59 S.Ct. 174, 83 L.Ed. 151, federal officers seized and searched packages of unstamped liquor found in the trunk of an automobile searched without a warrant. As described by a police officer who participated in the search: "I turned the handle and opened the trunk and found the trunk completely filled with packages wrapped in brown paper, and tied with twine; I think somewhere around thirty packages, each one containing six bottles." In these cases it was not contended that police officers needed a warrant to open the whiskey bags or to unwrap the brown paper packages. These decisions nevertheless "have much weight, as they show that this point neither occurred to the bar or the bench." Bank of the United States v. Deveaux, 5 Cranch 61, 88, 3 L.Ed. 38 (Marshall, C.J.). The fact that no such argument was even made illuminates the profession's understanding of the scope of the search permitted under *Carroll*. Indeed, prior to the decisions in *Chadwick* and *Sanders*, courts routinely had held that containers and packages found during a legitimate warrantless search of an automobile also could be searched without a warrant.

As we have stated, the decision in *Carroll* was based on the Court's appraisal of practical considerations viewed in the perspective of history. It is therefore significant that the practical consequences of the *Carroll* decision would be largely nullified if the permissible scope of a warrantless search of an automobile did not include containers and packages found inside the vehicle. Contraband goods rarely are strewn across the trunk or floor of a car; since by their very nature such goods must be withheld from public view, they rarely can be placed in an automobile unless they are enclosed within some form of container. The Court in *Carroll* held that "contraband goods *concealed* and illegally transported in an automobile or other vehicle may be searched for without a warrant." 267 U.S., at 153, 45 S.Ct., at 285 (emphasis added). As we noted in Henry v. United States, 361 U.S. 98, 104, 80 S.Ct. 168, 172, 4 L.Ed.2d 134, the decision in *Carroll* "merely relaxed the requirements for a warrant on grounds of impracticability." It neither broadened nor limited the scope of a lawful search based on probable cause.

A lawful search of fixed premises generally extends to the entire area in which the object of the search may be found and is not limited by the possibility that separate acts of entry or opening may be required to complete the search. Thus, a warrant that authorizes an officer to search a home for illegal weapons also provides authority to open closets, chests, drawers, and containers in which the weapon may be found. A warrant to open a footlocker to search for marijuana would also authorize the opening of packages found inside. A warrant to search a vehicle would support a search of every part of the vehicle that might contain the object of the search. When a legitimate search is under way, and when its purpose and its limits have been precisely defined, nice distinctions between closets, drawers, and containers, in the case of a home, or between glove compartments, upholstered seats, trunks, and wrapped packages, in the case of a vehicle, must give way to the interest in the prompt and efficient completion of the task at hand.[17]

---

[17] The practical considerations that justify a warrantless search of an automobile continue to apply until the entire search of the automobile and its contents has been

This rule applies equally to all containers, as indeed we believe it must. One point on which the Court was in virtually unanimous agreement in *Robbins* was that a constitutional distinction between "worthy" and "unworthy" containers would be improper. Even though such a distinction perhaps could evolve in a series of cases in which paper bags, locked trunks, lunch buckets, and orange crates were placed on one side of the line or the other,[18] the central purpose of the Fourth Amendment forecloses such a distinction. For just as the most frail cottage in the kingdom is absolutely entitled to the same guarantees of privacy as the most majestic mansion, so also may a traveler who carries a toothbrush and a few articles of clothing in a paper bag or knotted scarf claim an equal right to conceal his possessions from official inspection as the sophisticated executive with the locked attaché case.

As Justice Stewart stated in *Robbins,* the Fourth Amendment provides protection to the owner of every container that conceals its contents from plain view. 453 U.S., at 427, 101 S.Ct., at 2846 (plurality opinion). But the protection afforded by the Amendment varies in different settings. The luggage carried by a traveler entering the country may be searched at random by a customs officer; the luggage may be searched no matter how great the traveler's desire to conceal the contents may be. A container carried at the time of arrest often may be searched without a warrant and even without any specific suspicion concerning its contents. A container that may conceal the object of a search authorized by a warrant may be opened immediately; the individual's interest in privacy must give way to the magistrate's official determination of probable cause.

In the same manner, an individual's expectation of privacy in a vehicle and its contents may not survive if probable cause is given to believe that the vehicle is transporting contraband. Certainly the privacy interests in a car's trunk or glove compartment may be no less than those in a movable container. An individual undoubtedly has a significant interest that the upholstery of his automobile will not be ripped or a hidden compartment within it opened. These interests must yield to the authority of a search, however, which—in light of

completed. Arguably, the entire vehicle itself (including its upholstery) could be searched without a warrant, with all wrapped articles and containers found during that search then taken to a magistrate. But prohibiting police from opening immediately a container in which the object of the search is most likely to be found and instead forcing them first to comb the entire vehicle would actually exacerbate the intrusion on privacy interests. Moreover, until the container itself was opened the police could never be certain that the contraband was not secreted in a yet undiscovered portion of the vehicle; thus in every case in which a container was found, the vehicle would need to be secured while a warrant was obtained. Such a requirement would be directly inconsistent with

the rationale supporting the decisions in *Carroll* and *Chambers.*

[18] If the distinction is based on the proposition that the Fourth Amendment protects only those containers that objectively manifest an individual's reasonable expectation of privacy, however, the propriety of a warrantless search necessarily would turn on much more than the fabric of the container. A paper bag stapled shut and marked "private" might be found to manifest a reasonable expectation of privacy, as could a cardboard box stacked on top of two pieces of heavy luggage. The propriety of the warrantless search seemingly would turn on an objective appraisal of all the surrounding circumstances.

*Carroll*—does not itself require the prior approval of a magistrate. The scope of a warrantless search based on probable cause is no narrower— and no broader—than the scope of a search authorized by a warrant supported by probable cause. Only the prior approval of the magistrate is waived; the search otherwise is as the magistrate could authorize.

The scope of a warrantless search of an automobile thus is not defined by the nature of the container in which the contraband is secreted. Rather, it is defined by the object of the search and the places in which there is probable cause to believe that it may be found. Just as probable cause to believe that a stolen lawnmower may be found in a garage will not support a warrant to search an upstairs bedroom, probable cause to believe that undocumented aliens are being transported in a van will not justify a warrantless search of a suitcase. Probable cause to believe that a container placed in the trunk of a taxi contains contraband or evidence does not justify a search of the entire cab.

## V

Our decision today is inconsistent with the disposition in Robbins v. California and with the portion of the opinion in Arkansas v. Sanders on which the plurality in *Robbins* relied. Nevertheless, the doctrine of *stare decisis* does not preclude this action. Although we have rejected some of the reasoning in *Sanders,* we adhere to our holding in that case; although we reject the precise holding in *Robbins,* there was no Court opinion supporting a single rationale for its judgment and the reasoning we adopt today was not presented by the parties in that case. Moreover, it is clear that no legitimate reliance interest can be frustrated by our decision today. Of greatest importance, we are convinced that the rule we apply in this case is faithful to the interpretation of the Fourth Amendment that the Court has followed with substantial consistency throughout our history.

We reaffirm the basic rule of Fourth Amendment jurisprudence stated by Justice Stewart for a unanimous Court in Mincey v. Arizona, 437 U.S. 385, 390, 98 S.Ct. 2408, 2412, 57 L.Ed.2d 290:

> "The Fourth Amendment proscribes all unreasonable searches and seizures, and it is a cardinal principle that 'searches conducted outside the judicial process, without prior approval by judge or magistrate, are *per se* unreasonable under the Fourth Amendment—subject only to a few specifically established and well-delineated exceptions.' Katz v. United States, 389 U.S. 347, 357 [88 S.Ct. 507, 514, 19 L.Ed.2d 576] (footnotes omitted)."

The exception recognized in *Carroll* is unquestionably one that is "specifically established and well-delineated." We hold that the scope of the warrantless search authorized by that exception is no broader and no narrower than a magistrate could legitimately authorize by warrant. If probable cause justifies the search of a lawfully stopped vehicle, it justifies the search of every part of the vehicle and its contents that may conceal the object of the search.

The judgment of the Court of Appeals is reversed. The case is remanded for further proceedings consistent with this opinion.

It is so ordered.

JUSTICE WHITE, dissenting:

I would not overrule Robbins v. California, 453 U.S. 420, 101 S.Ct. 2841, 69 L.Ed.2d 744 (1981). For the reasons stated by Justice Stewart in that case, I would affirm the judgment of the Court of Appeals. I also agree with much of Justice Marshall's dissent in this case.

JUSTICE MARSHALL, with whom JUSTICE BRENNAN joins, dissenting.

The majority today not only repeals all realistic limits on warrantless automobile searches, it repeals the Fourth Amendment warrant requirement itself. * * *

# I

According to the majority, whenever police have probable cause to believe that contraband may be found within an automobile that they have stopped on the highway,[19] they may search not only the automobile but also any container found inside it, without obtaining a warrant. The scope of the search, we are told, is as broad as a magistrate could authorize in a warrant to search the automobile. The majority makes little attempt to justify this rule in terms of recognized Fourth Amendment values. The Court simply ignores the critical function that a magistrate serves. And although the Court purports to rely on the mobility of an automobile and the impracticability of obtaining a warrant, it never explains why these concerns permit the warrantless search of a *container,* which can easily be seized and immobilized while police are obtaining a warrant.

# A

* * *

Our cases do recognize a narrow exception to the warrant requirement for certain automobile searches. Throughout our decisions, two major considerations have been advanced to justify the automobile exception to the warrant requirement. We have upheld only those searches that are actually justified by those considerations.

First, these searches have been justified on the basis of the exigency of the mobility of the automobile. * * *

Because an automobile presents much of its contents in open view to police officers who legitimately stop it on a public way, is used for travel, and is subject to significant government regulation, this Court has determined that the intrusion of a warrantless search of an automobile is constitutionally less significant than a warrantless search of more private areas. * * *

---

[19] The Court confines its holding today to automobiles stopped on the highway which police have probable cause to believe contain contraband. I do not understand the Court to address the applicability of the automobile exception rule announced today to parked cars. Cf. Coolidge v. New Hampshire, 403 U.S. 443, 91 S.Ct. 2022, 29 L.Ed.2d 564 (1971).

## B

The majority's rule is flatly inconsistent with these established Fourth Amendment principles concerning the scope of the automobile exception and the importance of the warrant requirement. Historically, the automobile exception has been limited to those situations where its application is compelled by the justifications described above. Today, the majority makes no attempt to base its decision on these justifications. This failure is not surprising, since the traditional rationales for the automobile exception plainly do not support extending it to the search of a container found inside a vehicle.

The practical mobility problem—deciding what to do with both the car and the occupants if an immediate search is not conducted—is simply not present in the case of movable containers, which can easily be seized and brought to the magistrate. The lesser expectation of privacy rationale also has little force. A container, as opposed to the car itself, does not reflect diminished privacy interests. * * *

## C

\* \* \*

In light of these considerations, I conclude that any movable container found within an automobile deserves precisely the same degree of Fourth Amendment warrant protection that it would deserve if found at a location outside the automobile. *Chadwick,* as the majority notes, "reaffirmed the general principle that closed packages and containers may not be searched without a warrant." Although there is no need to describe the exact contours of that protection in this dissenting opinion, it is clear enough that closed, opaque containers—regardless of whether they are "worthy" or are always used to store personal items—are ordinarily fully protected.

Here, because appellant Ross had placed the evidence in question in a closed paper bag, the container could be seized, but not searched, without a warrant. No practical exigencies required the warrantless searches on the street or at the station: Ross had been arrested and was in custody when both searches occurred, and the police succeeded in transporting the bag to the station without inadvertently spilling its contents.

## II

\* \* \*

[T]he majority argues that *Carroll* and *Chambers* support its decisions because integral compartments of a car are functionally equivalent to containers found within a car, and because the practical advantages to the police of the *Carroll* doctrine "would be largely nullified if the permissible scope of a warrantless search of an automobile did not include containers and packages found inside the vehicle." Neither of these arguments is persuasive. First, the Court's argument that allowing warrantless searches of certain integral compartments of the car in *Carroll* and *Chambers,* while protecting movable containers within the car, would be "illogical" and "absurd," ignores the reason why this Court has allowed warrantless searches of automobile compartments. Surely an integral compartment within a car is just as mobile, and presents the same practical problems of safekeeping, as the car itself. This cannot be said of movable containers located within the car. The fact that there may be a high expectation of privacy in both containers and compartments is irrelevant, since the privacy rationale is not, and cannot be, the justification for the warrantless search of compartments.

The Court's second argument, which focuses on the practical advantages to police of the *Carroll* doctrine, fares no better. The practical considerations which concerned the *Carroll* Court involved the difficulty of immobilizing a vehicle while a warrant must be obtained. The Court had no occasion to address whether *containers* present the same practical difficulties as the car itself or integral compartments of the car. They do not. * * * [T]he burden to police departments of seizing a package or personal luggage simply does not compare to the burden of seizing and safeguarding automobiles. * * *

Finally, the majority's new rule is theoretically unsound and will create anomalous and unwarranted results. These consequences are readily apparent from the Court's attempt to reconcile its new rule with the holdings of *Chadwick* and *Sanders*. The Court suggests that probable cause to search only a container does not justify a warrantless search of an automobile in which it is placed, absent reason to believe that the contents could be secreted elsewhere in the vehicle. This, the majority asserts, is an indication that the new rule is carefully limited to its justification, and is not inconsistent with *Chadwick* and *Sanders*. But why is such a container more private, less difficult for police to seize and store, or in any other relevant respect more properly subject to the warrant requirement, than a container that police discover in a probable cause search in an entire automobile? This rule plainly has peculiar and unworkable consequences: the Government "must show that the investigating officer knew enough but not too much, that he had sufficient knowledge to establish probable cause but insufficient knowledge to know exactly where the contraband was located." United States v. Ross, 655 F.2d 1159, 1202 (CADC 1981) (en banc) (Wilkey, J., dissenting).

Alternatively, the majority may be suggesting that *Chadwick* and *Sanders* may be explained because the connection of the container to the vehicle was incidental in these two cases. That is, because police had preexisting probable cause to seize and search the containers, they were not entitled to wait until the item was placed in a vehicle to take advantage of the automobile exception. I wholeheartedly agree that police cannot employ a pretext to escape Fourth Amendment prohibitions and cannot rely on an exigency that they could easily have avoided. This interpretation, however, might well be an exception that swallows up the majority's rule. In neither *Chadwick* nor *Sanders* did the Court suggest that the delay of the police was a pretext for taking advantage of the automobile exception. For all that appears, the Government may have had legitimate reasons for not searching as soon as they had probable cause. In any event, asking police to rely on such an uncertain line in distinguishing between legitimate and illegitimate searches for containers in automobiles hardly indicates that the majority's approach has brought clarification to this area of the law. * * *

## III

* * *

This case will have profound implications for the privacy of citizens traveling in automobiles, as the Court well understands. "For countless vehicles are stopped on highways and public streets every day and our cases demonstrate that it is not uncommon for police officers to have probable cause to believe that contraband may be found in a stopped vehicle." A closed paper bag, a tool box, a knapsack, a suitcase, and an attache case can alike be searched without the protection of the judgment of a neutral magistrate, based only on the rarely disturbed decision of a police officer that he has probable cause to search for contraband in the vehicle. The Court derives satisfaction from the fact that its rule does not exalt the rights of the wealthy over the rights of the poor. A rule so broad that all citizens lose vital Fourth Amendment protection is no cause for celebration.

I dissent.

### NOTES

In United States v. Johns, 469 U.S. 478, 105 S.Ct. 881, 83 L.Ed.2d 890 (1985), federal Customs agents followed two pickup trucks from Tucson, Arizona to a remote airport located 50 miles from the Mexican border. Two small aircraft landed and then departed; officers conducting air surveillance reported that one of the trucks had driven to one of the planes. The officers on the ground approached the trucks and smelled what they believed was marihuana. In the back of the trucks they could see packages wrapped in dark green plastic, which they knew from experience was a common manner of packaging marihuana. All persons at the scene were arrested. The trucks were taken to local DEA headquarters in Tucson and the packages were removed from the trucks and placed in a warehouse. Three days later, some of the packages were opened and samples of the contents were taken. Analysis of these samples confirmed that the packages contained marihuana. A defense challenge to the admissibility of the marihuana failed and appeal followed. The Court of Appeals held the search of the packages improper because of the absence of a warrant. *Ross* did not control, in the court's view, because of the three day lapse after the packages were removed from the trucks. The Supreme Court reversed. Under *Ross*, the officers could have searched the packages when they were first discovered in the trucks at the air strip. The majority continued:

> The warrantless search of the packages was not unreasonable merely because the Customs officers returned to Tucson and placed the packages in a DEA warehouse rather than immediately open them. The practical effect of the opposite conclusion would only be to direct police officers to search immediately all containers that they discover in the course of a vehicle search. This result would be of little benefit to the person whose property is searched, and where police officers are entitled to seize the container and continue to have probable cause to believe that it contains contraband, we do not think that delay in the execution of the warrantless search is necessarily unreasonable.

We do not suggest that police officers may indefinitely retain possession of a vehicle and its contents before they complete a search. Nor do we foreclose the possibility that the owner of a vehicle or its contents might attempt to prove that delay in the completion of a vehicle search was unreasonable because it adversely affected a privacy or possessory interest. We note that in this case there was probable cause to believe the trucks contained contraband and there is no plausible argument that the object of the search could not have been concealed in the packages. Respondents do not challenge the legitimacy of the seizure of the trucks or the packages, and they never sought return of the property. Thus, respondents have not even alleged, much less proved, that the delay in the search of packages adversely affected legitimate interests protected by the Fourth Amendment. * * *

469 U.S. at 486–87, 105 S.Ct. at 886–87, 83 L.Ed.2d at 898–99. Justice Brennan, joined by Justice Marshall, dissented, reasoning that at the time of the search "no exigencies precluded reasonable efforts to obtain a warrant prior to a search of the packages in the warehouse." 469 U.S. at 489, 105 S.Ct. at 888, 83 L.Ed.2d at 900 (Brennan, J., dissenting).

## E. SEARCHES AND SEIZURES AT OR NEAR INTERNATIONAL BORDERS

Searches and other law enforcement activity related to the international border have traditionally given rise to substantial concern. Statutory authority to conduct activity of this sort consists of grants of authority to both the Bureau of Customs and the Department of Immigrations. Customs officers are authorized in 19 U.S.C.A. § 482 to "stop, search, and examine * * * any vehicle, beast, or person, on which or whom he or they shall suspect there is merchandise which is subject to duty, or shall have been introduced into the United States in any manner contrary to law * * *" Under 19 U.S.C.A. § 1581(a), customs officers are authorized to go on board any vessel or vehicle and to "search the vessel or vehicle and every part thereof and any person, trunk, package or cargo on board * * *." Immigration officers, on the other hand, are authorized by 8 U.S.C.A. § 1357(a)(1) to interrogate any person "believed to be an alien as to his right to be or remain in the United States * * *". They are also authorized to board any vessel, railway car or conveyance "within a reasonable distance" of any external border to search for persons who have illegally entered the country. 8 U.S.C.A. § 1357(a)(3). "Reasonable distance" is to be defined by regulation. Border patrol officers, as agents of the Department of Immigration, might be thought by the nature of their concern to have a somewhat more limited right to search than customs officials. But the Bureau of Customs has designated border patrol officers as customs agents and in this latter capacity they may search for things improperly brought over the border. See United States v. Thompson, 475 F.2d 1359 (5th Cir.1973).

Federal law enforcement activity conducted pursuant to this authority consists of several legally significant types. One, of course, is the process at the international border itself (and at the "functional equivalents" of the border) of searching and—in the case of persons—questioning persons and things actually then crossing the border. But in addition the Immigration and Naturalization Service conducts "area control" operations in the interior of the United States. These consist of traffic control operations and factory surveys to identify illegally entered aliens working at jobs. See Immigration and Naturalization Service v. Delgado, 466 U.S. 210, 225 n. 1, 104 S.Ct. 1758, 1767 n. 1, 80 L.Ed.2d 247, 261 n. 1 (1984) (Brennan, J., concurring in part and dissenting in part). In regard to the traffic control operations, the Court has noted:

> The Border Patrol conducts three types of surveillance along inland roadways, all in the asserted interest of detecting the illegal importation of aliens. Permanent checkpoints are maintained at certain nodal intersections; temporary checkpoints are established from time to time at various places; and finally, there are roving patrols * * *.

Almeida-Sanchez v. United States, 413 U.S. 266, 268, 93 S.Ct. 2535, 2537, 37 L.Ed.2d 596, 600 (1973). The first subsection of this section deals with law enforcement activity at the border or its functional equivalents. In the second, "area control" operations are considered.

## 1.  ENFORCEMENT ACTIVITY AT THE INTERNATIONAL BORDER

The Supreme Court has not had occasion to definitively address the limits, if any, that the federal constitution places upon law enforcement activity at the international border itself. But its basic position has often been made clear in dictum:

> That searches made at the border, pursuant to the long-standing right of the sovereign to protect itself by stopping and examining persons and property crossing into this country, are reasonable simply by virtue of the fact that they occur at the border, should, by now, require no extended demonstration.

United States v. Ramsey, 431 U.S. 606, 616, 97 S.Ct. 1972, 1978, 52 L.Ed.2d 617, 626 (1977). In *Ramsey,* the Court considered the constitutionality of a border search of mail conducted without a warrant and without probable cause. A customs inspector opened several letter size envelopes mailed from Thailand that felt unusually bulky. Heroin was discovered in each. A federal statute authorizes customs officials to open incoming international mail if there is "reasonable cause to suspect" that merchandise or contraband will be found. 19 U.S.C.A. § 482. A regulation prohibits reading any correspondence in such envelopes without judicial authorization. 19 C.F.R. § 145.3 (1976). Rejecting the argument that special Fourth Amendment considerations apply to "mailed letter size envelopes," the Court upheld the opening of the envelopes at issue.

There remains significant question as to the additional requirements that apply, if any do, when the search is one that is extraordinarily intrusive. Some lower court decisions impose at least minimal requirements upon personal searches that involve removal of clothing ("strip" searches) or probing or other inspection of body cavities or induced disgorging of the stomach contents for "inspection" ("body cavity" searches). The Ninth Circuit, for example, has held that information amounting to a "real suspicion" is required for a strip search but that there must be a "clear indication" or "plain suggestion" of contraband in a body cavity before a search of that body cavity is permissible. United States v. Shields, 453 F.2d 1235 (9th Cir.1972), cert. denied 406 U.S. 910, 92 S.Ct. 1615, 31 L.Ed.2d 821 (1972). Compare United States v. Asbury, 586 F.2d 973, 976 (2d Cir.1978) (adopting 5th Circuit requirement of "reasonable suspicion" for strip searches rather than "real suspicion").

The Court has also made clear that at least some activity permissible at the border itself may also take place at other locations within the country's borders:

> [R]outine border search[s] * * * may in certain circumstances take place not only at the border itself, but at its functional equivalents as well. For example, searches at an established station near the border, at a point marking the confluence of two or more roads that extend from the border, might be functional equivalents of border searches. For another example, a search of the passengers and cargo of an airplane arriving at a St. Louis airport after a nonstop flight from Mexico City would clearly be the functional equivalent of a border search.

Almeida-Sanchez v. United States, 413 U.S. 266, 272–73, 93 S.Ct. 2535, 2539, 37 L.Ed.2d 596, 602–03 (1973).

But the Court refused to expand the concept of the border in Torres v. Puerto Rico, 442 U.S. 465, 99 S.Ct. 2425, 61 L.Ed.2d 1 (1979). Upon Torres' arrival at San Juan's airport on a commercial flight from Miami, his luggage was searched pursuant to a Puerto Rican statute authorizing police to search the luggage of any person arriving in the Commonwealth from the United States. Emphasizing its "unique political status" as a commonwealth and its physical status as an island, Puerto Rico urged that the Court recognize an "intermediate border" between it and the rest of the United States at which its law enforcement officers have the same freedom to search as is possessed by United States officers at the international border. It stressed that such authority to search would enable it to deal with serious problems caused by the influx of weapons and narcotics. The Supreme Court rejected the argument:

> The authority of the United States to search the baggage of arriving international travelers is based on its inherent sovereign authority to protect its territorial integrity. By reason of that authority, it is entitled to require that whoever seeks entry must establish the right to enter and to bring into the country whatever he may carry. Puerto Rico has no sovereign authority to prohibit entry into its territory. * * * Congress has provided by statute that Puerto Rico must accord all citizens of the United States the privileges and immunities of its own residents. Act of Aug. 5, 1947, § 7, 61 Stat. 772, 48 U.S.C.A. § 737.

442 U.S. at 472–73, 99 S.Ct. at 2430–31, 61 L.Ed.2d at 9. Puerto Rico's law enforcement problems, the Court continued, are indistinguishable from those of many states that are isolated or have boundaries that coincide in part with the country's international boundaries. A "generalized urgency of law enforcement," such as that presented by the Commonwealth's argument, has not persuaded the Court to dispense with the fundamental requirements of the Fourth Amendment. 442 U.S. at 474, 99 S.Ct. at 2431, 61 L.Ed.2d at 9–10.

## UNITED STATES v. MONTOYA DE HERNANDEZ

Supreme Court of the United States, 1985.
473 U.S. 531, 105 S.Ct. 3304, 87 L.Ed.2d 381.

JUSTICE REHNQUIST delivered the opinion of the Court.

Respondent Rosa Elvira Montoya de Hernandez \* \* \* arrived at Los Angeles International Airport shortly after midnight, March 5, 1983, on Avianca Flight 080, a direct 10-hour flight from Bogota, Colombia. Her visa was in order so she was passed through Immigration and proceeded to the customs desk. At the customs desk she encountered Customs Inspector Talamantes, who reviewed her documents and noticed from her passport that she had made at least eight recent trips to either Miami or Los Angeles. Talamantes referred respondent to a secondary customs' desk for further questioning. At this desk Talamantes and another inspector asked respondent general questions concerning herself and the purpose of her trip. Respondent revealed that she spoke no English and had no family or friends in the United States. She explained in Spanish that she had come to the United States to purchase goods for her husband's store in Bogota. The customs inspectors recognized Bogota as a "source city" for narcotics. Respondent possessed $5,000 in cash, mostly $50 bills, but had no billfold. She indicated to the inspectors that she had no appointments with merchandise vendors, but planned to ride around Los Angeles in taxicabs visiting retail stores such as J.C. Penney and K–Mart in order to buy goods for her husband's store with the $5,000.

Respondent admitted that she had no hotel reservations, but stated that she planned to stay at a Holiday Inn. Respondent could not recall how her airline ticket was purchased. When the inspectors opened respondent's one small valise they found about four changes of "cold weather" clothing. Respondent had no shoes other than the high-heeled pair she was wearing. Although respondent possessed no checks, waybills, credit cards, or letters of credit, she did produce a Colombian business card and a number of old receipts, waybills, and fabric swatches displayed in a photo album.

At this point Talamantes and the other inspector suspected that respondent was a "balloon swallower," one who attempts to smuggle narcotics into this country hidden in her alimentary canal. Over the years Inspector Talamantes had apprehended dozens of alimentary canal smugglers arriving on Avianca Flight 080.

The inspectors requested a female customs inspector to take respondent to a private area and conduct a patdown and strip search.

During the search the female inspector felt respondent's abdomen area and noticed a firm fullness, as if respondent were wearing a girdle. The search revealed no contraband but the inspector noticed that respondent was wearing two pair of elastic underpants with a paper towel lining the crotch area.

When respondent returned to the customs area and the female inspector reported her discoveries, the inspector in charge told respondent that he suspected she was smuggling drugs in her alimentary canal. Respondent agreed to the inspector's request that she be x rayed at a hospital but in answer to the inspector's query stated that she was pregnant. She agreed to a pregnancy test before the x ray. Respondent withdrew the consent for an x ray when she learned that she would have to be handcuffed en route to the hospital. The inspector then gave respondent the option of returning to Colombia on the next available flight, agreeing to an x ray, or remaining in detention until she produced a monitored bowel movement that would confirm or rebut the inspectors' suspicions. Respondent chose the first option and was placed in a customs' office under observation. She was told that if she went to the toilet she would have to use a wastebasket in the women's restroom, in order that female customs inspectors could inspect her stool for balloons or capsules carrying narcotics. The inspectors refused respondent's request to place a telephone call.

Respondent sat in the customs office, under observation, for the remainder of the night. During the night customs officials attempted to place respondent on a Mexican airline that was flying to Bogota via Mexico City in the morning. The airline refused to transport respondent because she lacked a Mexican visa necessary to land in Mexico City. Respondent was not permitted to leave, and was informed that she would be detained until she agreed to an x ray or her bowels moved. She remained detained in the customs office under observation, for most of the time curled up in a chair leaning to one side. She refused all offers of food and drink, and refused to use the toilet facilities. The Court of Appeals noted that she exhibited symptoms of discomfort consistent with "heroic efforts to resist the usual calls of nature."

At the shift change at 4:00 p.m. the next afternoon, almost 16 hours after her flight had landed, respondent still had not defecated or urinated or partaken of food or drink. At that time customs officials sought a court order authorizing a pregnancy test, an x ray, and a rectal examination. The Federal Magistrate issued an order just before midnight that evening, which authorized a rectal examination and involuntary x ray, provided that the physician in charge considered respondent's claim of pregnancy. Respondent was taken to a hospital and given a pregnancy test, which later turned out to be negative. Before the results of the pregnancy test were known, a physician conducted a rectal examination and removed from respondent's rectum a balloon containing a foreign substance. Respondent was then placed formally under arrest. By 4:10 a.m. respondent had passed 6 similar balloons; over the next 4 days she passed 88 balloons containing a total of 528 grams of 80% pure cocaine hydrochloride.

After a suppression hearing the District Court admitted the cocaine in evidence against respondent. She was convicted of possession of cocaine with intent to distribute and unlawful importation of cocaine.

A divided panel of the United States Court of Appeals for the Ninth Circuit reversed respondent's convictions. The court noted that customs inspectors had a "justifiably high level of official skepticism" about respondent's good motives, but the inspectors decided to let nature take its course rather than seek an immediate magistrate's warrant for an x ray. Such a magistrate's warrant required a "clear indication" or "plain suggestion" that the traveler was an alimentary canal smuggler under previous decisions of the Court of Appeals. The court applied this required level of suspicion to respondent's case. The court questioned the "humanity" of the inspectors' decision to hold respondent until her bowels moved, knowing that she would suffer "many hours of humiliating discomfort" if she chose not to submit to the x-ray examination. The court concluded that under a "clear indication" standard "the evidence available to the customs officers when they decided to hold [respondent] for continued observation was insufficient to support the 16-hour detention."

The government contends that the customs inspectors reasonably suspected that respondent was an alimentary canal smuggler, and this suspicion was sufficient to justify the detention. In support of the judgment below respondent argues, *inter alia*, that reasonable suspicion would not support respondent's detention, and in any event the inspectors did not reasonably suspect that respondent was carrying narcotics internally.

The Fourth Amendment commands that searches and seizures be reasonable. What is reasonable depends upon all of the circumstances surrounding the search or seizure and the nature of the search or seizure itself. The permissibility of a particular law enforcement practice is judged by "balancing its intrusion on the individual's Fourth Amendment interests against its promotion of legitimate governmental interests." United States v. Villamonte-Marquez, 462 U.S. 579, 588, 103 S.Ct. 2573, 2579, 77 L.Ed.2d 22 (1983).

Here the seizure of respondent took place at the international border. Since the founding of our Republic, Congress has granted the Executive plenary authority to conduct routine searches and seizures at the border, without probable cause or a warrant, in order to regulate the collection of duties and to prevent the introduction of contraband into this country. This Court has long recognized Congress' power to police entrants at the border. * * * Consistently, therefore, with Congress' power to protect the Nation by stopping and examining persons entering this country, the Fourth Amendment's balance of reasonableness is qualitatively different at the international border than in the interior. Routine searches of the persons and effects of entrants are not subject to any requirement of reasonable suspicion, probable cause, or warrant, and first-class mail may be opened without a warrant on less than probable cause. Automotive travelers may be stopped at fixed check points near the border without individualized suspicion even if the stop is based largely on ethnicity, United States v. Martinez-Fuerte, 428 U.S. 543, 562–563, 96 S.Ct. 3074, 3085, 49 L.Ed.2d 1116 (1976), and boats on inland waters with ready access to the sea may be hailed and boarded with no suspicion whatever. United States v. Villamonte-Marquez, supra, 462 U.S. at 592–93, 103 S.Ct., at 2582.

These cases reflect longstanding concern for the protection of the integrity of the border. This concern is, if anything, heightened by the veritable national crisis in law enforcement caused by smuggling of illicit narcotics, and in particular by the increasing utilization of alimentary canal smuggling. This desperate practice appears to be a relatively recent addition to the smugglers' repertoire of deceptive practices, and it also appears to be exceedingly difficult to detect.
\* \* \*

Balanced against the sovereign's interests at the border are the Fourth Amendment rights of respondent. Having presented herself at the border for admission, and having subjected herself to the criminal enforcement powers of the Federal Government, respondent was entitled to be free from unreasonable search and seizure. But not only is the expectation of privacy less at the border than in the interior, but the Fourth Amendment balance between the interests of the Government and the privacy right of the individual is struck much more favorably to the Government at the border.

We have not previously decided what level of suspicion would justify a seizure of an incoming traveler for purposes other than a routine border search. The Court of Appeals held that the initial detention of respondent was permissible only if the inspectors possessed a "clear indication" of alimentary canal smuggling. This "clear indication" language comes from our opinion in Schmerber v. California, 384 U.S. 757, 86 S.Ct. 1826, 16 L.Ed.2d 908 (1966), but we think that the Court of Appeals misapprehended the significance of that phrase in the context in which it was used in *Schmerber*. The Court of Appeals for the Ninth Circuit viewed "clear indication" as an intermediate standard between "reasonable suspicion" and "probable cause." But we think that the words in *Schmerber* were used to indicate the necessity for particularized suspicion that the evidence sought might be found within the body of the individual, rather than as enunciating still a third Fourth Amendment threshold between "reasonable suspicion" and "probable cause."

No other court, including this one, has ever adopted *Schmerber*'s "clear indication" language as a Fourth Amendment standard. \* \* \* We do not think that the Fourth Amendment's emphasis upon reasonableness is consistent with the creation of a third verbal standard in addition to "reasonable suspicion" and "probable cause"; we are dealing with a constitutional requirement of reasonableness, \* \* \* and subtle verbal gradations may obscure rather than elucidate the meaning of the provision in question.

We hold that the detention of a traveler at the border, beyond the scope of a routine customs search and inspection, is justified at its inception if customs agents, considering all the facts surrounding the traveler and her trip, reasonably suspect that the traveler is smuggling contraband in her alimentary canal.[20]

The "reasonable suspicion" standard has been applied in a number of contexts and effects a needed balance between private and public interests when law enforcement officials must make a limited intrusion on less than probable cause. It thus fits well into the situations involving alimentary canal smuggling at the border: this type of smuggling gives no external signs and inspectors will rarely possess probable cause to arrest or search, yet governmental interests in stopping smuggling at the border are high indeed. Under this standard officials at the border must have a "particularized and objective basis for suspecting the particular person" of alimentary canal smuggling.

The facts, and their rational inferences, known to customs inspectors in this case clearly supported a reasonable suspicion that respondent was an alimentary canal smuggler. We need not belabor the facts, including respondent's implausible story, that supported this suspicion. The trained customs inspectors had encountered many alimentary canal smugglers and certainly had more than an "inchoate and unparticularized suspicion or 'hunch,'" that respondent was smuggling narcotics in her alimentary canal. The inspectors' suspicion was a "'common-sense conclusio[n] about human behavior' upon which 'practical people,'—including government officials, are entitled to rely."

The final issue in this case is whether the detention of respondent was reasonably related in scope to the circumstances which justified it initially. In this regard we have cautioned that courts should not indulge in "unrealistic second-guessing," United States v. Sharpe, 470 U.S. 675, 686, 105 S.Ct. 1568, 1576, 84 L.Ed.2d 605 (1985), and we have noted that "creative judge[s], engaged in *post hoc* evaluations of police conduct can almost always imagine some alternative means by which the objectives of the police might have been accomplished," Ibid. But "[t]he fact that the protection of the public might, in the abstract, have been accomplished by 'less intrusive' means does not, in itself, render the search unreasonable." Ibid. Authorities must be allowed "to graduate their response to the demands of any particular situation." United States v. Place, 462 U.S. 696, 709, n. 10, 103 S.Ct. 2637, 2646, n. 10, 77 L.Ed.2d 110 (1983). Here, respondent was detained *incommunicado* for almost 16 hours before inspectors sought a warrant; the warrant then took a number of hours to procure, through no apparent fault of the inspectors. This length of time undoubtedly exceeds any other detention we have approved under reasonable suspicion. But we have also consistently rejected hard-and-fast time limits. Instead, "common sense and ordinary human experience must govern over rigid criteria." *Sharpe,* supra, 470 U.S., at 685, 105 S.Ct., at 1575.

[20] It is also important to note what we do *not* hold. Because the issues are not presented today we suggest no view on what level of suspicion, if any, is required for nonroutine border searches such as strip, body cavity, or involuntary x-ray searches. Both parties would have us decide the issue of whether aliens possess lesser Fourth Amendment rights at the border; that question was not raised in either court below and we do not consider it today.

The rudimentary knowledge of the human body which judges possess in common with the rest of humankind tells us that alimentary canal smuggling cannot be detected in the amount of time in which other illegal activity may be investigated through brief *Terry*-type stops. It presents few, if any external signs; a quick frisk will not do, nor will even a strip search.  In the case of respondent the inspectors had available, as an alternative to simply awaiting her bowel movement, an x ray.  They offered her the alternative of submitting herself to that procedure.  But when she refused that alternative, the customs inspectors were left with only two practical alternatives: detain her for such time as necessary to confirm their suspicions, a detention which would last much longer than the typical *"Terry"* stop, or turn her loose into the interior carrying the reasonably suspected contraband drugs.

The inspectors in this case followed this former procedure.  They no doubt expected that respondent, having recently disembarked from a 10-hour direct flight with a full and stiff abdomen, would produce a bowel movement without extended delay.  But her visible efforts to resist the call of nature, which the court below labeled "heroic," disappointed this expectation and in turn caused her humiliation and discomfort.  Our prior cases have refused to charge police with delays in investigatory detention attributable to the suspect's evasive actions, and that principle applies here as well.  Respondent alone was responsible for much of the duration and discomfort of the seizure.

Under these circumstances, we conclude that the detention in this case was not unreasonably long.  It occurred at the international border, where the Fourth Amendment balance of interests leans heavily to the Government.  At the border, customs officials have more than merely an investigative law enforcement role.  They are also charged, along with immigration officials, with protecting this Nation from entrants who may bring anything harmful into this country, whether that be communicable diseases, narcotics, or explosives.  In this regard the detention of a suspected alimentary canal smuggler at the border is analogous to the detention of a suspected tuberculosis carrier at the border: both are detained until their bodily processes dispel the suspicion that they will introduce a harmful agent into this country.

Respondent's detention was long, uncomfortable, indeed, humiliating; but both its length and its discomfort resulted solely from the method by which she chose to smuggle illicit drugs into this country. * * * [I]n the presence of articulable suspicion of smuggling in her alimentary canal, the customs officers were not required by the Fourth Amendment to pass respondent and her 88 cocaine-filled balloons into the interior.  Her detention for the period of time necessary to either verify or dispel the suspicion was not unreasonable.  The judgment of the Court of Appeals is therefore

Reversed.

JUSTICE STEVENS, concurring in the judgment.

If a seizure and a search of the person of the kind disclosed by this record may be made on the basis of reasonable suspicion, we must assume that a significant number of innocent persons will be required to undergo similar procedures. The rule announced in this case cannot, therefore, be supported on the ground that respondent's prolonged and humiliating detention "resulted solely from the method by which she chose to smuggle illicit drugs into this country."

The prolonged detention of respondent was, however, justified by a different choice that respondent made; she withdrew her consent to an X-ray examination that would have easily determined whether the reasonable suspicion that she was concealing contraband was justified. I believe that Customs agents may require that a non-pregnant person reasonably suspected of this kind of smuggling submit to an X-ray examination as an incident to a border search. I therefore concur in the judgment.

JUSTICE BRENNAN, with whom JUSTICE MARSHALL joins, dissenting.

\* \* \*

## I

Travelers at the national border are routinely subjected to questioning, pat-downs, and thorough searches of their belongings. These measures, which involve relatively limited invasions of privacy and which typically are conducted on all incoming travelers, do not violate the Fourth Amendment given the interests of "national self-protection reasonably requiring one entering the country to identify himself as entitled to come in, and his belongings as effects which may lawfully be brought in." Carroll v. United States, 267 U.S. 132, 154, 45 S.Ct. 280, 285, 69 L.Ed. 543 (1925). Individual travelers also may be singled out on "reasonable suspicion" and briefly held for further investigation. Cf. Terry v. Ohio, 392 U.S. 1, 88 S.Ct. 1868, 20 L.Ed.2d 889 (1968). At some point, however, further investigation involves such severe intrusions on the values the Fourth Amendment protects that more stringent safeguards are required. For example, the length and nature of a detention may, at least when conducted for criminal-investigative purposes, ripen into something approximating a full-scale custodial arrest—indeed, the arrestee, unlike the detainee in cases such as this, is at least given such basic rights as a telephone call, *Miranda* warnings, a bed, a prompt hearing before the nearest federal magistrate, an appointed attorney, and consideration of bail. In addition, border detentions may involve the use of such highly intrusive investigative techniques as body-cavity searches, x-ray searches, and stomach-pumping.

I believe that detentions and searches falling into these more intrusive categories are presumptively "reasonable" within the meaning of the Fourth Amendment only if authorized by a judicial officer.

\* \* \*

We have, to be sure, held that executive officials need not obtain prior judicial authorization where exigent circumstances would make such authorization impractical and counterproductive. In so holding, however, we have reaffirmed the general rule that "the police must, whenever practicable, obtain advance judicial approval of searches and seizures through the warrant procedure." Terry v. Ohio, 392 U.S., at

20, 88 S.Ct., at 1879. And even where a person has permissibly been taken into custody without a warrant, we have held that a prompt probable-cause determination by a detached magistrate is a constitutional "prerequisite to extended restraint of liberty following arrest." Gerstein v. Pugh, 420 U.S. 103, 114, 95 S.Ct. 854, 863, 43 L.Ed.2d 54 (1975).

There is no persuasive reason not to apply these principles to lengthy and intrusive criminal-investigative detentions occurring at the nation's border. To be sure, the Court today invokes precedent stating that neither probable cause nor a warrant ever have been required for border searches. If this is the law as a general matter, I believe it is time that we reexamine its foundations. For while the power of Congress to authorize wide-ranging detentions and searches *for purposes of immigration and customs control* is unquestioned, the Court previously has emphasized that far different considerations apply when detentions and searches are carried out *for purposes of investigating suspected criminal activity.* And even if the Court is correct that such detentions for purposes of criminal investigation were viewed as acceptable a century or two ago, we repeatedly have stressed that "this Court has not simply frozen into constitutional law those law enforcement practices that existed at the time of the Fourth Amendment's passage." Payton v. New York, 445 U.S. 573, 591, n. 33, 100 S.Ct. 1371, 1382, n. 33, 63 L.Ed.2d 639 (1980).

The Government contends, however, that because investigative detentions of the sort that occurred in this case need not be supported by probable cause, no warrant is required given the phraseology of the Fourth Amendment's Warrant Clause. * * * Even assuming that border detentions and searches that become lengthy and highly intrusive need not be supported by probable cause, but see Part II, infra, this reasoning runs squarely contrary to the Court's administrative-warrant cases. * * *

Something has gone fundamentally awry in our constitutional jurisprudence when a neutral and detached magistrate's authorization is required before the authorities may inspect "the plumbing, heating, ventilation, gas, and electrical systems" in a person's home, investigate the back rooms of his workplace, or poke through the charred remains of his gutted garage, but *not* before they may hold him in indefinite involuntary isolation at the nation's border to investigate whether he might be engaged in criminal wrongdoing. * * *

* * * Although the Court previously has declined to require a warrant for border searches involving "minor interference with privacy resulting from the mere stop for questioning," surely there is no parallel between such "minor" intrusions and the extreme invasion of personal privacy and dignity that occurs in detentions and searches such as that before us today.

Moreover, the available evidence suggests that the number of highly intrusive border searches of suspicious-looking but ultimately innocent travelers may be very high. One physician who at the request of customs officials conducted many "internal searches"—rectal and vaginal examinations and stomach-pumping—estimated that he had found contraband in only 15 to 20 percent of the persons he had examined.[21]  It has similarly been estimated that only 16 percent of women subjected to body-cavity searches at the border were in fact found to be carrying contraband.[22]  It is precisely to minimize the risk of harassing so many innocent people that the Fourth Amendment requires the intervention of a judicial officer.  *  *  *

The Court argues, however, that the length and "discomfort" of de Hernandez' detention "resulted *solely* from the method by which she chose to smuggle illicit drugs into this country," and it speculates that only her " 'heroic' " efforts prevented the detention from being brief and to the point.  Although we now know that de Hernandez was indeed guilty of smuggling drugs internally, such *post hoc* rationalizations have no place in our Fourth Amendment jurisprudence, which demands that we "prevent hindsight from coloring the evaluation of the reasonableness of a search or seizure."  United States v. Martinez-Fuerte, [428 U.S. 543, 565, 96 S.Ct. 3074, 3086, 49 L.Ed.2d 1116 (1976)].  At the time the authorities simply had, at most, a reasonable suspicion that de Hernandez might be engaged in such smuggling.  *  *  *  [W]ith all respect to the Court, it is not " 'unrealistic second-guessing' " to predict that an innocent traveler, locked away in *incommunicado* detention in unfamiliar surroundings in a foreign land, might well be so frightened and exhausted as to be unable so to "cooperate" with the authorities.

*  *  *

Finally, I disagree with JUSTICE STEVENS that de Hernandez' alternative "choice" of submitting to abdominal x-irradiation at the discretion of customs officials made this detention "justified."  *  *  *  [T]he crux of my disagreement is this: We have learned in our lifetimes, time and again, the inherent dangers that result from coupling unchecked "law enforcement" discretion with the tools of medical technology.  *  *  *  This should be so whether the intrusion is by incision, by stomach-pumping, or by exposure to x-irradiation.  Because no exigent circumstances prevented the authorities from seeking a magistrate's authorization so to probe de Hernandez' abdominal cavity, the proffered alternative "choice" of a warrantless x-ray was just as impermissible as the 27-hour detention that actually occurred.

[21] Thompson v. United States, 411 F.2d 946, 948 (CA9 1969).

[22] United States v. Holtz, 479 F.2d, at 94 (Ely, J., dissenting) (citing testimony from congressional hearings).  It was suggested at oral argument that "with all the experience the government has had in the intervening years with increasing drug traffic" there might be "a little more skill in detection today."  Tr. of Oral Arg. 38.  There are, however, no published statistics more recent than the information discussed in text.  It is of course the Government's burden to muster facts demonstrating the reasonableness of its investigative practices.  The Government advised the Court at argument that it has more recent statistical evidence respecting the number of innocent travelers who are subjected to x-ray searches, but did not disclose that evidence because "it's not in the record and it's not public."  Tr. of Oral Arg. 23.

## II

I believe that de Hernandez' detention violated the Fourth Amendment for an additional reason: it was not supported by probable cause. In the domestic context, a detention of the sort that occurred here would be permissible only if there were probable cause at the outset.

To be sure, it is commonly asserted that as a result of the Fourth Amendment's "border exception" there is no requirement of probable cause for such investigations. But the justifications for the border exception necessarily limit its breadth. The exception derives from the unquestioned and paramount interest in "national self-protection reasonably requiring one entering the country to identify himself as entitled to come in, and his belongings as effects which may be lawfully brought in." Carroll v. United States, 267 U.S., at 154, 45 S.Ct., at 285. * * * Subject only to the other applicable guarantees of the Bill of Rights, this interest in "national self-protection" is plenary. Thus, as the Court notes, a suspected tuberculosis carrier may be detained at the border for medical testing and treatment as a condition of entry. As a condition of entry, the traveler may be subjected to exhaustive processing and examinations, and his belongings may be scrutinized with exacting care. I have no doubt as well that, *as a condition of entry,* travelers in appropriate circumstances may be required to excrete their bodily wastes for further scrutiny and to submit to diagnostic x-rays.

Contrary to the Court's reasoning, however, the Government in carrying out such immigration and customs functions does not simply have the two stark alternatives of either forcing a traveler to submit to such procedures or allowing him to "pass * * * into the interior." There is a third alternative: to instruct the traveler who refuses to submit to burdensome but reasonable conditions of entry that he is free to turn around and leave the country. In fact, I believe that the "reasonableness" of any burdensome requirement for entry is necessarily conditioned on the potential entrant's freedom to leave the country if he objects to that requirement. Surely the Government's manifest interest in preventing potentially excludable individuals carrying potential contraband from crossing our borders is fully vindicated if those individuals voluntarily decided not to cross the borders.

* * * If the traveler does not wish to consent to prolonged detentions or intrusive examinations, the nation's customs and immigration interests are fully served by sending the traveler on his way elsewhere. If the authorities nevertheless propose to detain the traveler for purposes of subjecting him to criminal investigation and possible arrest and punishment, they may do so only pursuant to constitutional safeguards applicable to everyone else in the country. Chief among those safeguards is the requirement that, except in limited circumstances not present here, custodial detentions occur only on probable cause. * * * That standard obviously is not met, and was not met here, simply by courier profiles, "common rumor or report, suspicion, or even 'strong reason to suspect.'" Because the contraband in this case was the fruit of the authorities' indefinite detention of Rosa de Her-

nandez without probable cause or a warrant, I would affirm the judgment of the Court of Appeals for the Ninth Circuit reversing her conviction.


## 2. BORDER–RELATED ENFORCEMENT ACTIVITY

Law enforcement activity conducted in the interior of the country may be viewed as less directly related to the federal government's interest in protecting the security of its borders. It also may intrude upon privacy and other concerns more significantly than activity occurring at the border itself. For these and perhaps other reasons, the Supreme Court has treated such law enforcement activity somewhat differently than law enforcement activity at the border or its functional equivalent. Most of the Court's case law, including the principal case in this subsection, has dealt with traffic control operations.

In United States v. Ortiz, 422 U.S. 891, 95 S.Ct. 2585, 45 L.Ed.2d 623 (1975), Border Patrol officers stopped Ortiz' automobile at a fixed checkpoint at San Clemente, California; the checkpoint is described and discussed in the principal case in this subsection. A search of the vehicle's trunk revealed three aliens and Ortiz was convicted of knowingly transporting aliens who were in the country illegally. A unanimous Supreme Court invalidated the search of the automobile because it was conducted without probable cause to believe that illegal aliens would be found. The government had urged that the probable cause requirement be found inapplicable for two reasons. First, careful selection of locations for checkpoints by high-level Border Patrol officials limited officers' discretion in stopping and searching cars. Second, checkpoints provided visible signs of the officers' authority and demonstrated to stopped motorists that others were being stopped and searched as well; motorists were, as a result, less likely to be frightened or annoyed by the search and consequently the search was less intrusive upon privacy than other law enforcement activities. Rejecting the government's argument, the Court stressed that a search of a car, even under the conditions at issue, remains a substantial invasion of privacy. Moreover, only a small portion of cars passing through checkpoints were searched; throughout the system, less than 3% were so examined. Officers manning the checkpoints exercised a degree of discretion in deciding which cars to search that is inconsistent with the Fourth Amendment. 422 U.S. at 896, 95 S.Ct. at 2588, 45 L.Ed.2d at 629.

The evidence showed that inspections of cars for the presence of illegal aliens typically included examinations of the trunk, under the hood, and beneath the chassis. Enclosed portions of trucks, campers and similar vehicles were also examined. But inspections sometimes because more rigorous. The Court noted that in one case previously before it officers had removed a back seat cushion because of reports that aliens had been found seated upright behind seats from which the springs had been removed. Not every aspect of the routine "inspections" necessarily constitutes a "search" for which probable cause is required, the Court noted, but it found no occasion in the case "to

define the exact limits of an automobile 'search.'"    422 U.S. at 897 n. 3,
95 S.Ct. at 2589 n. 2, 45 L.Ed.2d at 629 n. 3.

### UNITED STATES v. MARTINEZ–FUERTE

Supreme Court of the United States, 1976.
428 U.S. 543, 96 S.Ct. 3074, 49 L.Ed.2d 1116.

MR. JUSTICE POWELL delivered the opinion of the Court.

These cases involve criminal prosecutions for offenses relating to
the transportation of illegal Mexican aliens.    Each defendant was
arrested at a permanent checkpoint operated by the Border Patrol
away from the international border with Mexico, and each sought the
exclusion of certain evidence on the ground that the operation of the
checkpoint was incompatible with the Fourth Amendment.    In each
instance whether the Fourth Amendment was violated turns primarily
on whether a vehicle may be stopped at a fixed checkpoint for brief
questioning of its occupants even though there is no reason to believe
the particular vehicle contains illegal aliens.    We reserved this question last Term in United States v. Ortiz, 422 U.S. 891, 897 n. 3, 95 S.Ct.
2585, 2589, 45 L.Ed.2d 623 (1975).    We hold today that such stops are
consistent with the Fourth Amendment.    We also hold that the operation of a fixed checkpoint need not be authorized in advance by a
judicial warrant.

I

A

The respondents in No. 74–1560 are defendants in three separate
prosecutions resulting from arrests made on three different occasions at
the permanent immigration checkpoint on Interstate 5 near San Clemente, Cal.    Interstate 5 is the principal highway between San Diego
and Los Angeles, and the San Clemente checkpoint is 66 road miles
north of the Mexican border.    We previously have described the checkpoint as follows:

"'Approximately one mile south of the checkpoint is a large
black on yellow sign with flashing yellow lights over the highway
stating "ALL VEHICLES, STOP AHEAD, 1 MILE."    Three-
quarters of a mile further north are two black on yellow signs
suspended over the highway with flashing lights stating "WATCH
FOR BRAKE LIGHTS."    At the checkpoint, which is also the
location of a State of California weighing station, are two large
signs with flashing red lights suspended over the highway.    These
signs each state "STOP HERE—U.S. OFFICERS."    Placed on the
highway are a number of orange traffic cones funneling traffic into
two lanes where a Border Patrol agent in full dress uniform,
standing behind a white on red "STOP" sign checks traffic.    Block-
ing traffic in the unused lanes are official U.S. Border Patrol
vehicles with flashing red lights.    In addition, there is a permanent
building which houses the Border Patrol office and temporary
detention facilities.    There are also floodlights for nighttime opera-

tion.'" United States v. Ortiz, supra, at 893, 95 S.Ct., at 2587, quoting United States v. Baca, 368 F.Supp. 398, 410–411 (SD Cal. 1973).

The "point" agent standing between the two lanes of traffic visually screens all northbound vehicles, which the checkpoint brings to a virtual, if not a complete, halt. Most motorists are allowed to resume their progress without any oral inquiry or close visual examination. In a relatively small number of cases the "point" agent will conclude that further inquiry is in order. He directs these cars to a secondary inspection area, where their occupants are asked about their citizenship and immigration status. The Government informs us that at San Clemente the average length of an investigation in the secondary inspection area is three to five minutes. A direction to stop in the secondary inspection area could be based on something suspicious about a particular car passing through the checkpoint, but the Government concedes that [the stop] at issue in No. 74–1560 was [not] based on any articulable suspicion. During the period when these stops were made, the checkpoint was operating under a magistrate's "warrant of inspection," which authorized the Border Patrol to conduct a routine-stop operation at the San Clemente location.

We turn now to the particulars of the stops involved in No. 74–1560, and the procedural history of the case. Respondent Amado Martinez-Fuerte approached the checkpoint driving a vehicle containing two female passengers. The women were illegal Mexican aliens who had entered the United States at the San Ysidro port of entry by using false papers and rendezvoused with Martinez-Fuerte in San Diego to be transported northward. At the checkpoint their car was directed to the secondary inspection area. Martinez-Fuerte produced documents showing him to be a lawful resident alien, but his passengers admitted being present in the country unlawfully. He was charged, inter alia, with two counts of illegally transporting aliens in violation of 8 U.S.C. § 1324(a)(2). He moved before trial to suppress all evidence stemming from the stop on the ground that the operation of the checkpoint was in violation of the Fourth Amendment. The motion to suppress was denied, and he was convicted on both counts after a jury trial.

\* \* \*

Martinez-Fuerte appealed his conviction \* \* \*. The Court of Appeals held, with one judge dissenting, that [the stop] violated the Fourth Amendment, concluding that a stop for inquiry is constitutional only if the Border Patrol reasonably suspects the presence of illegal aliens on the basis of articulable facts. It reversed Martinez-Fuerte's conviction \* \* \*. 514 F.2d 308 (1975). We reverse and remand.

B

Petitioner in No. 75–5387, Rodolfo Sifuentes, was arrested at the permanent immigration checkpoint on U.S. Highway 77 near Sarita, Tex. Highway 77 originates in Brownsville, and it is one of the two major highways running north from the lower Rio Grande valley. The Sarita checkpoint is about 90 miles north of Brownsville, and 65–90 miles from the nearest points of the Mexican border. The physical arrangement of the checkpoint resembles generally that at San Clemente, but the checkpoint is operated differently in that the officers customarily stop all northbound motorists for a brief inquiry. Motorists whom the officers recognize as local inhabitants, however, are waved through the checkpoint without inquiry. Unlike the San Clemente checkpoint the Sarita operation was conducted without a judicial warrant.

Sifuentes drove up to the checkpoint without any visible passengers. When an agent approached the vehicle, however, he observed four passengers, one in the front seat and the other three in the rear, slumped down in the seats. Questioning revealed that each passenger was an illegal alien, although Sifuentes was a United States citizen. The aliens had met Sifuentes in the United States, by prearrangement, after swimming across the Rio Grande.

Sifuentes was indicted on four counts of illegally transporting aliens. He moved on Fourth Amendment grounds to suppress the evidence derived from the stop. The motion was denied and he was convicted after a jury trial. Sifuentes renewed his Fourth Amendment argument on appeal, contending primarily that stops made without reason to believe a car is transporting aliens illegally are unconstitutional. The United States Court of Appeals for the Fifth Circuit affirmed the conviction, 517 F.2d 1402 (1975), relying on its opinion in United States v. Santibanez, 517 F.2d 922 (1975). There the Court of Appeals had ruled that routine checkpoint stops are consistent with the Fourth Amendment. We affirm.

## II

The Courts of Appeals for the Ninth and the Fifth Circuits are in conflict on the constitutionality of a law enforcement technique considered important by those charged with policing the Nation's borders. Before turning to the constitutional question, we examine the context in which it arises.

## A

It has been national policy for many years to limit immigration into the United States. Since July 1, 1968, the annual quota for immigrants from all independent countries of the Western Hemisphere, including Mexico, has been 120,000 persons. Act of Oct. 3, 1965, § 21(e), 79 Stat. 921. Many more aliens than can be accommodated under the quota want to live and work in the United States. Consequently, large numbers of aliens seek illegally to enter or to remain in the United States. We noted last Term that "[e]stimates of the number of illegal immigrants [already] in the United States vary widely. A conservative estimate in 1972 produced a figure of about one million, but the Immigration and Naturalization Service now suggests there may be as many as 10 or 12 million aliens illegally in the country." United States v. Brignoni-Ponce, 422 U.S. 873, 878, 95 S.Ct. 2574, 2578, 45 L.Ed.2d 607 (1975) (footnote omitted). It is estimated that 85% of the illegal immigrants are from Mexico, drawn by the fact that economic opportunities are significantly greater in the United States than they are in Mexico. United States v. Baca, 368 F.Supp., at 402.

Interdicting the flow of illegal entrants from Mexico poses formidable law enforcement problems. The principal problem arises from surreptitious entries. Id., at 405. The United States shares a border with Mexico that is almost 2,000 miles long, and much of the border area is uninhabited desert or thinly populated arid land. Although the Border Patrol maintains personnel, electronic equipment, and fences along portions of the border, it remains relatively easy for individuals to enter the United States without detection. It also is possible for an alien to enter unlawfully at a port of entry by the use of falsified papers or to enter lawfully but violate restrictions of entry in an effort to remain in the country unlawfully. Once within the country, the aliens seek to travel inland to areas where employment is believed to be available, frequently meeting by prearrangement with friends or professional smugglers who transport them in private vehicles.

The Border Patrol conducts three kinds of inland traffic-checking operations in an effort to minimize illegal immigration. Permanent checkpoints, such as those at San Clemente and Sarita, are maintained at or near intersections of important roads leading away from the border. They operate on a coordinated basis designed to avoid circumvention by smugglers and others who transport the illegal aliens. Temporary checkpoints, which operate like permanent ones, occasionally are established in other strategic locations. Finally, roving patrols are maintained to supplement the checkpoint system. See Almeida-Sanchez v. United States, 413 U.S. 266, 268, 93 S.Ct. 2535, 2537, 37 L.Ed.2d 596 (1973). In fiscal 1973, 175,511 deportable aliens were apprehended throughout the Nation by "line watch" agents stationed at the border itself. Traffic-checking operations in the interior apprehended approximately 55,300 more deportable aliens. Most of the traffic-checking apprehensions were at checkpoints, though precise figures are not available. United States v. Baca, supra, at 405, 407, and n. 2.

### B

We are concerned here with permanent checkpoints, the locations of which are chosen on the basis of a number of factors. The Border Patrol believes that to assure effectiveness, a checkpoint must be (i) distant enough from the border to avoid interference with traffic in populated areas near the border, (ii) close to the confluence of two or more significant roads leading away from the border, (iii) situated in terrain that restricts vehicle passage around the checkpoint, (iv) on a stretch of highway compatible with safe operation, and (v) beyond the 25-mile zone in which "border passes" are valid.

The record in No. 74–1560 provides a rather complete picture of the effectiveness of the San Clemente checkpoint. Approximately 10 million cars pass the checkpoint location each year, although the checkpoint actually is in operation only about 70% of the time. In calendar year 1973, approximately 17,000 illegal aliens were apprehended there. During an eight-day period in 1974 that included the arrests involved in No. 74–1560, roughly 146,000 vehicles passed through the checkpoint during 124⅙ hours of operation.  Of these, 820 vehicles were referred to the secondary inspection area, where Border Patrol agents found 725 deportable aliens in 171 vehicles.  In all but two cases, the aliens were discovered without a conventional search of the vehicle.  A similar rate of apprehensions throughout the year would have resulted in an annual total of over 33,000, although the Government contends that many illegal aliens pass through the checkpoint undetected.  *  *  *

## IV

It is agreed that checkpoint stops are "seizures" within the meaning of the Fourth Amendment.  The defendants contend primarily that the routine stopping of vehicles at a checkpoint is invalid because *Brignoni-Ponce* must be read as proscribing any stops in the absence of reasonable suspicion.  Sifuentes alternatively contends in No. 75–5387 that routine checkpoint stops are permissible only when the practice has the advance judicial authorization of a warrant.  There was a warrant authorizing the stops at San Clemente but none at Sarita.  As we reach the issue of a warrant requirement only if reasonable suspicion is not required, we turn first to whether reasonable suspicion is a prerequisite to a valid stop, a question to be resolved by balancing the interests at stake.

## A

Our previous cases have recognized that maintenance of a traffic-checking program in the interior is necessary because the flow of illegal aliens cannot be controlled effectively at the border.  We note here only the substantiality of the public interest in the practice of routine stops for inquiry at permanent checkpoints, a practice which the Government identifies as the most important of the traffic-checking operations. These checkpoints are located on important highways;  in their absence such highways would offer illegal aliens a quick and safe route into the interior.  Routine checkpoint inquiries apprehend many smugglers and illegal aliens who succumb to the lure of such highways.  And the prospect of such inquiries forces others onto less efficient roads that are less heavily traveled, slowing their movement and making them more vulnerable to detection by roving patrols.

A requirement that stops on major routes inland always be based on reasonable suspicion would be impractical because the flow of traffic tends to be too heavy to allow the particularized study of a given car that would enable it to be identified as a possible carrier of illegal aliens.  In particular, such a requirement would largely eliminate any deterrent to the conduct of well-disguised smuggling operations, even though smugglers are known to use these highways regularly.

B

While the need to make routine checkpoint stops is great, the consequent intrusion on Fourth Amendment interests is quite limited. The stop does intrude to a limited extent on motorists' right to "free passage without interruption," Carroll v. United States, 267 U.S. 132, 154, 45 S.Ct. 280, 285, 69 L.Ed. 543 (1925), and arguably on their right to personal security. But it involves only a brief detention of travelers during which

> " '[a]ll that is required of the vehicle's occupants is a response to a brief question or two and possibly the production of a document evidencing a right to be in the United States.' " United States v. Brignoni-Ponce, supra, 422 U.S., at 880, 95 S.Ct., at 2579.

Neither the vehicle nor its occupants are searched, and visual inspection of the vehicle is limited to what can be seen without a search. This objective intrusion—the stop itself, the questioning, and the visual inspection—also existed in roving-patrol stops. But we view checkpoint stops in a different light because the subjective intrusion—the generating of concern or even fright on the part of lawful travelers—is appreciably less in the case of a checkpoint stop. * * *

In *Brignoni-Ponce*, we recognized that Fourth Amendment analysis in this context also must take into account the overall degree of interference with legitimate traffic. We concluded there that random roving-patrol stops could not be tolerated because they "would subject the residents of * * * [border] areas to potentially unlimited interference with their use of the highways, solely at the discretion of Border Patrol officers. * * * [They] could stop motorists at random for questioning, day or night, anywhere within 100 air miles of the 2,000-mile border, on a city street, a busy highway, or a desert road * * *." Ibid. There also was a grave danger that such unreviewable discretion would be abused by some officers in the field. Ibid.

Routine checkpoint stops do not intrude similarly on the motoring public. First, the potential interference with legitimate traffic is minimal. Motorists using these highways are not taken by surprise as they know, or may obtain knowledge of, the location of the checkpoints and will not be stopped elsewhere. Second, checkpoint operations both appear to and actually involve less discretionary enforcement activity. The regularized manner in which established checkpoints are operated is visible evidence, reassuring to law-abiding motorists, that the stops are duly authorized and believed to serve the public interest. The location of a fixed checkpoint is not chosen by officers in the field, but by officials responsible for making overall decisions as to the most effective allocation of limited enforcement resources. We may assume that such officials will be unlikely to locate a checkpoint where it bears arbitrarily or oppressively on motorists as a class. And since field officers may stop only those cars passing the checkpoint, there is less room for abusive or harassing stops of individuals than there was in the case of roving-patrol stops. Moreover, a claim that a particular exercise of discretion in locating or operating a checkpoint is unreasonable is subject to post-stop judicial review.

The defendants arrested at the San Clemente checkpoint suggest that its operation involves a significant extra element of intrusiveness in that only a small percentage of cars are referred to the secondary inspection area, thereby "stigmatizing" those diverted and reducing the assurances provided by equal treatment of all motorists. We think defendants overstate the consequences. Referrals are made for the sole purpose of conducting a routine and limited inquiry into residence status that cannot feasibly be made of every motorist where the traffic is heavy. The objective intrusion of the stop and inquiry thus remains minimal. Selective referral may involve some annoyance, but it remains true that the stops should not be frightening or offensive because of their public and relatively routine nature. Moreover, selective referrals—rather than questioning the occupants of every car—tend to advance some Fourth Amendment interests by minimizing the intrusion on the general motoring public.

C

The defendants note correctly that to accommodate public and private interests some quantum of individualized suspicion is usually a prerequisite to a constitutional search or seizure. But the Fourth Amendment imposes no irreducible requirement of such suspicion. This is clear from Camara v. Municipal Court, 387 U.S. 523, 87 S.Ct. 1727, 18 L.Ed.2d 930 (1967). In *Camara* the Court required an "area" warrant to support the reasonableness of inspecting private residences within a particular area for building code violations, but recognized that "specific knowledge of the condition of the particular dwelling" was not required to enter any given residence. In so holding, the Court examined the government interests advanced to justify such routine intrusions "upon the constitutionally protected interests of the private citizen," and concluded that under the circumstances the government interests outweighed those of the private citizen.

We think the same conclusion is appropriate here, where we deal neither with searches nor with the sanctity of private dwellings, ordinarily afforded the most stringent Fourth Amendment protection. As we have noted earlier, one's expectation of privacy in an automobile and of freedom in its operation are significantly different from the traditional expectation of privacy and freedom in one's residence. And the reasonableness of the procedures followed in making these checkpoint stops makes the resulting intrusion on the interests of motorists minimal. On the other hand, the purpose of the stops is legitimate and in the public interest, and the need for this enforcement technique is demonstrated by the records in the cases before us. Accordingly, we hold that the stops and questioning at issue may be made in the absence of any individualized suspicion at reasonably located checkpoints.[23]

---

[23] [W]e deem the argument by the defendants in No. 74–1560 * * * to raise the question whether, even though a warrant is not required, it is unreasonable to locate a checkpoint at San Clemente.

We further believe that it is constitutional to refer motorists selectively to the secondary inspection area at the San Clemente checkpoint on the basis of criteria that would not sustain a roving-patrol stop. Thus, even if it be assumed that such referrals are made largely on the basis of apparent Mexican ancestry, we perceive no constitutional violation. As the intrusion here is sufficiently minimal that no particularized reason need exist to justify it, we think it follows that the Border Patrol officers must have wide discretion in selecting the motorists to be diverted for the brief questioning involved.

## V

Sifuentes' alternative argument is that routine stops at a checkpoint are permissible only if a warrant has given judicial authorization to the particular checkpoint location and the practice of routine stops. A warrant requirement in these circumstances draws some support from *Camara,* where the Court held that, absent consent, an "area" warrant was required to make a building code inspection, even though the search could be conducted absent cause to believe that there were violations in the building searched.

We do not think, however, that *Camara* is an apt model. It involved the search of private residences, for which a warrant traditionally has been required. As developed more fully above, the strong Fourth Amendment interests that justify the warrant requirement in that context are absent here. The degree of intrusion upon privacy that may be occasioned by a search of a house hardly can be compared with the minor interference with privacy resulting from the mere stop for questioning as to residence. Moreover, the warrant requirement in *Camara* served specific Fourth Amendment interests to which a warrant requirement here would make little contribution. The Court there said:

> "[W]hen [an] inspector [without a warrant] demands entry, the occupant has no way of knowing whether enforcement of the municipal code involved requires inspection of his premises, no way of knowing the lawful limits of the inspector's power to search, and no way of knowing whether the inspector himself is acting under proper authorization." 387 U.S., at 532, 87 S.Ct., at 1732.

A warrant provided assurance to the occupant on these scores. We believe that the visible manifestations of the field officers' authority at a checkpoint provide substantially the same assurances in this case.

We answer this question in the negative. As indicated above, the choice of checkpoint locations is an administrative decision that must be left largely within the discretion of the Border Patrol. We think the decision to locate a checkpoint at San Clemente was reasonable. The location meets the criteria prescribed by the Border Patrol to assure effectiveness and the evidence supports the view that the needs of law enforcement are furthered by this location. The absolute number of apprehensions at the checkpoint is high confirming Border Patrol judgment that significant numbers of illegal aliens regularly use Interstate 5 at this point. Also, San Clemente was selected as the location where traffic is lightest between San Diego and Los Angeles, thereby minimizing interference with legitimate traffic.

No question has been raised about the reasonableness of the location of the Sarita checkpoint.

Other purposes served by the requirement of a warrant also are inapplicable here. One such purpose is to prevent hindsight from coloring the evaluation of the reasonableness of a search or seizure. The reasonableness of checkpoint stops, however, turns on factors such as the location and method of operation of the checkpoint, factors that are not susceptible to the distortion of hindsight, and therefore will be open to post-stop review notwithstanding the absence of a warrant. Another purpose for a warrant requirement is to substitute the judgment of the magistrate for that of the searching or seizing officer. But the need for this is reduced when the decision to "seize" is not entirely in the hands of the officer in the field, and deference is to be given to the administrative decisions of higher ranking officials.

## VI

In summary, we hold that stops for brief questioning routinely conducted at permanent checkpoints are consistent with the Fourth Amendment and need not be authorized by warrant. The principal protection of Fourth Amendment rights at checkpoints lies in appropriate limitations on the scope of the stop. We have held that checkpoint searches are constitutional only if justified by consent or probable cause to search. United States v. Ortiz, 422 U.S. 891, 95 S.Ct. 2585, 45 L.Ed. 2d 623 (1975). And our holding today is limited to the type of stops described in this opinion. "[A]ny further detention must be based on consent or probable cause." United States v. Brignoni-Ponce, supra, at 882, 95 S.Ct., at 2580. None of the defendants in these cases argues that the stopping officers exceeded these limitations. Consequently, we affirm the judgment of the Court of Appeals for the Fifth Circuit, which had affirmed the conviction of Sifuentes. We reverse the judgment of the Court of Appeals for the Ninth Circuit and remand the case with directions to affirm the conviction of Martinez-Fuerte * * *.

It is so ordered.

MR. JUSTICE BRENNAN, with whom MR. JUSTICE MARSHALL joins, dissenting.

* * *

The Court assumes, and I certainly agree, that persons stopped at fixed checkpoints, whether or not referred to a secondary detention area, are "seized" within the meaning of the Fourth Amendment. Moreover, since the vehicle and its occupants are subjected to a "visual inspection," the intrusion clearly exceeds mere physical restraint, for officers are able to see more in a stopped vehicle than in vehicles traveling at normal speeds down the highway. As the Court concedes, the checkpoint stop involves essentially the same intrusions as a roving-patrol stop, yet the Court provides no principled basis for distinguishing checkpoint stops.

Certainly that basis is not provided in the Court's reasoning that the subjective intrusion here is appreciably less than in the case of a stop by a roving patrol. *Brignoni-Ponce* nowhere bases the requirement of reasonable suspicion upon the subjective nature of the intrusion. In any event, the subjective aspects of checkpoint stops, even if different from the subjective aspects of roving-patrol stops, just as much require some principled restraint on law enforcement conduct. The motorist whose conduct has been nothing but innocent—and this is overwhelmingly the case—surely resents his own detention and inspection. And checkpoints, unlike roving stops, detain thousands of motorists, a dragnet-like procedure offensive to the sensibilities of free citizens. Also, the delay occasioned by stopping hundreds of vehicles on a busy highway is particularly irritating.

In addition to overlooking these dimensions of subjective intrusion, the Court, without explanation, also ignores one major source of vexation. In abandoning any requirement of a minimum of reasonable suspicion, or even articulable suspicion, the Court in every practical sense renders meaningless, as applied to checkpoint stops, the *Brignoni-Ponce* holding that "standing alone [Mexican appearance] does not justify stopping all Mexican-Americans to ask if they are aliens." 422 U.S., at 887, 95 S.Ct., at 2583. Since the objective is almost entirely the Mexican illegally in the country, checkpoint officials, uninhibited by any objective standards and therefore free to stop any or all motorists without explanation or excuse, wholly on whim, will perforce target motorists of Mexican appearance. The process will then inescapably discriminate against citizens of Mexican ancestry and Mexican aliens lawfully in this country for no other reason than that they unavoidably possess the same "suspicious" physical and grooming characteristics of illegal Mexican aliens.

\* \* \*

The Court argues \* \* \* that practicalities necessitate [upholding the stops]. \* \* \*

As an initial matter, whatever force this argument may have, it cannot apply to the secondary detentions that occurred in No. 74–1560. Once a vehicle has been slowed and observed at a checkpoint, ample opportunity exists to formulate the reasonable suspicion which, if it actually exists, would justify further detention. \* \* \*

The Court's rationale is also not persuasive because several of the factors upon which officers may rely in establishing reasonable suspicion are readily ascertainable, regardless of the flow of traffic. \* \* \*

Finally, the Court's argument fails for more basic reasons. There is no principle in the jurisprudence of fundamental rights which permits constitutional limitations to be dispensed with merely because they cannot be conveniently satisfied. \* \* \*

### NOTES

1. The Supreme Court has addressed the effect of Fourth Amendment considerations upon the technique often described as conducting "roving" border patrols. In Almeida-Sanchez v. United States, 413 U.S. 266, 93 S.Ct. 2535, 37 L.Ed.2d 596 (1973), Almeida-Sanchez' car was stopped and searched while traveling on highway 78 in California. Highway 78 runs east-west and although it meanders it does not touch the border; the point of the stop was 25 air miles north of the border. The Immigration and Nationality Act purports to authorize warrantless searches of automobiles or other conveyances for illegally entered aliens "within a reasonable distance from any external bound-

ary of the United States," as authorized by regulations promulgated by the Attorney General. "Reasonable distance" was defined in such regulations as within 100 air miles from any external boundary. 8 C.F.R. § 287.1. Rejecting the argument that the extraordinary needs of border enforcement justify searches such as that at issue in the case, the Court held that the absence of probable cause or consent rendered the search unreasonable. 413 U.S. at 273, 93 S.Ct. at 2540, 37 L.Ed.2d at 603.

Justice Powell, in a separate opinion, urged that the use of roving patrols might be permitted under a type of "area" warrant. Such a warrant would authorize the use of roving patrols on particular roads for a specific period of time; during the period, vehicles on those roads could be stopped despite the absence of any evidence focusing upon the particular vehicle. Warrants of this sort might be issued upon a general conclusion that the proposed action was "reasonable," considering—among other factors—the amount of illegal alien traffic on the roads, the proximity to the border, and the degree to which innocent persons' privacy would be invaded and the extent of those invasions. 413 U.S. at 283–84, 93 S.Ct. at 2544–45, 37 L.Ed.2d at 608–09.

In United States v. Brignoni-Ponce, 422 U.S. 873, 95 S.Ct. 2574, 45 L.Ed.2d 607 (1975), the car which Brignoni-Ponce was driving was stopped by Border Patrol officers on Interstate Highway 5 in California south of San Clemente. The only basis for the stop offered was that the three occupants of the vehicle appeared to be of Mexican decent. Questioning of the occupants revealed that the two passengers were aliens who had entered the country illegally. At Brignoni-Ponce's trial for transportation of illegally entered aliens, evidence obtained from the stop and questioning of the occupants was admitted over defense objection. The Supreme Court reversed the resulting conviction. It acknowledged that the important need to enforce border security created special problems, but it rejected the argument that this permitted law enforcement officers to stop motorists at random within 100 air miles of the border. Law enforcement needs are sufficiently met, the Court concluded, by officers' right to conduct brief field stops on reasonable suspicion. On the facts before it, however, the Government had failed to show that the officers harbored reasonable suspicion that Brignoni-Ponce's vehicle contained illegally entered aliens. In support of the stop, the Government offered only that the officers observed that the occupants were of apparent Mexican ancestry:

> [T]his factor alone would justify neither a reasonable belief that they were aliens, nor a reasonable belief that the car concealed other aliens who were illegally in the country. Large numbers of native-born and naturalized citizens have the physical characteristics identified with Mexican ancestry, and even in the border area a relatively small proportion of them are aliens. The likelihood that any given person of Mexican ancestry is an alien is high enough to make Mexican appearance a relevant factor, but standing alone it does not justify stopping all Mexican-Americans to ask if they are aliens.

422 U.S. at 886–87, 95 S.Ct. at 2583, 45 L.Ed.2d at 619–20. As to what other factors might contribute to the development of reasonable suspicion, the Court stated:

> Officers may consider the characteristics of the area in which they encounter a vehicle. Its proximity to the border, the usual patterns of traffic on the particular road, and previous experience with alien traffic are all relevant. They may also consider information about recent illegal border crossings in the area. The driver's behavior may be relevant, as erratic driving or obvious attempts to evade officers can support a reasonable suspicion. Aspects of the vehicle itself may justify suspicion. For instance,

officers say that certain station wagons, with large compartments for fold-down seats or spare tires, are frequently used for transporting concealed aliens. The vehicle may appear to be heavily loaded, it may have an extraordinary number of passengers, or the officers may observe persons trying to hide. The Government also points out that trained officers can recognize the characteristic appearance of persons who live in Mexico, relying on such factors as the mode of dress and haircut. In all situations the officer is entitled to assess the facts in light of his experience in detecting illegal entry and smuggling.

422 U.S. at 884–85, 95 S.Ct. at 2582, 45 L.Ed.2d at 618–19. Where the factors amount to reasonable suspicion, the Court has held that a stop of a vehicle and questioning of the driver is permissible. United States v. Cortez, 449 U.S. 411, 101 S.Ct. 690, 66 L.Ed.2d 621 (1981).

Substantial flexibility exists in the area, as was made clear in United States v. Villamonte-Marquez, 462 U.S. 579, 103 S.Ct. 2573, 77 L.Ed.2d 22 (1983). Customs officers boarded the Henry Morgan II, a 40 foot sailing vessel then anchored about 18 miles inland in the Calcasieu River Ship Channel. The channel connects Lake Charles (in Louisiana) with the Gulf of Mexico. 19 U.S. C.A. § 1581(a) authorizes the boarding of a vessel "at any place in the United States" to examine the manifest and other documents and papers. During the boarding, the officers came upon certain evidence in plain view and seized it. Finding no Fourth Amendment violation despite the absence of even reasonable suspicion, the Supreme Court stressed that the vessel was located on waters providing ready access to the open sea. Further, the boarding was relatively nonintrusive; it involved only a brief period of detention, the visiting of only public areas of the vessel, and the inspection of required documents more extensive than those demanded of automobiles. Stopping an automobile on a public highway near the border without reasonable suspicion would be unreasonable; but, the Court concluded, boardings of vessels in waters with ready access to the open sea, even in the absence of reasonable suspicion, are permissible. 462 U.S. at 588, 103 S.Ct. at 2579–80, 77 L.Ed.2d at 30–31.

2. To what, if any, extent is the validity of nonautomobile searches or seizures affected by the fact that the activity is related to border concerns? So-called "factory surveys" conducted by the Immigration and Naturalization Service were challenged in Immigration and Naturalization Service v. Delgado, 466 U.S. 210, 104 S.Ct. 1758, 80 L.Ed.2d 247 (1984). These surveys are conducted pursuant to warrants issued on the basis of a showing of probable cause to believe that illegal aliens are employed by certain employers. The warrants do not identify any particular illegal aliens. Armed agents execute the warrants. Some agents are positioned near the exits of the building. Others, displaying badges and carrying walkie-talkies, move through the workplace. These latter agents approach workers, identify themselves, and ask questions related to the workers' citizenship; apparently no effort is made to approach only workers suspected of being illegal aliens. If an employee admits being an alien or gives an unsatisfactory response to the questions, the worker is asked to produce immigration papers. Workers other than those actually being questioned continue their work and are free to move about the workplace. A suit challenging these surveys was brought in federal district court. The plaintiffs (who were the respondents before the Supreme Court) established that they had been questioned during previous surveys and in some cases had produced documentation to support their answers. In all cases, however, the agents had been satisfied with the plaintiffs' answers and ended the confrontations. A declaration that the surveys were unconstitutional and injunctive relief against future surveys was sought. The Court of Appeals ordered

summary judgment for the plaintiffs. It reasoned that the surveys involved unreasonable "seizures" of all employees of the workplaces being surveyed; moreover, it concluded, questioning of individual workers constituted seizures of them permissible only if supported by reasonable suspicion that they were illegal aliens.

The Supreme Court reversed. Justice Rehnquist, writing for the Court, read the tribunal's prior decisions as implying that neither interrogation relating to one's identity nor a request for identification, by itself, constitutes a Fourth Amendment seizure. Therefore, the Court of Appeals erred in concluding that all employees were seized in the surveys. Workers remained free to move about the places of work. Further:

> [T]he INS agents' conduct in this case consisted simply of questioning employees and arresting those they had probable cause to believe were unlawfully present in the factory. This conduct should have given respondents no reason to believe that they would be detained if they gave truthful answers to the questions put to them or if they refused to answer. If mere questioning does not constitute a seizure when it occurs outside the factory, it is no more a seizure when it occurs at the exits. \* \* \* [T]he mere possibility that [workers] would be questioned if they sought to leave the buildings should not have resulted in any reasonable apprehension by any of them that they would be seized or detained in any meaningful way. Since most workers could have had no reasonable fear that they would be detained upon leaving, we conclude that the work forces as a whole were not seized.

466 U.S. at 218–19, 104 S.Ct. at 1764, 80 L.Ed.2d at 256–57.

Whether the questioning of individual workers was proper under the Fourth Amendment would be presented, Justice Rehnquist continued, only if one of the respondents had been seized or detained. None had been, he concluded:

> Persons such as respondents who simply went about their business in the workplace were not detained in any way; nothing more occurred than that a question was put to them. While persons who attempted to flee or evade the agents may eventually have been detained for questioning, respondents did not do so and were not in fact detained. The manner in which respondents were questioned, given its obvious purpose, could hardly result in a reasonable fear that respondents were not free to continue working or to move about the factory. Respondents may only litigate what happened to them, and our review of their description of the encounters with the INS agents satisfies us that the encounters were classic consensual encounters rather than Fourth Amendment seizures.

466 U.S. at 220–21, 104 S.Ct. at 1765, 80 L.Ed.2d at 258.

Justice Powell concurred, preferring not to reach the "close" question of whether the surveys resulted in any Fourth Amendment seizures. Instead, he urged that any seizures as might have taken place were permissible under the reasoning of *Martinez-Fuerte:*

> The government's interest in using factory surveys is as great if not greater [than its interest in using permanent checkpoints to intercept traffic]. According to an affidavit by the INS's assistant director in Los Angeles contained in the record in this case, the surveys account for one-half to three-quarters of the illegal aliens identified and arrested away from the border every day in the Los Angeles district. In that district alone, over 20,000 illegal aliens were arrested in the course of factory surveys in one year. The surveys in this case resulted in the arrest of between 20% and

50% of the employees at each of the factories. * * * Factory surveys strike directly at [the] cause [of illegal entry into the country to seek employment], enabling the INS with relatively few agents to diminish the incentive for the dangerous passage across the border and to apprehend large numbers of those who come. Clearly, the government interest in this enforcement technique is enormous.

The intrusion into the Fourth Amendment interests of the employees, on the other hand, is about the same as it was in *Martinez-Fuerte*. The objective intrusion is actually less: there, cars often were stopped for up to five minutes, while here employees could continue work as the survey progressed. They were diverted briefly to answer a few questions or to display their registration cards. It is true that the initial entry into the plant in a factory survey is a surprise to the workers, but the obviously authorized character of the operation, the clear purpose of seeking illegal aliens, and the systematic and public nature of the survey serve to minimize any concern or fright on the part of lawful employees. Moreover, the employees' expectation of privacy in the plant setting here, like that in an automobile, certainly is far less than the traditional expectation of privacy in one's residence. Therefore, for the same reasons that we upheld the checkpoint stops in *Martinez-Fuerte* without any individualized suspicion, I would find the factory surveys here to be reasonable.

466 U.S. at 222–24, 104 S.Ct. at 1766–67, 80 L.Ed.2d at 259–60 (Powell, J., concurring in the result).

Justice Brennan, joined by Justice Marshall, agreed that the surveys did not result in seizures of the entire workforces of the factories being surveyed. But, in contrast to the Court, he concluded that workers "accosted" by INS agents reasonably felt compelled to stop and provide answers to the agents' questions. They were therefore "seized" within the meaning of the Fourth Amendment. To conclude that indiscriminate mass interrogation of workers of the sort at issue is constitutional, he commented, "makes a mockery of the words of the Fourth Amendment." 466 U.S. at 234, 104 S.Ct. at 1772, 80 L.Ed. 2d at 266 (Brennan, J., concurring in part and dissenting in part).

## F. EXTRAORDINARILY INTRUSIVE SEARCHES

In virtually all of the situations covered in the preceding sections of this chapter, the issues have been whether or to what extent the benchmark requirements of probable cause and a traditional search warrant should be abandoned or diluted. But in other situations, it is at least arguable that those requirements should not only be retained but also tightened so as to impose greater limitations upon the ability to "search" than are imposed in standard situations. One of those situations—surgical removal of evidence from the body of the suspect—is covered in this section.

### WINSTON v. LEE

Supreme Court of the United States, 1985.
470 U.S. 753, 105 S.Ct. 1611, 84 L.Ed.2d 662.

JUSTICE BRENNAN delivered the opinion of the Court.

* * *

I

A

At approximately 1 a.m. on July 18, 1982, Ralph E. Watkinson was closing his shop for the night. As he was locking the door, he observed someone armed with a gun coming toward him from across the street. Watkinson was also armed and when he drew his gun, the other person told him to freeze. Watkinson then fired at the other person, who returned his fire. Watkinson was hit in the legs, while the other individual, who appeared to be wounded in his left side, ran from the scene. The police arrived on the scene shortly thereafter, and Watkinson was taken by ambulance to the emergency room of the Medical College of Virginia (MCV) Hospital.

Approximately 20 minutes later, police officers responding to another call found respondent eight blocks from where the earlier shooting occurred. Respondent was suffering from a gunshot wound to his left chest area and told the police that he had been shot when two individuals attempted to rob him. An ambulance took respondent to the MCV Hospital. Watkinson was still in the MCV emergency room and, when respondent entered that room, said "[t]hat's the man that shot me." App. 14. After an investigation, the police decided that respondent's story of having been himself the victim of a robbery was untrue and charged respondent with attempted robbery, malicious wounding, and two counts of using a firearm in the commission of a felony.

B

The Commonwealth shortly thereafter moved in state court for an order directing respondent to undergo surgery to remove an object thought to be a bullet lodged under his left collarbone. The court conducted several evidentiary hearings on the motion. At the first hearing, the Commonwealth's expert testified that the surgical procedure would take 45 minutes and would involve a three to four percent chance of temporary nerve damage, a one percent chance of permanent nerve damage, and a one-tenth of one percent chance of death. At the second hearing, the expert testified that on re-examination of respondent, he discovered that the bullet was not "back inside close to the nerves and arteries," id., at 52, as he originally had thought. Instead, he now believed the bullet to be located "just beneath the skin." Id., at 57. He testified that the surgery would require an incision of only one and one-half centimeters (slightly more than one-half inch), could be performed under local anesthesia, and would result in "no danger on the basis that there's no general anesthesia employed." Id., at 51.

The state trial judge granted the motion to compel surgery. Respondent petitioned the Virginia Supreme Court for a writ of prohibition and/or a writ of habeas corpus, both of which were denied. Respondent then brought an action in the United States District Court for the Eastern District of Virginia to enjoin the pending operation on Fourth Amendment grounds. The court refused to issue a preliminary injunction, holding that respondent's cause had little likelihood of success on the merits. 551 F.Supp. 247, 247–253 (1982).

On October 18, 1982, just before the surgery was scheduled, the surgeon ordered that X rays be taken of respondent's chest. The X rays revealed that the bullet was in fact lodged two and one-half to three centimeters (approximately one inch) deep in muscular tissue in respondent's chest, substantially deeper than had been thought when the state court granted the motion to compel surgery. The surgeon now believed that a general anesthetic would be desirable for medical reasons.

Respondent moved the state trial court for a rehearing based on the new evidence. After holding an evidentiary hearing, the state trial court denied the rehearing and the Virginia Supreme Court affirmed. Respondent then returned to federal court, where he moved to alter or amend the judgment previously entered against him. After an evidentiary hearing, the District Court enjoined the threatened surgery. 551 F.Supp., at 253–261 (supplemental opinion). A divided panel of the Court of Appeals for the Fourth Circuit affirmed. 717 F.2d 888 (1983). We granted certiorari, 466 U.S. 935, 104 S.Ct. 1906, 80 L.Ed.2d 455 (1984), to consider whether a State may consistently with the Fourth Amendment compel a suspect to undergo surgery of this kind in a search for evidence of a crime.

II

The Fourth Amendment protects "expectations of privacy," see Katz v. United States, 389 U.S. 347, 88 S.Ct. 507, 19 L.Ed.2d 576 (1967)—the individual's legitimate expectations that in certain places and at certain times he has "the right to be let alone—the most comprehensive of rights and the right most valued by civilized men." Olmstead v. United States, 277 U.S. 438, 478, 48 S.Ct. 564, 572, 72 L.Ed. 944 (1928) (Brandeis, J., dissenting). Putting to one side the procedural protections of the warrant requirement, the Fourth Amendment generally protects the "security" of "persons, houses, papers, and effects" against official intrusions up to the point where the community's need for evidence surmounts a specified standard, ordinarily "probable cause." Beyond this point, it is ordinarily justifiable for the community to demand that the individual give up some part of his interest in privacy and security to advance the community's vital interests in law enforcement; such a search is generally "reasonable" in the Amendment's terms.

A compelled surgical intrusion into an individual's body for evidence, however, implicates expectations of privacy and security of such magnitude that the intrusion may be "unreasonable" even if likely to produce evidence of a crime. In Schmerber v. California, 384 U.S. 757, 86 S.Ct. 1826, 16 L.Ed.2d 908 (1966), we addressed a claim that the State had breached the Fourth Amendment's protection of the "right of the people to be secure in their *persons* . . . against unreasonable searches and seizures" (emphasis added) when it compelled an individual suspected of drunken driving to undergo a blood test. Schmerber had been arrested at a hospital while receiving treatment for injuries suffered when the automobile he was driving struck a tree. Id., at 758, 86 S.Ct., at 1829. Despite Schmerber's objection, a police officer at the hospital had directed a physician to take a blood sample from him. Schmerber subsequently objected to the introduction at trial of evidence obtained as a result of the blood test.

The authorities in *Schmerber* clearly had probable cause to believe that he had been driving while intoxicated, id., at 768, 86 S.Ct., at 1834, and to believe that a blood test would provide evidence that was exceptionally probative in confirming this belief. Id., at 770, 86 S.Ct., at 1835. Because the case fell within the exigent circumstances exception to the warrant requirement, no warrant was necessary. Ibid. The search was not more intrusive than reasonably necessary to accomplish its goals. Nonetheless, Schmerber argued that the Fourth Amendment prohibited the authorities from intruding into his body to extract the blood that was needed as evidence.

*Schmerber* noted that "[t]he overriding function of the Fourth Amendment is to protect personal privacy and dignity against unwarranted intrusion by the State." Id., at 767, 86 S.Ct., at 1834. Citing Wolf v. Colorado, 338 U.S. 25, 27, 69 S.Ct. 1359, 1361, 93 L.Ed. 1782 (1949), and Mapp v. Ohio, 367 U.S. 643, 81 S.Ct. 1684, 6 L.Ed.2d 1081 (1961), we observed that these values were "basic to a free society." We also noted that "[b]ecause we are dealing with intrusions into the human body rather than with state interferences with property relationships or private papers—'houses, papers, and effects'—we write on a clean slate." 384 U.S., at 767–768, 86 S.Ct., at 1833–1835. The intrusion perhaps implicated Schmerber's most personal and deep-rooted expectations of privacy, and the Court recognized that Fourth Amendment analysis thus required a discerning inquiry into the facts and circumstances to determine whether the intrusion was justifiable. The Fourth Amendment neither forbids nor permits all such intrusions; rather, the Amendment's "proper function is to constrain, not against all intrusions as such, but against intrusions which are not justified in the circumstances, or which are made in an improper manner." Id., at 768, 86 S.Ct., at 1834.

The reasonableness of surgical intrusions beneath the skin depends on a case-by-case approach, in which the individual's interests in privacy and security are weighed against society's interests in conducting the procedure. In a given case, the question whether the community's need for evidence outweighs the substantial privacy interests at stake is a delicate one admitting of few categorical answers. We believe that *Schmerber*, however, provides the appropriate framework of analysis for such cases.

*Schmerber* recognized that the ordinary requirements of the Fourth Amendment would be the threshold requirements for conducting this kind of surgical search and seizure. We noted the importance of probable cause. Id., at 768–769, 86 S.Ct., at 1834–1835. And we pointed out: "Search warrants are ordinarily required for searches of dwellings, and, absent an emergency, no less could be required where intrusions into the human body are concerned. . . . The importance of informed, detached and deliberate determinations of the issue whether or not to invade another's body in search of evidence of guilt is indisputable and great." Id., at 770, 86 S.Ct., at 1835.

Beyond these standards, *Schmerber*'s inquiry considered a number of other factors in determining the "reasonableness" of the blood test. A crucial factor in analyzing the magnitude of the intrusion in *Schmerber* is the extent to which the procedure may threaten the safety or health of the individual. "[F]or most people [a blood test] involves virtually no risk, trauma, or pain." Id., at 771, 86 S.Ct., at 1836. Moreover, all reasonable medical precautions were taken and no unusual or untested procedures were employed in *Schmerber*, the procedure was performed "by a physician in a hospital environment according to accepted medical practices." Ibid. Notwithstanding the existence of probable cause, a search for evidence of a crime may be unjustifiable if it endangers the life or health of the suspect.

Another factor is the extent of intrusion upon the individual's dignitary interests in personal privacy and bodily integrity. Intruding into an individual's living room, eavesdropping upon an individual's telephone conversations, or forcing an individual to accompany police officers to the police station typically do not injure the physical person of the individual. Such intrusions do, however, damage the individual's sense of personal privacy and security and are thus subject to the Fourth Amendment's dictates. In noting that a blood test was "a commonplace in these days of periodic physical examinations," 384 U.S., at 771, 86 S.Ct., at 1836, *Schmerber* recognized society's judgment that blood tests do not constitute an unduly extensive imposition on an individual's personal privacy and bodily integrity.

Weighed against these individual interests is the community's interest in fairly and accurately determining guilt or innocence. This interest is of course of great importance. We noted in *Schmerber* that a blood test is "a highly effective means of determining the degree to which a person is under the influence of alcohol." Id., at 771, 86 S.Ct., at 1836. Moreover, there was "a clear indication that in fact [desired] evidence [would] be found" if the blood test were undertaken. Id., at 770, 86 S.Ct., at 1835. Especially given the difficulty of proving drunkenness by other means, these considerations showed that results of the blood test were of vital importance if the State were to enforce its drunken driving laws. In *Schmerber*, we concluded that this state interest was sufficient to justify the intrusion, and the compelled blood test was thus "reasonable" for Fourth Amendment purposes.

### III

Applying the *Schmerber* balancing test in this case, we believe that the Court of Appeals reached the correct result. The Commonwealth plainly had probable cause to conduct the search. In addition, all parties apparently agree that respondent has had a full measure of procedural protections and has been able fully to litigate the difficult medical and legal questions necessarily involved in analyzing the rea-

sonableness of a surgical incision of this magnitude.[24]   Our inquiry
therefore must focus on the extent of the intrusion on respondent's
privacy interests and on the State's need for the evidence.

The threats to the health or safety of respondent posed by the
surgery are the subject of sharp dispute between the parties.   Before
the new revelations of October 18, the District Court found that the
procedure could be carried out "with virtually no risk to [respondent]."
551 F.Supp., at 252.   On rehearing, however, with new evidence before
it, the District Court held that "the risks previously involved have
increased in magnitude even as new risks are being added."   Id., at 260.

The Court of Appeals examined the medical evidence in the record
and found that respondent would suffer some risks associated with the
surgical procedure.   One surgeon had testified that the difficulty of
discovering the exact location of the bullet "could require extensive
probing and retracting of the muscle tissue," carrying with it "the
concomitant risks of injury to the muscle as well as injury to the
nerves, blood vessels and other tissue in the chest and pleural cavity."
717 F.2d, at 900.   The court further noted that "the greater intrusion
and the larger incisions increase the risks of infection."   Ibid.   Moreover, there was conflict in the testimony concerning the nature and the
scope of the operation.   One surgeon stated that it would take 15–20
minutes, while another predicted the procedure could take up to two
and one-half hours.   Ibid.   The court properly took the resulting
uncertainty about the medical risks into account.

Both lower courts in this case believed that the proposed surgery,
which for purely medical reasons required the use of a general anesthetic, would be an "extensive" intrusion on respondent's personal
privacy and bodily integrity.   Ibid.   When conducted with the consent
of the patient, surgery requiring general anesthesia is not necessarily
demeaning or intrusive.   In such a case, the surgeon is carrying out the
patient's own will concerning the patient's body and the patient's right
to privacy is therefore preserved.   In this case, however, the Court of
Appeals noted that the Commonwealth proposes to take control of
respondent's body, to "drug this citizen—not yet convicted of a criminal
offense—with narcotics and barbiturates into a state of unconscious-
ness," id., at 901, and then to search beneath his skin for evidence of a
crime.   This kind of surgery involves a virtually total divestment of
respondent's ordinary control over surgical probing beneath his skin.

The other part of the balance concerns the Commonwealth's need
to intrude into respondent's body to retrieve the bullet.   The Commonwealth claims to need the bullet to demonstrate that it was fired from
Watkinson's gun, which in turn would show that respondent was the
robber who confronted Watkinson.   However, although we recognize
the difficulty of making determinations in advance as to the strength of
the case against respondent, petitioners' assertions of a compelling need
for the bullet are hardly persuasive.   The very circumstances relied on

---

[24] Because the State has afforded respondent the benefit of a full adversary presentation and appellate review, we do not
reach the question whether the State may
compel a suspect to undergo a surgical
search of this magnitude for evidence absent such special procedural protections.

in this case to demonstrate probable cause to believe that evidence will be found tend to vitiate the Commonwealth's need to compel respondent to undergo surgery. The Commonwealth has available substantial additional evidence that respondent was the individual who accosted Watkinson on the night of the robbery. No party in this case suggests that Watkinson's entirely spontaneous identification of respondent at the hospital would be inadmissible. In addition, petitioners can no doubt prove that [respondent] was found a few blocks from Watkinson's store shortly after the incident took place. And petitioners can certainly show that the location of the bullet (under respondent's left collarbone) seems to correlate with Watkinson's report that the robber "jerked" to the left. App. 13. The fact that the Commonwealth has available such substantial evidence of the origin of the bullet restricts the need for the Commonwealth to compel respondent to undergo the contemplated surgery.[25]

In weighing the various factors in this case, we therefore reach the same conclusion as the courts below. The operation sought will intrude substantially on respondent's protected interests. The medical risks of the operation, although apparently not extremely severe, are a subject of considerable dispute: the very uncertainty militates against finding the operation to be "reasonable." In addition, the intrusion on respondent's privacy interests entailed by the operation can only be characterized as severe. On the other hand, although the bullet may turn out to be useful to the Commonwealth in prosecuting respondent, the Commonwealth has failed to demonstrate a compelling need for it. We believe that in these circumstances the Commonwealth has failed to demonstrate that it would be "reasonable" under the terms of the Fourth Amendment to search for evidence of this crime by means of the contemplated surgery.

## IV

The Fourth Amendment is a vital safeguard of the right of the citizen to be free from unreasonable governmental intrusions into any area in which he has a reasonable expectation of privacy. Where the Court has found a lesser expectation of privacy, or where the search involves a minimal intrusion on privacy interests, the Court has held that the Fourth Amendment's protections are correspondingly less

---

[25] There are also some questions concerning the probative value of the bullet, even if it could be retrieved. The evidentiary value of the bullet depends on a comparison between markings, if any, on the bullet in respondent's shoulder and markings, if any, found on a test bullet that the police could fire from Watkinson's gun. However, the record supports some doubt whether this kind of comparison is possible. This is because the bullet's markings may have been corroded in the time that the bullet has been in respondent's shoulder, thus making it useless for comparison purposes. See 717 F.2d, at 901, n. 15. In addition, respondent argues that any given gun may be incapable of firing bullets that have a consistent set of markings. See Joling, An Overview of Firearms Identification Evidence for Attorneys I: Salient Features of Firearms Evidence, 26 J. Forensic Sci. 153, 154 (1981). The record is devoid of any evidence that the police have attempted to test-fire Watkinson's gun, and there thus remains the additional possibility that a comparison of bullets is impossible because Watkinson's gun does not consistently fire bullets with the same markings. However, because the courts below made no findings on this point, we hesitate to give it significant weight in our analysis.

stringent.   Conversely, however, the Fourth Amendment's command that searches be "reasonable" requires that when the State seeks to intrude upon an area in which our society recognizes a significantly heightened privacy interest, a more substantial justification is required to make the search "reasonable."   Applying these principles, we hold that the proposed search in this case would be "unreasonable" under the Fourth Amendment.

Affirmed.

JUSTICE BLACKMUN and JUSTICE REHNQUIST concur in the judgment.

CHIEF JUSTICE BURGER, concurring.

I join because I read the Court's opinion as not preventing detention of an individual if there are reasonable grounds to believe that natural bodily functions will disclose the presence of contraband materials secreted internally.

# Chapter 6

# ELECTRONIC SURVEILLANCE

*Analysis*

---

Modern technology has resulted in the development of very sophisticated devices that can be used to enhance the effectiveness of the human senses, especially those of sight and hearing. The use of these devices—often referred to as "electronic surveillance"—in criminal investigations is the subject of this chapter. Most of the attention has been devoted to surveillance of the spoken word and this is the focus of the federal statute discussed in this chapter. But other law enforcement techniques may raise similar issues. Norwood, "Available Dark" Photography, Industrial Photography, Nov. 1971, at 24, for example, describes the electronic intensifier, which permits taking of photographs in very low light. This, he claims, permits law enforcement surveillance work to take place in "almost complete darkness." Excellent photographs of actual narcotics transactions have been taken, he continues, apparently in circumstances in which most persons would believe their actions are not subject to "capture" on film or even—given the darkness—to visual observation by others. See also, Canavor, The FBI: Surveillance Photography, Industrial Photography, May, 1973, at 26.

## A. THE CONSTITUTIONAL BACKGROUND

Electronic surveillance of communication is pervasively regulated by Title III of the Omnibus Crime Control and Safe Streets Act of 1968, codified as 18 U.S.C.A. § 2510 et seq. Although this statute is in part the product of legislation introduced earlier, it has clearly been molded by two important Supreme Court decisions.

In Berger v. New York, 388 U.S. 41, 87 S.Ct. 1873, 18 L.Ed.2d 1040 (1967), the Court considered the validity of New York's eavesdrop statute, which permitted eavesdropping pursuant to a court order issued under the statute. Assuming that the conduct which the statute authorized constituted a "search" under the Fourth Amendment, the Court found several defects in the New York statute. First, the statute did not require that the court order specify with particularity the crime under investigation, the "place" to be "searched," or the conversations to be "seized." Although the statute did require identification of the persons whose conversations were to be overheard, this was not sufficient. Second, the statute permitted officers serving the court order to "seize" all conversations of all persons coming into the area during a two-month period without regard to their connection to the crime under investigation. This authorized a series of intrusions pursuant to a single showing of probable cause, which might well not constitute an adequate basis for each of the numerous intrusions authorized by the court order. Third, the two-month period of eavesdropping which the statute authorized permitted avoidance of the requirement of prompt execution of the order. Fourth, two-month extensions of the eavesdropping order could be obtained upon a showing that this would be "in the public interest." This violated the requirement of probable cause, which demands a showing of present probable cause for such extensions. Fifth, there was no provision for termination of the "seizure" once the conversation sought was overheard. Sixth, the statute had neither a requirement of notice to persons whose conversations were seized nor any reasonable substitute. Finally, the statute provided for no return on the court order and consequently left the use of conversations overheard and information obtained completely within the discretion of the officer.

The New York statute permitted the issuance of an eavesdrop order upon the "oath" of a prosecutor or high police official that "there is probable cause to believe that evidence of a crime may thus be obtained." Whether this violated the Fourth Amendment's requirement that search warrants be issued only upon an adequate showing of probable cause was described by the Court as a serious question that did not have to be resolved at that time.

It is at least arguable that the Fourth Amendment requirements which *Berger* applied to the New York statutes are significantly more stringent than those which the Court has applied to regular search warrants. Cady v. Dombrowski, 413 U.S. 433, 93 S.Ct. 2523, 37 L.Ed.2d 706 (1973), for example, strongly suggests that there is no Fourth Amendment requirement of a return of a standard search warrant. Do each of the defects identified by the Court in the New York statute constitute application of separate and independent constitutional requirements, or did the statute fall because of the totality of the deficiencies?

The second case, Katz v. United States, 389 U.S. 347, 88 S.Ct. 507, 19 L.Ed.2d 576 (1967), was important because it established an expansive definition of the kinds of activities that the Fourth Amendment protected from unreasonable surveillance. In Olmstead v. United States, 277 U.S. 438, 48 S.Ct. 564, 72 L.Ed. 944 (1928), the Court found no infringement upon interests protected by the Fourth Amendment in the "tapping" of the defendant's telephone line accomplished without unlawful entry into (or onto) the defendant's premises. Section 605 of the Communications Act of 1934, however, barred "interception" of any interstate communication by wire and in Nardone v. United States, 302 U.S. 379, 58 S.Ct. 275, 82 L.Ed. 314 (1937) the Court held that this required the exclusion in federal criminal trials of the products of wiretaps that, under *Olmstead*, would not have involved searches under the Fourth Amendment. In Goldman v. United States, 316 U.S. 129, 62 S.Ct. 993, 86 L.Ed. 1322 (1942) the Court found no violation of the Fourth Amendment in the use of a "detectaphone" placed against an office wall to hear private conversations in the office next door because there was no "trespass" on the premises under surveillance. *Olmstead* and *Goldman* were generally regarded as establishing that surveillance did not amount to a search and therefore did not have to be "reasonable" in Fourth Amendment terms unless it involved some physical trespass on or into premises in which the subject had a privacy interest.

*Katz*, however, held that this trespass requirement was no longer controlling. In *Katz*, FBI agents had attached an electronic listening and recording device to the outside of a public telephone booth. This enabled them to overhear Katz' end of a telephone conversation he carried on in the booth, but involved no physical penetration of, or trespass into, the booth. Nevertheless, the Court held that this constituted a "search." The Fourth Amendment protects people—and not merely areas—against unreasonable searches and seizures, Justice Stewart explained for the majority, and consequently "the reach of that Amendment cannot turn upon the presence or absence of a physical intrusion into any given enclosure." Since Katz reasonably expected, when he used the booth, that the words he uttered into the mouthpiece would "not be broadcast to the world," he had a privacy interest in the content of those words that was infringed by the agents' use of the recording and listening device. The result of *Katz*, as Justice Harlan noted in his concurrence, appears to be that any surveillance that results in obtaining information that the subjects actually and reasonably believed was relatively private constitutes a "search" and must be scrutinized under Fourth Amendment reasonableness standards. 389 U.S. at 361, 88 S.Ct. at 516–17, 19 L.Ed.2d at 587–88 (Harlan, J., concurring).

The Senate Judiciary Report on Title III noted both *Berger* and *Katz*. It further commented that Title III was drafted to meet the constitutional criteria for electronic surveillance delineated in *Berger* and to "conform with" *Katz*. Senate Report No. 1097, 90th Congress, 2nd Session, 1968, U.S. Code Congressional and Administrative News, 1968, Vol. 2, 2112, at 2153.

The Supreme Court has not addressed the facial validity of the electronic surveillance statute, but there is no indication in its numerous decisions dealing with it that the Court regards the statute as suffering from the fatal defects found by the *Berger* Court in the New York statute. Lower courts have upheld the statute against constitutional attacks. E.g., United States v. Sklaroff, 506 F.2d 837 (5th Cir. 1975), cert. denied 423 U.S. 874, 96 S.Ct. 142, 46 L.Ed.2d 105; United States v. Tortorello, 480 F.2d 764 (2d Cir. 1973), cert. denied 414 U.S. 866, 94 S.Ct. 63, 38 L.Ed.2d 86; United States v. Cox, 449 F.2d 679 (8th Cir. 1971), cert. denied 406 U.S. 934, 92 S.Ct. 1783, 32 L.Ed.2d 136 (1972).

## B.  THE FEDERAL STATUTE AND ITS APPLICATION

### EDITORS' INTRODUCTION: A SUMMARY OF TITLE III

Title III was originally enacted in 1968, but has been amended frequently.  The following is a summary of the current provisions.

#### COVERAGE AND PROHIBITIONS

Title III distinguishes among "wire communications," "oral communications," and "electronic communications."  All three are covered, but in somewhat different ways.  A "wire communication" is defined as an aural transfer that in whole or part uses wire, cable or other "like connection."  It must at some point involve the human voice.  An "electronic communication," on the other hand, is a transfer of signs, signals, images, data or intelligence by means of wire, radio, or similar means.  Thus it includes such innovations as electronic mail, facsimile transmissions, and video teleconferences.  An "oral communication" is defined as "any oral communication uttered by a person exhibiting an expectation that such communication is not subject to interception under circumstances justifying such expectation."  18 U.S.C.A. § 2510.

"Intercept" is defined as "the aural or other acquisition of the contents of any wire, electronic, or oral communication through the use of any electronic, mechanical, or other device."  18 U.S.C.A. § 2510(4).  "Electronic, mechanical, or other device" is defined as "any device or apparatus which can be used to intercept a wire or oral communication."  Specifically designated as not such devices are telephone or telegraph equipment furnished to a user and used in the ordinary course of business (i.e., an extension phone) and a hearing aid or similar device being used to correct subnormal hearing to not better than normal.  18 U.S.C.A. § 2510(5).

#### EXCEPTIONS

Several exceptions to the statute's prohibition are created.  First, a party to the conversation or a person authorized by one of the parties to the communication may intercept the communication.  18 U.S.C.A. § 2511(2)(c).

Second, federal law enforcement officers may intercept communications in certain emergency situations.  The situations must be believed to involve "immediate danger of death or serious physical injury" or "conspiratorial activities threatening the national security interest or * * * characteristic of organized crime," and application for a court order approving the interception must be made within 48 hours.  18 U.S.C.A. § 2518(7).

Third—and most important—the statute provides for federal law enforcement agencies to obtain court orders from federal judges authorizing certain interceptions.  18 U.S.C.A. § 2516.  Further, the statute authorizes states to enact statutes permitting state law enforcement officers to obtain similar court orders from state judges "in conformity with" the provisions of Title III.  18 U.S.C.A. § 2516(2).  In the absence of an order obtained pursuant to a state "enabling" statute, the federal statute bars state law enforcement officers from engaging in the conduct prohibited by the statute.

### INTERCEPTIONS UNDER COURT ORDER

The process of applying for, obtaining, and serving a court order permitting otherwise prohibited interceptions under the statute is a complex one best considered in several steps.

#### (1) Offenses Involved

An application may be made to a federal court for interception of wire or oral communications only if the surveillance is sought to obtain evidence of certain enumerated offenses.  State statutes may authorize court orders only to obtain evidence regarding "murder, kidnapping, gambling, robbery, bribery, extortion, or dealing in narcotic drugs, marihuana or other dangerous drugs, or other crime dangerous to life, limb, or property, and punishable by imprisonment for more than one year  *  *  *  or any conspiracy to commit any of the foregoing offenses."  18 U.S.C.A. § 2516(2).  An application for authorization to intercept electronic communications may be made for any federal felony.

#### (2) Authorization

An application for interception of wire or oral communications may be made to a federal court for a surveillance order only if this is authorized by the Attorney General or an Assistant Attorney General specially designated by the Attorney General.  18 U.S.C.A. § 2516(1).  Any assistant United States Attorney may authorize application for an electronic communications intercept.  A state procedure must require authorization by the principal prosecuting attorney of the state or of a political subdivision of the state.  18 U.S.C.A. § 2516(2).

#### (3) Application Contents

The contents of the application are governed by 18 U.S.C.A. § 2518(1):

> Each application for an order authorizing or approving the interception of a wire, oral, or electronic communication . . . shall be made in writing upon oath or affirmation to a judge of competent jurisdiction and shall state the applicant's authority to make such application.  Each application shall include the following information:
>
> > (a) the identity of the investigative or law enforcement officer making the application, and the officer authorizing the application;
> >
> > (b) a full and complete statement of the facts and circumstances relied upon by the applicant, to justify his belief that an order should be issued, including (i) details as to the particular offense that has been, is being, or is about to be

committed, (ii) . . . a particular description of the nature and location of the facilities from which or the place where the communication is to be intercepted, (iii) a particular description of the type of communications sought to be intercepted, (iv) the identity of the person, if known, committing the offense and whose communications are to be intercepted;

(c) a full and complete statement as to whether or not other investigative procedures have been tried and failed or why they reasonably appear to be unlikely to succeed if tried or to be too dangerous;

(d) a statement of the period of time for which the interception is required to be maintained. If the nature of the investigation is such that the authorization for interception should not automatically terminate when the described type of communication has been first obtained, a particular description of facts establishing probable cause to believe that additional communications of the same type will occur thereafter;

(e) a full and complete statement of the facts concerning all previous applications known to the individual authorizing and making the application, made to any judge for authorization to intercept, or for approval of interceptions of, wire, oral, or electronic communications involving any of the same persons, facilities or places specified in the application, and the action taken by the judge on each such application; and

(f) where the application is for the extension of an order, a statement setting forth the results thus far obtained from the interception, or a reasonable explanation of the failure to obtain such results.

## (4) Judicial Function and Issuance of Order

The judge to whom the application is made may require the applicant to furnish additional testimony or evidence in support of the application. 18 U.S.C.A. § 2518(2). An *ex parte* order authorizing interception may be issued:

if the judge determines on the basis of the facts submitted by the applicant that—

(a) there is probable cause for belief that an individual is committing, has committed, or is about to commit [an offense for which an order may be issued];

(b) there is probable cause for belief that particular communications concerning that offense will be obtained through such interception;

(c) normal investigative procedures have been tried and have failed or reasonably appear to be unlikely to succeed if tried or to be too dangerous;

(d) there is probable cause for belief that the facilities from which, or the place where, the wire or oral communications are to be intercepted are being used, or are about to be used, in connection with the commission of such offense, or are leased to, listed in the name of, or commonly used by such person.

18 U.S.C.A. § 2518(3).

### (5) Contents of Order

Under 18 U.S.C.A. § 2518(4), each order shall specify:

(a) the identity of the person, if known, whose communications are to be intercepted;

(b) the nature and location of the communications facilities as to which, or the place where, authority to intercept is granted;

(c) a particular description of the type of communication sought to be intercepted, and a statement of the particular offense to which it relates;

(d) the identity of the agency authorized to intercept the communications, and of the person authorizing the application; and

(e) the period of time during which such interception is authorized, including a statement as to whether or not the interception shall automatically terminate when the described communication has been first obtained.

Where the order will authorize the interception of a wire or electronic communication, the requirement that the communication facilities to be intercepted be described specifically does not apply if the application identified the person whose communications are to be intercepted and the government makes a showing that the person has a "purpose * * * to thwart interception by changing facilities." The court must find that this purpose has been shown. If the order will authorize the interception of an oral communication, the application must identify the person whose communications are to be intercepted and explain why specification of the facilities is not practical. The judge must also find that such specification is not practical. 18 U.S.C.A. § 2518(11). Court orders authorizing interceptions of this sort are often referred to as permitting "roving taps."

Further, every order must contain a provision "that the authorization to intercept shall be executed as soon as practicable, [and] shall be conducted in such a way as to minimize the interception of communications not otherwise subject to interception under this chapter * * *" 18 U.S.C.A. § 2518(5).

The period of time during which interception may be authorized is only as long as is necessary to achieve the objective of the order, but never longer than thirty days. Each order must contain a directive that the interception "must terminate upon attainment of the authorized objective." 18 U.S.C.A. § 2518(5).

Upon request of the applicant, the judge "shall" include in the order a directive that a communication common carrier, landlord, custodian "or other person" shall furnish the officers with "all information, facilities, and technical assistance necessary to accomplish the interception unobtrusively." Such persons are to be compensated at prevailing rates. 18 U.S.C.A. § 2518(4).

The judge may also include a requirement that the officers submit progress reports at designated intervals. These reports may require a showing as to what progress has been made toward achievement of the authorized objective and the need for continued interception. 18 U.S. C.A. § 2518(6).

### (6) Service of the Intercept Order

The statute contains very few provisions relating directly to the manner in which the court order is to be served. Some can be read into the provisions discussed above. It is clear, for example, that the statute contemplates compliance with the order's provision that the interception occur as soon as practicable and that it be conducted in such a manner as to minimize the interception of communications not subject to interception. Further, assistance from landlords and other persons may be obtained.

It is specifically provided that the contents of any intercepted communications "shall, if possible, be recorded on tape or wire or other comparable device" and that this be done "in such way as will protect the recording from editing or other alteration." 18 U.S.C.A. § 2518(8) (a).

In Dalia v. United States, 441 U.S. 238, 99 S.Ct. 1682, 60 L.Ed.2d 177 (1979), the Supreme Court upheld covert entry of private premises by agents to install a listening device whose use was authorized by a court order. Such entries are not inherently unreasonable under the Fourth Amendment and the statute does not prohibit them. Nor is it necessary that the court order specifically authorize such covert entry. The precise manner in which search warrants are to be served, Justice Powell reasoned for the majority, has always been left to the discretion of the officers executing the order, subject to later judicial review for "reasonableness." There is no need, the Court concluded, to depart from this approach in the electronic surveillance area.

### (7) Extensions

Extensions of an intercept order may be granted. But an application for such an extension must comply with the requirements for applications for an initial order and an extension may be granted only if the judge makes the determinations required for an initial order. Extensions may be for no longer than is necessary to achieve the purposes for which they are granted and may never exceed thirty days. 18 U.S.C.A. § 2518(5).

### (8) Return to Court

The statute does not specifically impose a requirement of a return of the order to the issuing court. But immediately upon the expiration of the order, any recordings made of intercepted communications are to "be made available" to the judge and further shall be retained in custody as ordered by the court. 18 U.S.C.A. § 2518(8)(a). The provisions for notice (discussed below) appear to assume some sort of communication to the court from the serving agency or officers, if not a formal return.

### (9) Notice

The statute contains two provisions for notice to persons whose communications may have been intercepted. Within a reasonable time, but not more than ninety days after denial of an application or the termination of an interception authorized by an order, an inventory is to be served on certain persons. This inventory is to include notice of (a) the fact of the entry of the order or the application; (b) the date of the entry and the period of authorized, approved or disapproved interception, or the denial of the application; and (c) the fact that during the period communications were or were not intercepted. An inventory is to be served on the persons named in the application or order and "such other parties to the intercepted communications as the judge may determine in his discretion that is in the interest of justice." On an *ex parte* showing of good cause, the service of the inventory may be postponed. 18 U.S.C.A. § 2518(8)(d).

The second provision focuses upon the use of the results of surveillance. If the contents of an intercepted communication or evidence derived from such communications are to be used or disclosed in any trial, hearing or "other proceeding," each party must be given, no less than ten days before the proceedings, a copy of the court order and the application. 18 U.S.C.A. § 2518(9).

### INTERCEPTED COMMUNICATIONS CONCERNING NONTARGET OFFENSES

Officers serving a court order that authorizes the interception of communications related to a specified offense may, of course, overhear communications concerning other offenses as well. The statute provides that if this occurs while the officer is engaged in intercepting communications in the manner authorized by the federal statute, the officer may use the contents of these communications and may disclose those contents to other law enforcement officers to the extent that such action is appropriate to the proper performance of the intercepting officer's official duties. But the contents of communications concerning such nontarget offenses and information derived from them may be used in testimony only:

> when authorized or approved by a judge of competent jurisdiction where such judge finds on subsequent application that the contents were otherwise intercepted in accordance with the provisions of this chapter. Such application shall be made as soon as practicable.

18 U.S.C.A. § 2517(5).

This provision has created some confusion. It has been held, however, to authorize officers to apply for and federal courts to issue an order that does not purport to authorize future interceptions but rather embodies a determination that already intercepted communications were properly intercepted and thus may be used later in testimony.

See United States v. Agrusa, 541 F.2d 690 (8th Cir. 1976); cert. denied 429 U.S. 1045, 97 S.Ct. 751, 50 L.Ed.2d 759 (1977); United States v. Cox, 449 F.2d 679 (10th Cir. 1971), cert. denied 406 U.S. 934, 92 S.Ct. 1783, 32 L.Ed.2d 136 (1972).

## REMEDIES FOR VIOLATION OF THE STATUTE

The statute provides several remedies for a violation of its provisions. "Intentional" violations are punishable as criminal offenses and carry penalties of a fine of not more than $10,000 or imprisonment for not more than five years, or both. 18 U.S.C.A. § 2511. A civil cause of action is also created and provisions are made for recovery of attorney's fees, punitive damages, and actual damages not less than liquidated damages computed at the rate of $100 a day for each day of violation or $10,000, whichever is higher. 18 U.S.C.A. § 2520.

The statute also has its own exclusionary sanction in 18 U.S.C.A. § 2515:

> Whenever any wire or oral communication has been intercepted, no part of the contents of such communication and no evidence derived therefrom may be received in evidence in any trial, hearing, or other proceeding in or before any court, grand jury, department, officer, agency, regulatory body, legislative committee, or other authority of the United States, a State, or a political subdivision thereof if the disclosure of that information would be in violation of this chapter.

"Any aggrieved person" may move to suppress the contents of an intercepted communication or evidence derived from it on the following grounds:

> (i) the communication was unlawfully intercepted;

> (ii) the order of authorization or approval under which it was intercepted is insufficient on its face; or

> (iii) the interception was not made in conformity with the order of authorization or approval.

18 U.S.C.A. § 2518(10)(a). "Aggrieved person" is defined as "a person who was a party to any intercepted wire, oral, or electronic communication or a person against whom the interception was directed." 18 U.S.C.A. § 2510(11).

To some extent, this statutory exclusionary remedy is broader than that of the Fourth Amendment. In Gelbard v. United States, 408 U.S. 41, 92 S.Ct. 2357, 33 L.Ed.2d 179 (1972), the Court held that witnesses who had been subpoenaed before a grand jury could invoke 18 U.S.C.A. § 2515, and could not be cited for contempt for refusal to answer questions based upon information obtained in violation of the statute. It may not follow, however, that an indictment is subject to attack by a defendant on the basis that the grand jury considered or relied upon evidence obtained in violation of the statute.

Perhaps the most perplexing problem has been the determination as to what noncompliance with the statutory procedures requires suppression of the results of an interception. In United States v. Giordano,

416 U.S. 505, 94 S.Ct. 1820, 40 L.Ed.2d 341 (1974), the Supreme Court held that the Congressional intention was to provide for suppression where "there is failure to satisfy any of those statutory requirements that directly and substantially implement the congressional intent to limit the use of intercept procedures to those situations clearly calling for the employment of this extraordinary investigative device." 416 U.S. at 527, 94 S.Ct. at 1832, 40 L.Ed.2d at 342. In *Giordano*, the application for the court order recited that it had been approved by a designated Assistant Attorney General; evidence showed, however, that in fact the Executive Assistant to the Attorney General had approved it. Finding the requirement of approval by the Attorney General or a designated Assistant Attorney General was one that directly and substantially implemented the congressional purpose, the Court held that the products of the order had to be suppressed under 18 U.S.C.A. § 2515. In United States v. Chavez, 416 U.S. 562, 94 S.Ct. 1849, 40 L.Ed. 2d 380 (1974), however, the application recited that it had been approved by the Assistant Attorney General although the facts showed that the Attorney General himself had approved it. The statute's requirement that the application accurately state which of the several authorized persons approved it, held the Court, was not so directly and substantially related to the Congressional purpose as to require suppression of the products of the surveillance.

If there is a violation of a statutory requirement that does bring 18 U.S.C.A. § 2515 into play, does it require suppression of evidence or information obtained *before* that violation took place? In United States v. Donovan, 429 U.S. 413, 97 S.Ct. 658, 50 L.Ed.2d 652 (1977), the defendant did not receive post-interception notice because the government left the defendant's name off the list of persons whose conversations were intercepted that the government provided the court. This, the Supreme Court held, violated the statute, since the government had exclusive access to this information and thus was obligated to provide a full list to the court. But, it continued, this violation of the notice provision of the statute was not "retroactive" in the sense that it would not be held to render the earlier interceptions unlawful and therefore subject to suppression.

Section 2518(8)(a), which requires that officers record intercepted conversations and make the recording available to the judge, also directs that the recording be sealed under the judge's direction. This is to occur "[i]mmediately upon the expiration" of the order or any extensions that are authorized. In United States v. Ojeda Rios, ___ U.S. ___, 110 S.Ct. 1845, 109 L.Ed.2d 224 (1990), no seal was obtained immediately as the statute provides. The Supreme Court noted that § 2518(8)(a) contains its own "explicit exclusionary remedy" in language providing that the seal "or a satisfactory explanation for the absence thereof, shall be a prerequisite for the use or disclosure" of a communication intercepted under the statute or evidence derived from such a communication. In *Ojeda Rios*, the Court noted:

> The presence or absence of a seal does not in itself establish the integrity of electronic surveillance tapes [but] is a means of ensuring that subsequent to its placement on a tape, the Government

has no opportunity to tamper with, alter, or edit the conversations that have been recorded.

___ U.S. at ___, 110 S.Ct. at 1849, 109 L.Ed.2d at 234. It then rejected the Government's argument that evidence was admissible if the Government provided an explanation that was not "satisfactory" but in addition showed that the offered recording was authentic. Under the language of the statute, proof that no tampering with the recording occurred in the particular case is not an adequate substitute for a "satisfactory explanation" for the failure to have the recording sealed. There was also evidence that the attorney supervising the investigation had misconstrued the statute as requiring no effort on the Government's part to have the recording sealed until there was a "meaningful hiatus" in the investigation as a whole. This, the Court held, was an objectively reasonable—although ultimately incorrect—reading of the law and if offered to the trial court would constitute a "satisfactory explanation" for the absence of a seal timely secured. The case was remanded for a determination as to whether the Government had presented this to the trial court at the suppression hearing.

### PEN REGISTERS AND "TRAP AND TRACE" DEVICES

In United States v. New York Telephone Co., 434 U.S. 159, 98 S.Ct. 364, 54 L.Ed.2d 376 (1977) the Court addressed the issue of the applicability of Title III to pen registers—devices that record only the numbers called from the telephone on which they are installed. The Court held that they are not covered by Title III because they do not intercept communications.

As a result of 1986 legislation, federal law now covers pen registers. Also covered are "trap and trace" devices, which ascertain the number from which calls are placed to a particular telephone. These devices are now covered by Chapter 26 of Title 18 of the United States Code.

These provisions establish that no person may install or use a pen register or "trap and trace" device except as authorized by the statute. Knowingly violating this prohibition is a criminal offense. 18 U.S.C.A. § 3121. But apparently no statutory exclusionary rule, analogous to that in 18 U.S.C.A. § 2515 governing interception of wire, oral and electronic communications, applies.

The major exception permitting use of these devices is for their use under court orders. Specific provision is made for federal law enforcement to obtain such orders from federal courts, and state officers are authorized—unless prohibited from doing so by state law—to obtain such orders from state courts. 18 U.S.C.A. § 3122.

The court order procedure is a somewhat diluted version of the procedure for obtaining a court order authorizing electronic surveillance. Application for the court order can be made by any attorney for the government, who is defined as including any United States Attorney or any authorized assistant to a United States Attorney. The order may issue if the court finds that "the attorney for the Government * * * has certified to the court that the information likely to be obtained by [the] installation and use [of the pen register or "trace and trap" device] is relevant to an ongoing criminal investigation." 18 U.S. C.A. § 3123. The order is to contain a statement of the offense being investigated and is to specify, if this is known, the person to whom the telephone is listed, the person who is the subject of the investigation, and the number and physical location of the telephone line to which the device will be attached. The order is to be for a period not exceeding sixty days, but extensions are available.

## STATE STATUTES

Section 2516(2) authorizes states to enact legislation that would permit state court judges to issue to state law enforcement officers—"in conformity with section 2518 of [the federal statute] "—a court order authorizing interceptions otherwise barred by the federal statute. As of December 31, 1988, thirty-one states had enacted such legislation. Administrative Office of the United States Courts, Report on Applications for Orders Authorizing or Approving the Interception of Wire or Oral Communications for the Period January 1, 1988 to December 31, 1988 (April 1989). These statutes raise a number of issues, including the extent to which state legislation must embody provisions identical or similar to the federal statute.

In State v. Farha, 218 Kan. 394, 544 P.2d 341 (1975), cert. denied 426 U.S. 949, 96 S.Ct. 3170, 49 L.Ed.2d 1186 (1976), the Kansas Supreme Court held the state's former statute (repealed before the court's decision) unconstitutional for failure to comply with the federal statute. As read by the state court, the Kansas statute permitted an *assistant* attorney general to apply for an order, did not require that the applicant state a belief that any particular crime has been or is being committed, did not require that the order terminate when the conversations described were seized, and permitted extensions to be issued without a showing of present probable cause. But most state courts have been unwilling to find state statutes deficient on their faces. In Commonwealth v. Vitello, 367 Mass. 224, 327 N.E.2d 819 (1975), the court held that if the authorization sections of a state statute are valid, a court order and interception are valid if they meet federal constitutional requirements, notwithstanding inconsistencies between some provisions of the state statute and the federal legislation. Thus the court held that the failure of the state statute to require a minimization directive in each order did not invalidate an interception if minimization in fact took place. In State v. Siegel, 266 Md. 256, 292 A.2d 86 (1972), the court took the position that since a state statute authorizing an interception order existed, an order issued by a state judge would be valid if it complied with "whichever law is more constricting, be it federal or state." 266 Md. at 272, 292 A.2d at 95. It then found the order at issue to be invalid because it did not contain the elements demanded by the federal statute, including a directive to minimize interception of innocent conversations and to execute the order as soon as practicable. The court rejected the state's "substantial compliance" argument that the interception should be upheld if it was executed promptly and if minimization took place.

NOTE

Defendants not notified under Title III that electronic surveillance was used in the preparation of the government's case may experience difficulty in determining whether such surveillance was conducted. Unless this can be determined, of course, defendants are in no position to claim that government evidence is the "fruit" of impermissible surveillance. 18 U.S.C.A. § 3504(a) provides:

> upon a claim by a party aggrieved that evidence is admissible because it is the * * * product of an unlawful act * * * the opponent of the claim shall affirm or deny the occurrence of the alleged unlawful act.

Thus a defendant can claim illegal surveillance and the government must affirm or deny it. The specificity which lower courts have required of governmental claims that no such surveillance took place depends upon the specificity of and support for the defendant's assertion that it did. Where only a general unsupported claim is made by the defendant, a general denial by the government has been held to suffice. A more specific claim supported by facts indicating that surveillance was conducted may require the government to conduct a more comprehensive inquiry of agencies with surveillance capabilities before its denial that surveillance took place will be accepted. See Matter of Grand Jury, 529 F.2d 543 (3d Cir. 1976), cert. denied 425 U.S. 992, 96 S.Ct. 2203, 48 L.Ed.2d 816.

If it is established that illegal surveillance took place and that the defendant has "standing" to raise the matter, the defense is entitled to access to records of that surveillance. It is not sufficient for the trial judge to examine the records *in camera* and turn over to the defense those records the judge determines are "arguably relevant" to the proceedings. Alderman v. United States, 394 U.S. 165, 89 S.Ct. 961, 22 L.Ed.2d 176 (1969). But where the defendant did not establish which intercepted conversations he participated in and therefore had standing to challenge, the trial judge was held to have acted properly in examining the recordings of the intercepted conversations *in camera* and disclosing to the defense only those to which the defendant was a party. Taglianetti v. United States, 394 U.S. 316, 89 S.Ct. 1099, 22 L.Ed.2d 302 (1969).

## UNITED STATES v. KAHN

Supreme Court of the United States, 1974.
415 U.S. 143, 94 S.Ct. 977, 39 L.Ed.2d 225.

Mr. Justice Stewart delivered the opinion of the Court.

On March 20, 1970, an attorney from the United States Department of Justice submitted an application for an order authorizing a wiretap interception pursuant to Title III of the Omnibus Crime Control and Safe Streets Act of 1970, 18 U.S.C.A. §§ 2510–2520, to Judge William J. Campbell of the United States District Court for the Northern District of Illinois. The affidavit accompanying the application contained information indicating that the respondent, Irving Kahn, was a bookmaker who operated from his residence and used two home telephones to conduct his business. The affidavit also noted that the Government's informants had stated that they would refuse to testify against Kahn, that telephone company records alone would be insufficient to support a bookmaking conviction, and that physical surveillance or normal search-and-seizure techniques would be unlikely to produce useful evidence. The application therefore concluded that "normal investigative procedures reasonably appear to be unlikely to succeed," and asked for authorization to intercept wire communications of Irving Kahn and "others as yet unknown" over two named telephone lines, in order that information concerning the gambling offenses might be obtained.

Judge Campbell entered an order, pursuant to 18 U.S.C.A. § 2518, approving the application. He specifically found that there was probable cause to believe that Irving Kahn and "others as yet unknown" were using the two telephones to conduct an illegal gambling business, and that normal investigative techniques were unlikely to succeed in providing federal officials with sufficient evidence to successfully prosecute such crimes. The order authorized special agents of the F.B.I. to "intercept wire communications of Irving Kahn and others as yet unknown" to and from the two named telephones concerning gambling activities.

The authorization order further provided that status reports were to be filed with Judge Campbell on the fifth and 10th days following the date of the order, showing what progress had been made towards achievement of the order's objective, and describing any need for further interceptions. The first such report, filed with Judge Campbell on March 25, 1970, indicated that the wiretap had been terminated because its objectives had been attained. The status report gave a summary of the information garnered by the interceptions, stating in part that on March 21, Irving Kahn made two telephone calls from Arizona to his wife at their home in Chicago and discussed gambling wins and losses, and that on the same date Minnie Kahn, Irving's wife, made two telephone calls from the intercepted telephones to a person described in the status report as "a known gambling figure," with whom she discussed various kinds of betting information.

Both Irving and Minnie Kahn were subsequently indicted for using a facility in interstate commerce to promote, manage, and facilitate an illegal gambling business, in violation of 19 U.S.C.A. § 1952. The Government prosecutor notified the Kahns that he intended to introduce into evidence at trial the conversations intercepted under the court order. The Kahns in turn filed motions to suppress the conversations. These motions were heard by Judge Thomas R. McMillen in the Northern District of Illinois, who, in an unreported opinion, granted the motion to suppress. * * * [A]ll * * * conversations in which Minnie Kahn was a participant were suppressed as being outside the scope of Judge Campbell's order, on the ground that Minnie Kahn was not a person "as yet unknown" to the federal authorities at the time of the original application.

The Government filed an interlocutory appeal from the suppression order. A divided panel of the United States Court of Appeals for the Seventh Circuit affirmed that part of the District Court's order suppressing all conversations of Minnie Kahn, * * *. 471 F.2d 191. The court held that under the wiretap order all intercepted conversations had to meet two requirements before they could be admitted into evidence:

> "(1) that Irving Kahn be a party to the conversations, and (2) that his conversations intercepted be with 'others as yet unknown.'" Id., at 195.

The court then construed the statutory requirements of 18 U.S.C.A. §§ 2518(1)(b)(iv) and 2518(4)(a) that the person whose communications are to be intercepted is to be identified if known, as excluding from the term "others as yet unknown" any "persons whom careful investigation by the government would disclose were probably using the Kahn telephones in conversations for illegal activities." Id., at 196. Since the Government in this case had not shown that further investigation of Irving Kahn's activities would not have implicated Minnie in the gambling business, the Court of Appeals felt that Mrs. Kahn was not a "person as yet unknown" within the purview of Judge Campbell's order.

We granted the Government's petition for certiorari, 411 U.S. 980, in order to resolve a seemingly important issue involving the construction of this relatively new federal statute.

At the outset, it is worth noting what issues are not involved in this case. First, we are not presented with an attack upon the constitutionality of any part of Title III of the Omnibus Crime Control and Safe Streets Act of 1970. Secondly, review of this interlocutory order does not involve any questions as to the propriety of the Justice Department's internal procedures in authorizing the application for the wiretap. Finally, no argument is presented that the federal agents failed to conduct the wiretap here in such a manner as to minimize the interception of innocent conversations. The question presented is simply whether the conversations that the Government wishes to introduce into evidence at the respondents' trial are made inadmissible by the "others as yet unknown" language of Judge Campbell's order or by the corresponding statutory requirements of Title III.

In deciding that Minnie Kahn was not a person "as yet unknown" within the meaning of the wiretap order, the Court of Appeals relied heavily on an expressed objective of Congress in the enactment of Title III: the protection of the personal privacy of those engaging in wire communications. In light of this clear congressional concern, the Court of Appeals reasoned, the Government could not lightly claim that a person whose conversations were intercepted was "unknown" within the meaning of Title III. Thus, it was not enough that Mrs. Kahn was not known to be taking part in any illegal gambling business at the time that the Government applied for the wiretap order; in addition, the court held that the Government was required to show that such complicity would not have been discovered had a thorough investigation of Mrs. Kahn been conducted before the wiretap application.

In our view, neither the legislative history nor the specific language of Title III compels this conclusion. To be sure, Congress was concerned with protecting individual privacy when it enacted this statute. But it is also clear that Congress intended to authorize electronic surveillance as a weapon against the operations of organized crime. There is, of course, some tension between these two stated congressional objectives, and the question of how Congress struck the balance in any particular instance cannot be resolved simply through general reference to the statute's expressed concern for the protection of individual privacy. Rather, the starting point, as in all statutory construction, is the precise wording chosen by Congress in enacting Title III.

Section 2518(1) of Title 18, United States Code Annotated, sets out in detail the requirements for the information to be included in an application for an order authorizing the interception of wire communications. The sole provision pertaining to the identification of persons whose communications are to be intercepted is contained in § 2518(1)(b)(iv), which requires that the application state "the identity of the person, if known, *committing the offense* and whose communications are to be intercepted." (Emphasis supplied.) This statutory language would plainly seem to require the naming of a specific person in the wiretap application only when law enforcement officials believe that such an individual is actually committing one of the offenses specified in 18 U.S.C.A. § 2516. Since it is undisputed here that Minnie Kahn was not known to the Government to be engaging in gambling activities at the time the interception order was sought, the failure to include her name in the application would thus seem to comport with the literal language of § 2518(1)(b)(v).

Moreover, there is no reason to conclude that the omission of Minnie Kahn's name from the actual wiretap order was in conflict with any of the provisions of Title III. Section 2518(4)(a) requires that the order specify "the identity of the person, if known, whose communications are to be intercepted." Since the judge who prepares the order can only be expected to learn of the target individual's identity through reference to the original application, it can hardly be inferred that this statutory language imposes any broader requirement than the identification provisions of § 2518(1)(b)(iv).

In effect, the Court of Appeals read these provisions of § 2518 as if they required that the application and order identify "all persons, known or discoverable, who are committing the offense and whose communications are to be intercepted." But that is simply not what the statute says: identification is required only of those "known" to be "committing the offense." Had Congress wished to engraft a separate requirement of "discoverability" onto the provisions of Title III, it surely would have done so in language plainer than that now embodied in § 2518.

Moreover, the Court of Appeals' interpretation of § 2518 would have a broad impact. A requirement that the Government fully investigate the possibility that any likely user of a telephone was engaging in criminal activities before applying for an interception order would greatly subvert the effectiveness of the law enforcement mechanism that Congress constructed. In the case at hand, the Court of Appeals' holding would require the complete investigation not only of

Minnie Kahn, but also of the two teenaged Kahn children and other frequenters of the Kahn residence before a wiretap order could be applied for. If the telephone were in a store or an office, the Government might well be required to investigate everyone who had access to it—in some cases, literally hundreds of people—even though there was no reason to suspect that any of them were violating any criminal law. It is thus open to considerable doubt that such a requirement would ultimately serve the interests of individual privacy. In any event, the statute as actually drafted contains no intimation of such total investigative demands.

In arriving at its reading of § 2518, the Court of Appeals seemed to believe that taking the statute at face value would result in a wiretap order amounting to a "virtual general warrant," since the law enforcement authorities would be authorized to intercept communications of anyone who talked on the named telephone line. 471 F.2d, at 197. But neither the statute nor the wiretap order in this case would allow the federal agents such total unfettered discretion. By its own terms, the wiretap order in this case conferred authority to intercept only communications "concerning the above-described [gambling] offenses." Moreover, in accord with the statute the order required the agents to execute the warrant in such a manner as to minimize the interception of any innocent conversations. And the order limited the length of any possible interception to 15 days, while requiring status reports as to the progress of the wiretap to be submitted to the District Judge every five days, so that any possible abuses might be quickly discovered and halted. Thus, the failure of the order to specify that Mrs. Kahn's conversations might be the subject of interception hardly left the executing agents free to seize at will every communication that came over the wire—and there is no indication that such abuses took place in this case.[1]

We conclude, therefore, that Title III requires the naming of a person in the application or interception order only when the law enforcement authorities have probable cause to believe that that individual is "committing the offense" for which the wiretap is sought. Since it is undisputed that the Government had no reason to suspect Minnie Kahn of complicity in the gambling business before the wire interceptions here began, it follows that under the statute she was among the class of persons "as yet unknown" covered by Judge Campbell's order.

The remaining question is whether, under the actual language of Judge Campbell's order, only those intercepted conversations to which

---

[1] The fallacy in the Court of Appeals' "general warrant" approach may be illustrated by examination of an analogous conventional search and seizure. If a warrant had been issued, upon a showing of probable cause, to search the Kahn residence for physical records of gambling operations, there could be no question that a subsequent seizure of such records bearing Minnie Kahn's handwriting would be fully lawful, despite the fact that she had not been identified in the warrant nor independently investigated. In fact, as long as the property to be seized is described with sufficient specificity, even a warrant failing to name the owner of the premises at which a search is directed, while not the best practice, has been held to pass muster under the Fourth Amendment. * * *

Irving Kahn himself was a party are admissible in evidence at the Kahn's trial, as the Court of Appeals concluded. The effect of such an interpretation of the wiretap order in this case would be to exclude from evidence the intercepted conversations between Minnie Kahn and the "known gambling figure" concerning betting information. Again, we are unable to read either the District Court order or the underlying provisions of Title III as requiring such a result.

The order signed by Judge Campbell in this case authorized the Government to "intercept wire communications of Irving Kahn and others as yet unknown to and from two telephones, subscribed to by Irving Kahn." The order does not refer to conversations *between* Irving Kahn and others; rather, it describes "communications *of* Irving Kahn and others as yet unknown" to and from the target telephones. To read this language as requiring that Irving Kahn be a party to every intercepted conversation would not only involve a substantial feat of verbal gymnastics, but would also render the phrase "and others as yet unknown" quite redundant, since Kahn perforce could not communicate except with others.

Moreover, the interpretation of the wiretap authorization adopted by the Court of Appeals is at odds with one of the stated purposes of Judge Campbell's order. The District Judge specifically found that the wiretap was needed to "reveal the identities of [Irving Kahn's] confederates, their places of operation, and the nature of the conspiracy involved." It is evident that such information might be revealed in conversations to which Irving Kahn was not a party. For example, a confederate might call in Kahn's absence, and leave either a name, a return telephone number, or an incriminating message. Or, one of Kahn's associates might himself come to the family home and employ the target telephones to conduct the gambling business. It would be difficult under any circumstances to believe that a District Judge meant such intercepted conversations to be inadmissible at any future trial; given the specific language employed by Judge Campbell in the wiretap order today before us, such a conclusion is simply untenable.

Nothing in Title III requires that, despite the order's language, it must be read to exclude Minnie Kahn's communications. As already noted, 18 U.S.C.A. §§ 2518(1)(b)(iv) and 2518(4)(a) require identification of the person committing the offense only "if known." The clear implication of this language is that when there is probable cause to believe that a particular telephone is being used to commit an offense but no particular person is identifiable, a wire interception order may, nevertheless, properly issue under the statute. It necessarily follows that Congress could not have intended that the authority to intercept must be limited to those conversations *between* a party named in the order and others, since at least in some cases, the order might not name any specific party at all.

For these reasons, we hold that the Court of Appeals was in error when it interpreted the phrase "others as yet unknown" so as to exclude conversations involving Minnie Kahn from the purview of the wiretap order. We further hold that neither the language of Judge

Campbell's order nor that of Title III requires the suppression of legally intercepted conversations to which Irving Kahn was not himself a party.

Accordingly, the judgment of the Court of Appeals is reversed, and the case is remanded to that court for further proceedings consistent with this opinion.

It is so ordered.

MR. JUSTICE DOUGLAS, with whom MR. JUSTICE BRENNAN and MR. JUSTICE MARSHALL concur, dissenting. [omitted.]

## NOTES

1. Suppose the investigating officers had information indicating that Minnie Kahn was involved in the bookmaking operation. Would the failure to name her in the application have been improper? In United States v. Donovan, 429 U.S. 413, 97 S.Ct. 658, 50 L.Ed.2d 652 (1977), the Court rejected the argument that the statute required the applicant for a surveillance order to identify only the principal target of the surveillance. "[A] wiretap application," held the Court, "must name an individual if the Government has probable cause to believe that the individual is engaged in the criminal activity under investigation and expects to intercept the individual's conversations over the target telephone." 429 U.S. at 428, 97 S.Ct. at 668, 50 L.Ed.2d at 668. But suppose this requirement was not met, i.e., despite the existence of such probable cause, Minnie Kahn had not been named in the application. Would this require exclusion of the results of the surveillance? In *Donovan*, the Court held that the failure to name such a person did not require exclusion of the results of the surveillance. The majority concluded that § 2518(1)(b)(iv) does not play a "substantive role" with respect to judicial authorization of intercept orders:

> [Despite noncompliance with § 2518(1)(b)(iv)] the statutorily imposed preconditions to judicial authorization were satisfied, and the issuing judge was simply unaware that additional persons might be overheard engaging in incriminating conversations. In no meaningful sense can it be said that the presence of that information as to additional targets would have precluded judicial authorization of the intercept. * * * [T]he instant intercept is lawful because the application provided sufficient information to enable the issuing judge to determine that the statutory preconditions were satisfied.

429 U.S. at 436, 97 S.Ct. at 672, 50 L.Ed.2d at 673. The Court noted, however, that there was no suggestion that the Government agents "intentionally" failed to identify the person or that the failure to name this person resulted in the person's failure to receive the mandatory inventory notice required by § 2518(8) (d).

2. Under section 2518(3)(c), the judge who issued the intercept order in *Kahn* must have determined, "on the basis of the facts submitted by the applicant," that "normal investigative procedures have been tried and have failed or reasonably appear to be unlikely to succeed if tried or to be too dangerous." If Kahn had challenged the sufficiency of the evidence to support such a determination, should such a challenge have succeeded? The application apparently did not explain why the applicant believed that physical surveillance or "normal search and seizure techniques" would not produce useful evidence. Could the issuing judge have made an "independent" determination of the matter required by section 2518(3)(c)? If this determination was

not supported by adequate facts submitted by the applicant, would this invalidate the order and require the suppression of its "fruits"?

3. The Court notes that no argument was made in *Kahn* that the officers failed to conduct the wiretap in such a manner as to minimize the interception of innocent conversations. But suppose such an argument had been made? Were the officers justified in listening to the conversations between Irving and Minnie Kahn? Between Minnie and an unidentified person? Suppose the officers had listened to conversations between the two teenage Kahn children and their friends. Would it make any difference whether all of these conversations were listened to? Whether any effort was made to identify conversations that should not be listened to in the future, at least in their entirety? If the officers did violate the "minimization" requirement, what impact would this have upon the admissibility of information obtained during interception of conversations that were clearly within the order's authorization? Scott v. United States, 436 U.S. 128, 98 S.Ct. 1717, 56 L.Ed.2d 168 (1978), involved an investigation of a conspiracy to distribute heroin. An intercept order was issued and for the month of the surveillance the officers intercepted and recorded all conversations over the telephone described in the order. Forty percent of the calls were ultimately determined to relate to the conspiracy under investigation. The agent in charge of the investigation testified that although he was aware of the minimization requirement he made no effort to avoid the interception of innocent calls. The Court rejected the argument that this was bad faith which in itself violated the statute. Objective circumstances, not the officers' subjective intent, determine the legality of the actions:

> [B]lind reliance on the percentage of nonpertinent calls intercepted is not a sure guide * * *. Such percentages may provide assistance, but there are surely cases * * * where the percentage of nonpertinent calls is relatively high and yet their interception was still reasonable. Many of the nonpertinent calls may have been very short. Others may have been one-time-only calls. Still other calls may have been ambiguous in nature or apparently involved guarded or coded language. In all these circumstances agents can hardly be expected to know that the calls are not pertinent prior to their termination.
>
> * * * [I]t is also important to consider the circumstances of the wiretap. For example, when the investigation is focusing on what is thought to be a wide-spread conspiracy more extensive surveillance may be justified in an attempt to determine the precise scope of the enterprise. And it is possible that many more of the conversations will be permissibly interceptable because they will involve one or more of the co-conspirators. The type of use to which the telephone is normally put may also have some bearing on the extent of minimization required. For example, if the agents are permitted to tap a public telephone because one individual is thought to be placing bets over the phone, substantial doubts as to minimization may arise if the agents listen to every call which goes out over that phone regardless of who places the call. On the other hand, if the phone is located in the residence of a person thought to be the head of a major drug ring, a contrary conclusion may be indicated.
>
> * * * [I]t may be important to determine at exactly what point during the authorized period the investigation was made. During the early stages of surveillance the agents may be forced to intercept all calls to establish categories of nonpertinent calls which will not be intercepted thereafter. Interception of these same types of calls might be unreasonable later on, however, once the nonpertinent categories have been established and it is clear that this particular conversation is of that type. Other

situations may arise where patterns of nonpertinent calls do not appear. In these circumstances it may not be unreasonable to intercept almost every short conversation because the determination of relevancy cannot be made before the call is completed.

436 U.S. at 140–41, 98 S.Ct. at 1725, 56 L.Ed.2d at 179–80. On the facts of the case, the majority found no violation of the minimization requirement despite the high percentage of nonpertinent calls intercepted. Many of the nonpertinent calls were short and many were ambiguous in nature, making characterization impossible until the call was terminated. Further, the agents' conduct must be considered in light of the fact that the crime under investigation was a wide-ranging conspiracy with a large number of participants. The Court noted but did not reach the argument that if the agents violated the minimization requirements, suppression is required only of those conversations improperly intercepted, not of all intercepted conversations. 436 U.S. at 135, n. 10, 98 S.Ct. at 1722, n. 10, 56 L.Ed.2d at 176, n. 10. Justice Brennan, joined by Justice Marshall, dissented. Among other things, he accused the majority of undercutting that portion of the reasoning of *Kahn* which relied upon the minimization requirement to answer the contention that the holding in *Kahn* would authorize general search warrants. 436 U.S. at 147, 98 S.Ct. at 1728, 56 L.Ed.2d at 183–84.

4. The federal statute requires periodic reports by judges and prosecutors concerning applications, orders, and interceptions. This is apparently intended to develop and maintain a pool of information useful in evaluating the continued wisdom of making these law enforcement devices available under the limitations and restrictions imposed by present federal and state legislation. The reports are made to the Administrative Office of the United States Courts, which issues yearly reports summarizing the information collected for the previous year. See, e.g., Administrative Office of the United States Courts, Report on Applications for Orders Authorizing or Approving the Interception of Wire or Oral Communications for the Period January 1, 1988 to December 31, 1988 (April 1989), the latest available. Several aspects of this information for recent years is especially useful.

Statutory authorization of electronic surveillance exists in 31 states, the District of Columbia and the federal system.

During 1988, 738 applications were submitted for authorization of wire, oral, or electronic surveillance—293 were submitted to federal judges and 445 to state judges. Almost 60 percent of all state wiretap authorizations were approved by judges in New York and New Jersey. Only 2 applications were denied in 1988. During the 11 years from 1978 through 1988, a total of only 11 of the 7263 applications were denied by the judiciary.

Although intercept orders may be granted for any offense authorized by statute, the great majority (87 percent) fall within three offense categories. During 1988, 59 percent of all orders were for investigation of drug violations, 17 percent for gambling, and 11 percent for racketeering.

The majority of intercept orders were for conversations in dwellings. During 1988, 57 percent of all intercept orders were for dwellings, while 16 percent were for business establishments, such as hotels and restaurants. In 1988, there were only 3 applications for the "roving" taps authorized by Congress in 1986. Other applications were for public pay phones, paging devices and cellular phones.

Intercepts are expensive. During 1988, the average costs for the 652 intercepts in which costs were reported was $49,284, for a total cost for those intercepts of $32,133,168.

The great majority (81 percent) of intercepts were telephone wiretaps. Only 26 cases involved the interception only of electronic communications.

The average number of interceptions per day ranged from zero to 427 for each device. The average number of persons whose conversations were intercepted was 129 per installed intercept and the average number of conversations intercepted was 1,251. About 25 percent of those conversations produced incriminating evidence.

The best measure of the effectiveness of electronic surveillance would be the number of persons arrested and convicted as a result of intercepts who would not otherwise have been arrested and convicted. Those data are not available. Records are provided, however, on the numbers of arrests and convictions resulting from intercept orders. There is often considerable lapse of time from the year in which an intercept occurs and the time when an arrest, and especially, a conviction is obtained. Indeed, using the 1988 Report and earlier Reports, one can be confident of complete arrest and conviction figures resulting from intercepts installed only during the 1973 through 1983 period. The Percent column is the percentage of arrests that resulted in convictions.

| Year | No. of Intercepts | No. Arrests | No. Convictions | Percent |
|------|-------------------|-------------|-----------------|---------|
| 1973 | 812 | 3,030 | 1,833 | 60.5 |
| 1974 | 694 | 2,997 | 1,476 | 49.2 |
| 1975 | 676 | 3,053 | 1,552 | 50.8 |
| 1976 | 635 | 3,056 | 1,507 | 49.3 |
| 1977 | 601 | 2,865 | 1,251 | 43.7 |
| 1978 | 560 | 2,282 | 1,023 | 44.8 |
| 1979 | 533 | 2,552 | 1,370 | 53.7 |
| 1980 | 524 | 2,919 | 1,507 | 51.6 |
| 1981 | 562 | 2,901 | 1,808 | 62.3 |
| 1982 | 518 | 2,870 | 1,880 | 65.5 |
| 1983 | 602 | 2,864 | 1,987 | 69.4 |
| TOTALS | 6,717 | 31,389 | 17,193 | 54.8 |

# Chapter 7

# INTERROGATION AND CONFESSIONS

*Analysis*

## EDITORS' INTRODUCTION: CONFESSIONS IN THE CONTEXT OF MODERN LAW ENFORCEMENT

Among traditional law enforcement techniques have been the collection and preservation of out-of-court statements by suspects and, in scme situations, active elicitation or encouragement of such statements. These techniques and the legal issues raised by them are the subjects of this chapter.

When statements of this sort are offered as evidence against a defendant, a distinction has sometimes been drawn between a "confession"—a statement admitting or acknowledging all facts necessary for conviction of the crime charged—and an "admission"—an acknowledgement of one' or more facts that tend to establish guilt but not of all elements of the crime. Moreover, both of these are sometimes distinguished from an "exculpatory" statement, a statement which, at the time it was made, was intended to exculpate rather than incriminate the speaker, but which later is found to suggest the speaker's guilt. A common use of exculpatory statements by the prosecution consists of proving that a suspect gave a false explanation of incriminating circumstances; this is offered to prove that the suspect was conscious of his or her guilt and therefore that the suspect is in fact guilty. It is doubtful that these distinctions have much significance today. See McCormick, Evidence § 114 (E. Cleary ed., 2nd ed. 1972), and the discussion by the Supreme Court in Miranda v. Arizona at page 438, infra.

The legal doctrines related to the admissibility of confessions can helpfully be regarded as raising two different questions. First, when should a confession be excluded as a means of discouraging or punishing inappropriate law enforcement behavior? Second, when should a confession be excluded because—without regard to the existence or nonexistence of any "fault" on the part of law enforcement personnel—it was given in circumstances that make its use unacceptable? There is substantial overlap between these two matters, but it is also clear that the admissibility of confessions is sometimes attacked on the basis of factors which cannot be said to be the fault of law enforcement officers or other government agents.

In addressing the questions raised in this chapter—what rules should govern the admissibility of confessions and how should these rules be interpreted and applied—it is important to identify the various and sometimes competing policy considerations involved. The government, of course, has an obvious interest in being able to use reliable evidence of defendants' guilt of crimes. Confessions are traditionally regarded as exceptionally reliable evidence of guilt. In Hopt v. Utah, 110 U.S. 574, 584–85, 4 S.Ct. 202, 207, 28 L.Ed. 262, 267 (1884), the Court explained:

> A confession if freely and voluntarily made, is evidence of the most satisfactory character. Such a confession * * * "is deserving of the highest credit, because it is presumed to flow from the strongest sense of guilt, and, therefore, it is admitted as proof of the crime to which it refers." * * * [T]he presumption upon which

weight is given to such evidence [is]   *   *   *   that one who is innocent will not imperil his safety or prejudice his interests by an untrue statement   *   *   *.

How important confessions are to securing convictions is a matter of dispute. It is clear that in some cases, the evidence against the defendant other than the confession would result in conviction. In others, it seems certain that the confession is essential to proof of guilt. Project, Interrogation in New Haven: The Impact of Miranda, 76 Yale L.J. 1519 (1967), studied the investigation of 90 cases; in 49 questioning was successful, i.e., it resulted in a self-incriminating statement. But the researchers concluded that in only 4 of these 49 cases (8%) was questioning "necessary," in the sense that other evidence available would not have been sufficient to prove guilt. But Seeburger and Wettick, Miranda in Pittsburgh—A Statistical Study, 29 U.Pitt.L.Rev. 1 (1967), studied two samples of cases and concluded that confessions were necessary to conviction in 24.7% and 32.8% of those cases.

To some extent, legal requirements relating to interrogation and the admissibility of confessions are concerned with the reliability of the confessions. In this regard, why is *exclusion* of confessions appropriate? Defendants are entitled to the opportunity to persuade judges and juries that confessions should not be believed because of the manner in which they were elicited. This opportunity is a constitutional right. In Crane v. Kentucky, 476 U.S. 683, 106 S.Ct. 2142, 90 L.Ed.2d 636 (1986), the defense moved before trial to suppress Crane's confession to the murder for which he was to be tried. A pretrial hearing was held on the motion, at which Crane testified that he had been detained for questioning in a windowless room for some time, as many as six officers had been present during the questioning, he had unsuccessfully made repeated attempts to be allowed to contact his family and he had been badgered into making a false confession. Several police officers' testimony contradicted this version of the facts and the trial court held the confession admissible. At trial, the prosecution introduced the confession into evidence. The defense contended in response that contradictions in the confession and the circumstances under which it was given meant that the jury should not believe it. In support of this, the defense unsuccessfully attempted to introduce before the jury evidence concerning the interrogation during which the confession was given. The state supreme court affirmed the resulting conviction, reasoning that evidence relating only to the "voluntariness" of a confession is not admissible before the jury. While evidence relating to the "credibility" of the confession is admissible, the court reasoned, all of the evidence offered by Crane went only to voluntariness. A unanimous Supreme Court, speaking through Justice O'Connor, reversed:

> Whether rooted directly in the due process clause of the Fourteenth Amendment or in the Compulsory Process or Confrontation clauses of the Sixth Amendment, the Constitution guarantees criminal defendants "a meaningful opportunity to present a complete defense." We break no new ground in observing that an essential component of procedural fairness is an opportunity to be heard. That opportunity would be an empty one if the state were permit-

ted to exclude competent, reliable evidence bearing on the credibility of a confession when such evidence is central to the defendant's
claim of innocence.  *  *  *

Under these principles, the Kentucky courts erred in foreclos-
ing [Crane's] efforts to introduce testimony about the environment
in which the police secured his confession.  *  *  *  [E]vidence
about the manner in which a confession was obtained is often
highly relevant to its reliability and credibility.

476 U.S. at 690–91, 106 S.Ct. at 2146–47, 90 L.Ed.2d at 645.

In view of this, why is exclusion of a confession ever justified on
reliability grounds?  Are jurors likely to be insensitive to evidence that
should cause them to disregard a confession?  Perhaps the need to
discourage police actions that, in general, tend to result in inaccurate
confessions requires that the law provide an especially strong disincentive for engaging in such action.  Such a disincentive might best be
provided by completely excluding confessions rather than giving the
prosecution opportunities to convince juries that such confessions ought
to be credited.

The law concerning interrogation and confessions, of course, is also
concerned with matters completely divorced from the reliability of
confessions offered at trial by the prosecution.  To the extent that such
considerations are involved, defendants' right to an opportunity to
convince jurors to disregard the confession is probably of less significance.

Should confession law encourage police to elicit self-incriminating
admissions from suspects and prosecutors to use such confessions in
prosecuting cases?  Or, should it attempt to discourage either or both?
This may turn in part on whether reliance upon confessions discourages other and "better" investigative procedures.  Studies of homicide
investigations in Suffolk County, New York, provided some support for
concern that reliance upon confessions may lead officers to neglect
other avenues of investigation.  An investigation by Newsday staff
members indicated that in 94 percent of Suffolk County murder cases
the prosecution had evidence that the defendant had confessed.  In
other jurisdictions, this was the situation in only 50 to 70 percent of
cases.  Maier and Smith, Reliance on Getting Confessions Tied to
Abuses, Weakened Cases, Newsday, Dec. 7, 1986, at 5, 26–30 (Nassau
ed.).  An official investigation later concluded:

[T]he result of [this] unique incidence of confessions has been for
officers to rely on confessions and neglect both routine investigative steps and proper scientific and technical evidentiary practices.
The prevailing attitude has been that notetaking, forensic evidence,
neighborhood canvasses and crime-scene searches are not important because ultimately a defendant will confess.

State of New York Commission of Investigation, An Investigation of the
Suffolk County District Attorney's Office and Police Department 56
(April 1989).  As a result of this nearly exclusive reliance on confessions, the report concluded, "the chances of the guilty going free are
simply too high."  Id.

Confession law is complicated by the undeniable fact that interrogation and resulting statements may serve a number of law enforcement objectives other than securing admissible evidence of suspects' guilt of criminal offenses.  See Project, Interrogation in New Haven: The Impact of Miranda, 76 Yale L.J. 1519, 1593—96 (1967).   For example, confessions may be useful or necessary for identifying accomplices to an offense.  While a confession may not be admissible against the accomplice, it may direct law enforcement officers to other information and admissible evidence of the accomplice's guilt.  And statements may be used to "clear" crimes for purposes of internal police records. If a case is "cleared"—even if no prosecution results—the police books are closed and no further resources will be expended on it.  Further, the effectiveness of a law enforcement agency is often measured by this clearance rate, so the agency has a strong incentive to seek to close cases even if no criminal prosecution is possible or likely.  A variety of other purposes exist.  Statements may permit the recovery of stolen property or of weapons that might otherwise be available to persons for future crimes.  They may be used for "intelligence" purposes, to allocate resources most effectively, and to make various decisions as to how to proceed with the "policing" job.

In considering the matters raised in this chapter, consider whether the law should be concerned with police techniques that serve these various other functions as well as those designed to secure admissible evidence for courtroom use.  Is the exclusion of statements offered in criminal trials a sufficient answer to any such problems as exist?  Or should the law seek to discourage techniques such as interrogation even when those techniques are not intended to and will not result in the use against the suspect of a self-incriminating statement that is obtained? If so, how might this be done?

Are there, perhaps, considerations other than accuracy that should be accommodated in confession law?  Should some law enforcement techniques that pose no danger of eliciting inaccurate statements be barred or discouraged because suspects have a legitimate interest in not being subjected to them?  Should confessions made under certain circumstances be excluded even though no question can be raised concerning their accuracy because to permit a defendant to incriminate him or herself under such circumstances is inconsistent with the manner in which human beings should be treated?  There has been little brief made for the position that suspects should never be permitted to incriminate themselves or that all self-incriminating admissions should be rejected at trial.  As Justice Rehnquist recently commented, "[The Supreme Court] has never held that an accused is constitutionally protected from his inability to keep quiet  *  *  * ."  United States v. Henry, 447 U.S. 264, 297, 100 S.Ct. 2183, 2201, 65 L.Ed.2d 115, 140 (1980) (Rehnquist, J., dissenting).

But suspects may have a legitimate interest in being encouraged or permitted to incriminate themselves only when they have certain information concerning the results of doing so and the alternatives available to them.  Dix, Mistake, Ignorance, Expectation of Benefit, and the Modern Law of Confessions, 1975 Wash.U.L.Q. 275, 330–31, argued:

A major objective of the law of confessions  *  *  *  should be
*  *  *  assuring that a person who confesses does so with as
complete an understanding of his tactical position as possible.
This, of course, would require awareness not only of his abstract
legal rights, but also of his practical ability to implement those
rights in light of his factual situation and of the tactical wisdom of
asserting them.

Should this be at least one of the law's objectives in this area?  If
the act of making a confession as a practical matter assures conviction,
perhaps a confession should be regarded as a "waiver" of the right to
trial and the right to have the state prove guilt beyond a reasonable
doubt.  Waivers of important trial rights must, under prevailing law, be
"knowing" and "intelligent" as well as "voluntary."  Johnson v. Zerbst,
304 U.S. 458, 58 S.Ct. 1019, 82 L.Ed. 1461 (1938).  It may be argued that
the decision to confess, then, should be given legal effect only if it was
"knowing" and "intelligent" in this sense.  It may follow that legal
rules should discourage interrogation in situations likely to result in
confessions that fail to meet these requirements.  Further, perhaps
confessions should be regarded as admissible only if they meet these
standards.

But is the making of a confession the "functional equivalent" of
pleading guilty to the crime charged?  Neubauer, Confessions in Prairie
City, 65 J.Crim.L. & C. 103 (1974), investigated the effect of confession
upon the disposition of the charges against a sample of defendants.  As
might be expected, defendants who confessed were less likely to go to
trial than those who did not confess;  only 5 of 108 defendants who
made statements went to trial, while 23 of 117 nonconfessing defendants did so.  While he noted that the trials of the confessing defendants were "largely predetermined," he did not compare acquittal rates
of the two groups.  But since most cases were disposed of by pleas of
guilty, the effect of a confession upon the plea bargaining process is
obviously an important question.  Neubauer concluded that defendants
who did not confess received better plea bargains than those who did,
but nevertheless he noted that even confessing defendants received
substantial concessions in the bargaining process.  This, of course,
strongly suggests that the act of confessing is not always the functional
equivalent of pleading guilty to the most serious crime that might be
charged on the facts.

The material in this chapter reflects to some extent a progression
of developments.  The first part develops the requirement that a
confession be "voluntary," the traditional doctrine governing admissibility of confessions.  Consider the reasons why the Supreme Court may
have been dissatisfied with this doctrine as a means for dealing with
what the Court perceived to be the problems presented by confessions
in general and custodial interrogation in particular.  That such dissat-
isfaction existed is made clear by the Court's 1966 action in Miranda v.
Arizona, the subject of the second portion of the chapter.  Given the
nature of the *Miranda* rules and their subsequent development, have
they lived up to the Court's 1966 expectations?  Do they adequately
deal with the problems presented by custodial interrogation?  What

alternatives should be considered?  How should they be evaluated?
The third part of the chapter deals with suspects' Sixth Amendment
right to counsel.  Consider how this meshes with the voluntariness rule
and the *Miranda* requirements.

There have been relatively few legislative efforts to address confession issues.  The federal statute set out in this chapter is one of the few
such efforts.  The American Law Institute's Model Code of Pre-Arraignment Procedure (Official Draft, 1975) offers a more comprehensive
effort.  Article 150 deals with Exclusion of Statements and some
portions of Article 140, Conditions of Investigation During Custody of
an Arrested Person, are also relevant to confession issues.

## A.  THE REQUIREMENT OF "VOLUNTARINESS"

### EDITORS' INTRODUCTION: DEVELOPMENT, CONTENT, AND CURRENT SIGNIFICANCE OF THE VOLUNTARINESS REQUIREMENT

Because of the wide-spread publicity given the *Miranda* decision,
contemporary discussions of "confession law" tend to revolve around
the *Miranda* requirements.  An adequate understanding of the reasons
for what has been called the "*Miranda* revolution," however, demands
acquaintance with pre-*Miranda* voluntariness law.  In addition, the
voluntariness requirement is not without current significance.  If *Miranda* does not apply to a given situation, the voluntariness requirement is likely to be the major consideration in determining whether a
confession can be used in evidence.  If a confession is inadmissible to
prove a defendant's guilt because of the *Miranda* requirements, its
availability to impeach the defendant's credibility—should the defendant testify at trial—apparently depends in part upon the voluntariness of the admission.  Even if *Miranda* applies to a situation, there is
a high likelihood that among the issues will be the effectiveness of the
suspect's waiver of the rights to silence and to counsel.  Traditional
voluntariness law undoubtedly bears upon the appropriate resolution of
matters of this sort.  Further, if a suspect has given several confessions
and *Miranda* was violated only during the elicitation of the first, the
admissibility of the later confessions depends largely or entirely upon
their voluntariness.

*Development of the Federal Constitutional Requirement.*  In its first
confession case, Hopt v. Utah, 110 U.S. 574, 4 S.Ct. 202, 28 L.Ed. 262
(1884), the United States Supreme Court treated the admissibility of an
incriminating statement as a matter of federal evidence law.  The
admissibility of such statements, the Court noted, "so largely depends
upon the special circumstances connected with the confession, that it is
difficult, if not impossible, to formulate a rule that will comprehend all
cases."  But, it then held, the case before it could be resolved by "the
weight of authority," which it summarized as regarding a statement as
involuntary and inadmissible if "the confession appears to have been
made either in consequence of inducements of a temporal nature, held
out by one in authority, touching the charge preferred, or because of a
threat or promise by or in the presence of such person, which, operating

upon the fears or hopes of the accused, in reference to the charge, deprive him of that freedom of will or self-control essential to make the confession voluntary within the meaning of the law." 110 U.S. at 585, 4 S.Ct. at 207–08, 28 L.Ed. at 266–67.

Three years later, in Bram v. United States, 168 U.S. 532, 18 S.Ct. 183, 42 L.Ed. 568 (1897), the Court commented that "in criminal trials, in the courts of the United States, wherever a question arises whether a confession is incompetent because not voluntary, the issue is controlled by that portion of the fifth amendment to the constitution of the United States, commanding that no person 'shall be compelled in any criminal case, to be a witness against himself.'" 168 U.S. at 542, 18 S.Ct. at 187, 42 L.Ed. at 573. The Fifth Amendment privilege, in turn, was characterized as a crystallization of the common law voluntariness rule existing at the time of the adoption of the Constitution, and—after commenting that the "principle by which the admissibility of the confession of an accused person is to be determined is expressed in the textbooks"—the Court cited with approval the following passage from 3 Russell on Crimes 478 (6th ed.): "But a confession, in order to be admissible, must be free and voluntary; that is, must not be extracted by any sort of threats or violence, nor obtained by any direct or implied promises, however slight, nor by the exertion of any improper influence." 168 U.S. at 542–43, 18 S.Ct. at 187, 42 L.Ed. at 573.

The Fifth Amendment privilege against compelled self-incrimination was not held binding upon the states until Malloy v. Hogan, 378 U.S. 1, 84 S.Ct. 1489, 12 L.Ed.2d 653 (1964). But, beginning with Brown v. Mississippi, 297 U.S. 278, 56 S.Ct. 461, 80 L.Ed. 682 (1936), the Supreme Court imposed Constitutional limitations upon the use of confessions in state criminal trials through application of the Fourteenth Amendment's general requirement of due process of law. Although the earlier cases may have suggested some difference between the due process requirement and the *Bram* Fifth Amendment rules, in 1966 the Court commented that "the decisions of this Court have guaranteed the same procedural protection for the defendant whether his confession was used in a federal or state court." Miranda v. Arizona, 384 U.S. 436, 464 n. 33, 86 S.Ct. 1602, 1622 n. 33, 16 L.Ed.2d 694, 717–18 n. 33 (1966).

Not only has the "voluntariness" requirement been imposed as a matter of federal constitutional law, but state courts have universally accepted it as a matter of state constitutional doctrine. It is clear, then, that an understanding of this concept is basic to an appreciation of the need for and significance of subsequent developments in the legal standards governing the admissibility of confessions in American courts.

*Content of the Voluntariness Requirement.* In Blackburn v. Alabama, 361 U.S. 199, 80 S.Ct. 274, 4 L.Ed.2d 242 (1960), the Supreme Court observed that "a complex of values underlies the stricture against use by the state of confessions which, by way of convenient shorthand, this Court terms involuntary, and the role played by each in any situation varies according to the particular circumstances of the case." 361 U.S. at 207, 80 S.Ct. at 280, 4 L.Ed.2d at 248. In Spano v. New York, 360 U.S. 315, 79 S.Ct. 1202, 3 L.Ed.2d 1265 (1959), the Court commented upon these values:

> The abhorrence of society to the use of involuntary confessions does not turn alone on their inherent untrustworthiness. It also turns on the deep-rooted feeling that the police must obey the law while enforcing the law; that in the end life and liberty can be as much endangered from illegal methods used to convict those thought to be criminals as from the actual criminals themselves. Accordingly, the actions of police in obtaining confessions * * * come under scrutiny * * *.

360 U.S. at 320–21, 79 S.Ct. at 1205–06, 3 L.Ed.2d at 1270.

*Brown* itself and many of the early cases involved "coerced" confessions, that is, confessions stimulated by improper violence or the threat of such violence. In *Brown,* for example, the suspects were physically beaten and were told that such beatings would continue until they provided confessions of the substance desired by the law enforcement officers. But in subsequent cases the prohibition against involuntary confessions was extended far beyond such coerced statements.

*Overbearing of the Will.* In Blackburn v. Alabama, supra, the Court noted that "coercion can be mental as well as physical and * * * the blood of the accused is not the only hallmark of an unconstitutional inquisition." 361 U.S. at 206, 80 S.Ct. at 279, 4 L.Ed. 2d at 247. In Spano v. New York, supra, the Court observed:

> [A]s * * * the methods used to extract confessions [become] more sophisticated, our duty to enforce federal constitutional protections does not cease. It only becomes more difficult because of the more delicate judgments to be made.

360 U.S. at 321, 79 S.Ct. at 1206, 3 L.Ed.2d at 1271. In cases lacking overt brutality, the Court has applied a "totality of the circumstances" analysis. The classic statement of this approach is that of Justice Frankfurter in Culombe v. Connecticut, 367 U.S. 568, 81 S.Ct. 1860, 6 L.Ed.2d 1037 (1961):

> No single litmus-paper test for constitutionally-impermissible interrogation has been evolved: neither extensive cross questioning * * *; nor undue delay in arraignment * * *; nor failure to caution a prisoner * * *; nor refusal to permit communication with friends and legal counsel at stages in the proceeding when the prisoner is still only a suspect * * *.
>
> Each of these factors, in company with all of the surrounding circumstances—the duration and conditions of detention (if the confessor has been detained), the manifest attitude of the police towards him, his physical and mental state, the diverse pressures which sap or sustain his powers of resistance and self-control—is relevant. The ultimate test remains * * *: * * * Is the confession the product of an essentially free and unconstrained choice by its maker? * * * [I]f his will has been overborne and his

capacity for self-determination critically impaired, the use of his confession offends due process.

367 U.S. at 601–02, 81 S.Ct. at 1878–79, 6 L.Ed.2d at 1057–58.

Application of the test was illustrated by Greenwald v. Wisconsin, 390 U.S. 519, 88 S.Ct. 1152, 20 L.Ed.2d 77 (1968) (per curiam). Although the case was decided by the Supreme Court after *Miranda,* the nonretroactivity of *Miranda* meant that *Miranda* did not govern the admissibility of the confession. The facts were stated by the Court as follows:

[Greenwald], who has a ninth-grade education, was arrested on suspicion of burglary shortly before 10:45 on the evening of January 20, 1965. He was taken to a police station. He was suffering from high blood pressure, a condition for which he was taking medication twice a day. [He] had last taken food and medication, before his arrest, at 4 p.m. He did not have medication with him at the time of the arrest. At the police station [he] was interrogated from 10:45 until midnight. He was not advised of his constitutional rights. [He] repeatedly denied guilt. No incriminating statements were made at this time.

[He] was booked and fingerprinted and, sometime after 2 a.m., he was taken to a cell in the city jail. A plank fastened to the wall served as his bed. [He] claims he did not sleep. At 6 a.m., [he] was led from the cell to a "bullpen." At 8:30 he was placed in a lineup. At 8:45, his interrogation recommenced. It was conducted by several officers at a time, in a small room. [Greenwald] testified that in the course of the morning he was not offered food and that he continued to be without medication. For an hour or two he refused to answer any questions. When he did speak, it was to deny, once again, his guilt.

Sometime after 10 a.m., [Greenwald] was asked to write out a confession. He refused, stating that "it was against my constitutional rights" and that he was "entitled to have a lawyer." These statements were ignored. No further reference was made to an attorney, by [Greenwald] or by the police officers.

At about 11 a.m. [Greenwald] began a series of oral admissions culminating in a full oral confession at about 11:30. At noon he was offered food. The confession was reduced to writing about 1 p.m. Just before the confession was reduced to writing, [he] was advised of his constitutional rights. According to his testimony, he confessed because "I knew they weren't going to leave me alone until I did."

390 U.S. at 519–20, 88 S.Ct. at 1153, 20 L.Ed.2d at 79. Considering the totality of these circumstances, a majority of the Court concluded that the Wisconsin Supreme Court had erred in finding that Greenwald's statements "were the product of his free and rational choice." 390 U.S. at 521, 88 S.Ct. at 1154, 20 L.Ed.2d at 80. Justice Stewart, joined by two other members of the Court, read the circumstances as adequately supporting the state court's conclusion:

[Greenwald] was nearly 30 years old and was by no means a stranger to the criminal law. He was questioned for little more than an hour one evening and for less than four hours the next morning. He was neither abused nor threatened and was promised no benefits for confessing. * * * [H]e himself testified that, during his interrogation, "he knew he had a constitutional right to refuse to answer any questions, * * * he knew anything he said could be used against him, and * * * he knew he had a constitutional right to retain counsel." Moreover, * * * [he] himself testified that at no time between his arrest and his confession did he express to anyone a desire for food or for medication.

390 U.S. at 521–22, 88 S.Ct. at 1154, 20 L.Ed.2d at 80 (Stewart, J., dissenting).

As applied in cases such as *Greenwald,* does the voluntariness case law provide a meaningful standard for determining the admissibility of confessions? Judge Posner of the Seventh Circuit recently suggested not:

[W]hether a confession is voluntary is not really a fact, but a characterization. There is indeed no "faculty of will" inside our heads that has two states, on and off, such that through careful reconstruction of events the observer can determine whether the switch was on when the defendant was confessing. * * *

* * * [C]ourts have not been successful in devising a standard that will determine in a consistent fashion when confessions should be excluded on grounds of involuntariness. Of course if the confession is unreliable, it should go out, along with other unreliable evidence. It is on this basis that confessions extracted by torture are excluded. But in most cases in which a confession is sought to be excluded because involuntary, there is little likelihood that the inducements placed before the defendant were so overpowering as to induce an untrue confession. The courts in such cases retreat to the proposition that a confession, to be admissible, must be the product of a free choice. [B]ut [this] is just the faculty of will approach, and, as the courts are beginning to suspect, it leads nowhere. Taken seriously it would require the exclusion of virtually all fruits of custodial interrogation, since few choices to confess can be thought truly "free" when made by a person who is incarcerated and is being questioned by armed officers without the presence of counsel or anyone else to give him moral support. The formula is not taken seriously. * * * [V]ery few incriminating statements, custodial or otherwise, are held to be involuntary, though few are the product of a choice that the interrogators left completely free.

United States v. Rutledge, 900 F.2d 1127, 1128–29 (7th Cir.1990) (Posner, J.).

*Promises.* The traditional requirement of voluntariness mandated exclusion of a confession that was obtained as a result of a promise or inducement, made by a person in a position of authority, concerning the criminal charges to which the defendant confessed. See generally, Dix,

Mistake, Ignorance, Expectation of Benefit, and the Modern Law of Confessions, 1975 Wash.U.L.Q. 275 (1975). As the language from *Bram* set out above suggests, the Supreme Court appeared to incorporate this traditional requirement into the due process voluntariness standard. But this has not been developed in subsequent case law. It is consequently unclear how specific a promise of what sort would or might render a confession involuntary within the meaning of the due process requirement.

Some variation has developed in the manner in which the lower courts apply the requirement. Some courts have applied a rather rigid version of the traditional prohibition against promises. In State v. Woodruff, 259 N.C. 333, 130 S.E.2d 641 (1963), for example, the court held a murder confession inadmissible upon proof that the sheriff had promised to "help" the defendant. Other courts, however, have required that the promise be a quite specific one. In Hargett v. State, 235 Ark. 189, 357 S.W.2d 533 (1962), for example, a confession was found admissible despite evidence that an officer told the suspect the officer "would help him all I could." The court stressed that the statement was not explicitly conditioned upon a confession being made. And in People v. Hartgraves, 31 Ill.2d 375, 202 N.E.2d 33 (1964), cert. denied 380 U.S. 961, 85 S.Ct. 1104, 14 L.Ed.2d 152 (1965), a confession was held properly utilized despite testimony that an officer told the suspect that, "It would go easier for him in court if he made a statement." The court characterized the officer's statement as "a mere suggestion of the advisability of making a statement" rather than a fatal "direct promise of leniency." 31 Ill.2d at 381, 202 N.E.2d at 36. Some courts regard a confession stimulated by a promise as involuntary only if the promise was of a sort likely to induce an inaccurate or false confession, that is, one likely to cause an innocent person to confess to the crime. See Fisher v. State, 379 S.W.2d 900 (Tex.Crim.App.1964).

It is not always easy to determine whether a case presents a promise or a threat. In Payne v. Arkansas, 356 U.S. 560, 78 S.Ct. 844, 2 L.Ed.2d 975 (1958), for example, the suspect was made aware of the presence of a lynch mob outside the jail. The police chief then told the suspect that if the suspect wanted to make a confession, the chief would try to keep the mob out. Was this a threat to permit the suspect to be lynched or a promise to protect him if he confessed?

*Deception.* In contrast to the traditionally rigid prohibition against promises, no similar voluntariness mandate prohibiting deception of a suspect by police officers has existed. Some courts held that deception is simply not a basis for regarding a confession as involuntary. In Commonwealth v. Graham, 408 Pa. 155, 182 A.2d 727 (1962), for example, a female police employee attended a lineup, pointed to the defendant, and said, "That's the man." The Pennsylvania Supreme Court expressed emphatic disapproval of the action, but held that the deception did not amount to legal duress or coercion rendering the confession inadmissible. Some courts have stated the voluntariness requirement so as to leave open the possibility that at least some deception would affect admissibility. In People v. Everett, 10 N.Y.2d 500, 225 N.Y.S.2d 193, 180 N.E.2d 556 (1962), cert. denied 370 U.S. 963,

82 S.Ct. 1593, 8 L.Ed.2d 830 (1962), for example, an officer misrepresented to a murder suspect that the victim had only been injured and had identified the suspect as his assailant. "Deception alone will not render a confession invalid," the New York court held, "unless the deceiving acts amount to a deprivation of due process. 10 N.Y.2d at 507, 225 N.Y.S.2d at 198, 180 N.E.2d at 559. On the facts before it, the court found no aggravation of the sort necessary to violate due process.

Others courts have indicated that deception would render a confession involuntary if but only if the deception was of the sort likely to induce a false confession. In applying this test, the courts have been reluctant to find that particular deception created the required risk of a false statement by the suspect. E.g., People v. Castello, 194 Cal. 595, 229 P. 855 (1924) (inaccurate statement by officer that defendant had been seen stealing the property was not such as to produce an untrue confession and therefore did not render confession inadmissible).

The relationship between deception and the federal due process standard was not addressed until Frazier v. Cupp, 394 U.S. 731, 89 S.Ct. 1420, 22 L.Ed.2d 684 (1969). (Although *Frazier* was decided after *Miranda*, *Miranda's* requirements did not apply to the confession there at issue and therefore its admissibility turned upon its voluntariness.) Frazier was interrogated concerning a murder; he denied committing the offense and claimed to have been with his cousin, Rawls, on the night of the crime. The officer then falsely told Frazier that Rawls had confessed to the murder. Subsequently, Frazier decided to make a statement. This statement was used, over defense objection, at Frazier's trial.

The Supreme Court found no violation of the due process standard. It noted that Frazier had received a "partial warning" of his constitutional rights, the questioning was of short duration, and Frazier was "a mature individual of normal intelligence." Without citation of authority or discussion of the relevant considerations, the Court then commented, "The fact that the police misrepresented the statement that Rawls made is, while relevant, insufficient in our view to make this otherwise voluntary confession inadmissible." 394 U.S. at 739, 89 S.Ct. at 1425, 22 L.Ed.2d at 693. There were no dissents; Justice Fortas did not participate in the case, and Chief Justice Warren and Justice Douglas concurred in the result without separate opinions.

Does this mean that deception is at most one of the "totality of the circumstances" that is to be considered in determining whether the defendant's will was "overborne?" If so, how can this be justified in light of what appears to be the more specific and independent prohibition against promises?

*Burden of Proof.* If the prosecution offers a confession against a defendant, the prosecution must prove the voluntariness of that confession. But in Lego v. Twomey, 404 U.S. 477, 92 S.Ct. 619, 30 L.Ed.2d 618 (1972), the Court held that the federal Constitution required only that voluntariness be proved by a preponderance of the evidence. No basis existed, the majority reasoned, to believe that rulings made under the "preponderance of the evidence" standard have been unreliable or otherwise wanting in quality.  Consequently, the prosecution's ability to put confessions before juries need not be futher impeded by a need to prove voluntariness beyond a reasonable doubt.  States, of course, remain free to impose such a higher standard as a matter of state law. 404 U.S. at 488–89, 92 S.Ct. at 626–27, 30 L.Ed.2d at 627.

*Relationship to* Miranda *Requirements.*  How do the general voluntariness requirements compare to the requirements of effective waivers of Fifth Amendment rights under *Miranda?*  Some specific aspects of this are considered later in this chapter.  But at this point, it may be helpful to note that some courts have regarded the voluntariness requirement as demanding a more general and flexible analysis than is appropriate for *Miranda* waivers.  E.g., United States v. Doe, 819 F.2d 206, 209 (9th Cir.1985).  Drawing upon Justice O'Connor's discussion in Miller v. Fenton, 474 U.S. 104, 106 S.Ct. 445, 88 L.Ed.2d 405 (1985), this approach regards *Miranda* waiver analysis as involving an essentially factual inquiry into the suspect's state of mind.  But the voluntariness of a confession requires more subtle integration into the analysis of the underlying policy considerations and a balancing of the competing considerations.  Ultimately, it requires a relatively subjective conclusion as to whether the means used to elicit the confession are compatible with those underlying policy objectives.  *Doe,* supra, 819 F.2d at 209.

Under this approach, voluntariness remains an additional requirement where *Miranda* applies and is met.  A confession might meet all *Miranda* requirements but nevertheless be involuntary under a general due process analysis.

*The Requirement of Corroboration or "Independent" Proof of the Corpus Delicti.*  The requirement of voluntariness must be distinguished from the very different requirement that is often put as a demand that the prosecution, in order to prove guilt beyond a reasonable doubt, produce evidence other than an out-of-court confession by the defendant tending to show the *corpus delicti,* that is, that the crime charged was committed *by someone.*  The evidence independent of the confession need not tend to show that the defendant committed the crime charged.  Nor need it be sufficient in itself to prove commission of the crime beyond a reasonable doubt.  The confession can be the only evidence tending to show that the defendant committed the offense and the corroborating evidence can be considered together with the confession in determining whether the prosecution has proven guilt beyond a reasonable doubt.  In some states, the requirement has been incorporated into statute.  Section 60.50 of New York's Criminal Procedure Law, for example, provides that a conviction is not permitted "solely upon evidence of a confession made by [the defendant] without additional proof that the offense charged has been committed."

The requirement is sometimes stated as one addressing the admissibility of a confession—a confession is not admissible unless the prosecution has first introduced other evidence tending to show that the charged offense was committed.  But since trial judges have great discretion over the order of proof, it is unlikely to be reversible error even under this formulation of the requirement for a trial judge to admit a confession if the prosecution later in the case produces such evidence. See generally, McCormick on Evidence § 145 (3rd ed. 1984).

In some jurisdictions, the requirement is somewhat more flexible than one of independent proof of the *corpus delicti*. For purposes of federal litigation, the Supreme Court has held that in order for a conviction to be upheld the Government must have introduced "substantial independent evidence which would tend to establish the trustworthiness of the [defendant's] statement." Opper v. United States, 348 U.S. 84, 93, 75 S.Ct. 158, 164, 99 L.Ed. 101, 109 (1954). This is the requirement applied by the Court in Wong Sun v. United States, 371 U.S. 471, 83 S.Ct. 407, 9 L.Ed.2d 441 (1963), reprinted at page 28, supra. However the requirement is formulated, it is in effect a requirement that a confession be corroborated by some other evidence at trial in order to justify the conviction of the defendant.

Like the voluntariness rule, the requirement of corroboration is based upon concern regarding the accuracy of out-of-court self-incriminating statements. In *Opper* the Court explained:

> [O]ur concept of justice that finds no man guilty until proven has led our state and federal courts generally to refuse conviction on testimony concerning confessions of the accused not made by him at the trial of his case. * * * [T]he doubt persists that the zeal of the agencies of prosecution to protect the peace, the self-interest of the accomplice, the maliciousness of an enemy or the aberration or weakness of the accused under the strain of suspicion may tinge or warp the facts of the confession. Admissions, retold at trial, are much like hearsay, that is, statements not made at the pending trial. They had neither the compulsion of the oath nor the test of cross-examination.

348 U.S. at 89–90, 75 S.Ct. at 162–63, 99 L.Ed. at 106–07. Despite its concern with the accuracy of confessions and trials, however, the requirement of corroboration has not been incorporated into any federal constitutional doctrine and remains exclusively a matter of state or local definition of evidence sufficiency.

\* \* \*

The principal case in this section reflects a major conceptual development of the federal constitutional voluntariness doctrine. In addition to the statements raising the due process voluntariness concern discussed in those parts of the opinions reprinted here, the defendant had given other statements to which *Miranda* applied. The Supreme Court's holdings on the *Miranda* issues are discussed at pages 471–74, infra.

## COLORADO v. CONNELLY

Supreme Court of the United States, 1986.
479 U.S. 157, 107 S.Ct. 515, 93 L.Ed.2d 473.

CHIEF JUSTICE REHNQUIST delivered the opinion of the Court.

\* \* \*

I

On August 18, 1983, Officer Patrick Anderson of the Denver Police Department was in uniform, working in an off-duty capacity in downtown Denver. Respondent Francis Connelly approached Officer Anderson and, without any prompting, stated that he had murdered someone and wanted to talk about it. Anderson immediately advised respondent that he had the right to remain silent, that anything he said could be used against him in court, and that he had the right to an attorney prior to any police questioning. See Miranda v. Arizona, 384 U.S. 436, 86 S.Ct. 1602, 16 L.Ed.2d 694 (1966). Respondent stated that he understood these rights but he still wanted to talk about the murder. Understandably bewildered by this confession, Officer Anderson asked respondent several questions. Connelly denied that he had been drinking, denied that he had been taking any drugs, and stated that, in the past, he had been a patient in several mental hospitals. Officer Anderson again told Connelly that he was under no obligation to say anything. Connelly replied that it was "all right," and that he would talk to Officer Anderson because his conscience had been bothering him. To Officer Anderson, respondent appeared to understand fully the nature of his acts.

Shortly thereafter, Homicide Detective Stephen Antuna arrived. Respondent was again advised of his rights, and Detective Antuna asked him "what he had on his mind." Respondent answered that he had come all the way from Boston to confess to the murder of Mary Ann Junta, a young girl whom he had killed in Denver sometime during November 1982. Respondent was taken to police headquarters, and a search of police records revealed that the body of an unidentified female had been found in April 1983. Respondent openly detailed his story to Detective Antuna and Sergeant Thomas Haney, and readily agreed to take the officers to the scene of the killing. Under Connelly's sole direction, the two officers and respondent proceeded in a police vehicle to the location of the crime. Respondent pointed out the exact location of the murder. Throughout this episode, Detective Antuna perceived no indication whatsoever that respondent was suffering from any kind of mental illness.

Respondent was held overnight. During an interview with the public defender's office the following morning, he became visibly disoriented. He began giving confused answers to questions, and for the first time, stated that "voices" had told him to come to Denver and that he had followed the directions of these voices in confessing. Respondent was sent to a state hospital for evaluation. He was initially found incompetent to assist in his own defense. By March 1984, however, the doctors evaluating respondent determined that he was competent to proceed to trial.

At a preliminary hearing, respondent moved to suppress all of his statements. Doctor Jeffrey Metzner, a psychiatrist employed by the state hospital, testified that respondent was suffering from chronic schizophrenia and was in a psychotic state at least as of August 17,

1983, the day before he confessed.  Metzner's interviews with respondent revealed that respondent was following the "voice of God."  This voice instructed respondent to withdraw money from the bank, to buy an airplane ticket, and to fly from Boston to Denver.  When respondent arrived from Boston, God's voice became stronger and told respondent either to confess to the killing or to commit suicide.  Reluctantly following the command of the voices, respondent approached Officer Anderson and confessed.

Dr. Metzner testified that, in his expert opinion, respondent was experiencing "command hallucinations."  This condition interfered with respondent's "volitional abilities; that is, his ability to make free and rational choices."  Dr. Metzner further testified that Connelly's illness did not significantly impair his cognitive abilities.  Thus, respondent understood the rights he had when Officer Anderson and Detective Antuna advised him that he need not speak.  Dr. Metzner admitted that the "voices" could in reality be Connelly's interpretation of his own guilt, but explained that in his opinion, Connelly's psychosis motivated his confession.

On the basis of this evidence the Colorado trial court decided that respondent's statements must be suppressed because they were "involuntary."  *  *  *

The Colorado Supreme Court affirmed.  702 P.2d 722 (1985).
*  *  *

## II

The Due Process Clause of the Fourteenth Amendment provides that no State shall "deprive any person of life, liberty, or property, without due process of law."  Just last Term, in Miller v. Fenton, 474 U.S. 104, 109, 106 S.Ct. 445, 449, 88 L.Ed.2d 405 (1985), we held that by virtue of the Due Process Clause "certain interrogation techniques, either in isolation or as applied to the unique characteristics of a particular suspect, are so offensive to a civilized system of justice that they must be condemned."  *  *  * [T]he cases considered by this Court *  *  * have focused upon the crucial element of police overreaching.  While each confession case has turned on its own set of factors justifying the conclusion that police conduct was oppressive, all have contained a substantial element of coercive police conduct.  Absent police conduct causally related to the confession, there is simply no basis for concluding that any state actor has deprived a criminal defendant of due process of law.  Respondent correctly notes that as interrogators have turned to more subtle forms of psychological persuasion, courts have found the mental condition of the defendant a more significant factor in the "voluntariness" calculus.  But this fact does not justify a conclusion that a defendant's mental condition, by itself and apart from its relation to official coercion, should ever dispose of the inquiry into constitutional "voluntariness."

Respondent relies on Blackburn v. Alabama, 361 U.S. 199, 80 S.Ct. 274, 4 L.Ed.2d 242 (1960), and Townsend v. Sain, 372 U.S. 293, 83 S.Ct. 745, 9 L.Ed.2d 770 (1963), for the proposition that the "deficient mental condition of the defendants in those cases was sufficient to render their confessions involuntary." But respondent's reading of *Blackburn* and *Townsend* ignores the integral element of police overreaching present in both cases. In *Blackburn,* the Court found that the petitioner was probably insane at the time of his confession and the police learned during the interrogation that Blackburn had a history of mental problems. The police exploited this weakness with coercive tactics: "the eight-to nine-hour sustained interrogation in a tiny room which was upon occasion literally filled with police officers; the absence of Blackburn's friends, relatives, or legal counsel; [and] the composition of the confession by the Deputy Sheriff rather than by Blackburn." These tactics supported a finding that the confession was involuntary. Indeed, the Court specifically condemned police activity that "wrings a confession out of an accused against his will." *Townsend* presented a similar instance of police wrongdoing. In that case, a police physician had given Townsend a drug with truth-serum properties. The subsequent confession, obtained by officers who knew that Townsend had been given drugs, was held involuntary. These two cases demonstrate that while mental condition is surely relevant to an individual's susceptibility to police coercion, mere examination of the confessant's state of mind can never conclude the due process inquiry.

Our "involuntary confession" jurisprudence is entirely consistent with the settled law requiring some sort of "state action" to support a claim of violation of the Due Process Clause of the Fourteenth Amendment. The Colorado trial court, of course, found that the police committed no wrongful acts, and that finding has been neither challenged by the respondent nor disturbed by the Supreme Court of Colorado. The latter court, however, concluded that sufficient state action was present by virtue of the admission of the confession into evidence in a court of the State.

The difficulty with the approach of the Supreme Court of Colorado is that it fails to recognize the essential link between coercive activity of the State, on the one hand, and a resulting confession by a defendant, on the other. The flaw in respondent's constitutional argument is that it would expand our previous line of "voluntariness" cases into a far-ranging requirement that courts must divine a defendant's motivation for speaking or acting as he did even though there be no claim that governmental conduct coerced his decision.

The most outrageous behavior by a private party seeking to secure evidence against a defendant does not make that evidence inadmissible under the Due Process Clause. \* \* \* Moreover, suppressing respondent's statements would serve absolutely no purpose in enforcing constitutional guarantees. The purpose of excluding evidence seized in violation of the Constitution is to substantially deter future violations of the Constitution. Only if we were to establish a brand new constitutional right—the right of a criminal defendant to confess to his crime only when totally rational and properly motivated—could respondent's present claim be sustained.

We have previously cautioned against expanding "currently applicable exclusionary rules by erecting additional barriers to placing truthful and probative evidence before state juries. * * *" Lego v. Twomey, 404 U.S. 477, 488–489, 92 S.Ct. 619, 626, 30 L.Ed.2d 618 (1972). We abide by that counsel now. "[T]he central purpose of a criminal trial is to decide the factual question of the defendant's guilt or innocence," Delaware v. Van Arsdall, 475 U.S. 673, 680, 106 S.Ct. 1431, 1436, 89 L.Ed.2d 674 (1986), and while we have previously held that exclusion of evidence may be necessary to protect constitutional guarantees, both the necessity for the collateral inquiry and the exclusion of evidence deflect a criminal trial from its basic purpose. Respondent would now have us require sweeping inquiries into the state of mind of a criminal defendant who has confessed, inquiries quite divorced from any coercion brought to bear on the defendant by the State. We think the Constitution rightly leaves this sort of inquiry to be resolved by state laws governing the admission of evidence and erects no standard of its own in this area. A statement rendered by one in the condition of respondent might be proved to be quite unreliable, but this is a matter to be governed by the evidentiary laws of the forum, see, e.g., Fed.Rule Evid. 601, and not by the Due Process Clause of the Fourteenth Amendment. "The aim of the requirement of due process is not to exclude presumptively false evidence, but to prevent fundamental unfairness in the use of evidence, whether true or false." Lisenba v. California, 314 U.S. 219, 236, 62 S.Ct. 280, 290, 86 L.Ed. 166 (1941).

We hold that coercive police activity is a necessary predicate to the finding that a confession is not "voluntary" within the meaning of the Due Process Clause of the Fourteenth Amendment. We also conclude that the taking of respondent's statements, and their admission into evidence, constitute no violation of that Clause.

\* \* \*

## IV

The judgment of the Supreme Court of Colorado is accordingly reversed, and the cause remanded for further proceedings not inconsistent with this opinion.

JUSTICE BLACKMUN, concurring in part and concurring in the judgment.

I join Parts I [and] II * * * of the Court's opinion and its judgment.

\* \* \*

JUSTICE STEVENS, concurring in the judgment in part and dissenting in part.

Respondent made incriminatory statements both before and after he was handcuffed and taken into custody. The only question presented by the Colorado district attorney in his certiorari petition concerned the admissibility of respondent's precustodial statements. I agree with the State of Colorado that the United States Constitution does not require suppression of those statements, but in reaching that conclusion, unlike the Court, I am perfectly willing to accept the state trial court's finding that the statements were involuntary.

The state trial court found that, in view of the "overwhelming evidence presented by the Defense," the prosecution did not meet its burden of demonstrating that respondent's initial statements to Officer Anderson were voluntary. Nevertheless, in my opinion, the use of these involuntary precustodial statements does not violate the Fifth Amendment because they were not the product of state compulsion. Although they may well be so unreliable that they could not support a conviction, at this stage of the proceeding I could not say that they have no probative force whatever. The fact that the statements were involuntary—just as the product of Lady Macbeth's nightmare was involuntary—does not mean that their use for whatever evidentiary value they may have is fundamentally unfair or a denial of due process.

* * *

Accordingly, I concur in the judgment insofar as it applies to respondent's precustodial statements * * *.

JUSTICE BRENNAN, with whom JUSTICE MARSHALL joins, dissenting.

Today the Court denies Mr. Connelly his fundamental right to make a vital choice with a sane mind, involving a determination that could allow the State to deprive him of liberty or even life. This holding is unprecedented * * *. Because I believe that the use of a mentally ill person's involuntary confession is antithetical to the notion of fundamental fairness embodied in the Due Process Clause, I dissent.

I

The respondent's seriously impaired mental condition is clear on the record of this case. * * *

II

The absence of police wrongdoing should not, by itself, determine the voluntariness of a confession by a mentally ill person. The requirement that a confession be voluntary reflects a recognition of the importance of free will and of reliability in determining the admissibility of a confession, and thus demands an inquiry into the totality of the circumstances surrounding the confession.

A

Today's decision restricts the application of the term "involuntary" to those confessions obtained by police coercion. Confessions by mentally ill individuals or by persons coerced by parties other than police officers are now considered "voluntary." The Court's failure to recognize all forms of involuntariness or coercion as antithetical to due process reflects a refusal to acknowledge free will as a value of constitutional consequence. But due process derives much of its meaning from a conception of fundamental fairness that emphasizes the right to make vital choices voluntarily: "The Fourteenth Amendment secures against state invasion * * * the right of a person to remain silent unless he

chooses to speak in the unfettered exercise of his own will. ＊ ＊ ＊ ”
Malloy v. Hogan, 378 U.S. 1, 8, 84 S.Ct. 1489, 1493, 12 L.Ed.2d 653
(1964). ＊ ＊ ＊

We have never confined our focus to police coercion, because the
value of freedom of will has demanded a broader inquiry. The confession cases decided by this Court over the 50 years since Brown v.
Mississippi, 297 U.S. 278, 56 S.Ct. 461, 80 L.Ed. 682 (1936), have focused
upon both police overreaching and free will. While it is true that
police overreaching has been an element of every confession case to
date, it is also true that in every case the Court has made clear that
ensuring that a confession is a product of free will is an independent
concern. The fact that involuntary confessions have always been
excluded in part because of police overreaching, signifies only that this
is a case of first impression. Until today, we have never upheld the
admission of a confession that does not reflect the exercise of free will.

＊ ＊ ＊

This Court abandons this precedent in favor of the view that only
confessions rendered involuntary by some state action are inadmissible,
and that the only relevant form of state action is police conduct. But
even if state action is required, police overreaching is not its only
relevant form. The Colorado Supreme Court held that the trial court's
admission of the involuntary confession into evidence is also state
action. The state court's analysis is consistent with Brown v. Mississippi, 297 U.S. 278, 56 S.Ct. 461, 80 L.Ed. 682 (1936), on which this Court
so heavily relies. *Brown,* a case involving the use of confessions at
trial, makes clear that "[t]he due process clause requires 'that state
action, *whether through one agency or another,* shall be consistent with
the fundamental principles of liberty and justice which lie at the base
of all our civil and political institutions.' " Id., at 286, 56 S.Ct., at 465
(emphasis added), citing Hebert v. Louisiana, 272 U.S. 312, 316, 47 S.Ct.
103, 104, 71 L.Ed. 270 (1926). Police conduct constitutes but one form
of state action. ＊ ＊ ＊

The only logical "flaw" which the Court detects in this argument is
that it would require courts to "divine a defendant's motivation for
speaking or acting as he did even though there be no claim that
governmental conduct coerced his decision." Such a criticism, however,
ignores the fact that we have traditionally examined the totality of the
circumstances, including the motivation and competence of the defendant, in determining whether a confession is voluntary.

## B

Since the Court redefines voluntary confessions to include confessions by mentally ill individuals, the reliability of these confessions
becomes a central concern. A concern for reliability is inherent in our
criminal justice system, which relies upon accusatorial rather than
inquisitorial practices. ＊ ＊ ＊.[1]

---

[1] Even if police knowledge of the defendant's insanity is required to exclude an
involuntary confession, the record supports
a finding of police knowledge in this case.
The Court accepts the trial court's finding
of no police wrongdoing since, in the trial
judge's view, none of the police officers
knew that Mr. Connelly was insane. After

Because the admission of a confession so strongly tips the balance against the defendant in the adversarial process, we must be especially careful about a confession's reliability. We have to date not required a finding of reliability for involuntary confessions only because *all* such confessions have been excluded upon a finding of involuntariness, regardless of reliability. The Court's adoption today of a restrictive definition of an "involuntary" confession will require heightened scrutiny of a confession's reliability.

The instant case starkly highlights the danger of admitting a confession by a person with a severe mental illness. The trial court made no findings concerning the reliability of Mr. Connelly's involuntary confession, since it believed that the confession was excludable on the basis of involuntariness. However, the overwhelming evidence in the record points to the unreliability of Mr. Connelly's delusional mind. Mr. Connelly was found incompetent to stand trial because he was unable to relate accurate information, and the court-appointed psychiatrist indicated that Mr. Connelly was actively hallucinating and exhibited delusional thinking at the time of his confession. The Court, in fact, concedes that "[a] statement rendered by one in the condition of respondent might be proved to be quite unreliable. * * *"

Moreover, the record is barren of any corroboration of the mentally ill defendant's confession. No physical evidence links the defendant to the alleged crime. Police did not identify the alleged victim's body as the woman named by the defendant. Mr. Connelly identified the alleged scene of the crime, but it has not been verified that the unidentified body was found there or that a crime actually occurred there. There is not a shred of competent evidence in this record linking the defendant to the charged homicide. There is only Mr. Connelly's confession.

Minimum standards of due process should require that the trial court find substantial indicia of reliability, on the basis of evidence extrinsic to the confession itself, before admitting the confession of a mentally ill person into evidence. I would require the trial court to make such a finding on remand. To hold otherwise allows the State to imprison and possibly to execute a mentally ill defendant based solely upon an inherently unreliable confession.

\* \* \*

plenary review of the record, I conclude that this finding is clearly erroneous.

When the defendant confessed to Officer Anderson, the officer's first thought was that Mr. Connelly was a "crackpot." Today's Court describes Officer Anderson as "[u]nderstandably bewildered." After giving *Miranda* warnings, the officer questioned the defendant about whether he used drugs or alcohol. He also asked Mr. Connelly if he had been treated for any mental disorders, and the defendant responded that he had been treated in five different mental hospitals. While this Court concludes that "Detective Antuna perceived no indication whatsoever that respondent was suffering from any kind of mental illness," the record indicates that Officer Anderson informed the detective about the defendant's five hospitalizations in mental institutions. Thus, even under this Court's test requiring police wrongdoing, the record indicates that the officers here had sufficient knowledge about the defendant's mental incapacity to render the confession "involuntary."

## NOTES

1. In Rogers v. Richmond, 365 U.S. 534, 81 S.Ct. 735, 5 L.Ed.2d 760 (1961), the police, among other things, misrepresented to defendant that they were about to bring his wife into the stationhouse for questioning. The trial judge held the resulting confession admissible because the police pretense "had no tendency to produce a confession that was not in accord with the truth." The United States Supreme Court reversed the conviction:

> From a fair reading of * * * [the record] we cannot but conclude that the question whether Rogers' confessions were admissible was answered by reference to a legal standard which took into account the circumstance of probable truth or falsity. And this is not a permissible standard under the Due Process Clause of the Fourteenth Amendment. The attention of the trial court should have been focused * * * on the question whether the behavior of the State's law enforcement officials was such as to overbear petitioner's will to resist and to bring about confessions not freely self-determined—a question to be answered with complete disregard of whether or not petitioner in fact spoke the truth.

365 U.S. at 543–44, 81 S.Ct. at 741, 5 L.Ed.2d at 768.

2. Rule 5(a) of the Federal Rules of Criminal Procedure demands presentation of an arrested person before a judicial officer without "unnecessary delay." Most if not all states have similar requirements of "prompt presentation" of arrested suspects. In part, prompt presentation can be regarded as minimizing the opportunity for coercive or otherwise improper interrogation techniques. At the arrestee's appearance before the magistrate, the arrestee may be given information concerning the charges pending and may be informed regarding legal rights by the judge. Moreover, provision may be made for pretrial release. In McNabb v. United States, 318 U.S. 332, 63 S.Ct. 608, 87 L.Ed. 819 (1943), the Supreme Court held that under its supervisory power it would require exclusion of a confession made by a defendant after federal officers who had the defendant in custody failed to comply with a statutory predecessor to Rule 5(a) that demanded prompt presentation. The Court later applied the same exclusionary rule to Rule 5(a). Upshaw v. United States, 335 U.S. 410, 69 S.Ct. 170, 93 L.Ed. 100 (1948). In Mallory v. United States, 354 U.S. 449, 77 S.Ct. 1356, 1 L.Ed.2d 1479 (1957), the Court considered the meaning of "unnecessary delay" under Rule 5(a), and made clear that this was to be defined so as to minimize the opportunity for custodial interrogation:

> Circumstances may justify a brief delay between arrest and arraignment, as for instance, where the story volunteered by the accused is susceptible of quick verification through third parties. But the delay must not be of a nature to give opportunity for the extraction of a confession.

354 U.S. at 455, 77 S.Ct. at 1360, 1 L.Ed.2d at 1483. The delay in the case before it, the Court held, was "unnecessary" because a magistrate was readily available and the defendant was not presented only because the officers desired the opportunity for interrogation.

The Supreme Court has never held that this so-called *McNabb-Mallory* rule is in any way binding on the states, and the fact that a confession was obtained during an improper delay in presenting the defendant before a magistrate has always been regarded as merely one factor to consider in determining the voluntariness of the confession. Columbe v. Connecticut (quoted above). Of course, this is no bar to states adopting, as a matter of state law, an exclusionary rule requiring the suppression of confessions made during a period of delay violative of the state's prompt presentation requirement. As a matter of federal law, Congress has modified the *McNabb-Mallory* rule. Under 18 U.S. C.A. § 3501(c), a confession offered against a federal criminal defendant is not to be excluded solely because of delay in presenting a defendant before a magistrate if the confession is voluntary and was made within six hours immediately following the defendant's taking into custody. Further, a confession obtained after a six-hour period is not to be excluded on delay grounds alone if the delay is found to be reasonable, considering the distance to be traveled to a judicial officer and the means of transportation available to the officers.

3. Was the voluntariness requirement insufficient to protect suspects' interests during custodial interrogation? Schulhofer, Confessions and the Court, 79 Mich.L.Rev. 865, 869–72 (1981), summarizes a number of defects which critics found in the due process voluntariness requirement. It failed to provide specific guidance to law enforcement on which questioning tactics were and which were not permissible. The "elusive task of balancing" invited trial judges to give weight to their subjective preferences and discouraged appellate review; judicial review of police activity was therefore impaired. Often, the critical issue was one of fact—what happened in the interrogation room— resulting in "swearing matches" between officers and defendants; defendants generally lost. And despite the requirement, considerable pressure was placed on suspects to confess, those with special weaknesses were especially susceptible to such pressure, and even physical brutality was not effectively enough discouraged.

For a general discussion of the voluntariness requirement which concludes that it is the only constitutional restraint that can justifiably be imposed upon police interrogation, see Grano, Voluntariness, Free Will and the Law of Confessions, 65 Va.L.Rev. 859 (1979).

## B.  SELF–INCRIMINATION AND *MIRANDA'S* RIGHT TO COUNSEL

Beginning with Escobedo v. Illinois, 378 U.S. 478, 84 S.Ct. 1758, 12 L.Ed.2d 977 (1964), the Supreme Court began to shift away from the voluntariness requirement as a means of addressing what it perceived to be the continuing problems posed by police questioning of suspects. This shift was completed two years later in Miranda v. Arizona, 384 U.S. 436, 86 S.Ct. 1602, 16 L.Ed.2d 694 (1966). The so-called *Miranda* requirements have to some extent superceded the voluntariness requirement as the major vehicle for imposing federal constitutional limits upon police questioning and the admissibility of resulting admissions and confession. *Miranda* was among the most controversial of the Supreme Court's decisions and it continues to be the subject of vigorous and heated discussion.

The decision itself is presented in the first subsection of this section. The second subsection addresses the task of determining those situations to which *Miranda* applies. The next considers what has become a major problem area in *Miranda* law—the existence and validity of waivers of the *Miranda* rights. In the fourth subsection, attention is turned to a particularly troublesome problem concerning remedy—a defendant's potential right to exclusion of evidence obtained as a factual result of an inadmissible confession. Finally, the last subsection considers the impact of the *Miranda* rules and the Congressional effort to "overrule" the decision.

In considering the *Miranda* holding, its development and its wisdom, address specifically the extent to which it has superceded the voluntariness requirement. To what, if any, extent have the *Miranda* requirements eliminated the need to evaluate the voluntariness of confessions or eased the task of doing so?

The *Miranda* decision has been explored in L. Baker, Miranda: Crime, Law and Politics (1983). Reviews of the Baker book also contain interesting commentary. See, Belsky, Book Review, 62 Tex.L.Rev. 1341 (1984); Caplan, Book Review, 93 Yale L.J. 1375 (1984); Kamisar, Book Review, 82 Mich.L.Rev. 1074 (1984); MacKerron, Book Review, 35 Hastings, L.J. 551 (1984). For a recent discussion calling for rethinking of *Miranda*, see Caplan, Questioning *Miranda*, 38 Vand.L.Rev. 1417 (1985).

## 1.  THE *MIRANDA* DECISION

### EDITORS' INTRODUCTION: THE *MIRANDA* RIGHTS

To put *Miranda* in doctrinal perspective, it is necessary to understand that before the decision there was substantial support for the proposition that police interrogation did not—directly, at least—implicate the Fifth Amendment privilege against compelled self-incrimination. The privilege, it was widely considered, applied only where the suspect could be the subject of "legal compulsion," that is, compulsion authorized by law, to answer questions. In a courtroom or before a grand jury a witness could be penalized for contempt of court for refusing to respond to questions; thus "legal" compulsion could be exerted and the privilege was implicated by questioning in these situations. Police officers, on the other hand, have no legal right to impose penalties upon suspects who refuse to answer the officers' questions. Consequently, although police interrogation could give rise to an involuntary confession it could not directly violate the Fifth Amendment privilege. See McCormick on Evidence § 125 (3rd ed. 1984).

In addition, even where the privilege against compelled self-incrimination applies, it is, as a general rule, violated only if a person first specifically claims a right under the privilege to refuse to answer a question and then is nevertheless encouraged to answer. Unless the person first claims the privilege, he has not been "compelled" to incriminate himself within the meaning of the privilege. It follows from this, of course, that—again, as a general rule—the government has no obligation before or during the questioning of a citizen to inform the citizen of the privilege. The citizen has the obligation to assert the privilege. See Minnesota v. Murphy, 465 U.S. 420, 427, 104 S.Ct. 1136, 1142, 79 L.Ed.2d 409, 418–19 (1984).

After determining that custodial interrogation of a citizen by police officers implicated interests of the citizen protected by the Fifth Amendment, the *Miranda* Court then proceeded to define the requirements of the Fifth Amendment in this context. Consider how the resulting "*Miranda* rights" differ from the demands of the voluntariness rule.

Subsequent judicial discussion and development of *Miranda* has sometimes emphasized the identification of "*per se*" rules. See, for example, North Carolina v. Butler, 441 U.S. 369, 374, 99 S.Ct. 1755, 1758, 60 L.Ed.2d 286, 293 (1979), rejecting a lower court's holding that *Miranda* created a *per se* rule that the suspect must make an explicit waiver of the right to counsel, and Justice Powell's comment in Oregon v. Bradshaw, 462 U.S. 1039, 1047, 103 S.Ct. 2830, 2836, 77 L.Ed.2d 405, 413 (1983) (Powell, J., concurring in the judgment), that members of the Court disagree as to whether Edwards v. Arizona, 451 U.S. 477, 101 S.Ct. 1880, 68 L.Ed.2d 378 (1981) (reprinted at page 484, infra), "announced a new *per se* rule." In *Bradshaw,* Justice Rehnquist described *Edwards* as setting out "in effect a prophylactic rule * * *." 462 U.S. at 1044, 103 S.Ct. at 2834, 77 L.Ed.2d at 411 (Rehnquist, J., announcing the judgment of the Court).

The precise meaning of these characterizations is not always clear. Perhaps, however, they are best considered as describing the relationship between a legal requirement and the exclusionary remedy. A *per se* requirement, then, may be one that, when violated, automatically demands the exclusion of any resulting evidence. Violation by police of other requirements, on the other hand, may not require exclusion of resulting evidence unless other considerations apply. In the *Miranda* context, for example, violation of some requirements announced in the *Miranda* decision or subsequent case law might require the exclusion of resulting evidence only if it rendered the suspect's waiver of the right to remain silent involuntary or otherwise ineffective.

Whatever the terminology used, it is important in identifying and understanding the *Miranda* rights to separate two matters. One, of course, is the contents of the requirements which the case law places upon law enforcement officers. The other, however, is the relationship between violation of these requirements and the admissibility of self-incriminating statements from the suspect and other evidence obtained as the result of such statements.

### MIRANDA v. ARIZONA

Supreme Court of the United States, 1966.

384 U.S. 436, 86 S.Ct. 1602, 16 L.Ed.2d 694.

MR. CHIEF JUSTICE WARREN delivered the opinion of the Court.

The cases before us raise questions which go to the roots of our concepts of American criminal jurisprudence: the restraints society must observe consistent with the Federal Constitution in prosecuting individuals for crime. More specifically, we deal with the admissibility of statements obtained from an individual who is subjected to custodial police interrogation and the necessity for procedures which assure that the individual is accorded his privilege under the Fifth Amendment to the Constitution not to be compelled to incriminate himself.

* * *

Our holding will be spelled out with some specificity in the pages which follow but briefly stated it is this: the prosecution may not use statements, whether exculpatory or inculpatory, stemming from custodial interrogation of the defendant unless it demonstrates the use of procedural safeguards effective to secure the privilege against self-incrimination. By custodial interrogation, we mean questioning initiated by law enforcement officers after a person has been taken into custody or otherwise deprived of his freedom of action in any significant way. As for the procedural safeguards to be employed, unless other fully effective means are devised to inform accused persons of their right of silence and to assure a continuous opportunity to exercise it, the following measures are required. Prior to any questioning, the person must be warned that he has a right to remain silent, that any statement he does make may be used as evidence against him, and that he has a right to the presence of an attorney, either retained or appointed. The defendant may waive effectuation of these rights, provided the waiver is made voluntarily, knowingly and intelligently. If, however, he indicates in any manner and at any stage of the process that he wishes to consult with an attorney before speaking there can be no questioning. Likewise, if the individual is alone and indicates in any manner that he does not wish to be interrogated, the police may not question him. The mere fact that he may have answered some questions or volunteered some statements on his own does not deprive him of the right to refrain from answering any further inquiries until he has consulted with an attorney and thereafter consents to be questioned.

## I.

The constitutional issue we decide in each of these cases is the admissibility of statements obtained from a defendant questioned while in custody or otherwise deprived of his freedom of action in any significant way. In each, the defendant was questioned by police officers, detectives, or a prosecuting attorney in a room in which he was cut off from the outside world. In none of these cases was the defendant given a full and effective warning of his rights at the outset of the interrogation process. In all the cases, the questioning elicited oral admissions, and in three of them, signed statements as well which were admitted at their trials. They all thus share salient features—incommunicado interrogation of individuals in a police-dominated atmosphere, resulting in self-incriminating statements without full warnings of constitutional rights.

An understanding of the nature and setting of this in-custody interrogation is essential to our decisions today. The difficulty in depicting what transpires at such interrogations stems from the fact that in this country they have largely taken place incommunicado. From extensive factual studies undertaken in the early 1930's, including the famous Wickersham Report to Congress by a Presidential Commission, it is clear that police violence and the "third degree" flourished at that time. In a series of cases decided by this Court long after these studies, the police resorted to physical brutality—beatings, hanging, whipping—and to sustained and protracted questioning incommunicado in order to extort confessions. The Commission on Civil Rights in 1961 found much evidence to indicate that "some policemen still resort to physical force to obtain confessions," 1961 Comm'n on Civil Rights Rep., Justice, pt. 5, 17. The use of physical brutality and violence is not, unfortunately, relegated to the past or to any part of the country. Only recently in Kings County, New York, the police brutally beat, kicked and placed lighted cigarette butts on the back of a potential witness under interrogation for the purpose of securing a statement incriminating a third party. People v. Portelli, 15 N.Y.2d 235, 257 N.Y.S.2d 931, 205 N.E.2d 857 (1965).

The examples given above are undoubtedly the exception now, but they are sufficiently widespread to be the object of concern. Unless a proper limitation upon custodial interrogation is achieved—such as these decisions will advance—there can be no assurance that practices of this nature will be eradicated in the foreseeable future.

\* \* \*

\* \* \* [T]he modern practice of in-custody interrogation is psychologically rather than physically oriented. As we have stated before, "Since Chambers v. State of Florida, 309 U.S. 227, 60 S.Ct. 472, 84 L.Ed. 716, this Court has recognized that coercion can be mental as well as physical, and that the blood of the accused is not the only hallmark of an unconstitutional inquisition." Blackburn v. State of Alabama, 361 U.S. 199, 206, 80 S.Ct. 274, 279, 4 L.Ed.2d 242 (1960). Interrogation still takes place in privacy. Privacy results in secrecy and this in turn results in a gap in our knowledge as to what in fact goes on in the interrogation rooms. A valuable source of information about present police practices, however, may be found in various police manuals and texts which document procedures employed with success in the past, and which recommend various other effective tactics. These texts are used by law enforcement agencies themselves as guides. It should be noted that these texts professedly present the most enlightened and effective means presently used to obtain statements through custodial interrogation. By considering these texts and other data, it is possible to describe procedures observed and noted around the country.

The officers are told by the manuals that the "principal psychological factor contributing to a successful interrogation is privacy—being alone with the person under interrogation." The efficacy of this tactic has been explained as follows:

"If at all practicable, the interrogation should take place in the investigator's office or at least in a room of his own choice. The subject should be deprived of every psychological advantage. In his own home he may be confident, indignant, or recalcitrant. He is more keenly aware of his rights and more reluctant to tell of his indiscretions or criminal behavior within the walls of his home. Moreover his family and other friends are nearby, their presence lending moral support. In his office, the investigator possesses all the advantages. The atmosphere suggests the invincibility of the forces of the law."

To highlight the isolation and unfamiliar surroundings, the manuals instruct the police to display an air of confidence in the suspect's guilt and from outward appearance to maintain only an interest in confirming certain details.  The guilt of the subject is to be posited as a fact.  The interrogator should direct his comments toward the reasons why the subject committed the act, rather than court failure by asking the subject whether he did it.  Like other men, perhaps the subject has had a bad family life, had an unhappy childhood, had too much to drink, had an unrequited desire for women.  The officers are instructed to minimize the moral seriousness of the offense, to cast blame on the victim or on society.  These tactics are designed to put the subject in a psychological state where his story is but an elaboration of what the police purport to know already—that he is guilty.  Explanations to the contrary are dismissed and discouraged.

The texts thus stress that the major qualities an interrogator should possess are patience and perseverance.  One writer describes the efficacy of these characteristics in this manner:

> "In the preceding paragraphs emphasis has been placed on kindness and stratagems.  The investigator will, however, encounter many situations where the sheer weight of his personality will be the deciding factor.  Where emotional appeals and tricks are employed to no avail, he must rely on an oppressive atmosphere of dogged persistence.  He must interrogate steadily and without relent, leaving the subject no prospect of surcease.  He must dominate his subject and overwhelm him with his inexorable will to obtain the truth.  He should interrogate for a spell of several hours pausing only for the subject's necessities in acknowledgment of the need to avoid a charge of duress that can be technically substantiated.  In a serious case, the interrogation may continue for days, with the required intervals for food and sleep, but with no respite from the atmosphere of domination.  It is possible in this way to induce the subject to talk without resorting to duress or coercion.  The method should be used only when the guilt of the subject appears highly probable."

The manuals suggest that the suspect be offered legal excuses for his actions in order to obtain an initial admission of guilt.  Where there is a suspected revenge-killing, for example, the interrogator may say:

> "Joe, you probably didn't go out looking for this fellow with the purpose of shooting him.  My guess is, however, that you expected something from him and that's why you carried a gun—for your own protection.  You knew him for what he was, no good.  Then when you met him he probably started using foul, abusive language and he gave some indication that he was about to pull a gun on you, and that's when you had to act to save your own life.  That's about it, isn't it, Joe?"

Having then obtained the admission of shooting, the interrogator is advised to refer to circumstantial evidence which negates the self-defense explanation.  This should enable him to secure the entire story.  One text notes that "Even if he fails to do so, the inconsistency between the subject's original denial of the shooting and his present admission of at least doing the shooting will serve to deprive him of a self-defense 'out' at the time of trial."

When the techniques described above prove unavailing, the texts recommend they be alternated with a show of some hostility.  One ploy often used has been termed the "friendly-unfriendly" or the "Mutt and Jeff" act:

> " *   *   * In this technique, two agents are employed.  Mutt, the relentless investigator, who knows the subject is guilty and is not going to waste any time.  He's sent a dozen men away for this crime and he's going to send the subject away for the full term. Jeff, on the other hand, is obviously a kindhearted man.  He has a family himself.  He has a brother who was involved in a little scrape like this.  He disapproves of Mutt and his tactics and will arrange to get him off the case if the subject will cooperate.  He can't hold Mutt off for very long.  The subject would be wise to make a quick decision.  The technique is applied by having both investigators present while Mutt acts out his role.  Jeff may stand by quietly and demur at some of Mutt's tactics.  When Jeff makes his plea for cooperation, Mutt is not present in the room."

The interrogators sometimes are instructed to induce a confession out of trickery.  The technique here is quite effective in crimes which require identification or which run in series.  In the identification situation, the interrogator may take a break in his questioning to place the subject among a group of men in a line-up.  "The witness or complainant (previously coached, if necessary) studies the line-up and confidently points out the subject as the guilty party."  Then the questioning resumes "as though there were now no doubt about the guilt of the subject."  A variation on this technique is called the "reverse line-up":

> "The accused is placed in a line-up, but this time he is identified by several fictitious witnesses or victims who associated him with different offenses.  It is expected that the subject will become desperate and confess to the offense under investigation in order to escape from the false accusations."

The manuals also contain instructions for police on how to handle the individual who refuses to discuss the matter entirely or who asks for an attorney or relatives.  The examiner is to concede him the right to remain silent.  "This usually has a very undermining effect.  First of all, he is disappointed in his expectation of an unfavorable reaction on the part of the interrogator.  Secondly, a concession of this right to remain silent impresses the subject with the apparent fairness of his interrogator."  After this psychological conditioning, however, the officer is told to point out the incriminating significance of the suspect's refusal to talk:

> "Joe, you have a right to remain silent.  That's your privilege and I'm the last person in the world who'll try to take it away from you. If that's the way you want to leave this, O. K.  But let me ask you this.  Suppose you were in my shoes and I were in yours and you

called me in to ask me about this and I told you, 'I don't want to answer any of your questions.' You'd think I had something to hide, and you'd probably be right in thinking that. That's exactly what I'll have to think about you, and so will everybody else. So let's sit here and talk this whole thing over."

Few will persist in their initial refusal to talk, it is said, if this monologue is employed correctly.

In the event that the subject wishes to speak to a relative or an attorney, the following advice is tendered:

"[T]he interrogator should respond by suggesting that the subject first tell the truth to the interrogator himself rather than get anyone else involved in the matter. If the request is for an attorney, the interrogator may suggest that the subject save himself or his family the expense of any such professional service, particularly if he is innocent of the offense under investigation. The interrogator may also add, 'Joe, I'm only looking for the truth, and if you're telling the truth, that's it. You can handle this by yourself.' "

From these representative samples of interrogation techniques, the setting prescribed by the manuals and observed in practice becomes clear. In essence, it is this: To be alone with the subject is essential to prevent distraction and to deprive him of any outside support. The aura of confidence in his guilt undermines his will to resist. He merely confirms the preconceived story the police seek to have him describe. Patience and persistence, at times relentless questioning, are employed. To obtain a confession, the interrogator must "patiently maneuver himself or his quarry into a position from which the desired objective may be attained." When normal procedures fail to produce the needed result, the police may resort to deceptive stratagems such as giving false legal advice. It is important to keep the subject off balance, for example, by trading on his insecurity about himself or his surroundings. The police then persuade, trick, or cajole him out of exercising his constitutional rights.

Even without employing brutality, the "third degree" or the specific stratagems described above, the very fact of custodial interrogation exacts a heavy toll on individual liberty and trades on the weakness of individuals. * * *

In the cases before us today * * * we might not find the defendants' statements to have been involuntary in traditional terms. Our concern for adequate safeguards to protect precious Fifth Amendment rights is, of course, not lessened in the slightest. In each of the cases, the defendant was thrust into an unfamiliar atmosphere and run through menacing police interrogation procedures. The potentiality for compulsion is forcefully apparent, for example, in *Miranda*, where the indigent Mexican defendant was a seriously disturbed individual with pronounced sexual fantasies * * *. To be sure, the records do not evince overt physical coercion or patent psychological ploys. The fact remains that in none of these cases did the officers undertake to afford appropriate safeguards at the outset of the interrogation to insure that the statements were truly the product of free choice.

It is obvious that such an interrogation environment is created for no purpose other than to subjugate the individual to the will of his examiner.  This atmosphere carries its own badge of intimidation.  To be sure, this is not physical intimidation, but it is equally destructive of human dignity.  The current practice of incommunicado interrogation is at odds with one of our Nation's most cherished principles—that the individual may not be compelled to incriminate himself.  Unless adequate protective devices are employed to dispel the compulsion inherent in custodial surroundings, no statement obtained from the defendant can truly be the product of his free choice.

From the foregoing, we can readily perceive an intimate connection between the privilege against self-incrimination and police custodial questioning.  It is fitting to turn to history and precedent underlying the Self-Incrimination Clause to determine its applicability in this situation.

## II.

\* \* \*

[W]e may view the historical development of the privilege as one which groped for the proper scope of governmental power over the citizen.  \* \* \*  [T]he constitutional foundation underlying the privilege is the respect a government—state or federal—must accord to the dignity and integrity of its citizens.  \* \* \*  [O]ur accusatory system of criminal justice demands that the government seeking to punish an individual produce the evidence against him by its own independent labors, rather than by the cruel, simple expedient of compelling it from his own mouth.  \* \* \*  In sum, the privilege is fulfilled only when the person is guaranteed the right "to remain silent until he chooses to speak in the unfettered exercise of his own will."  Malloy v. Hogan, 378 U.S. 1, 8, 84 S.Ct. 1489, 1493, 12 L.Ed.2d 653 (1964).

The question in these cases is whether the privilege is fully applicable during a period of custodial interrogation.  \* \* \*  We are satisfied that all the principles embodied in the privilege apply to informal compulsion exerted by law-enforcement officers during in-custody questioning.  An individual swept from familiar surroundings into police custody, surrounded by antagonistic forces, and subjected to the techniques of persuasion described above cannot be otherwise than under compulsion to speak.  As a practical matter, the compulsion to speak in the isolated setting of the police station may well be greater than in courts or other official investigations, where there are often impartial observers to guard against intimidation or trickery.

\* \* \*

## III.

Today, then, there can be no doubt that the Fifth Amendment privilege is available outside of criminal court proceedings and serves to protect persons in all settings in which their freedom of action is curtailed in any significant way from being compelled to incriminate themselves. We have concluded that without proper safeguards the process of in-custody interrogation of persons suspected or accused of crime contains inherently compelling pressures which work to undermine the individual's will to resist and to compel him to speak where he would not otherwise do so freely. In order to combat these pressures and to permit a full opportunity to exercise the privilege against self-incrimination, the accused must be adequately and effectively apprised of his rights and the exercise of those rights must be fully honored.

It is impossible for us to foresee the potential alternatives for protecting the privilege which might be devised by Congress or the States in the exercise of their creative rule-making capacities. Therefore we cannot say that the Constitution necessarily requires adherence to any particular solution for the inherent compulsions of the interrogation process as it is presently conducted. Our decision in no way creates a constitutional straitjacket which will handicap sound efforts at reform, nor is it intended to have this effect. We encourage Congress and the States to continue their laudable search for increasingly effective ways of protecting the rights of the individual while promoting efficient enforcement of our criminal laws. However, unless we are shown other procedures which are at least as effective in apprising accused persons of their right of silence and in assuring a continuous opportunity to exercise it, the following safeguards must be observed.

At the outset, if a person in custody is to be subjected to interrogation, he must first be informed in clear and unequivocal terms that he has the right to remain silent. For those unaware of the privilege, the warning is needed simply to make them aware of it—the threshold requirement for an intelligent decision as to its exercise. More important, such a warning is an absolute prerequisite in overcoming the inherent pressures of the interrogation atmosphere. It is not just the subnormal or woefully ignorant who succumb to an interrogator's imprecations, whether implied or expressly stated, that the interrogation will continue until a confession is obtained or that silence in the face of accusation is itself damning and will bode ill when presented to a jury. Further, the warning will show the individual that his interrogators are prepared to recognize his privilege should he choose to exercise it.

The Fifth Amendment privilege is so fundamental to our system of constitutional rule and the expedient of giving an adequate warning as to the availability of the privilege so simple, we will not pause to inquire in individual cases whether the defendant was aware of his rights without a warning being given. Assessments of the knowledge the defendant possessed, based on information as to his age, education, intelligence, or prior contact with authorities, can never be more than speculation; a warning is a clearcut fact. More important, whatever the background of the person interrogated, a warning at the time of the interrogation is indispensable to overcome its pressures and to insure that the individual knows he is free to exercise the privilege at that point in time.

The warning of the right to remain silent must be accompanied by the explanation that anything said can and will be used against the individual in court.   This warning is needed in order to make him aware not only of the privilege, but also of the consequences of forgoing it.   It is only through an awareness of these consequences that there can be any assurance of real understanding and intelligent exercise of the privilege.   Moreover, this warning may serve to make the individual more acutely aware that he is faced with a phase of the adversary system—that he is not in the presence of persons acting solely in his interest.

The circumstances surrounding in-custody interrogation can operate very quickly to overbear the will of one merely made aware of his privilege by his interrogators.   Therefore, the right to have counsel present at the interrogation is indispensable to the protection of the Fifth Amendment privilege under the system we delineate today.   Our aim is to assure that the individual's right to choose between silence and speech remains unfettered throughout the interrogation process. A once-stated warning, delivered by those who will conduct the interrogation, cannot itself suffice to that end among those who most require knowledge of their rights.   A mere warning given by the interrogators is not alone sufficient to accomplish that end.   Prosecutors themselves claim that the admonishment of the right to remain silent without more "will benefit only the recidivist and the professional."   Brief for the National District Attorneys Association as *amicus curiae*, p. 14. Even preliminary advice given to the accused by his own attorney can be swiftly overcome by the secret interrogation process.   *   *   *   Thus, the need for counsel to protect the Fifth Amendment privilege comprehends not merely a right to consult with counsel prior to questioning, but also to have counsel present during any questioning if the defendant so desires.

The presence of counsel at the interrogation may serve several significant subsidiary functions as well.   If the accused decides to talk to his interrogators, the assistance of counsel can mitigate the dangers of untrustworthiness.   With a lawyer present the likelihood that the police will practice coercion is reduced, and if coercion is nevertheless exercised the lawyer can testify to it in court.   The presence of a lawyer can also help to guarantee that the accused gives a fully accurate statement to the police and that the statement is rightly reported by the prosecution at trial.

An individual need not make a pre-interrogation request for a lawyer.   While such request affirmatively secures his right to have one, his failure to ask for a lawyer does not constitute a waiver.   No effective waiver of the right to counsel during interrogation can be recognized unless specifically made after the warnings we here delineate have been given.   The accused who does not know his rights and therefore does not make a request may be the person who most needs counsel.   *   *   *

Accordingly we hold that an individual held for interrogation must be clearly informed that he has the right to consult with a lawyer and to have the lawyer with him during interrogation under the system for protecting the privilege we delineate today. As with the warnings of the right to remain silent and that anything stated can be used in evidence against him, this warning is an absolute prerequisite to interrogation. No amount of circumstantial evidence that the person may have been aware of this right will suffice to stand in its stead. Only through such a warning is there ascertainable assurance that the accused was aware of this right.

If an individual indicates that he wishes the assistance of counsel before any interrogation occurs, the authorities cannot rationally ignore or deny his request on the basis that the individual does not have or cannot afford a retained attorney. The financial ability of the individual has no relationship to the scope of the rights involved here. The privilege against self-incrimination secured by the Constitution applies to all individuals. The need for counsel in order to protect the privilege exists for the indigent as well as the affluent. In fact, were we to limit these constitutional rights to those who can retain an attorney, our decisions today would be of little significance. The cases before us as well as the vast majority of confession cases with which we have dealt in the past involve those unable to retain counsel. While authorities are not required to relieve the accused of his poverty, they have the obligation not to take advantage of indigence in the administration of justice.   *   *   *

In order fully to apprise a person interrogated of the extent of his rights under this system then, it is necessary to warn him not only that he has the right to consult with an attorney, but also that if he is indigent a lawyer will be appointed to represent him. Without this additional warning, the admonition of the right to consult with counsel would often be understood as meaning only that he can consult with a lawyer if he has one or has the funds to obtain one. The warning of a right to counsel would be hollow if not couched in terms that would convey to the indigent—the person most often subjected to interrogation—the knowledge that he too has a right to have counsel present. As with the warnings of the right to remain silent and of the general right to counsel, only by effective and express explanation to the indigent of this right can there be assurance that he was truly in a position to exercise it.[2]

Once warnings have been given, the subsequent procedure is clear. If the individual indicates in any manner, at any time prior to or during questioning, that he wishes to remain silent, the interrogation must cease.[3] At this point he has shown that he intends to exercise his Fifth Amendment privilege; any statement taken after the person

---

[2] While a warning that the indigent may have counsel appointed need not be given to the person who is known to have an attorney or is known to have ample funds to secure one, the expedient of giving a warning is too simple and the rights involved too important to engage in *ex post facto* inquiries into financial ability when there is any doubt at all on that score.

[3] If an individual indicates his desire to remain silent, but has an attorney present, there may be some circumstances in which further questioning would be permissible. In the absence of evidence of overbearing, statements then made in the presence of counsel might be free of the compelling influence of the interrogation process and might fairly be construed as a waiver of

invokes his privilege cannot be other than the product of compulsion, subtle or otherwise. Without the right to cut off questioning, the setting of in-custody interrogation operates on the individual to overcome free choice in producing a statement after the privilege has been once invoked. If the individual states that he wants an attorney, the interrogation must cease until an attorney is present. At that time, the individual must have an opportunity to confer with the attorney and to have him present during any subsequent questioning. If the individual cannot obtain an attorney and he indicates that he wants one before speaking to police, they must respect his decision to remain silent.

This does not mean, as some have suggested, that each police station must have a "station house lawyer" present at all times to advise prisoners. It does mean, however, that if police propose to interrogate a person they must make known to him that he is entitled to a lawyer and that if he cannot afford one, a lawyer will be provided for him prior to any interrogation. If authorities conclude that they will not provide counsel during a reasonable period of time in which investigation in the field is carried out, they may refrain from doing so without violating the person's Fifth Amendment privilege so long as they do not question him during that time.

If the interrogation continues without the presence of an attorney and a statement is taken, a heavy burden rests on the government to demonstrate that the defendant knowingly and intelligently waived his privilege against self-incrimination and his right to retained or appointed counsel. * * * This Court has always set high standards of proof for the waiver of constitutional rights, Johnson v. Zerbst, 304 U.S. 458, 58 S.Ct. 1019, 82 L.Ed. 1461 (1938), and we reassert these standards as applied to in-custody interrogation. Since the State is responsible for establishing the isolated circumstances under which the interrogation takes place and has the only means of making available corroborated evidence of warnings given during incommunicado interrogation, the burden is rightly on its shoulders.

An express statement that the individual is willing to make a statement and does not want an attorney followed closely by a statement could constitute a waiver. But a valid waiver will not be presumed simply from the silence of the accused after warnings are given or simply from the fact that a confession was in fact eventually obtained. * * * Moreover, where in-custody interrogation is involved, there is no room for the contention that the privilege is waived if the individual answers some questions or gives some information on his own prior to invoking his right to remain silent when interrogated.

Whatever the testimony of the authorities as to waiver of rights by an accused, the fact of lengthy interrogation or incommunicado incarceration before a statement is made is strong evidence that the accused did not validly waive his rights. In these circumstances the fact that the individual eventually made a statement is consistent with the

the privilege for purposes of these statements.

conclusion that the compelling influence of the interrogation finally forced him to do so. It is inconsistent with any notion of a voluntary relinquishment of the privilege. Moreover, any evidence that the accused was threatened, tricked, or cajoled into a waiver will, of course, show that the defendant did not voluntarily waive his privilege. The requirement of warnings and waiver of rights is a fundamental with respect to the Fifth Amendment privilege and not simply a preliminary ritual to existing methods of interrogation.

The warnings required and the waiver necessary in accordance with our opinion today are, in the absence of a fully effective equivalent, prerequisites to the admissibility of any statement made by a defendant. No distinction can be drawn between statements which are direct confessions and statements which amount to "admissions" of part or all of an offense. The privilege against self-incrimination protects the individual from being compelled to incriminate himself in any manner; it does not distinguish degrees of incrimination. Similarly, for precisely the same reason, no distinction may be drawn between inculpatory statements and statements alleged to be merely "exculpatory." If a statement made were in fact truly exculpatory it would, of course, never be used by the prosecution. In fact, statements merely intended to be exculpatory by the defendant are often used to impeach his testimony at trial or to demonstrate untruths in the statement given under interrogation and thus to prove guilt by implication. These statements are incriminating in any meaningful sense of the word and may not be used without the full warnings and effective waiver required for any other statement. In *Escobedo* itself, the defendant fully intended his accusation of another as the slayer to be exculpatory as to himself.

The principles announced today deal with the protection which must be given to the privilege against self-incrimination when the individual is first subjected to police interrogation while in custody at the station or otherwise deprived of his freedom of action in any significant way. It is at this point that our adversary system of criminal proceedings commences, distinguishing itself at the outset from the inquisitorial system recognized in some countries. Under the system of warnings we delineate today or under any other system which may be devised and found effective, the safeguards to be erected about the privilege must come into play at this point.

Our decision is not intended to hamper the traditional function of police officers in investigating crime. When an individual is in custody on probable cause, the police may, of course, seek out evidence in the field to be used at trial against him. Such investigation may include inquiry of persons not under restraint. General on-the-scene questioning as to facts surrounding a crime or other general questioning of citizens in the fact-finding process is not affected by our holding. It is an act of responsible citizenship for individuals to give whatever information they may have to aid in law enforcement. In such situations the compelling atmosphere inherent in the process of in-custody interrogation is not necessarily present.

In dealing with statements obtained through interrogation, we do not purport to find all confessions inadmissible. Confessions remain a proper element in law enforcement. Any statement given freely and voluntarily without any compelling influences is, of course, admissible in evidence. The fundamental import of the privilege while an individual is in custody is not whether he is allowed to talk to the police without the benefit of warnings and counsel, but whether he can be interrogated. There is no requirement that police stop a person who enters a police station and states that he wishes to confess to a crime, or a person who calls the police to offer a confession or any other statement he desires to make. Volunteered statements of any kind are not barred by the Fifth Amendment and their admissibility is not affected by our holding today.

*     *     *

## V.

Because of the nature of the problem and because of its recurrent significance in numerous cases, we have to this point discussed the relationship of the Fifth Amendment privilege to police interrogation without specific concentration on the facts of the cases before us. We turn now to these facts to consider the application to these cases of the constitutional principles discussed above. In each instance, we have concluded that statements were obtained from the defendant under circumstances that did not meet constitutional standards for protection of the privilege.

### No. 759.  *Miranda v. Arizona*

On March 13, 1963, petitioner, Ernesto Miranda, was arrested at his home and taken in custody to a Phoenix police station. He was there identified by the complaining witness. The police then took him to "Interrogation Room No. 2" of the detective bureau. There he was questioned by two police officers. The officers admitted at trial that Miranda was not advised that he had a right to have an attorney present. Two hours later, the officers emerged from the interrogation room with a written confession signed by Miranda. At the top of the statement was a typed paragraph stating that the confession was made voluntarily, without threats or promises of immunity and "with full knowledge of my legal rights, understanding any statement I make may be used against me."

At his trial before a jury, the written confession was admitted into evidence over the objection of defense counsel, and the officers testified to the prior oral confession made by Miranda during the interrogation. Miranda was found guilty of kidnapping and rape. He was sentenced to 20 to 30 years' imprisonment on each count, the sentences to run concurrently. On appeal, the Supreme Court of Arizona held that Miranda's constitutional rights were not violated in obtaining the confession and affirmed the conviction. 98 Ariz. 18, 401 P.2d 721. In reaching its decision, the court emphasized heavily the fact that Miranda did not specifically request counsel.

We reverse.  From the testimony of the officers and by the admission of respondent, it is clear that Miranda was not in any way apprised of his right to consult with an attorney and to have one present during the interrogation, nor was his right not to be compelled to incriminate himself effectively protected in any other manner.  Without these warnings the statements were inadmissible.  The mere fact that he signed a statement which contained a typed-in clause stating that he had "full knowledge" of his "legal rights" does not approach the knowing and intelligent waiver required to relinquish constitutional rights.

\* \* \*

[The Court's discussion of the facts of the other cases is omitted. Editors.]

Judgment of Supreme Court of California in No. 584 affirmed.

MR. JUSTICE CLARK, dissenting in Nos. 759, 760, and 761, and concurring in the result in No. 584.

\* \* \* Since there is at this time a paucity of information and an almost total lack of empirical knowledge on the practical operation of requirements truly comparable to those announced by the majority, I would be more restrained lest we go too far too fast.

\* \* \*

Custodial interrogation has long been recognized as "undoubtedly an essential tool in effective law enforcement."  Haynes v. State of Washington, 373 U.S. 503, 515, 83 S.Ct. 1336, 1344, 10 L.Ed.2d 513 (1963).  Recognition of this fact should put us on guard against the promulgation of doctrinaire rules.  \* \* \*

The rule prior to today—as Mr. Justice Goldberg, the author of the Court's opinion in *Escobedo*, stated it in Haynes v. Washington— depended upon "a totality of circumstances evidencing an involuntary \* \* \* admission of guilt."  373 U.S. at 514, 83 S.Ct. at 1343.  \* \* \*

\* \* \*

I would continue to follow that rule.  Under the "totality of circumstances" rule of which my Brother Goldberg spoke in *Haynes*, I would consider in each case whether the police officer prior to custodial interrogation added the warning that the suspect might have counsel present at the interrogation, and further, that a court would appoint one at his request if he was too poor to employ counsel.  In the absence of warnings, the burden would be on the State to prove that counsel was knowingly and intelligently waived or that in the totality of the circumstances, including the failure to give the necessary warnings, the confession was clearly voluntary.

Rather than employing the arbitrary Fifth Amendment rule which the Court lays down I would follow the more pliable dictates of Due Process Clauses of the Fifth and Fourteenth Amendments which we are accustomed to administering and which we know from our cases are effective instruments in protecting persons in police custody.  In this way we would not be acting in the dark nor in one full sweep changing the traditional rules of custodial interrogation which this Court has for so long recognized as a justifiable and proper tool in balancing individual rights against the rights of society. It will be soon enough to go further when we are able to appraise with somewhat better accuracy the effect of such a holding.

*   *   *

[The dissenting opinions of Justice Harlan, with whom Justices Stewart and White joined, and of Justice White, with whom Justices Harlan and Stewart joined, are omitted.]

NOTES

1. How much deviation from the language used by the majority in *Miranda* is permissible in giving suspects the *Miranda* warnings? In California v. Prysock, 453 U.S. 355, 101 S.Ct. 2806, 69 L.Ed.2d 696 (1981) (per curiam) the sixteen year old suspect was warned and questioned in the presence of his mother. The officer first told Prysock that "you have the right to remain silent," that "if you give up your right to remain silent, anything you say can and will be used as evidence against you in a court of law," and that "you have the right to talk to a lawyer before you are questioned, have him present with you while you are being questioned, and all during the questioning." He was also told, "you have the right to have a lawyer appointed to represent you at no cost to yourself." This was all tape recorded. There was then a brief off-the-record discussion between the suspect's mother and the officer. The officer later testified that in this discussion, the mother asked if a lawyer would be available later if the suspect did not request one at this time. According to the officer, he responded to this by saying:

> That he would have an attorney when he went to Court. And that he could have one at this time if he wished one. He could terminate the statement at any time he so desired.

Following the warnings, Prysock consented to questioning without an attorney and admitted the killing. This confession was later used against him in his trial for murder, and he was convicted. On appeal, however, the intermediate California appellate court (in an unreported opinion) reversed. Emphasizing its view that the rigidity of the *Miranda* requirements affords police clear guidance, the court held that Prysock had not been adequately informed that the services of a free attorney were available to him prior to the impending questioning. The Supreme Court reversed. Reading the state appellate court's decision as establishing "a flat rule that the content of *Miranda* warnings be a virtual incantation of the precise language contained in the *Miranda* opinion" and as holding that the warnings here were defective because of the order in which they were given, the majority stressed that "no talismanic incantation" is required to satisfy *Miranda*. The warnings given Prysock conveyed to him that he had a right to an appointed attorney prior to and during questioning. The Court stressed, however, that the warnings might well be inadequate if the reference to the right to counsel was linked with some future point in time after the police interrogation. United States v. Garcia, 431 F.2d 134 (9th Cir. 1970), holding inadequate a statement to the defendant that she could "have an attorney appointed to represent you when you first appear before the U.S. Commissioner or the Court," was cited with apparent approval. 453 U.S. at 360, 101 S.Ct. at 2810, 59 L.Ed.2d at 701–02. Justice Stevens, joined by Justices Marshall and Brennan, dissented. He argued that the warning was sufficiently ambigious to provide adequate support for what he read as the California court's holding that the warning did not convey to Prysock that he had a right to the services of a free lawyer before questioning. The state court's conclusion, he urged, "is at least reasonable, and is clearly not so patently erroneous as to warrant summary reversal." 453 U.S. at 364, 101 S.Ct. at 2812, 69 L.Ed. 2d at 704.

2. In Duckworth v. Eagan, ___ U.S. ___, 109 S.Ct. 2875, 106 L.Ed.2d 166 (1989), Eagan had been given warnings that, in regard to the right to counsel, included:

> You have a right to talk to a lawyer for advice before we ask you any questions, and to have him with you during questioning. You have this right to the advice and presence of a lawyer even if you cannot afford to hire one. We have no way of giving you a lawyer, but one will be appointed for you, if you wish, if and when you go to court. If you wish to answer questions now without a lawyer present, you have the right to stop answering questions at any time. You also have the right to stop answering at any time until you've talked to a lawyer.

By a 5-to-4 vote, the Supreme Court held that this complied with *Miranda*. Chief Justice Rehnquist wrote for the Court rejecting Eagan's argument that the "if and when you go to court" phrase rendered the warning confusing and insufficient:

> First, this instruction accurately described the procedure for the appointment of counsel in Indiana. Under Indiana law, counsel is appointed at the defendant's initial appearance in court, and formal charges must be filed at or before that hearing. We think it must be relatively commonplace for a suspect, after receiving *Miranda* warnings, to ask when he will obtain counsel. The "if and and when you go to court" advice simply anticipates that question. Second, *Miranda* does not require that attorneys be producible on call, but only that the suspect be informed, as here, that he has the right to an attorney before and during questioning, and that an attorney would be appointed for him if he could not afford one. The Court in *Miranda* emphasized that it was not suggesting that "each police station must have a 'station house lawyer' present at all times to advise prisoners." If the police cannot provide appointed counsel, *Miranda* requires only that the police not question a suspect unless he waives his right to counsel. Here, [Eagan] did just that.

___ U.S. at ___, 109 S.Ct. at 2880, 106 L.Ed.2d at 177–78. Justice Marshall, speaking for the four dissenters, disagreed:

> In concluding that the first warning given to respondent Eagan * * * satisfies the dictates of *Miranda,* the majority makes a mockery of that decision. Eagan was initially advised that he had the right to the presence of counsel before and during questioning. But in the very next breath, the police informed Eagan that, if he could not afford a lawyer, one would be appointed to represent him only "if and when" he went to court. As the Court of Appeals found, Eagan could easily have concluded from the "if and when" caveat that only "those accused who can afford an attorney have the right to have one present before answering any questions; those who are not so fortunate must wait." 843 F.2d 1554, 1557 (CA7 1988). Eagan was, after all, never told that questioning would be delayed until a lawyer was appointed "if and when" Eagan did, in fact, go to court. Thus, the "if and when" caveat may well have had the effect of negating the initial promise that counsel could be present. At best, a suspect like Eagan "would not know * * * whether or not he had a right to the services of a lawyer." Emler v. State, 286 N.E.2d 408, 412 (Ind.1972) (DeBruler, J., dissenting).
>
> In lawyer-like fashion, the Chief Justice parses the initial warnings given Eagan and finds that the most plausible interpretation is that Eagan would not be questioned until a lawyer was appointed when he later

appeared in court. What goes wholly overlooked in the Chief Justice's analysis is that the recipients of police warnings are often frightened suspects unlettered in the law, not lawyers or judges or others schooled in interpreting legal or semantic nuance. Such suspects can hardly be expected to interpret, in as facile a manner as the Chief Justice, "the pretzel-like warnings here—intertwining, contradictory, and ambiguous as they are." Commonwealth v. Johnson, 484 Pa. 349, 356, 399 A.2d 111, 115 (Pa.1979).

___ U.S. at ___, 109 S.Ct. at 2886–87, 106 L.Ed.2d at 185–86 (Marshall, J. dissenting). Even a suspect who understood the warning as the Chief Justice read it, Justice Marshall continued, might well believe that "go[ing] to court" meant trial and thus that no appointed lawyer would be available until then. Moreover, he argued, perceiving counsel as available only after significant delay might itself be coercive:

> [T]he negative implication of the caveat is that, if the suspect is never taken to court, he "is not entitled to an attorney at all." 843 F.2d, at 1557. An unwitting suspect harboring uncertainty on this score is precisely the sort of person who may feel compelled to talk "voluntarily" to the police, without the presence of counsel, in an effort to extricate himself from his predicament: "[The suspect] is effectively told that he can talk now or remain in custody—in an alien, friendless, harsh world—for an indeterminate length of time. To the average accused, still hoping at this stage to be home on time for dinner or to make it to work on time, the implication that his choice is to answer questions right away or remain in custody until that nebulous time "if and when" he goes to court is a coerced choice of the most obvious kind." Dickerson v. State, 276 N.E.2d 845, 852 (Ind.1972) (DeBruler, J., concurring in result) ∗ ∗ ∗ *Miranda*, it is true, does not require the police to have a "station house lawyer" ready at all times to counsel suspects taken into custody. But if a suspect does not understand that a lawyer will be made available within a reasonable period of time after he has been taken into custody and advised of his rights, the suspect may decide to talk to the police *for that reason alone*. The threat of an indefinite deferral of interrogation, in a system like Indiana's, thus constitutes an effective means by which the police can pressure a suspect to speak without the presence of counsel. Sanctioning such police practices simply because the warnings given do not misrepresent state law does nothing more than let the state-law tail wag the federal constitutional dog.

___ U.S. at ___, 109 S.Ct. at 2887–88, 106 L.Ed.2d at 186–87.

3. The "impeachment exception" to many exclusionary sanctions, see pages 59–61, supra, has been applied to confessions in a manner which requires distinguishing between the requirements of *Miranda* and other prerequisites to the admissibility of a confession. In Harris v. New York, 401 U.S. 222, 91 S.Ct. 643, 28 L.Ed.2d 1 (1971), the majority acknowledged language in *Miranda* that could be read as barring the use of a confession obtained in violation of *Miranda* for any purpose. Nevertheless, the Court held that a statement obtained after a warning which failed to inform the defendant of his right to appointed counsel could be used to impeach the defendant when he took the stand at trial and testified in a manner inconsistent with the statement. "[T]he trustworthiness of the evidence satisfies legal standards," the majority commented, and the confession would undoubtedly aid the jury in evaluating the defendant's credibility as well as determining whether he perjured himself during the testimony. Turning to the need to exclude such confessions as a means of deterring violation of the *Miranda* requirements, the majority concluded that "sufficient deterrence flows when the evidence in question is made

unavailable to the prosecution in its case in chief." 401 U.S. at 225, 91 S.Ct. at 645, 28 L.Ed.2d at 4.

In Oregon v. Hass, 420 U.S. 714, 95 S.Ct. 1215, 43 L.Ed.2d 570 (1975), Hass had been arrested and given complete *Miranda* warnings. After he indicated that he would like to telephone a lawyer, however, the officer continued to interrogate him without the presence of counsel; an incriminating statement resulted, and was used for impeachment at trial after Hass took the stand and testified to facts contrary to those contained in the confession. The Supreme Court affirmed Hass' conviction. The dissent urged that the case was distinguishable from *Harris*:

> [A]fter *Harris*, police had some incentive for following *Miranda* by warning an accused of his right to remain silent and his right to counsel. If the warnings were given, the accused might still make a statement which could be used in the prosecution's case in chief. [But where the warnings are given and the suspect indicates a desire for counsel], police have almost no incentive for following *Miranda's* requirement that "[i]f the individual states that he wants an attorney, the interrogation must cease until an attorney is present." * * * If the requirement is followed there will almost surely be no statement since the attorney will advise the accused to remain silent. If, however, the requirement is disobeyed, the police may obtain a statement which can be used for impeachment if the accused has the temerity to testify in his own defense.

420 U.S. at 725, 95 S.Ct. at 1222, 43 L.Ed.2d at 579 (Brennan, J., dissenting). Thus the need to exclude the confession to encourage compliance with *Miranda* was greater in the case before the Court than it had been in *Harris*. The majority, however, characterized the possibility of an officer proceeding on the basis suggested by the dissent as "speculative." "If, in a given case," it concluded, "the officer's conduct amounts to an abuse, that case, like those involving coercion or duress, may be taken care of when it arises measured by the traditional standards for evaluating voluntariness and trustworthiness." 420 U.S. at 723, 95 S.Ct. at 1221, 43 L.Ed.2d at 578.

Mincey v. Arizona, 437 U.S. 385, 98 S.Ct. 2408, 57 L.Ed.2d 290 (1978), involved a significantly different situation. Mincey had been seriously injured in a gun battle and was in a hospital intensive care unit. Because of a tube in his mouth, he was unable to speak, but could communicate by writing answers to questions on pieces of paper. A detective visited Mincey in the hospital, informed him that he was under arrest for the murder of a police officer, and gave him full *Miranda* warnings. He then proceeded to question Mincey, although he temporarily ceased several times when Mincey lost consciousness or received treatment. Several times during the four-hour period Mincey asked that the questioning stop until he could obtain representation, but the detective continued to question him. A nurse who was present "suggested" that it would be "best" if Mincey answered the detective's questions. At trial Mincey testified in his own behalf; the trial court held that his statements given during the interrogation were inadmissible as part of the state's case-in-chief but, relying on *Harris* and *Hass*, permitted them to be used for impeachment. Mincey was convicted; the Supreme Court reversed. Mincey's statements were not, the Court concluded, the result of his free and rational choice and therefore were involuntary. And *any* use of involuntary statements against a defendant constitutes a denial of due process, apparently because such statements—unlike the statements at issue in *Harris* and *Hass*—do not satisfy legal standards of trustworthiness. 437 U.S. at 397–98, 98 S.Ct. at 2416, 57 L.Ed.2d at 303.

4. A defendant's silence under circumstances in which a reasonable, innocent person would have denied guilt is, generally speaking, admissible to

prove the defendant's guilt as a "tacit" confession. See McCormick, Evidence § 160 (3rd ed. 1984). *Miranda*, however, imposes some limitations upon the admissibility of such silence. In Doyle v. Ohio, 426 U.S. 610, 96 S.Ct. 2240, 49 L.Ed.2d 91 (1976), Doyle was charged with sale of marijuana based on a transaction arranged by one Bonnell, a police informant. None of the narcotics agents who had the transaction under surveillance actually saw the alleged transfer of the marijuana from Doyle to Bonnell. At trial, Doyle took the stand and testified that the arrangement had actually been for Bonnell to sell marijuana to Doyle. On cross examination, the prosecution elicited Doyle's admission that after being arrested and given the *Miranda* warnings he had not told this version of the incident to the arresting officers. Reversing Doyle's conviction, the Supreme Court held that silence after being given the *Miranda* warnings could not be used even for impeachment:

> Silence in the wake of [the *Miranda*] warnings may be nothing more than the arrestee's exercise of these *Miranda* rights. Thus, every post-arrest silence is insolubly ambiguous because of what the State is required to advise the person arrested. * * * Moreover, while it is true that the *Miranda* warnings contain no express assurance that silence will carry no penalty, such assurance is implicit to any person who receives the warnings. In such circumstances, it would be fundamentally unfair and a deprivation of due process to allow the arrested person's silence to be used to impeach an explanation subsequently offered at trial.

426 U.S. at 617–18, 96 S.Ct. at 2244–45, 49 L.Ed.2d at 97–98.

But in Fletcher v. Weir, 455 U.S. 603, 102 S.Ct. 1309, 71 L.Ed.2d 490 (1982) (per curiam), the Court found no federal constitutional barrier to the use of a defendant's silence after arrest but before *Miranda* warnings, at least where the silence was used to impeach the defendant after he took the witness stand at trial and testified to an exculpatory version of the events. *Doyle* was characterized as resting not upon the ambiguity of suspects' silence but rather upon the fundamental unfairness of using silence against defendants after they have received governmental assurances that there is a right to remain silent. Where the *Miranda* warnings have not been given, the Court reasoned, no such assurances have been given and there is no unfairness in using the defendants' silence. Whether in such situations a defendant's silence is a sufficiently reliable indicator that the defendant has lied during his direct examination, the Court commented, is a decision each State is entitled to make as a matter of State evidence law policy.

In South Dakota v. Neville, 459 U.S. 553, 103 S.Ct. 916, 74 L.Ed.2d 748 (1983), the prosecution used at trial testimony concerning the defendant's refusal to submit to a blood-alcohol test. After finding no self-incrimination problem, the Court turned to the defendant's argument that use of his refusal was impermissible under *Doyle* because he had not been fully warned of the consequences of his refusal, that is, he had not been told that his refusal could itself be used in evidence against him. The officers had told Neville that if he took the test he had a right to know the results and to have an additional test administered by a person chosen by him. They also told him that if he refused the test, he might lose his driver's license; no further explanation as to the effect of refusal was offered. Rejecting Neville's argument, the Court explained:

> [W]e think it unrealistic to say that the warnings given here implicitly assure a suspect that no consequences other than those mentioned will occur. Importantly, the warning that he could lose his driver's license

made it clear that refusing the test was not a "safe harbor," free of adverse consequences.

459 U.S. at 565, 103 S.Ct. at 924, 74 L.Ed.2d at 760.

No federal constitutional bar exists to the use of prearrest silence to impeach a testifying defendant. Jenkins v. Anderson, 447 U.S. 231, 100 S.Ct. 2124, 65 L.Ed.2d 86 (1980). Nor does *Miranda* bar questioning of a testifying defendant concerning inconsistent statements made after arrest and receipt of *Miranda* warnings. Such a defendant has chosen to speak rather than remain silent so there is no impermissible use of silence as prohibited by *Doyle*. Anderson v. Charles, 447 U.S. 404, 100 S.Ct. 2180, 65 L.Ed.2d 222 (1980) (per curiam).

In Wainwright v. Greenfield, 474 U.S. 284, 106 S.Ct. 634, 88 L.Ed.2d 623 (1986), Greenfield was tried for sexual battery; he asserted a defense of insanity. In its case in chief, the State was permitted to introduce evidence that after his arrest, Greenfield was given his *Miranda* warnings and then stated that he understood his rights and wished to talk with a lawyer before making any statement. This, the prosecution argued, showed "a degree of comprehension" on his part inconsistent with insanity. A majority of the Supreme Court held that *Doyle* was violated. Given the promise in the *Miranda* warnings, it reasoned, use of silence to overcome a defendant's claim of insanity is as unfair as the use of silence in *Doyle*. 474 U.S. at 292, 106 S.Ct. at 639, 88 L.Ed.2d at 631. Justice Rehnquist, joined by the Chief Justice, disagreed. The case involved not silence, he urged, but an affirmative request for a lawyer, which was quite probative with regard to Greenfield's sanity. No *Doyle* unfairness was caused by the use of Greenfield's silence, he continued, because the "promise" of the *Miranda* warnings refers only to silence. It does not indicate that words affirmatively used by the suspect in responding to the notice of the right to representation will not be used by the State. 474 U.S. at 298, 106 S.Ct. at 642, 88 L.Ed.2d at 634 (Rehnquist, J., concurring in the result). He joined the majority's result, however, because the prosecutor had, in addition to using Greenfield's affirmative response to the *Miranda* warnings, also relied upon Greenfield's failure to make a statement after consulting with an attorney. 474 U.S. at 300–01, 106 S.Ct. at 643, 88 L.Ed.2d at 636.

## 2. APPLICABILITY OF *MIRANDA*

### EDITORS' INTRODUCTION: "THRESHOLD" ISSUES

The *Miranda* opinion itself made clear that the requirements established by the case did not apply to all out-of-court confessions or statements by defendants. When those demands have to be met, however, has become the subject of extensive post-*Miranda* litigation.

In Orozco v. Texas, 394 U.S. 324, 89 S.Ct. 1095, 22 L.Ed.2d 311 (1969), four officers were admitted to the bedroom where Orozco was sleeping. They awoke, arrested, and questioned him. Urging that *Miranda* did not apply, the state argued that the requirements should be limited to stationhouse interrogation or at least not applied to questioning conducted in surroundings familiar to the suspect. A majority of the Court rejected this and held *Miranda* applicable. The decision in *Miranda* that the warnings there set out were required before custodial interrogation "was reached after careful considera-tion," it reasoned, and "there is no need to canvass those arguments again." 394 U.S. at 327, 89 S.Ct. at 1097, 22 L.Ed.2d at 315.

Eight years later, in Oregon v. Mathiason, 429 U.S. 492, 97 S.Ct. 711, 50 L.Ed.2d 714 (1977) (per curiam), the suspect had responded to a request that he appear at the state patrol office and was questioned there. The state court held that because the questioning took place in a "coercive environment," *Miranda* applied. Finding that the suspect was not "in custody," the Supreme Court reversed. "[A] noncustodial situation is not converted to one in which *Miranda* applies," the majority explained, "simply because a reviewing court concludes that * * * the questioning took place in a 'coercive environment.'" 429 U.S. at 495, 97 S.Ct. at 714, 50 L.Ed.2d at 719.

*Orozco* and *Mathiason* confirm that the Court adheres to the position that *Miranda* applies only when the self-incriminating statement was the result of custodial interrogation. The Court's insistence upon these two requirements seems motivated in part by a majority's belief that the requirements provide adequate guidance for law enforcement officers concerning the need to comply with the *Miranda* requirements. This section addresses the content of the requirements of "custody" and "interrogation." Consider after covering this material whether the requirements do in fact adequately inform officers as to when they need to comply with *Miranda*.

It is also clear, however, that *Miranda* does not apply in at least some situations in which there is both custody and interrogation. A "public safety" exception to the *Miranda* requirements was adopted and applied in New York v. Quarles, 467 U.S. 649, 104 S.Ct. 2626, 81 L.Ed.2d 550 (1984). A woman approached two New York police officers and reported that she had just been raped by a man who entered a nearby supermarket and who was carrying a gun. Upon arrival at the supermarket, one officer (Kraft) entered the store and the other radioed for assistance. Officer Kraft quickly observed Quarles, who met the description given by the woman. Apparently upon seeing Officer Kraft, Quarles ran towards the rear of the store. Kraft drew his weapon and pursued Quarles. Although he lost sight of Quarles for several seconds, Officer Kraft soon saw him again and ordered Quarles to stop and place his hands over his head. Several other officers had since arrived. Kraft approached Quarles and upon frisking him discovered that he was wearing an empty shoulder holster. Quarles was handcuffed. Kraft then, without providing any *Miranda* warnings, asked Quarles where the gun was. Quarles responded by nodding in the direction of some empty cartons and saying, "The gun is over there." Kraft searched the area and found a loaded .38 caliber revolver. Quarles was then warned under *Miranda* and agreed to answer questions without an attorney present. In response to questions by Kraft, Quarles admitted ownership of the gun and explained how he had acquired it. The revolver, his pre-warning statement, "The gun is over there," and his post-warning admissions were all offered in his prosecution for criminal possession of a weapon. Both the gun and the pre-warning statement were excluded because of Officer Kraft's failure to comply with *Miranda* before asking about the gun's location; the post-warning admissions were excluded as tainted by the preceding *Miranda* violation.

By a five-to-four vote, the Supreme Court reversed. *Miranda* had not been violated, it held, because Officer Kraft's actions came within a "narrow exception" to *Miranda* for situations in which the officer's question is prompted by concern for the public safety. This exception, Justice Rehnquist explained for the Court, is consistent with the rationale for *Miranda*. Where the only "cost" of the pre-interrogation procedures at issue in *Miranda* is the possibility of fewer convictions, this cost is acceptable given the value of the procedures in protecting the underlying right to be free from compelled self-incrimination. But where in addition these procedures pose an immediate risk to the public safety, the cost becomes unacceptably high:

> We decline to place officers such as Officer Kraft in the untenable position of having to consider, often in a matter of seconds, whether it best serves society for them to ask the necessary questions without the *Miranda* warnings and render whatever probative evidence they uncover inadmissible, or for them to give the warnings in order to preserve the admissibility of evidence they might uncover but possibly damage or destroy their ability to obtain that evidence and neutralize the volatile situation confronting them.

467 U.S. at 657–58, 104 S.Ct. at 2632, 81 L.Ed.2d at 558. On the facts before it, the Court found sufficient risk to the public safety. Officer Kraft had reason to believe that the gun was somewhere in the store, where it might be retrieved by an accomplice of Quarles or come upon by a store employee or customer.

The state court had declined to apply a public safety exception because of its perception that there was no indication that Officer Kraft was actually motivated by a desire to protect himself or the public. This, the Court reasoned, was not controlling:

> [T]he availability of the exception does not depend upon the motivation of the individual officer involved. In a kaleidoscopic situation such as the one confronting these officers, where spontaneity rather than adherence to a police manual is necessarily the order of the day, the application of the exception * * * should not be made to depend on *post hoc* findings at a suppression hearing concerning the subjective motivation of the arresting officer.

467 U.S. at 656, 104 S.Ct. at 2631, 81 L.Ed.2d at 557.

The Court observed that it had been presented with no claim that Quarles' pre-warning statement was "actually compelled by police conduct which overcame his will to resist." Quarles was free to argue on remand that his statement was "coerced under traditional due process standards." The Court's holding, Justice Rehnquist emphasized, was not a rejection of this argument; "we merely reject the * * * argument * * * that the statement must be *presumed* compelled because of Officer Kraft's failure to read [Quarles] his *Miranda* warnings." 467 U.S. at 655 n. 5, 104 S.Ct. at 2631 n. 5, 81 L.Ed.2d at 556 n. 5 (emphasis in original).

Justice Marshall, joined by Justices Brennan and Stevens, dissented. The majority's public safety exception, he asserted, destroys *Miranda's* valuable clarity. Moreover, its effect is to permit the use of coerced confessions in violation of the Fifth Amendment. Officer Kraft's critical question was asked in the middle of the night at the rear of an empty supermarket when Quarles was surrounded by four armed officers; to contend that this questioning was not coercive "would strain credulity." Finally, he argued, no exception is necessary to accommodate the Fifth Amendment and public safety. Under *Miranda*, the Fifth Amendment simply prohibits use of the products of such questioning to prove the suspects' guilt. 467 U.S. at 686, 104 S.Ct. at 2648, 81 L.Ed.2d at 577 (Marshall, J., dissenting). Justice O'Connor also dissented from the majority's recognition of a public safety exception. Were the Court "writing from a clean slate," she commented, she would agree with its holding. "But *Miranda* is now the law and * * * the Court has not provided sufficient justification for departing from it or for blurring its now clear strictures." 467 U.S. at 660, 104 S.Ct. at 2634, 81 L.Ed.2d at 560 (O'Connor, J., concurring in part and dissenting in part).

A plurality of the Court recognized another exception in Pennsylvania v. Muniz, ___ U.S. ___, 110 S.Ct. 2638, 110 L.Ed.2d 528 (1990). After his arrest for drunk-driving, Muniz was taken to the stationhouse and, in the ensuing procedure, asked his name, address, height, weight, eye color, date of birth, and current age; this was videotaped, but no *Miranda* warnings were provided. Justice Brennan, writing for a plurality of four justices, explained:

> We agree with amicus United States * * * that Muniz's answers to these * * * questions are * * * admissible because the questions fall within a "routine booking question" exception which exempts from *Miranda's* coverage questions to secure the "biographical data necessary to complete booking or pretrial services." Brief for the United States as Amicus Curiae 12, quoting United States v. Horton, 873 F.2d 180, 181, n. 2 (CA8 1989). The state court found that the first seven questions were "requested for record-keeping purposes only," and therefore the questions appear reasonably related to the police's administrative concerns. In this context, therefore, the * * * questions * * * fall outside the protections of *Miranda* and the answers thereto need not be suppressed.

___ U.S. at ___, 110 S.Ct. at 2650, 110 L.Ed.2d at 552. He added:

> As amicus United States explains, "[r]ecognizing a 'booking exception' to *Miranda* does not mean, of course, that any question asked during the booking process falls within that exception. Without obtaining a waiver of the suspect's *Miranda* rights, the police may not ask questions, even during booking, that are designed to elicit incriminatory admissions." Brief for United States as Amicus Curiae 13.

___ U.S. at ___ n. 14, 110 S.Ct. at 2650 n. 14, 110 L.Ed.2d at 552 n. 14. Justice Marshall argued against such an exception:

> Such exceptions undermine *Miranda's* fundamental principle that the doctrine should be clear so that it can be easily applied by both police and courts. The plurality's position, were it adopted by a

majority of the Court, would necessitate difficult, time-consuming litigation over whether particular questions asked during booking are "routine," whether they are necessary to secure biographical information, whether that information is itself necessary for rec-ordkeeping purposes, and whether the questions are—despite their routine nature—designed to elicit incriminating testimony. The far better course would be to maintain the clarity of the doctrine by requiring police to preface all direct questioning of a suspect with *Miranda* warnings if they want his responses to be admissible at trial.

___ U.S. at ___, 110 S.Ct. at 2654–55, 110 L.Ed.2d at 557 (Marshall, J., dissenting). If such an exception is recognized, he continued, it should not apply to questions the police should know are reasonably likely to elicit incriminating responses. Officers should know that questions such as those asked in *Muniz* are reasonably likely to elicit an incrimi-nating response from an intoxicated subject and thus the plurality erred in finding its exception applicable here. ___ U.S. at ___, 110 S.Ct. at 2655, 110 L.Ed.2d at 558. Four members of the Court conclud-ed that the answers to the questions were not testimonial and therefore "it is unnecessry to determine whether the questions fall within the 'routine booking question' exception to *Miranda* Justice Brennan recog-nizes." ___ U.S. at ___, 110 S.Ct. at 2654, 110 L.Ed.2d at 556 (Rehn-quist, C.J., concurring in part, concurring in the result in part and dissenting in part).

### a.    THE REQUIREMENT OF "INTERROGATION"

Unless a suspect who is in custody is subjected to "interrogation," *Miranda* has no applicability. Thus when a statement is "volunteered" by a suspect, it is admissible despite the failure to comply with *Miranda* requirements.

### RHODE ISLAND v. INNIS

Supreme Court of the United States, 1980.
446 U.S. 291, 100 S.Ct. 1682, 64 L.Ed.2d 297.

MR. JUSTICE STEWART delivered the opinion of the Court.

In Miranda v. Arizona, 384 U.S. 436, 474, 86 S.Ct. 1602, 1627, 16 L.Ed.2d 694, the Court held that, once a defendant in custody asks to speak with a lawyer, all interrogation must cease until a lawyer is present. The issue in this case is whether the respondent was "interro-gated" in violation of the standards promulgated in the *Miranda* opinion.

I.

On the night of January 12, 1975, John Mulvaney, a Providence, R. I., taxicab driver, disappeared after being dispatched to pick up a customer. His body was discovered four days later buried in a shallow grave in Coventry, R. I. He had died from a shotgun blast aimed at the back of his head.

On January 17, 1975, shortly after midnight, the Providence police received a telephone call from Gerald Aubin, also a taxicab driver, who reported that he had just been robbed by a man wielding a sawed-off shotgun. Aubin further reported that he had dropped off his assailant near Rhode Island College in a section of Providence known as Mount Pleasant. While at the Providence police station waiting to give a statement, Aubin noticed a picture of his assailant on a bulletin board. Aubin so informed one of the police officers present. The officer prepared a photo array, and again Aubin identified a picture of the same person. That person was the respondent. Shortly thereafter, the Providence police began a search of the Mount Pleasant area.

At approximately 4:30 a. m. on the same date, Patrolman Lovell, while cruising the streets of Mount Pleasant in a patrol car, spotted the respondent standing in the street facing him. When Patrolman Lovell stopped his car, the respondent walked towards it. Patrolman Lovell then arrested the respondent, who was unarmed, and advised him of his so-called *Miranda* rights. While the two men waited in the patrol car for other police officers to arrive, Patrolman Lovell did not converse with the respondent other than to respond to the latter's request for a cigarette.

Within minutes, Sergeant Sears arrived at the scene of the arrest, and he also gave the respondent the *Miranda* warnings. Immediately thereafter, Captain Leyden and other police officers arrived. Captain Leyden advised the respondent of his *Miranda* rights. The respondent stated that he understood those rights and wanted to speak with a lawyer. Captain Leyden then directed that the respondent be placed in a "caged wagon," a four-door police car with a wire screen mesh between the front and rear seats, and be driven to the central police station. Three officers, Patrolmen Gleckman, Williams, and McKenna, were assigned to accompany the respondent to the central station. They placed the respondent in the vehicle and shut the doors. Captain Leyden then instructed the officers not to question the respondent or intimidate or coerce him in any way. The three officers then entered the vehicle, and it departed.

While enroute to the central station, Patrolman Gleckman initiated a conversation with Patrolman McKenna concerning the missing shotgun. As Patrolman Gleckman later testified:

> "A. At this point, I was talking back and forth with Patrolman McKenna stating that I frequent this area while on patrol and [that because a school for handicapped children is located nearby,] there's a lot of handicapped children running around in this area, and God forbid one of them might find a weapon with shells and they might hurt themselves." App., at 43–44.

Patrolman McKenna apparently shared his fellow officer's concern:

> "A. I more or less concurred with him [Gleckman] that it was a safety factor and that we should, you know, continue to search for the weapon and try to find it." Id., at 53.

While Patrolman Williams said nothing, he overheard the conversation between the two officers:

"A.  He [Gleckman] said it would be too bad if the little—I believe he said girl—would pick up the gun, maybe kill herself." Id., at 59.

The respondent then interrupted the conversation, stating that the officers should turn the car around so he could show them where the gun was located.  At this point, Patrolman McKenna radioed back to Captain Leyden that they were returning to the scene of the arrest, and that the respondent would inform them of the location of the gun.  At the time the respondent indicated that the officers should turn back, they had traveled no more than a mile, a trip encompassing only a few minutes.

The police vehicle then returned to the scene of the arrest where a search for the shotgun was in progress.  There, Captain Leyden again advised the respondent of his *Miranda* rights.  The respondent replied that he understood those rights but that he "wanted to get the gun out of the way because of the kids in the area in the school."  The respondent then led the police to a nearby field, where he pointed out the shotgun under some rocks by the side of the road.

On March 20, 1975, a grand jury returned an indictment charging the respondent with the kidnapping, robbery, and murder of John Mulvaney.  Before trial, the respondent moved to suppress the shotgun and the statements he had made to the police regarding it.  After an evidentiary hearing at which the respondent elected not to testify, the trial judge found that the respondent had been "repeatedly and completely advised of his *Miranda* rights."  He further found that it was "entirely understandable that [the officers in the police vehicle] would voice their concern [for the safety of the handicapped children] to each other."  The judge then concluded that the respondent's decision to inform the police of the location of the shotgun was "a waiver, clearly, and on the basis of the evidence that I have heard, and [*sic*] intelligent waiver, of his [*Miranda*] right to remain silent."  Thus, without passing on whether the police officers had in fact "interrogated" the respondent, the trial court sustained the admissibility of the shotgun and testimony related to its discovery.  That evidence was later introduced at the respondent's trial, and the jury returned a verdict of guilty on all counts.

\* \* \*

## II

\* \* \*

In the present case, the parties are in agreement that the respondent was fully informed of his *Miranda* rights and that he invoked his *Miranda* right to counsel when he told Captain Leyden that he wished to consult with a lawyer.  It is also uncontested that the respondent was "in custody" while being transported to the police station.

The issue, therefore, is whether the respondent was "interrogated" by the police officers in violation of the respondent's undisputed right under *Miranda* to remain silent until he had consulted with a lawyer.

In resolving this issue, we first define the term "interrogation" under *Miranda* before turning to a consideration of the facts of this case.

## A

The starting point for defining "interrogation" in this context is, of course, the Court's *Miranda* opinion. There the Court observed that "[b]y custodial interrogation, we mean *questioning* initiated by law enforcement officers after a person has been taken into custody or otherwise deprived of his freedom of action in any significant way." 384 U.S., at 444 (emphasis added). This passage and other references throughout the opinion to "questioning" might suggest that the *Miranda* rules were to apply only to those police interrogation practices that involve express questioning of a defendant while in custody.

We do not, however, construe the *Miranda* opinion so narrowly. The concern of the Court in *Miranda* was that the "interrogation environment" created by the interplay of interrogation and custody would "subjugate the individual to the will of his examiner" and thereby undermine the privilege against compulsory self-incrimination. Id., at 457–458, 86 S.Ct., at 1619. The police practices that evoked this concern included several that did not involve express questioning. For example, one of the practices discussed in *Miranda* was the use of lineups in which a coached witness would pick the defendant as the perpetrator. This was designed to establish that the defendant was in fact guilty as a predicate for futher interrogation. Id., at 453, 86 S.Ct., at 1602. A variation on this theme discussed in *Miranda* was the so-called "reverse line-up" in which a defendant would be identified by coached witnesses as the perpetrator of a fictitious crime, with the object of inducing him to confess to the actual crime of which he was suspected in order to escape the false prosecution. Ibid. The Court in *Miranda* also included in its survey of interrogation practices the use of psychological ploys, such as to "posit[ ] " "the guilt of the subject," to "minimize the moral seriousness of the offense," and "to cast blame on the victim or on society." Id., at 450, 86 S.Ct., at 1615. It is clear that these techniques of persuasion, no less than express questioning, were thought, in a custodial setting, to amount to interrogation.

This is not to say, however, that all statements obtained by the police after a person has been taken into custody are to be considered the product of interrogation. * * * It is clear therefore that the special procedural safeguards outlined in *Miranda* are required not where a suspect is simply taken into custody, but rather where a suspect in custody is subjected to interrogation. "Interrogation," as conceptualized in the *Miranda* opinion, must reflect a measure of compulsion above and beyond that inherent in custody itself.

We conclude that the *Miranda* safeguards come into play whenever a person in custody is subjected to either express questioning or its functional equivalent. That is to say, the term "interrogation" under *Miranda* refers not only to express questioning, but also to any words or actions on the part of the police (other than those normally attendant to arrest and custody) that the police should know are reasonably likely to elicit an incriminating response from the suspect.  The latter portion of this definition focuses primarily upon the perceptions of the suspect, rather than the intent of the police.  This focus reflects the fact that the *Miranda* safeguards were designed to vest a suspect in custody with an added measure of protection against coercive police practices, without regard to objective proof of the underlying intent of the police.  A practice that the police should know is reasonably likely to evoke an incriminating response from a suspect thus amounts to interrogation.[4]  But, since the police surely cannot be held accountable for the unforeseeable results of their words or actions, the definition of interrogation can extend only to words or actions on the part of police officers that they *should have known* were reasonably likely to elicit an incriminating response.[5]

B

Turning to the facts of the present case, we conclude that the respondent was not "interrogated" within the meaning of *Miranda*.  It is undisputed that the first prong of the definition of "interrogation" was not satisfied, for the conversation between Patrolmen Gleckman and McKenna included no express questioning of the respondent.  Rather, that conversation was, at least in form, nothing more than a dialogue between the two officers to which no response from the respondent was invited.

Moreover, it cannot be fairly concluded that the respondent was subjected to the "functional equivalent" of questioning.  It cannot be said, in short, that Patrolmen Gleckman and McKenna should have known that their conversation was reasonably likely to elicit an incriminating response from the respondent.  There is nothing in the record to suggest that the officers were aware that the respondent was peculiarly susceptible to an appeal to his conscience concerning the safety of handicapped children.  Nor is there anything in the record to suggest that the police knew that the respondent was unusually disoriented or upset at the time of his arrest.[6]

The case thus boils down to whether, in the context of a brief conversation, the officers should have known that the respondent would suddenly be moved to make a self-incriminating response.  Given the fact that the entire conversation appears to have consisted of no more than a few off-hand remarks, we cannot say that the officers should

---

[4] This is not to say that the intent of the police is irrelevant, for it may well have a bearing on whether the police should have known that their words or actions were reasonably likely to evoke an incriminating response.  In particular, where a police practice is designed to elicit an incriminating response from the accused, it is unlikely that the practice will not also be one which the police should have known was reasonably likely to have that effect.

[5] Any knowledge the police may have had concerning the unusual susceptibility of a defendant to a particular form of persuasion might be an important factor in determining whether the police should have known that their words or actions were reasonably likely to elicit an incriminating response from the suspect.

[6] The record in no way suggests that the officers' remarks were *designed* to elicit a response.  It is significant that the trial judge, after hearing the officers' testimony, concluded that it was "entirely understandable that [the officers] would voice their concern [for the safety of the handicapped children] to each other."

have known that it was reasonably likely that Innis would so respond. This is not a case where the police carried on a lengthy harangue in the presence of the suspect. Nor does the record support the respondent's contention that, under the circumstances, the officers' comments were particularly "evocative." It is our view, therefore, that the respondent was not subjected by the police to words or actions that the police should have known were reasonably likely to elicit an incriminating response from him.

The Rhode Island Supreme Court erred  *  *  *  in equating "subtle compulsion" with interrogation. That the officers' comments struck a responsive cord is readily apparent. Thus, it may be said, as the Rhode Island Supreme Court did say, that the respondent was subjected to "subtle compulsion." But that is not the end of the inquiry. It must also be established that a suspect's incriminating response was the product of words or actions on the part of the police that they should have known were reasonably likely to elicit an incriminating response.[7] This was not established in the present case.

*  *  *

[The opinions of Justice White, concurring, Chief Justice Burger, concurring in the judgment, and Justice Marshall, joined by Justice Brennan, dissenting, are omitted.]

MR. JUSTICE STEVENS, dissenting.

*  *  *

*  *  *  [I]n order to give full protection to a suspect's right to be free from any interrogation at all [after he has invoked his right to cut off questioning], the definition of "interrogation" must include any police statement or conduct that has the same purpose or effect as a direct question. Statements that appear to call for a response from the suspect, as well as those that are designed to do so, should be considered interrogation. By prohibiting only those relatively few statements or actions that a police officer should know are likely to elicit an incriminating response, the Court today accords a suspect considerably less protection. Indeed, since I suppose most suspects are unlikely to incriminate themselves even when questioned directly, this new definition will almost certainly exclude every statement that is not punctuated with a question mark from the concept of "interrogation."

*  *  *

In any event, I think the Court is clearly wrong in holding, as a matter of law, that Officer Gleckman should not have realized that his statement was likely to elicit an incriminating response. The Court implicitly assumes that, at least in the absence of a lengthy harangue, a criminal suspect will not be likely to respond to indirect appeals to his humanitarian impulses. It then goes on to state that the officers in this case had no reason to believe that respondent would be unusually

---

[7] By way of example, if the police had done no more than to drive past the site of the concealed weapon while taking the most direct route to the police station, and if the respondent, upon noticing for the first time the proximity of the school for handicapped children, had blurted out that he would show the officers where the gun was located, it could not seriously be argued that this "subtle compulsion" would have constituted "interrogation" within the meaning of the *Miranda* opinion.

susceptible to such appeals. Finally, although the significance of the officer's intentions is not clear under its objective test, the Court states in a footnote that the record "in no way suggests" that Officer Gleckman's remarks were designed to elicit a response.

The Court's assumption that criminal suspects are not susceptible to appeals to conscience is directly contrary to the teachings of police interrogation manuals, which recommend appealing to a suspect's sense of morality as a standard and often successful interrogation technique. Surely the practical experience embodied in such manuals should not be ignored in a case such as this in which the record is devoid of any evidence—one way or the other—as to the susceptibility of suspects in general or of Innis in particular.

Moreover, there is evidence in the record to support the view that Officer Gleckman's statement was intended to elicit a response from Innis. Officer Gleckman, who was not regularly assigned to the caged wagon, was directed by a police captain to ride with respondent to the police station. Although there is a dispute in the testimony, it appears that Gleckman may well have been riding in the back seat with Innis. The record does not explain why, notwithstanding the fact that respondent was handcuffed, unarmed, and had offered no resistance when arrested by an officer acting alone, the captain ordered Officer Gleckman to ride with respondent. It is not inconceivable that two professionally trained police officers concluded that a few well-chosen remarks might induce respondent to disclose the whereabouts of the shotgun. This conclusion becomes even more plausible in light of the emotionally charged words chosen by Officer Gleckman ("God forbid" that a "little girl" should find the gun and hurt herself).

### NOTES

1. *Innis* was applied in Arizona v. Mauro, 481 U.S. 520, 107 S.Ct. 1931, 95 L.Ed.2d 458 (1987). Mauro had been arrested after he had approached authorities, volunteered that he had killed his young son, and led authorities to the victim's body. At the stationhouse, he was advised of his *Miranda* rights. He told officers that he did not want to make any more statements until his lawyer was present. Questioning then ceased. Meanwhile, Mauro's wife, who had been questioned by other officers, asked to speak to Mauro. After discussion, the officer in charge (Sergeant Allen) permitted this. Mrs. Mauro was taken to the office in which Mauro was being held. The couple was told that they could speak only if an officer remained present and the officer—Detective Manson— then placed a tape recorder in plain sight. A brief conversation ensued in which Mrs. Mauro expressed despair regarding the situation and Mauro urged his wife not to answer questions until a lawyer was present. At trial, Mauro presented a defense of insanity. The state then in rebuttal offered to prove the conversation between Mauro and his wife as tending to show that Mauro was at that time functioning in a sane fashion. The defense objected that the conversation was the result of "interrogation" conducted in violation of *Miranda,* because Mauro had invoked his right to counsel which barred further "interrogation" until a lawyer was present. Nevertheless, the evidence was admitted. By a 5–4 vote, the Supreme Court found no *Miranda* defect. The majority noted some uncertainty in the record as to whether Mauro was given

advance notice that his wife would be coming to speak with him. Assuming that no such notice was provided, however, the Court explained:

> The sole issue  *  *  * is whether the officers'  *  *  * actions rose to the level of interrogation—that is, in the language of *Innis,* whether they were the "functional equivalent" of police interrogation. We think it is clear under both *Miranda* and *Innis* that Mauro was not interrogated.  *  *  * Detective Manson asked Mauro no questions about the crime or his conduct. Nor is it suggested—or supported by any evidence—that Sergeant Allen's decision to allow Mauro's wife to see him was the kind of psychological ploy that properly could be treated as the functional equivalent of interrogation.
>
> There is no evidence that the officers sent Mrs. Mauro in to see her husband for the purpose of eliciting incriminating statements. As the trial court found, the officers tried to discourage her from talking to her husband, but finally "yielded to her insistent demands." Nor was Detective Manson's presence improper. His testimony, that the trial court found credible, indicated a number of legitimate reasons—not related to securing incriminating statements—for having a police officer present. [These included concern that a weapon might be smuggled or some other method of escape planned or that the couple might "cook up a lie or swap statements."] Finally, the weakness of Mauro's claim that he was interrogated is underscored by examining the situation from his perspective. We doubt that a suspect, told by officers that his wife will be allowed to speak to him, would feel that he was being coerced to incriminate himself in any way.  *  *  * [T]here was a "possibility" that Mauro would incriminate himself while talking to his wife.  *  *  * [T]he officers were aware of that possibility when they agreed to allow the Mauros to talk to each other. But the actions in this case were far less questionable than the "subtle compulsion" that was held *not* to be interrogation in *Innis.* Officers do not interrogate a suspect simply by hoping that he will incriminate himself.  *  *  * Mauro was not subjected to compelling influences, psychological ploys, or direct questioning. Thus, his volunteered statements cannot properly be considered the result of police interrogation.
>
> In deciding whether particular police conduct is interrogation, we must remember the purpose behind our [decision] in *Miranda*  *  *  *: preventing government officials from using the coercive nature of confinement to extract confessions that would not be given in an unrestrained environment. The government actions in this case do not implicate this purpose in any way. Police departments need not adopt inflexible rules barring suspects from speaking with their spouses, nor must they ignore legitimate security concerns by allowing spouses to meet in private. In short, the officers in this case acted reasonably and lawfully by allowing Mrs. Mauro to speak with her husband. In this situation, the Federal Constitution does not forbid use of Mauro's subsequent statements at his criminal trial.

481 U.S. at 527–30, 107 S.Ct. at 1935–37, 95 L.Ed.2d at 467–68. Justice Stevens, joined by Justices Brennan, Marshall and Blackmun, dissented:

> The record indicates  *  *  * that the police employed a powerful psychological ploy; they failed to give [Mauro] any advance warning that Mrs. Mauro was coming to talk to him, that a police officer would accompany her, or that their conversation would be recorded. As the transcript of the conversation reveals, [Mauro] would not have freely chosen to speak with her. These facts compel the conclusion that the police took advantage of Mrs. Mauro's request to visit her husband, setting up a confrontation between them at a time when he manifestly desired to remain silent.

Because they allowed [Mauro's] conversation with his wife to commence at a time when they knew it was reasonably likely to produce an incriminating statement, the police interrogated him. * * *

The State should not be permitted to [avoid this] conclusion with testimony that merely indicates that the evidence-gathering purpose of the police was mixed with other motives. For example, it is irrelevant to the inquiry whether the police had legitimate security reasons for having an officer present * * *.

481 U.S. at 531, 536, 107 S.Ct. at 1937, 1940, 95 L.Ed.2d at 469, 472 (Stevens, J., dissenting).

2. In *Innis*, the Court indicated that "interrogation" did not include police words or activity "normally attendant to arrest and custody." In South Dakota v. Neville, 459 U.S. 553, 103 S.Ct. 916, 74 L.Ed.2d 748 (1983), the Court held that a request that a suspect submit to a blood alcohol test is not "interrogation." Emphasizing the *Innis* dictum, Justice O'Connor explained:

The police inquiry * * * is highly regulated by state law, and is presented in virtually the same words to all suspects. It is similar to a police request to submit to fingerprinting or photography.

459 U.S. at 564 n. 15, 103 S.Ct. at 923 n. 15, 74 L.Ed.2d at 759 n. 15. This qualification of the definition of interrogation obviously supports arguments for a "routine booking question" exception to *Miranda;* see the discussion at pages 449–50, supra.

### b.   THE REQUIREMENT OF "CUSTODY"

The requirement of custody has given rise to more Supreme Court consideration than the requirement of interrogation. In Mathis v. United States, 391 U.S. 1, 88 S.Ct. 1503, 20 L.Ed.2d 381 (1968), the suspect was questioned while in prison serving a sentence for an offense unrelated to that under investigation. Rejecting the argument that *Miranda* applied only to suspects "in custody" in connection with the case under investigation, the majority explained that such a limitation would "[go] against the whole purpose of the *Miranda* decision * * *." 391 U.S. at 4, 88 S.Ct. at 1505, 20 L.Ed.2d at 385.

When custody exists has presented a more troublesome situation. In Oregon v. Mathiason, 429 U.S. 492, 97 S.Ct. 711, 50 L.Ed.2d 714 (1977) (per curiam), the Court reaffirmed the requirement of custody and concluded that a parolee who appeared at a police station in response to an officer's request for a discussion was not in custody for purposes of *Miranda*. The majority explained, "*Miranda* warnings are required only where there has been such a restriction on a person's freedom as to render him 'in custody.'" 429 U.S. at 495, 97 S.Ct. at 714, 50 L.Ed.2d at 719.

The requirement of custody was again applied in California v. Beheler, 463 U.S. 1121, 103 S.Ct. 3517, 77 L.Ed.2d 1275 (1983) (per curiam). Beheler himself called police after he and several others attempted to rob a drug dealer and one of the others killed the dealer. He admitted his participation and consented to a search of his backyard; the murder weapon was located there, as he said it would be. That evening, he agreed to accompany officers to the stationhouse. The officers told him he was not under arrest. During a thirty minute interview, he again acknowledged his participation.  He was told that his statement would be evaluated by the district attorney and he was then permitted to leave.  The stationhouse statement was admitted over defense objection at Beheler's trial for aiding and abetting first degree murder.  An intermediate California appellate court, however, held admission of the statement to violate *Miranda,* reasoning that the prosecution had failed to meet its burden of establishing lack of custody.  *Mathiason* was distinguished on several grounds:  (a) the interview with Beheler took place soon after the offense, while that with Mathiason occurred 25 days after the crime under investigation; (b) the officers had more information implicating Beheler than had been available against Mathiason at the time of his interview;  (c) Beheler had been drinking and was emotionally upset; and (d) Beheler was not a parolee and therefore lacked a parolee's incentive to cooperate with law enforcement officers by voluntarily consenting to an interview.

The Supreme Court reversed.  Under *Mathiason,* it stated, "the ultimate inquiry is simply whether there is a 'formal arrest or restraint on freedom of movement' of the degree associated with a formal arrest."  463 U.S. at 1125, 103 S.Ct. at 3520, 77 L.Ed.2d at 1279. Considerations (a) and (b) summarized above, it continued, are irrelevant to this inquiry.  Properly framed, the issue presented "is whether *Miranda* warnings are required if the suspect is not placed under arrest, voluntarily comes to the police station, and is allowed to leave unhindered by the police after a brief interview."  Since the Court's past decisions clearly settled this in the negative, the decision of the California appellate tribunal was reversed.

"Custody" was revisited in Minnesota v. Murphy, 465 U.S. 420, 104 S.Ct. 1136, 79 L.Ed.2d 409 (1984).  Murphy had been placed on probation.  The terms of this probation directed that he report to his probation officer and be truthful with that officer "in all matters." When Murphy's probation officer learned that during a therapy session Murphy had admitted to a rape and murder, she wrote to him and asked him to contact her to discuss a treatment plan for the remainder of his probationary period.  He contacted the officer and arranged for a meeting.  At that meeting, the officer confronted Murphy with the information; during the session, Murphy admitted to the officer his commission of the rape and murder.  No warnings were given.  At Murphy's later trial for murder, the State was permitted to use Murphy's admissions made to the probation officer to prove his guilt.  A majority of the Supreme Court found no constitutional error.  Despite Murphy's probationary status, he was not—under *Mathiason* and *Beheler*—"in custody" and therefore *Miranda* did not apply:

> He was, to be sure, subject to a number of restrictive conditions governing various aspects of his life, and he would be regarded as "in custody" for purposes of federal habeas corpus.  But * * * custody for *Miranda* purposes has been more narrowly circumscribed.  Under the narrower standard appropriate in the *Miranda* context, it is clear that Murphy was not "in custody" * * * since

there was no " 'formal arrest or restraint on freedom of movement' of the degree associated with a formal arrest."

465 U.S. at 430, 104 S.Ct. at 1144, 79 L.Ed.2d at 421 (citing *Beheler* and *Mathiason*). The majority also rejected Murphy's argument that despite the absence of custody, a *Miranda*-like warning requirement should be imposed in such situations as a means of adequately protecting probationers' privilege against compelled self-incrimination:

Even a cursory comparison of custodial interrogation and probation interviews reveals the inaptness of the \* \* \* analogy to *Miranda*. Custodial arrest is said to convey to the suspect a message that he has no choice but to submit to the officers' will and to confess. It is unlikely that a probation interview, arranged by appointment at a mutually convenient time, would give rise to a similar impression. Moreover, custodial arrest thrusts an individual into "an unfamiliar atmosphere" or "an interrogation environment \* \* \* created for no purpose other than to subjugate the individual to the will of his examiner." Many of the psychological ploys discussed in *Miranda* capitalize on the suspect's unfamiliarity with the officers and the environment. Murphy's regular meetings with his probation officer should have served to familiarize him with her and her office and to insulate him from psychological intimidation that might overbear his desire to claim the privilege. Finally, the coercion inherent in custodial interrogation derives in large measure from an interrogator's insinuations that the interrogation will continue until a confession is obtained. Since Murphy was not physically restrained and could have left the office, any compulsion he might have felt from the possibility that terminating the meeting would have led to revocation of his probation was not comparable to the pressure on a suspect who is painfully aware that he literally cannot escape a persistent custodial interrogator.

465 U.S. at 433, 104 S.Ct. at 1145–46, 79 L.Ed.2d at 423.

As the principal case in this subsection indicates, the Court has chosen the requirement of custody as the vehicle for accommodating the *Miranda* requirements with what it perceives to be the realities of certain nonarrest detentions consisting of "traffic stops." Has the Court already resolved the applicability of *Miranda* to other nonarrest detentions such as investigatory field stops made for the specific purpose of questioning the suspect?

## BERKEMER v. McCARTY

Supreme Court of the United States, 1984.
468 U.S. 420, 104 S.Ct. 3138, 82 L.Ed.2d 317.

JUSTICE MARSHALL delivered the opinion of the Court.

This case presents two related questions: First, does our decision in Miranda v. Arizona, 384 U.S. 436, 86 S.Ct. 1602, 16 L.Ed.2d 694 (1966), govern the admissibility of statements made during custodial interrogation by a suspect accused of a misdemeanor traffic offense? Second, does the roadside questioning of a motorist detained pursuant to a traffic stop constitute custodial interrogation for the purposes of the doctrine enunciated in *Miranda?*

## I

### A

The parties have stipulated to the essential facts. On the evening of March 31, 1980, Trooper Williams of the Ohio State Highway Patrol observed respondent's car weaving in and out of a lane on Interstate Highway 270. After following the car for two miles, Williams forced respondent to stop and asked him to get out of the vehicle. When respondent complied, Williams noticed that he was having difficulty standing. At that point, "Williams concluded that [respondent] would be charged with a traffic offense and, therefore, his freedom to leave the scene was terminated." However, respondent was not told that he would be taken into custody. Williams then asked respondent to perform a field sobriety test, commonly known as a "balancing test." Respondent could not do so without falling.

While still at the scene of the traffic stop, Williams asked respondent whether he had been using intoxicants. Respondent replied that "he had consumed two beers and had smoked several joints of marijuana a short time before." Respondent's speech was slurred, and Williams had difficulty understanding him. Williams thereupon formally placed respondent under arrest and transported him in the patrol car to the Franklin County Jail.

At the jail, respondent was given an intoxilyzer test to determine the concentration of alcohol in his blood. The test did not detect any alcohol whatsoever in respondent's system. Williams then resumed questioning respondent in order to obtain information for inclusion in the State Highway Patrol Alcohol Influence Report. Respondent answered affirmatively a question whether he had been drinking. When then asked if he was under the influence of alcohol, he said, "I guess, barely." Williams next asked respondent to indicate on the form whether the marihuana he had smoked had been treated with any chemicals. In the section of the report headed "Remarks," respondent wrote, "No ang[el] dust or PCP in the pot. Rick McCarty."

At no point in this sequence of events did Williams or anyone else tell respondent that he had a right to remain silent, to consult with an attorney, and to have an attorney appointed for him if he could not afford one.

### B

Respondent was charged with operating a motor vehicle while under the influence of alcohol and/or drugs in violation of Ohio Rev. Code Ann. § 4511.19 (Supp.1983). Under Ohio law, that offense is a first-degree misdemeanor and is punishable by fine or imprisonment for up to 6 months. § 2929.21 (1982). Incarceration for a minimum of 3 days is mandatory. § 4511.99 (Supp.1983).

Respondent moved to exclude the various incriminating statements he had made to Patrolman Williams on the ground that introduction into evidence of those statements would violate the Fifth Amendment insofar as he had not been informed of his constitutional rights prior to his interrogation. When the trial court denied the motion, respondent pleaded "no contest" and was found guilty. He was sentenced to 90 days in jail, 80 of which were suspended, and was fined $300, $100 of which were suspended.

On appeal [in the state courts, respondent's conviction was affirmed.]

Respondent then filed an action for a writ of habeas corpus in the District Court for the Southern District of Ohio. The District Court dismissed the petition *   *   *.

A divided panel of the Court of Appeals for the Sixth Circuit reversed, holding that "*Miranda* warnings must be given to *all* individuals prior to custodial interrogation, whether the offense investigated be a felony or a misdemeanor traffic offense." McCarty v. Herdman, 716 F.2d 361, 363 (1983) (emphasis in original). *   *   *

We granted certiorari *   *   *.

## II

*   *   *

In the years since the decision in *Miranda*, we have frequently reaffirmed the central principle established by that case: if the police take a suspect into custody and then ask him questions without informing him of the rights enumerated above, his responses cannot be introduced into evidence to establish his guilt.

Petitioner asks us to carve an exception out of the foregoing principle. When the police arrest a person for allegedly committing a misdemeanor traffic offense and then ask him questions without telling him his constitutional rights, petitioner argues, his responses should be admissible against him. We cannot agree.

One of the principal advantages of the doctrine that suspects must be given warnings before being interrogated while in custody is the clarity of that rule.

*   *   *

The exception to *Miranda* proposed by petitioner would substantially undermine this crucial advantage of the doctrine. The police often are unaware when they arrest a person whether he may have committed a misdemeanor or a felony. *   *   * It would be unreasonable to expect the police to make guesses as to the nature of the criminal conduct at issue before deciding how they may interrogate the suspect.

Equally important, the doctrinal complexities that would confront the courts if we accepted petitioner's proposal would be byzantine. Difficult questions quickly spring to mind: For instance, investigations into seemingly minor offenses sometimes escalate gradually into investigations into more serious matters; at what point in the evolution of an affair of this sort would the police be obliged to give *Miranda* warnings to a suspect in custody?  What evidence would be necessary to establish that an arrest for a misdemeanor offense was merely a pretext to enable the police to interrogate the suspect (in hopes of obtaining information about a felony) without providing him the safeguards prescribed by *Miranda?*  The litigation necessary to resolve such matters would be time-consuming and disruptive of law enforcement. And the end result would be an elaborate set of rules, interlaced with exceptions and subtle distinctions, discriminating between different kinds of custodial interrogations.  Neither the police nor criminal defendants would benefit from such a development.

Absent a compelling justification we surely would be unwilling so seriously to impair the simplicity and clarity of the holding of *Miranda.* Neither of the two arguments proffered by petitioner constitutes such a justification.  Petitioner first contends that *Miranda* warnings are unnecessary when a suspect is questioned about a misdemeanor traffic offense, because the police have no reason to subject such a suspect to the sort of interrogation that most troubled the Court in *Miranda.*  We cannot agree that the dangers of police abuse are so slight in this context.  For example, the offense of driving while intoxicated is increasingly regarded in many jurisdictions as a very serious matter. Especially when the intoxicant at issue is a narcotic drug rather than alcohol, the police sometimes have difficulty obtaining evidence of this crime.  Under such circumstances, the incentive for the police to try to induce the defendant to incriminate himself may well be substantial. Similar incentives are likely to be present when a person is arrested for a minor offense but the police suspect that a more serious crime may have been committed.

We do not suggest that there is any reason to think improper efforts were made in this case to induce respondent to make damaging admissions.  More generally, we have no doubt that, in conducting most custodial interrogations of persons arrested for misdemeanor traffic offenses, the police behave responsibly and do not deliberately exert pressures upon the suspect to confess against his will.  But the same might be said of custodial interrogations of persons arrested for felonies.  The purposes of the safeguards prescribed by *Miranda* are to *ensure* that the police do not coerce or trick captive suspects into confessing, to relieve the " 'inherently compelling pressures' " generated by the custodial setting itself, " 'which work to undermine the individual's will to resist,' " and as much as possible to free courts from the task of scrutinizing individual cases to try to determine, after the fact, whether particular confessions were voluntary.  Those purposes are implicated as much by in-custody questioning of persons suspected of misdemeanors as they are by questioning of persons suspected of felonies.

Petitioner's second argument is that law enforcement would be more expeditious and effective in the absence of a requirement that persons arrested for traffic offenses be informed of their rights.  Again, we are unpersuaded.  The occasions on which the police arrest and then interrogate someone suspected only of a misdemeanor traffic offense are rare.  The police are already well accustomed to giving

*Miranda* warnings to persons taken into custody. Adherence to the principle that *all* suspects must be given such warnings will not significantly hamper the efforts of the police to investigate crimes.

We hold therefore that a person subjected to custodial interrogation is entitled to the benefit of the procedural safeguards enunciated in *Miranda*,[8] regardless of the nature or severity of the offense of which he is suspected or for which he was arrested.

The * * * statements made by respondent at the County Jail were inadmissible. There can be no question that respondent was "in custody" at least as of the moment he was formally placed under arrest and instructed to get into the police car. Because he was not informed of his constitutional rights at that juncture, respondent's subsequent admissions should not have been used against him.

### III

To assess the admissibility of the self-incriminating statements made by respondent prior to his formal arrest, we are obliged to address a second issue concerning the scope of our decision in *Miranda:* whether the roadside questioning of a motorist detained pursuant to a routine traffic stop should be considered "custodial interrogation." Respondent urges that it should, on the ground that *Miranda* by its terms applies whenever "a person has been taken into custody *or otherwise deprived of his freedom of action in any significant way,*" 384 U.S., at 444, 86 S.Ct., at 1612 (emphasis added); see id., at 467, 86 S.Ct., at 1624. Petitioner contends that a holding that every detained motorist must be advised of his rights before being questioned would constitute an unwarranted extension of the *Miranda* doctrine.

It must be acknowledged at the outset that a traffic stop significantly curtails the "freedom of action" of the driver and the passengers, if any, of the detained vehicle. Under the law of most States, it is a crime either to ignore a policeman's signal to stop one's car or, once having stopped, to drive away without permission. Certainly few motorists would feel free either to disobey a directive to pull over or to leave the scene of a traffic stop without being told they might do so. * * *

However, we decline to accord talismanic power to the phrase in the *Miranda* opinion emphasized by respondent. Fidelity to the doctrine announced in *Miranda* requires that it be enforced strictly, but only in those types of situations in which the concerns that powered the decision are implicated. Thus, we must decide whether a traffic stop exerts upon a detained person pressures that sufficiently impair his

---

[8] * * * [I]t is suggested that we decide whether an indigent suspect has a right, under the Fifth Amendment, to have an attorney appointed to advise him regarding his responses to custodial interrogation when the alleged offense about which he is being questioned is sufficiently minor that he would not have a right, under the Sixth Amendment, to the assistance of appointed counsel at trial, see Scott v. Illinois, 440 U.S. 367, 99 S.Ct. 1158, 59 L.Ed.2d 383 (1979). We prefer to defer resolution of [this matter] to a case in which law enforcement authorities have at least attempted to inform the suspect of rights to which he is indisputably entitled.

free exercise of his privilege against self-incrimination to require that he be warned of his constitutional rights.

Two features of an ordinary traffic stop mitigate the danger that a person questioned will be induced "to speak where he would not otherwise do so freely," Miranda v. Arizona, 384 U.S., at 467, 86 S.Ct., at 1624. First, detention of a motorist pursuant to a traffic stop is presumptively temporary and brief. The vast majority of roadside detentions last only a few minutes. A motorist's expectations, when he sees a policeman's light flashing behind him, are that he will be obliged to spend a short period of time answering questions and waiting while the officer checks his license and registration, that he may then be given a citation, but that in the end he most likely will be allowed to continue on his way. In this respect, questioning incident to an ordinary traffic stop is quite different from stationhouse interrogation, which frequently is prolonged, and in which the detainee often is aware that questioning will continue until he provides his interrogators the answers they seek.[9]

Second, circumstances associated with the typical traffic stop are not such that the motorist feels completely at the mercy of the police. To be sure, the aura of authority surrounding an armed, uniformed officer and the knowledge that the officer has some discretion in deciding whether to issue a citation, in combination, exert some pressure on the detainee to respond to questions. But other aspects of the situation substantially offset these forces. Perhaps most importantly, the typical traffic stop is public, at least to some degree. Passersby, on foot or in other cars, witness the interaction of officer and motorist. This exposure to public view both reduces the ability of an unscrupulous policeman to use illegitimate means to elicit self-incriminating statements and diminishes the motorist's fear that, if he does not cooperate, he will be subjected to abuse. The fact that the detained motorist typically is confronted by only one or at most two policemen further mutes his sense of vulnerability. In short, the atmosphere surrounding an ordinary traffic stop is substantially less "police dominated" than that surrounding the kinds of interrogation at issue in Miranda itself, see 384 U.S., at 445, 491–498, 86 S.Ct., at 1612, 1636–1640, and in the subsequent cases in which we have applied Miranda.

In both of these respects, the usual traffic stop is more analogous to a so-called "Terry stop," see Terry v. Ohio, 392 U.S. 1, 88 S.Ct. 1868, 20 L.Ed.2d 889 (1968), than to a formal arrest. Under the Fourth Amendment, we have held, a policeman who lacks probable cause but whose "observations lead him reasonably to suspect" that a particular person has committed, is committing, or is about to commit a crime, may detain that person briefly in order to "investigate the circumstances that provoke suspicion." United States v. Brignoni-Ponce, 422 U.S.

[9] The brevity and spontaneity of an ordinary traffic stop also reduces the danger that the driver through subterfuge will be made to incriminate himself. One of the investigative techniques that Miranda was designed to guard against was the use by police of various kinds of trickery—such as "Mutt and Jeff" routines—to elicit confessions from suspects. A police officer who stops a suspect on the highway has little chance to develop or implement a plan of this sort.

873, 881, 95 S.Ct. 2574, 2580, 45 L.Ed.2d 607 (1975). "[T]he stop and inquiry must be 'reasonably related in scope to the justification for their initiation.'" Ibid. (quoting Terry v. Ohio, supra, 392 U.S., at 29, 88 S.Ct., at 1884.) Typically, this means that the officer may ask the detainee a moderate number of questions to determine his identity and to try to obtain information confirming or dispelling the officer's suspicions. But the detainee is not obliged to respond. And, unless the detainee's answers provide the officer with probable cause to arrest him, he must then be released. The comparatively nonthreatening character of detentions of this sort explains the absence of any suggestion in our opinions that *Terry* stops are subject to the dictates of *Miranda*. The similarly noncoercive aspect of ordinary traffic stops prompts us to hold that persons temporarily detained pursuant to such stops are not "in custody" for the purposes of *Miranda*.

Respondent contends that to "exempt" traffic stops from the coverage of *Miranda* will open the way to widespread abuse. Policemen will simply delay formally arresting detained motorists, and will subject them to sustained and intimidating interrogation at the scene of their initial detention. * * * The net result, respondent contends, will be a serious threat to the rights that the *Miranda* doctrine is designed to protect.

We are confident that the state of affairs projected by respondent will not come to pass. It is settled that the safeguards prescribed by *Miranda* become applicable as soon as a suspect's freedom of action is curtailed to a "degree associated with formal arrest." California v. Beheler, 463 U.S. 1121, 1125, 103 S.Ct. 3517, 3520, 77 L.Ed.2d 1275 (1983) (per curiam). If a motorist who has been detained pursuant to a traffic stop thereafter is subjected to treatment that renders him "in custody" for practical purposes, he will be entitled to the full panoply of protections prescribed by *Miranda*.

Admittedly, our adherence to the doctrine just recounted will mean that the police and lower courts will continue occasionally to have difficulty deciding exactly when a suspect has been taken into custody. Either a rule that *Miranda* applies to all traffic stops or a rule that a suspect need not be advised of his rights until he is formally placed under arrest would provide a clearer, more easily administered line. However, each of these two alternatives has drawbacks that make it unacceptable. The first would substantially impede the enforcement of the nation's traffic laws—by compelling the police either to take the time to warn all detained motorists of their constitutional rights or to forgo use of self-incriminating statements made by those motorists—while doing little to protect citizens' Fifth Amendment rights. The second would enable the police to circumvent the constraints on custodial interrogations established by *Miranda*.

Turning to the case before us, we find nothing in the record that indicates that respondent should have been given *Miranda* warnings at any point prior to the time Trooper Williams placed him under arrest. For the reasons indicated above, we reject the contention that the initial stop of respondent's car, by itself, rendered him "in custody."

And respondent has failed to demonstrate that, at any time between the initial stop and the arrest, he was subjected to restraints comparable to those associated with a formal arrest. Only a short period of time elapsed between the stop and the arrest. At no point during that interval was respondent informed that his detention would not be temporary. Although Trooper Williams apparently decided as soon as respondent stepped out of his car that respondent would be taken into custody and charged with a traffic offense, Williams never communicated his intention to respondent. A policeman's unarticulated plan has no bearing on the question whether a suspect was "in custody" at a particular time; the only relevant inquiry is how a reasonable man in the suspect's position would have understood his situation. Nor do other aspects of the interaction of Williams and respondent support the contention that respondent was exposed to "custodial interrogation" at the scene of the stop. From aught that appears in the stipulation of facts, a single police officer asked respondent a modest number of questions and requested him to perform a simple balancing test at a location visible to passing motorists. Treatment of this sort cannot fairly be characterized as the functional equivalent of formal arrest.

We conclude, in short, that respondent was not taken into custody for the purposes of *Miranda* until Williams arrested him. Consequently, the statements respondent made prior to that point were admissible against him.

## IV

\* \* \* [W]e agree with the Court of Appeals that respondent's postarrest statements should have been suppressed but conclude that respondent's prearrest statements were admissible \* \* \*.

Accordingly, the judgment of the Court of Appeals is

Affirmed.

## NOTES

1. Insofar as a suspect subjected to a nonarrest detention is not "in custody," *Miranda* is rendered entirely inapplicable. But are there—or should there be—any requirements for interrogation in such circumstances, other than the apparent demand that any resulting admissions be "voluntary?" Should, for example, the Court have considered whether a modified version of the *Miranda* rights might be required by the risks posed to suspects' Fifth Amendment interests in traffic stop situations? Might this be required when the nonarrest detention is rather an investigatory field stop concerning a serious offense?

The American Law Institute's Model Code of Pre-arraignment Procedure proposed the following alternatives to govern questioning during nonarrest stops for investigation:

(5) *Questioning of Suspects.*

(a) *Warnings.* If a law enforcement officer stops any person who he suspects or has reasonable cause to suspect may have committed a crime, the officer shall warn such person as promptly as is reasonable under the circumstances, and in any case before engaging in any sustained questioning

(i) that such person is not obligated to say anything, and anything he says may be used in evidence against him,

(ii) that within twenty minutes he will be released unless he is arrested.[,]

[ (iii) that if he is arrested he will be taken to a police station where he may promptly communicate by telephone with counsel, relatives or friends, and

(iv) that he will not be questioned unless he wishes, and that if he wishes to consult a lawyer or have a lawyer present during questioning, he will not be questioned at this time, and that after being taken to the stationhouse a lawyer will be furnished him prior to questioning if he is unable to obtain one.]

(b) *Limitations on Questioning.* No law enforcement officer shall question a person detained pursuant to the authority of this Section who he suspects or has reasonable cause to suspect may have committed a crime, if such person has indicated in any manner that he does not wish to be questioned, or that he wishes to consult counsel before submitting to any questioning.

A Model Code of Pre-arraignment Procedure § 110.2 (Official Draft 1975).

2. In Brown v. Texas, 443 U.S. 47, 99 S.Ct. 2637, 61 L.Ed.2d 357 (1979), Brown had been convicted under a Texas statute which made it a criminal offense for a person to refuse to give his name and address to an officer "who has lawfully stopped him and requested the information." Vernon's Texas Code Ann., Penal Code § 38.02(a). The Supreme Court found that the officers who stopped Brown had insufficient information to amount to reasonable suspicion that Brown was engaged or had engaged in criminal conduct. Under these circumstances, it concluded, Brown could not be punished for refusing to identify himself. The Court specifically noted, however, that it was not addressing whether a person could be punished for refusing to identify himself "in the context of a lawful investigatory stop which satisfies Fourth Amendment requirements." 443 U.S. at 52 n. 3, 99 S.Ct. at 2641 n. 3, 61 L.Ed.2d at 363 n. 3.

### 3. WAIVER OF THE *MIRANDA* RIGHTS

### EDITORS' INTRODUCTION: WAIVER ISSUES

As *Miranda* makes clear, the constitutionally-required foundation for the admissibility of a self-incriminating statement made by the defendant during custodial interrogation is proof that he "knowingly and intelligently waived his privilege against self-incrimination and [unless a lawyer was present during the interrogation] his right to retained or appointed counsel. 384 U.S. at 475, 86 S.Ct. at 1602, 16 L.Ed.2d at 724. In most—perhaps almost all—cases, counsel will not have been present so the issue of waiver takes on extreme importance. Consequently, waiver issues have tended to take on more and more importance in *Miranda* law. Two preliminary distinctions may be helpful.

First, issues of waiver need to be distinguished from so-called *per se* rules. The latter, if violated, require exclusion of a resulting confession without inquiry into the defendant's decisions to submit to questioning or to confess. As the principal cases in this section indicate, the Court's decisions have not always been clear as to whether *per se* rules are being announced.

Second, analysis is helped by distinguishing between proving—first—that the defendant made some sort of choice that might constitute waiver, and—second—that a proven choice by the defendant was effective. The two inquiries raise different concerns. What evidence is necessary to prove a choice, for example, is a much different question than what is necessary to prove that a choice was sufficiently voluntary and intelligent to be effective.

*Express Waivers.* No "express" waiver is required. In North Carolina v. Butler, 441 U.S. 369, 99 S.Ct. 1755, 60 L.Ed.2d 286 (1979), the North Carolina Supreme Court was held to have erred in applying a *per se* rule that required an express waiver. "[A] court may find an intelligent and understanding rejection of counsel in situation where the defendant did not expressly state as much," Justice Stewart explained for the Court. He continued:

> The question is not one of form, but rather whether the defendant in fact knowingly and voluntarily waived the right delineated in *Miranda.* * * * [M]ere silence is not enough. That does not mean that the defendant's silence, coupled with an understanding of his rights and a course of conduct indicating waiver, may never support a conclusion that a defendant has waived his rights. * * * [I]n at least some cases waiver can be clearly inferred from the actions and words of the person interrogated.

441 U.S. at 373, 99 S.Ct. at 1757, 60 L.Ed.2d at 292.

Justice Brennan, joined by Justices Marshall and Stevens, dissented, arguing that the case before the Court demonstrated the need for an express waiver requirement:

> Faced with "actions and words" of uncertain meaning, some judges may find waivers where none occurred. Others may fail to find them where they did. In the former case, the defendant's rights will have been violated; in the latter, society's interest in effective law enforcement will have been frustrated. A simple prophylactic rule requiring the police to obtain an express waiver of the right to counsel before proceeding with the interrogation eliminates these difficulties. And since the Court agrees that *Miranda* requires the police to obtain some kind of waiver—whether express or implied—the requirement of an express waiver would impose no burden on the police not imposed by the Court's interpretation. It would merely make that burden explicit.

441 U.S. at 378–79, 99 S.Ct. at 1760, 60 L.Ed.2d at 295–96.

*Burden of Proof.* The burden of proof on waiver was addressed in Colorado v. Connelly, 479 U.S. 157, 107 S.Ct. 515, 93 L.Ed.2d 473 (1986) (reprinted in part, supra page 416, and other aspects discussed, infra, page 471), in which the state court had held that the prosecution must establish waivers of the rights to counsel and to remain silent by "clear and convincing evidence." Lego v. Twomey, 404 U.S. 477, 92 S.Ct. 619,

30 L.Ed.2d 618 (1972) (discussed at page 414, supra), the Court noted, established that the voluntariness of a confession need only be proved by a preponderance of the evidence. After reaffirming that position, the majority reasoned that "a waiver of the auxiliary protections established in *Miranda* should require no higher a burden of proof." 479 U.S. at 169, 107 S.Ct. at 523, 93 L.Ed.2d at 485. Justice Blackmun declined to join this part of the Court's opinion on the ground that the issue was neither raised nor briefed by the parties. Justice Stevens concurred in the judgment. Justice Brennan, joined by Justice Marshall, dissented from the holding on the waiver burden. He indicated continuing disagreement with the Court's resolution of the *Lego* issue, reasoning that the prosecution should have to prove voluntariness by proof beyond a reasonable doubt. But assuming that *Lego* correctly held otherwise, he found the *Miranda* situation distinguishable:

> *Lego* involved a situation in which the defendant was not in custody. By contrast, a *Miranda* waiver is found while a defendant is in police custody. The coercive custodial interrogation atmosphere poses an increased danger of police overreaching. The police establish the isolated conditions of custody and can document the voluntary waiver of *Miranda* rights through disinterested witnesses or recordings. It is therefore appropriate to place a higher burden of proof on the government in establishing a waiver of *Miranda* rights.

469 U.S. at 187, 107 S.Ct. at 532, 93 L.Ed.2d at 497 (Brennan, J., dissenting). Proof beyond a reasonable doubt, he concluded, "constitutes the appropriate standard." Id.

*Distinguishing Different Waivers.* Often discussions assume that only one waiver or set of waivers is at issue. But is this always or even often the case? Suppose that a suspect, after being given the required warnings, agrees to talk with officers in the absence of an attorney. After two hours of discussion, the suspect makes a self-incriminating admission. Can the suspect's waiver of the right to counsel and his waiver of the right to silence be regarded as identical? Or did the waiver of the right to counsel occur before interrogation began and the waiver of the right to remain silent occur only when he made the admission?

This may be important because intervening events may bear upon the effectiveness of one waiver but not the other. Suppose, for example, that during the two hour discussion the officers inform the suspect that he will not be presented before a judge until the officers have what they regard as a satisfactory statement from him. If the suspect had already waived his right to counsel during interrogation, this "threat" could not affect the effectiveness of this waiver. (Perhaps, however, his continued willingness to undergo questioning without a lawyer is a "continuing waiver" of the right to counsel which is rendered involuntary after the threat was made.) But if, in response to this threat, the suspect decides to give an incriminating statement and thereby waive his right to be free from self-incrimination, it is arguable that his waiver of this right was fatally tainted by the threat.

*Effectiveness of Waivers: Voluntariness. Miranda* itself as well as other waiver discussions made clear that a suspect's waiver must be "voluntary." But what does that mean? How does the standard for determining voluntariness in this context compare with the criterion used under the due process standard for determining the voluntariness of a confession?

In Colorado v. Connelly, 479 U.S. 157, 107 S.Ct. 515, 93 L.Ed.2d 473 (1986) (reprinted in part, supra page 416), after addressing the voluntariness of the confessions there at issue, the Court assumed that once officer Anderson handcuffed Connelly *Miranda* became applicable. It then turned to the state court's determination that Connelly had not effectively waived his *Miranda* rights:

> The Supreme Court of Colorado in addressing this question relied on the testimony of the court-appointed psychiatrist to the effect that [Connelly] was not capable of making a "free decision with respect to his constitutional right of silence . . . and his constitutional right to confer with a lawyer before talking to the police."
>
> We think that the Supreme Court of Colorado erred in importing into this area of constitutional law notions of "free will" that have no place there. There is obviously no reason to require more in the way of a "voluntariness" inquiry in the *Miranda* waiver context than in the Fourteenth Amendment confession context. The sole concern of the Fifth Amendment, on which *Miranda* was based, is governmental coercion. * * * The voluntariness of a waiver of this privilege has always depended on the absence of police overreaching, not on "free choice" in any broader sense of the word. * * *
>
> [Connelly] urges this Court to adopt his "free will" rationale, and to find an attempted waiver invalid whenever the defendant feels compelled to waive his rights by reason of any compulsion, even if the compulsion does not flow from the police. But such treatment of the waiver issue would "cut this Court's holding in [*Miranda*] completely loose from its own explicitly stated rationale." Beckwith v. United States, 425 U.S. 341, 345, 96 S.Ct. 1612, 1615, 48 L.Ed.2d 1 (1976). *Miranda* protects defendants against government coercion leading them to surrender rights protected by the Fifth Amendment; it goes no further than that. [Connelly's] perception of coercion flowing from the "voice of God," however important or significant such a perception might be in other disciplines, is a matter to which the United States Constitution does not speak.

479 U.S. at 169–71, 107 S.Ct. at 523–24, 93 L.Ed.2d at 486–87. As the reprinted portion of the Court's opinion, supra, makes clear, the Court then reversed the judgment of the Colorado Supreme Court and remanded the cause "for further proceedings not inconsistent with this opinion."

Justice Brennan, joined by Justice Marshall, dissented. He urged that his objections to the majority's analysis of the voluntariness of a confession (see that portion of his dissent, reprinted supra) also applied

to analysis of the voluntariness of a waiver of *Miranda* rights. 479 U.S.
at 186, 107 S.Ct. at 533, 93 L.Ed.2d at 498 (Brennan, J., dissenting).
Justice Stevens concurred in the majority's conclusion that use of
Connelly's precustodial statements did not violate federal Constitutional requirements. But he dissented from the majority's disposition of
the question raised by Connelly's post-custodial statements:

> [Since *Miranda* applied,] the questioning could not thereafter go
> forward in the absence of a valid waiver of [Connelly's] constitu-
> tional rights unless he was provided with counsel. Since it is
> undisputed that [Connelly] was not then competent to stand trial, I
> would also conclude that he was not competent to waive his
> constitutional right to remain silent.
>
> The Court seems to believe that a waiver can be voluntary
> even if it is not the product of an exercise of the defendant's "free
> will." The Court's position is not only incomprehensible to me; it
> is also foreclosed by the Court's recent pronouncement that in
> Moran v. Burbine, 475 U.S. 412, 421, 106 S.Ct. 1135, 1141, 89 L.Ed.
> 2d 410 (1986) [reprinted at page 492, infra] that "the relinquish-
> ment of the right must have been voluntary in the sense that it
> was the product of a free and deliberate choice . . . ." Because
> [Connelly's] waiver was not voluntary in that sense, his custodial
> interrogation was presumptively coercive. The Colorado Supreme
> Court was unquestionably correct in concluding that his post-
> custodial incriminatory statements were inadmissible.

479 U.S. at 173, 107 S.Ct. at 525, 93 L.Ed.2d at 488–89 (Stevens, J.,
concurring in the judgment in part and dissenting in part).

*Effectiveness of Waivers: Intelligence.* The Supreme Court has
made clear that the requirement of an intelligent or "knowing" waiver
is separate from, and requires different proof than, the need for
voluntariness.

In Tague v. Louisiana, 444 U.S. 469, 100 S.Ct. 652, 62 L.Ed.2d 622
(1980), Tague's confession given during custodial interrogation was
offered at his trial for robbery. At a pretrial hearing on the admissibility of the statement, the officer who had taken the confession testified
that he had read Tague the *Miranda* rights from a card, that he could
not presently remember what those rights were, that he could not
recall whether he had asked Tague whether he understood the rights,
and that he "couldn't say yes or no" whether he rendered any tests to
determine whether Tague was literate or otherwise capable of understanding the rights. The confession was admitted and Tague was
convicted. On appeal, the Supreme Court of Louisiana affirmed, reasoning that "absent a clear and readily apparent lack thereof, it can be
presumed that a person has capacity to understand [the *Miranda*
rights], and the burden is on the one claiming a lack of capacity to show
that lack." State v. Tague, 372 So.2d 555, 558 (La.1979). Without oral
argument and in a *per curiam* opinion, the Supreme Court reversed.
The Louisiana courts had impermissibly relied upon a presumption that
one given the *Miranda* warnings understands the rights involved; such
a presumption is inconsistent with the burden placed by *Miranda* on

the state to show a knowing and intelligent waiver of the rights. Turning to the facts of the case, the Court continued:

> In this case no evidence at all was introduced to prove that [Tague] knowingly and intelligently waived his rights before making the inculpatory statement. The statement was therefore inadmissible.

441 U.S. at 471, 100 S.Ct. at 653, 62 L.Ed.2d at 625. Justice Rehnquist dissented, arguing that the Louisiana court's result was "fully consistent" with the Supreme Court's cases. The Chief Justice indicated he favored setting the case for oral argument.

The criterion to be used in determining the effectiveness of a waiver under *Miranda* was further developed in Edwards v. Arizona, 451 U.S. 477, 101 S.Ct. 1880, 68 L.Ed.2d 378 (1981) (reprinted in part at page 484, infra). Before making his oral confession, given during a custodial interrogation, Edwards insisted that he did not want it recorded because it could be used against him in court. The interrogating detectives attempted to explain that an unrecorded oral confession could be used against him. Edwards then made an incriminating statement. Prior to trial, defense counsel moved to suppress the confession on the ground that despite the detectives' efforts Edwards did not understand the admissibility of an oral confession and therefore the waiver of his rights was not knowingly made. Denying the motion to suppress, the trial judge found the confession to have been "voluntary." On appeal, the Arizona Supreme Court cited Schneckloth v. Bustamonte, 412 U.S. 218, 93 S.Ct. 2041, 36 L.Ed.2d 854 (1973) (reprinted at page 296, supra), dealing with the voluntariness of a consent to search, and posed the question as whether the trial court's conclusions, based on the totality of the circumstances, that the defendant's action in confessing was knowing and intelligent and that his will had not been overborne were "clear and manifest error." It found no such error. State v. Edwards, 122 Ariz. 206, 212, 594 P.2d 72, 78 (1979). The Supreme Court held that the Arizona Supreme Court had not adequately considered whether Edwards had effectively relinquished his right to counsel. The "voluntariness" of a consent or an admission, on the one hand, and the existence of a knowing and intelligent waiver, on the other, "are discrete inquiries." However sound the state court's conclusion regarding the "voluntariness" of Edwards' confession might be, the state court did not adequately address the *Miranda* waiver issue:

> [W]aivers of counsel must not only be voluntary, but must also constitute a knowing and intelligent relinquishment or abandonment of a known right or privilege * * *. [N]either the trial court nor the Arizona Supreme Court undertook to focus on whether Edwards understood his right to counsel and intelligently and knowingly relinquished it. It is thus apparent that the decision below misunderstood the requirement for finding a valid waiver of the right to counsel * * *.

451 U.S. at 482–84, 101 S.Ct. at 1883–84, 68 L.Ed.2d at 385–86.

But what precisely must a suspect know or understand in order to render effective his decision to forego the assistance of counsel, his right to remain silent, or both? Consider this in light of the cases reprinted and discussed in this section.

Suppose a defendant's waiver is "unintelligent" but for reasons not attributable to misconduct by law enforcement officers. *Connelly* made clear that a *Miranda* waiver cannot be rendered involuntary by the defendant's mental impairment, where there is no law enforcement misconduct. Is it possible, however, that even in the absence of police misconduct, such mental impairment might prevent a suspect from adequately understanding his right to counsel and intelligently and knowingly relinquishing it?

In *Connelly,* the Supreme Court noted that the Colorado Supreme Court's opinion could be read as finding Connelly's waiver invalid "on other grounds." This was apparently a reference to the state court's comment that Connelly's mental impairment had rendered him unable to make an "intelligent" decision. The Colorado court's analysis was influenced by "its mistaken view of 'voluntariness' in the constitutional sense," the *Connelly* majority stated. It thus reversed the state court's judgment "in its entirety," although it commented that on remand the state court was free to reconsider other issues in a manner not inconsistent with the opinion of the Court. 479 U.S. at 171 n. 4, 107 S.Ct. at 524 n. 4, 93 L.Ed.2d at 487 n. 4. Justice Brennan construed this as permitting the state court to find that despite the absence of any official compulsion, Connelly's mental illness demonstrated that *Miranda's* requirement of a knowing and intelligent waiver was not met. 479 U.S. at 188, 107 S.Ct. at 533, 93 L.Ed.2d at 498 (Brennan, J., dissenting).

*Scope of Waivers.* The scope of an effective waiver, especially of the right to counsel, was presented by Wyrick v. Fields, 459 U.S. 42, 103 S.Ct. 394, 74 L.Ed.2d 214 (1982). Fields had agreed to a polygraph test and had waived his right to counsel during that procedure. After the examination, the agent who administered the examination told Fields that there had been some deceit and asked Fields if he could explain why his answers were bothering him. In the resulting discussion, Fields made incriminating admissions. He argued that neither he nor the lawyer who advised him prior to the waiver anticipated questioning after the examination and therefore his waiver of counsel had not extended to such post-examination questioning. Rejecting this, the Court explained:

> [I]t would have been unreasonable for Fields and his attorneys to assume that Fields would not be informed of the polygraph readings and asked to explain any unfavorable results. Moreover, Fields had been informed that he could stop the questioning at any time, and could request at any time that his lawyer join him. Merely disconnecting the polygraph equipment could not remove this knowledge from Fields' mind.

459 U.S. 47–48, 103 S.Ct. at 396, 74 L.Ed.2d at 219. Does this mean that the scope of a waiver is not defined by what the defendant actually understood it would cover but rather by what he should, in the exercise of reasonable care, have known it would be treated by police as covering?

*Empirical Information.* It may be useful, in addressing *Miranda* waiver issues, to consider some available information concerning the actual making of waivers by suspects. Medalie, Zeitz and Alexander, Custodial Police Interrogation in Our Nation's Capitol: The Attempt to Implement *Miranda,* 66 Mich.L.Rev. 1347 (1968), gave 85 arrested persons the *Miranda* warnings and then questioned them concerning their understanding of the rights involved. The interviewers concluded that 15 percent failed to understand the right to the presence of counsel. Leiken, Police Interrogation in Colorado: The Implementation of *Miranda,* 47 Denver L.J. 1 (1970), interviewed 50 defendants who had been interrogated by the police. About 60 percent indicated a belief that signing the waiver forms had no legal effect. Id. at 33. 45 percent expressed the view that an oral statement could not be used against them in court. Id. at 15–16.

Leiken reported that half of the defendants he interviewed told him of promises or threats, such as the threat to charge a more serious offense unless the subject waived his rights. Id. at 22. Medalie, Zeitz and Alexander reported that a wide variety of factors appeared to have influenced suspects to waive their rights. One suspect indicated that he simply did not believe a lawyer would be provided; another expressed distrust of any lawyer provided by the police. Some suspects were apparently too preoccupied with other matters—such as personal problems related to the investigation—to recognize the value of a lawyer. Others, however, appeared to have made a reasonably well-informed tactical choice. One was reported to have explained: "I wouldn't want [a lawyer]. That's the worst place to have a lawyer because the police play it straight then. I wanted them to make a mistake." Medalie, Zeitz and Alexander, supra, at 1378.

More recent information was developed by Grisso, Juveniles' Capacity to Waive Miranda Rights: An Empirical Analysis, 68 Cal.L.Rev. 1134 (1980). For purposes of comparison with juveniles, Grisso studied the results of giving *Miranda* warnings to 203 adult parolees and 57 adults employed in custodial services and university and hospital maintenance crews. He concluded that a significant proportion of these adults did not learn the underlying rights from the *Miranda* warnings. Id., at 1165 n. 114. 42.3% of the subjects were able accurately to paraphrase all four of the *Miranda* rights after the warning; 57.7% were not. Id. at, 1152. The most commonly misunderstood part of the warning concerned the right to the presence of counsel; 14.6% of the subjects were totally unable to paraphrase this. Id. In an effort to avoid the effect of facility in verbal expression, Geiss administered a true-false test containing 12 questions to the subjects. 76.5% received a score of 10–12 correct responses; another 18.9% scored 7 to 9 correct answers. But 4.6% of the subjects scored only 5 or 6 correct answers. Id., at 1154. A further test consisted of questioning the subjects concerning a hypothetical interrogation situation. 89–95% of the subjects recognized the adversarial nature of the interrogation, the role of the subject's lawyer in it, and the lawyers' need for full information concerning the events. Id., at 1157–58. But many of the subjects failed to understand the effect which the privilege against self-incrimination would have later in the courtroom. 42.9% believed that they would have to later explain their criminal involvement in court if questioned by the judge. Id., at 1158–59. Does this mean that a significant proportion of *Miranda* waivers may be influenced by the subjects' perception that they will later be compelled to answer questions concerning the situation and therefore might as well do it during police questioning?

\* \* \*

The first principal case in this subsection, Michigan v. Mosley, contains as an editors' insertion rather extensive portions of the transcription of the examination of the interrogating officers at the hearing on the admissibility of the confession. Consider in connection with this what should be required of the prosecution to establish at least a prima facie case for its position that effective waivers occurred. What answers of the witness established the voluntariness of Mosley's waivers? What answers established the intelligence of them? Might the prosecutor have asked better questions on either of these matters?

### MICHIGAN v. MOSLEY

Supreme Court of the United States, 1975.
423 U.S. 96, 96 S.Ct. 321, 46 L.Ed.2d 313.

MR. JUSTICE STEWART delivered the opinion of the Court.

The respondent, Richard Bert Mosley, was arrested in Detroit, Michigan, on the early afternoon of April 8, 1971, in connection with robberies that had recently occurred at the Blue Goose Bar and the White Tower Restaurant on that city's lower east side. The arresting officer, Detective James Cowie of the Armed Robbery Section of the Detroit Police Department, was acting on a tip implicating Mosley and three other men in the robberies.[10] After effecting the arrest, Detective Cowie brought Mosley to the Robbery, Breaking and Entering Bureau of the Police Department, located on the fourth floor of the departmental headquarters building. The officer advised Mosley of his rights under this Court's decision in Miranda v. Arizona, 384 U.S. 436, 86 S.Ct. 1602, 16 L.Ed.2d 694, and had him read and sign the department's constitutional rights notification certificate. After filling out the necessary arrest papers, Cowie began questioning Mosley about the robbery of the White Tower Restaurant. When Mosley said he did not want to answer any questions about the robberies, Cowie promptly ceased the interrogation. The completion of the arrest papers and the questioning of Mosley together took approximately 20 minutes. At no time during the questioning did Mosley indicate a desire to consult with a lawyer, and there is no claim that the procedures followed to this point did not fully comply with the strictures of the *Miranda* opinion. Mosley was then taken to a ninth-floor cell block.

Shortly after 6 p. m., Detective Hill of the Detroit Police Department Homicide Bureau brought Mosley from the cell block to the fifth-

[10] The officer testified that information supplied by an anonymous caller was the sole basis for his arrest of Mosley.

floor office of the Homicide Bureau for questioning about the fatal shooting of a man named Leroy Williams. Williams had been killed on January 9, 1971, during a holdup attempt outside the 101 Ranch Bar in Detroit. Mosley had not been arrested on this charge nor interrogated about it by Detective Cowie.[11] Before questioning Mosley about this homicide, Detective Hill carefully advised him of his "Miranda rights." Mosley read the notification form both silently and aloud, and Detective Hill then read and explained the warnings to him and had him sign the form. Mosley at first denied any involvement in the Williams murder, but after the officer told him that Anthony Smith had confessed to participating in the slaying and had named him as the "shooter," Mosley made a statement implicating himself in the homicide.[12] The interrogation by Detective Hill lasted approximately 15 minutes, and at no time during its course did Mosley ask to consult with a lawyer or indicate that he did not want to discuss the homicide. In short, there is no claim that the procedures followed during Detective Hill's interrogation of Mosley, standing alone, did not fully comply with the strictures of the *Miranda* opinion.

Mosley was subsequently charged in a one-count information with first-degree murder. Before the trial he moved to suppress his incriminating statement on a number of grounds, among them the claim that under the doctrine of the *Miranda* case it was constitutionally impermissible for Detective Hill to question him about the Williams murder after he had told Detective Cowie that he did not want to answer any questions about the robberies.[13]

[An evidentiary hearing was held on the motion. At the hearing, Detective Hill testified. In response to the prosecutor's questions on direct examination, he stated that between 4:00 and 6:30 on April 8, he had talked with Anthony Smith, who had been arrested for the Williams murder. Smith told Hill that he had been in the bar when Mosley and one Charles Little had discussed robbing another patron. Smith admitted approaching the victim and reporting to the others that the victim had "a roll." He also admitted agreeing to help rob the victim outside the tavern. But he claimed that he refused to participate, that Mosley and Little had robbed the victim, and that Mosley had panicked and shot the victim. Hill testified that he then got Mosley for purposes of questioning:

Q: And what did you do   *   *   * ?

A: The first thing I did was I got two Miranda warning forms out.   *   *   *   I told him to read [one] to himself.   *   *   *   After I asked him if he could read.

---

[11] The original tip to Officer Cowie had, however, implicated Mosley in the Williams murder.

[12] During cross-examination by Mosley's counsel at the subsequent trial, Detective Hill conceded that Smith in fact had not confessed but had "denied a physical participation in the robbery."

[13] In addition to the claim that Detective Hill's questioning violated *Miranda*, Mosley contended that the statement was the product of an illegal arrest, that the statement was inadmissible because he had not been taken before a judicial officer without unnecessary delay, and that it had been obtained through trickery and promises of leniency. He argued that these circumstances, either independently or in combination, required the suppression of his incriminating statement.

Q: And did he relay that he could read?

A: Yes, sir.

Q: Did you ask him how far he had gone in school?

A: Yes, sir?

Q: And what did he say to that?

A: He told me he went through the 10–A at Southeastern High.

Q: And did he appear to be reading that particular form?

A: Yes, sir.

\* \* \*

Q: By that, his eyes scanned the particular paper?

A: Right. \* \* \* When he said he was through, then I told him to read it out loud.

Q: And did he read it out loud?

A: Yes, sir. \* \* \* [At another point, Detective Hill explained, "I wanted him to do that so I could know that he could read."] I read it to him as I explained it to him. [Later, Detective Hill explained, "I had him hold [one] form while I read the other form \* \* \* to him, so that he would be looking at this while I was explaining this to him \* \* \*"]

\* \* \*

Q: Did he ask for any explanation \* \* \*?

A: Nothing specific. I made it plain.

Q: \* \* \* Did he indicate to you that he understood his rights?

A: Yes, sir, he did.

Q: And did he sign that form in front of you?

A: Yes, sir, he did.

\* \* \*

Q: Now, at any time did he ask for an attorney?

A: No, sir, he did not.

Q: At any time during your questioning did he ask to make a telephone call?

A: He did not ask to make a phone call. I think he stated he had already made one \* \* \*

Q: Did he ask at any time that the questioning be terminated?

A: No, sir, he did not.

Q: Now, did you take a statement from him?

A: Yes, sir, I did.

Q: Prior to taking that statement from him, did you promise him anything in return for that statement?

A: No, sir, I did not.

Q: Did you physically mistreat him in any way?

A: No, sir, I did not.

On cross examination by defense counsel the following occurred, with the trial judge interjecting himself into the questioning:

Q: Do you recall what the very first thing you said to Mr. Mosley was?

\* \* \*

A: Yes. That he was accused of \* \* \* being the shooter in the holdup shooting of Mr. Leroy Williams, and I asked him if he wanted to tell me about it.

\* \* \*

Q: When did you first mention Anthony Smith's name to Mr. Mosley?

A: When Mr. Mosley denied being involved at all.

Q: And when did Mr. Mosley deny being involved at all?

A: Almost right away.

Q: And to his denial you rejoined with the information that Anthony Smith had confessed, is that true?

A: Yes, sir. \* \* \* And that Anthony Smith had admitted that they had planned the holdup inside the bar, and that Anthony Smith and Charles Little were to grab the man and hold him, and he was to put the gun on him, and that he had panicked and shot the man.

\* \* \*

Q: Do you recall whether Mr. Mosley made any comment or reply \* \* \*?

A: No. I seem to remember [a "]what is the use["] look on his face. \* \* \* Then he decided to tell me about it. Then he said that he \* \* \* was not trying to kill the man \* \* \*.

\* \* \*

Q: When you were finished talking to Anthony Smith \* \* \* did you feel that you had a confession of guilt from Anthony Smith?

A: \* \* \* I knew we had an accomplice, and I knew we had a witness.

Q: Can you answer the question, Mr. Hill?

\* \* \*

A: No, that's not what I thought at that time.

\* \* \*

Q: But I think your testimony was that \* \* \* you told Richard Mosley that Anthony Smith had confessed and implicated Richard Mosley?

A: I did.

The Court: Was there any particular reason why you would tell him that if you didn't think the man had confessed?

\* \* \*

The Witness: I have done it a lot of times when there had been no confession.

The Court: Yes, but why do you do that? Are you trying to get him to confess by telling him that?

The Witness: I wasn't trying to get him to confess in this instance, but I have done that.

* * *

The Court: In other words, you are going to trick him into it?

The Witness: Well, I would tell them their partners have confessed.

The Court: I mean, you are going to trick him into it?

The Witness: To see if he would deny it. No, sir, I don't always tell a prisoner the truth.

The Court: You don't think you should?

The Witness: I would tell him sometimes we have their fingerprints, and we don't have it, or something along this nature.

The Court: All right.

The defendant then testified that Detective Hill had told him he was charged with first degree murder, which carried life. Further:

> He told me that Anthony Smith already made a statement, and that to go ahead, and if I go ahead and tell what I know, that I might get off light. That he would talk to the Judge to try and get it knocked down to Manslaughter.

Mosley testified further that Hill told him that he could get probation for manslaughter. Editors.] The trial court denied the motion * * * and the incriminating statement was subsequently introduced in evidence against Mosley at his trial. The jury convicted Mosley of first-degree murder, and the court imposed a mandatory sentence of life imprisonment.

On appeal to the Michigan Court of Appeals, Mosley renewed his previous objections to the use of his incriminating statement in evidence. The appellate court reversed the judgment of conviction, holding that Detective Hill's interrogation of Mosley had been a *per se* violation of the *Miranda* doctrine. Accordingly, without reaching Mosley's other contentions, the Court remanded the case for a new trial with instructions that Mosley's statement be suppressed as evidence. 51 Mich.App. 105, 214 N.W.2d 564. * * *

The issue in this case * * * is whether the conduct of the Detroit police that led to Mosley's incriminating statement did in fact violate the *Miranda* "guidelines," so as to render the statement inadmissible in evidence against Mosley at his trial. Resolution of the question turns almost entirely on the interpretation of a single passage in the *Miranda* opinion, upon which the Michigan appellate court relied in finding a *per se* violation of *Miranda*:

> "Once warnings have been given, the subsequent procedure is clear. If the individual indicates in any manner, at any time prior to or during questioning, that he wishes to remain silent, the interrogation must cease. At this point he has shown that he intends to exercise his Fifth Amendment privilege; any statement taken after the person invokes his privilege cannot be other than the product of compulsion, subtle or otherwise. Without the right

to cut off questioning, the setting of in-custody interrogation operates on the individual to overcome free choice in producing a
statement after the privilege has been once invoked." 384 U.S., at
473–474, 86 S.Ct., at 1627.[14]

This passage states that "the interrogation must cease" when the
person in custody indicates that "he wishes to remain silent." It does
not state under what circumstances, if any, a resumption of questioning
is permissible. The passage could be literally read to mean that a
person who has invoked his "right to silence" can never again be
subjected to custodial interrogation by any police officer at any time or
place on any subject. Another possible construction of the passage
would characterize "any statement taken after the person invokes his
privilege" as "the product of compulsion" and would therefore mandate
its exclusion from evidence, even if it were volunteered by the person in
custody without any further interrogation whatever. Or the passage
could be interpreted to require only the immediate cessation of questioning, and to permit a resumption of interrogation after a momentary
respite.

It is evident that any of these possible literal interpretations would
lead to absurd and unintended results. To permit the continuation of
custodial interrogation after a momentary cessation would clearly frustrate the purposes of *Miranda* by allowing repeated rounds of questioning to undermine the will of the person being questioned. At the other
extreme, a blanket prohibition against the taking of voluntary statements or a permanent immunity from further interrogation, regardless
of the circumstances, would transform the *Miranda* safeguards into
wholly irrational obstacles to legitimate police investigative activity,
and deprive suspects of an opportunity to make informed and intelligent assessments of their interests. Clearly, therefore, neither this
passage nor any other passage in the *Miranda* opinion can sensibly be
read to create a *per se* proscription of indefinite duration upon any
further questioning by any police officer on any subject, once the person
in custody has indicated a desire to remain silent.

A reasonable and faithful interpretation of the *Miranda* opinion
must rest on the intention of the Court in that case to adopt "fully
effective means  *  *  *  to notify the person of his right of silence and
to assure that the exercise of the right will be scrupulously honored.
*  *  *"  384 U.S., at 479, 86 S.Ct., at 1630. The critical safeguard
identified in the passage at issue is a person's "right to cut off questioning." Id., at 474, 86 S.Ct., at 1627. Through the exercise of his option
to terminate questioning he can control the time at which questioning
occurs, the subjects discussed, and the duration of the interrogation.
The requirement that law enforcement authorities must respect a
person's exercise of that option counteracts the coercive pressures of
the custodial setting. We therefore conclude that the admissibility of
statements obtained after the person in custody has decided to remain

[14] The present case does not involve the
procedures to be followed if the person in
custody asks to consult with a lawyer,
since Mosley made no such request at any
time.  *  *  *

silent depends under *Miranda* on whether his "right to cut off questioning" was "scrupulously honored." [15]

A review of the circumstances leading to Mosley's confession reveals that his "right to cut off questioning" was fully respected in this case. Before his initial interrogation, Mosley was carefully advised that he was under no obligation to answer any questions and could remain silent if he wished. He orally acknowledged that he understood the *Miranda* warnings and then signed a printed notification of rights form. When Mosley stated that he did not want to discuss the robberies, Detective Cowie immediately ceased the interrogation and did not try either to resume the questioning or in any way to persuade Mosley to reconsider his position. After an interval of more than two hours, Mosely was questioned by another police officer at another location about an unrelated holdup murder. He was given full and complete *Miranda* warnings at the outset of the second interrogation. He was thus reminded again that he could remain silent and could consult with a lawyer, and was carefully given a full and fair opportunity to exercise these options. The subsequent questioning did not undercut Mosley's previous decision not to answer Detective Cowie's inquiries. Detective Hill did not resume the interrogation about the White Tower Restaurant robbery or inquire about the Blue Goose Bar robbery, but instead focused exclusively on the Leroy Williams homicide, a crime different in nature and in time and place of occurrence from the robberies for which Mosley had been arrested and interrogated by Detective Cowie. Although it is not clear from the record how much Detective Hill knew about the earlier interrogation, his questioning of Mosley about an unrelated homicide was quite consistent with a reasonable interpretation of Mosley's earlier refusal to answer any questions about the robberies.

This is not a case, therefore, where the police failed to honor a decision of a person in custody to cut off questioning, either by refusing to discontinue the interrogation upon request or by persisting in repeated efforts to wear down his resistance and make him change his mind. In contrast to such practices, the police here immediately ceased the interrogation, resumed questioning only after the passage of a significant period of time and the provision of a fresh set of warnings, and restricted the second interrogation to a crime that had not been a subject of the earlier interrogation.

\* \* \*

For these reasons, we conclude that the admission in evidence of Mosley's incriminating statement did not violate the principles of Miranda v. Arizona, supra. Accordingly, the judgment of the Michigan Court of Appeals is vacated, and the case is remanded to that court for further proceedings not inconsistent with this opinion.

---

[15] The dissenting opinion asserts that *Miranda* established a requirement that once a person has indicated a desire to remain silent, questioning may be resumed only when counsel is present. \* \* \* But clearly the Court in *Miranda* imposed no such requirement, for it distinguished between the procedural safeguards triggered by a request to remain silent and a request for an attorney and directed that "the interrogation must cease until an attorney is present" only "[i]f the individual states that he wants an attorney." 384 U.S., at 474, 86 S.Ct. at 1628.

It is so ordered.

MR. JUSTICE WHITE, concurring in the result.

I concur in the result and in much of the majority's reasoning. However, it appears to me that, in an effort to make only a limited holding in this case, the majority has implied that some custodial confessions will be suppressed even though they follow an informed and voluntary waiver of the defendant's rights.  *  *  *  I disagree.  I do not think the majority's conclusion is compelled by Miranda v. Arizona, 384 U.S. 436, 86 S.Ct. 1602, 16 L.Ed.2d 694 and I suspect that in the final analysis the majority will adopt voluntariness as the standard by which to judge the waiver of the right to silence by a properly informed defendant.  I think the Court should say so now.

*  *  *

MR. JUSTICE BRENNAN, with whom MR. JUSTICE MARSHALL joins, dissenting.

*  *  *

[T]he consideration in the task confronting the Court is not whether voluntary statements will be excluded, but whether the procedures approved will be sufficient to assure with reasonable certainty that a confession is not obtained under the influence of the compulsion inherent in interrogation and detention.  The procedures approved by the Court today fail to provide that assurance.

*  *  *

The Court's formulation  *  *  *  assumes the very matter at issue here: whether renewed questioning following a lengthy period of detention acts to overbear the suspect's will, irrespective of giving the *Miranda* warnings a second time (and scrupulously honoring them), thereby rendering inconsequential any failure to exercise the right to remain silent.  For the Court it is enough conclusorily to assert that "[t]he subsequent questioning did not undercut Mosley's previous decision not to answer Detective Cowie's inquiries."  *  *  *  Under *Miranda*, however, Mosley's failure to exercise the right upon renewed questioning is presumptively the consequence of an overbearing in which detention and that subsequent questioning played central roles.

I agree that *Miranda* is not to be read, on the one hand, to impose an absolute ban on resumption of questioning "at any time or place on any subject,"  *  *  *  or on the other hand, "to permit a resumption of interrogation after a momentary respite,"  *  *  *.  But this surely cannot justify adoption of a vague and ineffective procedural standard that falls somewhere between those absurd extremes  *  *  *.

The fashioning of guidelines for this case is an easy task.  Adequate procedures are readily available.  Michigan law requires that the suspect be arraigned before a judicial officer "without unnecessary delay," certainly not a burdensome requirement.  Alternatively, a requirement that resumption of questioning should await appointment and arrival of counsel for the suspect would be an acceptable and readily satisfied precondition to resumption.  *Miranda* expressly held that "[t]he presence of counsel  *  *  *  would be the adequate protective device necessary to make the process of police interrogation conform to the dictates of the privilege [against self-incrimination]." Id., at 466, 86 S.Ct. at 1623. The Court expediently bypasses this alternative in its search for circumstances where renewed questioning would be permissible.[16]

\* \* \*

My concern with the Court's opinion does not end with its treatment of *Miranda*, but extends to its treatment of the facts in this case. The Court's effort to have the Williams homicide appear as "an unrelated holdup murder," \* \* \* is patently unsuccessful. The anonymous tip received by Detective Cowie, conceded by the Court to be the sole basis for Mosley's arrest, \* \* \* embraced both the robberies covered in Cowie's interrogation and the robbery-murder of Williams, \* \* \* about which Detective Hill questioned Mosley. Thus, when Mosley was apprehended, Cowie suspected him of being involved in the Williams robbery in addition to the robberies about which he tried to examine Mosley. On another matter, the Court treats the second interrogation as being "at another location," \* \* \*. Yet the fact is that it was merely a different floor of the same building \* \* \*.

I also find troubling the Court's finding that Mosley never indicated that he did not want to discuss the robbery-murder \* \* \*. I cannot read Cowie's testimony as the Court does. Cowie testified that Mosley declined to answer "[a]nything about robberies," \* \* \*. That can be read only against the background of the anonymous tip that implicated Mosley in the Williams incident. Read in that light, it may reasonably be inferred that Cowie understood "[a]nything" to include the Williams episode, since the anonymous tip embraced that episode. More than this, the Court's reading of Cowie's testimony is not even faithful to the standard it articulates here today. "Anything about robberies" may more than reasonably be interpreted as comprehending the Williams murder which occurred during a robbery. To interpret Mosley's alleged statement to the contrary, therefore, hardly honors "scrupulously" the suspect's rights.

\* \* \*

## EDWARDS v. ARIZONA

Supreme Court of the United States, 1981.
451 U.S. 477, 101 S.Ct. 1880, 68 L.Ed.2d 378.

JUSTICE WHITE delivered the opinion of the Court.

\* \* \*

### I.

On January 19, 1976, a sworn complaint was filed against Edwards in Arizona state court charging him with robbery, burglary, and first-degree murder. An arrest warrant was issued pursuant to the com-

---

[16] I do not mean to imply that counsel may be forced on a suspect who does not request an attorney. I suggest only that either arraignment or counsel must be provided before resumption of questioning to eliminate the coercive atmosphere of in- custody interrogation. The Court itself apparently proscribes resuming questioning until counsel is present if an accused has exercised the right to have an attorney present at questioning. \* \* \*

plaint, and Edwards was arrested at his home later that same day. At the police station, he was informed of his rights as required by Miranda v. Arizona, 384 U.S. 436, 86 S.Ct. 1602, 16 L.Ed.2d 694 (1966). Petitioner stated that he understood his rights, and was willing to submit to questioning. After being told that another suspect already in custody had implicated him in the crime, Edwards denied involvement and gave a taped statement presenting an alibi defense. He then sought to "make a deal." The interrogating officer told him that he wanted a statement, but that he did not have the authority to negotiate a deal. The officer provided Edwards with the number of a county attorney. Petitioner made the call, but hung up after a few moments. Edwards then said, "I want an attorney before making a deal." At that point, questioning ceased and Edwards was taken to county jail.

At 9:15 the next morning, two detectives, colleagues of the officer who had interrogated Edwards the previous night, came to the jail and asked to see Edwards. When the detention officer informed Edwards that the detectives wished to speak with him, he replied that he did not want to talk to anyone. The guard told him that "he had" to talk and then took him to meet with the detectives. The officers identified themselves, stated they wanted to talk to him, and informed him of his *Miranda* rights. Edwards was willing to talk, but he first wanted to hear the taped statement of the alleged accomplice who had implicated him. After listening to the tape for several minutes, petitioner said that he would make a statement so long as it was not tape recorded. The detectives informed him that the recording was irrelevant since they could testify in court concerning whatever he said. Edwards replied "I'll tell you anything you want to know, but I don't want it on tape." He thereupon implicated himself in the crime.

Prior to trial, Edwards moved to suppress his confession on the ground that his *Miranda* rights had been violated when the officers returned to question him after he had invoked his right to counsel. The trial court initially granted the motion to suppress, but reversed its ruling * * *. Edwards was * * * convicted. * * *

On appeal, the Arizona Supreme Court held that Edwards had invoked both his right to remain silent and his right to counsel during the interrogation conducted on the night of January 19. The court then went on to determine, however, that Edwards had waived both rights during the January 20 meeting * * *.

Because the use of Edwards' confession against him at his trial violated his rights under the Fifth and Fourteenth Amendments as construed in Miranda v. Arizona, supra, we reverse the judgment of the Arizona Supreme Court.[17]

II.

* * *

*Miranda* * * * declared that an accused has a Fifth and Fourteenth Amendment right to have counsel present during custodial

---

[17] We thus need not decide Edwards' claim that the State deprived him of his right to counsel under the Sixth and Fourteenth Amendments * * *.

interrogation. Here, the critical facts as found by the Arizona Supreme Court are that Edwards asserted his right to counsel and his right to remain silent on January 19, but that the police, without furnishing him counsel, returned the next morning to confront him and as a result of the meeting secured incriminating oral admissions. Contrary to the holdings of the state courts, Edwards insists that having exercised his right on the 19th to have counsel present during interrogation, he did not validly waive that right on the 20th. * * * [W]e agree.

[The Court's holding that the Arizona courts had applied an erroneous standard in evaluating the effectiveness of Edwards' waiver is discussed at page 473, supra.]

* * *

[A]lthough we have held that after initially being advised of his *Miranda* rights, the accused may himself validly waive his rights and respond to interrogation, the Court has strongly indicated that additional safeguards are necessary when the accused asks for counsel; and we now hold that when an accused has invoked his right to have counsel present during custodial interrogation, a valid waiver of that right cannot be established by showing only that he responded to further police-initiated custodial interrogation even if he has been advised of his rights. We further hold that an accused, such as Edwards, having expressed his desire to deal with the police only through counsel, is not subject to further interrogation by the authorities until counsel has been made available to him, unless the accused himself initiates further communication, exchanges or conversations with the police.

*Miranda* itself indicated that the assertion of the right to counsel was a significant event and that once exercised by the accused, "the interrogation must cease until an attorney is present." 384 U.S., at 474, 86 S.Ct., at 1627. Our later cases have not abandoned that view. In Michigan v. Mosley, 423 U.S. 96, 96 S.Ct. 321, 46 L.Ed.2d 313 (1975), the Court noted that *Miranda* had distinguished between the procedural safeguards triggered by a request to remain silent and a request for an attorney and had required that interrogation cease until an attorney was present only if the individual stated that he wanted counsel. 423 U.S., at 104, n.10, 96 S.Ct., at 326, n.10 * * *. We reconfirm these views and to lend them substance, emphasize that it is inconsistent with *Miranda* and its progeny for the authorities, at their instance, to reinterrogate an accused in custody if he has clearly asserted his right to counsel.

In concluding that the fruits of the interrogation initiated by the police on January 20 could not be used against Edwards, we do not hold or imply that Edwards was powerless to countermand his election or that the authorities could in no event use any incriminating statements made by Edwards prior to his having access to counsel. Had Edwards initiated the meeting on January 20, nothing in the Fifth and Fourteenth Amendments would prohibit the police from merely listening to his voluntary, volunteered statements and using them against him at the trial. The Fifth Amendment right identified in *Miranda* is the right to have counsel present at any custodial interrogation. Absent such interrogation, there would have been no infringement of the right that Edwards invoked and there would be no occasion to determine whether there had been a valid waiver.   *   *   * 18

But this is not what the facts of this case show.   Here, the officers conducting the interrogation on the evening of January 19, ceased interrogation when Edwards requested counsel as he had been advised he had the right to do.   The Arizona Supreme Court was of the opinion that this was a sufficient invocation of his *Miranda* rights, and we are in accord.   It is also clear that without making counsel available to Edwards, the police returned to him the next day.   This was not at his suggestion or request.   Indeed, Edwards informed the detention officer that he did not want to talk to anyone.   At the meeting, the detectives told Edwards that they wanted to talk to him and again advised him of his *Miranda* rights.   Edwards stated that he would talk, but what prompted this action does not appear.   He listened at his own request to part of the taped statement made by one of his alleged accomplices and then made an incriminating statement, which was used against him at his trial.   We think it is clear that Edwards was subjected to custodial interrogation on January 20 within the meaning of Rhode Island v. Innis, [446 U.S. 291, 100 S.Ct. 1682, 64 L.Ed.2d 297 (1980)] and that this occurred at the instance of the authorities.   His statement made without having had access to counsel, did not amount to a valid waiver and hence was inadmissible.

Accordingly, the holding of the Arizona Supreme Court that Edwards had waived his right to counsel was infirm and the judgment of that court is reversed.

So ordered.

CHIEF JUSTICE BURGER, concurring in the judgment.

*   *   *   For me, the inquiry in this setting is whether resumption of interrogation is a result of a voluntary waiver, and that inquiry should be resolved under the traditional standards established in Johnson v. Zerbst, 304 U.S. 458, 464, 58 S.Ct. 1019, 1023, 82 L.Ed. 1461 (1938)   *   *   *.   [O]n this record the Supreme Court of Arizona erred in holding that the resumption of interrogation was the product of a voluntary waiver   *   *   *.

JUSTICE POWELL, with whom JUSTICE REHNQUIST joins, concurring in the result.

Although I agree that the judgment of the Arizona Supreme Court must be reversed, I do not join the Court's opinion because I am not sure what it means.

*   *   *

18 If, as frequently would occur in the course of a meeting initiated by the accused, the conversation is not wholly one-sided, it is likely that the officers will say or do something that clearly would be "interrogation."   In that event, the question would be whether a valid waiver of the right to counsel and the right to silence had occurred, that is, whether the purported waiver was knowing and intelligent and found to be so under the totality of the circumstances, including the necessary fact that the accused, not the police, reopened the dialogue with the authorities.

*   *   *

In its opinion today  \*  \*  \*  the Court—after reiterating the familiar principles of waiver—goes on to say:

> "We further hold that an accused, such as Edwards, having expressed his desire to deal with the police only through counsel, is not subject to further interrogation by the authorities until counsel has been made available to him, *unless the accused has himself initiated further communication, exchanges, or conversations with the police.*" (emphasis added).

In view of the emphasis placed on "initiation," I find the Court's opinion unclear. If read to create a new *per se* rule, requiring a threshold inquiry as to precisely who opened any conversation between an accused and state officials, I cannot agree. I would not superimpose a new element of proof on the established doctrine of waiver of counsel.

\*  \*  \*

\*  \*  \* [O]nce warnings have been given and the right to counsel has been invoked, the relevant inquiry—whether the suspect now desires to talk to police without counsel—is a question of fact to be determined in light of all of the circumstances. Who "initiated" a conversation may be relevant to the question of waiver, but it is not the *sine qua non* to the inquiry. The ultimate question is whether there was a free and knowing waiver of counsel before interrogation commenced.

If the Court's opinion does nothing more than restate these principles, I am in agreement with it. I hesitate to join the opinion only because of what appears to be an undue and undefined, emphasis on a single element: "initiation."  \*  \*  \* Waiver always has been evaluated under the general formulation at the *Zerbst* standard  \*  \*  \*. My concern is that the Court's opinion today may be read as "constitutionalizing" not the generalized *Zerbst* standard but a *single element of fact* among the various facts that may be relevant to determining whether there has been a valid waiver.[19]

## NOTES

1. *Edwards* was substantially extended in Arizona v. Roberson, 486 U.S. 675, 108 S.Ct. 2093, 100 L.Ed.2d 704 (1988). Officers called to the scene of a breakin arrested Roberson for the burglary. This took place on April 16, 1985. After the arresting officer gave him his *Miranda* warnings, Roberson responded that he "wanted a lawyer before answering any questions." This was noted by the officer in his written report. Three days later, another officer approached Roberson, who was still in custody, regarding a burglary committed on April 15. This officer had not read the arresting officer's report and was unaware that Roberson had invoked his right to counsel. After warning Roberson and questioning him, the second officer obtained from Roberson an admission to the April 15 offense. A majority of the Supreme Court held this was inadmissible under *Edwards*. Once a suspect invokes his right to counsel, Justice Stevens reasoned for the Court, *Edwards* bars further interrogation (until a lawyer is provided) even if that subsequent interrogation concerns an offense unrelated

---

[19] Such a step should be taken only if it is demonstrably clear that the traditional waiver standard is ineffective. There is no indication, in the multitude of cases that come to us each Term, that *Zerbst* and its progeny have failed to protect constitutional rights.

to the offense involved in the first interrogation session. Roberson's invocation of his right to counsel during questioning about the April 15 breakin, therefore, barred the second officer from reapproaching him even though that reapproach concerned the separate April 15 offense. The rationale for *Edwards*—that a suspect's invocation of the right to counsel raises a "presumption" that the suspect believes himself not capable of undergoing questioning without the help of an attorney—does not disappear because the officers' further interrogation concerns a different offense. The rigid *Edwards* rule is justified in order to vigorously discourage police activity that creates an especially high risk of an involuntary waiver; the Court found no basis for concluding "that police engaged in separate investigations will be any less eager than police involved in only one inquiry to question a suspect in custody." 486 U.S. at 686, 108 S.Ct. at 2100, 100 L.Ed.2d at 716. Unlike Connecticut v. Barrett (discussed at page 504, infra), Roberson did not involve a "limited" request for counsel; the Court stressed that Roberson told the arresting officer he wanted an attorney before answering *any* questions. Suspects like Roberson might have good reason to speak with police about a different offense or at least to learn from police what the new investigation concerns so they can decide whether or not to make a statement, the Court acknowledged. But:

> the suspect, having requested counsel, can determine how to deal with the separate investigations with counsel's advice. Further, even if the police have decided temporarily not to provide counsel, they are free to inform the suspect of the facts of the second investigation as long as such communication does not constitute interrogation.

486 U.S. at 687, 108 S.Ct. at 2101, 100 L.Ed.2d at 717. It was of no significance that the second officer was unaware that Roberson had invoked his right to counsel. *Edwards* focuses upon the state of mind of the suspect rather than that of the officer. *Miranda* creates a "need to determine whether the suspect has requested counsel," and this applies whether further investigation concerns the same or a different offense. Failure to honor a request for counsel "cannot be justified by the lack of diligence of a particular officer." 486 U.S. at 688, 108 S.Ct. at 2101, 100 L.Ed.2d at 717–18.

Justice Kennedy, joined by the Chief Justice, dissented. When officers reapproach a suspect concerning a separate crime, he reasoned, "the danger of badgering is minimal and insufficient to justify a rigid *per se* rule." Suspects' interests, in this type of situation, are adequately protected by the officers' need to provide the "known and tested warnings" and the prosecution's obligation to prove any waivers by the suspect were voluntary. When persons are arrested for one offense, it is frequently learned that they are "wanted for questioning" with regard to other offenses. The majority's approach, Justice Kennedy complained, will often bar officers, even those representing a jurisdiction other than the arresting one, from such questioning. "The majority's rule is not necessary to protect the rights of suspects, and it will in many instances deprive our nationwide law enforcement network of a legitimate investigative technique now routinely used to resolve major crimes." 486 U.S. at 688, 108 S.Ct. at 2102, 100 L.Ed.2d at 718 (Kennedy, J., dissenting).

2. In Oregon v. Bradshaw, 462 U.S. 1039, 103 S.Ct. 2830, 77 L.Ed.2d 405 (1983), Bradshaw had been asked to accompany a police officer to the station for further investigation of a traffic accident in which one Reynolds, a minor, had been killed. After being given full *Miranda* warnings, Bradshaw acknowledged furnishing Reynolds with liquor but denied other involvement. He was then placed under arrest for furnishing liquor to a minor and again advised of his *Miranda* rights. A police officer informed him that the officer believed that Bradshaw had been driving the vehicle in which Reynolds had been killed.

After denying this, Bradshaw said, "I do want an attorney before it goes very much further." The officer immediately stopped the conversation.

"Sometime later" Bradshaw was transported about ten or fifteen miles to a jail. Just before or during this trip, he inquired of a police officer, "Well, what is going to happen to me?" The officer responded, "You do not have to talk to me. You have requested an attorney and I don't want you talking to me unless you so desire because anything you say—because—since you have requested an attorney, you know, it has to be at your own free will." Bradshaw stated that he understood. A conversation then took place between Bradshaw and the officer concerning where Bradshaw would be taken and the offense that would be charged. The officer suggested that Bradshaw take a lie detector test and Bradshaw agreed. The next day, after another reading of the *Miranda* rights, the test was performed. Following it, Bradshaw admitted driving the vehicle and passing out because of intoxication. At his subsequent trial, his post-polygraph test statement was admitted into evidence. A state appellate tribunal, however, held that admission of the confession violated *Edwards* and reversed.

Without an opinion of the Court, the Supreme Court found no violation of *Miranda* and *Edwards*. The judgment of the Court was announced in an opinion authored by Justice Rehnquist and joined in by three other justices. In this opinion, Justice Rehnquist explained:

> [In *Edwards*,] we held that after the right to counsel had been asserted by an accused, further interrogation of the accused should not take place "unless the accused himself initiates further communication, exchanges, or conversations with the police." This was in effect a prophylactic rule, designed to protect an accused in police custody from being badgered by police officers * * *.
>
> But even if a conversation taking place after the accused had "expressed his desire to deal with the police only through counsel," is initiated by the accused, where reinterrogation follows, the burden remains upon the prosecution to show that subsequent events indicated a waiver of the Fifth Amendment right to have counsel present during the interrogation.

462 U.S. at 1044, 103 S.Ct. at 2834, 77 L.Ed.2d at 411–12. A suspect "initiates" a conversation under *Edwards* only by inquiries which can "be fairly said to represent a desire on the part of an accused to open up a more generalized discussion relating directly or indirectly to the investigation." Other inquiries by a suspect, such as requests for water to drink or access to a telephone, are "routine incidents of the custodial relationship" and generally do not amount to an initiation of a conversation within the meaning of *Edwards*. No violation of the *Edwards* "rule" took place, Justice Rehnquist then concluded:

> Although ambiguous, [Bradshaw's] question in this case as to what was going to happen to him evinced a willingness and a desire for a generalized discussion about the investigation; it was not merely a necessary inquiry arising out of the incidents of the custodial relationship. It could reasonably have been interpreted by the officer as relating generally to the investigation.

462 U.S. at 1045–46, 103 S.Ct. at 2835, 77 L.Ed.2d at 412–13. Progressing to whether the waiver was valid, Justice Rehnquist found no reason to dispute the conclusions of the lower courts that the waiver was voluntary and intelligent.

Justice Marshall, joined by three other members of the Court, dissented. He agreed with Justice Rehnquist that under *Edwards* an accused "initiates" furthe. communication with police only by conduct demonstrating a desire to discuss the subject matter of the investigation. But, he added, this "obviously" means "communication or dialogue *about the subject matter of the criminal investigation.*"  462 U.S. at 1052, 103 S.Ct. at 2839, 77 L.Ed.2d at 418 (Marshall, J., dissenting) (emphasis in original).  As applied to the facts before the Court, Justice Marshall construed Bradshaw's inquiry as expressing no more than a desire to find out where he was being taken.  It did not concern the subject matter of the investigation and therefore did not express a desire to discuss that subject matter.  As a result, the officer's actions violated *Edwards' per se* rule and the subsequent confession was inadmissible under *Miranda.*  He further suggested that the opinions in the case appeared to reflect conclusions of eight members of the Court that *Edwards* created a *per se* rule.  462 U.S. at 1054 n. 2, 103 S.Ct. at 2840 n. 2, 77 L.Ed.2d at 418 n. 2.

Justice Powell concurred in the judgment, commenting that the opinions "reflect the ambiguity of some of the *Edwards* language, particularly on the meaning of 'initiation.' "  462 U.S. at 1048, 103 S.Ct. at 2836, 77 L.Ed.2d at 414 (Powell, J., concurring in the judgment).  But, he noted, both other opinions agreed that the initiation question under *Edwards* is "the first step of a two-step analysis, the second step being the application of the [Johnson v. Zerbst, 304 U.S. 458 (1938)] standard that requires examination of the 'totality of the circumstances.' "  Such a two-step analysis, he urged, might confound the confusion already generated by *Edwards.*  Instead, the only question should be whether, given the totality of the circumstances, the waiver met the *Zerbst* standard.  Because he found that on the totality of the circumstances Bradshaw knowingly and intelligently waived his right to counsel, he concluded the confession was admissible.

3.  Under *Edwards*, what may an officer do if, before or during custodial interrogation, a suspect says or does something that *might* mean that he wishes to invoke his right to counsel but does not necessarily mean this?  In Smith v. Illinois, 469 U.S. 91, 95–96, 105 S.Ct. 490, 493, 83 L.Ed.2d 488, 494 (1984), the Court noted but did not address the problem of what is often called the "ambiguous" or "equivocal" request for counsel.  While some lower courts require that all police inquiries cease when the suspect says anything that might indicate a desire for representation, most take a more flexible approach under which officers may not continue (or begin) "interrogation" but may inquire further into whether the suspect in fact wishes representation.  E.g., Towne v. Dugger, 899 F.2d 1104, 1107 (11th Cir.1990); State v. Griffin, 754 P.2d 965 (Utah App.1988).  The scope of further inquiries "is immediately limited to one subject and one subject only.  Further questioning * * * must be limited to clarifying [the suspect's possible] request * * *."  Towne v. Dugger, 899 F.2d at 1107.  When, under this approach, is there sufficient ambiguity so that officers can inquire into the suspect's meaning?  Sufficient ambiguity was found in *Dugger* where the suspect responded to the admonition concerning the right to counsel by asking the interrogating officer what the officer thought about whether the suspect should get a lawyer, and in *Griffin* where the suspect, upon being told of the accusation against him, said, "That's a lie.  I'm going to talk to an attorney."  In *Smith,* the suspect—when told of his *Miranda* right to counsel—said, "Uh, yeah.  I'd like to do that."  This, the Court held, was on its face an unambiguous invocation of the right to counsel and the officer's further inquiries violated *Miranda* and *Edwards.*  It rejected the State's argument that Smith's responses to the officer's completion of the *Miranda* warnings showed that in fact Smith was willing to discuss the matter with the officer in the absence of counsel.  Statements made by a defendant *after* his facially unambiguous request for counsel, the majority held, "may not be used to cast doubt on the clarity of the initial request itself."  469 U.S. at 95–100, 105 S.Ct. at 492–95, 83 L.Ed.2d at 493–96.

## MORAN v. BURBINE

Supreme Court of the United States, 1986.
475 U.S. 412, 106 S.Ct. 1135, 89 L.Ed.2d 410.

JUSTICE O'CONNOR delivered the opinion of the Court.

After being informed of his rights pursuant to Miranda v. Arizona, 384 U.S. 436, 86 S.Ct. 1602, 16 L.Ed.2d 694 (1966), and after executing a series of written waivers, respondent confessed to the murder of a young woman. * * * The question presented is whether either the conduct of the police or respondent's ignorance of the attorney's efforts to reach him taints the validity of the waivers and therefore requires exclusion of the confessions.

I

On the morning of March 3, 1977, Mary Jo Hickey was found unconscious in a factory parking lot in Providence, Rhode Island. Suffering from injuries to her skull apparently inflicted by a metal pipe found at the scene, she was rushed to a nearby hospital. Three weeks later she died from her wounds.

Several months after her death, the Cranston, Rhode Island police arrested respondent and two others in connection with a local burglary. Shortly before the arrest, Detective Ferranti of the Cranston police force had learned from a confidential informant that the man responsible for Ms. Hickey's death lived at a certain address and went by the name of "Butch." Upon discovering that respondent lived at that address and was known by that name, Detective Ferranti informed respondent of his Miranda rights. When respondent refused to execute a written waiver, Detective Ferranti spoke separately with the two other suspects arrested on the breaking and entering charge and obtained statements further implicating respondent in Ms. Hickey's murder. At approximately 6:00 p.m., Detective Ferranti telephoned the police in Providence to convey the information he had uncovered. An hour later, three officers from that department arrived at the Cranston headquarters for the purpose of questioning respondent about the murder.

That same evening, at about 7:45 p.m., respondent's sister telephoned the Public Defender's Office to obtain legal assistance for her brother. Her sole concern was the breaking and entering charge, as she was unaware that respondent was then under suspicion for murder. She asked for Richard Casparian who had been scheduled to meet with respondent earlier that afternoon to discuss another charge unrelated to either the break-in or the murder. As soon as the conversation ended, the attorney who took the call attempted to reach Mr. Casparian. When those efforts were unsuccessful, she telephoned Allegra Munson, another Assistant Public Defender, and told her about respondent's arrest and his sister's subsequent request that the office represent him.

At 8:15 p.m., Ms. Munson telephoned the Cranston police station and asked that her call be transferred to the detective division. In the words of the Supreme Court of Rhode Island * * * the conversation proceeded as follows:

"A male voice responded with the word 'Detectives.' Ms. Munson identified herself and asked if Brian Burbine was being held; the person responded affirmatively. Ms. Munson explained to the person that Burbine was represented by attorney Casparian who was not available; she further stated that she would act as Burbine's legal counsel in the event that the police intended to place him in a lineup or question him. The unidentified person told Ms. Munson that the police would not be questioning Burbine or putting him in a lineup and that they were through with him for the night. Ms. Munson was not informed that the Providence Police were at the Cranston police station or that Burbine was a suspect in Mary's murder." State v. Burbine, 451 A.2d 22, 23–24 (1982).

At all relevant times, respondent was unaware of his sister's efforts to retain counsel and of the fact and contents of Ms. Munson's telephone conversation.

Less than an hour later, the police brought respondent to an interrogation room and conducted the first of a series of interviews concerning the murder. Prior to each session, respondent was informed of his Miranda rights, and on three separate occasions he signed a written form acknowledging that he understood his right to the presence of an attorney and explicitly indicating that he "[did] not want an attorney called or appointed for [him]" before he gave a statement. Uncontradicted evidence at the suppression hearing indicated that at least twice during the course of the evening, respondent was left in a room where he had access to a telephone, which he apparently declined to use. Eventually, respondent signed three written statements fully admitting to the murder.

Prior to trial, respondent moved to suppress the statements. The court denied the motion, finding that respondent had received the *Miranda* warnings and had "knowingly, intelligently, and voluntarily waived his privilege against self-incrimination [and] his right to counsel." Rejecting the contrary testimony of the police, the court found that Ms. Munson did telephone the detective bureau on the evening in question, but concluded that "there was no * * * conspiracy or collusion on the part of the Cranston Police Department to secrete this defendant from his attorney." In any event, the court held, the constitutional right to request the presence of an attorney belongs solely to the defendant and may not be asserted by his lawyer. Because the evidence was clear that respondent never asked for the services of an attorney, the telephone call had no relevance to the validity of the waiver or the admissibility of the statements.

The jury found respondent guilty of murder in the first degree, and he appealed to the Supreme Court of Rhode Island. A divided court rejected his contention that the Fifth and Fourteenth Amendments to the Constitution required the suppression of the inculpatory statements and affirmed the conviction. * * *

After unsuccessfully petitioning the United States District Court for the District of Rhode Island for a writ of habeas corpus, 589 F.Supp. 1245 (1984), respondent appealed to the Court of Appeals for the First Circuit.  That court reversed.  753 F.2d 178 (1985).  *  *  *

We granted certiorari to decide whether a pre-arraignment confession preceded by an otherwise valid waiver must be suppressed either because the police misinformed an inquiring attorney about their plans concerning the suspect or because they failed to inform the suspect of the attorney's efforts to reach him.  We now reverse.

*  *  *

## II

Respondent *  *  * contends *  *  * that the confessions must be suppressed because the police's failure to inform him of the attorney's telephone call deprived him of information essential to his ability to knowingly waive his Fifth Amendment rights.  In the alternative, he suggests that to fully protect the Fifth Amendment values served by *Miranda,* we should extend that decision to condemn the conduct of the Providence police.  We address each contention in turn.

## A

Echoing the standard first articulated in Johnson v. Zerbst, 304 U.S. 458, 464, 58 S.Ct. 1019, 1023, 82 L.Ed. 1461 (1938), *Miranda* holds that "[t]he defendant may waive effectuation" of the rights conveyed in the warnings "provided the waiver is made voluntarily, knowingly and intelligently."  384 U.S., at 444, 475, 86 S.Ct., at 1612, 1628.  The inquiry has two distinct dimensions.  First the relinquishment of the right must have been voluntary in the sense that it was the product of a free and deliberate choice rather than intimidation, coercion or deception.  Second, the waiver must have been made with a full awareness both of the nature of the right being abandoned and the consequences of the decision to abandon it.  Only if the "totality of the circumstances surrounding the interrogation" reveal both an uncoerced choice and the requisite level of comprehension may a court properly conclude that the *Miranda* rights have been waived.  Fare v. Michael C., 442 U.S. 707, 725, 99 S.Ct. 2560, 2572, 61 L.Ed.2d 197 (1979).

Under this standard, we have no doubt that respondent validly waived his right to remain silent and to the presence of counsel.  The voluntariness of the waiver is not at issue.  As the Court of Appeals correctly acknowledged, the record is devoid of any suggestion that police resorted to physical or psychological pressure to elicit the statements.  Indeed it appears that it was respondent, and not the police, who spontaneously initiated the conversation that led to the first and most damaging confession.  Nor is there any question about respondent's comprehension of the full panoply of rights set out in the *Miranda* warnings and of the potential consequences of a decision to relinquish them.  Nonetheless, the Court of Appeals believed that the "[d]eliberate or reckless" conduct of the police, in particular their failure to inform respondent of the telephone call, fatally undermined the validity of the otherwise proper waiver. We find this conclusion untenable as a matter of both logic and precedent.

Events occurring outside of the presence of the suspect and entirely unknown to him surely can have no bearing on the capacity to comprehend and knowingly relinquish a constitutional right. Under the analysis of the Court of Appeals, the same defendant, armed with the same information and confronted with precisely the same police conduct, would have knowingly waived his *Miranda* rights had a lawyer not telephoned the police station to inquire about his status. Nothing in any of our waiver decisions or in our understanding of the essential components of a valid waiver requires so incongruous a result. No doubt the additional information would have been useful to respondent; perhaps even it might have affected his decision to confess. But we have never read the Constitution to require that the police supply a suspect with a flow of information to help him calibrate his self interest in deciding whether to speak or stand by his rights. Once it is determined that a suspect's decision not to rely on his rights was uncoerced, that he at all times knew he could stand mute and request a lawyer, and that he was aware of the state's intention to use his statements to secure a conviction, the analysis is complete and the waiver is valid as a matter of law. The Court of Appeals' conclusion to the contrary was in error.

Nor do we believe that the level of the police's culpability in failing to inform respondent of the telephone call has any bearing on the validity of the waiver. In light of the state-court findings that there was no "conspiracy or collusion" on the part of the police, 451 A.2d, at 30, n. 5, we have serious doubts about whether the Court of Appeals was free to conclude that their conduct constituted "deliberate or reckless irresponsibility." But whether intentional or inadvertent, the state of mind of the police is irrelevant to the question of the intelligence and voluntariness of respondent's election to abandon his rights. Although highly inappropriate, even deliberate deception of an attorney could not possibly affect a suspect's decision to waive his *Miranda* rights unless he were at least aware of the incident. Compare Escobedo v. Illinois, 378 U.S. 478, 481, 84 S.Ct. 1758, 1760, 12 L.Ed.2d 977 (1964) (excluding confession where police incorrectly told the *suspect* that his lawyer " 'didn't want to see' him"). Nor was the failure to inform respondent of the telephone call the kind of "trick[ery]" that can vitiate the validity of a waiver. *Miranda*, 384 U.S., at 476, 86 S.Ct., at 1629. Granting that the "deliberate or reckless" withholding of information is objectionable as a matter of ethics, such conduct is only relevant to the constitutional validity of a waiver if it deprives a defendant of knowledge essential to his ability to understand the nature of his rights and the consequences of abandoning them. Because respondent's voluntary decision to speak was made with full awareness and comprehension of all the information *Miranda* requires the police to convey, the waivers were valid.

B

At oral argument respondent acknowledged that a constitutional rule requiring the police to inform a suspect of an attorney's efforts to reach him would represent a significant extension of our precedents. He contends, however, that the conduct of the Providence police was so inimical to the Fifth Amendment values *Miranda* seeks to protect that we should read that decision to condemn their behavior. Regardless of any issue of waiver, he urges, the Fifth Amendment requires the reversal of a conviction if the police are less than forthright in their dealings with an attorney or if they fail to tell a suspect of a lawyer's unilateral efforts to contact him. Because the proposed modification ignores the underlying purposes of the *Miranda* rules and because we think that the decision as written strikes the proper balance between society's legitimate law enforcement interests and the protection of the defendant's Fifth Amendment rights, we decline the invitation to further extend *Miranda's* reach.

At the outset, while we share respondent's distaste for the deliberate misleading of an officer of the court, reading *Miranda* to forbid police deception of an *attorney* "would cut [the decision] completely loose from its own explicitly stated rationale." Beckwith v. United States, 425 U.S. 341, 345, 96 S.Ct. 1612, 1615, 48 L.Ed.2d 1 (1976). As is now well established, "[t]he * * * *Miranda* warnings are 'not themselves rights protected by the Constitution but [are] instead measures to insure that the [suspect's] right against compulsory self-incrimination [is] protected.'" New York v. Quarles, 467 U.S. 649, 654, 104 S.Ct. 2626, 2631, 81 L.Ed.2d 550 (1984), quoting Michigan v. Tucker, 417 U.S. 433, 444, 94 S.Ct. 2357, 2364, 41 L.Ed.2d 182 (1974). Their objective is not to mold police conduct for its own sake. Nothing in the Constitution vests in us the authority to mandate a code of behavior for state officials wholly unconnected to any federal right or privilege. The purpose of the *Miranda* warnings instead is to dissipate the compulsion inherent in custodial interrogation and, in so doing, guard against abridgement of the suspect's Fifth Amendment rights. Clearly, a rule that focuses on how the police treat an attorney—conduct that has no relevance at all to the degree of compulsion experienced by the defendant during interrogation—would ignore both *Miranda's* mission and its only source of legitimacy.

Nor are we prepared to adopt a rule requiring that the police inform a suspect of an attorney's efforts to reach him. While such a rule might add marginally to *Miranda's* goal of dispelling the compulsion inherent in custodial interrogation, overriding practical considerations counsel against its adoption. As we have stressed on numerous occasions, "[o]ne of the principal advantages" of *Miranda* is the ease and clarity of its application. Berkemer v. McCarty, 468 U.S. 420, 430, 104 S.Ct. 3138, 3145, 82 L.Ed.2d 317 (1984). We have little doubt that the approach urged by respondent and endorsed by the Court of Appeals would have the inevitable consequence of muddying *Miranda's* otherwise relatively clear waters. The legal questions it would spawn are legion: To what extent should the police be held accountable for knowing that the accused has counsel?  Is it enough that someone in the station house knows, or must the interrogating officer himself know of counsel's efforts to contact the suspect?  Do counsel's efforts to talk to the suspect concerning one criminal investigation trigger the obligation to inform the defendant before interrogation may proceed on a wholly separate matter?  We are unwilling to modify *Miranda* in manner that would so clearly undermine the decision's central "virtue of informing police and prosecutors with specificity ＊  ＊  ＊ what they may do in conducting [a] custodial interrogation, and of informing courts under what circumstances statements obtained during such interrogation are not admissible."  Fare v. Michael C., supra, at 718, 99 S.Ct., at 2568.

Moreover, problems of clarity to one side, reading *Miranda* to require the police in each instance to inform a suspect of an attorney's efforts to reach him would work a substantial and, we think, inappropriate shift in the subtle balance struck in that decision.  Custodial interrogations implicate two competing concerns.  On the one hand, "the need for police questioning as a tool for effective enforcement of criminal laws" cannot be doubted.  Schneckloth v. Bustamonte, 412 U.S. 218, 225, 93 S.Ct. 2041, 2046, 36 L.Ed.2d 854 (1973).  Admissions of guilt are more than merely "desirable"; they are essential to society's compelling interest in finding, convicting and punishing those who violate the law.  On the other hand, the Court has recognized that the interrogation process is "inherently coercive" and that, as a consequence, there exists a substantial risk that the police will inadvertently traverse the fine line between legitimate efforts to elicit admissions and constitutionally impermissible compulsion.  *Miranda* attempted to reconcile these opposing concerns by giving the *defendant* the power to exert some control over the course of the interrogation.  Declining to adopt the more extreme position that the actual presence of a lawyer was necessary to dispel the coercion inherent in custodial interrogation, the Court found that the suspect's Fifth Amendment rights could be adequately protected by less intrusive means.  Police questioning, often an essential part of the investigatory process, could continue in its traditional form, the Court held, but only if the suspect clearly understood that, at any time, he could bring the proceeding to a halt or, short of that, call in an attorney to give advice and monitor the conduct of his interrogators.

The position urged by respondent would upset this carefully drawn approach in a manner that is both unnecessary for the protection of the Fifth Amendment privilege and injurious to legitimate law enforcement.  Because, as *Miranda* holds, full comprehension of the rights to remain silent and request an attorney are sufficient to dispel whatever coercion is inherent in the interrogation process, a rule requiring the police to inform the suspect of an attorney's efforts to contact him would contribute to the protection of the Fifth Amendment privilege only incidentally, if at all.  This minimal benefit, however, would come at a substantial cost to society's legitimate and substantial interest in securing admissions of guilt.  Indeed, the very premise of the Court of Appeals was not that awareness of Ms. Munson's phone call would have dissipated the coercion of the interrogation room, but that it might have convinced respondent not to speak at all. Because neither the letter nor purposes of *Miranda* require this additional handicap on otherwise permissible investigatory efforts, we are unwilling to expand the *Miranda* rules to require the police to keep the suspect abreast of the status of his legal representation.

We acknowledge that a number of state courts have reached a contrary conclusion. * * * Nothing we say today disables the States from adopting different requirements for the conduct of its employees and officials as a matter of state law. We hold only that the Court of Appeals erred in construing the Fifth Amendment to the Federal Constitution to require the exclusion of respondent's three confessions.

## IV

Finally, respondent contends that the conduct of the police was so offensive as to deprive him of the fundamental fairness guaranteed by the Due Process Clause of the Fourteenth Amendment. Focusing primarily on the impropriety of conveying false information to an attorney, he invites us to declare that such behavior should be condemned as violative of canons fundamental to the " 'traditions and conscience of our people.' " Rochin v. California, 342 U.S. 165, 169, 72 S.Ct. 205, 208, 96 L.Ed. 183 (1952), quoting Snyder v. Massachusetts, 291 U.S. 97, 105, 54 S.Ct. 330, 332, 78 L.Ed. 674 (1934). We do not question that on facts more egregious than those presented here police deception might rise to a level of a due process violation. * * * We hold only that, on these facts, the challenged conduct falls short of the kind of misbehavior that so shocks the sensibilities of civilized society as to warrant a federal intrusion into the criminal processes of the States.

We hold therefore that the Court of Appeals erred in finding that the Federal Constitution required the exclusion of the three inculpatory statements. Accordingly, we reverse and remand for proceedings consistent with this opinion.

So ordered.

JUSTICE STEVENS, with whom JUSTICE BRENNAN and JUSTICE MARSHALL join, dissenting.

* * *

## II

Well-settled principles of law lead inexorably to the conclusion that the failure to inform Burbine of the call from his attorney makes the subsequent waiver of his constitutional rights invalid. Analysis should begin with an acknowledgment that the burden of proving the validity of a waiver of constitutional rights is always on the *government.* When such a waiver occurs in a custodial setting, that burden is an especially heavy one because custodial interrogation is inherently coercive, because disinterested witnesses are seldom available to describe what actually happened, and because history has taught us that the danger of overreaching during incommunicado interrogation is so real.

In applying this heavy presumption against the validity of waivers, this Court has sometimes relied on a case-by-case totality of the circumstances analysis. We have found, however, that some custodial interrogation situations require strict presumptions against the validity of a waiver. *Miranda* established that a waiver is not valid in the absence of certain warnings. Edwards v. Arizona, 451 U.S. 477, 101 S.Ct. 1880, 68 L.Ed.2d 378 (1981), similarly established that a waiver is not valid if police initiate questioning after the defendant has invoked his right to counsel. In these circumstances, the waiver is invalid as a matter of law even if the evidence overwhelmingly establishes, as a matter of fact, that "a suspect's decision not to rely on his rights was uncoerced, that he at all times knew that he could stand mute and request a lawyer, and that he was aware of the state's intention to use his statement to secure a conviction." * * * Like the failure to give warnings and like police initiation of interrogation after a request for counsel, police deception of a suspect through omission of information regarding attorney communications greatly exacerbates the inherent problems of incommunicado interrogation and requires a clear principle to safeguard the presumption against the waiver of constitutional rights. As in those situations, the police deception should render a subsequent waiver invalid.

* * *

### III

The Court makes the alternative argument that requiring police to inform a suspect of his attorney's communications to and about him is not required because it would upset the careful "balance" of *Miranda*. Despite its earlier notion that the attorney's call is an "outside event" that has "no bearing" on a knowing and intelligent waiver, the majority does acknowledge that information of attorney Munson's call "would have been useful to respondent" and "might have affected his decision to confess." Thus, a rule requiring the police to inform a suspect of an attorney's call would have two predictable effects. It would serve "*Miranda's* goal of dispelling the compulsion inherent in custodial interrogation" and it would disserve the goal of custodial interrogation because it would result in fewer confessions. By a process of balancing these two concerns, the Court finds the benefit to the individual outweighed by the "substantial cost to society's legitimate and substantial interest in securing admissions of guilt."

The Court's balancing approach is profoundly misguided. The cost of suppressing evidence of guilt will always make the value of a procedural safeguard appear "minimal," "marginal," or "incremental." Indeed, the value of any trial at all seems like a "procedural technicality" when balanced against the interest in administering prompt justice to a murderer or a rapist caught redhanded. The individual interest in procedural safeguards that minimize the risk of error is easily discounted when the fact of guilt appears certain beyond doubt.

What is the cost of requiring the police to inform a suspect of his attorney's call? It would decrease the likelihood that custodial interrogation will enable the police to obtain a confession. This is certainly a real cost, but it is the same cost that this Court has repeatedly found necessary to preserve the character of our free society and our rejection of an inquisitorial system.  *  *  *

If the Court's cost benefit analysis were sound, it would justify a repudiation of the right to a warning about counsel itself.  There is only a difference in degree between a presumption that advice about the immediate availability of a lawyer would not affect the voluntariness of a decision to confess, and a presumption that every citizen knows that he has a right to remain silent and therefore no warnings of any kind are needed.  In either case, the withholding of information serves precisely the same law enforcement interests.  And in both cases, the cost can be described as nothing more than an incremental increase in the risk that an individual will make an unintelligent waiver of his rights.

\*  \*  \*

## IV

The Court also argues that a rule requiring the police to inform a suspect of an attorney's efforts to reach him would have an additional cost: it would undermine the "clarity" of the rule of the *Miranda* case. This argument is not supported by any reference to the experience in the States that have adopted such a rule.  The Court merely professes concern about its ability to answer three quite simple questions.

\*  \*  \*

## V

At the time attorney Munson made her call to the Cranston Police Station, she was acting as Burbine's attorney.  Under ordinary principles of agency law the deliberate deception of Munson was tantamount to deliberate deception of her client.  If an attorney makes a mistake in the course of her representation of her client, the client must accept the consequences of that mistake.  It is equally clear that when an attorney makes an inquiry on behalf of her client, the client is entitled to a truthful answer.  Surely the client must have the same remedy for a false representation to his lawyer that he would have if he were acting *pro se* and had propounded the question himself.

\*  \*  \*

In my view, as a matter of law, the police deception of Munson was tantamount to deception of Burbine himself.  It constituted a violation of Burbine's right to have an attorney present during the questioning that began shortly thereafter.  *  *  *

The possible reach of the Court's opinion is stunning.  For the majority seems to suggest that police may deny counsel all access to a client who is being held.  At least since *Escobedo v. Illinois,* it has been widely accepted that police may not simply deny attorneys access to their clients who are in custody.  *  *  * The Court today seems to assume that this view was error—that, from the federal constitutional perspective, the lawyer's access is, as a question from the Court put it in oral argument, merely "a matter of prosecutorial grace."   Tr. of Oral Arg. 32.   *   *   *

## VI

The Court devotes precisely five sentences to its conclusion that the police interference in the attorney's representation of Burbine did not violate the Due Process Clause.   In the majority's view, the due process analysis is a simple "shock the conscience" test.   Finding its conscience troubled, but not shocked, the majority rejects the due process challenge.

*   *   *

In my judgment, police interference in the attorney-client relationship is the type of governmental misconduct on a matter of central importance to the administration of justice that the Due Process Clause prohibits.   Just as the police cannot impliedly promise a suspect that his silence will not be used against him and then proceed to break that promise, so too police cannot tell a suspect's attorney that they will not question the suspect and then proceed to question him.   Just as the government cannot conceal from a suspect material and exculpatory evidence, so too the government cannot conceal from a suspect the material fact of his attorney's communication.

*   *   *

## VII

This case turns on a proper appraisal of the role of the lawyer in our society.   If a lawyer is seen as a nettlesome obstacle to the pursuit of wrongdoers—as in an inquisitorial society—then the Court's decision today makes a good deal of sense.   If a lawyer is seen as an aid to the understanding and protection of constitutional rights—as in an accusatorial society—then today's decision makes no sense at all.

Like the conduct of the police in the Cranston station on the evening of June 29, 1977, the Court's opinion today serves the goal of insuring that the perpetrator of a vile crime is punished.   Like the police on that June night as well, however, the Court has trampled on well-established legal principles and flouted the spirit of our accusatorial system of justice.

I respectfully dissent.

## NOTES

1.   In Colorado v. Spring, 479 U.S. 564, 107 S.Ct. 851, 93 L.Ed.2d 954 (1987), an informant told officers of the federal Bureau of Alcohol, Tobacco, and Firearms (ATF) that John Spring was engaged in the transportation of stolen firearms and had admitted to the informant that he had once shot a companion during a hunting trip in Colorado.   The agents set up a "sting" operation in Kansas City, Missouri, and during a purchase of firearms from Spring the agents arrested him.   He was advised of his *Miranda* rights at the scene of the arrest.   After being taken to the ATF office in Kansas City, he was again advised of his rights and signed a written form stating that he understood and waived his rights and that he was willing to answer questions and make a statement.   After questioning him about the firearms transaction, the ATF

agents asked Spring about homicides. He "ducked his head" and mumbled, "I shot another guy once." But when asked specifically about the Colorado killing, he "paused," "ducked his head again," and denied the shooting. The interview ended.

About two months later, Colorado law enforcement officials interviewed Spring while he remained in custody on the federal charges. He was given his *Miranda* warnings and signed another written form indicating he understood his rights and was willing to waive them. When the officers told him they wished to question him about the Colorado homicide, Spring responded that he wanted to "get it off his chest" and confessed to the murder. A written statement was prepared and Springs read, edited and signed it. The Colorado Supreme Court held that admission of Spring's written statement in his trial for the murder violated *Miranda*. His waiver of *Miranda* rights during the interview with ATF agents was not voluntary and intelligent, the state tribunal reasoned, because the agents failed to inform Spring that the questioning would involve the homicide and such a failure to inform the suspect of the offenses at issue is a factor to consider in evaluating voluntariness and intelligence. His written statement during the later interview with state officers, in turn, was the "fruit" of his earlier and improper interrogation. Spring v. State, 713 P.2d 865 (Colo.1985).

The Supreme Court reversed, reasoning in an opinion by Justice Powell that no violation of *Miranda* occurred during the interview of Spring by the ATF agents:

> The Court's fundamental aim in designing the *Miranda* warnings was "to assure that the individual's right to choose between silence and speech remains unfettered throughout the interrogation process." [Miranda v. Arizona, 384 U.S. 436, 469, 86 S.Ct. 1602, 1625, 16 L.Ed.2d 694 (1966)].

* * *

> The *Miranda* warnings protect [the] privilege [against compelled self-incrimination] by ensuring that a suspect knows that he may choose not to talk to law enforcement officers, to talk only with counsel present, or to discontinue talking at any time * * * [T]here is no allegation that Spring failed to understand the basic privilege guaranteed by the Fifth Amendment. Nor is there any allegation that he misunderstood the consequences of speaking freely to the law enforcement officials. * * * [T]he trial court was indisputably correct in finding that Spring's waiver was made knowingly and intelligently within the meaning of *Miranda*.

* * *

> Once *Miranda* warnings are given, it is difficult to see how official silence could cause a suspect to misunderstand the nature of his constitutional right * * *. We have held that a valid waiver does not require that an individual be informed of all information "useful" in making his decision or all information that "might . . . affec[t] his decision to confess." Moran v. Burbine, 475 U.S. [412, 422, 106 S.Ct. 1135, 1142, 89 L.Ed.2d 410 (1986)]. * * * [This] additional information could affect only the wisdom of a *Miranda* waiver, not its essentially voluntary and knowing nature. Accordingly, the failure of law enforcement officials to inform Spring of the subject matter of the interrogation could not affect Spring's decision to waive his Fifth Amendment privilege in a constitutionally significant manner.

* * *

> Accordingly, we hold that a suspect's awareness of all the possible subjects of questioning in advance of interrogation is not relevant to

determining whether the suspect voluntarily, knowingly, and intelligently waived his Fifth Amendment privilege.

479 U.S. at 572, 574–77, 107 S.Ct. at 856, 857–59, 93 L.Ed.2d at 966–68.

Justice Marshall, joined by Justice Brennan, dissented:

It seems to me self-evident that a suspect's decision to waive [the privilege against compelled self-incrimination] will necessarily be influenced by his awareness of the scope and seriousness of the matters under investigation.

To attempt to minimize the relevance of such information by saying that it "could affect only the wisdom of" the suspect's waiver, as opposed to the validity of that waiver, ventures an inapposite distinction. Wisdom and validity in this context are overlapping concepts, as circumstances relevant to assessing the validity of a waiver may also be highly relevant to its wisdom in any given context. * * * The Court offers no principled basis for concluding that [the suspect's awareness that whatever he says may be used as evidence against him] is a relevant factor for determining the validity of a waiver but that * * * a suspect's knowledge of the specific crimes and other topics previously identified for questioning can never be.

* * *

I would include among the relevant factors for consideration whether before waiving his Fifth Amendment rights the suspect was aware, either through the circumstances surrounding his arrest or through a specific advisement from the arresting or interrogating officers, of the crime or crimes he was suspected of committing and about which they intended to ask questions. * * *

The interrogation tactics utilized in this case demonstrate the relevance of the information Spring did not receive. The agents evidentially hoped to obtain from Spring a valid confession to the federal firearms charge for which he was arrested and then parlay this admission into an additional confession of first degree murder. Spring could not have expected questioning about the latter, separate offense when he agreed to waive his rights, as it occurred in a different state and was a violation of state law outside the normal investigative focus of federal Alcohol, Tobacco and Firearms agents. * * The coercive aspects of the psychological ploy intended in this case, when combined with an element of surprise which may far too easily rise to a level of deception, cannot be justified in light of *Miranda*'s strict requirements that the suspect's waiver and confession be voluntary, intelligent and knowing. * * * [Under the majority's approach] once [a] waiver is given and the intended statement made, the protections afforded by *Miranda* against the "inherently compelling pressures" of the custodial interrogation have effectively dissipated. Additional questioning about entirely separate and more serious suspicions of criminal activity can take unfair advantage of the suspect's psychological state, as the unexpected questions cause the compulsive pressures suddenly to reappear. * * * It is reasonable to conclude that, had Spring known of the federal agents' intent to ask questions about a murder unrelated to the offense for which he was arrested, he would not have consented to interrogation without first consulting his attorney. In this case, I would therefore accept the determination of the Colorado Supreme Court that Spring did not voluntarily, knowingly, and intelligently waive his Fifth Amendment rights.

479 U.S. at 578–82, 107 S.Ct. at 860–62, 93 L.Ed.2d at 969–71 (Marshall, J., dissenting).

2. The requirements of an intelligent *Miranda* waiver are also addressed in Oregon v. Elstad, reprinted in the next subsection. Reevaluate what is necessary for a waiver to be effective after considering *Elstad*.

3. In Connecticut v. Barrett, 479 U.S. 523, 107 S.Ct. 828, 93 L.Ed.2d 920 (1987), Barrett signed an acknowledgment that he had been given the *Miranda* warnings and then stated to the officers several times that he would not give the police any written statement, at least until his lawyer was present. He added, however, that he had "no problem" in talking with them about the incident for which he had been arrested. During the interrogation sessions that followed, he made oral admissions of involvement in a sexual assault. At trial, testimony concerning these admissions was permitted over defense objection. The state appellate court—emphasizing that requests for counsel are not to be narrowly construed—held that Barrett's response to his *Miranda* warnings invoked *Edwards*. Since the subsequent conversations resulting in his oral admissions were not initiated by Barrett himself, it reasoned, those admissions had to be excluded under *Edwards*. The Supreme Court reversed:

> Barrett's limited requests for counsel * * * were accompanied by affirmative announcements of his willingness to speak with the authorities. The fact that officials took the opportunity provided by Barrett to obtain an oral confession is quite consistent with the Fifth Amendment. *Miranda* gives the defendant a right to choose between speech and silence, and Barrett chose to speak. * * * We do not denigrate the "settled approach to questions of waiver [that] requires use to give a broad, rather than a narrow, interpretation to a defendant's request for counsel," Michigan v. Jackson, 475 U.S. 625, 633, 106 S.Ct. 1404, 1409, 89 L.Ed.2d 631 (1986), when we observe that this approach does little to aid [Barrett's] cause. Interpretation is only required where the defendant's words, understood as ordinary people would understand them, are ambiguous. Here, however, Barrett made clear his intentions, and they were honored by police. To conclude that [Barrett] invoked his right to counsel for all purposes requires not a broad interpretation of an ambiguous statement, but a disregard of the ordinary meaning of [Barrett's] statement.

479 U.S. at 529–30, 107 S.Ct. at 832, 93 L.Ed.2d at 928. Justice Brennan concurred, explaining that "a partial waiver of the right to counsel, without more, invariably will be ambiguous." But here, Barrett's partial waiver was accompanied by an express waiver of his right to silence, which removed the ambiguity and rendered *Edwards* inapplicable. 479 U.S. at 533–34, 107 S.Ct. at 834–35, 93 L.Ed.2d at 932 (Brennan, J., concurring in the judgment). Justices Stevens and Marshall would have dismissed the writ of certiorari as improvidently granted.

The Court did not address directly whether Barrett's waivers were "intelligent" within the meaning of the *Miranda* requirements. It did, however, consider and reject the contention that Barrett's distinction between oral and written statements indicated a sufficiently "incomplete" understanding of the consequences of forgoing the right to counsel that his action should be construed as invoking the *Edwards* rule:

> This * * * ignores Barrett's testimony * * * that [he] fully understood the *Miranda* warnings. These warnings, of course, made clear to Barrett that "[if] you talk to any police officers, anything you say can and will be used against you." The fact that some might find Barrett's decision illogical is irrelevant, for we have never "embraced the theory that a defendant's ignorance of the full consequences of his decisions vitiates their voluntariness." [Oregon v.] Elstad, [470 U.S. 298, 316, 105 S.Ct. 1285, 1297, 84 L.Ed.2d 222 (1984)].

479 U.S. at 530, 107 S.Ct. at 832–33, 93 L.Ed.2d at 929. The Court added:

> We do not suggest that the distinction drawn by Barrett is in fact illogical, for there may be several strategic reasons why a defendant willing to speak to the police would still refuse to write out his answers to questions, or to sign a transcript of his answers prepared by the police, a statement that might be used against him.

479 U.S. at 530 n. 4, 107 S.Ct. at 832 n. 4, 93 L.Ed.2d at 929 n. 4. Justice Brennan addressed directly the effectiveness of Barrett's waiver:

> Barrett's statement to police—that he would talk to them, but allow nothing in writing without counsel—created doubt about whether he actually understood that anything he *said* could be used against him. In other words, the statement is not, on its face, a knowing and intelligent waiver of the right to silence. * * * But Barrett's testimony revealed that he understood that he had rights to remain silent and to have an attorney present, and that anything he said could be used against him; nevertheless he chose to speak.
>
> In sum, the State has carried its "heavy burden" of demonstrating waiver.
>
> * * *

479 U.S. at 532–33, 107 S.Ct. at 834, 93 L.Ed.2d at 930–31 (Brennan, J., concurring in the judgment).

3. What is the effect of deception by police officers before or during interrogation to which *Miranda* applies? The issue was urged in *Spring* but the Court held that it was not raised. The ATF agents' failure to inform Spring that he would be questioned about the homicide did not constitute "trickery":

> This Court has never held that mere silence by law enforcement officials as to the subject matter of an interrogation is "trickery" sufficient to invalidate a suspect's waiver of *Miranda* rights, and we expressly decline to so hold today.

479 U.S. at 572, 107 S.Ct. at 858, 93 L.Ed.2d at 967. Therefore it was not addressing, the Court noted, the validity of waivers when law enforcement officials make "an affirmative misrepresentation * * * as to the scope of the interrogation * * *." 479 U.S. at 576 n. 8, 107 S.Ct. at 858 n. 8, 93 L.Ed.2d at 967 n. 8.

*Miranda* itself contains language suggesting that waivers will be rendered ineffective by proof that the defendant "was * * * tricked * * * into [the] waiver;" see text supra, at page 438. Frazier v. Cupp, discussed supra at page 414, addressed the effect of deception upon due process voluntariness. Although it was decided after *Miranda, Frazier* did not acknowledge potential tension between its holding and the discussion in *Miranda.* Perhaps, then, *Frazier's* approach is not necessarily applicable when the issue is the validity of a *Miranda* waiver. See Santiago Ortiz v. Kelly, 687 F.Supp. 64, 65–66 (E.D.N.Y. 1988). Most lower courts, however, have assumed that the *Frazier* approach applies under *Miranda* and consequently that deception is merely a factor to be considered along with all other relevant information, in deciding whether, on the totality of the circumstances, the defendant's decisions were "voluntary." See United States v. Velasquez, 885 F.2d 1076, 1088 (3d Cir.1989), cert. denied ___ U.S. ___, 110 S.Ct. 1321, 108 L.Ed.2d 497 (1990).

Some courts have indicated that deception will render a confession inadmissible if it affects the reliability of the confession, State v. Worley, ___ W.Va. ___, 369 S.E.2d 706, 717 (1988), cert. denied 488 U.S. 895, 109 S.Ct. 236, 102 L.Ed.2d 226, or if the deception "is likely to procure an untrustworthy confession." State v. Wilson, 755 S.W.2d 707, 709 (Mo.App.1988). To the extent that such a test represents an application of due process voluntariness, it may be inconsistent with Rogers v. Richmond, discussed supra at page 424, holding that the reliability of a confession cannot be considered in determining voluntariness. See Santiago Ortiz v. Kelly, supra, at 66.

Many courts are obviously uncomfortable with police deception of suspects and sometimes find that deception renders statements inadmissible, usually pursuant to some sort of voluntariness analysis. E.g., Ex parte McCary, 528 So. 2d 1133 (Ala.1988) (confession rendered involuntary when police told robbery suspect that his suspected companion in the robbery had been found dead "with a bullet between his eyes"). In State v. Cayward, 552 So.2d 971 (Fla.App.1989), the police prepared two documents falsely purporting to be scientific reports indicating that semen found on the clothing of the nine year old murder victim was that of Cayward. He confessed. The court upheld the trial court's finding that this rendered the confession involuntary under both the state and federal constitutions but certified the question to the Florida Supreme Court. Among other considerations, it emphasized that sanctioning this sort of police action would open the door to law enforcement fabrication of even court documents and erosion of public confidence in the judicial system and would greatly lessen public respect for the criminal justice system and the police in particular. 552 So.2d at 975. The proceeding to obtain the Florida Supreme Court's evaluation of the certified question was dismissed by the Florida Supreme Court upon motion of the state. State v. Cayward, 562 So.2d 347 (Fla.1990).

4. What is, or should be, the effect of a showing that the defendant was made "promises" prior to waiving his right to counsel or before confessing? The traditional formulation of the voluntariness requirement as apparently incorporated into Fourteenth Amendment due process required that a confession not have been "obtained by any direct or implied promises, however slight." Bram v. United States, 168 U.S. 532, 543, 18 S.Ct. 183, 187, 42 L.Ed. 568, 573 (1897) (discussed supra on page 409). *Bram* itself can be read as holding a confession involuntary in part because the defendant was told that he might receive more lenient treatment if he disclosed the identity of those who committed the crime with him.

A plea of guilty is constitutionally voluntary although it was made in return for a specific promise of lenient treatment. But in the course of so holding, the Supreme Court appeared to reaffirm *Bram's* holding that a promise of leniency renders an out-of-court confession involuntary. Confessions, the Court explained, are given by suspects "in custody, alone and unrepresented by counsel." A confession made by such a suspect ·ॄ rendered inadmissible by "even a mild promise of leniency . . . because defendants at such times are too sensitive to inducement and the possible impact on them too great to ignore and too difficult to assess." Brady v. United States, 397 U.S. 742, 754, 90 S.Ct. 1463, 1472, 25 L.Ed.2d 747, 759 (1970).

Whatever the due process voluntariness standard, should effective *Miranda* waivers require the same, more, or perhaps less?

If *Bram* incorporated a rigid *per se* rule barring promises into due process voluntariness, later lower court decisions have generally abandoned that approach or at least defined "promises" in such a limited manner as to greatly limit the rule. State v. Findling, 456 N.W.2d 3 (Iowa App.1990) illustrated the latter approach. A videotape of the interrogation disclosed that the officer, Ames, said to Findling:

> Now's the time to help yourself. Not six months down the road. So, if you've got something to tell me, I don't want anything that isn't the truth, and I don't want you to tell me that you did something if you didn't do it,

but I would like you to give me the truth. So if you want to tell me your story, now is the time to do it.

Finding the subsequent statement admissible, the court explained:

> We find this contention without merit. "An officer can ordinarily tell a suspect that it is better to tell the truth. The line between admissibility and exclusion seems to be crossed, however, if the officer also tells the suspect what advantage is to be gained or is likely from making a confession." State v. Hodges, 326 N.W.2d 345, 349 (Iowa 1982). Officer Ames at no time told Findling he would gain some advantage by making a confession. We hold that the statement was voluntarily given because it was not induced by a promise of leniency.

456 N.E.2d at 8. Some courts, however, are more strict. In Dunn v. State, 547 So.2d 42 (Miss.1989), for example, a confession was held inadmissible because the officer testified that he told the defendant "I would do whatever was legal within my realms to help [him]."

More often, courts read *Bram* as meaning that a confession is rendered involuntary if the specific representations or promises made in the case, considered with the "totality of the circumstances," overbore the defendant's will. They also assume that the same approach is appropriate to determining the effectiveness of *Miranda* waivers. See Miller v. Fenton, 796 F.2d 598, 608 (3rd Cir.1986), cert. denied sub nom. Miller v. Neubert, 479 U.S. 989, 107 S.Ct. 585, 93 L.Ed.2d 587. If a defendant initiates the discussion of possible benefits from confessing, many courts regard this as requiring that the evidence of "promises" be given even less effect. See Drew v. State, 503 N.E.2d 613, 617 (Ind.1987). As a result of this approach, a suspect's confession decisions are not automatically rendered ineffective by evidence that the officers offered to communicate his cooperation to the prosecutor or the judge, especially if they disclaim any authority of their own to "make a deal" or assure any particular disposition of the case. United States v. Fraction, 795 F.2d 12, 14 (3d Cir.1986).

Perhaps the basic question is whether the law should seek to discourage what amounts to preliminary plea bargaining at the early police interrogation stages of an investigation/prosecution. If the *Brady* discussion reflects the rationale for distinguishing between guilty pleas and out-of-court confessions, perhaps suspects' right to representation during custodial interrogation renders them no longer so sensitive to inducement as to require the extraordinary protection of the traditional rule against promises. The Second Circuit seemed to adopt this position:

> [A] confession is not involuntary merely because the suspect was promised leniency if he cooperated with law enforcement officials. So long as the characteristics of the suspect and the conduct of the law enforcement officials do not otherwise suggest that the suspect could not freely and independently decide whether to cooperate or remain silent, a confession made pursuant to a cooperation agreement is not the product of coercion.

United States v. Guarno, 819 F.2d 28, 31 (2d Cir.1987).

Should it make any difference whether the officers discourage the suspect from consulting counsel concerning a proposed "deal?" In *Guarno*, the officers told the suspect that they would withdraw their offer of leniency if he consulted a lawyer. This, the court commented, did not render the cooperation agreement "less voluntary." "[L]aw enforcement officials," the court explained, "have legitimate reasons for protecting the secrecy of ongoing investigations and the identity of the targets of those investigations." Id.

In contrast, the Pennsylvania court treated differently a case in which the suspect, after being warned, said to the officer:

Maybe I should talk to a lawyer.  What good would it do me to tell you?

The officer responded that he didn't know what good it would do and

> The only thing is I would tell the District Attorney you cooperated for whatever good that would be, but I would have no idea whether it would help your case or not.

This, the court held, was an "impermissible inducement" that tainted the suspect's later confession.  It stressed the need to avoid police frustration of the *Miranda* warning process.  Promises by the police during the initial employment of *Miranda*, it explained, "choke off the legal process at the very moment which *Miranda* was desinged to protect."  Commonwealth v. Gibbs, 520 Pa. 151, 155, 553 A.2d 409, 411 (1989), cert. denied ___ U.S. ___, 110 S.Ct. 403, 107 L.Ed.2d 369.

5.  What effect does a suspect's intoxication have upon the effectiveness of a waiver of the *Miranda* rights?  In Berkemer v. McCarty, 468 U.S. 420, 104 S.Ct. 3138, 82 L.Ed.2d 317 (1984), reprinted supra at page 460, the Court noted:

> [W]e are asked to consider what a State must do in order to demonstrate that a suspect who might have been under the influence of drugs or alcohol when subjected to custodial interrogation nevertheless understood and freely waived his constitutional rights.  *  *  *  We prefer to defer resolution of [this matter] to a case in which law enforcement authorities have at least attempted to inform the suspect of rights to which he is indisputably entitled.

468 U.S. at 434 n. 21, 104 S.Ct. at 3147 n. 21, 82 L.Ed.2d at 331 n. 21.  In light of *Connelly,* see supra page 416, is intoxication relevant at all in the absence of law enforcement overreaching of some sort?

### 4.  "FRUITS" OF AN INADMISSIBLE CONFESSION

Fourth Amendment case law has firmly established that when a defendant shows a violation of his Fourth Amendment rights, Mapp v. Ohio and its progeny require exclusion of what is often called all "fruit of the poisonous tree."  This requirement, and various limitations and exceptions, were developed in Part B of Chapter 1, and are illustrated by Wong Sun v. United States, reprinted in that portion of the material.  As the principal case in this subsection suggests, however, the "fruit of the poisonous tree" rule does not always apply where the primary illegality consists of a violation not of the Fourth Amendment but rather of those rules derived from the federal constitution but applicable to elicitation of confessions.

#### OREGON v. ELSTAD
Supreme Court of the United States, 1985.
470 U.S. 298, 105 S.Ct. 1285, 84 L.Ed.2d 222.

JUSTICE O'CONNOR delivered the opinion of the Court.

This case requires us to decide whether an initial failure of law enforcement officers to administer the warnings required by Miranda v. Arizona, 384 U.S. 436, 86 S.Ct. 1602, 16 L.Ed.2d 694 (1966), without more, "taints" subsequent admissions made after a suspect has been fully advised of and has waived his *Miranda* rights.  *  *  *

I

In December, 1981, the home of Mr. and Mrs. Gilbert Gross, in the town of Salem, Polk County, Ore., was burglarized. Missing were art objects and furnishings valued at $150,000. A witness to the burglary contacted the Polk County Sheriff's Office, implicating respondent Michael Elstad, an 18-year-old neighbor and friend of the Grosses' teenage son. Thereupon, Officers Burke and McAllister went to the home of respondent Elstad, with a warrant for his arrest. Elstad's mother answered the door. She led the officers to her son's room where he lay on his bed, clad in shorts and listening to his stereo. The officers asked him to get dressed and to accompany them into the living room. Officer McAllister asked respondent's mother to step into the kitchen, where he explained that they had a warrant for her son's arrest for the burglary of a neighbor's residence. Officer Burke remained with Elstad in the living room. He later testified:

> "I sat down with Mr. Elstad and I asked him if he was aware of why Detective McAllister and myself were there to talk with him. He stated no, he had no idea why we were there. I then asked him if he knew a person by the name of Gross, and he said yes, he did, and also added that he heard that there was a robbery at the Gross house. And at that point I told Mr. Elstad that I felt he was involved in that, and he looked at me and stated, 'Yes, I was there.'"  App. 19–20.

The officers then escorted Elstad to the back of the patrol car. As they were about to leave for the Polk County Sheriff's office, Elstad's father arrived home and came to the rear of the patrol car. The officers advised him that his son was a suspect in the burglary. Officer Burke testified that Mr. Elstad became quite agitated, opened the rear door of the car and admonished his son: "I told you that you were going to get into trouble. You wouldn't listen to me. You never learn." Id., at 21.

Elstad was transported to the Sheriff's headquarters and approximately one hour later, Officers Burke and McAllister joined him in McAllister's office. McAllister then advised respondent for the first time of his *Miranda* rights, reading from a standard card. Respondent indicated he understood his rights, and, having these rights in mind, wished to speak with the officers. Elstad gave a full statement, explaining that he had known that the Gross family was out of town and had been paid to lead several acquaintances to the Gross residence and show them how to gain entry through a defective sliding glass door. The statement was typed, reviewed by respondent, read back to him for correction, initialed and signed by Elstad and both officers. As an afterthought, Elstad added and initialed the sentence, "After leaving the house Robby & I went back to [the] van & Robby handed me a small bag of grass." App. 42. Respondent concedes that the officers made no threats or promises either at his residence or at the Sheriff's office.

Respondent was charged with first-degree burglary. He was represented at trial by retained counsel. Elstad waived his right to a jury and his case was tried by a Circuit Court Judge. Respondent moved at once to suppress his oral statement and signed confession. He contended that the statement he made in response to questioning at his house "let the cat out of the bag," citing United States v. Bayer, 331 U.S. 532, 67 S.Ct. 1394, 91 L.Ed. 1654 (1947), and tainted the subsequent confession as "fruit of the poisonous tree," citing Wong Sun v. United States, 371 U.S. 471, 83 S.Ct. 407, 9 L.Ed.2d 441 (1963). The judge ruled that the statement, "I was there," had to be excluded because the defendant had not been advised of his *Miranda* rights. The written confession taken after Elstad's arrival at the Sheriff's office, however, was admitted in evidence. The court found:

> "[H]is written statement was given freely, voluntarily and knowingly by the defendant after he had waived his right to remain silent and have counsel present which waiver was evidenced by the card which the defendant had signed. [It] was not tainted in any way by the previous brief statement between the defendant and the Sheriff's Deputies that had arrested him." App. 45.

Elstad was found guilty of burglary in the first degree. He received a 5-year sentence and was ordered to pay $18,000 in restitution.

Following his conviction, respondent appealed to the Oregon Court of Appeals * * *. The Court of Appeals reversed respondent's conviction, identifying the crucial constitutional inquiry as "whether there was a sufficient break in the stream of events between [the] inadmissible statement and the written confession to insulate the latter statement from the effect of what went before." 61 Ore.App. 673, 676, 658 P.2d 552, 554 (1983). The Oregon court concluded:

> "Regardless of the absence of actual compulsion, the coercive impact of the unconstitutionally obtained statement remains, because in a defendant's mind it has sealed his fate. It is this impact that must be dissipated in order to make a subsequent confession admissible. In determining whether it has been dissipated, lapse of time, and change of place from the original surroundings are the most important considerations." Id., at 677, 658 P.2d, at 554.

Because of the brief period separating the two incidents, the "cat was sufficiently out of the bag to exert a coercive impact on [respondent's] later admissions." Id., at 678, 658 P.2d, at 555.

The State of Oregon petitioned the Oregon Supreme Court for review, and review was declined. This Court granted certiorari to consider the question whether the Self-Incrimination Clause of the Fifth Amendment requires the suppression of a confession, made after proper *Miranda* warnings and a valid waiver of rights, solely because the police had obtained an earlier voluntary but unwarned admission from the defendant.

## II

The arguments advanced in favor of suppression of respondent's written confession rely heavily on metaphor. One metaphor, familiar from the Fourth Amendment context, would require that respondent's confession, regardless of its integrity, voluntariness, and probative value, be suppressed as the "tainted fruit of the poisonous tree" of the *Miranda* violation. A second metaphor questions whether a confession can be truly voluntary once the "cat is out of the bag." Taken out of context, each of these metaphors can be misleading. They should not be used to obscure fundamental differences between the role of the Fourth Amendment exclusionary rule and the function of *Miranda* in guarding against the prosecutorial use of compelled statements as prohibited by the Fifth Amendment. The Oregon court assumed and respondent here contends that a failure to administer *Miranda* warnings necessarily breeds the same consequences as police infringement of a constitutional right, so that evidence uncovered following an unwarned statement must be suppressed as "fruit of the poisonous tree." We believe this view misconstrues the nature of the protections afforded by *Miranda* warnings and therefore misreads the consequences of police failure to supply them.

A

*   *   *

Respondent's contention that his confession was tainted by the earlier failure of the police to provide *Miranda* warnings and must be excluded as "fruit of the poisonous tree" assumes the existence of a constitutional violation. This figure of speech is drawn from Wong Sun v. United States, 371 U.S. 471, 83 S.Ct. 407, 9 L.Ed.2d 441 (1963), in which the Court held that evidence and witnesses discovered as a result of a search in violation of the Fourth Amendment must be excluded from evidence. The *Wong Sun* doctrine applies as well when the fruit of the Fourth Amendment violation is a confession. It is settled law that "a confession obtained through custodial interrogation after an illegal arrest should be excluded unless intervening events break the causal connection between the illegal arrest and the confession so that the confession is 'sufficiently an act of free will to purge the primary taint.'" Taylor v. Alabama, 457 U.S. 687, 690, 102 S.Ct. 2664, 2667, 73 L.Ed.2d 314 (1982) (quoting Brown v. Illinois, 422 U.S. 590, 602, 95 S.Ct. 2254, 2261, 45 L.Ed.2d 416 (1975)).

But * * * a procedural *Miranda* violation differs in significant respects from violations of the Fourth Amendment, which have traditionally mandated a broad application of the "fruits" doctrine. * * *

The *Miranda* exclusionary rule * * * serves the Fifth Amendment and sweeps more broadly than the Fifth Amendment itself. It may be triggered even in the absence of a Fifth Amendment violation. The Fifth Amendment prohibits use by the prosecution in its case in chief only of *compelled* testimony. Failure to administer *Miranda* warnings creates a presumption of compulsion. Consequently, unwarned statements that are otherwise voluntary within the meaning of the Fifth Amendment must nevertheless be excluded from evidence under *Miranda*. Thus, in the individual case, *Miranda's* preventive medicine provides a remedy even to the defendant who has suffered no identifiable constitutional harm.

But the *Miranda* presumption, though irrebutable for purposes of the prosecution's case in chief, does not require that the statements and their fruits be discarded as inherently tainted. Despite the fact that patently *voluntary* statements taken in violation of *Miranda* must be excluded from the prosecution's case, the presumption of coercion does not bar their use for impeachment purposes on cross-examination. Harris v. New York, 401 U.S. 222, 91 S.Ct. 643, 28 L.Ed.2d 1 (1971).

\*   \*   \*

In Michigan v. Tucker, [417 U.S. 433, 94 S.Ct. 2357, 41 L.Ed.2d 182 (1974)], the Court was asked to extend the *Wong Sun* fruits doctrine to suppress the testimony of a witness for the prosecution whose identity was discovered as the result of a statement taken from the accused without benefit of full *Mircnda* warnings. \*   \*   \* [T]he *Tucker* Court noted that neither the general goal of deterring improper police practices nor the Fifth Amendment goal of assuring trustworthy evidence would be served by suppression of the witness' testimony. The unwarned confession must, of course, be suppressed, but the Court ruled that introduction of the third-party witness' testimony did not violate Tucker's Fifth Amendment rights.

We believe that this reasoning applies with equal force when the alleged "fruit" of a noncoercive *Miranda* violation is neither a witness nor an article of evidence but the accused's own voluntary testimony. As in *Tucker,* the absence of any coercion or improper tactics undercuts the twin rationales—trustworthiness and deterrence—for a broader rule. \*   \*   \* If errors are made by law enforcement officers in administering the prophylactic *Miranda* procedures, they should not breed the same irremediable consequences as police infringement of the Fifth Amendment itself. It is an unwarranted extension of *Miranda* to hold that a simple failure to administer the warnings, unaccompanied by any actual coercion or other circumstances calculated to undermine the suspect's ability to exercise his free will so taints the investigatory process that a subsequent voluntary and informed waiver is ineffective for some indeterminate period. Though *Miranda* requires that the unwarned admission must be suppressed, the admissibility of any subsequent statement should turn in these circumstances solely on whether it is knowingly and voluntarily made.

### B

The Oregon court, however, believed that the unwarned remark compromised the voluntariness of respondent's later confession. It was the court's view that the prior *answer* and not the unwarned questioning impaired respondent's ability to give a valid waiver and that only lapse of time and change of place could dissipate what it termed the "coercive impact" of the inadmissible statement. When a prior statement is actually coerced, the time that passes between confessions, the change in place of interrogations, and the change in identity of the interrogators all bear on whether that coercion has carried over into the second confession. The failure of police to administer *Miranda* warnings does not mean that the statements received have actually been coerced, but only that courts will presume the privilege against compulsory self-incrimination has not been intelligently exercised. Of the courts that have considered whether a properly warned confession must be suppressed because it was preceded by an unwarned but clearly voluntary admission, the majority have explicitly or implicitly recognized that [the] requirement of a break in the stream of events is inapposite. In these circumstances, a careful and thorough administration of *Miranda* warnings serves to cure the condition that rendered the unwarned statement inadmissible. The warning conveys the relevant information and thereafter the suspect's choice whether to exercise his privilege to remain silent should ordinarily be viewed as an "act of free will." Wong Sun v. United States, 371 U.S., at 486, 83 S.Ct., at 416.

The Oregon court nevertheless identified a subtle form of lingering compulsion, the psychological impact of the suspect's conviction that he has let the cat out of the bag and, in so doing, has sealed his own fate. But endowing the psychological effects of *voluntary* unwarned admissions with constitutional implications would, practically speaking, disable the police from obtaining the suspect's informed cooperation even when the official coercion proscribed by the Fifth Amendment played no part in either his warned or unwarned confessions. * * *

This Court has never held that the psychological impact of voluntary disclosure of a guilty secret qualifies as state compulsion or compromises the voluntariness of a subsequent informed waiver. The Oregon court, by adopting this expansive view of Fifth Amendment compulsion, effectively immunizes a suspect who responds to pre-*Miranda* warning questions from the consequences of his subsequent informed waiver of the privilege of remaining silent. This immunity comes at a high cost to legitimate law enforcement activity, while adding little desirable protection to the individual's interest in not being *compelled* to testify against himself. When neither the initial nor the subsequent admission is coerced, little justification exists for permitting the highly probative evidence of a voluntary confession to be irretrievably lost to the factfinder.

There is a vast difference between the direct consequences flowing from coercion of a confession by physical violence or other deliberate means calculated to break the suspect's will and the uncertain consequences of disclosure of a "guilty secret" freely given in response to an unwarned but noncoercive question, as in this case. * * * Certainly, in respondent's case, the causal connection between any psychological disadvantage created by his admission and his ultimate decision to cooperate is speculative and attenuated at best. It is difficult to tell with certainty what motivates a suspect to speak. A suspect's confession may be traced to factors as disparate as "a prearrest event such as a visit with a minister," Dunaway v. New York, [442 U.S. 200, 220, 99 S.Ct. 2248, 2261, 60 L.Ed.2d 824, 841 (1979)] (STEVENS, J., concurring), or an intervening event such as the exchange of words respondent had with his father. We must conclude that, absent deliberately coercive or improper tactics in obtaining the initial statement, the mere fact that a suspect has made an unwarned admission does not warrant a presumption of compulsion.  A subsequent administration of *Miranda* warnings to a suspect who has given a voluntary but unwarned statement ordinarily should suffice to remove the conditions that precluded admission of the earlier statement.  In such circumstances, the finder of fact may reasonably conclude that the suspect made a rational and intelligent choice whether to waive or invoke his rights.

III

Though belated, the reading of respondent's rights was undeniably complete.  McAllister testified that he read the *Miranda* warnings aloud from a printed card and recorded Elstad's responses.  There is no question that respondent knowingly and voluntarily waived his right to remain silent before he described his participation in the burglary.  It is also beyond dispute that respondent's earlier remark was voluntary, within the meaning of the Fifth Amendment.  Neither the environment nor the manner of either "interrogation" was coercive.  The initial conversation took place at midday, in the living room area of respondent's own home, with his mother in the kitchen area, a few steps away.  Although in retrospect the officers testified that respondent was then in custody, at the time he made his statement he had not been informed that he was under arrest.  The arresting officers' testimony indicates that the brief stop in the living room before proceeding to the station house was not to interrogate the suspect but to notify his mother of the reason for his arrest.  App. 9–10.

The state has conceded the issue of custody and thus we must assume that Burke breached *Miranda* procedures in failing to administer *Miranda* warnings before initiating the discussion in the living room.  This breach may have been the result of confusion as to whether the brief exchange qualified as "custodial interrogation" or it may simply have reflected Burke's reluctance to initiate an alarming police procedure before McAllister had spoken with respondent's mother.  Whatever the reason for Burke's oversight, the incident had none of the earmarks of coercion.  Nor did the officers exploit the unwarned admission to pressure respondent into waiving his right to remain silent.

Respondent, however, has argued that he was unable to give a fully *informed* waiver of his rights because he was unaware that his prior statement could not be used against him.  Respondent suggests that Deputy McAllister, to cure this deficiency, should have added an additional warning to those given him at the Sheriff's office.  Such a requirement is neither practicable nor constitutionally necessary.  In many cases, a breach of *Miranda* procedures may not be identified as such until long after full *Miranda* warnings are administered and a valid confession obtained.  The standard *Miranda* warnings explicitly inform the suspect of his right to consult a lawyer before speaking.  Police officers are ill equipped to pinch-hit for counsel, construing the murky and difficult questions of when "custody" begins or whether a given unwarned statement will ultimately be held admissible.

This Court has never embraced the theory that a defendant's ignorance of the full consequences of his decisions vitiates their voluntariness. If the prosecution has actually violated the defendant's Fifth Amendment rights by introducing an inadmissible confession at trial, compelling the defendant to testify in rebuttal, the rule announced in Harrison v. United States precludes use of that testimony on retrial. 392 U.S. 219, 88 S.Ct. 2008, 20 L.Ed.2d 1047 (1968). "Having 'released the spring' by using the petitioner's unlawfully obtained confessions against him, the Government must show that its illegal action did not induce his testimony." Id., at 224–225, 88 S.Ct., at 2011. But the Court has refused to find that a defendant who confesses, after being falsely told that his codefendant has turned state's evidence, does so involuntarily. Frazier v. Cupp, 394 U.S. 731, 739, 89 S.Ct. 1420, 1424, 22 L.Ed.2d 684 (1969). The Court has also rejected the argument that a defendant's ignorance that a prior coerced confession could not be admitted in evidence compromised the voluntariness of his guilty plea. McMann v. Richardson, [397 U.S. 759, 769, 90 S.Ct. 1441, 1448, 25 L.Ed.2d 763, 772 (1970)]. Likewise, in California v. Beheler, [463 U.S. 1121, 103 S.Ct. 3517, 77 L.Ed.2d 1275 (1983)], the Court declined to accept defendant's contention that, because he was unaware of the potential adverse consequences of statements he made to the police, his participation in the interview was involuntary. Thus we have not held that the *sine qua non* for a knowing and voluntary waiver of the right to remain silent is a full and complete appreciation of all of the consequences flowing from the nature and the quality of the evidence in the case.

## IV

When police ask questions of a suspect in custody without administering the required warnings, *Miranda* dictates that the answers received be presumed compelled and that they be excluded from evidence at trial in the State's case in chief. The Court has carefully adhered to this principle, permitting a narrow exception only where pressing public safety concerns demanded. The Court today in no way retreats from the bright line rule of *Miranda*. We do not imply that good faith excuses a failure to administer *Miranda* warnings; nor do we condone inherently coercive police tactics or methods offensive to due process that render the initial admission involuntary and undermine the suspect's will to invoke his rights once they are read to him. A handful of courts has, however, applied our precedents relating to confessions obtained under coercive circumstances to situations involving wholly voluntary admissions, requiring a passage of time or break in events before a second, fully warned statement can be deemed voluntary. Far from establishing a rigid rule, we direct courts to avoid one; there is no warrant for presuming coercive effect where the suspect's initial inculpatory statement, though technically in violation of *Miranda*, was voluntary. The relevant inquiry is whether, in fact, the second statement was also voluntarily made. As in any such inquiry, the finder of fact must examine the surrounding circumstances and the entire course of police conduct with respect to the suspect in evaluating the voluntariness of his statements. The fact that a suspect chooses to speak after being informed of his rights is, of course, highly probative. We find that the dictates of *Miranda* and the goals of the Fifth Amendment proscription against use of compelled testimony are fully satisfied in the circumstances of this case by barring use of the unwarned statement in the case in chief. No further purpose is served by imputing "taint" to subsequent statements obtained pursuant to a voluntary and knowing waiver. We hold today that a suspect who has once responded to unwarned yet uncoercive questioning is not thereby disabled from waiving his rights and confessing after he has been given the requisite *Miranda* warnings.

The judgment of the Court of Appeals of Oregon is reversed, and the case is remanded for further proceedings not inconsistent with this opinion.

It is so ordered.

JUSTICE BRENNAN, with whom JUSTICE MARSHALL joins, dissenting.

\* \* \*

This Court has had long experience with the problem of confessions obtained after an earlier confession has been illegally secured. Subsequent confessions in these circumstances are not *per se* inadmissible, but the prosecution must demonstrate facts "sufficient to insulate the [subsequent] statement from the effect of all that went before." Clewis v. Texas, 386 U.S. 707, 710, 87 S.Ct. 1338, 1340, 18 L.Ed.2d 423 (1967).

\* \* \*

One of the factors that can vitiate the voluntariness of a subsequent confession is the hopeless feeling of an accused that he has nothing to lose by repeating his confession, even where the circumstances that rendered his first confession illegal have been removed. As the Court observed in United States v. Bayer, 331 U.S., at 540, 67 S.Ct., at 1398:

> "[A]fter an accused has once let the cat out of the bag by confessing, no matter what the inducement, he is never thereafter free of the psychological and practical disadvantages of having confessed. He can never get the cat back in the bag. The secret is out for good. In such a sense, a later confession always may be looked upon as a fruit of the first."

\* \* \*

Our precedents did not develop in a vacuum. They reflect an understanding of the realities of police interrogation and the everyday experience of lower courts. Expert interrogators, far from dismissing a first admission or confession as creating merely a "speculative and attenuated" disadvantage for a suspect, understand that such revelations frequently lead directly to a full confession. Standard interrogation manuals advise that "[t]he securing of the first admission is the biggest stumbling block. \* \* \*" A. Aubry & R. Caputo, Criminal Interrogation 290 (3d ed. 1980). If this first admission can be obtained, "there is every reason to expect that the first admission will lead to others, and eventually to the full confession." Ibid.

> "For some psychological reason which does not have to concern us at this point 'the dam finally breaks as a result of the first leak'

with regards to the tough subject.  \*  \*  \* Any structure is only as strong as its weakest component, and total collapse can be anticipated when the weakest part first begins to sag." Id., at 291.

\*  \*  \*

One police practice that courts have frequently encountered involves the withholding of *Miranda* warnings until the end of an interrogation session.  Specifically, the police escort a suspect into a room, sit him down and, without explaining his Fifth Amendment rights or obtaining a knowing and voluntary waiver of those rights, interrogate him about his suspected criminal activity.  If the police obtain a confession, it is then typed up, the police hand the suspect a pen for his signature, and—just before he signs—the police advise him of his *Miranda* rights and ask him to proceed.  Alternatively, the police may call a stenographer in after they have obtained the confession, advise the suspect for the first time of his *Miranda* rights, and ask him to repeat what he has just told them.  In such circumstances, the process of giving *Miranda* warnings and obtaining the final confession is " 'merely a formalizing, a setting down almost as a scrivener does, [of] what ha[s] already taken [place].' "  People v. Raddatz, 91 Ill.App.2d 425, 430, 235 N.E.2d 353, 356 (1968) (quoting trial court).  In such situations, where "it was all over except for reading aloud and explaining the written waiver of the *Miranda* safeguards," courts have time and again concluded that "[t]he giving of the *Miranda* warnings before reducing the product of the day's work to written form could not undo what had been done or make legal what was illegal."  People v. Bodner, 75 App.Div.2d 440, 448, 430 N.Y.S.2d 433, 438 (1980).

There are numerous variations on this theme.  Police may obtain a confession in violation of *Miranda* and then take a break for lunch or go home for the evening.  When questioning is resumed, this time preceded by *Miranda* warnings, the suspect is asked to "clarify" the earlier illegal confession and to provide additional information.  Or he is led by one of the interrogators into another room, introduced to another official, and asked to repeat his story.  The new officer then gives the *Miranda* warnings and asks the suspect to proceed.  Alternatively, the suspect might be questioned by arresting officers "in the field" and without *Miranda* warnings, as was young Elstad in the instant case.  After making incriminating admissions or a confession, the suspect is then brought into the stationhouse and either questioned by the same officers again or asked to repeat his earlier statements to another officer.

\*  \*  \*

I would have thought that the Court, instead of dismissing the "cat out of the bag" presumption out of hand, would have accounted for these practical realities.  \*  \*  \* Expert interrogators and experienced lower-court judges will be startled, to say the least, to learn that the connection between multiple confessions is "speculative" and that a subsequent rendition of *Miranda* warnings "ordinarily" enables the accused in these circumstances to exercise his "free will" and to make "a rational and intelligent choice whether to waive or invoke his rights."  \*  \*  \*

The correct approach, administered for almost 20 years by most courts with no untoward results, is to presume that an admission or confession obtained in violation of *Miranda* taints a subsequent confession unless the prosecution can show that the taint is so attenuated as to justify admission of the subsequent confession.   *   *   *

The Court today refuses to apply the derivative-evidence rule even to the extent necessary to deter objectively unreasonable failures by the authorities to honor a suspect's *Miranda* rights.   Incredibly, faced with an obvious violation of *Miranda*, the Court asserts that it will not countenance suppression of a subsequent confession in such circumstances where the authorities have acted "legitimate[ly]" and have not used "improper tactics."   One can only respond: whither went *Miranda*?

*   *   *

I dissent.

JUSTICE STEVENS, dissenting.

The Court concludes its opinion with a carefully phrased statement of its holding:

> "We hold today that a suspect who has once responded to unwarned yet uncoercive questioning is not thereby disabled from waiving his rights and confessing after he has been given the requisite *Miranda* warnings."

I find nothing objectionable in such a holding.   Moreover, because the Court expressly endorses the "bright line rule of *Miranda*," which conclusively presumes that incriminating statements obtained from a suspect in custody without administering the required warnings are the product of compulsion, and because the Court places so much emphasis on the special facts of this case, I am persuaded that the Court intends its holding to apply only to a narrow category of cases in which the initial questioning of the suspect was made in a totally uncoercive setting and in which the first confession obviously had no influence on the second.   I nevertheless dissent because even such a narrowly confined exception is inconsistent with the Court's prior cases, because the attempt to identify its boundaries in future cases will breed confusion and uncertainty in the administration of criminal justice, and because it denigrates the importance of one of the core constitutional rights that protects every American citizen from the kind of tyranny that has flourished in other societies.

*   *   *

For me, the most disturbing aspect of the Court's opinion is its somewhat opaque characterization of the police misconduct in this case. The Court appears ambivalent on the question whether there was any constitutional violation.   This ambivalence is either disingenuous or completely lawless.   This Court's power to require state courts to exclude probative self-incriminatory statements rests entirely on the premise that the use of such evidence violates the Federal Constitution. The same constitutional analysis applies whether the custodial interrogation is actually coercive or irrebuttably presumed to be coercive.   If the Court does not accept that premise, it must regard the holding in the *Miranda* case itself, as well as all of the Federal jurisprudence that has evolved from that decision, as nothing more than an illegitimate exercise of raw judicial power. If the Court accepts the proposition that respondent's self-incriminatory statement was inadmissible, it must also acknowledge that the Federal Constitution protected him from custodial police interrogation without first being advised of his right to remain silent.

The source of respondent's constitutional protection is the Fifth Amendment's privilege against compelled self-incrimination that is secured against state invasion by the Due Process Clause of the Fourteenth Amendment. Like many other provisions of the Bill of Rights, that provision is merely a procedural safeguard. It is, however, the specific provision that protects all citizens from the kind of custodial interrogation that was once employed by the Star Chamber, by "the Germans of the 1930's and early 1940's," and by some of our own police departments only a few decades ago. Custodial interrogation that violates that provision of the Bill of Rights is a classic example of a violation of a constitutional right.

I respectfully dissent.

### NOTES

1. Suppose, as a result of a confession obtained after incomplete *Miranda* warnings, police locate tangible evidence such as the weapon with which the crime was committed. Does *Elstad* hold or suggest that the weapon may be admitted even if the prosecution fails to show the applicability of an exception, such as attenuation of taint? See, e.g., United States v. Sangineto–Miranda, 859 F.2d 1501, 1516 (6th Cir.1988) (opinion announcing the judgment) (*Elstad* does not resolve issue but suggests that such evidence is admissible because physical, tangible "fruits" of *Miranda* violations need not be excluded).

2. Suppose that the *Miranda* violation in *Elstad* had consisted of a failure to halt interrogation after Elstad had invoked either or both his right to silence or his right to counsel. Would this violation have triggered application of a version of the "fruit of the poisonous tree" rule and required suppression of the second statement?

### 5.　IMPACT OF *MIRANDA* AND EFFORTS AT LEGISLATIVE CHANGE

#### EDITORS' INTRODUCTION: THE EFFECT OF *MIRANDA*

Despite the outcry that followed the *Miranda* decision, the available evidence suggests that its impact was relatively slight. Early research efforts and the problems of such studies are summarized and discussed in The American Law Institute's, A Model Code of Pre-Arraignment Procedure Part II (Study Draft No. 1, 1968). See also Medalie, Zeitz and Alexander, Custodial Police Interrogation in our Nation's Capitol: The Attempt to Implement Miranda, 66 Mich.L.Rev. 1347 (1968).

Project, Interrogations in New Haven: The Impact of Miranda, 76 Yale L.J. 1519 (1965), compared the success of interrogations involving warnings and others in which no warning was given. Paradoxically, the questioning was *more* successful in those cases in which the subject was warned. The conduct of 81 warned suspects was analyzed, and the researchers concluded that the warning affected the interrogation result for only eight. Three refused to talk; two of these had received advice of counsel. Three others made oral incriminating statements but refused to sign written statements. One admitted his own guilt but refused to sign a statement implicating others, and another confessed after consulting an attorney and being advised to do so. The minor impact of the warnings, the study concluded, was not surprising in light of the process observed:

> In the first place, although most interrogations were not intimidating, they were designed to discourage any initiative on the part of the suspect. * * * [T]he warnings * * * were often intoned in a manner designed to minimize or negate their importance and effectiveness. * * * [U]nless the detectives made it absolutely clear what the warning meant—which they rarely did—most suspects appeared unable to grasp their significance.
>
> Perhaps equally important, almost every person arrested * * * had committed the crime for which he was arrested and knew that the police had evidence of this. When he remained silent, the police would confront him with the evidence. Most suspects apparently felt compelled to give some alibi. Usually they lied and in doing so were caught in their lie. From then on the process was all downhill—from the suspect's point of view. Once a suspect said anything he usually had taken the first step towards incriminating himself.
>
> In addition * * *, the warnings did not have an impact on a number of suspects who, knowing they were guilty, apparently saw no point in denying their guilt. Perhaps previous exposure to the process made them believe silence was futile—several of the defendants we interviewed expressed this belief.
>
> Finally, the warnings had no apparent impact on the behavior of the suspects who seemingly believed they were giving exculpatory statements. * * * Most of those who began by attempting to justify their actions ended by incriminating themselves to some degree.

Id. at 1571–72.

Seeburger and Wettick, Miranda in Pittsburgh—A Statistical Study, 29 U.Pitt.L.Rev. 1 (1967), compared cases before and after *Miranda* and produced somewhat different results. The percentage of cases in which confessions were obtained dropped from 54.4% to 37.5% after *Miranda*; in robbery cases, the drop was from 62.4% to 36.7%. The percentage of cases in which confessions were necessary for conviction did not drop after *Miranda*. But the conviction rate did not drop significantly after *Miranda*. This, the study suggested, might be explained by refusal of the grand jury to indict in the post-*Miranda* cases in which no confession was obtained and in which a confession was essential to conviction, or by the dismissal of these cases at arraignment. Turning to the clearance rate for the crimes studied, the authors concluded that the post-*Miranda* clearance rate actually exceeded the pre-*Miranda* rate by a small percentage.

These studies were conducted soon after the *Miranda* decision. They may, then, reflect in part problems of transition as law enforcement adjusted to the new requirements. Certainly the studies do not reflect the effects, if any, of post-*Miranda* decisions reducing the effect of the seminal case. Nevertheless, some changes seem certain to have occurred after—and perhaps—because of *Miranda*. Gerald Caplan has noted widespread agreement (although no firm evidence) on some matters:

> Before *Miranda*, charges of physical force, questioning in relays, and sustained incommunicado detention were common; after *Miranda*, they became far less frequent.

Caplan, Book Review, 93 Yale L.J. 1375, 1382–83 (1984).

Whatever the "real" facts, there was after *Miranda* widespread pressure for some countermeasures to the decision. In 1968, Congress passed legislation—reprinted in this subsection—designed "to offset the harmful effects of the [Supreme] Court decisions" dealing with the admissibility of confessions, primarily *Miranda*. S.Rep. No. 1097, 90th Cong., 2nd S. (1968), U.S.Code Cong. & Adm.News. Vol. 2, p. 2112, at 2127. Explaining the need for the legislation, the Senate Judiciary Committee stated:

> The committee is convinced * * * that the rigid and inflexible requirements of the majority opinion in the Miranda case are unreasonable, unrealistic, and extremely harmful to law enforcement. Instance after instance are documented in the transcript [of the subcommittee hearings] where the most vicious criminals have gone unpunished, even though they had voluntarily confessed their guilt.

Id. at 2132.

## OMNIBUS CRIME CONTROL AND SAFE
## STREETS ACT OF 1968
18 U.S.C.A.

### § 3501. ADMISSIBILITY OF CONFESSIONS

(a) In any criminal prosecution brought by the United States or by the District of Columbia, a confession * * * shall be admissible in evidence if it is voluntarily given. Before such confession is received in evidence, the trial judge shall, out of the presence of the jury, determine any issue as to voluntariness. If the trial judge determines that the confession was voluntarily made it shall be admitted in evidence and the trial judge shall permit the jury to hear relevant evidence on the issue of voluntariness and shall instruct the jury to give such weight to the confession as the jury feels it deserves under all the circumstances.

(b) The trial judge in determining the issue of voluntariness shall take into consideration all the circumstances surrounding the giving of the confession, including (1) the time elapsing between arrest and arraignment of the defendant making the confession, if it was made after arrest and before arraignment, (2) whether such defendant knew the nature of the offense with which he was charged or of which he was suspected at the time of making the confession, (3) whether or not such defendant was advised or knew that he was not required to make any statement and that any such statement could be used against him, (4) whether or not such defendant had been advised prior to questioning of his right to the assistance of counsel; and (5) whether or not such defendant was without the assistance of counsel when questioned and when giving such confession.

The presence or absence of any of the above-mentioned factors to be taken into consideration by the judge need not be conclusive on the issue of voluntariness of the confession.

*   *   *

NOTES

1.  Is this legislation constitutionally valid?  The Senate Judiciary Committee's report on the bill cited the passage in the *Miranda* majority opinion which encouraged legislative searches "for increasingly effective ways of protecting the rights of the individual while promoting efficient enforcement of our criminal laws."  384 U.S. at 467, 86 S.Ct. at 1624, 16 L.Ed.2d at 720.  It then concluded:

> The committee feels that it is obvious  *   *   *  that the overwhelming weight of judicial opinion in this country is that the voluntariness test does not offend the Constitution or deprive a defendant of any Constitutional right.  No one can predict with any assurance what the Supreme Court might at some future date decide if these provisions are enacted.  The committee has concluded that this approach to the balancing of the rights of society and the rights of the individual served us well over the years, that it is constitutional and that Congress should adopt it.  After all, the *Miranda* decision itself was by a bare majority of one, and with increasing frequency the Supreme Court has reversed itself.  The committee feels that by the time the issue of constitutionality would reach the Supreme Court, the probability rather is that this legislation would be upheld.

S.Rep. No. 1097, supra, at 2138.  The Supreme Court has not yet addressed the issue.  In fact, no reported decision addresses the constitutionality of admitting a confession that would not be admissible under *Miranda* but is under the legislation.  Might this be because prosecutors are reluctant to risk reliance upon the statute?

2.  An alternative approach would be to authorize interrogation by or under the supervision of a judicial officer.  An early brief for such a procedure was Kauper, Judicial Examination of the Accused—A Remedy for the Third Degree, 30 Mich.L.Rev. 1224 (1932).  A "modernized" version of Kauper's proposal is contained in Kamisar, Kauper's "Judicial Examination of the Accused" Forty Years Later—Some Comments on a Remarkable Article, 73 Mich.L.Rev. 15, 23–24, 27, 32 (1974):

> 1.  A person taken into custody because of, or charged with, a crime to which an interrogation relates, may be questioned only in the presence of and under the supervision of a judicial officer.

2.   The person shall immediately (that is, as soon as humanly possible) be brought before a judicial officer who shall, before questioning begins, determine the existence of the grounds for detention or arrest.

3.   The judicial officer shall give the person the familiar *Miranda* warnings and, in addition, inform him that if he is subsequently prosecuted his refusal to answer any questions will be disclosed at trial.

4.   A complete written record shall be kept of the judicial examinations; the information of rights, any waiver thereof, and any questioning shall be recorded upon a sound recording device; and the suspect shall be so informed.

5.   The questions shall be asked by police officers or prosecuting attorneys rather than the judicial officer, but only in the presence of the judicial officer, who may intervene to prevent abuse.

Would such a procedure be desirable?   Would it be constitutional?

3.   Another reform urged by many is the recording of custodial interrogation and suspects' resulting statements.   The Model Code of Pre–Arraignment Procedure, for example, proposed a requirement that sound recordings be made of warnings, waivers, questioning, and statements made in response to questioning.   Model Code of Pre–Arraignment Procedure § 130.4(3) (Official Draft 1975).   Increased availability of videotaping equipment has led to proposals that recordings be by videotape.   Dix, Putting Suspects' Confessions on Videotape, Manhattan Lawyer, April 25–May 1, 1189, pp. 12, 14–15.   The Alaska Supreme Court has read the state's constitutional due process demand as requiring electronic recording of custodial interrogations.   Stephan v. State, 711 P.2d 1156, 1162 (Alaska 1985).   Other courts, however, have refused to find such a constitutional requirement.   E.g., Jimenez v. State, 775 P.2d 694, 595–97 (Nev.1989).

Should the Supreme Court permit evidentiary use of voluntary confessions despite officers' failure to give the suspects full *Miranda* warnings if the interrogation is so recorded?   Perhaps such recordings would permit sufficiently accurate and reliable application of the voluntariness requirement to remove the need for *Miranda's* rigid exclusionary sanction.

## C.   SIXTH AMENDMENT RIGHT TO COUNSEL

### EDITORS' INTRODUCTION: SIXTH AMENDMENT RIGHT TO COUNSEL DURING POLICE QUESTIONING

In a series of cases beginning with Massiah v. United States, 377 U.S. 201, 84 S.Ct. 1199, 12 L.Ed.2d 246 (1964), the Supreme Court held that the Sixth Amendment right to counsel applied to law enforcement undercover efforts to elicit self-incriminating statements, where that occurred after the investigation had progressed to a certain point.   This is considered further in Chapter 8.   In Brewer v. Williams, 430 U.S. 387, 97 S.Ct. 1232, 51 L.Ed.2d 424 (1977), however, the Court held that the Sixth Amendment also applied to overt interrogations by officers when that occurred after the case had progressed far enough to trigger the Sixth Amendment.   As the principal case in this section makes clear, this presents the difficult task of determining how suspects' rights are affected when their *Miranda* rights are supplemented (or perhaps preempted) by the Sixth Amendment right to counsel.

Several other aspects of the Sixth Amendment right as developed in *Williams* and its progeny should first be considered.

*Attachment of the Sixth Amendment.* In *Williams,* the Court noted some uncertainty as to the scope of the Sixth Amendment but stated that it certainly provides its protection "at or after the time that judicial proceedings have been initiated against [a suspect]—'whether by way of formal charge, preliminary hearing, information or arraignment.' Kirby v. Illinois, [406 U.S. 682, 689, 92 S.Ct. 1877, 1882, 32 L.Ed. 2d 411 (1972)]." 430 U.S. at 398, 97 S.Ct. at 1239, 51 L.Ed.2d at 436. As the Court's citation to *Kirby* indicates, this raises here the same problem created by application of the Sixth Amendment to lineups and similar law enforcement techniques; see Chapter 10, infra. In *Williams,* an arrest warrant had been issued for Williams and he had been taken into custody. Then he was presented before a judge and was "committed" to confinement in jail. Thus judicial proceedings had been initiated. But in Edwards v. Arizona, 451 U.S. 477, 480 n. 7, 101 S.Ct. 1880, 1882–83 n. 7, 68 L.Ed.2d 378, 383 n. 7 (1981), the Court did not reach the prosecution's contention that under state law adversary judicial proceedings began only with the filing of an indictment or information or perhaps at a preliminary hearing if one was held.

Michigan v. Jackson, 475 U.S. 625, 106 S.Ct. 1404, 89 L.Ed.2d 631 (1986), made clear that "arraignment" triggers the Sixth Amendment right.[a] The defendant had been arrested and "arraigned," and then questioned. The State challenged that this reflected the initiation of formal legal proceedings, but the Court responded, "In view of the clear language in our decisions about the significance of arraignment, the State's argument is untenable." 475 U.S. at 629 n. 3, 106 S.Ct. at 1407 n. 3, 89 L.Ed.2d at 638 n. 3.

In Moran v. Burbine, 475 U.S. 412, 106 S.Ct. 1135, 89 L.Ed.2d 410 (1986) (reprinted in part at page 492, supra), the defendant argued that the interrogation there invoked his Sixth Amendment rights and that those rights were violated. He acknowledged that "adversary judicial proceedings" had not yet begun, but urged that in some situations at least the Sixth Amendment comes into operation before that point. The importance of custodial interrogation is such, he argued, that the

[a] In *Jackson,* the Court used the term "arraignment" without defining it. Apparently, however, the term refers in the *Jackson* context to the defendant's appearance required by Mich.Comp.Laws Anno. § 764.13:

A peace officer who has arrested a person for an offense without a warrant shall without unnecessary delay take the person arrested before a magistrate of the judicial district in which the offense is charged to have been committed, and shall present to the magistrate a complaint stating the charge against the person arrested.

The Michigan courts have referred to this appearance as an "arraignment." E.g., People v. White, 392 Mich. 404, 424, 221 N.W.2d 357, 366 (1974). In Brewer v. Williams, however, the Court quoted language from Powell v. Alabama, 287 U.S. 45, 47, 53 L.Ed. 55, 59, 77 L.Ed. 158 (1932) that used the word "arraignment" in a different sense. Under the Alabama procedure at issue in *Powell,* the arraignment was a post-indictment appearance before the trial court at which the defendants entered pleas. This appearance or its equivalent continues to be formally designated the "arraignment" under the procedural law of many jurisdictions. E.g., Fed.R.Crim.P. 10 (arraignment "shall consist of reading the indictment or information to the defendant * * * and calling on him to plead thereto").

Sixth Amendment creates a right to non-interference with an attorney's dealings with a client-suspect if the attorney-client relationship has been formed and custodial interrogation begins. According to the state court, no attorney-client relationship had been established as a matter of state law. If the Sixth Amendment's applicability was affected by the existence of such a relationship, the majority observed, when such a relationship existed "would certainly have a federal definition." 475 U.S. at 429 n. 3, 106 S.Ct. at 1145 n. 3, 89 L.Ed.2d at 426 n. 3. But the majority rejected the proposition that an attorney-client relationship independently triggered the Sixth Amendment right to counsel:

> As a practical matter, it makes little sense to say that the Sixth Amendment right to counsel attaches at different times depending on the fortuity of whether the suspect or his family happened to have retained counsel prior to interrogation. More importantly, the suggestion that the existence of an attorney-client relationship itself triggers the protections of the Sixth Amendment misconceives the underlying purpose of the right to counsel. The Sixth Amendment's intended function is not to wrap a protective cloak around the attorney-client relationship for its own sake any more than it is to protect a suspect from the consequences of his own candor. Its purpose, rather, is to assure than in any "criminal prosecutio[n]," U.S. Const., Amdt. 6, the accused shall not be left to his own devices in facing the " 'prosecutorial forces of organized society.' " Maine v. Moulton, [474 U.S. 159, 169, 106 S.Ct. 477, 484, 88 L.Ed.2d 481 (1985)]. By its very terms, it becomes applicable only when the government's role shifts from investigation to accusation. * * * [L]ooking to the initiation of adversary judicial proceedings, far from being mere formalism, is fundamental to the proper application of the Sixth Amendment right to counsel. * * * [U]ntil such time as the " 'government has committed itself to prosecute, and . . . the adverse positions of the government and defendant have solidified' " the Sixth amendment right to counsel does not attach. [United States v. Gouveia, 467 U.S. 180, 189, 104 S.Ct. 2292, 2298, 81 L.Ed.2d 146 (1984)].

475 U.S. at 430–32, 106 S.Ct. at 1146–47, 89 L.Ed.2d at 427–28.

*Application of* Edwards *Rule.* In *Jackson,* the Court held that the *Edwards* rule as developed in the *Miranda* context, see page 484, supra, also applied in Sixth Amendment situations. The two respondent-defendants had been arrested, and at "arraignment" requested that counsel be appointed for them. It is not clear whether this was in response to an offer by the magistrate to appoint counsel or in what terms the requests (and any preceding offers) were made. Later, while the defendants were still in custody, they were approached by police officers, given *Miranda* warnings, and—apparently after agreeing to submit to questioning without counsels' presence—made incriminating statements. A majority of the Supreme Court agreed with the Michigan Supreme Court that the Sixth Amendment required the suppression of these statements. The "arraignment" caused the defendants' Sixth Amendment right to counsel to attach. At issue in the case "is

whether respondents validly waived their right to counsel at the postarraignment custodial interrogations." The Sixth Amendment right, the
Court continued, is subject to the *Edwards* rule, because "the Sixth
Amendment right to counsel at a postarraignment interrogation requires at least as much protection as does the Fifth Amendment right
to counsel at any custodial interrogation." 475 U.S. at 632, 106 S.Ct. at
1409, 89 L.Ed.2d at 639. The State argued that the defendants may
have intended their request for counsel to refer only to counsel for trial
and other formal legal purposes and not for purposes of representation
during further questioning. But the Court responded:

> [I]t is the State that has the burden of establishing a valid waiver.
> Doubts must be resolved in favor of protecting the constitutional
> claim. This settled approach to questions of waiver requires us to
> give a broad, rather than a narrow, interpretation to a defendant's
> request for counsel—we presume that the defendant requests the
> lawyer's services at every critical stage of the prosecution. We
> thus reject the State's suggestion * * *.

475 U.S. at 633, 106 S.Ct. at 1409, 89 L.Ed.2d at 640. In a footnote, the
Court commented further:

> In construing respondents' request for counsel, we do not, of
> course, suggest that the right to counsel turns on such a request.
> Rather, we construe the defendant's request for counsel as an
> extremely important fact in considering the validity of a subse-
> quent waiver in response to police-initiated interrogation.

475 U.S. at 633 n. 6, 106 S.Ct. at 1409 n. 6, 89 L.Ed.2d at 640 n. 6. The
Court summarized its holding:

> We * * * hold that, if police initiate interrogation after a defen-
> dant's assertion, at an arraignment or similar proceeding, of his
> right to counsel, any waiver of the defendant's right to counsel for
> that police-initiated interrogation is invalid.

475 U.S. at 636, 106 S.Ct. at 1411, 89 L.Ed.2d at 642.

Justice Rehnquist, joined by Justices Powell and O'Connor, dissented:

> The dispositive question * * * is whether the same kind of
> prophylactic rule [as was created in *Miranda* and *Edwards*] is
> needed to protect a defendant's right to counsel under the Sixth
> Amendment. The answer to this question, it seems to me, is
> clearly "no." The Court does not even suggest that the police
> commonly deny defendants their Sixth Amendment right to coun-
> sel. Nor, I suspect, would such a claim likely be borne out by
> empirical evidence. Thus, the justification for the prophylactic
> rules this Court created in *Miranda* and *Edwards,* namely the
> perceived widespread problem that the police were violating, and
> would probably continue to violate, the Fifth Amendment rights of
> defendants during the course of custodial interrogation, is conspicu-
> ously absent in the Sixth Amendment context. To put it simply,
> the prophylactic rule set forth in *Edwards* makes no sense at all

except when linked to the Fifth Amendment's prohibition against compelled self-incrimination.

475 U.S. at 639–40, 106 S.Ct. at 1413, 89 L.Ed.2d at 644–45 (Rehnquist, J., dissenting). Chief Justice Burger concurred in the judgment, reasoning that "*Stare decisis* calls for my following the rule of *Edwards* in this context, but plainly the subject calls for re-examination." 475 U.S. at 637, 106 S.Ct. at 1411, 89 L.Ed.2d at 643 (Burger, C.J., concurring in the judgment).

\* \* \*

When the Sixth Amendment is triggered, what effect does it have upon the legal status of a suspect undergoing custodial interrogation, above and beyond what is dictated by *Miranda* and the Fifth Amendment? Justice Marshall has suggested that waivers of the Sixth Amendment right to counsel should be subjected to greater scrutiny than waivers of *Miranda* rights. A waiver of the former, he urged, should require a greater comprehension of the consequences than does a waiver of the former. See Fields v. Wyrick, 464 U.S. 1020, 1022–23, 104 S.Ct. 556, 557, 78 L.Ed.2d 728, 729 (1983) (Marshall, J., dissenting from denial of certiorari). The following case, to some extent, confronts this general question.

## PATTERSON v. ILLINOIS

Supreme Court of the United States, 1988.
487 U.S. 285, 108 S.Ct. 2389, 101 L.Ed.2d 261.

JUSTICE WHITE delivered the opinion of the Court.

In this case, we are called on to determine whether the interrogation of petitioner after his indictment violated his Sixth Amendment right to counsel.

### I

Before dawn on August 21, 1983, petitioner and other members of the "Vice Lords" street gang became involved in a fight with members of a rival gang, the "Black Mobsters." Some time after the fight, a former member of the Black Mobsters, James Jackson, went to the home where the Vice Lords had fled. A second fight broke out there, with petitioner and three other Vice Lords beating Jackson severely. The Vice Lords then put Jackson into a car, drove to the end of a nearby street, and left him face down in a puddle of water. Later that morning, police discovered Jackson, dead, where he had been left.

That afternoon, local police officers obtained warrants for the arrest of the Vice Lords, on charges of battery and mob action, in connection with the first fight. One of the gang members who was arrested gave the police a statement concerning the first fight; the statement also implicated several of the Vice Lords (including petitioner) in Jackson's murder. A few hours later, petitioner was apprehended. Petitioner was informed of his rights under Miranda v. Arizona, 384 U.S. 436, 86 S.Ct. 1602, 16 L.Ed.2d 694 (1966), and volunteered to answer questions put to him by the police. Petitioner gave a statement concerning the initial fight between the rival gangs, but denied knowing anything about Jackson's death. Petitioner was held in custody the following day, August 22, as law enforcement authorities completed their investigation of the Jackson murder.

On August 23, a Cook County grand jury indicted petitioner and two other gang members for the murder of James Jackson. Police officer Michael Gresham, who had questioned petitioner earlier, removed him from the lockup where he was being held, and told petitioner that because he had been indicted he was being transferred to the Cook County jail. Petitioner asked Gresham which of the gang members had been charged with Jackson's murder, and upon learning that one particular Vice Lord had been omitted from the indictments, asked: "[W]hy wasn't he indicted, he did everything." Petitioner also began to explain that there was a witness who would support his account of the crime.

At this point, Gresham interrupted petitioner, and handed him a *Miranda* waiver form. The form contained five specific warnings, as suggested by this Court's *Miranda* decision, to make petitioner aware of his right to counsel and of the consequences of any statement he might make to police. Gresham read the warnings aloud, as petitioner read along with him. Petitioner initialed each of the five warnings, and signed the waiver form. Petitioner then gave a lengthy statement to police officers concerning the Jackson murder; petitioner's statement described in detail the role of each of the Vice Lords—including himself—in the murder of James Jackson.

Later that day, petitioner confessed involvement in the murder for a second time. This confession came in an interview with Assistant State's Attorney (ASA) George Smith. At the outset of the interview, Smith reviewed with petitioner the *Miranda* waiver he had previously signed, and petitioner confirmed that he had signed the waiver and understood his rights. Smith went through the waiver procedure once again: reading petitioner his rights, having petitioner initial each one, and sign a waiver form. In addition, Smith informed petitioner that he was a lawyer working with the police investigating the Jackson case. Petitioner then gave another inculpatory statement concerning the crime.

Before trial, petitioner moved to suppress his statements, arguing that they were obtained in a manner at odds with various constitutional guarantees. The trial court denied these motions, and the statements were used against petitioner at his trial. The jury found petitioner guilty of murder, and petitioner was sentenced to a 24–year prison term.

On appeal, petitioner argued that he had not "knowingly and intelligently" waived his Sixth Amendment right to counsel before he gave his uncounseled postindictment confessions. Petitioner contended that the warnings he received, while adequate for the purposes of protecting his *Fifth* Amendment rights as guaranteed by *Miranda*, did not adequately inform him of his *Sixth* Amendment right to counsel. The Illinois Supreme Court, however, rejected, this theory * * *.

## II

There can be no doubt that petitioner had the right to have the assistance of counsel at his postindictment interviews with law enforcement authorities. Our cases make it plain that the Sixth Amendment guarantees this right to criminal defendants. Michigan v. Jackson, 475 U.S. 625, 629–630, 106 S.Ct. 1404, 1407–1408, 89 L.Ed.2d 631 (1986); Brewer v. Williams, 430 U.S. 387, 398–401, 97 S.Ct. 1232, 1239–1241, 51 L.Ed.2d 424 (1977); Massiah v. United States, 377 U.S. 201, 205–207, 84 S.Ct. 1199, 1202–1204, 12 L.Ed.2d 246 (1964).[20] Petitioner asserts that the questioning that produced his incriminating statements violated his Sixth Amendment right to counsel in two ways.

## A

Petitioner's first claim is that because his Sixth Amendment right to counsel arose with his indictment, the police were thereafter barred from initiating a meeting with him. He equates himself with a preindictment suspect who, while being interrogated, asserts his Fifth Amendment right to counsel; under Edwards v. Arizona, 451 U.S. 477, 101 S.Ct. 1880, 68 L.Ed.2d 378 (1981), such a suspect may not be questioned again unless he initiates the meeting.

\* \* \*

At bottom, petitioner's theory cannot be squared with our rationale in *Edwards,* the case he relies on for support. \* \* \* Preserving the integrity of an accused's choice to communicate with police only through counsel is the essence of *Edwards* and its progeny—not barring an accused from making an *initial* election as to whether he will face the State's officers during questioning with the aid of counsel, or go it alone. If an accused "knowingly and intelligently" pursues the latter course, we see no reason why the uncounseled statements he then makes must be excluded at his trial.

## B

Petitioner's principal and more substantial claim is that questioning him without counsel present violated the Sixth Amendment because he did not validly waive his right to have counsel present during the interviews. Since it is clear that after the *Miranda* warnings were given to petitioner, he not only voluntarily answered questions without claiming his right to silence or his right to have a lawyer present to advise him but also executed a written waiver of his right to counsel during questioning, the specific issue posed here is whether this waiver was a "knowing and intelligent" waiver of his Sixth Amendment

---

[20] We note as a matter of some significance that petitioner had not retained, or accepted by appointment, a lawyer to represent him at the time he was questioned by authorities. Once an accused has a lawyer, a distinct set of constitutional safeguards aimed at preserving the sanctity of the attorney-client relationship takes effect. See Maine v. Moulton, 474 U.S. 159, 176, 106 S.Ct. 477, 487–88, 88 L.Ed.2d 481 (1985). The State conceded as much at argument.

right.[21] See *Brewer v. Williams,* supra, at 401, 404, 97 S.Ct. at 1240–41, 1242; Johnson v. Zerbst, 304 U.S. 458, 464–465, 58 S.Ct. 1019, 1023, 82 L.Ed.2d 1461 (1938).

In the past, this Court has held that a waiver of the Sixth Amendment right to counsel is valid only when it reflects "an intentional relinquishment or abandonment of a known right or privilege." *Johnson v. Zerbst,* supra, at 464, 58 S.Ct. at 1023. In other words, the accused must "kno[w] what he is doing" so that "his choice is made with eyes open." Adams v. United States ex rel. McCann, 317 U.S. 269, 279, 63 S.Ct. 236, 242, 87 L.Ed.2d 268 (1942). In a case arising under the Fifth Amendment, we described this requirement as "a full awareness [of] both the nature of the right being abandoned and the consequences of the decision to abandon it." Moran v. Burbine, 475 U.S. 412, 421, 106 S.Ct. 1135, 1141, 89 L.Ed.2d 410 (1986). Whichever of these formulations is used, the key inquiry in a case such as this one must be: Was the accused, who waived his Sixth Amendment rights during postindictment questioning, made sufficiently aware of his right to have counsel present during the questioning, and of the possible consequences of a decision to forgo the aid of counsel? In this case, we are convinced that by admonishing petitioner with the *Miranda* warnings, respondent has met this burden and that petitioner's waiver of his right to counsel at the questioning was valid.

First, the *Miranda* warnings given petitioner made him aware of his right to have counsel present during the questioning. By telling petitioner that he had a right to consult with an attorney, to have a lawyer present while he was questioned, and even to have a lawyer appointed for him if he could not afford to retain one on his own, Officer Gresham and ASA Smith conveyed to petitioner the sum and substance of the rights that the Sixth Amendment provided him. * * * There is little more petitioner could have possibly been told in an effort to satisfy this portion of the waiver inquiry.

Second, the *Miranda* warnings also served to make petitioner aware of the consequences of a decision by him to waive his Sixth Amendment rights during postindictment questioning. Petitioner knew that any statement that he made could be used against him in subsequent criminal proceedings. This is the ultimate adverse consequence petitioner could have suffered by virtue of his choice to make uncounseled admissions to the authorities. This warning also sufficed—contrary to petitioner's claim here—to let him know what a lawyer could "do for him" during the postindictment questioning: namely, advise petitioner to refrain from making any such statements. By knowing what could be done with any statements he might make, and therefore, what benefit could be obtained by having the aid of counsel while making such statements, petitioner was essentially informed of the possible consequences of going without counsel during questioning. If petitioner nonetheless lacked "a full and complete appreciation of all of the consequences flowing" from his waiver, it does

---

[21] * * * [T]he voluntariness of petitioner's confession is not before us.

not defeat the State's showing that the information it provided to him satisfied the constitutional minimum.

Our conclusion is supported by petitioner's inability, in the proceedings before this Court, to articulate with precision what additional information should have been provided to him before he would have been competent to waive his right to counsel. All that petitioner's brief and reply brief suggest is petitioner should have been made aware of his "right under the Sixth Amendment to the broad protection of counsel"—a rather nebulous suggestion—and the "gravity of [his] situation." But surely this latter "requirement" (if it is one) was met when Officer Gresham informed petitioner that he had been formally charged with the murder of James Jackson. Under close questioning on this same point at argument, petitioner likewise failed to suggest any meaningful additional information that he should have been, but was not, provided in advance of his decision to waive his right to counsel.

*   *   *

As a general matter, then, an accused who is admonished with the warnings prescribed by this Court in *Miranda,* has been sufficiently apprised of the nature of his Sixth Amendment rights, and of the consequences of abandoning those rights, so that his waiver on this basis will be considered a knowing and intelligent one.[22]

## C

We consequently reject petitioner's argument, which has some acceptance from courts and commentators that since "the sixth amendment right [to counsel] is far superior to that of the fifth amendment right" and since "[t]he greater the right the greater the loss from a waiver of that right," waiver of an accused's Sixth Amendment right to counsel should be "more difficult" to effectuate than waiver of a suspect's Fifth Amendment rights. Brief for Petitioner 23. While our cases have recognized a "difference" between the Fifth Amendment and Sixth Amendment rights to counsel, and the "policies" behind these Constitutional guarantees, we have never suggested that one right is "superior" or "greater" than the other, nor is there any support in our cases for the notion that because a Sixth Amendment right may be

---

[22] This does not mean, of course, that all Sixth Amendment challenges to the conduct of postindictment questioning will fail whenever the challenged practice would pass constitutional muster under *Miranda.* For example, we have permitted a *Miranda* waiver to stand where a suspect was not told that his lawyer was trying to reach him during questioning; in the Sixth Amendment context, this waiver would not be valid. See Moran v. Burbine, 475 U.S., at 424, 428, 106 S.Ct. at 1142–43, 1145. Likewise a surreptitious conversion between an undercover police officer and an undicted suspect would not give rise to any *Miranda* violation as long as the "interrogation" was not in a custodial setting, see *Miranda,* 384 U.S., at 475, 86 S.Ct. at 1628;

however, once the accused is indicted, such questioning would be prohibited. See United States v. Henry, 447 U.S. 264, 273, 274–275, 100 S.Ct. 2183, 2188–2189, 65 L.Ed.2d 115 (1980).

Thus, because the Sixth Amendment's protection of the attorney-client relationship—"the right to rely on counsel as a 'medium' between [the accused] and the State"—extends beyond *Miranda's* protection of the Fifth Amendment right to counsel, see Maine v. Moulton, 474 U.S., at 176, 106 S.Ct. at 487–88, there will be cases where a waiver which would be valid under *Miranda* will not suffice for Sixth Amendment purposes.

involved, it is more difficult to waive than the Fifth Amendment counterpart.

Instead, we have taken a more pragmatic approach to the waiver question—asking what purposes a lawyer can serve at the particular stage of the proceedings in question, and what assistance he could provide to an accused at that stage—to determine the scope of the Sixth Amendment right to counsel, and the type of warnings and procedures that should be required before a waiver of that right will be recognized.

At one end of the spectrum, we have concluded there is no Sixth Amendment right to counsel whatsoever at a postindictment photographic display identification, because this procedure is not one at which the accused "require[s] aid in coping with legal problems or assistance in meeting his adversary." See United States v. Ash, 413 U.S. 300, 313–320, 93 S.Ct. 2568, 2575, 37 L.Ed.2d 619 (1973). At the other extreme, recognizing the enormous importance and role that an attorney plays at a criminal trial, we have imposed the most rigorous restrictions on the information that must be conveyed to a defendant, and the procedures that must be observed, before permitting him to waive his right to counsel at trial. See Faretta v. California, 422 U.S. 806, 835–836, 95 S.Ct. 2525, 2541–2542, 45 L.Ed.2d 562 (1975). In these extreme cases, and in others that fall between these two poles, we have defined the scope of the right to counsel by a pragmatic assessment of the usefulness of counsel to the accused at the particular proceeding, and the dangers to the accused of proceeding without counsel. An accused's waiver of his right to counsel is "knowing" when he is made aware of these basic facts.

Applying this approach, it is our view that whatever warnings suffice for *Miranda's* purposes will also be sufficient in the context of postindictment questioning. The State's decision to take an additional step and commence formal adversarial proceedings against the accused does not substantially increase the value of counsel to the accused at questioning, or expand the limited purpose that an attorney serves when the accused is questioned by authorities. With respect to this inquiry, we do not discern a substantial difference between the usefulness of a lawyer to a suspect during custodial interrogation, and his value to an accused at postindictment questioning.

Thus, we require a more searching or formal inquiry before permitting an accused to waive his right to counsel at trial than we require for a Sixth Amendment waiver during postindictment questioning—*not* because postindictment questioning is "less important" than a trial (the analysis that petitioner's "hierarchical" approach would suggest)—but because the full "dangers and disadvantages of self-representation," during questioning are less substantial and more obvious to an accused than they are at trial. Because the role of counsel at questioning is relatively simple and limited, we see no problem in having a waiver procedure at that stage which is likewise simple and limited. So long as the accused is made aware of the "dangers and disadvantages of self-representation" during postindictment questioning, by use of the *Mi-*

*randa* warnings, his waiver of his Sixth Amendment right to counsel at such questioning is "knowing and intelligent."

## III

Before confessing to the murder of James Jackson, petitioner was meticulously informed by authorities of his right to counsel, and of the consequences of any choice not to exercise that right. On two separate occasions, petitioner elected to forgo the assistance of counsel, and speak directly to officials concerning his role in the murder. Because we believe that petitioner's waiver of his Sixth Amendment rights was "knowing and intelligent," we find no error in the decision of the trial court to permit petitioner's confessions to be used against him. Consequently, the judgment of the Illinois Supreme Court is

Affirmed.

---

JUSTICE BLACKMUN, dissenting.

I agree with most of what Justice Stevens says in his dissenting opinion. I, however, merely would hold that after formal adversary proceedings against a defendant have been commenced, the Sixth Amendment mandates that the defendant not be " 'subject to further interrogation by the authorities until counsel has been made available to him, unless the accused himself initiates further communication, exchanges, or conversations with the police.' " Michigan v. Jackson, 475 U.S. 625, 626, 106 S.Ct. 1404, 1406, 89 L.Ed.2d 631 (1986), quoting Edwards v. Arizona, 451 U.S. 477, 484–485, 101 S.Ct. 1880, 1884–1885, 68 L.Ed.2d 378 (1981).

\* \* \*

JUSTICE STEVENS, with whom JUSTICE BRENNAN and JUSTICE MARSHALL join, dissenting.

The Court should not condone unethical forms of trial preparation by prosecutors or their investigators. In civil litigation it is improper for a lawyer to communicate with his or her adversary's client without either notice to opposing counsel or the permission of the court. An attempt to obtain evidence for use at trial by going behind the back of one's adversary would be not only a serious breach of professional ethics but also a manifestly unfair form of trial practice. In the criminal context, the same ethical rules apply and, in my opinion, notions of fairness that are at least as demanding should also be enforced.

\* \* \*

The question that this case raises \* \* \* is at what point in the adversary process does it become impermissible for the prosecutor, or his or her agents, to conduct such private interviews with the opposing party? Several alternatives are conceivable: when the trial commences, when the defendant has actually met and accepted representation by his or her appointed counsel, when counsel is appointed, or when the adversary process commences. In my opinion, the Sixth

Amendment right to counsel demands that a firm and unequivocal line be drawn at the point at which adversary proceedings commence.

*      *      *

Today, however * * * the Court backs away from the significance previously attributed to the initiation of formal proceedings. In the majority's view, the purported waiver of counsel in this case is properly equated with that of an unindicted suspect. Yet, * * * important differences separate the two. The return of an indictment, or like instrument, substantially alters the relationship between the state and the accused. Only after a formal accusation has "the government * * * committed itself to prosecute, and only then [have] the adverse positions of government and defendant * * * solidified." Moreover, the return of an indictment also presumably signals the government's conclusion that it has sufficient evidence to establish a prima facie case. As a result, any further interrogation can only be designed to buttress the government's case; authorities are no longer simply attempting " 'to solve a crime.' " Given the significance of the initiation of formal proceedings and the concomitant shift in the relationship between the state and the accused, I think it quite wrong to suggest that *Miranda* warnings—or for that matter, any warnings offered by an adverse party—provide a sufficient basis for permitting the undoubtedly prejudicial—and, in my view, unfair—practice of permitting trained law enforcement personnel and prosecuting attorneys to communicate with as-of-yet unrepresented criminal defendants.

It is well settled that there is a strong presumption against waiver of Sixth Amendment protections. Warnings offered by an opposing party, whether detailed or cursory, simply cannot satisfy this high standard.

The majority premises its conclusion that *Miranda* warnings lay a sufficient basis for accepting a waiver of the right to counsel on the assumption that those warnings make clear to an accused "what a lawyer could 'do for him' during the postindictment questioning: namely, advise [him] to refrain from making any [incriminating] statements." Yet, this is surely a gross understatement of the disadvantage of proceeding without a lawyer and an understatement of what a defendant must understand to make a knowing waiver. The *Miranda* warnings do not, for example, inform the accused that a lawyer might examine the indictment for legal sufficiency before submitting his or her client to interrogation or that a lawyer is likely to be considerably more skillful at negotiating a plea bargain and that such negotiations may be most fruitful if initiated prior to any interrogation. Rather, the warnings do not even go so far as to explain to the accused the nature of the charges pending against him—advice that a court would insist upon before allowing a defendant to enter a guilty plea with or without the presence of an attorney. Without defining precisely the nature of the inquiry required to establish a valid waiver of the Sixth Amendment right to counsel, it must be conceded that at least minimal advice is necessary—the accused must be told of the "dangers and disadvantages of self-representation."

Yet, once it is conceded that certain advice is required and that after indictment the adversary relationship between the state and the accused has solidified, it inescapably follows that a prosecutor may not conduct private interviews with a charged defendant. * * * [T]here are ethical constraints that prevent a prosecutor from giving legal advice to an uncounseled adversary. Thus, neither the prosecutor nor his or her agents can ethically provide the unrepresented defendant with the kind of advice that should precede an evidence-gathering interview after formal proceedings have been commenced. Indeed, in my opinion even the *Miranda* warnings themselves are a species of legal advice that is improper when given by the prosecutor after indictment.

Moreover, there are good reasons why such advice is deemed unethical, reasons that extend to the custodial, postindictment setting with unequaled strength. First, the offering of legal advice may lead an accused to underestimate the prosecuting authorities' true adversary posture. For an incarcerated defendant—in this case, a 17–year–old who had been in custody for 44 hours at the time he was told of the indictment—the assistance of someone to explain why he is being held, the nature of the charges against him, and the extent of his legal rights, may be of such importance as to overcome what is perhaps obvious to most, that the prosecutor is a foe and not a friend. Second, the adversary posture of the parties, which is not fully solidified until formal charges are brought, will inevitably tend to color the advice offered. As hard as a prosecutor might try, I doubt that it is possible for one to wear the hat of an effective advisor to a criminal defendant while at the same time wearing the hat of a law enforcement authority. Finally, regardless of whether or not the accused actually understands the legal and factual issues involved and the state's role as an adversary party, advice offered by a lawyer (or his or her agents) with such an evident conflict of interest cannot help but create a public perception of unfairness and unethical conduct. And as we held earlier this Term, "courts have an independent interest in ensuring that criminal trials are conducted within the ethical standards of the profession and that legal proceedings appear fair to all who observe them." Wheat v. United States, 486 U.S. 153, 160, 108 S.Ct. 1692, 1697, 100 L.Ed.2d 140 (1988). This interest is a factor that may be considered in deciding whether to override a defendant's waiver of his or her Sixth Amendment right to conflict free representation, and likewise, should be considered in determining whether a waiver based on advice offered by the criminal defendant's adversary is ever appropriate.

In sum, without a careful discussion of the pitfalls of proceeding without counsel, the Sixth Amendment right cannot properly be waived. An adversary party, moreover, cannot adequately provide such advice. As a result, once the right to counsel attaches and the adversary relationship between the state and the accused solidifies, a prosecutor cannot conduct a private interview with an accused party without "dilut[ing] the protection afforded by the right to counsel," Maine v. Moulton, 474 U.S. 159, 171, 106 S.Ct. 477, 485, 88 L.Ed.2d 481 (1985). Although this ground alone is reason enough to never permit such private interviews, the rule also presents the added virtue of drawing a clear and easily identifiable line at the point between the investigatory and adversary stages of a criminal proceeding. Such clarity in definition of constitutional rules that govern criminal proceedings is important to the law enforcement profession as well as to the private citizen. It is true, of course, that the interest in effective law enforcement would benefit from an opportunity to engage in incommunicado questioning of defendants who, for reasons beyond their control, have not been able to receive the legal advice from counsel to which they are constitutionally entitled. But the Court's singleminded concentration on that interest might also lead to the toleration of similar practices at any stage of the trial. I think it clear that such private communications are intolerable not simply during trial, but at any point after adversary proceedings have commenced.

I therefore respectfully dissent.

## NOTE

In footnote 22, *Patterson* cited Moran v. Burbine, 475 U.S. 412, 428, 106 S.Ct. 1135, 1144, 89 L.Ed.2d 410, 425 (1986), where the Court "readily agreed" that once the Sixth Amendment right to counsel did attach, "it follows that the police may not interfere with the efforts of a defendant's attorney to act as a ' "medium" between [the suspect] and the State' during the interrogation." Burbine's waiver, apparently, would not have been effective if the events had occurred after his Sixth Amendment right to counsel had attached. Why? In general terms, how are a suspect's rights during custodial interrogation increased by a showing that he had not only Fifth Amendment rights during that interrogation but Sixth Amendment rights as well?

# Chapter 8

# UNDERCOVER INVESTIGATIONS

*Analysis*

Police undercover investigations present a sufficiently unique situation to deserve separate consideration. To some extent this is because some perceive the deception inherent in such investigations as infringing more than other types of investigations upon the subjects' interest in privacy. In addition, however, because of their inherently covert nature, undercover investigations involve "low visibility" decisionmaking and the decisions to conduct such investigations or to use particular investigatory techniques are therefore comparatively less open to scrutiny, evaluation, and control.

An unfortunate characteristic of many analyses of undercover investigations—both legal discussions and others—is a failure to identify the underlying concern or concerns. This may be that the undercover investigations will stimulate criminal acts which would not otherwise be committed. Or, it may be that such investigation is regarded as unjustifiably infringing upon what is perceived as the subjects' interest in privacy. Deception—or other activities always or sometimes involved in undercover work—may be opposed because of what is perceived as a tendency to bring the law enforcement agency involved into public disrepute, or because such tactics are inherently "wrong" and should simply not be used by government agencies. Of course, these concerns might be subjected to further refinement—what the subjects' interest in "privacy" is, for example, obviously can be more carefully defined—and others might well be added. But too often discussions fail to make any effort whatsoever to define and evaluate the "real" underlying concern.

Perhaps because of this, the legal situation of undercover investigations and specific techniques used in such investigations is confused. Many doctrines do—or may—relate to undercover police work but judicial opinions and other discussions often suggest that the available legal "tools" are inadequate to deal with problems that are regarded as presented by some undercover police activity. In part to emphasize what might be described as this doctrinal chaos, this chapter is divided into sections each dealing primarily with a doctrine that does or might affect undercover investigations. First, descriptions of several actual undercover investigations are presented in the format of "problems." The "traditional" law of entrapment is then presented. The Sixth Amendment right to counsel and its effect upon the elicitation and overhearing by undercover personnel of self-incriminating admissions made by defendants is explored next. Finally, the application of the Fourth Amendment's right to be free from unreasonable searches and seizures in this context is considered.

In considering undercover investigations, it may be helpful to distinguish two categories of activities. The first involves surveillance by an undercover investigator. This may be visual observation or it may involve overhearing communications. It may even lead to the officer gaining possession of physical evidence, if the subject of the surveillance—unaware of the agent's official status—entrusts items to the agent. But this must be contrasted with the other category of investigation which consists of the undercover investigator actively stimulating the subject of the investigation to commit an offense at a time and place which make it feasible or easier for law enforcement officers—including the undercover investigator—to obtain proof of commission of the offense. L. Tiffany, D. McIntyre and D. Rotenberg, Detection of Crime 273 (1967) and Rotenberg, The Police Detection Practice of Encouragement: Lewis v. United States and Beyond, 4 Hous.L.Rev. 609 (1967), use the phrase "encouragement" to describe this tactic. Dix, Undercover Investigations and Police Rulemaking, 53 Texas L.Rev. 203, 215 (1975), prefers the phrase, "an offer * * * of the opportunity to commit an offense under controlled conditions." Whatever the practice is called, however, it involves some different—or perhaps additional—potential objections. Although tactics within both categories involve deception and therefore some invasion of the subject's expectation of privacy, it is arguable that the manipulation of the subject involved in "encouragement" constitutes a significantly greater invasion of that interest. In addition, "encouragement" arguably creates a greater danger of stimulating the commission of offenses that would not otherwise have been committed and of involving police agents themselves in the commission of criminal acts.

## A. PROBLEMS

The following "problems" represent actual undercover investigations that have been recently conducted in the United States. In considering them, identify what interests of what persons have arguably been infringed by the investigation. Then consider whether that infringement is such as to deserve protection—not necessarily prohibition, but perhaps limitation—by the law. Finally, consider the extent to which existing legal doctrine as presented in the remainder of this chapter provides any such protection that should be afforded.

(1)

University police at The University of Texas at Austin placed an undercover officer on the campus for seven months to combat traffic in marijuana. During some—but not all—of that period, he enrolled as a student. While living at a university dormitory, he befriended the head resident, who hired him as a "resident assistant" for the fall semester. Neither the head resident nor other dormitory officials were aware of the agent's official capacity. A resident assistant's job entails keeping order in his assigned portion of the dormitory as well as advising those students living in that portion. The agent made contact with students and purchased marijuana from them. There is evidence that certain students, concerned with the traffic in marijuana, had contacted the university police who placed them in contact with the undercover officer. These students were instrumental in introducing the undercover officer to at least some of those students from whom he purchased marijuana. In addition to the marijuana sales, the undercover agent's surveillance provided the basis for a number of more serious charges, including possession and sale of cocaine, LSD, and amphetamines. An official of the dormitory staff stated that they would never accept an undercover agent as a resident assistant because the investigatory role of such an agent "is completely incompatible with the job of" a resident assistant. Following the arrest of those students involved in the offenses uncovered by the agent, a sign appeared on one dormitory door reading, "If you can't trust your RA then who can you trust." [a]

(2)

F.B.I. agents, working out of the Hauphaug, Long Island, office of the Bureau, solicited the assistance of one Melvin Weinberg in developing an investigation to identify corrupt or corruptable public officials. Weinberg was about to be sentenced on a federal mail fraud conviction and faced a substantial prison term; the agents interceded with the sentencing judge and Weinberg was placed on probation.

The investigation was organized with agents posing as representatives of supposedly wealthy Arab sheiks who wanted to invest large sums of money in American ventures. Pursuant to arrangements made with the Chase Manhattan Bank, inquiries concerning the sheiks' financial status would result in a representation that they had more than $400 million on deposit with the bank. Weinberg was to spread the word through his underworld and shady connections that the sheiks were available for funding projects. Those who expressed an interest would be carefully screened. Apparently legitimate deals would be rejected; if proposed projects appeared to hold promise of disclosing criminality, however, they would be pursued.

As part of the scheme, Weinberg and the agents presented a realistic picture of great wealth. They entertained on a yacht in

---

[a] The incident was extensively covered in the student newspaper, The Daily Texan.   See especially those issues for January 24 and 25, 1972 and July 6, 1973.

Florida, occupied expensive townhouses and hotel suites, and traveled by private jet and chauffeur-driven limousines. Weinberg also received substantial compensation for his time during the investigation. Video-tape and other electronic recording techniques were used to preserve many of the meetings.

The agents represented that the sheiks were concerned with "the Arab way of doing business" and would not undertake any project unless they were assured of the "friendship" of those with whom they were dealing. The sheiks were said to be especially impressed by persons with official titles and who held positions of power and influ-ence. Their concept of friendship involved payment of substantial sums to those involved. The agents were not to elicit any specific promises of official conduct in return for the payments; they were to emphasize that their objective was to be able to represent to the sheiks that payment had been made to persons in high places and therefore the friendship of those persons was assured. On some occasions, the subjects were introduced to an agent who was represented as one of the sheiks. Before such meetings, the subject might be told that it would be helpful in securing the sheik's help if the subject were to emphasize his or her importance, contacts, and similar matters. These meetings with the "sheik" were videotaped; the pre-meeting "coaching sessions" were apparently not.

The investigation—which came to be known as "Abscam"—devel-oped a number of localized aspects. One of these, focusing upon Philadelphia, unfolded as follows. Two Philadelphia lawyers, Howard Criden and Louis Johanson, had been employed on a contingent fee basis to secure financing for the development of a site in Atlantic City, New Jersey, which might be appropriate for a casino. They heard of one of the sheik's interests through Mayor Angelo Errichetti of Cam-den, a major focus of the investigation. Contact was made with the agents and all three were invited to the Florida yacht to discuss the matter. Perhaps during the sessions on the yacht and clearly later during discussions with Errichetti, the lawyers learned that the sheik was interested in becoming a permanent resident of the United States and would like to meet Congressmen and others who might provide assistance with immigration problems. Errichetti and the lawyers subsequently arranged meetings between several congressmen and the sheik's representatives. For some of these meetings, they received direct payment for their services in making the arrangements.

In addition, Weinberg told lawyer Criden that the sheik was interested in establishing a "base of operations" in Philadelphia and Criden would be contacted concerning this. Criden was contacted by Agent Wald, who indicated that the sheik was interested in building a hotel complex and perhaps in some projects concerning the coal indus-try and Philadelphia's waterfront. It would be necessary, Wald cau-tioned, for the sheik to be assured of the friendship of important governmental officials. Criden then arranged for meetings between agent Wald and the president and two other members of the city council, including his law partner, Johanson. Payments were made to them of sums ranging from $10,000 to $30,000. Wald indicated an interest in their support and in assurances that the project would encounter no "problems." As represented, the project was apparently one which a conscientious city official could easily support on its merits.[b]

### (3)

From September, 1975, into February, 1976, District of Columbia Metropolitan Police and Federal Bureau of Investigation officers, posing as underworld characters, operated a "fencing" business in Washington, D. C. Stolen goods and contraband were purchased with government funds. All transactions between the officers posing as employees of the business and their customers were recorded by hidden cameras and microphones. The public name of the business was P.F.F., Inc.; in law enforcement inner circles, it was known as "Police-FBI Fencing Incognito." The detective who posed as the head of the operation, Patrick Lilly, assumed the name of Pasqualle LaRoca; at least some of the customers understood they were dealing with a Mafia-affiliated business.

A prime objective of the operation was to get unregistered and stolen guns off the street. Pursuant to this purpose, the detectives often urged their customers to bring guns and represented that they would pay "top dollar" for firearms. There was some evidence that even if a customer disclaimed any interest in securing firearms, the officers would affirmatively reiterate their interest in purchasing such items. Customers were given a bonus—about $10.00—for bringing in a new customer to the operation.

On some occasions, the detectives made loans to their customers. This provided an excuse to obtain the customers' identification and telephone numbers. The evidence concerning the amount of these loans was in conflict. The officers acknowledged loans of about $20.00; other evidence indicated that the amounts were as high as $200.00. There was also evidence that the detectives represented that customers who failed to repay these loans would suffer physical harm; the customers' perception of the detectives as affiliated with organized crime may have lent credence to these representations.

On February 26, 1976, hundreds of persons who had done business with P.F.F., Inc., were invited to a party at the warehouse used as the primary place of business. After guests arrived, they were informed of the true nature of P.F.F., Inc., and were placed under arrest. The entire program received extensive press coverage and became known as "Operation Sting."[c]

### B. ENTRAPMENT

Consideration of undercover investigations almost automatically brings to mind the phrase "entrapment." Yet the doctrine—certainly as developed by the United States Supreme Court under federal sub-

---

[b] These facts are taken from United States v. Jannotti, 501 F.Supp. 1182 (E.D. Pa.1980).

[c] See United States v. Borum, 584 F.2d 424 (D.C.Cir.1978); United States v. Brooks, 567 F.2d 134 (D.C.Cir.1977).

stantive criminal law doctrine—arguably deals with only a small portion of the concerns that many harbor over use of undercover investigations. In evaluating the use of entrapment doctrine, consider the extent to which it deals—or should deal—with undercover tactics not involving encouragement or the offer of an opportunity to commit an offense under controlled conditions. Is there evidence of judicial willingness to distort the doctrine in an effort to deal with other concerns related to undercover investigations? If so, would it be appropriate to use other legal doctrines to impose limits upon undercover investigations?

## UNITED STATES v. RUSSELL

Supreme Court of the United States, 1973.
411 U.S. 423, 93 S.Ct. 1637, 36 L.Ed.2d 366.

MR. JUSTICE REHNQUIST delivered the opinion of the Court.

Respondent Richard Russell was charged in three counts of a five count indictment returned against him and codefendants John and Patrick Connolly. After a jury trial in the District Court, in which his sole defense was entrapment, respondent was convicted on all three counts of having unlawfully manufactured and processed methamphetamine ("speed") and of having unlawfully sold and delivered that drug in violation of 21 U.S.C.A. §§ 331(q)(1), (2), 360a(a), (b). He was sentenced to concurrent terms of two years in prison for each offense, the terms to be suspended on the condition that he spend six months in prison and be placed on probation for the following three years. On appeal the United States Court of Appeals for the Ninth Circuit, one judge dissenting, reversed the conviction solely for the reason that an undercover agent supplied an essential chemical for manufacturing the methamphetamine which formed the basis of respondent's conviction. The court concluded that as a matter of law "a defense to a criminal charge may be founded upon an intolerable degree of governmental participation in the criminal enterprise." United States v. Russell, 459 F.2d 671, 673 (C.A.9 1972). We granted certiorari, 409 U.S. 911, 93 S.Ct. 226, 34 L.Ed.2d 172 (1972), and now reverse that judgment.

There is little dispute concerning the essential facts in this case. On December 7, 1969, Joe Shapiro, an undercover agent for the Federal Bureau of Narcotics and Dangerous Drugs, went to respondent's home on Whidbey Island in the State of Washington where he met with respondent and his two codefendants, John and Patrick Connolly. Shapiro's assignment was to locate a laboratory where it was believed that methamphetamine was being manufactured illicitly. He told the respondent and the Connollys that he represented an organization in the Pacific Northwest that was interested in controlling the manufacture and distribution of methamphetamine. He then made an offer to supply the defendants with the chemical phenyl–2–propanone, an essential ingredient in the manufacture of methamphetamine, in return for one-half of the drug produced. This offer was made on the condition that Agent Shapiro be shown a sample of the drug which they were making and the laboratory where it was being produced.

During the conversation Patrick Connolly revealed that he had been making the drug since May 1969 and since then had produced three pounds of it. John Connolly gave the agent a bag containing a quantity of methamphetamine that he represented as being from "the last batch that we made." Shortly thereafter, Shapiro and Patrick Connolly left respondent's house to view the laboratory which was located in the Connolly house on Whidbey Island. At the house Shapiro observed an empty bottle bearing the chemical label phenyl-2-propanone.

By prearrangement Shapiro returned to the Connolly house on December 9, 1969, to supply 100 grams of propanone and observe the chemical reaction. When he arrived he observed Patrick Connolly and the respondent cutting up pieces of aluminum foil and placing them in a large flask. There was testimony that some of the foil pieces accidentally fell on the floor and were picked up by the respondent and Shapiro and put into the flask.[1] Thereafter Patrick Connolly added all of the necessary chemicals, including the propanone brought by Shapiro, to make two batches of methamphetamine. The manufacturing process having been completed the following morning, Shapiro was given one-half of the drug and respondent kept the remainder. Shapiro offered to buy, and the respondent agreed to sell, part of the remainder for $60.

About a month later Shapiro returned to the Connolly house and met with Patrick Connolly to ask if he was still interested in their "business arrangement." Connolly replied that he was interested but that he had recently obtained two additional bottles of phenyl-2-propanone and would not be finished with them for a couple of days. He provided some additional methamphetamine to Shapiro at that time. Three days later Shapiro returned to the Connolly house with a search warrant and, among other items, seized an empty 500-gram bottle of propanone and a 100-gram bottle, not the one he had provided, that was partially filled with the chemical.

There was testimony at the trial of respondent and Patrick Connolly that phenyl-2-propanone was generally difficult to obtain. At the request of the Bureau of Narcotics and Dangerous Drugs, some chemical supply firms had voluntarily ceased selling the chemical.

At the close of the evidence, and after receiving the District Judge's standard entrapment instruction,[2] the jury found the respondent guilty on all counts charged. On appeal the respondent conceded that the jury could have found him predisposed to commit the offenses, 459 F.2d at 672, but argued that on the facts presented there was entrapment as a matter of law. The Court of Appeals agreed, although it did not find

---

[1] Agent Shapiro did not otherwise participate in the manufacture of the drug or direct any of the work.

[2] The District Judge stated the governing law on entrapment as follows: "Where a person has the willingness and the readiness to break the law, the mere fact that the government agent provides what appears to be a favorable opportunity is not entrapment." He then instructed the jury to acquit respondent if it had a "reasonable doubt whether the defendant had the previous intent or purpose to commit the offense * * * and did so only because he was induced or persuaded by some officer or agent of the government." No exception was taken by respondent to this instruction.

the District Court had misconstrued or misapplied the traditional standards governing the entrapment defense. Rather, the court in effect expanded the traditional notion of entrapment, which focuses on the predisposition of the defendant, to mandate dismissal of a criminal prosecution whenever the court determines that there has been "an intolerable degree of governmental participation in the criminal enterprise." In this case the court decided that the conduct of the agent in supplying a scarce ingredient essential for the manufacture of a controlled substance established that defense.

This new defense was held to rest on either of two alternative theories. One theory is based on two lower court decisions which have found entrapment, regardless of predisposition, whenever the government supplies contraband to the defendants. United States v. Bueno, 447 F.2d 903 (C.A.5 1971); United States v. Chisum, 312 F.Supp. 1307 (C.D.Cal.1970). The second theory, a nonentrapment rationale, is based on a recent Ninth Circuit decision that reversed a conviction because a government investigator was so enmeshed in the criminal activity that the prosecution of the defendants was held to be repugnant to the American criminal justice system. Greene v. United States, 454 F.2d 783 (C.A.9 1971). The court below held that these two rationales constitute the same defense and that only the label distinguishes them. In any event, it held that "[b]oth theories are premised on fundamental concepts of due process and evince the reluctance of the judiciary to countenance 'overzealous law enforcement.'" 459 F.2d, at 674, quoting Sherman v. United States, 356 U.S. 369, 381, 78 S.Ct. 819, 825, 2 L.Ed. 2d 848 (1958) (Frankfurter, J., concurring).

This Court first recognized and applied the entrapment defense in Sorrells v. United States, 287 U.S. 435, 53 S.Ct. 210, 77 L.Ed. 413 (1932). In *Sorrells* a federal prohibition agent visited the defendant while posing as a tourist and engaged him in conversation about their common war experiences. After gaining the defendant's confidence the agent asked for some liquor, was twice refused, but upon asking a third time the defendant finally capitulated, and was subsequently prosecuted for violating the National Prohibition Act.

Chief Justice Hughes, speaking for the Court, held that as a matter of statutory construction the defense of entrapment should have been available to the defendant. Under the theory propounded by the Chief Justice, the entrapment defense prohibits law enforcement officers from instigating criminal acts by persons "otherwise innocent in order to lure them to its commission and to punish them." 287 U.S., at 448, 53 S.Ct., at 215. Thus, the thrust of the entrapment defense was held to focus on the intent or predisposition of the defendant to commit the crime. "[I]f the defendant seeks acquittal by reason of entrapment he cannot complain of an appropriate and searching inquiry into his own conduct and predisposition as bearing upon that issue." 287 U.S., at 451, 53 S.Ct., at 216.

Justice Roberts concurred in the result but was of the view "that courts must be closed to the trial of a crime instigated by the government's own agents." 287 U.S., at 459, 53 S.Ct., at 219. The difference in the view of the majority and the concurring opinions is that in the former the inquiry focuses on the predisposition of the defendant, whereas in the latter the inquiry focuses on whether the government "instigated the crime."

In 1958 the Court again considered the theory underlying the entrapment defense and expressly reaffirmed the view expressed by the *Sorrells* majority. Sherman v. United States, 356 U.S. 369, 78 S.Ct. 819, 2 L.Ed.2d 848 (1958). In *Sherman* the defendant was convicted of selling narcotics to a government informer. As in *Sorrells* it appears that the government agent gained the confidence of the defendant and, despite initial reluctance, the defendant finally acceded to the repeated importunings of the agent to commit the criminal act. On the basis of *Sorrells*, this Court reversed the affirmance of the defendant's conviction.

In affirming the theory underlying *Sorrells*, Chief Justice Warren for the Court, held that "[t]o determine whether entrapment has been established, a line must be drawn between the trap for the unwary innocent and the trap for the unwary criminal." 356 U.S., at 372, 78 S.Ct., at 821. Justice Frankfurter stated in a concurring opinion that he believed Justice Roberts had the better view in *Sorrells* and would have framed the question to be asked in an entrapment defense in terms of "whether the police conduct revealed in the particular case falls below standards  *  *  *  for the proper use of governmental power." 356 U.S., at 382, 78 S.Ct., at 825.

In the instant case respondent asks us to reconsider the theory of the entrapment defense as it is set forth in the majority opinions in *Sorrells* and *Sherman*. His principal contention is that the defense should rest on constitutional grounds. He argues that the level of Shapiro's involvement in the manufacture of the methamphetamine was so high that a criminal prosecution for the drug's manufacture violates the fundamental principles of due process. The respondent contends that the same factors that led this Court to apply the exclusionary rule to illegal searches and seizures, Weeks v. United States, 232 U.S. 383, 34 S.Ct. 341, 58 L.Ed. 652 (1914); Mapp v. Ohio, 367 U.S. 643, 81 S.Ct. 1684, 6 L.Ed.2d 1081 (1961), and confessions, Miranda v. Arizona, 384 U.S. 436, 86 S.Ct. 1602, 16 L.Ed.2d 694 (1966), should be considered here. But he would have the Court go further in deterring undesirable official conduct by requiring that any prosecution be barred absolutely because of the police involvement in criminal activity. The analogy is imperfect in any event, for the principal reason behind the adoption of the exclusionary rule was the government's "failure to observe its own laws." Mapp v. Ohio, supra, 367 U.S., at 659, 81 S.Ct., at 1694. Unlike the situations giving rise to the holdings in *Mapp* and *Miranda*, the government's conduct here violated no independent constitutional right of the respondent. Nor did Shapiro violate any federal statute or rule or commit any crime in infiltrating the respondent's drug enterprise.

Respondent would overcome this basic weakness in his analogy to the exclusionary rule cases by having the Court adopt a rigid constitutional rule that would preclude any prosecution when it is shown that the criminal conduct would not have been possible had not an undercover agent "supplied an indispensable means to the commission of the crime that could not have been obtained otherwise, through legal or illegal channels." Even if we were to surmount the difficulties attending the notion that due process of law can be embodied in fixed rules, and those attending respondent's particular formulation, the rule he proposes would not appear to be of significant benefit to him. For on the record presented it appears that he cannot fit within the terms of the very rule he proposes.

The record discloses that although the propanone was difficult to obtain it was by no means impossible. The defendants admitted making the drug both before and after those batches made with the propanone supplied by Shapiro. Shapiro testified that he saw an empty bottle labeled phenyl-2-propanone on his first visit to the laboratory on December 7, 1969. And when the laboratory was searched pursuant to a search warrant on January 10, 1970, two additional bottles labeled phenyl-2-propanone were seized. Thus, the facts in the record amply demonstrate that the propanone used in the illicit manufacture of methamphetamine not only *could* have been obtained without the intervention of Shapiro but was in fact obtained by these defendants.

While we may some day be presented with a situation in which the conduct of law enforcement agents is so outrageous that due process principles would absolutely bar the government from invoking judicial processes to obtain a conviction, cf. Rochin v. California, 342 U.S. 165, 72 S.Ct. 205, 96 L.Ed. 183 (1952), the instant case is distinctly not of that breed. Shapiro's contribution of propanone to the criminal enterprise already in process was scarcely objectionable. The chemical is by itself a harmless substance and its possession is legal. While the government may have been seeking to make it more difficult for drug rings, such as that of which respondent was a member, to obtain the chemical, the evidence described above shows that it nonetheless was obtainable. The law enforcement conduct here stops far short of violating that "fundamental fairness, shocking to the universal sense of justice," mandated by the Due Process Clause of the Fifth Amendment. Kinsella v. United States ex rel. Singleton, 361 U.S. 234, 246, 80 S.Ct. 297, 304, 4 L.Ed.2d 268 (1960).

The illicit manufacture of drugs is not a sporadic, isolated criminal incident, but a continuing, though illegal, business enterprise. In order to obtain convictions for illegally manufacturing drugs, the gathering of evidence of past unlawful conduct frequently proves to be an all but impossible task. Thus in drug-related offenses law enforcement personnel have turned to one of the only practicable means of detection: the infiltration of drug rings and a limited participation in their unlawful present practices. Such infiltration is a recognized and permissible means of apprehension; if that be so, then the supply of some item of value that the drug ring requires must, as a general rule, also be permissible. For an agent will not be taken into the confidence of the illegal entrepreneurs unless he has something of value to offer them. Law enforcement tactics such as this can hardly be said to violate "fundamental fairness" or "shocking to the universal sense of justice," *Kinsella,* supra.

Respondent also urges, as an alternative to his constitutional argument, that we broaden the nonconstitutional defense of entrapment in order to sustain the judgment of the Court of Appeals. This Court's opinions in Sorrells v. United States, supra, and Sherman v. United States, supra, held that the principal element in the defense of entrapment was the defendant's predisposition to commit the crime. Respondent conceded in the Court of Appeals, as well he might, "that he may have harbored a predisposition to commit the charged offenses." 459 F.2d, at 672. Yet he argues that the jury's refusal to find entrapment under the charge submitted to it by the trial court should be overturned and the views of Justices Roberts and Frankfurter, concurring in *Sorrells* and *Sherman,* respectively, which make the essential element of the defense turn on the type and degree of governmental conduct, be adopted as the law.

We decline to overrule these cases. *Sorrells* is a precedent of long standing that has already been once reexamined in *Sherman* and implicitly there reaffirmed. Since the defense is not of a constitutional dimension, Congress may address itself to the question and adopt any substantive definition of the defense that it may find desirable.

Critics of the rule laid down in *Sorrells* and *Sherman* have suggested that its basis in the implied intent of Congress is largely fictitious, and have pointed to what they conceive to be the anomalous difference between the treatment of a defendant who is solicited by a private individual and one who is entrapped by a government agent. Questions have been likewise raised as to whether "predisposition" can be factually established with the requisite degree of certainty. Arguments such as these, while not devoid of appeal, have been twice previously made to this Court, and twice rejected by it, first in *Sorrells* and then in *Sherman.*

We believe that at least equally cogent criticism has been made of the concurring views in these cases. Commenting in *Sherman* on Justice Roberts' position in *Sorrells* that "although the defendant could claim that the Government had induced him to commit the crime, the Government could not reply by showing that the defendant's criminal conduct was due to his own readiness and not to the persuasion of government agents," Sherman v. United States, supra, 356 U.S., at 376–377, 78 S.Ct., at 823, 2 L.Ed.2d 848, Chief Justice Warren quoted the observation of Judge Learned Hand in an earlier stage of that proceeding:

> " 'Indeed, it would seem probable that, if there were no reply [to the claim of inducement], it would be impossible ever to secure convictions of any offences which consist of transactions that are carried on in secret.' United States v. Sherman, 2 Cir., 200 F.2d 880, 882." Sherman v. United States, supra, 356 U.S., at 377 n. 7, 78 S.Ct., at 823.

Nor does it seem particularly desirable for the law to grant complete immunity from prosecution to one who himself planned to commit a crime, and then committed it, simply because government undercover agents subjected him to inducements which might have seduced a hypothetical individual who was not so predisposed. * * *

Several decisions of the United States district courts and courts of appeals have undoubtedly gone beyond this Court's opinions in *Sorrells* and *Sherman* in order to bar prosecutions because of what they thought to be for want of a better term "overzealous law enforcement." But the defense of entrapment enunciated in those opinions was not intended to give the federal judiciary a "chancellor's foot" veto over law enforcement practices of which it did not approve. The execution of the federal laws under our Constitution is confined primarily to the Executive Branch of the Government, subject to applicable constitutional and statutory limitations and to judicially fashioned rules to enforce those limitations. We think that the decision of the Court of Appeals in this case quite unnecessarily introduces an unmanageably subjective standard which is contrary to the holdings of this Court in *Sorrells* and *Sherman*.

Those cases establish that entrapment is a relatively limited defense. It is rooted not in any authority of the Judicial Branch to dismiss prosecutions for what it feels to have been "overzealous law enforcement," but instead in the notion that Congress could not have intended criminal punishment for a defendant who has committed all the elements of a prescribed offense, but who was induced to commit them by the government.

* * *

Respondent's concession in the Court of Appeals that the jury finding as to predisposition was supported by the evidence is, therefore, fatal to his claim of entrapment. He was an active participant in an illegal drug manufacturing enterprise which began before the government agent appeared on the scene, and continued after the government agent had left the scene. He was, in the words of *Sherman*, supra, not an "unwary innocent" but an "unwary criminal." The Court of Appeals was wrong, we believe, when it sought to broaden the principle laid down in *Sorrells* and *Sherman*. Its judgment is therefore reversed.

Reversed.

[The dissenting opinion of Mr. Justice Douglas, with whom Mr. Justice Brennan concurs, is omitted.]

MR. JUSTICE STEWART, with whom MR. JUSTICE BRENNAN and MR. JUSTICE MARSHALL join, dissenting.

It is common ground that "[t]he conduct with which the defense of entrapment is concerned is the *manufacturing* of crime by law enforcement officials and their agents." Lopez v. United States, 373 U.S. 427, 434, 83 S.Ct. 1381, 1385, 10 L.Ed.2d 462 (1963). For the Government cannot be permitted to instigate the commission of a criminal offense in order to prosecute someone for committing it. * * * It is to prevent this situation from occurring in the administration of federal criminal justice that the defense of entrapment exists. But the Court has been sharply divided as to the proper basis, scope, and focus of the entrapment defense, and as to whether, in the absence of a conclusive showing, the issue of entrapment is for the judge or the jury to determine.

I.

In Sorrells v. United States, supra, and Sherman v. United States, supra, the Court took what might be called a "subjective" approach to the defense of entrapment. In that view, the defense is predicated on an unexpressed intent of Congress to exclude from its criminal statutes the prosecution and conviction of persons, "otherwise innocent," who have been lured to the commission of the prohibited act through the Government's instigation. Sorrells v. United States, supra, 287 U.S., at 448, 53 S.Ct., at 215. * * * The Court today adheres to this approach.

The concurring opinion of Mr. Justice Roberts, joined by Justices Brandeis and Stone, in the *Sorrells* case, and that of Mr. Justice Frankfurter, joined by Justices Douglas, Harlan, and Brennan, in the *Sherman* case, took a different view of the entrapment defense. In their concept, the defense is not grounded on some unexpressed intent of Congress to exclude from punishment under its statutes those otherwise innocent persons tempted into crime by the Government, but rather on the belief that "the methods employed on behalf of the Government to bring about conviction cannot be countenanced." Sherman v. United States, supra, 356 U.S., at 380, 78 S.Ct., at 324. Thus, the focus of this approach is not on the propensities and predisposition of a specific defendant, but on "whether the police conduct revealed in the particular case falls below [the] standards, to which common feelings respond, for the proper use of governmental power." Id., at 382, 78 S.Ct., at 825. Phrased another way, the question is whether—regardless of the predisposition to crime of the particular defendant involved—the governmental agents have acted in such a way as is likely to instigate or create a criminal offense. Under this approach, the determination of the lawfulness of the Government's conduct must be made—as it is on all questions involving the legality of law enforcement methods—by the trial judge, not the jury.

In my view, this objective approach to entrapment, advanced by the concurring opinions in *Sorrells* and *Sherman* is the only one truly consistent with the underlying rationale of the defense. Indeed, the very basis of the entrapment defense itself demands adherence to an approach that focuses on the conduct of the governmental agents, rather than on whether the defendant was "predisposed" or "otherwise innocent." I find it impossible to believe that the purpose of the defense is to effectuate some unexpressed congressional intent to exclude from its criminal statutes persons who committed a prohibited act, but would not have done so except for the Government's inducements. * * *

The purpose of the entrapment defense, then, cannot be to protect persons who are "otherwise innocent." Rather, it must be to prohibit unlawful governmental activity in instigating crime. * * * If that

is so, then whether the particular defendant was "predisposed" or
"otherwise innocent" is irrelevant; and the important question becomes whether the Government's conduct in inducing the crime was
beyond judicial toleration.

Moreover, a test that makes the entrapment defense depend on
whether the defendant had the requisite predisposition permits the
introduction into evidence of all kinds of hearsay, suspicion, and rumor—all of which would be inadmissible in any other context—in order
to prove the defendant's predisposition. It allows the prosecution, in
offering such proof, to rely on the defendant's bad reputation or past
criminal activities, including even rumored activities of which the
prosecution may have insufficient evidence to obtain an indictment,
and to present the agent's suspicions as to why they chose to tempt this
defendant. This sort of evidence is not only unreliable, as the hearsay
rule recognizes; but it is also highly prejudicial, especially if the matter
is submitted to the jury, for, despite instructions to the contrary, the
jury may well consider such evidence as probative not simply of the
defendant's predisposition, but of his guilt of the offense with which he
stands charged.

More fundamentally, focusing on the defendant's innocence or
predisposition has the direct effect of making what is permissible or
impermissible police conduct depend upon the past record and propensities of the particular defendant involved. Stated another way, this
subjective test means that the Government is permitted to entrap a
person with a criminal record or bad reputation, and then to prosecute
him for the manufactured crime, confident that his record or reputation itself will be enough to show that he was predisposed to commit the
offense anyway.

\* \* \*

\* \* \* [W]hen the agents' involvement in criminal activities goes
beyond the mere offering of such an opportunity and when their
conduct is of a kind that could induce or instigate the commission of a
crime by one not ready and willing to commit it, then—regardless of
the character or propensities of the particular person induced—I think
entrapment has occurred. For in that situation, the Government has
engaged in the impermissible manufacturing of crime, and the federal
courts should bar the prosecution in order to preserve the institutional
integrity of the system of federal criminal justice.

## II.

In the case before us, I think that the District Court erred in
submitting the issue of entrapment to the jury, with instructions to
acquit only if it had a reasonable doubt as to the respondent's predisposition to committing the crime. Since, under the objective test of
entrapment, predisposition is irrelevant and the issue is to be decided
by the trial judge, the Court of Appeals, I believe, would have been
justified in reversing the conviction on this basis alone. But since the
appellate court did not remand for consideration of the issue by the
District Judge under an objective standard, but rather found entrap-

ment as a matter of law and directed that the indictment be dismissed, we must reach the merits of the respondent's entrapment defense.

Since, in my view, it does not matter whether the respondent was predisposed to commit the offense of which he was convicted, the focus must be, rather, on the conduct of the undercover government agent. What the agent did here was to meet with a group of suspected producers of methamphetamine, including the respondent; to request the drug; to offer to supply the chemical phenyl-2-propanone in exchange for one-half of the methamphetamine to be manufactured therewith; and, when that offer was accepted, to provide the needed chemical ingredient, and to purchase some of the drug from the respondent.

It is undisputed that phenyl-2-propanone is an essential ingredient in the manufacture of methamphetamine; that it is not used for any other purpose; and that, while its sale is not illegal, it is difficult to obtain, because a manufacturer's license is needed to purchase it, and because many suppliers, at the request of the Federal Bureau of Narcotics and Dangerous Drugs, do not sell it at all. It is also undisputed that the methamphetamine which the respondent was prosecuted for manufacturing and selling was all produced on December 10, 1969, and that all the phenyl-2-propanone used in the manufacture of that batch of the drug was provided by the government agent. In these circumstances, the agent's undertaking to supply this ingredient to the respondent, thus making it possible for the Government to prosecute him for manufacturing an illicit drug with it, was, I think, precisely the type of governmental conduct that the entrapment defense is meant to prevent.

\*    \*    \*

### NOTES

1. Two Congressional units have recently issued reports based upon study of undercover activities by federal law enforcement agencies. House Subcomm. on Civil and Constitutional Rights of the Committee on the Judiciary, 98th Cong., 2nd Sess., FBI Undercover Operations (Comm.Print 1984) ("House Subcommittee Report"); Senate Select Comm. to Study Undercover Activities of Components of the Department of Justice, Final Report, S.Doc. No. 97–682, 97th Cong., 2nd Sess. (1982) ("Senate Select Committee Report"). Among the Senate Select Committee's proposals was that Congress consider adoption of a version of the "objective" standard for entrapment:

> A defendant should be acquitted on entrapment grounds when a law enforcement agent—or a private party acting under the direction or with the approval of law enforcement authorities—induces the defendant to commit an offense, using methods that would be likely to cause a normally law-abiding citizen to commit a similar offense.

Senate Select Committee Report, at 373. It further urged that the legislation provide that entrapment *per se* is established in certain situations, including those in which the defendant shows that "federal law enforcement agents manipulated the defendant's personal, economic, or vocational situation to increase the likelihood of his committing [the] crime \* \* \*." Id., at 362. The House Subcommittee's recommendations included the following:

A judicial warrant should be required for initiating and continuing undercover operations. Like other intrusive methods which pose a threat to important individual and societal interests, the use of undercover operations ought to be limited to those situations where an independent judicial officer has determined that sufficient evidence exists to believe that crime of a particular sort is on-going and that the individual targets (when known) are part of that activity. The federal law requiring warrants for wiretapping may provide an appropriate model for such an approach.

House Subcommittee Report, at 10.

2. The phenyl-2-propanone provided to the defendants by the officers in *Russell* was not contraband, i.e., its possession by persons like the defendants was not itself criminal. Suppose officers provide contraband for use in the commission of an offense? In Hampton v. United States, 425 U.S. 484, 96 S.Ct. 1646, 48 L.Ed.2d 113 (1976), Hampton and one Hutton, a Drug Enforcement Administration informant, sold heroin to federal undercover officers. At his trial for distribution of heroin, Hampton testified that Hutton had provided the heroin and had suggested selling it; other testimony suggested that Hampton provided the drug. The defense requested an instruction that Hampton was entitled to acquittal if the jury found that the heroin sold had been supplied to Hampton by a government informer. This was denied, Hampton was convicted, and appeal followed. The Supreme Court, with Justice Stevens not participating, affirmed. Justice Rehnquist, joined by the Chief Justice and Justice White, concluded that *Russell* "ruled out the possibility that the defense of entrapment could ever be based upon governmental misconduct in a case, such as this one, where the predisposition of the defendant to commit the crime was established." 425 U.S. at 488–89, 96 S.Ct. at 1649, 48 L.Ed.2d at 118. He continued:

> The limitations of the Due Process Clause of the Fifth Amendment come into play only when the Government activity in question violates some protected right of the *defendant*. Here, * * * the police, the Government informant, and the defendant acted in concert with one another. * * * If the police engage in illegal activity in concert with a defendant beyond the scope of their duties the remedy lies, not in freeing the equally culpable defendant, but in prosecuting the police under the applicable provisions of state or federal law. But the police conduct here no more deprived defendant of any right secured to him by the United States Constitution than did the police conduct in *Russell* deprive Russell of any rights.

425 U.S. at 490–91, 96 S.Ct. at 1650, 48 L.Ed.2d at 119. Justice Powell, joined by Justice Blackmun, concurred in the judgment. Given that the phenyl-2-propanone in *Russell* was difficult to obtain and useful only in the manufacture of methamphetamine, he found no difference between providing that substance and in providing heroin. *Russell*, he concluded, controlled. Turning to the Due Process argument, he acknowledged "the doctrinal and practical difficulties of delineating limits to police involvement in crimes that do not focus upon predisposition, as Government participation ordinarily will be fully justified in society's 'war with the criminal classes.' " 425 U.S. at 493–94, 96 S.Ct. at 1652, 48 L.Ed.2d at 121–22. But given that Hampton's Due Process claim can be rejected as controlled by *Russell*, he was unwilling to join the plurality's broad language rejecting such claims in all cases of government involvement in crime. 425 U.S. at 493, 96 S.Ct. at 1541–52, 48 L.Ed.2d at 121.

Justice Brennan, joined by Justices Stewart and Marshall, dissented. He urged adoption of the objective approach to entrapment and concluded that under this approach Hampton's claims showed entrapment as a matter of law.

But he also argued that the subjective approach followed by a majority of the Court mandated reversal and that either Due Process or the Court's supervisory power required the same result. Evaluating the police activity in the case before the Court, Justice Brennan found two distinctions between it and the conduct involved in *Russell*:

> First, the chemical supplied in [*Russell*] was not contraband. * * * In contrast, [Hampton] claims that the very narcotic he is accused of selling was supplied by an agent of the Government.
>
> Second, the defendant in *Russell* "was an active participant in an illegal drug manufacturing enterprise which began before the Government had left the scene." * * * [Russell's] crime was participation in an ongoing enterprise. In contrast, the two sales for which [Hampton] was convicted were allegedly instigated by Government agents and completed by the Government's purchase. The beginning and end of this crime thus coincided exactly with the Government's entry into and withdrawal from the criminal activity involved in this case, while the Government was not similarly involved in Russell's crime.

425 U.S. at 497–98, 96 S.Ct. at 1654, 48 L.Ed.2d at 123.

3. The Supreme Court of Alaska adopted an objective standard for entrapment in Grossman v. State, 457 P.2d 226 (Alaska 1969):

> [U]nlawful entrapment occurs when a public law enforcement official * * * induces another person to commit * * * an offense by persuasion which would be effective to persuade an average person, other than one who is ready and willing, to commit such an offense.

457 P.2d at 229. In Pascu v. State, 577 P.2d 1064 (Alaska 1978), the Court observed that since *Grossman*, "we have come to realize there are certain difficulties in applying the [*Grossman*] standard." Id., at 1066–67. The court continued:

> An "average person" probably cannot be induced to commit a serious crime except under circumstances so extreme as to amount to duress. Yet it is clear that entrapment may occur where the degree of inducement falls short of actual duress. What is prohibited, by *Grossman*, is unreasonable or unconscionable efforts on the part of the police to induce one to commit a crime so that he may be arrested and prosecuted for the offense. In determining whether entrapment has occurred, the trial court must focus "upon the particular conduct of the police in the case presented." The question is really whether that conduct falls below an acceptable standard for the fair and honorable administration of justice.

Id., at 1067. The facts of the case were as follows: Pascu, a heroin addict, was approached by Blair, a good friend he had known for four or five years. Blair represented that he was suffering from heroin withdrawal and needed a "fix" for himself and a friend who was also "sick." Pascu refused, saying that he was trying to stop using heroin and was feeling "sick," too. Blair became "agitated" and continued his efforts to persuade Pascu, reminding Pascu that he had done similar favors for Pascu in the past when Pascu had suffered withdrawal symptoms. When Pascu indicated he did not want to expose himself to the temptation of heroin, Blair continued his persuasive efforts and offered to give Pascu a "hit" if Pascu would obtain the heroin. He finally offered Pascu enough heroin to "get down", and for the next morning, about $200 worth of the drug. Pascu yielded, obtained the heroin, and give it to Blair and one Geiger. He was then arrested and charged with the sale of heroin. This, if uncontradicted, the court held, was sufficient to establish entrapment under the *Grossman* standard as construed in the present case. The matter was remanded to the trial court, however, to give the state an opportunity to contest the accuracy of Pascu's version of the facts leading to the sale.

4. Does a showing that an informer who arranged or made a purchase of prohibited substances had a "contingent fee" arrangement with the government tend to show or perhaps establish entrapment? In Williamson v. United States, 311 F.2d 441 (5th Cir. 1962), (*Williamson I*), the informant, Moye, had purchased "moonshine" from the defendants. He testified at trial that in addition to a $10 per day "fee" and expenses, he was to be paid specific sums ($100 to $200) for each of the three targets of the investigation. A three-judge panel of the Fifth Circuit reversed Williamson's conviction. An opinion by Judge Rives noted that contingent fee arrangements such as the evidence showed here encouraged informants to entrap undisposed persons into committing offenses and, "without some  *  *  *  justification or explanation," could not be sanctioned. Citing McNabb v. United States, 318 U.S. 332, 63 S.Ct. 608, 87 L.Ed. 819 (1943) in which the Supreme Court exercised its supervisory power to exclude a confession made during improper delay in presenting a defendant before a magistrate, Judge Rives noted a duty of federal courts "to require fair and lawful conduct from federal agents" and reversed. Judge Brown, concurring specially, agreed with this disposition of the case but noted that he did not think the conduct of Moye was "an aspect of entrapment." 311 F.2d at 445. Judge Cameron, the third member of the panel, dissented. On remand, Williamson was again tried for the same offense but the testimony of Moye was not used. He was convicted and the conviction was affirmed on appeal. Williamson v. United States, 340 F.2d 612 (5th Cir. 1965), cert. denied 381 U.S. 950, 85 S.Ct. 1803, 14 L.Ed.2d 724 (*Williamson II*).

Even in the Fifth Circuit, *Williamson I* has been applied narrowly. Contingent fee arrangements have been held to be "justified" within the meaning of the case by a showing of careful instructions to the informer to avoid entrapment and by a demonstration that in light of special investigation problems there is an exceptional need for a contingent fee arrangement. Sears v. United States, 343 F.2d 139 (5th Cir. 1965). It has been held that *Williamson I* is limited to those situations in which an informant is offered a specific sum to implicate a particular person. United States v. Lane, 693 F.2d 385, 387–88 (5th Cir. 1982) In a Fifth Circuit's recent discussion of *Williamson I*, it indicated that the case is limited to "a narrow set of circumstances." Among the factors that militate against application of *Williamson I* are showings of a "possibility" that the informer was instructed in the law of entrapment, that a government agent rather than the informer made the actual purchase from the defendant, and that the government agent was unaware of the identity of the seller under investigation and therefore did not "target" any specific person for the informer. United States v. McClure, 546 F.2d 670 (5th Cir. 1977), on appeal from conviction following retrial on remand 577 F.2d 1021, 1022 (1978).

Other circuits have rejected *Williamson I*. See, e.g., United States v. Reynoso-Ulloa, 548 F.2d 1329, 1338 (9th Cir. 1977), cert. denied 436 U.S. 926, 98 S.Ct. 2820, 56 L.Ed.2d 769 (1978), declining to follow the rationale of *Williamson I* in light of *Russell* and *Hampton*.

5. Even the "objective" entrapment formulation, advocated by the dissenters in *Russell*, is limited to law enforcement conduct which is objectionable because of its tendency to cause criminal acts where none would otherwise be committed. But should entrapment be expanded to cover situations where the law enforcement conduct is objectionable on other grounds? A few formulations of the defense appear to provide for it on this basis. In State v. Sainz, 84 N.M. 259, 501 P.2d 1247 (App.1972), the court held that entrapment exists where the state's participation in a criminal enterprise, even if not likely to

induce the commission of crime in law-abiding citizens, "is such that if allowed to continue would shake the public's confidence in the fair and honorable administration of justice." 84 N.M. at 261, 501 P.2d at 1249. See also, State v. Molnar, 81 N.J. 475, 410 A.2d 37 (1980) (entrapment is established by a showing of "official conduct in inducing a crime  *  *  * so egregious as to impugn the integrity of a court that permits a conviction"). The New Mexico Court of Appeals formulation of entrapment in *Sainz* was overruled by the New Mexico Supreme Court in State v. Fiechter, 89 N.M. 74, 547 P.2d 557 (1976).

## C. ELICITATION OF SELF–INCRIMINATING STATEMENTS

The elicitation or overhearing by an undercover agent of self-incriminating admissions made by a suspect is obviously distinguishable from custodial police interrogation. In Hoffa v. United States, 385 U.S. 293, 87 S.Ct. 408, 17 L.Ed.2d 374 (1966) (reprinted in part in section D of this Chapter), the Supreme Court addressed the argument that testimony by a government informer concerning incriminating admissions made by the defendant in the former's presence violated the defendant's Fifth Amendment privilege against compelled self-incrimination. It was clear that if the informer had disclosed his status he would not have been permitted to overhear conversations. The Court held:

> [A] necessary element of compulsory self-incrimination is some kind of compulsion.  *  *  * [No] claim has been or could be made that [Hoffa's] incriminating statements were the product of any sort of coercion, legal or factual. The  *  *  * conversations  *  *  * were wholly voluntary. For that reason, if for no other, it is clear that no right protected by the Fifth Amendment privilege against compulsory self-incrimination was violated in this case.

384 U.S. at 304, 87 S.Ct. at 414–15, 17 L.Ed.2d at 383.

Constitutional regulation of law enforcement conduct in this area, to the extent that it exists, is achieved through the Sixth and Fourteenth Amendments right to counsel. The seminal case is Massiah v. United States, 377 U.S. 201, 84 S.Ct. 1199, 12 L.Ed.2d 246 (1964). Massiah, one Colson, and others had been arrested and indicted for certain drug offenses; Massiah and Colson were released on bail. Massiah had retained a lawyer. Unknown to Massiah, Colson decided to cooperate with the government agents in their continuing investigation, and permitted the installation of a radio transmitter in his car. One evening, Colson and Massiah had a lengthy conversation while sitting in Colson's parked automobile. A federal agent was nearby and listened over his radio to the conversation, including several incriminating admissions made by Massiah. At Massiah's trial, the agent was permitted to testify as to these admissions. The Supreme Court held this constitutional error:

> We hold that [Massiah] was denied the basic protection of [the Sixth Amendment right to counsel] when there was used against him at his trial evidence of his own incriminating words, which

federal agents had deliberately elicited from him after he had been indicted and in the absence of his counsel.

377 U.S. at 206, 84 S.Ct. at 1203, 12 L.Ed.2d at 250. The principal case in this section explores the ramifications of *Massiah*. Other aspects are explored in that portion of *Hoffa* reprinted in the next section.

### UNITED STATES v. HENRY

Supreme Court of the United States, 1980.
447 U.S. 264, 100 S.Ct. 2183, 65 L.Ed.2d 115.

MR. CHIEF JUSTICE BURGER delivered the opinion of the Court.

We granted certiorari to consider whether respondent's Sixth Amendment right to the assistance of counsel was violated by the admission at trial of incriminating statements made by respondent to his cellmate, an undisclosed government informant, after indictment and while in custody.

I.

The Janaf Branch of the United Virginia Bank/Seaboard National in Norfolk, Va., was robbed in August 1972. Witnesses saw two men wearing masks and carrying guns enter the bank while a third man waited in the car. No witnesses were able to identify respondent Henry as one of the participants. About an hour after the robbery, the getaway car was discovered. Inside was found a rent receipt signed by one "Allen R. Norris" and a lease, also signed by Norris, for a house in Norfolk. Two men, who were subsequently convicted of participating in the robbery, were arrested at the rented house. Discovered with them were the proceeds of the robbery and the guns and masks used by the gunman.

Government agents traced the rent receipt to Henry; on the basis of this information, Henry was arrested in Atlanta, Ga., in November 1972. Two weeks later he was indicted for armed robbery under 18 U.S.C.A. § 2113(a) and (d). He was held pending trial in the Norfolk City Jail. Counsel was appointed on November 27.

On November 21, 1972, shortly after Henry was incarcerated, government agents working on the Janaf robbery contacted one Nichols, an inmate at the Norfolk City Jail, who for some time prior to this meeting had been engaged to provide confidential information to the Federal Bureau of Investigation as a paid informant. Nichols was then serving a sentence on local forgery charges. The record does not disclose whether the agent contacted Nichols specifically to acquire information about Henry or the Janaf robbery.

Nichols informed the agent that he was housed in the same cellblock with several federal prisoners awaiting trial, including Henry. The agent told him to be alert to any statements made by the federal prisoners, but not to initiate any conversation with or question Henry regarding the bank robbery. In early December, after Nichols had been released from jail, the agent again contacted Nichols, who reported that he and Henry had engaged in conversation and that Henry had told him about the robbery of the Janaf bank.  Nichols was paid for furnishing the information.

When Henry was tried in March 1973, an agent of the Federal Bureau of Investigation testified concerning the events surrounding the discovery of the rental slip and the evidence uncovered at the rented house.  Other witnesses also connected Henry to the rented house, including the rental agent who positively identified Henry as the "Allen R. Norris" who had rented the house and had taken the rental receipt described earlier.  A neighbor testified that prior to the robbery she saw Henry at the rented house with John Luck, one of the two men who had by the time of Henry's trial been convicted for the robbery.  In addition, palm prints found on the lease agreement matched those of Henry.

Nichols testified at trial that he had "an opportunity to have some conversations with Mr. Henry while he was in the jail," and that Henry told him that on several occasions he had gone to the Janaf Branch to see which employees opened the vault.  Nichols also testified that Henry described to him the details of the robbery and stated that the only evidence connecting him to the robbery was the rental receipt. The jury was not informed that Nichols was a paid government informant.

On the basis of this testimony, Henry was convicted of bank robbery and sentenced to a term of imprisonment of 25 years.  On appeal he raised no Sixth Amendment claims.  His conviction was affirmed, 483 F.2d 1401 (C.A.4 1973), and his petition to this Court for a writ of certiorari was denied.  421 U.S. 915, 95 S.Ct. 1575, 43 L.Ed.2d 781 (1975).

On August 28, 1975, Henry moved to vacate his sentence pursuant to 28 U.S.C.A. § 2255.  At this stage, he stated that he had just learned that Nichols was a paid government informant and alleged that he had been intentionally placed in the same cell with Nichols so that Nichols could secure information about the robbery.  Thus, Henry contended that the introduction of Nichols' testimony violated his Sixth Amendment right to the assistance of counsel.  The District Court denied the motion without a hearing.  The Court of Appeals, however, reversed and remanded for an evidentiary inquiry into "whether the witness [Nichols] was acting as a government agent during his interviews with Henry."

On remand, the District Court requested affidavits from the government agents.  An affidavit was submitted describing the agent's relationship with Nichols and relating the following conversation:

> "I recall telling Nichols at this time to be alert to any statements made by these individuals [the federal prisoners] regarding the charges against them.  I specifically recall telling Nichols that he was not to question Henry or these individuals about the charges against them, however, if they engaged him in conversation or talked in front of him, he was requested to pay attention to their statements.  I recall telling Nichols not to initiate any conversations with Henry regarding the bank robbery charges against

Henry, but that if Henry initiated the conversations with Nichols, I requested Nichols to pay attention to the information furnished by Henry."

The agent's affidavit also stated that he never requestd anyone affiliated with the Norfolk City Jail to place Nichols in the same cell with Henry.

The District Court again denied Henry's § 2255 motion, concluding that Nichols' testimony at trial did not violate Henry's Sixth Amendment right to counsel. The Court of Appeals reversed and remanded, holding that the actions of the government impaired the Sixth Amendment rights of the defendant under Massiah v. United States, 377 U.S. 201, 84 S.Ct. 1199, 12 L.Ed.2d 246 (1964). The court noted that Nichols had engaged in conversation with Henry and concluded that if by association, by general conversation, or both, Nichols had developed a relationship of trust and confidence with Henry such that Henry revealed incriminating information, this constituted interference with the right to the assistance of counsel under the Sixth Amendment. 590 F.2d 544 (1978).

## II.

\* \* \*

The question here is whether under the facts of this case, a government agent "deliberately elicited" incriminating statements from Henry within the meaning of Massiah. Three factors are important. First, Nichols was acting under instructions as a paid informant for the government; second, Nichols was ostensibly no more than a fellow inmate of Henry; and third, Henry was in custody and under indictment at the time he was engaged in conversation by Nichols.

The Court of Appeals viewed the record as showing that Nichols deliberately used his position to secure incriminating information from Henry when counsel was not present and held that conduct attributable to the government. Nichols had been a paid government informant for more than a year; moreover, the FBI agent was aware that Nichols had access to Henry and would be able to engage him in conversations without arousing Henry's suspicion. The arrangement between Nichols and the agent was on a contingent fee basis; Nichols was to be paid only if he produced useful information. This combination of circumstances is sufficient to support the Court of Appeals' determination. Even if the agent's statement is accepted that he did not intend that Nichols would take affirmative steps to secure incriminating information, he must have known that such propinquity likely would lead to that result.

The Government argues that the federal agents instructed Nichols not to question Henry about the robbery. Yet according to his own testimony, Nichols was not a passive listener; rather, he had "some conversations with Mr. Henry" while he was in jail and Henry's incriminatory statements were "the product of this conversation."

\* \* \*

\* \* \*

It is undisputed that Henry was unaware of Nichols' role as a government informant.  The Government argues that this Court should apply a less rigorous standard under the Sixth Amendment where the accused is prompted by an undisclosed undercover informant than where the accused is speaking in the hearing of persons he knows to be government officers.  That line of argument, however, seeks to infuse Fifth Amendment concerns against compelled self-incrimination into the Sixth Amendment protection of the right to the assistance of counsel.  An accused speaking to a known government agent is typically aware that his statements may be used against him.  The adversary positions at that stage are well established; the parties are then "arms length" adversaries.

When the accused is in the company of a fellow inmate who is acting by prearrangement as a government agent, the same cannot here be said.  Conversation stimulated in such circumstances may elicit information that an accused would not intentionally reveal to persons known to be government agents.  Indeed, the *Massiah* Court noted that if the Sixth Amendment "is to have any efficacy it must apply to indirect and surreptitious interrogations as well as those conducted in the jailhouse."  The Court pointedly observed that Massiah was more seriously imposed upon because he did not know that his codefendant was a government agent.

Moreover, the concept of a knowing and voluntary waiver of Sixth Amendment rights does not apply in the context of communications with an undisclosed undercover informant acting for the government.  In that setting Henry, being unaware that Nichols was a government agent expressly commissioned to secure evidence, cannot be held to have waived his right to the assistance of counsel.

Finally Henry's incarceration at the time he was engaged in conversation by Nichols is also a relevant factor.  As a ground for imposing the prophylactic requirements in Miranda v. Arizona, 384 U.S. 436, 467, 86 S.Ct. 1602, 1624, 16 L.Ed.2d 694 (1964), this Court noted the powerful psychological inducements to reach for aid when a person is in confinement.  While the concern in *Miranda* was limited to custodial police interrogation, the mere fact of custody imposes pressures on the accused; confinement may bring into play subtle influences that will make him particularly susceptible to the ploys of undercover government agents.  The Court of Appeals determined that on this record the incriminating conversations between Henry and Nichols were facilitated by Nichols' conduct and apparent status as a person sharing a common plight.  That Nichols had managed to gain the confidence of Henry, as the Court of Appeals determined, is confirmed by Henry's request that Nichols assist him in his escape plans when Nichols was released from confinement.

Under the strictures of the Court's holdings on the exclusion of evidence, we conclude that the Court of Appeals did not err in holding that Henry's statements to Nichols should not have been admitted at trial.  By intentionally creating a situation likely to induce Henry to make incriminating statements without the assistance of counsel, the government violated Henry's Sixth Amendment right to counsel. This is not a case where, in Justice Cardozo's words, "the constable blundered," People v. DeFore, 242 N.Y. 13, 21, 150 N.E. 585, 587 (1926); rather, it is one where the "constable" planned an impermissible interference with the right to the assistance of counsel.

The judgment of the Court of Appeals for the Fourth Circuit is affirmed.

MR. JUSTICE POWELL, concurring.  [omitted]

MR. JUSTICE BLACKMUN, with whom MR. JUSTICE WHITE joins, dissenting.

\*   \*   \*

## I.

*Massiah* mandates exclusion only if a federal agent "deliberately elicited" statements from the accused in the absence of counsel. 377 U.S., at 206, 84 S.Ct., at 1203. The word "deliberately" denotes intent. *Massiah* ties this intent to the act of elicitation, that is, to conduct that draws forth a response. Thus *Massiah*, by its own terms, covers only action undertaken with the specific intent to evoke an inculpatory disclosure.

\*   \*   \*

\*   \*   \* [W]hile claiming to retain the "deliberately elicited" test, the Court really forges a new test that saps the word "deliberately" of all significance. The Court's extension of *Massiah* would cover even a "negligent" triggering of events resulting in reception of disclosures. This approach, in my view, is unsupported and unwise.

\*   \*   \*

## II.

In my view, the Court not only missteps in forging a new *Massiah* test; it proceeds to misapply the very test it has created. The new test requires a showing that the agent created a situation "likely to induce" the production of incriminatory remarks, and that the informant in fact "prompted" the defendant. Even accepting the most capacious reading of both this language and the facts, I believe that neither prong of the Court's test is satisfied.

A.  *"Likely to Induce."* In holding that Coughlin's actions were likely to induce Henry's statements, the Court relies on three facts: a contingent fee arrangement; Henry's assumption that Nichols was just a cellmate; and Henry's incarceration.

\*   \*   \*

\*   \*   \* I question whether the existence of a contingent fee arrangement is at all significant. The reasonable conclusion of an informant like Nichols would be that, whatever the arrangement, he would *not* be remunerated if he breached his promise; yet the Court asks us to infer that Coughlin's conversation with Nichols "likely would lead" Nichols to engage in the very conduct which Coughlin told him to avoid.

The Court also emphasizes that Henry was "unaware that Nichols was a government agent." One might properly assign this factor some importance, were it not for Brewer v. Williams, 430 U.S. 387, 97 S.Ct. 1232, 51 L.Ed.2d 424 (1977). In that case, the Court explicitly held that the fact "[t]hat the incriminating statements were elicited surreptitiously in the *Massiah* case, and otherwise here, is *constitutionally irrelevant.*" 430 U.S., at 400, 97 S.Ct., at 1240. (Emphasis added.) The Court's teeter-tottering with this factor in *Massiah* analysis can only induce confusion.

Finally, the Court notes that Henry was incarcerated when he made his statements to Nichols. The Court's emphasis of the "subtle influences" exerted by custody, however, is itself too subtle for me. This is not a case of a custodial encounter with police, in which the Government's display of power might overcome the free will of the accused. The relationship here was "social" and relaxed. Henry did not suspect that Nichols was connected with the FBI. Moreover, even assuming that "subtle influences" might encourage a detainee to talk about his crime, there are certainly counterbalances of at least equal weight. Since, in jail, "official surveillance has traditionally been the order of the day," Lanza v. New York, 370 U.S. 139, 143, 82 S.Ct. 1218, 1221, 8 L.Ed.2d 1234 (1962), and a jailmate has obvious incentives to assist authorities, one may expect a detainee to act with corresponding circumspection.     *     *     *

*     *     *

B. *"Prompting."* All Members of the Court agree that Henry's statements were properly admitted if Nichols did not "prompt" him. The record, however, gives no indication that Nichols "stimulated" Henry's remarks with "affirmative steps to secure incriminating information." Certainly the known facts reveal nothing more than "a jailhouse informant who had been instructed to overhear conversations and to engage a criminal defendant in some conversations." The scant record demonstrates only that Nichols "had 'an opportunity to have some conversations with Mr. Henry while he was in the jail.'" "Henry had engaged [Nichols] in conversation," "had requested Nichols' assistance," and "had talked to Nichols about the bank robbery charges against him." App. to Pet. for Cert. 58a. Thus, we know only that Nichols and Henry had conversations, hardly a startling development, given their location in the same cellblock in a city jail. We know nothing about the nature of these conversations, particularly whether Nichols subtly or otherwise focused attention on the bank robberies. Indeed, to the extent the record says anything at all, it supports the inference that it was Henry, not Nichols, who "engaged" the other "in some conversations," and who was the moving force behind any mention of the crime. I cannot believe that *Massiah* requires exclusion when a cellmate previously unknown to the defendant and asked only to keep his ears open says: "It's a nice day," and the defendant responds: "It would be nicer if I hadn't robbed that bank."     *     *     *

*     *     *

MR. JUSTICE REHNQUIST, dissenting.

\* \* \*

The doctrinal underpinnings of *Massiah* have been largely left unexplained, and the result in this case, as in *Massiah*, is difficult to reconcile with the traditional notions of the role of an attorney. Here, as in *Massiah*, the accused was not prevented from consulting with his counsel as often as he wished. No meetings between the accused and his counsel were disturbed or spied upon. And preparation for trial was not obstructed. \* \* \*

Once the accused has been made aware of his rights, it is his responsibility to decide whether or not to exercise them. If he voluntarily relinquishes his rights by talking to authorities, or if he decides to disclose incriminating information to someone whom he mistakenly believes will not report it to the authorities, he is normally accountable for his actions and must bear any adverse consequences that result. Such information has not in any sense been obtained because the accused's will has been overborne, nor does it result from any "unfair advantage" that the State has over the accused: the accused is free to keep quiet and to consult with his attorney if he so chooses. In this sense, the decision today and the result in *Massiah* are fundamentally inconsistent with traditional notions of the role of the attorney that underlie the Sixth Amendment right to counsel.

\* \* \*

\* \* \* This Court has never held that an accused is constitutionally protected from his inability to keep quiet, whether or not he has been encouraged by third party citizens to voluntarily make incriminating remarks. I do not think the result should be different merely because the government has encouraged a third party informant to report remarks obtained in this fashion. When an accused voluntarily chooses to make an incriminatory remark in these circumstances, he knowingly assumes the risk that his confidant may be untrustworthy.

\* \* \*

The fact that police carry on undercover activities should not automatically be transmuted because formal criminal proceedings have begun. It is true that once such proceedings have commenced, there is an "adversary" relationship between the government and the accused. But an adversary relationship may very well exist prior to the commencement of formal proceedings. And, as this Court has previously recognized, many events, while perhaps "adversarial," are not of such a nature that an attorney can provide any special knowledge or assistance to the accused as a result of his legal expertise. \* \* \* When an attorney has no such special knowledge or skill, the Sixth Amendment does not give the accused a right to have an attorney present.

In addition, the mere bringing of formal proceedings does not necessarily mean that an undercover investigation or the need for it has terminated. A person may be arrested on the basis of probable cause arising in the immediate aftermath of an offense and during early stages of investigation, but before the authorities have had an opportunity to investigate fully his connection with the crime. And for the criminal, there is no rigid dichotomy between the time before commencement of former criminal proceedings and the time after such proceedings have begun. Once out on bail the accused remains free to continue his criminal activity, and very well may decide to do so. * * * I would hold that the Government's activity here is merely a continuation of their lawful authority to use covert operations in investigating a criminal case after formal proceedings have commenced.

## NOTES

1. In Maine v. Moulton, 474 U.S. 159, 106 S.Ct. 477, 88 L.Ed.2d 481 (1985), both Moulton and one Colson had been indicted for theft by receiving stolen property. Colson contacted police; he reported that he had received anonymous threatening telephone calls and that Moulton had suggested that the two kill Gary Elwell, a state witness. Other witnesses in the case had reported to authorities that they had received threats. The police made and Colson accepted a deal under which Colson would cooperate with the authorities in return for no further charges being brought against him. During later telephone conversations with Colson, Moulton suggested that the two meet to plan their defense to the charges. For purposes of this meeting, Colson was equipped with a body wire transmitter to record what was said at the meeting; according to police testimony, this was done for Colson's safety in the event Moulton realized Colson was cooperating with authorities and to record any further threats to witnesses that Moulton might make. During the conversation, Moulton offered that the plan for killing Elwell would not work. There was extended discussion concerning the falsification of alibis and Colson encouraged Moulton to make a number of incriminating admissions concerning the crime for which he had been indicted. At Moulton's later theft trial, the state successfully offered into evidence those portions of the recorded conversations in which Moulton made admissions concerning the crime charged. One portion of the discussion concerning false alibis was admitted, but no part of the conversation concerning the killing of the witness was offered. Moulton was convicted.

The Supreme Court reversed, reasoning that admission of the conversations violated Moulton's Sixth Amendment rights as developed in *Massiah* and *Henry*. First, it rejected the argument that the Sixth Amendment was inapplicable because Moulton rather than the authorities set up the meeting. If police knowingly exploit an opportunity to secure incriminating admissions from an accused in violation of the right to counsel, the Sixth Amendment is violated regardless of who initiated the events. Here, the police knew that Moulton would make statements to Colson concerning the offense for which he had been indicted. Therefore, by concealing the fact that Colson was an agent of the State, the officers denied Moulton his Sixth Amendment right to counsel.

The majority also rejected the argument that the evidence was admissible because the police activity was legitimately intended to investigate matters other than the theft offense for which Moulton had been indicted—the threats to Colson and Moulton's plan to kill Elwell:

> To allow the admission of evidence obtained from the accused in violation of his Sixth Amendment right whenever the police assert an alternative, legitimate reason for their surveillance invites abuse by law enforcement personnel in the form of fabricated investigations and risks the evisceration of the Sixth Amendment right recognized in *Massiah*. * * * Consequently, incriminating statements pertaining to pending charges are inadmissible at the trial of those charges, notwithstanding the fact that the police were also investigating other crimes, if, in obtaining this evidence,

the State violated the Sixth Amendment by knowingly circumventing the accused's right to the assistance of counsel.

474 U.S. at 180, 106 S.Ct. at 489, 88 L.Ed.2d at 498–99. Because Moulton's *Massiah* right was violated, the use of the evidence in his theft trial was improper. The Court also offered:

> On the other hand, to exclude evidence pertaining to charges as to which the Sixth Amendment right to counsel had not attached at the time the evidence was obtained, simply because other charges were pending at that time, would unnecessarily frustrate the public's interest in the investigation of criminal activities.

474 U.S. at 180, 106 S.Ct. at 489, 88 L.Ed.2d at 498. It added:

> Incriminating statements pertaining to other crimes, as to which the Sixth Amendment right has not yet attached are, of course, admissible at the trial of those offenses.

474 U.S. at 180 n. 16, 106 S.Ct. at 489 n. 16, 88 L.Ed.2d at 499 n. 16. Suppose Moulton, at his theft trial, had testified to a fabricated alibi. Would his statements to Colson indicating the false nature of this testimony be admissible at a later trial for perjury based on his testimony at the theft trial? It is clear that at the time of the meeting, Moulton had no Sixth Amendment right to counsel concerning the yet-uncommitted perjury. Suppose in his recorded conversation with Colson, Moulton had admitted threatening the State's witnesses in the theft prosecution. Would that part of the conversation be admissible against Moulton in a prosecution based upon those threats?

Chief Justice Burger, joined by three other justices, dissented in *Moulton*. In addition to other concerns, he expressed "serious doubt" about extending the exclusionary rule to the case. Given the concerns regarding Colson's safety and Moulton's plans to kill Elwell, the investigation that resulted in securing the evidence was proper:

> Since the State was not trying to build its theft case against [Moulton] in obtaining the evidence, excluding the evidence from the theft trial will not affect police behavior at all. The exclusion of evidence "cannot be expected, and should not be applied, to deter objectively reasonable law enforcement activity." [United States v.] Leon, [468 U.S. 897, 919, 104 S.Ct. 3405, 3419, 82 L.Ed.2d 677 (1984)]. Indeed, * * * it is impossible to identify any police "misconduct" to deter in this case.

474 U.S. at 192, 106 S.Ct. at 495, 88 L.Ed.2d at 506 (Burger, C.J., dissenting).

2. In Kuhlmann v. Wilson, 477 U.S. 436, 106 S.Ct. 2616, 91 L.Ed.2d 364 (1986), Wilson was arrested and arraigned on charges relating to a robbery-murder. He was placed in a cell with a prisoner named Benny Lee; the cell provided its occupants with a view of the garage at which the crimes were committed. Unknown to Wilson, Lee had entered into an arrangement under which he agreed to listen to Wilson's conversations and to report Wilson's remarks to police. Lee was instructed not to ask Wilson any questions but to "keep his ears open." Wilson soon told Lee that although he had been present at the robbery and murder, he did not know the perpetrators and was not involved in the crime. According to Lee's later testimony at one point, Lee responded that the story "didn't sound too good" and that "things didn't look too good for him." At another point, Lee testified that he had told Wilson, "[Y]ou better come up with a better story because that one doesn't sound too cool to me * * *." Several days later, Wilson told Lee another version of the events, admitting guilty participation. At Wilson's state trial, the trial judge found that Wilson's admissions to Lee were "spontaneous" and "unsolicited"

and admitted them. In subsequent federal habeas corpus litigation, the Supreme Court held that Wilson was entitled to no relief. Acknowledging that it had never expressly addressed whether the Sixth Amendment bars the admission of statements overheard by an informant who made no effort to stimulate those statements, the majority resolved the issue:

> [T]he primary concern of the *Massiah* line of decisions is secret interrogation by investigatory techniques that are the equivalent of direct police interrogation. Since "the Sixth Amendment is not violated whenever—by luck or happenstance—the State obtains incriminating statements from the accused after the right to counsel has attached," [Maine v. Moulton, 474 U.S. 159, 176, 106 S.Ct. 477, 487, 88 L.Ed.2d 481 (1985)], a defendant does not make out a violation of that right simply by showing that an informant, either through prior arrangement or voluntarily, reported his incriminating statements to the police. Rather, the defendant must demonstrate that the police and their informant took some action, beyond merely listening, that was designed deliberately to elicit incriminating remarks.

477 U.S. at 459, 106 S.Ct. at 2630, 91 L.Ed.2d at 384–85. The record in the case, the majority concluded, did not permit a federal habeas corpus court to find, under this standard, that Wilson's Sixth Amendment rights were violated. Three members of the Court disagreed with the majority's application of the "deliberate elicitation" standard: I think that the deliberate elicitation standard requires consideration of the entire course of government behavior.

> The State intentionally created a situation in which it was forseeable that [Wilson] would make incriminating statements without the assistance of counsel—it assigned [Wilson] to a cell overlooking the scene of the crime and designated a secret informant to be [Wilson's] cellmate. The informant, while avoiding direct questions, nonetheless developed a relationship of cellmate camaraderie with [Wilson] and encouraged him to talk about his crime. * * * Clearly the State's action had a sufficient nexus with [Wilson's] admission of guilt to constitute deliberate elicitation * * *.

477 U.S. at 476, 106 S.Ct. at 2639, 91 L.Ed.2d at 395–96 (Brennan, J., dissenting). See also, 477 U.S. at 476, 106 S.Ct. at 2639, 91 L.Ed.2d at 396 (Stevens, J., dissenting).

3. Whether *Miranda* has any application to undercover elicitation of self-incriminating statements was addressed in Illinois v. Perkins, 495 U.S. ___, 110 S.Ct. 2394, 110 L.Ed.2d 243 (1990). Police learned from a former prison acquaintance of Perkins that Perkins had admitted a homicide. Upon locating Perkins in a local jail, police placed the former acquaintance and an undercover officer in the same cellblock. After the former acquaintance introduced them, the officer engaged Perkins in conversations and encouraged Perkins to admit the offense and relate details of its commission. Failure to comply with *Miranda* in this process, the Court held, did not render Perkins' admissions subject to suppression.

> Conversations between suspects and undercover agents do not implicate the concerns underlying *Miranda*. The essential ingredients of a "police-dominated atmosphere" and compulsion are not present when an incarcerated person speaks freely to someone he believes to be a fellow inmate. Coercion is determined from the perspective of the suspect. . . . When a suspect considers himself in the company of cellmates and not officers, the coercive atmosphere is lacking. * * * When the suspect has no reason to think that the listeners have official power over him, it should not be assumed that his words are motivated by the reaction he expects from his listeners. * * *

*Miranda* forbids coercion, not mere strategic deception by taking advantage of a suspect's misplaced trust in one he supposes to be a fellow prisoner. ＊ ＊ ＊

495 U.S. at ＿＿, 110 S.Ct. at 2397, 110 L.Ed.2d at 251. *Massiah* and its progeny were distinguished as applicable only after charges have been filed against the suspect. 495 U.S. at ＿＿, 110 S.Ct. at 2399, 110 L.Ed.2d at 253.

Justice Brennan concurred, but suggested that on remand the lower court could find that although *Miranda* was not violated, "under the totality of the circumstances, [Perkins'] confession was elicited in a manner that violated the Due Process Clause." 495 U.S. at ＿＿, 110 S.Ct. at 2400–01, 110 L.Ed.2d at 255 (Brennan, J., concurring). Justice Marshall dissented, arguing that *Miranda* should be applied to the situation. Persons incarcerated are subject to pressures, he reasoned, that render them susceptible to efforts by officials to elicit admissions. The risk that these circumstances will render particular confessions involuntary is not eliminated simply because the suspect is ignorant of his interrogator's identity. Consequently, *Miranda's* rationale suggests that no exception be recognized for situations like *Perkins*.

## D. UNDERCOVER SURVEILLANCE AS A "SEARCH" (AND RELATED MATTERS)

Given the prominence of the Fourth Amendment in federal constitutional regulation of other aspects of law enforcement investigatory behavior, it is appropriate to consider its use as a means of limiting, but not prohibiting, certain aspects of undercover investigations. This, of course, would be possible only if some or all of the activities of undercover officers and agents constituted "searches" or "seizures" within the meaning of the Fourth Amendment. Those issues are addressed in the principal case in this section, which also explores an additional aspect of the *Massiah* Sixth Amendment right to counsel and the general Fifth and Fourteenth Amendments right to due process of law.

### HOFFA v. UNITED STATES

Supreme Court of the United States, 1966.
385 U.S. 293, 87 S.Ct. 408, 17 L.Ed.2d 374.

MR. JUSTICE STEWART delivered the opinion of the Court.

Over a period of several weeks in the late autumn of 1962 there took place in a federal court in Nashville, Tennessee, a trial by jury in which James Hoffa was charged with violating a provision of the Taft-Hartley Act. That trial, known in the present record as the Test Fleet trial, ended with a hung jury. The petitioners now before us—James Hoffa, Thomas Parks, Larry Campbell, and Ewing King—were tried and convicted in 1964 for endeavoring to bribe members of that jury. The convictions were affirmed by the Court of Appeals. A substantial element in the Government's proof that led to the convictions of these four petitioners was contributed by a witness named Edward Partin, who testified to several incriminating statements which he said petitioners Hoffa and King had made in his presence during the course of the Test Fleet trial. Our grant of certiorari was limited to the single issue of whether the Government's use in this case of evidence supplied by Partin operated to invalidate these convictions.

\* \* \*

The controlling facts can be briefly stated. The Test Fleet trial, in which James Hoffa was the sole individual defendant, was in progress between October 22 and December 23, 1962, in Nashville, Tennessee. James Hoffa was president of the International Brotherhood of Teamsters. During the course of the trial he occupied a three-room suite in the Andrew Jackson Hotel in Nashville. One of his constant companions throughout the trial was the petitioner King, president of the Nashville local of the Teamsters Union. Edward Partin, a resident of Baton Rouge, Louisiana, and a local Teamsters Union official there, made repeated visits to Nashville during the period of the trial. On these visits he frequented the Hoffa hotel suite, and was continually in the company of Hoffa and his associates, including King, in and around the hotel suite, the hotel lobby, the courthouse, and elsewhere in Nashville. During this period Partin made frequent reports to a federal agent named Sheridan concerning conversations he said Hoffa and King had had with him and with each other, disclosing endeavors to bribe members of the Test Fleet jury. Partin's reports and his subsequent testimony at the petitioners' trial unquestionably contributed, directly or indirectly, to the convictions of all four of the petitioners.

The chain of circumstances which led Partin to be in Nashville during the Test Fleet trial extended back at least to September of 1962. At that time Partin was in jail in Baton Rouge on a state criminal charge. He was also under a federal indictment for embezzling union funds, and other indictments for state offenses were pending against him. Between that time and Partin's initial visit to Nashville on October 22 he was released on bail on the state criminal charge, and proceedings under the federal indictment were postponed. On October 8, Partin telephoned Hoffa in Washington, D. C., to discuss local union matters and Partin's difficulties with the authorities. In the course of this conversation Partin asked if he could see Hoffa to confer about these problems, and Hoffa acquiesced. Partin again called Hoffa on October 18 and arranged to meet him in Nashville. During this period Partin also consulted on several occasions with federal law enforcement agents, who told him that Hoffa might attempt to tamper with the Test Fleet jury, and asked him to be on the lookout in Nashville for such attempts and to report to the federal authorities any evidence of wrongdoing that he discovered. Partin agreed to do so.

After the Test Fleet trial was completed, Partin's wife received four monthly installment payments of $300 from government funds, and the state and federal charges against Partin were either dropped or not actively pursued.

Reviewing these circumstances in detail, the Government insists the fair inference is that Partin went to Nashville on his own initiative to discuss union business and his own problems with Hoffa, that Partin ultimately cooperated closely with federal authorities only after he discovered evidence of jury tampering in the Test Fleet trial, that the payments to Partin's wife were simply in partial reimbursement of Partin's subsequent out-of-pocket expenses, and that the failure to prosecute Partin on the state and federal charges had no necessary connection with his services as an informer. The findings of the trial ccurt support this version of the facts, and these findings were accepted by the Court of Appeals as "supported by substantial evidence." 349 F.2d at 36. But whether or not the Government "placed" Partin with Hoffa in Nashville during the Test Fleet trial, we proceed upon the premise that Partin was a government informer from the time he first arrived in Nashville on October 22, and that the Government compensated him for his services as such. It is upon that premise that we consider the constitutional issues presented.

*　*　*

I.

It is contended that only by violating the petitioner's rights under the Fourth Amendment was Partin able to hear the petitioner's incriminating statements in the hotel suite, and that Partin's testimony was therefore inadmissible under the exclusionary rule of Weeks v. United States, 232 U.S. 383, 34 S.Ct. 341, 58 L.Ed. 652. The argument is that Partin's failure to disclose his role as a government informer vitiated the consent that the petitioner gave to Partin's repeated entries into the suite, and that by listening to the petitioner's statements Partin conducted an illegal "search" for verbal evidence.

The preliminary steps of this argument are on solid ground. A hotel room can clearly be the object of Fourth Amendment protection as much as a home or an office. United States v. Jeffers, 342 U.S. 48, 72 S.Ct. 93, 96 L.Ed. 59. The Fourth Amendment can certainly be violated by guileful as well as by forcible intrusions into a constitutionally protected area. Gouled v. United States, 255 U.S. 298, 41 S.Ct. 261, 65 L.Ed. 647. And the protections of the Fourth Amendment are surely not limited to tangibles, but can extend as well to oral statements. Silverman v. United States, 365 U.S. 505, 81 S.Ct. 679, 5 L.Ed. 2d 734.

Where the argument falls is in its misapprehension of the fundamental nature and scope of Fourth Amendment protection. What the Fourth Amendment protects is the security a man relies upon when he places himself or his property within a constitutionally protected area, be it his home or his office, his hotel room or his automobile. There he is protected from unwarranted governmental intrusion. And when he puts something in his filing cabinet, in his desk drawer, or in his pocket, he has the right to know it will be secure from an unreasonable search or an unreasonable seizure. So it was that the Fourth Amendment could not tolerate the warrantless search of the hotel room in *Jeffers*, the purloining of the petitioner's private papers in *Gouled*, or the surreptitious electronic surveillance in *Silverman*. Countless other cases which have come to this Court over the years have involved a myriad of differing factual contexts in which the protections of the Fourth Amendment have been appropriately invoked. No doubt the future will bring countless others. By nothing we say here do we either foresee or foreclose factual situations to which the Fourth Amendment may be applicable.

In the present case, however, it is evident that no interest legitimately protected by the Fourth Amendment is involved. It is obvious that the petitioner was not relying on the security of his hotel suite when he made the incriminating statements to Partin or in Partin's presence. Partin did not enter the suite by force or by stealth. He was not a surreptitious eavesdropper. Partin was in the suite by invitation, and every conversation which he heard was either directed to him or knowingly carried on in his presence. The petitioner, in a word, was not relying on the security of the hotel room; he was relying upon his misplaced confidence that Partin would not reveal his wrongdoing. As counsel for the petitioner himself points out, some of the communications with Partin did not take place in the suite at all, but in the "hall of the hotel," in the "Andrew Jackson Hotel lobby," and "at the courthouse."

Neither this Court nor any member of it has ever expressed the view that the Fourth Amendment protects a wrongdoer's misplaced belief that a person to whom he voluntarily confides his wrongdoing will not reveal it. Indeed, the Court unanimously rejected that very contention less than four years ago in Lopez v. United States, 373 U.S. 427, 83 S.Ct. 1381, 10 L.Ed.2d 462. * * * In the words of the dissenting opinion in *Lopez*, "The risk of being overheard by an eavesdropper or betrayed by an informer or deceived as to the identity of one with whom one deals is probably inherent in the conditions of human society. It is the kind of risk we necessarily assume whenever we speak." Id., 373 U.S. at 465, 83 S.Ct. at 1402, 10 L.Ed.2d 462. See also Lewis v. United States, 385 U.S. 206, 87 S.Ct. 424, 17 L.Ed.2d 312.

Adhering to these views, we hold that no right protected by the Fourth Amendment was violated in the present case.

\* \* \*

## III.

The petitioner makes two separate claims under the Sixth Amendment, and we give them separate consideration.

### A.

During the course of the Test Fleet trial the petitioner's lawyers used his suite as a place to confer with him and with each other, to interview witnesses, and to plan the following day's trial strategy. Therefore, argues the petitioner, Partin's presence in and around the suite violated the petitioner's Sixth Amendment right to counsel, because an essential ingredient thereof is the right of a defendant and his counsel to prepare for trial without intrusion upon their confidential relationship by an agent of the government, the defendant's trial adversary. Since Partin's presence in the suite thus violated the Sixth Amendment, the argument continues, any evidence acquired by reason of his presence there was constitutionally tainted and therefore inadmissible against the petitioner in this case.  We reject this argument.

\*    \*    \*

It is possible to imagine a case in which the prosecution might so pervasively insinuate itself into the councils of the defense as to make a new trial on the same charges impermissible under the Sixth Amendment.  But even if it were further arguable that a situation could be hypothesized in which the Government's previous activities in undermining a defendant's Sixth Amendment rights at one trial would make evidence obtained thereby inadmissible in a different trial on other charges, the case now before us does not remotely approach such a situation.

This is so because of the clinching basic fact in the present case that none of the petitioner's incriminating statements which Partin heard were made in the presence of counsel, in the hearing of counsel, or in connection in any way with the legitimate defense of the Test Fleet prosecution.  The petitioner's statements related to the commission of a quite separate offense—attempted bribery of jurors—and the statements were made to Partin out of the presence of any lawyers.

Even assuming, therefore, as we have, that there might have been a Sixth Amendment violation which might have made invalid a conviction, if there had been one, in the Test Fleet case, the evidence supplied by Partin in the present case was in no sense the "fruit" of any such violation.   \*    \*    \*

### B.

The petitioner's second argument under the Sixth Amendment needs no extended discussion.  That argument goes as follows:  Not later than October 25, 1962, the Government had sufficient ground for taking the petitioner into custody and charging him with endeavors to tamper with the Test Fleet jury.  Had the Government done so, it could not have continued to question the petitioner without observance of his Sixth Amendment right to counsel.  Massiah v. United States, 377 U.S. 201, 84 S.Ct. 1199, 12 L.Ed.2d 246.  Therefore, the argument concludes, evidence of statements made by the petitioner subsequent to October 25 was inadmissible, because the Government acquired that evidence only by flouting the petitioner's Sixth Amendment right to counsel.

Nothing in *Massiah*   \*   \*   \*   or in any other case that has come to our attention, even remotely suggests this novel and paradoxical constitutional doctrine, and we decline to adopt it now.  There is no constitutional right to be arrested.  The police are not required to guess at their peril the precise moment at which they have probable cause to arrest a suspect, risking a violation of the Fourth Amendment if they act too soon, and a violation of the Sixth Amendment if they wait too long.  Law enforcement officers are under no constitutional duty to call a halt to a criminal investigation the moment they have the minimum evidence to establish probable cause, a quantum of evidence which may fall far short of the amount necessary to support a criminal conviction.

## IV.

Finally, the petitioner claims that even if there was no violation— "as separately measured by each such Amendment"—of the Fourth Amendment, the compulsory self-incrimination clause of the Fifth Amendment, or of the Sixth Amendment in this case, the judgment of conviction must nonetheless be reversed. The argument is based upon the Due Process Clause of the Fifth Amendment. The "totality" of the Government's conduct during the Test Fleet trial operated, it is said, to " 'offend those canons of decency and fairness which express the notions of justice of English-speaking peoples even toward those charged with the most heinous offenses' (Rochin v. [People of] California, 342 U.S. 165, 169 [72 S.Ct. 205, 208, 96 L.Ed. 183])."

The argument boils down to a general attack upon the use of a government informer as "a shabby thing in any case," and to the claim that in the circumstances of this particular case the risk that Partin's testimony might be perjurious was very high. Insofar as the general attack upon the use of informers is based upon historic "notions" of "English-speaking peoples," it is without historical foundation. In the words of Judge Learned Hand, "Courts have countenanced the use of informers from time immemorial; in cases of conspiracy, or in other cases when the crime consists of preparing for another crime, it is usually necessary to rely upon them or upon accomplices because the criminals will almost certainly proceed covertly.   *   *   *"   United States v. Dennis, 2 Cir., 183 F.2d 201, at 224.

This is not to say that a secret government informer is to the slightest degree more free from all relevant constitutional restrictions than is any other government agent. See Massiah v. United States, 377 U.S. 201, 84 S.Ct. 1199, 12 L.Ed.2d 246. It *is* to say that the use of secret informers is not *per se* unconstitutional.

The petitioner is quite correct in the contention that Partin, perhaps even more than most informers, may have had motives to lie. But it does not follow that his testimony was untrue, nor does it follow that his testimony was constitutionally inadmissible. The established safeguards of the Anglo-American legal system leave the veracity of a witness to be tested by cross-examination, and the credibility of his testimony to be determined by a properly instructed jury. At the trial of this case, Partin was subjected to rigorous cross-examination, and the extent and nature of his dealings with federal and state authorities were insistently explored. The trial judge instructed the jury, both specifically and generally, with regard to assessing Partin's credibility. The Constitution does not require us to upset the jury's verdict.

Affirmed.

[The dissenting opinion of CHIEF JUSTICE WARREN and the dissenting opinion of JUSTICE CLARK, joined in by JUSTICE DOUGLAS, are omitted.]

## NOTES

1. If an undercover agent uses electronic devices, does the investigation involve a "search"? Should it make any difference whether the undercover

agent merely records a conversation with the suspect on one hand, or, on the other, causes it to be transmitted for hearing (and perhaps recording) by others? In United States v. White, 401 U.S. 745, 91 S.Ct. 1122, 28 L.Ed.2d 453 (1971), White was charged with drug transactions with a government informer, Harvey Jackson. Jackson had carried a radio transmitter concealed on his person and nearby government agents listened to the transaction by this means. At trial, Jackson was not available and over objection the trial judge permitted the government agents to testify to what they had overheard; White was convicted. On appeal, the Court of Appeals read On Lee v. United States, 343 U.S. 747, 72 S.Ct. 967, 96 L.Ed. 1270 (1952), as holding that use of such a transmitting device did not make Jackson's conduct a search. But it further read Katz v. United States, 389 U.S. 347, 88 S.Ct. 507, 19 L.Ed.2d 576 (1967), as overruling On Lee and held that under Katz Jackson's activity was a search conducted without a warrant and therefore the agents' testimony was inadmissible. The Supreme Court reversed. In an opinion announcing the judgment of the Court and joined by three other members of the Court, Justice White relied upon two grounds. First, the Court of Appeals erred in reading Katz as overruling On Lee:

> If the conduct and revelations of an agent operating without electronic equipment do not invade the defendant's constitutionally justifiable expectations of privacy, neither does a simultaneous recording of the same conversation made by the agent or by others from transmissions received from the agent to whom the defendant is talking and whose trustworthiness the defendant necessarily risks.

401 U.S. at 751, 91 S.Ct. at 1126, 28 L.Ed.2d at 458. Second, under Desist v. United States, 394 U.S. 244, 89 S.Ct. 1030, 22 L.Ed.2d 248 (1969), Katz is not to be applied to surveillance which took place before the decision in Katz. Judged by pre-Katz law, i.e., On Lee, the facts presented no search.

Justices Harlan, Marshall, and Douglas dissented separately; each expressed the view that Desist was wrongly decided and should not be followed. All also took the further position that On Lee should no longer be regarded as controlling, and that Jackson's activity did implicate the Fourth Amendment. Justice Harlan explained:

> The critical question  *  *  *  is whether under our system of government, as reflected in the Constitution, we should impose on our citizens the risk of the electronic listener or observer without at least the protection of a warrant requirement.
>
> This question must, in my view, be answered by assessing the nature of a particular practice and the likely extent of its impact on the individual's sense of security balanced against the utility of the conduct as a technique of law enforcement.  *  *  *
>
> The impact of the practice of third-party bugging must, I think, be considered such as to undermine that confidence and sense of security in dealing with one another that is characteristic of individual relationships between citizens in a free society. It goes beyond the impact on privacy occasioned by the ordinary type of "informer" investigation  *  *  *. The argument of the plurality opinion, to the effect that it is irrelevant whether secrets are revealed by the mere tattletale or the transistor, ignores the differences occasioned by third-party monitoring and recording which insures full and accurate disclosure of all that is said, free of the possibility of error and oversight that inheres in human reporting.

401 U.S. at 786–87, 91 S.Ct. at 1143, 28 L.Ed.2d at 478–79. Abolition of On Lee, he stressed, would not end third-party monitoring of informants but would

merely prevent law enforcement officers from engaging in the practice "unless they first had probable cause to suspect an individual of involvement in illegal activities and had tested their version of the facts before a detached judicial officer." 401 U.S. at 790, 91 S.Ct. at 1145, 28 L.Ed.2d at 480. Justice Harlan noted that recording of a transaction by an informer-participant (without transmission of it to others) was not at issue. He observed, however, that such a situation might be distinguished on the ground that the informer may renege and not provide the recording to the Government; where transmission of the conversation is involved, however, the intrusion involved in providing the government with a documented record of the conversation "is instantaneous." 401 U.S. at 788 n. 24, 91 S.Ct. at 1144 n. 24, 28 L.Ed.2d at 479 n. 24. Justice Marshall expressed the view that in light of *Katz, On Lee* "cannot be considered viable." 401 U.S. at 795, 91 S.Ct. at 1148, 28 L.Ed.2d at 483.

Justice Douglas' discussion was general but strongly suggested that he would regard either participant recording or transmission as a search. 401 U.S. at 756, 91 S.Ct. at 1128, 28 L.Ed.2d at 461. Justice Brennan concurred in the result on the ground that under *Desist* the case was controlled by *On Lee*. But he further stated that in his view "current Fourth Amendment jurisprudence interposes a warrant requirement not only in cases of third-party electronic monitoring * * * but also in cases of electronic recording by a government agent of a face-to-face conversation with a criminal suspect." 401 U.S. at 755, 91 S.Ct. at 1128, 28 L.Ed.2d at 461. Justice Black also concurred in the result only. He expressed disagreement with the plurality's reliance upon *Desist*, because in his view exclusionary rule cases should be applied retroactively. But relying upon his dissent in *Katz*, he took the position that eavesdropping by electronic means cannot constitute a search (i.e., *Katz* was wrongly decided) and therefore Jackson's activities did not constitute a search for Fourth Amendment purposes. 401 U.S. at 754, 91 S.Ct. at 1127, 28 L.Ed.2d at 460.

Does *White* settle the issue of transmission of a conversation by an undercover agent? Justices Brennan, Douglas, Marshall and Harlan all expressed the view that Jackson's conduct constituted a search under the Fourth Amendment; the four Justices in the plurality were obviously committed to the opposite position. Can Justice Black's action be characterized as a refusal to address the effect of *Katz* upon this situation because he regarded *Katz* itself as wrongly decided?

2. Despite the Government's apparent victory in *White*, on October 16, 1972, the United States Attorney General issued a memorandum which requires Department of Justice approval for all consensual monitoring of nontelephone conversations by federal departments or agencies. If less than 48 hours are available to obtain such approval or if exigent circumstances preclude an effort to secure Department of Justice approval, the head of the department or agency (or someone designated by the head) may authorize the action. In United States v. Caceres, 440 U.S. 741, 99 S.Ct. 1465, 59 L.Ed.2d 733 (1979), the Supreme Court refused to require the exclusion in a federal criminal trial of evidence obtained in violation of Internal Revenue Service regulations adopted pursuant to the Attorney General's memorandum.

3. State law may, however, require the suppression of the results of participant recording or monitoring even if federal law does not. In State v. Glass, 583 P.2d 872 (Alaska 1978), the court held that the right of privacy established in Alaska Const. art. 1, § 22 ("The right of the people to privacy is recognized and shall not be infringed * * *.") prohibited law enforcement officers, without first securing a warrant, from recording a drug sale by means of a transmitting device concealed on the informant's person. In State v.

Williams, 94 Wn.2d 531, 617 P.2d 1012 (1980), federal law enforcement agents investigating alleged racketeering activities recorded various conversations between an informant and the subjects of the investigation. This, of course, was not in violation of the federal electronic surveillance statute; see 18 U.S. C.A. § 2511(2)(c), discussed in Chapter 6, supra. It was, however, in violation of the state privacy act, which requires judicial approval for the interception of a conversation unless all parties to the conversation give consent. Wash.Rev. Code Ann. § 9.73.030. Evidence concerning these conversations was the subject of a motion to suppress in later state criminal proceedings. Rejecting arguments that the federal statute preempted the field and that the state statute did not apply to federal law enforcement officers engaged in a legitimate investigation, the Washington Supreme Court held that the recordings violated the state statute and were inadmissible in state criminal proceedings. Further, the court held that in view of the legislative intent to protect persons from public dissemination of illegally obtained information, the state could not use in the criminal trial testimony by participants in conversations that were illegally recorded even if it did not seek to use the recordings themselves.

4. Does the Fourth Amendment have any applicability if the undercover officer engages in a more traditional "search," as contrasted with the efforts to overhear conversations involved in *Hoffa?* Perhaps the leading case is Gouled v. United States, 255 U.S. 298, 41 S.Ct. 261, 65 L.Ed. 647 (1921). Army intelligence personnel suspected Gouled of involvement in a scheme to defraud the Government. They discovered that an enlisted man assigned to intelligence, Cohen, was a business associate of Gouled and directed him to visit Gouled to see what he could learn. The formal certificate before the Supreme Court stated that Cohen came to Gouled's office during Gouled's absence on the pretense of making a friendly call, gained admission to the office, and—in a manner not detailed—found and seized a certain document later admitted at trial. The Solicitor General, however, urged that this version of the facts was not supported by the only evidence directly bearing upon the matter, Cohen's own testimony. Cohen testified that Gouled was in his office when Cohen arrived and the two chatted; when Gouled stepped out for a moment, Cohen took the document at issue from the top of Gouled's desk. Brief for the United States 8, Appendix (pp. 58–59). The Court's opinion states that Cohen "pretending to make a friendly call upon the defendant gained admission to his office and in his absence * * * seized and carried away" the document. 255 U.S. at 304, 41 S.Ct. at 263, 65 L.Ed. at 650. It is not clear whether Gouled, if he was present at the time of Cohen's visit, was aware of Cohen's status as an army intelligence agent. The Court held that the manner in which the document was obtained constituted an unreasonable search within the meaning of the Fourth Amendment. "[W]hether entrance to the home or office of a person suspected of crime be obtained * * * by stealth, or through social acquaintance, or in the guise of a business call, and whether the owner be present or not when [the officer] enters, any search and seizure subsequently and secretly made in his absence falls within the scope of the prohibition of the Fourth Amendment * * *." 255 U.S. at 306, 41 S.Ct. at 264, 65 L.Ed. at 651. *Gouled* can be read as holding only that if an undercover officer obtains consent to enter premises or to inspect items through deception, the officer cannot exceed the scope of that consent. Thus the decision may rest upon the proposition that Cohen's entry into the office, although pursuant to consent obtained by deception, was permissible; when he approached the desk, rummaged through the papers there (if he did so), or seized the document he exceeded the scope of that consent and his conduct was no longer supportable on the basis of the consent. It is also possible, however, to read *Gouled* more

broadly as imposing or at least suggesting more stringent limitations upon some undercover activities.

In 1975, Memphis police officer Joseph Hoing was assigned the task of conducting surveillance of Arthur Baldwin, operator of several local nightclubs. Hoing gained Baldwin's confidence and secured employment as Baldwin's chauffeur and general handyman; he also worked in one of Baldwin's clubs as a bartender and later as club manager. The two shared a two-bedroom apartment until Baldwin moved to a house, at which time Hoing began to occupy a downstairs bedroom. On four occasions, Hoing obtained samples of a white powder he observed Baldwin use and distribute. Two samples were obtained from a tabletop in Baldwin's bedroom; one was found by Hoing on the floorboard of Baldwin's car while Hoing was cleaning it. The fourth sample was taken from a substance which Hoing delivered to Baldwin in response to Baldwin's request that Hoing bring some "coke" from a dresser drawer to one of Baldwin's clubs. All four samples were determined to be cocaine. Baldwin was charged and prosecuted for possession of the cocaine; the defense moved to suppress the three samples obtained by Hoing which the Government intended to use at trial. In opposition to the motion, Hoing testified that he had free access to all parts of both of Baldwin's residences, including Baldwin's bedroom; the District Court found that Hoing had not exceeded his "authority" in entering the bedrooms and cleaning the car and denied the motion. Baldwin was convicted. On appeal, the conviction was affirmed with extensive reliance being placed on *Hoffa*. United States v. Baldwin, 621 F.2d 251 (6th Cir. 1980). "The fact that Baldwin would not knowingly have invited a police agent to share his house," the court reasoned, "does not render Hoing's presence there illegal." Id., at 253. Since Hoing's presence in the various locations was permissible, he came upon the cocaine in "plain view" and could therefore seize it. Id. Over the vigorous dissent of two members of the court, rehearing en banc was denied. 632 F.2d 1 (6th Cir. 1980).

The Supreme Court denied review. 450 U.S. 1045, 101 S.Ct. 1767, 68 L.Ed. 2d 244 (1981). Justice Brennan indicated he would grant review. Justice Marshall dissented from the Court's action in a written opinion. Not only does *Gouled* apply, he reasoned, but the law enforcement conduct here

> is arguably more objectionable in constitutional terms than that condemned in *Gouled*; the search was of a home rather than a business office, lasted for six months instead of several minutes, and appears to have been undertaken for the general purpose of gathering any incriminating evidence rather than the specific purpose of seizing certain incriminating documents.

450 U.S. at 1047, 101 S.Ct. at 1769, 68 L.Ed.2d at 645. Lewis v. United States, 385 U.S. 206, 87 S.Ct. 424, 17 L.Ed.2d 312 (1966) involved only entry and not a search for evidence. Lewis had invited a federal agent, working undercover, into his home and sold narcotics to him there. Baldwin, unlike Lewis, did not relinquish any of his interest in privacy by inviting Hoing into his home for the purpose of an illegal transaction or by converting his residence into "a center of unlawful business." 450 U.S. at 1048, 101 S.Ct. at 1769, 68 L.Ed.2d at 246. Further, the rationale of *Hoffa* is inapplicable because *Hoffa* involved only the misplaced confidence that an associate would not reveal orally communicated information; "[Hoffa's] claim—unlike [Baldwin's] here—was not based on any asserted violation of his right of privacy." 450 U.S. at 1049, 101 S.Ct. at 1770, 68 L.Ed.2d at 246. In concluding, Justice Marshall observed:

> If the decision of the Memphis police to place an undercover agent in [Baldwin's] home for a six-month period, during which the agent rifled through his belongings in the search for incriminating evidence, does not

implicate the "right of the people to be secure in their persons, houses, papers, and effects, against unreasonable searches and seizures," it is hard to imagine what sort of undercover activity would. Indeed, under the Sixth Circuit's approach, the Government need never satisfy the probable cause and warrant requirements of the Fourth Amendment if, by disguising its officers as repairmen, babysitters, neighbors, maids, and the like, it is able to gain entry into an individual's home by ruse rather than force in order to conduct a search.

450 U.S. at 1049, 101 S.Ct. at 1770, 68 L.Ed.2d at 246.

5. Can it be argued that at least some types of undercover surveillance sufficiently intrude upon the "privacy" protected by the Fourth Amendment that it would be desirable and appropriate to impose upon them the traditional requirements of "reasonableness?" This might mean, for example, that before an undercover officer could feign friendship with a suspect (or perhaps exploit an existing friendship), probable cause to believe that such action would lead to incriminating evidence would have to exist and perhaps that—in the absence of exigent circumstances—the adequacy of the available information would have to be determined by a judicial officer in a warrant procedure. Would it be possible to define with reasonable precision what activities by law enforcement officers would be subject to such limitations? It would clearly be unacceptable, would it not, to hold all observations by ununiformed law enforcement personnel unreasonable under the Fourth Amendment unless probable cause existed and a warrant was obtained or the failure to get one justified?

If surveillance activities are excluded from the definition of search—as seems to be the case under *Hoffa*—should the offer of an opportunity to commit an offense under controlled conditions or "encouragement" nevertheless be regarded as "search" subject to Fourth Amendment reasonableness scrutiny? Dix, Undercover Investigations and Police Rulemaking, 53 Texas L.Rev. 203, 247 (1975), suggests so:

> The interest in personal privacy  *  *  *  is arguably more significantly infringed when an undercover investigator not only engages in surveillance but also creates the opportunity for the commission of a controlled offense. To some extent this aggravated infringement is due to the personal affront to the subject; the "straight" who is solicited for homosexual conduct, for example, may experience substantial discomfort. In addition, most persons probably regard the manipulation of their environment to create a controlled opportunity as inherently more offensive than mere surveillance.

6. If Hoffa had been convicted in the Test Fleet trial, what showing would have been necessary to establish that Partin's activity violated Hoffa's right to counsel in regard to that proceeding? In Weatherford v. Bursey, 429 U.S. 545, 97 S.Ct. 837, 51 L.Ed.2d 30 (1977), Weatherford and Bursey had, with two others, vandalized a selective service office. Weatherford, a state undercover agent, informed officials of the act. In order to preserve his capacity to continue functioning as an undercover agent, he was arrested along with the other participants. Both Weatherford and Bursey were released on bond and retained separate attorneys. On two occasions Weatherford met with Bursey and Bursey's attorney, at the attorney's request. Bursey and his attorney apparently were unaware of Weatherford's status as a law enforcement agent until Weatherford was called as a Government witness during Bursey's criminal trial. Bursey was convicted and sentenced to imprisonment. He then brought a civil action for damages against Weatherford and his superior under 18 U.S.C.A. § 1983, alleging that Weatherford's actions violated his Sixth and Fourteenth Amendment right to counsel. The District Court found that at the meetings with Bursey and his attorney Weatherford did not seek information

from the others and did not pass on to his superiors or to prosecutors any information concerning Bursey's trial plans or the criminal incident. It found for the defendants and entered judgment in their favor. On appeal, this was reversed by the Fourth Circuit, which applied a *per se* rule establishing a violation of the right to counsel whenever the prosecution knowingly arranges and permits intrusion into the attorney-client relationship. 528 F.2d 483, 486 (4th Cir. 1975).

The Supreme Court reversed, rejecting the *per se* approach of the lower court. Weatherford's testimony at Bursey's trial revealed nothing said or done at the meetings between Bursey and his attorney, no evidence introduced by the Government was obtained as a consequence of his participation at those meetings, Weatherford communicated nothing at all to his superiors or to prosecutors concerning defense plans, strategy, or preparation, and Weatherford's intrusion into the relationship was not "purposeful." While Weatherford may have obtained information which, if communicated, would have established a violation of Bursey's right to counsel, "as long as the information possessed by Weatherford remained uncommunicated, he posed no substantial threat to Bursey's Sixth Amendment rights." 429 U.S. at 556, 97 S.Ct. at 844, 51 L.Ed.2d at 40. Justice Marshall, joined by Justice Brennan, dissented, emphasizing the difficulty of proving, in a particular case, such matters as a desire on the agent's part to intercept confidential communications between a lawyer and his client and actual communication to the prosecution of information obtained during the investigation. Given these problems, he urged a *per se* approach which would absolutely bar—at least "absent a compelling justification for doing so"—interception of confidential communications as in the case before the Court. 429 U.S. at 565–66, 97 S.Ct. at 848–49, 51 L.Ed.2d at 46.

In United States v. Morrison, 449 U.S. 361, 101 S.Ct. 665, 66 L.Ed.2d 564 (1981), federal agents urged that the defendant abandon the lawyer she had retained. Assuming a violation of the Sixth Amendment, the Court found no "prejudice" because Morrison had not followed the agents' advice. Would similar entreaties by undercover agents to discharge a lawyer or to ignore the lawyer's advice violate the Sixth Amendment?

# Chapter 9

# GRAND JURY INVESTIGATIVE FUNCTIONS

*Analysis*

---

## EDITORS' INTRODUCTION: GRAND JURY
## INVESTIGATIVE POWERS

The grand jury serves—or may serve—two distinct functions. One is a screening function; the grand jury evaluates evidence supporting possible charges and returns an indictment only in those cases in which the evidence amounts to at least probable cause. The other is an investigatorial function: the grand jury sometimes develops information that is of value in determining whether grounds for a charge exist and—perhaps incidentally—in proving that charge at the defendant's later criminal trial. It is this second function that is the subject of the present chapter.

The unique advantage that the grand jury has as an investigatorial agency is the subpoena power. Unlike the police or the prosecution, the grand jury can compel persons, under threat of contempt, to appear, be sworn, and—in absence of a legal privilege—to accurately answer questions. Note, The Grand Jury—Its Investigatory Powers and Limitations, 37 Minn.L.Rev. 586, 606 (1953). See also, Note, The Grand Jury as an Investigatory Body, 74 Harv.L.Rev. 590 (1961). In addition, the subpoena can direct persons to bring with them papers, documents, or physical items for production to the grand jury. A subpoena directing appearance for oral testimony is often referred to as a subpoena *ad testificandum*, while a subpoena directing the production of items is labeled a subpoena *duces tecum*. See State ex rel. Pollard v. Criminal Court, 263 Ind. 236, 329 N.E.2d 573 (1975).

### INVESTIGATORY ROLE

The investigatory role of grand juries developed out of their function in screening charges. Although the government often presented a proposed criminal charge to the grand jury for its consideration, it is clear that traditionally grand juries were free to act on their own knowledge and to return charges based upon this sort of information.

Costello v. United States, 350 U.S. 359, 362, 76 S.Ct. 406, 408, 100 L.Ed. 397, 402 (1956). Moreover, the grand jury could properly act to develop such information even in the absence of a proposed criminal charge submitted by the government. See Hale v. Henkel, 201 U.S. 43, 26 S.Ct. 370, 50 L.Ed. 652 (1906). The authority to subpoena witnesses and documents appears to have developed as an aid in performing the duty to develop information to use in deciding whether to return formal criminal charges. The Supreme Court has commented,

> [T]he grand jury  *  *  *  plays an important role in fair and effective law enforcement  *  *  *. Because its task is to inquire into the existence of possible criminal conduct and to return only well-founded indictments, its investigative powers are necessarily broad. "It is a grand inquest, a body with powers of investigation and inquisition, the scope of whose inquiries is not to be limited narrowly by questions of propriety or forecasts of the probable results of the investigation, or by doubts whether any particular individual will be found properly subject to an accused action of crime." Blair v. United States, 250 U.S. 273, 282, 39 S.Ct. 468, 471, 63 L.Ed. 979 (1919). Hence, the grand jury's authority to subpoena witnesses is not only historic  *  *  *  but essential to its task.

Branzburg v. Hayes, 408 U.S. 665, 687–88, 92 S.Ct. 2646, 2660, 33 L.Ed. 2d 626, 643–44 (1972).

The traditional absence of legal limitations upon the grand jury's inquiries—both their scope and method—has been justified on what has been perceived to be the need for full information, the absence of danger of abuse of the power due in large part to the lay composition of the groups, and the difficulty of imposing such limitations without unduly disrupting or impeding the work of the bodies. In Costello v. United States, supra, the grand jury was described as "a body of laymen, free from technical rules, acting in secret, pledged to indict no one because of prejudice and to free no one because of special favor." 350 U.S. at 362, 76 S.Ct. at 408, 100 L.Ed. at 402. The solemn nature of the special responsibilities which service on the grand jury entails and the absence of a professional or occupational bias in favor of law enforcement have been regarded as sufficient to prevent abuse of the grand jury's investigatorial powers, at least in light of the disruption and cost entailed in any efforts to regulate those powers by legal means.

### GRAND JURY SUBPOENA POWER

The grand jury typically has the authority to call into operation the subpoena power of the court which called the grand jury into existence. In theory, the grand jury decides whether to seek to subpoena witnesses and the court determines whether to issue the subpoena. But in practice the situation may be far different:

> [A]lthough like all federal court subpoenas grand jury subpoenas are issued in the name of the district court over the signature of the clerk, they are issued pro forma and in blank to anyone requesting them. The court exercises no prior control whatsoever over their use.  *  *  *  [A]lthough grand jury subpoenas are

occasionally discussed as if they were instrumentalities of the grand jury, they are in fact almost universally instrumentalities of the United States Attorney's office or of some other investigative or prosecutorial department of the executive branch.

In re Grand Jury Proceedings, 486 F.2d 85, 90 (3d Cir. 1973).

A grand jury may not itself punish an actual or potential witness for failing to respond to the subpoena or for declining to answer questions. Only the court which called the grand jury into existence can exercise the contempt power. See 28 U.S.C.A. § 1826. In the federal system, the scenario often develops as follows: A witness appears before the grand jury but refuses to answer questions put. This is brought to the attention of the district judge, who considers the witness's reasons, if any, for refusing to answer. The judge then orders the witness to testify. The witness is returned to the grand jury room. If the witness persists in refusing to respond, the matter is returned to the district judge and contempt proceedings are begun. See Note, Coercive Contempt and the Federal Grand Jury, 79 Colum.L.Rev. 735, 746 n. 83 (1979). In this contempt proceeding, the witness has an opportunity to assert any defenses the witness may have, i.e., any legal reason for declining to answer the questions put. 28 U.S.C.A. § 1826(a) provides for contempt sanctions if a witness has refused to comply with a court order "without just cause." If found in contempt, the witness may be confined until s/he is willing to comply. But such confinement cannot, generally, extend beyond the term of the grand jury. Shillitani v. United States, 384 U.S. 364, 86 S.Ct. 1531, 16 L.Ed.2d 622 (1966). A witness found in contempt can also be given a "criminal contempt" penalty, which generally provides no provision for escape from the penalty by complying with the initial order or directive. The Supreme Court, however, has indicated that the lower federal courts should regard so-called "civil" contempt as the preferred response to an uncooperative witness. Shillitani v. United States, supra.

### INDEPENDENCE OF GRAND JURY

Perhaps the major issue in structuring grand jury investigation tools is the extent to which some characteristics of the body render it less susceptible to abuse than other law enforcement agencies. It is traditionally regarded as an independent body, in part because its screening and indictment functions assume such independence and because the independence which the body is regarded as having for indictment purposes is presumed to carry over into its use of the subpoena power for purposes of investigation.

But detractors of the grand jury assert that this independence is nonexistent, largely because of prosecution dominance over the grand jury. Prosecutors are generally given the right to be present during the investigatory stages of the grand jury process, although they may not remain in the chamber for the jury's deliberation and vote on a proposed indictment. E.g., Fed.R.Crim.Pro. 6(d). Although prosecutors have no formal legal power to control the grand jury, they may have immense practical authority. See Note, The Grand Jury—Its Investigatory Powers and Limitations, 37 Minn.L.Rev. 586, 600 (1953). The prosecutor generally proposes avenues of inquiry, subpoenas witnesses, questions witnesses when they appear, and advises the grand jurors concerning all matters. One commentator, after noting the "plain fact" of the prosecutor's dominance over the grand jury, concluded:

> The real evil of the grand jury system—its viciousness, if you will—lies not so much in the fact that the grand jury is　*　*　* the prosecutor's alter ego, as it does in our pretensions that it is actually an informed and independent quasi-judicial organ, a pretension which misrepresents the prosecutor's unilateral action as the product of stately proceedings conducted by judicial standards. Therefore,　*　*　*　the grand jury　*　*　* ironically　*　*　* encourages abuses by allowing the prosecuting authority to carry on its work with complete anonymity and with effects greatly magnified by the accompanying judicial rites.

Antell, The Modern Grand Jury: Benighted Supergovernment, 51 A.B. A.J. 153, 156 (1965).

## "ONE MAN" GRAND JURIES

A number of jurisdictions have a curious procedure for judicial participation in the investigation of suspected criminal offenses that somewhat resembles the traditional grand jury but is substantially more streamlined because it consists of an inquiry by a single judge. See Conn.Gen.Stat. § 54–47; Mich.Stat.Ann. §§ 28.943–28.945. In some jurisdictions, a judge functioning in this capacity is labeled a "special inquiry" judge. See Idaho Code §§ 19.1116–19.1123 (enacted in 1980); Wash.Rev.Code Ann. § 10.27.170; Okla.Stat.Ann. § 21–951 (limited to possible violation of gambling laws). More traditionally, judges operating under such a procedure are referred to as "one man" grand juries. See In re Slattery, 310 Mich. 458, 461, 17 N.W.2d 251, 252 (1945), cert. denied 325 U.S. 876, 65 S.Ct. 1553, 89 L.Ed. 1993. The judge typically has the power to subpoena witnesses, to compel testimony with the contempt power, and to grant immunity to witnesses. At the conclusion of the inquiry, the judge may issue a report or direct the apprehension of the suspect (if probable cause is found), but does not appear to have authority to return formal charges. This authority remains in the traditional grand jury, if the jurisdiction retains a defendant's right to grand jury indictment, or in the prosecutor. See State v. Manning, 86 Wn.2d 272, 543 P.2d 632 (1975).

The rationale for this procedure was discussed by the Michigan Supreme Court in In re Colacasides, 379 Mich. 69, 150 N.W.2d 1 (1967):

> Experience has demonstrated　*　*　* that regularly constituted law enforcement agencies sometimes are unable effectively and lawfully to enforce the laws, particularly with respect to corrupt conduct by officers of government and conspiratorial criminal activity on an organized and continuing basis. Our experience has also demonstrated that the common-law 23-man grand jury is unwieldy and ineffective for the investigation of such crimes in a modern, industrialized, and mobile society. It has demonstrated

also that corruption in government and organized crime are susceptible to discovery and prosecution if the investigative body has the power to compel some participants therein to testify by enforcing attendance of witness by subpoena and granting immunity from prosecution, but police agencies in this country do not possess such extraordinary power. * * * Traditionally in this country, such extraordinary power has been entrusted only to judicial officers. * * *

This dilemma has been resolved * * * by [the] unique one-man grand jury, comprised of a judicial officer who can properly exercise the subpoena power and the power to grant immunity to compel testimony. * * *

379 Mich. at 89–90, 150 N.W.2d at 11.

If procedural protections for suspects applicable in police investigations are properly relaxed in traditional grand jury inquiries, is such relaxation also appropriate when the inquiry is being conducted by such a one man grand jury or special inquiry judge? A Michigan court has read that state's statutes as permitting a witness to have counsel present during questioning by a one man grand jury but not during an appearance before a traditional grand jury. Responding to the argument that this violated the equal protection rights of persons appearing before traditional grand juries, the court summarily concluded that "the significant differences" between the two types of proceedings justified the different rights to counsel. People v. Blachura, 59 Mich. App. 664, 667, 229 N.W.2d 877, 878 (1975).

* * *

The present chapter contains two sections addressing two aspects of the grand jury's investigatory function. The first addresses the subpoena power and the extent to which this is subject to Fourth Amendment requirements placed upon law enforcement investigation. The second considers the applicability of the Fifth Amendment privilege against compelled self-incrimination in this context and more specifically the need to afford grand jury witnesses the procedural incidents of that privilege that apply in traditional law enforcement investigations.

In connection with these issues, consider the recommendation of the National Advisory Commission on Criminal Justice Standards and Goals that the subpoena power presently reposing in the grand jury be given to the prosecutor who, in the Commission's judgment, already exercises it as a practical matter. The Commission's proposal would require a prosecutor using the subpoena power to permit the subject's attorney to be present during the questioning, to provide an attorney if the subject desires one but is unable to provide any, and to warn the subject concerning his rights including the privilege against self-incrimination. The result, according to the Commission, would be a "workable and efficient alternative to the grand jury in many criminal cases," which could be used "at even less danger to the interests of the subjects, who often are inadequately protected by existing grand jury procedures." National Advisory Commission on Criminal Justice Standards and Goals, Courts 244–45 (1973). In some jurisdictions, prosecutors already have subpoena power under certain circumstances. Del.Code Ann. tit. 19 § 2504(4); Kan.Stat.Ann. § 22–3101(2). Under the Comprehensive Drug Abuse Prevention and Control Act of 1970, the Attorney General is given the power to subpoena witnesses, compel testimony, and require the production of records. 21 U.S.C.A. § 876. This authority has been delegated to special agents in charge of the Drug Enforcement Administration. Exercise of the subpoena power by these agents was upheld in United States v. Hossbach, 518 F.Supp. 759 (E.D.Pa. 1980).

## A. THE SUBPOENA POWER

When a person is required by subpoena to appear before a grand jury to testify or to engage in some activities in assistance of the grand jury's investigation, it could reasonably be said that the person has been subjected to a "seizure" within the meaning of the Fourth Amendment. If compelled appearance and participation is so characterized, it is necessary to consider the circumstances under which such seizures are "reasonable" within Fourth Amendment meaning. That is the major issue addressed by the cases in this section.

### UNITED STATES v. DIONISIO

Supreme Court of the United States, 1973.
410 U.S. 1, 93 S.Ct. 764, 35 L.Ed.2d 67.

MR. JUSTICE STEWART delivered the opinion of the Court.

A special grand jury was convened in the Northern District of Illinois in February 1971, to investigate possible violations of federal criminal statutes relating to gambling. In the course of its investigation the grand jury received in evidence certain voice recordings that had been obtained pursuant to court orders.

The grand jury subpoenaed approximately 20 persons, including the respondent Dionisio, seeking to obtain from them voice exemplars for comparison with the recorded conversations that had been received in evidence. Each witness was advised that he was a potential defendant in a criminal prosecution. Each was asked to examine a transcript of an intercepted conversation, and to go to a nearby office of the United States Attorney to read the transcript into a recording device. The witnesses were advised that they would be allowed to have their attorneys present when they read the transcripts. Dionisio and other witnesses refused to furnish the voice exemplars, asserting that these disclosures would violate their rights under the Fourth and Fifth Amendments.

The Government then filed separate petitions in the United States District Court to compel Dionisio and the other witnesses to furnish the voice exemplars to the grand jury. The petitions stated that the examplars were "essential and necessary" to the grand jury investigation, and that they would "be used solely as a standard of comparison in order to determine whether or not the witness is the person whose voice was intercepted  *  *  *  *."

Following a hearing, the district judge rejected the witnesses' constitutional arguments and ordered them to comply with the grand jury's request. He reasoned * * * there would be no Fourth Amendment violation, because the grand jury subpoena did not itself violate the Fourth Amendment, and the order to produce the voice exemplars would involve no unreasonable search and seizure within the proscription of that Amendment * * *. When Dionisio persisted in his refusal to respond to the grand jury's directive, the District Court adjudged him in civil contempt and ordered him committed to custody until he obeyed the court order, or until the expiration of 18 months.

The Court of Appeals for the Seventh Circuit reversed. 442 F.2d 276. It * * * concluded that to compel the voice recordings would violate the Fourth Amendment. In the Court's view, the grand jury was "seeking to obtain the voice exemplars of the witnesses by the use of its subpoena powers because probable cause did not exist for their arrest or for some other, less unusual, method of compelling the production of the exemplars." Id., at 280. The Court found that the Fourth Amendment applied to grand jury process, and that "under the fourth amendment law enforcement officials may not compel the production of physical evidence absent a showing of the reasonableness of the seizure. Davis v. Mississippi, 394 U.S. 721, 89 S.Ct. 1394, 22 L.Ed. 2d 676 * * *." Ibid.

* * *

The Court of Appeals held that the Fourth Amendment required a preliminary showing of reasonableness before a grand jury witness could be compelled to furnish a voice exemplar, and that in this case the proposed "seizures" of the voice exemplars would be unreasonable because of the large number of witnesses summoned by the grand jury and directed to produce such exemplars. We disagree.

The Fourth Amendment guarantees that all people shall be "secure in their persons, houses, papers, and effects, against unreasonable searches and seizures * * *." Any Fourth Amendment violation in the present setting must rest on a lawless governmental intrusion upon the privacy of "persons" rather than on interference with "property relationships or private papers." Schmerber v. California, 384 U.S. 757, 767, 86 S.Ct. 1826, 1833, 16 L.Ed.2d 908; see United States v. Doe (Schwartz), 2 Cir., 457 F.2d 895, 897. In Terry v. Ohio, 392 U.S. 1, 88 S.Ct. 1868, 20 L.Ed.2d 889, the Court explained the protection afforded to "persons" in terms of the statement in Katz v. United States, 389 U.S. 347, 88 S.Ct. 507, 19 L.Ed.2d 576, that "the Fourth Amendment protects people, not places," id., at 351, 88 S.Ct., at 511, and concluded that "wherever an individual may harbor a reasonable 'expectation of privacy,' * * * he is entitled to be free from unreasonable governmental intrusion." Terry v. Ohio, 392 U.S., at 9, 88 S.Ct., at 1873.

As the Court made clear in *Schmerber*, supra, the obtaining of physical evidence from a person involves a potential Fourth Amendment violation at two different levels—the "seizure" of the "person" necessary to bring him into contact with government agents, and the subsequent search for and seizure of the evidence. * * * The constitutionality of the compulsory production of exemplars from a grand jury witness necessarily turns on the same dual inquiry—whether either the initial compulsion of the person to appear before the grand jury, or the subsequent directive to make a voice recording is an unreasonable "seizure" within the meaning of the Fourth Amendment.

It is clear that a subpoena to appear before a grand jury is not a "seizure" in the Fourth Amendment sense, even though that summons may be inconvenient or burdensome. Last Term we again acknowledged what has long been recognized, that "[c]itizens generally are not constitutionally immune from grand jury subpoenas   *   *   *." Branzburg v. Hayes, 408 U.S. 665, 682, 92 S.Ct. 2646, 2656, 33 L.Ed.2d 626.

*   *   *

These are recent reaffirmations of the historically grounded obligation of every person to appear and give his evidence before the grand jury. "The personal sacrifice involved is a part of the necessary contribution of the individual to the welfare of the public." Blair v. United States, 250 U.S. 273, 281, 39 S.Ct. 468, 471, 63 L.Ed. 979. See also Garland v. Torre, 2 Cir., 259 F.2d 545, 549. And while the duty may be "onerous" at times, it is "necessary to the administration of justice." Blair v. United States, supra, at 281, 39 S.Ct., at 471.

The compulsion exerted by a grand jury subpoena differs from the seizure effected by an arrest or even an investigative "stop" in more than civic obligation. For, as Judge Friendly wrote for the Court of Appeals for the Second Circuit:

> "The latter is abrupt, is effected with force or the threat of it and often in demeaning circumstances, and, in the case of arrest, results in a record involving social stigma. A subpoena is served in the same manner as other legal process; it involves no stigma whatever; if the time for appearance is inconvenient, this can generally be altered; and it remains at all times under the control and supervision of a court." United States v. Doe (Schwartz) 457 F.2d 895, 898.

*   *   *

This is not to say that a grand jury subpoena is some talisman that dissolves all constitutional protections. The grand jury cannot require a witness to testify against himself. It cannot require the production by a person of private books and records that would incriminate him. See Boyd v. United States, 116 U.S. 616, 633–635, 6 S.Ct. 524, 533–535, 29 L.Ed. 746. The Fourth Amendment provides protection against a grand jury subpoena *duces tecum* too sweeping in its terms "to be regarded as reasonable." Hale v. Henkel, 201 U.S. 43, 76, 26 S.Ct. 370, 379, 50 L.Ed. 652; cf. Oklahoma Press Publishing Co. v. Walling, 327 U.S. 186, 208, 217, 66 S.Ct. 494, 505, 509, 90 L.Ed. 614. And last Term, in the context of a First Amendment claim, we indicated that the Constitution could not tolerate the transformation of the grand jury into an instrument of oppression: "Official harassment of the press undertaken not for purposes of law enforcement but to disrupt a reporter's relationship with his news sources would have no justification. Grand juries are subject to judicial control and subpoenas to motions to quash. We do not expect courts will forget that grand juries must operate within the limits of the First Amendment as well as the Fifth." Branzburg v. Hayes, 408 U.S. 665, 707–708, 92 S.Ct. 2646, 2669–2670, 33 L.Ed.2d 626. See also, id., at 710, 92 S.Ct., at 2671 (Powell, J., concurring).

But we are here faced with no such constitutional infirmities in the subpoena to appear before the grand jury or in the order to make the voice recordings. There is  *   *   *  no valid Fifth Amendment claim. There was no order to produce private books and papers, and no sweeping subpoena *duces tecum*. And even if *Branzburg* be extended beyond its First Amendment moorings and tied to a more generalized due process concept, there is still no indication in this case of the kind of harassment that was of concern there.

The Court of Appeals found critical significance in the fact that the grand jury had summoned approximately 20 witnesses to furnish voice exemplars. We think that fact is basically irrelevant to the constitutional issues here. The grand jury may have been attempting to identify a number of voices on the tapes in evidence, or it might have summoned the 20 witnesses in an effort to identify one voice. But whatever the case, "[a] grand jury's investigation is not fully carried out until every available clue has been run down and all witnesses examined in every proper way to find if a crime has been committed *   *   *." United States v. Stone, 2 Cir., 429 F.2d 138, 140. See also Wood v. Georgia, 370 U.S. 375, 392, 82 S.Ct. 1364, 1374, 8 L.Ed.2d 569. As the Court recalled last Term, "Because its task is to inquire into the existence of possible criminal conduct and to return only well-founded indictments, its investigative powers are necessarily broad." Branzburg v. Hayes, 408 U.S., at 688, 92 S.Ct., at 2659. The grand jury may well find it desirable to call numerous witnesses in the course of an investigation. It does not follow that each witness may resist a subpoena on the ground that too many witnesses have been called. Neither the order to Dionisio to appear, nor the order to make a voice recording was rendered unreasonable by the fact that many others were subjected to the same compulsion.

But the conclusion that Dionisio's compulsory appearance before the grand jury was not an unreasonable "seizure" is the answer to only the first part of the Fourth Amendment inquiry here. Dionisio argues that the grand jury's subsequent directive to make the voice recording was itself an infringement of his rights under the Fourth Amendment. We cannot accept that argument.

In Katz v. United States, supra, we said that the Fourth Amendment provides no protection for what "a person knowingly exposes to the public, even in his own home or office  *   *   *." 389 U.S. 347, 351, 88 S.Ct. 507, 511, 19 L.Ed.2d 576. The physical characteristics of a person's voice, its tone and manner, as opposed to the content of a specific conversation, are constantly exposed to the public. Like a man's facial characteristics, or handwriting, his voice is repeatedly produced for others to hear. No person can have a reasonable expectation that others will not know the sound of his voice, any more than he can reasonably expect that his face will be a mystery to the world. As the Court of Appeals for the Second Circuit stated:

> "Except for the rare recluse who chooses to live his life in complete solitude, in our daily lives we constantly speak and write, and while the content of a communication is entitled to Fourth Amendment protection,  *  *  *  the underlying identifying characteristics—the constant factor throughout both public and private communications—are open for all to see or hear. There is no basis for constructing a wall of privacy against the grand jury which does not exist in casual contacts with strangers. Hence no intrusion into an individual's privacy results from compelled execution of handwriting or voice exemplars; nothing is being exposed to the grand jury that has not previously been exposed to the public at large." United States v. Doe (Schwartz), 2 Cir., 457 F.2d 895, 898–899.

The required disclosure of a person's voice is thus immeasurably further removed from the Fourth Amendment protection than was the intrusion into the body effected by the blood extraction in *Schmerber*. "The interests in human dignity and privacy which the Fourth Amendment protects forbid any such intrusions on the mere chance that desired evidence might be obtained." Schmerber v. California, 384 U.S. 757, 769–770, 86 S.Ct. 1826, 1835, 16 L.Ed.2d 908. Similarly, a seizure of voice exemplars does not involve the "severe, though brief, intrusion upon cherished personal security," effected by the "pat down" in *Terry*—"surely  *  *  *  an annoying, frightening, and perhaps humiliating experience." Terry v. Ohio, 392 U.S. 1, 24–25, 88 S.Ct. 1868, 1882, 20 L.Ed.2d 889. Rather, this is like the fingerprinting in *Davis*, where, though the initial dragnet detentions were constitutionally impermissible, we noted that the fingerprinting itself, "involves none of the probing into an individual's private life and thoughts that marks an interrogation or search." Davis v. Mississippi, 394 U.S. 721, 727, 89 S.Ct. 1394, 1398, 22 L.Ed.2d 676; cf. Thom v. New York Stock Exchange, D.C., 306 F.Supp. 1002, 1009.

Since neither the summons to appear before the grand jury, nor its directive to make a voice recording infringed upon any interest protected by the Fourth Amendment, there was no justification for requiring the grand jury to satisfy even the minimal requirement of "reasonableness" imposed by the Court of Appeals. See United States v. Doe (Schwartz), 2 Cir., 457 F.2d 895, 899–900. A grand jury has broad investigative powers to determine whether a crime has been committed and who has committed it. The jurors may act on tips, rumors, evidence offered by the prosecutor, or their own personal knowledge. Branzburg v. Hayes, 408 U.S. 665, 701, 92 S.Ct. 2646, 2666, 33 L.Ed.2d 626. No grand jury witness is "entitled to set limits to the investigation that the grand jury may conduct." Blair v. United States, 250 U.S. 273, 282, 39 S.Ct. 468, 471, 63 L.Ed. 979. And a sufficient basis for an indictment may only emerge at the end of the investigation when all the evidence has been received.

"It is impossible to conceive that * * * the examination of witnesses must be stopped until a basis is laid by an indictment formally preferred, when the very object of the examination is to ascertain who shall be indicted." Hale v. Henkel, 201 U.S. 43, 65, 26 S.Ct. 370, 375, 50 L.Ed. 652.

Since Dionisio raised no valid Fourth Amendment claim, there is no more reason to require a preliminary showing of reasonableness here than there would be in the case of any witness who, despite the lack of any constitutional or statutory privilege, declined to answer a question or comply with a grand jury request. Neither the Constitution nor our prior cases justify any such interference with grand jury proceedings.[1]

The Fifth Amendment guarantees that no civilian may be brought to trial for an infamous crime "unless on a presentment or indictment of a Grand Jury." This constitutional guarantee presupposes an investigative body "acting independently of either prosecuting attorney or judge," Stirone v. United States, 361 U.S. 212, 218, 80 S.Ct. 270, 273, 4 L.Ed.2d 252, whose mission is to clear the innocent, no less than to bring to trial those who may be guilty. Any holding that would saddle a grand jury with mini-trials and preliminary showings would assuredly impede its investigation and frustrate the public's interest in the fair and expeditious administration of the criminal laws. * * * The grand jury may not always serve its historic role as a protective bulwark standing solidly between the ordinary citizen and an overzealous prosecutor, but if it is even to approach the proper performance of its constitutional mission, it must be free to pursue its investigations unhindered by external influence or supervision so long as it does not trench upon the legitimate rights of any witness called before it.

Since the Court of Appeals found an unreasonable search and seizure where none existed, and imposed a preliminary showing of reasonableness where none was required, its judgment is reversed and this case is remanded to that Court for further proceedings consistent with this opinion.

It is so ordered.

## UNITED STATES v. MARA

Supreme Court of the United States, 1973.
410 U.S. 19, 93 S.Ct. 774, 35 L.Ed.2d 99.

MR. JUSTICE STEWART delivered the opinion of the Court.

The respondent, Richard J. Mara, was subpoenaed to appear before the September 1971 Grand Jury in the Northern District of Illinois that

---

[1] Mr. Justice Marshall in dissent suggests that a preliminary showing of "reasonableness" is required where the grand jury subpoenas a witness to appear and produce handwriting or voice exemplars, but not when it subpoenas him to appear and testify. Such a distinction finds no support in the Constitution. The dissent argues that there is a potential Fourth Amendment violation in the case of a subpoenaed grand jury witness because of the asserted intrusiveness of the initial subpoena to appear—the possible stigma from a grand jury appearance and the inconvenience of the official restraint. But the initial directive to appear is as intrusive if the witness is called simply to testify as it is if he is summoned to produce physical evidence.

was investigating thefts of interstate shipments. On two separate occasions he was directed to produce handwriting and printing exemplars to the grand jury's designated agent. Each time he was advised that he was a potential defendant in the matter under investigation. On both occasions he refused to produce the exemplars.

The Government then petitioned the United States District Court to compel Mara to furnish the handwriting and printing exemplars to the grand jury. * * * The District Judge rejected the respondent's contention that the compelled production of such exemplars would constitute an unreasonable search and seizure, and he ordered the respondent to provide them. When the witness continued to refuse to do so, he was adjudged to be in civil contempt and was committed to custody until he obeyed the court order or until the expiration of the grand jury term.

The Court of Appeals for the Seventh Circuit reversed. 454 F.2d 580. * * *

We have held today in *Dionisio*, that a grand jury subpoena is not a "seizure" within the meaning of the Fourth Amendment, and further, that that Amendment is not violated by a grand jury directive compelling production of "physical characteristics" which are "constantly exposed to the public." Handwriting, like speech, is repeatedly shown to the public, and there is no more expectation of privacy in the physical characteristics of a person's script than there is in the tone of his voice. * * * Consequently the Government was under no obligation here, any more than in *Dionisio*, to make a preliminary showing of "reasonableness."

Indeed, this case lacks even the aspects of an expansive investigation that the Court of Appeals found significant in *Dionisio*. In that case 20 witnesses were summoned to give exemplars; here there was only one. The specific and narrowly drawn directive requiring the witness to furnish a specimen of his handwriting violated no legitimate Fourth Amendment interest. The District Court was correct, therefore, in ordering the respondent to comply with the grand jury's request.

Accordingly, the judgment of the Court of Appeals is reversed, and this case is remanded to that court for further proceedings consistent with this opinion.

It is so ordered.

[The dissenting opinions of Mr. Justice Brennan and Mr. Justice Douglas are omitted.]

MR. JUSTICE MARSHALL, dissenting [in both *Dionisio* and *Mara*.]

\* \* \*

The Court concludes that the exemplars sought from the respondents are not protected by the Fourth Amendment because respondents have surrendered their expectation of privacy with respect to voice and handwriting by knowingly exposing these to the public, see Katz v. United States, 389 U.S. 347, 351, 88 S.Ct. 507, 511, 19 L.Ed.2d 576 (1967). But even accepting this conclusion, it does not follow that the investigatory seizures of respondents, accomplished through the use of subpoenas ordering them to appear before the grand jury—and thereby necessarily interfering with their personal liberty—are outside the protection of the Fourth Amendment. To the majority, though, "[i]t is clear that a subpoena to appear before a grand jury is not a 'seizure' in the Fourth Amendment sense, even though that summons may be inconvenient or burdensome." With due respect, I find nothing "clear" about so sweeping an assertion.

There can be no question that investigatory seizures effected by the police are subject to the constraints of the Fourth and Fourteenth Amendments. * * * [T]he present cases involve official investigatory seizures which interfere with personal liberty. The Court considers dispositive, however, the fact that the seizures were effected by the grand jury, rather than the police. I cannot agree.

* * *

In the present cases * * * it was not testimony that the grand juries sought from respondents, but physical evidence. The Court glosses over this important distinction from its prior decisions, however, by artificially bifurcating its analysis of what is taking place in these cases—that is, by effectively treating what is done with individuals once they are before the grand jury as irrelevant in determining what safeguards are to govern the procedures by which they are initially compelled to appear. Nonetheless, the fact remains that the historic exception to which the Court resorts is not necessarily as broad as the context in which it is now employed. Hence, I believe that the question we must consider is whether an extension of that exception is warranted, and if so, under what conditions.

* * *

The Court seems to reason that the exception to the Fourth Amendment for grand jury subpoenas directed at persons is justified by the relative unintrusiveness of the grand jury process on an individual's liberty. The Court, adopting Chief Judge Friendly's analysis in United States v. Doe (Schwartz), 457 F.2d 895, 898 (C.A.2 1972), suggests that arrests or even investigatory "stops" are inimical to personal liberty because they may involve the use of force; they may be carried out in demeaning circumstances; and at least an arrest may yield the social stigma of a record. By contrast, we are told, a grand jury subpoena is a simple legal process, which is served in an unoffensive manner; it results in no stigma; and a convenient time for appearance may always be arranged. The Court would have us believe, in short, that, unlike an arrest or an investigatory "stop," a grand jury subpoena entails little more inconvenience than a visit to an old friend. Common sense and practical experience indicate otherwise.

It may be that service of a grand jury subpoena does not involve the same potential for momentary embarrassment as does an arrest or investigatory "stop." But this difference seems inconsequential in comparison to the substantial stigma which—contrary to the Court's assertion—may result from a grand jury appearance as well as from an arrest or investigatory seizure. Public knowledge that a man has been summoned by a federal grand jury investigating, for instance, organized criminal activity can mean loss of friends, irreparable injury to business, and tremendous pressures on one's family life. Whatever nice legal distinctions may be drawn between police and prosecutor, on the one hand, and the grand jury, on the other, the public often treats an appearance before a grand jury as tantamount to a visit to the station house. Indeed, the former is frequently more damaging than the latter, for a grand jury appearance has an air of far greater gravity than a brief visit "downtown" for a "talk." The Fourth Amendment was placed in our Bill of Rights to protect the individual citizen from such potentially disruptive governmental intrusion into his private life unless conducted reasonably and with sufficient cause.

Nor do I believe that the constitutional problems inherent in such governmental interference with an individual's person are substantially alleviated because one may seek to appear at a "convenient time." * * * No matter how considerate a grand jury may be in arranging for an individual's appearance, the basic fact remains that his liberty has been officially restrained for some period of time. In terms of its effect on the individual, this restraint does not differ meaningfully from the restraint imposed on a suspect compelled to visit the police station house. Thus, the nature of the intrusion on personal liberty caused by a grand jury subpoena cannot, without more, be considered sufficient basis for denying respondents the protection of the Fourth Amendment.

* * *

Thus, the Court's decisions today can serve only to encourage prosecutorial exploitation of the grand jury process, at the expense of both individual liberty and the traditional neutrality of the grand jury. Indeed, by holding that the grand jury's power to subpoena these respondents for the purpose of obtaining exemplars is completely outside the purview of the Fourth Amendment, the Court fails to appreciate the essential difference between real and testimonial evidence in the context of these cases, and thereby hastens the reduction of the grand jury into simply another investigative device of law enforcement officials. By contrast, the Court of Appeals, in proper recognition of these dangers, imposed narrow limitations on the subpoena power of the grand jury which are necessary to guard against unreasonable official interference with individual liberty but which would not impair significantly the traditional investigatory powers of that body.

The Court of Appeals in *Mara*, No. 71–850, did not impose a requirement that the Government establish probable cause to support a grand jury's request for examplars. It correctly recognized that "examination of witnesses by a grand jury need not be preceded by a formal charge against a particular individual," since the very purpose of the grand jury process is to ascertain probable cause. Consistent with the Court's decision in Hale v. Henkel, it ruled only that the request for physical evidence such as exemplars should be subject to a showing of reasonableness. See 201 U.S., at 76, 26 S.Ct., at 379. This "reasonableness" requirement has previously been explained by this Court, albeit in a somewhat different context, to require a showing by the Government that: (1) "the investigation is authorized by Congress"; (2) the investigation "is for a purpose Congress can order"; (3) the evidence sought is "relevant"; and (4) the request is "adequate, but not excessive, for the purposes of the relevant inquiry." See Oklahoma Press Publishing Co. v. Walling, 327 U.S. 186, 209, 66 S.Ct. 494, 506, 90 L.Ed. 614 (1946). This was the interpretation of the "reasonableness" requirement properly adopted by the Court of Appeals. See In re September 1971 Grand Jury, 7 Cir., 454 F.2d 580, 584–585. And, in elaborating on the requirement that the request not be "excessive," it added that the Government would bear the burden of showing that it was not conducting "a general fishing expedition under grand jury sponsorship." Id., at 585.

These are not burdensome limitations to impose on the grand jury when it seeks to secure physical evidence, such as exemplars, that has traditionally been gathered directly by law enforcement officials. The essence of the requirement would be nothing more than a showing that the evidence sought is relevant to the purpose of the investigation and that the particular grand jury is not the subject of prosecutorial abuse—a showing that the Government should have little difficulty making, unless it is in fact acting improperly. Nor would the requirement interfere with the power of the grand jury to call witnesses before it, to take their testimony, and to ascertain their knowledge concerning criminal activity. It would only discourage prosecutorial abuse of the grand jury process. The "reasonableness" requirement would do no more in the context of these cases than the Constitution compels— protect the citizen from unreasonable and arbitrary governmental interference, and ensure that the broad subpoena powers of the grand jury which the Court now recognizes are not turned into a tool of prosecutorial oppression.

I would therefore affirm the Court of Appeals' decisions reversing the judgments of contempt against respondents and order the cases remanded to the District Court to allow the Government an opportunity to make the requisite showing of "reasonableness" in each case. To do less is to invite the very sort of unreasonable governmental intrusion on individual liberty that the Fourth Amendment was intended to prevent.[2]

### NOTES

1. In two major opinions, the United States Court of Appeals for the Third Circuit has developed what may be significant limitations upon the grand jury subpoena process. Invoking its supervisory power and developing a district court's authority to deal individually with each request to enforce a subpoena, the court held that in each case in which enforcement of a subpoena is sought the Government must, by affidavit, make a showing that the item or information sought is relevant to an investigation being conducted by the grand jury and properly within its jurisdiction and is not sought primarily for another purpose. In re Grand Jury Proceedings, 486 F.2d 85, 93 (3d Cir. 1973)

---

[2] * * * [A] requirement that the Government establish the "reasonableness" of the request for an exemplar would hardly be so burdensome as the Court suggests. As matters stand, if the suspect resists the request, the Government must seek a judicial order directing that he comply with the request. Thus, a formal judicial proceeding is already necessary. The question whether the request is "reasonable" would simply be one further matter to consider in such a proceeding.

(Schofield I).  After the government complies, the trial judge has "considerable discretion" as to whether to conduct further inquiry into the propriety of enforcing the subpoena.  It might require additional affidavits or even hold a hearing.  In re Grand Jury Proceedings, 507 F.2d 963 (3d Cir. 1975), cert. denied 421 U.S. 1015, 95 S.Ct. 2424, 44 L.Ed.2d 685 (Schofield II).  In the second decision, the court took pains to make clear that *Schofield I* "did not require a showing of reasonableness, it did not require any determination of probable cause and it clearly did not require a hearing in every case."  507 F.2d at 966.  A number of courts have declined to follow these decisions.  United States v. Wilson, 614 F.2d 1224 (9th Cir. 1980); In re Liberatore, 574 F.2d 78 (2d Cir. 1978); In re Grand Jury Proceedings, 567 F.2d 281 (5th Cir. 1978).  But at least one state court has adopted the *Schofield* approach pursuant to its own supervisory powers.  See Robert Hawthorne, Inc. v. County Investigating Grand Jury, 488 Pa. 373, 412 A.2d 556 (1980).

2.  A few limitations upon the grand jury's investigatory power are widely acknowledged.  It is improper for a grand jury to take testimony for purposes of pursuing civil remedies available to the government.  United States v. Procter & Gamble Co., 356 U.S. 677, 78 S.Ct. 983, 2 L.Ed.2d 1077 (1958), on remand 175 F.Supp. 198 (D.N.J.1959), 187 F.Supp. 55 (D.N.J.1960).  If, for example, during a grand jury antitrust investigation the Government decides that criminal sanctions will not be sought, it is improper for the grand jury to continue to take testimony on the matter for purposes of pursuing the Government's civil antitrust remedies.  175 F.Supp. at 199.  Further, courts frequently state that a grand jury may not be used after indictment to strengthen the Government's case or to secure evidence for use at trial.  E.g., Beverly v. United States, 468 F.2d 732 (5th Cir. 1972).  But if a legitimate primary purpose for the grand jury's inquiry exists, the fact that the Government's case against an indicted defendant will benefit from the inquiry as an incidental matter does not render the grand jury's further inquiry improper.  United States v. Beasley, 550 F.2d 261 (5th Cir. 1977).

3.  In United States v. Sells Engineering, Inc., 463 U.S. 418, 103 S.Ct. 3133, 77 L.Ed.2d 743 (1983) the Supreme Court held that under Fed.R.Crim.P. 6, not all attorneys in the Justice Department are entitled to automatic disclosure of federal grand jury materials.  Rather, such automatic disclosure is limited to those Justice Department attorneys who conduct the criminal investigations to which the materials pertain.  The Court's construction of Rule 6 was influenced by its perception of "the general purposes and policies of grand jury secrecy." Permitting Justice Department lawyers automatic access to grand jury materials where these materials are sought for use in civil litigation, the majority explained, poses several problems:

First, disclosure  *   *   *  raises much the same concerns that underlie the rule of secrecy in other contexts.  Not only does disclosure increase the number of persons to whom the information is available (thereby increasing the risk of inadvertent or illegal release to others), but it renders considerably more concrete the threat to the willingness of witnesses to come forward and to testify fully and candidly.  *   *   *

Second,  *   *   *  disclosure to government attorneys for civil use poses a significant threat to the integrity of the grand jury itself.  If prosecutors in a given case knew that their colleagues would be free to use the materials generated by the grand jury for a civil case, they might be tempted to manipulate the grand jury's powerful investigative tools to root out additional evidence useful in the civil suit, or even to start or continue a grand jury inquiry where no criminal prosecution seemed likely.  *   *   *

463 U.S. at 432, 103 S.Ct. at 3142, 77 L.Ed.2d at 757. A Department of Justice attorney not entitled to automatic disclosure, the Court continued, is entitled to disclosure under Rule 6(e)(3)(C)(i) only upon a showing of "particularized need." Four members of the Court dissented. See also, United States v. Baggot, 463 U.S. 476, 103 S.Ct. 3164, 77 L.Ed.2d 785 (1983) (disclosure of grand jury materials cannot be ordered under Rule 6(e)(3)(C)(i) for purposes of determining a taxpayer's civil tax liability because such an investigation is not "preliminar[y] to or in connection with a judicial proceeding" within meaning of the Rule); Illinois v. Abbott & Associates, Inc., 460 U.S. 557, 103 S.Ct. 1356, 75 L.Ed.2d 281 (1983) (state attorney general seeking materials generated by federal grand jury must meet "particularized need" under Rule 6(e)).

4. One court has indicated that a witness subpoenaed before a grand jury might be entitled to have the subpoena quashed if the witness establishes that "the grand jury has lost its independence which is essential to the historical assumption of neutrality that underlies the grand jury process." United States v. Doe, 541 F.2d 490, 492 (5th Cir. 1976). What sort of showing would suffice under this standard is, of course, not clear.

5. When if ever does the Fifth Amendment privilege against compelled self-incrimination justify one upon whom a subpoena *duces tecum* is served in refusing to produce the described documents or items for the grand jury? The matter is clearly affected by Fisher v. United States, 425 U.S. 391, 96 S.Ct. 1569, 48 L.Ed.2d 39 (1976), involving an Internal Revenue Service summons. The mechanics of the IRS administrative summons process are almost identical to the grand jury subpoena process. 26 U.S.C.A. §§ 7602, 7604. It seems clear that the Fifth Amendment right to resist compulsory production of documents, to the extent that it exists, will be the same in the summons and subpoena contexts. In *Fisher*, the taxpayers had obtained certain workpapers from their accountants and transferred these papers to the taxpayers' attorneys. The Service then issued summonses directing the lawyers to produce the papers; the lawyers refused on the ground that to do so would violate their clients' privilege against compelled self-incrimination. Speaking through Justice White, a majority of the Supreme Court held that the lawyers must comply with the summonses. Because the summonses were directed to the lawyers, there was no compulsion exerted upon the taxpayers to do anything; consequently, "the taxpayers' Fifth Amendment privilege is not violated by enforcement of the summonses directed towards their attorneys." 425 U.S. at 397, 96 S.Ct. at 1574, 48 L.Ed.2d at 48. But, the Court continued, the attorney-client privilege requires that a client be free to transfer to an attorney items and documents in order to obtain legal advice. If, therefore, the documents at issue could not have been obtained by summons from the taxpayers, the attorney-client privilege requires that they be held unavailable when in the possession of the attorneys. Despite language to the contrary in Boyd v. United States, 116 U.S. 616, 634–35, 6 S.Ct. 524, 534, 29 L.Ed.2d 746, 752 (1886), the majority held that the nature of the items sought did not render them unavailable from the taxpayer:

> A subpoena served on a taxpayer requiring him to produce an accountant's workpapers in his possession without doubt involves substantial compulsion. But it does not compel oral testimony; nor would it ordinarily require the taxpayer to restate, repeat, or affirm the truth of the contents of the documents sought. Therefore, the Fifth Amendment would not be violated by the fact alone that the papers on their face might incriminate the taxpayer, for the privilege protects a person only against being incriminated by his own compelled testimonial communications. * * * The accountant's workpapers are not the taxpayer's. They were not prepared

by the taxpayer and they contain no testimonial declarations by him. Furthermore, as far as this record demonstrates, the preparation of all of the papers sought in these cases was wholly voluntary, and they cannot be said to contain compelled testimonial evidence, either of the taxpayers or of anyone else.

425 U.S. at 409–10, 96 S.Ct. at 1580, 48 L.Ed.2d at 55. Further, the Court observed:

> The fact that the documents may have been written by the person asserting the privilege is insufficient to trigger the privilege. And, unless the Government has compelled the subpoenaed person to write the document, the fact that it was written by him is not controlling with respect to the Fifth Amendment issue. Conversations may be seized and introduced in evidence under proper safeguards if not compelled. In the case of a documentary subpoena the only thing compelled is the act of producing the document and the compelled act is the same as the one performed when a chattel or document not authored by the producer is demanded.

425 U.S. at 410 n. 11, 96 S.Ct. at 150 n. 11, 48 L.Ed.2d at 55 n. 11.

Compliance with a summons or subpoena for documents may itself have communicative aspects, Justice White continued. The act of complying may constitute tacit acknowledgments: (1) that the documents described in the subpoena exist and are in the person's possession; and (2) that the produced documents are the ones described and thus constitute an "implicit authentication" of the documents produced. Compliance is clearly "compelled," he observed. But whether the tacit averments are both "testimonial" and "incriminating" are questions not lending themselves to categorical answers. Both matters may depend upon the facts and circumstances of particular cases or classes of cases. Turning to tax cases like the ones before the Court, Justice White reasoned that the Government will already know of the existence of the papers and of the subjects' access to them; the Government will not rely on any tacit acknowledgment by the person as to these matters and in this regard compliance has no testimonial significance. Seeking preparation of the papers and their delivery by the accountant is not illegal; any such testimonial communication as might be involved, therefore, poses no realistic threat of incrimination of the taxpayer. Tacit acknowledgment of the described documents' existence and their possession by the subject will not justify noncompliance. 425 U.S. at 412, 96 S.Ct. at 1581, 48 L.Ed.2d at 56–57.

Turning to the danger of implicit authentication, the Court noted that the taxpayers lacked first-hand knowledge as to the preparation of the documents, could not vouch for their accuracy, and therefore would not be competent to authenticate them. If the documents were eventually offered as evidence of the taxpayers' guilt in a criminal trial, they would not be admissible without authenticating testimony other than evidence that the taxpayer produced them in response to the subpoena. "Without more," Justice White reasoned, "responding to the subpoena in the circumstance before us would not appear to represent a substantial threat of self-incrimination." 425 U.S. at 413, 96 S.Ct. at 1582, 48 L.Ed.2d at 57. He concluded:

> Whether the Fifth Amendment would shield the taxpayer from producing his own tax records in his possession is a question not involved here; for the papers demanded here are not his "private papers." We do hold that compliance with a summons directing the taxpayer to produce the accountant's documents involved in these cases would involve no incriminating testimony within the protection of the Fifth Amendment.

425 U.S. at 414, 96 S.Ct. at 1582, 48 L.Ed.2d at 58.

Justice Brennan concurred, reasoning that the Fifth Amendment prohibits the compelled production of certain private papers but that the papers sought in the case before the Court were not "private." He also questioned the majority's rejection of the argument that the tacit acknowledgments involved in compliance were insufficient to invoke the privilege. 425 U.S. at 428–29, 96 S.Ct. at 1589–90, 48 L.Ed.2d at 66–67. Justice Marshall also concurred, expressing hope that the majority's approach, "properly understood and applied," would preclude the compelled production of many private papers. He read the majority's analysis as prohibiting compulsory production of papers if there is significant doubt as to the existence of those papers or their possession by the person subpoenaed or summoned; in such cases, the tacit acknowledgment of the papers' existence and location would be both "testimonial" and "incriminating." The more private the paper, he concluded, the less permissible an assumption concerning its existence (and location) and the greater the likelihood that under the majority's analysis compelled production would be barred. 425 U.S. at 432–33, 96 S.Ct. at 1591–92, 48 L.Ed.2d at 68–69.

6. The application of the privilege to subpoenas for production of documents was again addressed in United States v. Doe, 465 U.S. 605, 104 S.Ct. 1237, 79 L.Ed.2d 552 (1984). Grand jury subpoenas were issued, directing Doe to produce certain records of businesses which he owned. The government conceded that these records were or might be incriminating. Doe sought to quash the subpoenas on the ground that they would compel him to engage in self-incrimination. A majority of the Supreme Court held that the subpoenas were properly quashed. *Fisher,* it noted, did not directly address whether the Fifth Amendment makes privileged incriminating documents in a person's possession. But the reasoning of the case compels a negative answer; since the documents were already prepared when the subpoenas were issued, those subpoenas could not have compelled the preparation of the documents. The "contents" of the documents, then, were not privileged.

But the majority next turned to whether the privilege barred the compelled production of those documents. The lower courts had found that the act of producing the documents would involve testimonial self-incrimination. By producing any described documents he had in his possession, Doe would be acknowledging—in a testimonial fashion—that such documents did in fact exist and that they were in his possession. Further, his acknowledgments might relieve the government of the need for other evidence to authenticate those documents should they be offered against Doe in a criminal prosecution. The Court noted that the Government was not foreclosed from rebutting this by producing evidence that existence, possession and authentication of the documents was a "foregone conclusion." But no such evidence had been produced. Unlike the situation in *Fisher,* the record in *Doe* failed to establish that the act of production would have only minimal testimonial value and would not operate to incriminate. As a result, Doe's actions in producing the described documents were privileged by the Fifth Amendment and could not be compelled.

The majority further commented that production of the documents could be compelled if Doe was granted immunity from the use of evidence which might be created by his acts in producing the documents. 465 U.S. at 614–15, 104 S.Ct. at 1245, 79 L.Ed.2d at 563. Immunity as a means of eliminating the risk of "incrimination" is discussed later in this Chapter.

7. Self-incrimination limits upon grand juries' subpoena power were again explored in Doe v. United States, 487 U.S. 201, 108 S.Ct. 2341, 101 L.Ed.2d 184 (1988). Doe, the target of a grand jury investigation, was directed by a grand jury subpoena to produce records of transactions in accounts at three specified

foreign banks. He produced some records and testified that no additional records within the subpoena's demand were in his possession. When he was questioned about the existence or location of additional records, he invoked his Fifth Amendment right to refuse to answer. The three foreign banks were served with subpoenas directing them to produce records of accounts over which Doe has signatory authority. They refused, on the basis that their local law prohibited the disclosure of such records without the customers' consents. The District Court ordered Doe to sign a form, purporting to give his consent to the disclosure of records of any and all accounts in the three banks over which he had a right of withdrawal. He refused, in reliance upon his privilege against self-incrimination, and was found in contempt. The Supreme Court affirmed. At issue, the majority concluded, was whether the act of executing the form is a "testimonial communication" within the meaning of the privilege. If it is, it is clearly "incriminating" and Doe could not be compelled to do it. Reviewing *Fisher* and other decisions, the majority concluded that:

> [I]n order to be testimonial, an accused's communication must itself, explicitly or implicitly, relate a factual assertion or disclose information. Only then is a person compelled to be a "witness" against himself.

487 U.S. at 210, 108 S.Ct. at 2347, 101 L.Ed.2d at 197. The majority acknowledged that Doe's act of signing the form might lead the Government to incriminating evidence it did not already have. But nevertheless that form was not such that signing it would be "testimonial." The form contained no acknowledgment that any accounts or records exist; it referred only to any records concerning any accounts as might exist. Nothing in the form directed the Government to hidden accounts or other information that might enable the Government to locate evidence. Doe's act of executing the form would not be a statement that any accounts or records exist or an admission as to the authenticity of any records the Government might get as a result of its use of the signed form. Given the terms of the form, his execution of it does not admit or assert that he has "consented" to disclosure. It does not state that Doe "consents" but merely represents that he is signing it under court directive; thus it does not purport to reveal his actual state of mind or "consent." The majority concluded:

> We read the directive as equivalent to a statement by Doe that, although he expresses no opinion about the existence of, or his control over, any such accounts, he is authorizing the bank to disclose information relating to accounts over which, in the bank's opinion, Doe can exercise a right of withdrawal.

487 U.S. at 218, 108 S.Ct. at 2351, 101 L.Ed.2d at 202. In light of this characterization of the form, its execution by Doe would not be "testimonial" and can be compelled by grand jury subpoena. Justice Stevens suggested in dissent that the form purported to evidence a reasoned decision by Doe to authorize the banks to release the records. To compel him to execute it, Justice Stevens reasoned, is to compel him to "use his mind to assist the prosecution in convicting him of a crime." This, he concluded, should be barred by the Fifth Amendment. 487 U.S. at 219, 108 S.Ct. at 2352–53, 101 L.Ed.2d at 203–05 (Stevens, J., dissenting).

8. In Baltimore City Department of Social Services v. Bouknight, 493 U.S. ___, 110 S.Ct. 900, 107 L.Ed.2d 992 (1990), Bouknight's child had been placed within the jurisdiction of the juvenile court. She assumed custody, subject to various conditions including further orders of the court. Later, fearing that the child had again been abused or even killed, the court ordered her to produce the child. She resisted on the basis that by doing so she would be testimonially acknowledging custody of the child and this might assist later prosecution of

her. Finding that Bouknight had no Fifth Amendment right to resist, the Supreme Court invoked the principle underlying the "required records" exception to the Fifth Amendment: "When a person assumes control over items that are the legitimate object of the government's non-criminal regulatory powers, the ability to invoke the privilege is reduced." 493 U.S. at ___, 110 S.Ct. at 906, 107 L.Ed.2d at 1002. When Bouknight accepted custody, she did so subject to subsequent court-ordered production. The Supreme Court suggested, however, that the prosecution in any later trial might not be able to use against her evidence of her act of producing the child. 493 U.S. at ___, 110 S.Ct. at 908, 107 L.Ed.2d at 1004–05.

## B.  QUESTIONING AND THE PRIVILEGE AGAINST COMPELLED SELF–INCRIMINATION

As the Supreme Court's opinion in *Dionisio* recognizes, there is universal agreement that the Fifth Amendment privilege against compelled self-incrimination is available to a witness appearing before a grand jury and that the witness can, in reliance upon this privilege, decline to answer specific questions put by the jurors or the prosecutor. The major questions concern the extent to which, if any, the privilege or sound policy requires that various procedures be followed to assist implementation of the right to remain silent. Given the holding in Miranda v. Arizona, that a suspect undergoing custodial interrogation by police must be afforded the right to the presence of counsel and to warnings designed to assure that the suspect is aware of the right to silence and to counsel, perhaps the major issue is whether these requirements should be relaxed when a suspect is interrogated before a grand jury. But there are also additional questions raised by the grand jury process. One who has been taken into custody and who is questioned by police may generally have adequate notice that he or she is a suspect in the investigation. But given the right and practice of grand jurors to subpoena witnesses who are thought to have information relevant to the investigation but who are not even suspected of criminal involvement, does or should one who is suspected of involvement have the right to a warning of that fact when called to testify before the grand jury?

### UNITED STATES v. WASHINGTON

Supreme Court of the United States, 1977.
431 U.S. 181, 97 S.Ct. 1814, 52 L.Ed.2d 238.

MR. CHIEF JUSTICE BURGER delivered the opinion of the Court.

The question presented in this case is whether testimony given by a grand jury witness suspected of wrongdoing may be used against him in a later prosecution for a substantive criminal offense when the witness was not informed in advance of his testimony that he was a potential defendant in danger of indictment.

(1)

The facts are not in dispute. Zimmerman and Woodard were driving respondent's van truck when a Washington, D. C., policeman stopped them for a traffic offense. Seeing a motorcycle in the rear of the van which he identified as stolen, the officer arrested both men and impounded respondent's vehicle. When respondent came to reclaim the van, he told police that Zimmerman and Woodard were friends who were driving the van with his permission.

He explained the presence of the stolen motorcycle by saying that while driving the van himself he had stopped to assist an unknown motorcyclist whose machine had broken down. Respondent then allowed the motorcycle to be placed in his van to take it for repairs. Soon after this the van stalled and he walked to a nearby gasoline station to call Zimmerman and Woodard for help, leaving the van with the unknown motorcyclist. After reaching Zimmerman by phone, respondent waited at the gasoline station for his friends, then returned to the spot he had left the van when they failed to appear; by that time the van had disappeared. Respondent said he was not alarmed, assuming his friends had repaired the van and driven it away. Shortly thereafter, Zimmerman and Woodard were arrested with the stolen motorcycle in the van.

Not surprisingly, the officer to whom respondent related this tale was more than a little skeptical; he told respondent he did not believe his story, and advised him not to repeat it in court, "because you're liable to be in trouble if you [do so]." The officer also declined to release the van. Respondent then repeated this story to an Assistant United States Attorney working on the case. The prosecutor, too, was dubious of the account; nevertheless, he released the van to respondent. At the same time, he served respondent with a subpoena to appear before the grand jury investigating the motorcycle theft.

When respondent appeared before the grand jury, the Assistant United States Attorney in charge had not yet decided whether to seek an indictment against him. The prosecutor was aware of respondent's explanation, and was also aware of the possibility that respondent could be indicted by the grand jury for the theft if his story was not believed.

The prosecutor did not advise respondent before his appearance that he might be indicted on a criminal charge in connection with the stolen motorcycle. But respondent, after reciting the usual oath to tell the truth, was given a series of other warnings, as follows:

"Q.   *   *   *

"You have a right to remain silent. You are not required to say anything to us in this Grand Jury at any time or to answer any question.[3]

"Anything you say can be used against you in Court.

---

[3] This was an obvious overstatement of respondent's constitutional rights; the very purpose of the grand jury is to elicit testimony, and it can compel answers, by use of contempt powers, to all except self-incriminating questions.

After the oral warnings, respondent was also handed a card containing all the warnings prescribed by Miranda v. Arizona, 384 U.S. 436, 86 S.Ct. 1602, 16 L.Ed.2d 694 (1966), and a waiver form acknowledging that the witness waived the privilege against compelled self-incrimination. Respondent signed the waiver.

"You have the right to talk to a lawyer for advice before we question you and have him outside the Grand Jury during any questioning.

"If you cannot afford a lawyer and want one a lawyer will be provided for you.

"If you want to answer questions now without a lawyer present you will still have the right to stop answering at any time.

"You also have the right to stop answering at any time until you talk to a lawyer.

"Now, do you understand those rights, sir?

"A. Yes, I do.

"Q. And do you want to answer questions of the Grand Jury in reference to a stolen motorcycle that was found in your truck?

"A. Yes, sir.

"Q. And do you want a lawyer here or outside the Grand Jury room while you answer those questions?

"A. No, I don't think so."

In response to questions, respondent again related his version of how the stolen motorcycle came to be in the rear of his van. Subsequently, the grand jury indicted respondent, Zimmerman, and Woodard for grand larceny and receiving stolen property.

Respondent moved to suppress his testimony and quash the indictment, arguing that it was based on evidence obtained in violation of his Fifth Amendment privilege against compelled self-incrimination. The Superior Court for the District of Columbia suppressed the testimony * * * holding that before the Government could use respondent's grand jury testimony at trial, it had first to demonstrate that respondent had knowingly waived his privilege against compelled self-incrimination. Notwithstanding the comprehensive warnings described earlier, the court found no effective waiver had been made, holding that respondent was not properly advised of his Fifth Amendment rights. The court thought the Constitution required, at a minimum, that

"inquiry be made of the suspect to determine what his educational background is, and what his formal education is and whether or not he understands that this is a constitutional privilege and whether he fully understands the consequences of what might result in the event that he does waive his constitutional right and in the event that he does make incriminatory statements * * * ."

The court also held that respondent should have been told that his testimony could lead to his indictment by the grand jury before which he was testifying, and could then be used to convict him in a criminal prosecution.

The District of Columbia Court of Appeals affirmed the suppression order. 328 A.2d 98 (1974). That court also took the position that "the most significant failing of the prosecutor was in not advising [respondent] that he was a potential defendant. Another shortcoming was in the prosecutor's waiting until after administering the oath in the cloister of the grand jury before undertaking to furnish what advice was given." Id., at 100.[4]

(2)

The implicit premise of the District of Columbia Court of Appeals' holding is that a grand jury inquiry, like police custodial interrogation, is an "interrogation of persons suspected or accused of crime [that] contains inherently compelling pressures which work to undermine the individual's will to resist and to compel him to speak where he would not otherwise do so freely." Miranda v. Arizona, 384 U.S. 436, 467, 86 S.Ct. at 1624 (1966). But this Court has not decided that the grand jury setting presents coercive elements which compel witnesses to incriminate themselves. Nor have we decided whether any Fifth Amendment warnings whatever are constitutionally required for grand jury witnesses; moreover, we have no occasion to decide these matters today, for even assuming that the grand jury setting exerts some pressures on witnesses generally or on those who may later be indicted, the comprehensive warnings respondent received in this case plainly satisfied any possible claim to warnings. Accordingly, respondent's grand jury testimony may properly be used against him in a subsequent trial for theft of the motorcycle.

Although it is well settled that the Fifth Amendment privilege extends to grand jury proceedings, Counselman v. Hitchcock, 142 U.S. 547, 12 S.Ct. 195, 35 L.Ed. 1110 (1892), it is also axiomatic that the Amendment does not automatically preclude self-incrimination, whether spontaneous or in response to questions put by government officials. * * * Absent some officially coerced self-accusation, the Fifth Amendment privilege is not violated by even the most damning admissions. Accordingly, unless the record reveals some compulsion, respondent's incriminating testimony cannot conflict with any constitutional guarantees of the privilege.[5]

The Constitution does not prohibit every element which influences a criminal suspect to make incriminating admissions. * * * Of course, for many witnesses the grand jury room engenders an atmosphere conducive to truth telling, for it is likely that upon being brought before such a body of neighbors and fellow citizens, and having been placed under a solemn oath to tell the truth, many witnesses will feel obliged to do just that. But it does not offend the guarantees of the Fifth Amendment if in that setting a witness is more likely to tell the

---

[4] Though both courts below found no effective waiver of Fifth Amendment rights, neither court found, and no one suggests here, that respondent's signing of the waiver-of-rights form was involuntary or was made without full appreciation of all the rights of which he was advised. The Government does not challenge, and we do not disturb, the finding that at the time of his grand jury appearance respondent was a potential defendant whose indictment was considered likely by the prosecution.

[5] In *Miranda*, the Court saw as inherently coercive any police custodial interrogation conducted by isolating the suspect with police officers; therefore, the Court established a *per se* rule that all incriminating statements made during such interrogation are barred as "compelled." All *Miranda's* safeguards, which are designed to avoid the coercive atmosphere, rest on the overbearing compulsion which the Court thought was caused by isolation of a suspect in police custody. * * *

truth than in less solemn surroundings. The constitutional guarantee is only that the witness be not *compelled* to give self-incriminating testimony. The test is whether, considering the totality of the circumstances, the free will of the witness was overborne.

(3)

After being sworn, respondent was explicitly advised that he had a right to remain silent and that any statements he did make could be used to convict him of crime. It is inconceivable that such a warning would fail to alert him to his right to refuse to answer any question which might incriminate him. This advice also eliminated any possible compulsion to self-incrimination which might otherwise exist. To suggest otherwise is to ignore the record and reality. Indeed, it seems self-evident that one who is told he is free to refuse to answer questions is in a curious posture to later complain that his answers were compelled. Moreover, any possible coercion or unfairness resulting from a witness' misimpression that he must answer truthfully even questions with incriminatory aspects is completely removed by the warnings given here. Even in the presumed psychologically coercive atmosphere of police custodial interrogation, *Miranda* does not require that any additional warnings be given simply because the suspect is a potential defendant; indeed, such suspects are potential defendants more often than not. United States v. Binder, 453 F.2d 805, 810 (CA2 1971), cert. denied, 407 U.S. 920, 92 S.Ct. 2458, 32 L.Ed.2d 805 (1972).

Respondent points out that unlike one subject to custodial interrogation, whose arrest should inform him only too clearly that he is a potential criminal defendant, a grand jury witness may well be unaware that he is targeted for possible prosecution. While this may be so in some situations, it is an overdrawn generalization. In any case, events here clearly put respondent on notice that he was a suspect in the motorcycle theft. He knew that the grand jury was investigating that theft and that his involvement was known to the authorities. Respondent was made abundantly aware that his exculpatory version of events had been disbelieved by the police officer, and that his friends, whose innocence his own story supported, were to be prosecuted for the theft. The interview with the prosecutor put him on additional notice that his implausible story was not accepted as true. The warnings he received in the grand jury room served further to alert him to his own potential criminal liability. In sum, by the time he testified respondent knew better than anyone else of his potential defendant status.

However, all of this is largely irrelevant, since we do not understand what constitutional disadvantage a failure to give potential defendant warnings could possibly inflict on a grand jury witness, whether or not he has received other warnings. It is firmly settled that the prospect of being indicted does not entitle a witness to commit perjury, and witnesses who are not grand jury targets are protected from compulsory self-incrimination to the same extent as those who are. Because target witness status neither enlarges nor diminishes the constitutional protection against compelled self-incrimination, potential-defendant warnings add nothing of value to protection of Fifth Amendment rights.

\*    \*    \*

(4)

Since warnings were given, we are not called upon to decide whether such warnings were constitutionally required. However, the District of Columbia Court of Appeals held that whatever warnings are required are insufficient if given "in the cloister of the grand jury." 328 A.2d at 100. That court gave no reason for its view that warnings must be given outside the presence of the jury, but respondent now advances two justifications. First, it could be thought that warnings given to respondent before the grand jury came too late, because of the short time to assimilate their significance, and because of the presence of the grand jurors. But respondent does not contend that he did not understand the warnings given here. In any event, it is purely speculative to attribute any such effects to warnings given in the presence of the jury immediately before taking the stand. If anything, the proximity of the warnings to respondent's testimony and the solemnity of the grand jury setting seem likely to increase their effectiveness.

Second, respondent argues that giving the oath in the presence of the grand jury undermines assertion of the Fifth Amendment privilege by placing the witness in fear that the grand jury will infer guilt from invocation of the privilege. But this argument entirely overlooks that the grand jury's historic role is an investigative body; it is not the final arbiter of guilt or innocence. Moreover, it is well settled that invocation of the Fifth Amendment privilege in a grand jury proceeding is not admissible in a criminal trial, where guilt or innocence is actually at stake.

The judgment of the Court of Appeals is reversed, and the cause is remanded for further proceedings not inconsistent with this opinion.

Reversed and remanded.

Mr. Justice Brennan, with whom Mr. Justice Marshall joins, dissenting.

\*    \*    \*

I would hold that a failure to warn the witness that he is a potential defendant is fatal to an indictment of him when it is made unmistakably to appear, as here, that the grand jury inquiry became an investigation directed against the witness and was pursued with the purpose of compelling him to give self-incriminating testimony upon which to indict him. I would further hold that without such prior warning and the witness' subsequent voluntary waiver of his privilege, there is such gross encroachment upon the witness' privilege as to render worthless the values protected by it unless the self-incriminating testimony is unavailable to the Government for use at any trial brought pursuant to even a valid indictment.

## NOTES

1. In United States v. Wong, 431 U.S. 174, 97 S.Ct. 1823, 52 L.Ed.2d 231 (1977), the defendant had been called before a grand jury investigating police corruption. She was warned of her privilege against self-incrimination and then denied having given money to police officers or having discussed gambling activities with them. Subsequently, she was indicted for perjury on the basis of these statements, which were false. At a hearing on her motion to dismiss the indictment, she convinced the District Judge that because of her limited command of English she had not understood the warning concerning the Fifth Amendment privilege and, in fact, had believed she was required to answer all questions. Her testimony before the grand jury was ordered suppressed by the District Judge and this was affirmed by the Court of Appeal. A unanimous Supreme Court reversed:

> [T]he Fifth Amendment privilege does not condone perjury. It grants a privilege to remain silent without risking contempt but it "does not endow the person who testifies with a license to commit perjury." * * * The failure to provide a warning of the privilege, in addition to the oath to tell the truth, does not call for a different result.

431 U.S. at 178, 97 S.Ct. at 1825, 52 L.Ed.2d 235. The Court also rejected the argument that the failure to provide an effective warning violated due process requirements of fundamental fairness: "perjury is not a permissible way of objecting to the Government's [unfair or oppressive] questions." 431 U.S. at 180, 97 S.Ct. at 1827, 52 L.Ed.2d at 237.

2. There is wide variation concerning the rights, if any, that a target of a grand jury investigation has under state case law and legislation concerning testimony before the grand jury. In State v. Vinegra, 73 N.J. 484, 376 A.2d 150 (1977), the New Jersey Supreme Court noted that its cases have "approved" the "principle" that the target of a grand jury investigation must, if called as a witness, be advised that he is a target and that he has a right not to incriminate himself. But the court found no need to resolve whether such rights existed as a matter of self-incrimination law, because it found the remedy for violation of any such rights as might exist to be the exclusion at trial of evidence given by the target before the grand jury, not the dismissal of the indictment as the appellant before it contended. New Mexico statutes require that a person who is a target of a grand jury inquiry be advised of that fact and be given an opportunity to testify. N.M.Stat.Ann. § 31–6–11(B). Further, the target is not to be subpoenaed "except where it is found by the prosecuting attorney to be essential to the investigation." N.M.Stat.Ann. § 31–6–12. Rule 12.6 of the Arizona Rules of Criminal Procedure provides that "a person under investigation by the grand jury," if s/he appears as a witness, is to be advised of the right to remain silent and to have counsel present.

It may be argued that such "target warnings" would, to some extent, require disclosure of the grand jury's purpose and thus breach grand jury secrecy. Consequently the bases for grand jury secrecy might militate against such a warning. These bases include the needs to prevent the flight of persons under investigation, to protect the grand jurors from those under scrutiny, to prevent subornation of perjury and tampering with witnesses, to protect innocent persons from unfounded accusations, and to assure prospective witnesses of secrecy so they will be willing to testify freely. See Additional January 1979 Grand Jury v. Doe, 50 N.Y.2d 14, 427 N.Y.S.2d 950, 405 N.E.2d 194 (1980). To what extent do these concerns argue against a target warning?

3. Under *Miranda*, a suspect has the right to the presence of counsel during custodial police interrogation. As the discussion in *Washington* suggests, the Supreme Court has given no indication of a willingness to extend this right to questioning before the grand jury. In United States v. Mandujano, 425 U.S. 564, 96 S.Ct. 1768, 48 L.Ed.2d 212 (1976), the grand jury witness (and subsequent perjury defendant) had been informed that if he desired he could have the assistance of counsel but that counsel could not be inside the grand jury room. The Supreme Court commented, "that statement was plainly a correct recital of the law." 425 U.S. at 581, 96 S.Ct. at 1779, 48 L.Ed.2d at 225.

A number of jurisdictions presently provide for at least some grand jury witnesses to have counsel present during their questioning. The Colorado statute providing for representation clearly attempts to address a number of potential problems that counsel might create:

> Any witness subpoenaed to appear and testify before a grand jury or to produce books, papers, documents, or other objects before such grand jury shall be entitled to assistance of counsel during any such time that such witness is being questioned in the presence of such grand jury, and counsel may be present in the grand jury room with his client during such questioning. However, counsel for the witness shall be permitted only to counsel the witness and shall not make objections, arguments, or address the grand jury. Such counsel may be retained by the witness or may, for any person financially unable to obtain adequate assistance, be appointed * * *. An attorney present in the grand jury room shall take an oath of secrecy. * * *

Colo.Rev.Stat. § 16–5–204(4)(d). The Massachusetts statute, Mass.Rev.Stat. ch. 277, § 14A, provides further, "no witness may refuse to appear for reason of unavailability of counsel for that witness." See also, Ariz.Rules Crim.Pro., Rule 12.6 and N.M.Stat.Ann. § 31–6–4(B) and (C) (target witnesses may have counsel present during grand jury testimony). The Massachusetts provision was declared constitutionally valid in an advisory opinion. See Opinion of the Justices to the Governor, 373 Mass. 915, 371 N.E.2d 422 (1977). The court held that the provision for counsel's presence did not violate grand jury secrecy required by the state constitution. Further, the absence of any provision for appointed counsel for indigent witnesses was held not to invalidate the statute on its face. But the court observed that failure in practice to provide counsel for such persons would present a clear issue concerning the application of the statute.

4. It is clear that a person's Fifth Amendment right to decline to respond to questions in the grand jury context as well as in other situations depends upon the "incriminatory" nature of the answers. If no danger of incrimination exists, there is no privilege to refuse an answer. The danger of incrimination can be removed by the expiration of the period of limitations for the offenses at issue, an executive pardon for them or—as is more frequently the case—an effective grant of immunity from prosecution. Brown v. Walker, 161 U.S. 591, 16 S.Ct. 644, 40 L.Ed. 819 (1896). In Ullmann v. United States, 350 U.S. 422, 76 S.Ct. 497, 100 L.Ed. 511 (1956), for example, the petitioner urged that despite a grant of immunity from prosecution he had a right to refuse to provide information to a grand jury because to do so would result in loss of his job, expulsion from a labor union, ineligibility for a passport and general public opprobrium. Rejecting the argument, the Court stressed that the Fifth Amendment protects only against criminal liability and, for a grant of immunity to be effective, "the immunity granted need only remove those sanctions which generate the fear justifying invocation of the privilege * * *." 350 U.S. at 431, 76 S.Ct. at 502, 100 L.Ed. at 520.

5. The major question presented by grants of immunity is the type of immunity required to render the privilege inapplicable. Specifically, the issue is whether the immunity must be from prosecution for the offenses which the answers concern (so-called "transactional immunity" because the immunity is from criminal prosecution for the transaction as to which the person is required to testify) or whether immunity from the use of the answers (so-called "use immunity") is sufficient. The matter was addressed in Kastigar v. United States, 406 U.S. 441, 92 S.Ct. 1653, 32 L.Ed.2d 212 (1972). Kastigar had been called before a federal grand jury and was granted immunity under 18 U.S.C.A. §§ 6002, 6003. If a person has refused to give testimony or provide information in a proceeding before a court or grand jury of the United States, Section 6003 authorizes a federal district judge, upon the request of a United States attorney, to issue an order requiring the person to give the testimony or provide the information. A person who testifies or provides information under such an order is entitled to certain immunity under Section 6002, which provides as follows:

> Whenever a witness refuses, on the basis of his privilege against self-incrimination, to testify or provide other information in a proceeding before or ancillary to—

> (1) a court or grand jury of the United States, * * *.

> and the person presiding over the proceeding communicates to the witness an order issued under [Section 6003], the witness may not refuse to comply with the order on the basis of his privilege against self-incrimination; but no testimony or other information compelled under the order (or any information directly or indirectly derived from such testimony or other information) may be used against the witness in any criminal case, except a prosecution for perjury, giving a false statement, or otherwise failing to comply with the order.

He nevertheless declined to answer the questions and consequently was found in contempt of court. The Supreme Court upheld the contempt citation, concluding that the grant of immunity was sufficiently broad and, therefore, Kastigar had no Fifth Amendment basis for refusing to answer the questions:

> The statute's explicit proscription of the use in any criminal case of "testimony or other information compelled under the order (or any information directly or indirectly derived from such testimony or other information)" is consonant with Fifth Amendment standards. We hold that such immunity from use and derivative use is coextensive with the scope of the privilege against self-incrimination, and therefore is sufficient to compel testimony over a claim of the privilege. While a grant of immunity must afford protection commensurate with that afforded by the privilege, it need not be broader. Transactional immunity, which accords full immunity from prosecution for the offense to which the compelled testimony relates, affords the witness considerably broader protection than does the Fifth Amendment privilege. The privilege has never been construed to mean that one who invokes it cannot subsequently be prosecuted. Its sole concern is to afford protection against being "forced to give testimony leading to the infliction of 'penalties affixed to * * * criminal acts.'" Immunity from the use of compelled testimony, as well as evidence derived directly and indirectly therefrom, affords this protection. It prohibits the prosecutorial authorities from using the compelled testimony in any respect, and it therefore insures that the testimony cannot lead to the infliction of criminal penalties on the witness.

406 U.S. at 453, 92 S.Ct. at 1661, 32 L.Ed.2d at 222.  Kastigar had argued that persons compelled to testify and later prosecuted would experience difficulty in determining whether evidence offered against them was derived from their compelled testimony.  The Court, however, responded by holding that once a defendant demonstrates in a criminal prosecution that the prosecution concerns a matter as to which he was compelled to testify under a grant of use immunity, the prosecution has the burden of showing that its evidence has an independent legitimate source and is therefore not tainted by the compelled testimony.  406 U.S. at 460, 92 S.Ct. at 1665, 32 L.Ed.2d at 226.  Justice Marshall, dissenting, urged that a defendant, as a practical matter, would have such a difficult task in challenging the prosecution's claim that evidence offered at trial had a source independent of prior compelled testimony that only transactional immunity would effectively protect such persons from the use of their testimony and its "fruits."

    6.  Immunity grants may have interjurisdictional aspects which present special problems.  In Murphy v. Waterfront Commission, 378 U.S. 52, 84 S.Ct. 1594, 12 L.Ed.2d 678 (1964), the petitioners had been granted immunity from prosecution under state law.  They persisted in their refusals to answer on the ground that their testimony would incriminate them under federal law and the grant of immunity did not address this problem.  The Supreme Court held that the Fifth Amendment privilege protects state witnesses against incrimination under federal as well as state law and federal witnesses against incrimination under state as well as federal law.  Consequently, a state witness can only be compelled to give testimony which may be incriminating under federal law if the testimony and its fruits cannot be used in a federal criminal prosecution:

> We conclude  *  *  *  that in order to implement this constitutional rule and accommodate the interests of the State and Federal Government in investigating and prosecuting crime, the Federal Government must be prohibited from making any such use of compelled testimony and its fruits.

378 U.S. at 79, 94 S.Ct. at 1609, 12 L.Ed.2d at 695.  But suppose a person is prosecuted in one state for a matter as to which he was compelled to testify under a grant of immunity in another state?  Must the prosecution satisfy the Kastigar standard in regard to its evidence, i.e., must it establish that its evidence has a source independent of the testimony compelled in the other state?  Murphy does not address the issue.  Perhaps, however, the federal constitutional bar against the use of "involuntary" confessions and their fruit compels this result.

    This was strongly suggested by New Jersey v. Portash, 440 U.S. 450, 99 S.Ct. 1292, 59 L.Ed.2d 501 (1979).  Portash had testified before a grand jury after his lawyers and prosecuting attorneys agreed that neither his statements nor any evidence obtained as a result of those statements could under state statutory law be used in a subsequent criminal proceeding, except a prosecution for perjury or false swearing.  Subsequently, Portash was indicted and tried for misconduct in office and extortion by a public official.  In response to defense motions, the trial judge ruled that if Portash took the stand at trial and gave testimony materially inconsistent with his grand jury testimony, the grand jury testimony could be used in the prosecutor's cross examination.  Portash did not testify and was convicted.  The Supreme Court reversed.  The Court distinguished Harris v. New York, 401 U.S. 222, 91 S.Ct. 643, 28 L.Ed.2d 1 (1971) and Oregon v. Hass, 420 U.S. 714, 95 S.Ct. 1215, 43 L.Ed.2d 570 (1975) in which confessions obtained in violation of Miranda v. Arizona, 384 U.S. 436, 86 S.Ct. 1602, 16 L.Ed.2d 694 (1966) were held admissible to impeach the confessing defendants after they took the stand at their trials.  Unlike the confessions at issue in Harris and Hass, Justice Stewart wrote for the Court, the testimony at issue in *Portash* was involuntary and therefore under the Fifth and Fourteenth Amendments could not be put to any use whatever against the defendant in a criminal trial:

> Testimony given in response to a grant of legislative immunity is the essence of coerced testimony. In such cases there is no question whether physical or psychological pressures overrode the defendant's will; the witness is told to talk or face the government's coercive sanctions, notably, a citation for contempt.

440 U.S. at 458, 99 S.Ct. at 1297, 59 L.Ed.2d at 510. Since the case presented the privilege against self-incrimination "in its most pristine form," the Court continued, there is no room for balancing policy considerations that might favor the admissibility of such testimony for limited purposes of impeachment and the privilege unqualifiedly directs that the testimony be excluded. Justice Blackmun, joined by the Chief Justice, dissented on the ground that the issue should not be reached since Portash did not actually take the stand at trial and therefore his grand jury testimony was never actually used against him.

7. The Supreme Court has permitted rather extensive use of compelled testimony in perjury proceedings. United States v. Apfelbaum, 445 U.S. 115, 100 S.Ct. 948, 63 L.Ed.2d 250 (1980). Apfelbaum had been called before a federal grand jury to testify concerning a suspected robbery and extortion. He invoked his privilege against self-incrimination, was granted immunity under 18 U.S.C.A. § 6002, and testified concerning a number of matters. Subsequently, he was charged with perjury on the basis that during his grand jury testimony he had falsely denied attempting to locate one Harry Brown during December, 1975, and making a loan to Brown. At trial, the government introduced over objection portions of Apfelbaum's grand jury testimony other than the testimony charged in the indictment as perjured testimony. This testimony concerned his relationship and discussions with Brown, a trip on another occasion to Florida to visit Brown, and similar matters; the government argued that this evidence put the allegedly perjured statements "in context" and tended to prove that Apfelbaum knew they were false. Apfelbaum was convicted. On appeal, he successfully argued that the federal statute and the Fifth Amendment prohibited, even in a perjury trial, the use of immunized testimony that was not specifically the basis for the perjury charge. The Supreme Court reversed the Court of Appeals.

After considering the legislative history of the immunity statute, the Court concluded that Congress intended to permit use of both truthful and false statements made during immunized testimony, if this was permitted by the Fifth Amendment. It then turned to defendant's argument that the Fifth Amendment prohibited the use of immunized testimony except for the "corpus delicti" or "core" of a perjury charge. The Court of Appeals below had held that use of defendant's immunized testimony must be limited to that charged as perjury on the following rationale: A grant of immunity must be coextensive with Fifth Amendment protection; this means that a defendant must be placed in as near a position as possible to that which he would have occupied had he retained the privilege. Because of the need to prevent perjury, a narrow exception to this rule permitting the use of perjured testimony in a prosecution for that perjury is necessary. But because an immunized witness would not have given the other testimony had he retained the privilege, this other, i.e., nonperjured, testimony must not be used even in a perjury prosecution where it is relevant to guilt. The Supreme Court rejected this, reasoning that for a grant of immunity to provide protection coextensive with that of the privilege, it need not treat the witness as if he had remained silent. As long as the use of immunized testimony is limited to perjury prosecution, the exception is sufficiently narrow. "[W]e hold," the Court concluded, "that neither the statute nor the Fifth Amendment requires that the admissibility of immunized testimony be governed by any different rules than other testimony at a trial for making false statements." 445 U.S. at 117, 100 S.Ct. at 950, 63 L.Ed.2d at 254. Justices Brennan, Blackmun, and Marshall concurred, preferring to withhold comment on situations not before the Court. Specifically, they expressed reservation concerning the admissibility of immunized testimony in a prosecution for perjury allegedly committed after the immunized testimony rather than, as in the present case, during the immunized testimony.

8. Increased utilization of "use" rather than "transactional" immunity presents some difficult questions concerning the scope of immunity granted. Where use rather than transactional immunity is granted, the Government maintains a great deal of control over the information which it elicits under the grant of immunity and which it consequently loses the right to use later in criminal proceedings. It may, for example, seek immunity and compel testimony from a witness concerning only some of the relevant matters concerning which the Government believes the witness has information. Information concerning other matters about which the witness is not compelled to testify under the grant of immunity remain unaffected by the process, since no testimony concerning them has been elicited from the witness pursuant to a grant of use immunity.

In Pillsbury Co. v. Conboy, 459 U.S. 248, 103 S.Ct. 608, 74 L.Ed.2d 430 (1983), Conboy had been granted use immunity for testimony before a federal grand jury. In a subsequent civil suit, a plaintiff sought to take a deposition of Conboy. In this deposition proceeding, Conboy was asked the same questions he had been asked before the grand jury; he was then read his answers before the grand jury and was asked whether he had "so testified." He refused to respond, relying on his privilege against compelled self-incrimination. Conboy was held in contempt, apparently on the ground that the earlier grant of immunity compelled him in the civil deposition proceeding to again testify to the same things to which he had testified before the grand jury. The Supreme Court held that the Fifth Amendment precluded penalizing Conboy for his refusal to answer. At the crux of the case, the Court concluded, was whether the original grant of immunity not only compelled Conboy to answer questions during his appearance before the grand jury but also later in other contexts when he was asked the same questions. If he was compelled to again respond to the questions, the Court continued, there was a substantial risk that during cross examination or otherwise he would disclose further information which, under the terms of the grant of immunity, could not then be used against him by the Government. Whether or not such further disclosure occurred would be beyond the control of the Government. In other words, a party to private litigation might be able to increase the amount of information which a grant of use immunity makes unavailable to the Government for use in criminal litigation. Should the Government in a later criminal trial seek to introduce evidence similar to the defendant's answers in the civil deposition, it would be required to prove that its evidence was from an independent source, which it might be unable to do because of lack of notice as to what answers would be given in the deposition proceedings.

# Chapter 10

# EYEWITNESS IDENTIFICATION

### Analysis

## EDITORS' INTRODUCTION: THE PERSUASIVE POWERS AND RISKS OF EYEWITNESS IDENTIFICATION

Although this chapter focuses primarily on the constitutional issues that arise from eyewitness identifications, evidentiary issues may also arise from the use of some kinds of identification evidence. Traditionally the rule against hearsay would have prevented the introduction of testimony regarding an out-of-court identification, but there is now a trend toward admissibility of such evidence because it can be of greater probative value than the courtroom identification. 4 Wigmore, Evidence § 1130 (Chadborn rev. 1972). Often, between the time of the crime and the time of the trial, events occur that tend to make the courtroom identification an inevitable and empty formality. In contrast, the pretrial identification, if made under the proper circumstances, can be a much more significant indication that the witness recognized the defendant. For that reason, most jurisdictions now admit evidence of out-of-court identifications at least for the limited purposes of rehabilitating or corroborating in-court identifications by the same witnesses. See, e.g., Virgil v. State, 84 Wis.2d 166, 267 N.W.2d 852 (1978). Several jurisdictions, including the federal courts, go further and admit testimony regarding prior identifications as independent evidence that the defendant is the person in question. Fed.R. Evid. 801(d)(1)(C).

This liberalizing of the evidentiary rules reflects the view that eyewitness identification testimony is an unusually persuasive form of evidence tending to show a defendant's guilt. But recent research and commentary has suggested that this emphasis upon eyewitness identification may lead to questionable results. Elizabeth Loftus, Ph.D., recently wrote:

> The danger of eyewitness identification is clear: anyone in the world can be convicted of a crime he or she did not commit

\* \* \* based solely on the evidence of a witness who convinced a jury that his or her memory about what was seen is correct. Eyewitness testimony is so powerful that it can sway a jury even after it has been shown to be largely false. Jurors appear to respond more to the confidence with which an eyewitness responds than to the circumstances surrounding the original event and subsequent recollection of it.

People in general and jurors in particular are probably so ready to believe eyewitness testimony because for the most part our memories serve us reasonably well. But precise memory is rarely demanded of us. If errors are made, they go unnoticed and uncorrected, and belief in an accurate memory is reaffirmed by default.

Loftus, The Eyewitness on Trial, Trial, Oct. 1980, at 31. Among the factors hindering accurate memory, she suggests, is stress at the time of the original observation, which disrupts perception and thus the ability to recall accurately what was perceived. Id., at 32. In addition, however, she emphasizes the impact of "new information," especially information suggesting that a particular version of a previously observed incident was most likely observed. She reports the results of a study in which subjects were shown a film of an automobile accident and later asked whether they had observed a barn along the road on which the cars were traveling. No barn appeared in the film. Some of the subjects had previously been asked the question, "How fast was the white sports car going when it passed the barn?" Others were asked instead, "How fast was the sports car going?" Those subjects asked the question containing the new (and false) information that a barn was present tended more than the others to report that they had observed a barn on the film. Loftus' studies and analysis are developed in more detail in E. Loftus, Eyewitness Testimony (1979).

Traditionally any problems that these tendencies might create in regard to eyewitness identification have been left to triers of fact as part of their task of evaluating the credibility of witnesses. Counsel for both sides have been given substantial leeway in developing information that supports and detracts from a witness's credibility and the matter is then left to the jury to resolve. In 1967, however, the United States Supreme Court decided a trilogy of cases that found federal constitutional problems in the admission of testimony of eyewitnesses that had been subject to certain procedures during the pretrial investigatory process. These constitutional issues are the focus of this chapter. The first two cases, United States v. Wade, 388 U.S. 218, 87 S.Ct. 1926, 18 L.Ed.2d 1149 (1967), and Gilbert v. California, 388 U.S. 263, 87 S.Ct. 1951, 18 L.Ed.2d 1178 (1967), dealt with the right to counsel, the subject of the first section. The third case of the trilogy, Stovall v. Denno, 388 U.S. 293, 87 S.Ct. 1967, 18 L.Ed.2d 1199 (1967), suggested the availability of an argument that a pretrial procedure could be so suggestive that use of the later testimony of the witness would violate due process of law. This is explored in the second section.

## A.  WHEN IS COUNSEL REQUIRED?

Particular attention should be paid to the kind of identification procedure that was used, the timing of that procedure, and the type of evidence that is in issue—whether it is an in-court identification or testimony regarding the out-of-court identification procedure itself.  In conjunction with the requirement that counsel be present at certain identification confrontations, consideration should be given to proper role for the attorney at those confrontations.  Should he be a passive observer or an active advocate?  May he obstruct the investigation process by advising his client not to participate in the lineup or other procedure?  If not, what sanctions may be applied to prevent this kind of obstruction?  More fundamentally, can the attorney actually detect whatever unfair suggestiveness exists at the confrontation, particularly if the police purposely try to abuse the identification process?  See generally, Note, Lawyers and Lineups, 77 Yale L.J. 390 (1967).

### UNITED STATES v. WADE

Supreme Court of the United States, 1967.
388 U.S. 218, 87 S.Ct. 1926, 18 L.Ed.2d 1149.

MR. JUSTICE BRENNAN delivered the opinion of the Court.

The question here is whether courtroom identifications of an accused at trial are to be excluded from evidence because the accused was exhibited to the witnesses before trial at a post-indictment line-up conducted for identification purposes without notice to and in the absence of the accused's appointed counsel.

The federally insured bank in Eustace, Texas, was robbed on September 21, 1964.  A man with a small strip of tape on each side of his face entered the bank, pointed a pistol at the female cashier and the vice president, the only persons in the bank at the time, and forced them to fill a pillowcase with the bank's money.  The man then drove away with an accomplice who had been waiting in a stolen car outside the bank.  On March 23, 1965, an indictment was returned against respondent, Wade, and two others for conspiring to rob the bank, and against Wade and the accomplice for the robbery itself.  Wade was arrested on April 2, and counsel was appointed to represent him on April 26.  Fifteen days later an FBI agent, without notice to Wade's lawyer, arranged to have the two bank employees observe a lineup made up of Wade and five or six other prisoners and conducted in a courtroom of the local county courthouse.  Each person in the line wore strips of tape such as allegedly worn by the robber and upon direction each said something like "put the money in the bag," the words allegedly uttered by the robber.  Both bank employees identified Wade in the lineup as the bank robber.

At trial the two employees, when asked on direct examination if the robber was in the courtroom, pointed to Wade.  The prior lineup identification was then elicited from both employees on cross-examination.  At the close of testimony, Wade's counsel moved for a judgment of acquittal or, alternatively, to strike the bank officials' courtroom identifications on the ground that conduct of the lineup, without notice to and in the absence of his appointed counsel, violated his Fifth Amendment privilege against self-incrimination and his Sixth Amendment right to the assistance of counsel. The motion was denied, and Wade was convicted. The Court of Appeals for the Fifth Circuit reversed the conviction and ordered a new trial at which the in-court identification evidence was to be excluded, holding that, though the lineup did not violate Wade's Fifth Amendment rights, "the lineup, held as it was, in the absence of counsel, already chosen to represent appellant, was a violation of his Sixth Amendment rights    *    *    *." 358 F.2d 557, 560.   *   *   * We reverse the judgment of the Court of Appeals and remand to that court with direction to enter a new judgment vacating the conviction and remanding the case to the District Court for further proceedings consistent with this opinion.

## I.

Neither the lineup itself nor anything shown by this record that Wade was required to do in the lineup violated his privilege against self-incrimination.   *   *   * Schmerber v. State of California, 384 U.S. 757, 761, 86 S.Ct. 1826, 1830, 16 L.Ed.2d 908. [This part of the Court's holding is discussed at page 71, supra.  Editors.]

*   *   *

## II.

The fact that the lineup involved no violation of Wade's privilege against self-incrimination does not, however, dispose of his contention that the courtroom identifications should have been excluded because the lineup was conducted without notice to and in the absence of his counsel.  Our rejection of the right to counsel claim in *Schmerber* rested on our conclusion in that case that "[n]o issue of counsel's ability to assist petitioner in respect of any rights he did possess is presented." 384 U.S., at 766, 86 S.Ct. at 1833.  In contrast, in this case it is urged that the assistance of counsel at the lineup was indispensable to protect Wade's most basic right as a criminal defendant—his right to a fair trial at which the witnesses against him might be meaningfully cross-examined.

The Framers of the Bill of Rights envisaged a broader role for counsel than under the practice then prevailing in England of merely advising his client in "matters of law," and eschewing any responsibility for "matters of fact."  The constitutions in at least 11 of the 13 States expressly or impliedly abolished this distinction.  Powell v. State of Alabama, 287 U.S. 45, 60–65, 53 S.Ct. 55, 60–62, 77 L.Ed. 158; Note, 73 Yale L.J. 1000, 1030–1033 (1964).  "Though the colonial provisions about counsel were in accord on few things, they agreed on the necessity of abolishing the facts-law distinction; the colonists appreciated that if a defendant were forced to stand alone against the state, his case was foredoomed."  73 Yale L.J., supra, at 1033–1034.  This background is reflected in the scope given by our decisions to the Sixth Amendment's guarantee to an accused of the assistance of counsel for his defense. When the Bill of Rights was adopted, there were no organized police forces as we know them today. The accused confronted the prosecutor and the witnesses against him, and the evidence was marshalled, largely at the trial itself. In contrast, today's law enforcement machinery involves critical confrontations of the accused by the prosecution at pretrial proceedings where the results might well settle the accused's fate and reduce the trial itself to a mere formality. In recognition of these realities of modern criminal prosecution, our cases have construed the Sixth Amendment guarantee to apply to "critical" stages of the proceedings. The guarantee reads: "In all criminal prosecutions, the accused shall enjoy the right * * * to have the Assistance of Counsel *for his defence."* (Emphasis supplied.) The plain wording of this guarantee thus encompasses counsel's assistance whenever necessary to assure a meaningful "defence."

As early as Powell v. State of Alabama, supra, we recognized that the period from arraignment to trial was "perhaps the most critical period of the proceedings * * *," id., at 57, 53 S.Ct. at 59, during which the accused "requires the guiding hand of counsel * * *," id., at 69, 53 S.Ct. at 64 if the guarantee is not to prove an empty right. That principle has since been applied to require the assistance of counsel at the type of arraignment—for example, that provided by Alabama—where certain rights might be sacrificed or lost: "What happens there may affect the whole trial. Available defenses may be irretrievably lost, if not then and there asserted * * *." Hamilton v. State of Alabama, 368 U.S. 52, 54, 82 S.Ct. 157, 159, 7 L.Ed.2d 114. See White v. State of Maryland, 373 U.S. 59, 83 S.Ct. 1050, 10 L.Ed.2d 193. The principle was also applied in Massiah v. United States, 377 U.S. 201, 84 S.Ct. 1199, 12 L.Ed.2d 246, where we held that incriminating statements of the defendant should have been excluded from evidence when it appeared that they were overheard by federal agents who, without notice to the defendant's lawyer, arranged a meeting between the defendant and an accomplice turned informant. We said, quoting a concurring opinion in Spano v. People of State of New York, 360 U.S. 315, 326, 79 S.Ct. 1202, 1209, 3 L.Ed.2d 1265, that "[a]nything less * * * might deny a defendant 'effective representation by counsel at the only stage when legal aid and advice would help him.'" 377 U.S., at 204, 84 S.Ct. at 1202.

In Escobedo v. State of Illinois, 378 U.S. 478, 84 S.Ct. 1758, 12 L.Ed. 2d 977, we drew upon the rationale of *Hamilton* and *Massiah* in holding that the right to counsel was guaranteed at the point where the accused, prior to arraignment, was subjected to secret interrogation despite repeated requests to see his lawyer. We again noted the necessity of counsel's presence if the accused was to have a fair opportunity to present a defense at the trial itself:

> "The rule sought by the State here, however, would make the trial no more than an appeal from the interrogation; and the 'right to use counsel at the formal trial [would be] a very hollow thing [if], for all practical purposes, the conviction is already assured by pretrial examination'. * * * 'One can imagine a cynical prosecutor saying: "Let them have the most illustrious counsel, now.

They can't escape the noose. There is nothing that counsel can do for them at the trial." ' " 378 U.S., at 487–488, 84 S.Ct. at 1763.

Finally in Miranda v. State of Arizona, 384 U.S. 436, 86 S.Ct. 1602, 16 L.Ed.2d 694, the rules established for custodial interrogation included the right to the presence of counsel. The result was rested on our finding that this and the other rules were necessary to safeguard the privilege against self-incrimination from being jeopardized by such interrogation.

Of course, nothing decided or said in the opinions in the cited cases links the right to counsel only to protection of Fifth Amendment rights. Rather those decisions "no more than [reflect] a constitutional principle established as long ago as Powell v. Alabama   *   *   * ." Massiah v. United States, supra, 377 U.S. at 205, 84 S.Ct. at 1202. It is central to that principle that in addition to counsel's presence at trial, the accused is guaranteed that he need not stand alone against the State at any stage of the prosecution, formal or informal, in court or out, where counsel's absence might derogate from the accused's right to a fair trial. The security of that right is as much the aim of the right to counsel as it is of the other guarantees of the Sixth Amendment—the right of the accused to a speedy and public trial by an impartial jury, his right to be informed of the nature and cause of the accusation, and his right to be confronted with the witnesses against him and to have compulsory process for obtaining witnesses in his favor. The presence of counsel at such critical confrontations, as at the trial itself, operates to assure that the accused's interests will be protected consistently with our adversary theory of criminal prosecution. Cf. Pointer v. State of Texas, 380 U.S. 400, 35 S.Ct. 1065, 13 L.Ed.2d 923.

In sum, the principle of Powell v. Alabama and succeeding cases requires that we scrutinize *any* pretrial confrontation of the accused to determine whether the presence of his counsel is necessary to preserve the defendant's basic right to a fair trial as affected by his right meaningfully to cross-examine the witnesses against him and to have effective assistance of counsel at the trial itself. It calls upon us to analyze whether potential substantial prejudice to defendant's rights inheres in the particular confrontation and the ability of counsel to help avoid that prejudice.

## III.

The Government characterizes the lineup as a mere preparatory step in the gathering of the prosecution's evidence, not different—for Sixth Amendment purposes—from various other preparatory steps, such as systematized or scientific analyzing of the accused's fingerprints, blood sample, clothing, hair, and the like. We think there are differences which preclude such stages being characterized as critical stages at which the accused has the right to the presence of his counsel. Knowledge of the techniques of science and technology is sufficiently available, and the variables in techniques few enough, that the accused has the opportunity for a meaningful confrontation of the Government's case at trial through the ordinary processes of cross-examination

of the Government's expert witnesses and the presentation of the
evidence of his own experts. The denial of a right to have his counsel
present at such analyses does not therefore violate the Sixth Amendment; they are not critical stages since there is minimal risk that his
counsel's absence at such stages might derogate from his right to a fair
trial.

IV.

But the confrontation compelled by the State between the accused
and the victim or witnesses to a crime to elicit identification evidence is
peculiarly riddled with innumerable dangers and variable factors which
might seriously, even crucially, derogate from a fair trial. The vagaries
of eyewitness identification are well-known; the annals of criminal law
are rife with instances of mistaken identification. Mr. Justice Frankfurter once said: "What is the worth of identification testimony even
when uncontradicted? The identification of strangers is proverbially
untrustworthy. The hazards of such testimony are established by a
formidable number of instances in the records of English and American
trials. These instances are recent—not due to the brutalities of ancient
criminal procedure." The Case of Sacco and Vanzetti 30 (1927). A
major factor contributing to the high incidence of miscarriage of justice
from mistaken identification has been the degree of suggestion inherent
in the manner in which the prosecution presents the suspect to witnesses for pretrial identification. A commentator has observed that "[t]he
influence of improper suggestion upon identifying witnesses probably
accounts for more miscarriages of justice than any other single factor—
perhaps it is responsible for more such errors than all other factors
combined." Wall, Eye-Witness Identification in Criminal Cases 26.
Suggestion can be created intentionally or unintentionally in many
subtle ways. And the dangers for the suspect are particularly grave
when the witness' opportunity for observation was insubstantial, and
thus his susceptibility to suggestion the greatest.

Moreover, "[i]t is a matter of common experience that, once a
witness has picked out the accused at the line-up, he is not likely to go
back on his word later on, so that in practice the issue of identity may
(in the absence of other relevant evidence) for all practical purposes be
determined there and then, before the trial."

The pretrial confrontation for purpose of identification may take
the form of a lineup, also known as an "identification parade" or
"showup," as in the present case, or presentation of the suspect alone to
the witness, as in Stovall v. Denno, supra. It is obvious that risks of
suggestion attend either form of confrontation and increase the dangers
inhering in eyewitness identification. But as is the case with secret
interrogations, there is serious difficulty in depicting what transpires at
lineups and other forms of identification confrontations. "Privacy
results in secrecy and this in turn results in a gap in our knowledge as
to what in fact goes on *  *  * ." Miranda v. State of Arizona, supra,
384 U.S. at 448, 86 S.Ct. at 1614. For the same reasons, the defense can
seldom reconstruct the manner and mode of lineup identification for

judge or jury at trial. Those participating in a lineup with the accused may often be police officers; in any event, the participants' names are rarely recorded or divulged at trial. The impediments to an objective observation are increased when the victim is the witness. Lineups are prevalent in rape and robbery prosecutions and present a particular hazard that a victim's understandable outrage may excite vengeful or spiteful motives. In any event, neither witnesses nor lineup participants are apt to be alert for conditions prejudicial to the suspect. And if they were, it would likely be of scant benefit to the suspect since neither witnesses nor lineup participants are likely to be schooled in the detection of suggestive influences.[1] Improper influences may go undetected by a suspect, guilty or not, who experiences the emotional tension which we might expect in one being confronted with potential accusers. Even when he does observe abuse, if he has a criminal record he may be reluctant to take the stand and open up the admission of prior convictions. Moreover any protestations by the suspect of the fairness of the lineup made at trial are likely to be in vain; the jury's choice is between the accused's unsupported version and that of the police officers present. In short, the accused's inability effectively to reconstruct at trial any unfairness that occurred at the lineup may deprive him of his only opportunity meaningfully to attack the credibility of the witness' courtroom identification.

What facts have been disclosed in specific cases about the conduct of pretrial confrontations for identification illustrate both the potential for substantial prejudice to the accused at that stage and the need for its revelation at trial. A commentator provides some striking examples:

> "In a Canadian case   *   *   *   the defendant had been picked out of a lineup of six men, of which he was the only Oriental. In other cases, a black-haired suspect was placed among a group of light-haired persons, tall suspects have been made to stand with short non-suspects, and, in a case where the perpetrator of the crime was known to be a youth, a suspect under twenty was placed in a lineup with five other persons, all of whom were forty or over."

Similarly state reports, in the course of describing prior identifications admitted as evidence of guilt, reveal numerous instances of suggestive procedures, for example, that all in the lineup but the suspect were known to the identifying witness, that the other participants in a lineup were grossly dissimilar in appearance to the suspect, that only the suspect was required to wear distinctive clothing which the culprit allegedly wore, that the witness is told by the police that they have caught the culprit after which the defendant is brought before the witness alone or is viewed in jail, that the suspect is pointed out before or during a lineup, and that the participants in the lineup are asked to try on an article of clothing which fits only the suspect.

---

[1] An additional impediment to the detection of such influences by participants, including the suspect, is the physical conditions often surrounding the conduct of the lineup. In many, lights shine on the stage in such a way that the suspect cannot see the witness. See Gilbert v. United States, 366 F.2d 923 (9th Cir.1966). In some a one-way mirror is used and what is said on the witness' side cannot be heard.

The potential for improper influence is illustrated by the circumstances, insofar as they appear, surrounding the prior identifications in the three cases we decide today. In the present case, the testimony of the identifying witnesses elicited on cross-examination revealed that those witnesses were taken to the courthouse and seated in the courtroom to await assembly of the lineup. The courtroom faced on a hallway observable to the witnesses through an open door. The cashier testified that she saw Wade "standing in the hall" within sight of an FBI agent. Five or six other prisoners later appeared in the hall. The vice president testified that he saw a person in the hall in the custody of the agent who "resembled the person that we identified as the one that had entered the bank."

The lineup in *Gilbert*, supra, was conducted in an auditorium in which some 100 witnesses to several alleged state and federal robberies charged to Gilbert made wholesale identifications of Gilbert as the robber in each other's presence, a procedure said to be fraught with dangers of suggestion. And the vice of suggestion created by the identification in *Stovall*, supra, was the presentation to the witness of the suspect alone handcuffed to police officers. It is hard to imagine a situation more clearly conveying the suggestion to the witness that the one presented is believed guilty by the police. See Frankfurter, The Case of Sacco and Vanzetti 31–32.

The few cases that have surfaced therefore reveal the existence of a process attended with hazards of serious unfairness to the criminal accused and strongly suggest the plight of the more numerous defendants who are unable to ferret out suggestive influences in the secrecy of the confrontation. We do not assume that these risks are the result of police procedures intentionally designed to prejudice an accused. Rather we assume they derive from the dangers inherent in eyewitness identification and the suggestibility inherent in the context of the pretrial identification. Williams & Hammelmann, in one of the most comprehensive studies of such forms of identification, said "[T]he fact that the police themselves have, in a given case, little or no doubt that the man put up for identification has committed the offense, and that their chief preoccupation is with the problem of getting sufficient proof, because he has not 'come clean,' involves a danger that this persuasion may communicate itself even in a doubtful case to the witness in some way  *   *   *." Identification Parades, Part I, [1963] Crim.L.Rev. 479, 483.

Insofar as the accused's conviction may rest on a courtroom identification in fact the fruit of a suspect pretrial identification which the accused is helpless to subject to effective scrutiny at trial, the accused is deprived of that right of cross-examination which is an essential safeguard to his right to confront the witnesses against him. Pointer v. State of Texas, 380 U.S. 400, 85 S.Ct. 1065, 13 L.Ed.2d 923. And even though cross-examination is a precious safeguard to a fair trial, it cannot be viewed as an absolute assurance of accuracy and reliability. Thus in the present context, where so many variables and pitfalls exist, the first line of defense must be the prevention of unfairness and the lessening of the hazards of eye-witness identification at the lineup itself. The trial which might determine the accused's fate may well not be that in the courtroom but that at the pretrial confrontation, with the State aligned against the accused, the witness the sole jury, and the accused unprotected against the overreaching, intentional or unintentional, and with little or no effective appeal from the judgment there rendered by the witness—"that's the man."

Since it appears that there is grave potential for prejudice, intentional or not, in the pretrial lineup, which may not be capable of reconstruction at trial, and since presence of counsel itself can often avert prejudice and assure a meaningful confrontation at trial,[2] there can be little doubt that for Wade the post-indictment lineup was a critical stage of the prosecution at which he was "as much entitled to such aid [of counsel]  *  *  *  as at the trial itself." Powell v. State of Alabama, 287 U.S. 45, at 57, 53 S.Ct. 55, at 60, 77 L.Ed. 158. Thus both Wade and his counsel should have been notified of the impending lineup, and counsel's presence should have been a requisite to conduct of the lineup, absent an "intelligent waiver." See Carnley v. Cochran, 369 U.S. 506, 82 S.Ct. 884, 8 L.Ed.2d 70. No substantial countervailing policy considerations have been advanced against the requirement of the presence of counsel. Concern is expressed that the requirement will forestall prompt identifications and result in obstruction of the confrontations. As for the first, we note that in the two cases in which the right to counsel is today held to apply, counsel had already been

[2] One commentator proposes a model statute providing not only for counsel, but other safeguards as well:

"Most, if not all, of the attacks on the lineup process could be averted by a uniform statute modeled upon the best features of the civilian codes. Any proposed statute should provide for the right to counsel during any lineup or during any confrontation. Provision should be made that any person, whether a victim or a witness, must give a description of the suspect before he views any arrested person. A written record of this description should be required, and the witness should be made to sign it. This written record would be available for inspection by defense counsel for copying before the trial and for use at the trial in testing the accuracy of the identification made during the lineup and during the trial.

"This ideal statute would require at least six persons in addition to the accused in a lineup, and these persons would have to be of approximately the same height, weight, coloration of hair and skin, and bodily types as the suspect. In addition, all of these men should, as nearly as possible, be dressed alike. If distinctive garb was used during the crime, the suspect should not be forced to wear similar clothing in the lineup unless all of the other persons are similarly garbed. A complete written report of the names, addresses, descriptive details of the other persons in the lineup, and of everything which transpired during the identification would be mandatory. This report would include everything stated by the identifying witness during this step, including any reasons given by him as to what features, etc., have sparked his recognition.

"This statute should permit voice identification tests by having each person in the lineup repeat identical innocuous phrases, and it would be impermissible to force the use of words allegedly used during a criminal act.

"The statute would enjoin the police from suggesting to any viewer that one or more persons in the lineup had been arrested as a suspect. If more than one witness is to make an identification, each witness should be required to do so separately and should be forbidden to speak to another witness until all of them have completed the process.

"The statute could require the use of movie cameras and tape recorders to record the lineup process in those states which are financially able to afford these devices. Finally, the statute should provide that any evidence obtained as the result of a violation of this statute would be inadmissible." Murray, The Criminal Lineup at Home and Abroad, 1966 Utah L.Rev. 610, 627–628.

appointed and no argument is made in either case that notice to counsel would have prejudicially delayed the confrontations. Moreover, we leave open the question whether the presence of substitute counsel might not suffice where notification and presence of the suspect's own counsel would result in prejudicial delay.[3]  And to refuse to recognize the right to counsel for fear that counsel will obstruct the course of justice is contrary to the basic assumptions upon which this Court has operated in Sixth Amendment cases.  We rejected similar logic in Miranda v. State of Arizona, concerning presence of counsel during custodial interrogation, 384 U.S. at 480–481, 86 S.Ct. at 1631, 16 L.Ed.2d 694:

> "[A]n attorney is merely exercising the good professional judgment he has been taught.  This is not cause for considering the attorney a menace to law enforcement.  He is merely carrying out what he is sworn to do under his oath—to protect to the extent of his ability the rights of his client.  In fulfilling this responsibility the attorney plays a vital role in the administration of criminal justice under our Constitution."

In our view counsel can hardly impede legitimate law enforcement; on the contrary, for the reasons expressed, law enforcement may be assisted by preventing the infiltration of taint in the prosecution's identification evidence.[4]  That result cannot help the guilty avoid conviction but can only help assure that the right man has been brought to justice.

Legislative or other regulations, such as those of local police departments, which eliminate the risks of abuse and unintentional suggestion at lineup proceedings and the impediments to meaningful confrontation at trial may also remove the basis for regarding the stage as "critical."  But neither Congress nor the federal authorities have seen fit to provide a solution.  What we hold today "in no way creates a constitutional straitjacket which will handicap sound efforts at reform, nor is it intended to have this effect."  Miranda v. State of Arizona, supra, at 467, 86 S.Ct. at 1624.

## V.

We come now to the question whether the denial of Wade's motion to strike the courtroom identification by the bank witnesses at trial because of the absence of his counsel at the lineup required, as the Court of Appeals held, the grant of a new trial at which such evidence is to be excluded.  We do not think this disposition can be justified without first giving the Government the opportunity to establish by clear and convincing evidence that the in-court identifications were

---

[3] Although the right to counsel usually means a right to the suspect's own counsel, provision for substitute counsel may be justified on the ground that the substitute counsel's presence may eliminate the hazards which render the lineup a critical stage for the presence of the suspect's *own* counsel.

[4] Concern is also expressed that the presence of counsel will force divulgence of the identity of government witnesses whose identity the Government may want to conceal.  To the extent that this is a valid or significant state interest there are police practices commonly used to effect concealment, for example, masking the face.

based upon observations of the suspect other than the lineup identification. See Murphy v. Waterfront Commission, 378 U.S. 52, 79, n. 18, 84 S.Ct. 1594, 1609, 12 L.Ed.2d 678. Where, as here, the admissibility of evidence of the lineup identification itself is not involved, a per se rule of exclusion of courtroom identification would be unjustified.[5] See Nardone v. United States, 308 U.S. 338, 341, 60 S.Ct. 266, 267, 84 L.Ed. 307. A rule limited solely to the exclusion of testimony concerning identification at the lineup itself, without regard to admissibility of the courtroom identification, would render the right to counsel an empty one. The lineup is most often used, as in the present case, to crystallize the witnesses' identification of the defendant for future reference. We have already noted that the lineup identification will have that effect. The State may then rest upon the witnesses' unequivocal courtroom identification, and not mention the pretrial identification as part of the State's case at trial. Counsel is then in the predicament in which Wade's counsel found himself—realizing that possible unfairness at the lineup may be the sole means of attack upon the unequivocal courtroom identification, and having to probe in the dark in an attempt to discover and reveal unfairness, while bolstering the government witness' courtroom identification by bringing out and dwelling upon his prior identification. Since counsel's presence at the lineup would equip him to attack not only the lineup identification but the courtroom identification as well, limiting the impact of violation of the right to counsel to exclusion of evidence only of identification at the lineup itself disregards a critical element of that right.

We think it follows that the proper test to be applied in these situations is that quoted in Wong Sun v. United States, 371 U.S. 471, 488, 83 S.Ct. 407, 417, 9 L.Ed.2d 441. " '[W]hether, granting establishment of the primary illegality, the evidence to which instant objection is made has been come at by exploitation of that illegality or instead by means sufficiently distinguishable to be purged of the primary taint.' Maguire, Evidence of Guilt, 221 (1959)." See also Hoffa v. United States, 385 U.S. 293, 309, 87 S.Ct. 408, 17 L.Ed.2d 374. Application of this test in the present context requires consideration of various factors; for example, the prior opportunity to observe the alleged criminal act, the existence of any discrepancy between any pre-lineup description and the defendant's actual description, any identification prior to lineup of another person, the identification by picture of the defendant prior to the lineup, failure to identify the defendant on a prior occasion, and the lapse of time between the alleged act and the lineup identification. It is also relevant to consider those facts which, despite the absence of counsel, are disclosed concerning the conduct of the lineup.[6]

[5] We reach a contrary conclusion in Gilbert v. California, supra, as to the admissibility of the witness' testimony that he also identified the accused at the lineup.

[6] Thus it is not the case that "[i]t matters not how well the witness knows the suspect, whether the witness is the suspect's mother, brother, or long-time associate, and no matter how long or well the witness observed the perpetrator at the scene of the crime." Such factors will have an important bearing upon the true basis of the witness' in-court identification. Moreover, the State's inability to bolster the witness' courtroom identification by introduction of the lineup identification itself, see Gilbert v. California, supra, will become less significant the more the evidence of other opportunities of the witness to observe the defendant. Thus where the witness is a "kidnap

We doubt that the Court of Appeals applied the proper test for exclusion of the in-court identification of the two witnesses. The court stated that "it cannot be said with any certainty that they would have recognized appellant at the time of trial if this intervening lineup had not occurred," and that the testimony of the two witnesses "may well have been colored by the illegal procedure [and] was prejudicial." 358 F.2d at 560. Moreover, the court was persuaded, in part, by the "compulsory verbal responses made by Wade at the instance of the Special Agent." Ibid. This implies the erroneous holding that Wade's privilege against self-incrimination was violated so that the denial of counsel required exclusion.

On the record now before us we cannot make the determination whether the in-court identifications had an independent origin. This was not an issue at trial, although there is some evidence relevant to a determination. That inquiry is most properly made in the District Court. We therefore think the appropriate procedure to be followed is to vacate the conviction pending a hearing to determine whether the in-court identifications had an independent source, or whether, in any event, the introduction of the evidence was harmless error, Chapman v. State of California, 386 U.S. 18, 87 S.Ct. 824, 17 L.Ed.2d 705, and for the District Court to reinstate the conviction or order a new trial, as may be proper. See United States v. Shotwell Mfg. Co., 355 U.S. 233, 245–246, 78 S.Ct. 245, 253, 2 L.Ed.2d 234.

The judgment of the Court of Appeals is vacated and the case is remanded to that court with direction to enter a new judgment vacating the conviction and remanding the case to the District Court for further proceedings consistent with this opinion. It is so ordered.

Judgment of Court of Appeals vacated and case remanded with direction.

THE CHIEF JUSTICE joins the opinion of the Court except for Part I, from which he dissents for the reasons expressed in the opinion of MR. JUSTICE FORTAS.

MR. JUSTICE DOUGLAS joins the opinion of the Court except for Part I. On that phase of the case he adheres to the dissenting views in Schmerber v. State of California, 384 U.S. 757, 772–779, 86 S.Ct. 1826, 16 L.Ed.2d 908, since he believes that compulsory lineup violates the privilege against self-incrimination contained in the Fifth Amendment.

MR. JUSTICE CLARK, concurring [omitted].

MR. JUSTICE BLACK, dissenting in part and concurring in part [omitted].

MR. JUSTICE WHITE, whom MR. JUSTICE HARLAN and MR. JUSTICE STEWART join, dissenting in part and concurring in part [omitted].

MR. JUSTICE FORTAS, with whom THE CHIEF JUSTICE and MR. JUSTICE DOUGLAS join, concurring in part and dissenting in part [omitted].

victim who has lived for days with his abductor" the value to the State of admission of the lineup identification is indeed marginal, and such identification would be a mere formality.

## NOTES

1. In his dissenting and concurring opinion in *Wade*, Justice White disagreed with that portion of the Court's opinion that requires the prosecutor to show by clear and convincing evidence that the courtroom identification is based on observation of the defendant other than that made at the counselless lineup. He characterized that requirement as a very difficult, if not impossible one for the prosecutor to meet and expressed concern that it would almost always result in the exclusion of an in-court identification after there has been a counselless pretrial identification. 388 U.S. at 250–51, 87 S.Ct. at 1944, 18 L.Ed.2d at 1170–71. But, in fact, commentators have noted that the lower courts so often find that the courtroom identification has an independent source that there is actually little pressure on the police or prosecutor to have counsel present at the pretrial confrontation. Levine and Tapp, The Psychology of Criminal Identification: The Gap from Wade to Kirby, 121 U.Penn.L.Rev. 1079, 1083 (1973); Quinn, In the Wake of Wade: The Dimensions of Eyewitness Identification Cases, 42 U.Colo.L.Rev. 135, 140–143 (1970). Even the Supreme Court would seem likely to apply the test very broadly. In Coleman v. Alabama, 399 U.S. 1, 90 S.Ct. 1999, 26 L.Ed.2d 387 (1970), the Court stated that the trial court would have been justified in finding that the courtroom identification of the defendant was based entirely on the witness's observations of his assailant at the time of the crime. The evidence showed that the witness had only a fleeting glimpse of his assailant as he ran across the highway and was caught briefly in the headlights of an oncoming car, that the witness's description of his assailant did not match the defendant's description and that the lineup was conducted over two months after the crime.

2. In Gilbert v. California, 388 U.S. 263, 87 S.Ct. 1951, 18 L.Ed.2d 1178 (1967), a companion case to *Wade*, the Court concluded that a pre-trial lineup had been conducted in violation of Gilbert's Sixth Amendment right to counsel. Unlike in *Wade*, however, one of the eyewitnesses in *Gilbert* testified on direct examination at the trial that he had picked Gilbert out of the pre-trial lineup that the Court had judged defective. The Court characterized that testimony as "the direct result of the illegal lineup 'come at by exploitation of [the primary] illegality.' Wong Sun v. United States  *  *  *. The State is therefore not entitled to an opportunity to show that that testimony had an independent source. Only a *per se* exclusionary rule as to such testimony can be an effective sanction to assure that law enforcement authorities will respect the accused's constitutional right to the presence of his counsel at the critical lineup." 388 U.S. at 272–73, 87 S.Ct. at 1956–57, 18 L.Ed.2d at 1186.

3. In Kirby v. Illinois, 406 U.S. 682, 92 S.Ct. 1877, 32 L.Ed.2d 411 (1972), the Court considered whether counsel is required at an identification procedure that takes place before the defendant is charged or indicted. The police legitimately stopped Kirby and a companion and found that they had in their possession traveller's checks and papers belonging to a man who had been robbed the day before. The officers arrested the two men and took them to the police station. They also had the robbery victim brought to the station where he immediately identified the two suspects as the men who had robbed him. Neither of the suspects had been advised of his right to counsel and no counsel was present. At trial the victim testified during the state's case-in-chief about the police station identification and he identified Kirby in court as one of the robbers. Kirby's conviction of robbery was sustained by the Illinois Appellate Court. The United States Supreme Court held that the identification evidence was properly admitted even though there had been no attorney present at the

pretrial confrontation because the right to counsel does not attach until prosecution has been initiated:

> The initiation of judicial criminal proceedings is far from a mere formalism. It is the starting point of our whole system of adversary criminal justice. For it is only then that the government has committed itself to prosecute, and only then that the adverse positions of government and defendant have solidified. It is then that a defendant finds himself faced with the prosecutorial forces of organized society, and immersed in the intricacies of substantive and procedural criminal law. It is this point, therefore, that marks the commencement of the "criminal prosecutions" to which alone the explicit guarantees of the Sixth Amendment are applicable.

*      *      *

> In this case we are asked to import into a routine police investigation an absolute constitutional guarantee historically and rationally applicable only after the onset of formal prosecutorial proceedings. We decline to do so. Less than a year after *Wade* and *Gilbert* were decided, the Court explained the rule of those decisions as follows: "The rationale of those cases was that an accused is entitled to counsel at any 'critical state of the *prosecution*,' and that a post-indictment lineup is such a 'critical stage.' " (Emphasis supplied.) Simmons v. United States, 390 U.S. 377, 382–383, 88 S.Ct. 967, 970, 19 L.Ed.2d 1247. We decline to depart from that rationale today by imposing a *per se* exclusionary rule upon testimony concerning an identification that took place long before the commencement of any prosecution whatever.

Id. at 689–90, 92 S.Ct. at 1882–83, 32 L.Ed.2d at 418.

No effort was made by the *Kirby* majority to define "commencement of the criminal prosecution" which apparently signaled the attachment of the right to counsel. Lower courts, however, widely assumed that only formal indictment (or, in some jurisdictions, the filing of an information) constituted "commencement" under *Kirby*. Several state courts rejected this approach and required, as a matter of state law, that counsel be present at pre-indictment lineups. In People v. Jackson, 391 Mich. 323, 217 N.W.2d 22 (1974), the Michigan court, exercising its "constitutional power to establish rules of evidence applicable to judicial proceedings in Michigan courts," rejected *Kirby* outright and held that absent exigent circumstances counsel is required in all pretrial identification procedures. In Blue v. State, 558 P.2d 636 (Alas.1977), the court held that the state constitution requires counsel at all pretrial confrontations. In Commonwealth v. Richman, 458 Pa. 167, 320 A.2d 351 (1974), the court held that arrest, with or without a warrant, marks the initiation of adversary judicial proceedings in Pennsylvania and that counsel is required at any post-arrest identification confrontation.

The assumption that indictment or information is necessary for attachment of the right to counsel under *Wade* and *Gilbert*, however, was proved erroneous by Moore v. Illinois, 434 U.S. 220, 98 S.Ct. 458, 54 L.Ed.2d 424 (1977). Petitioner Moore was arrested for a rape and robbery that had occurred one week earlier. The evidence indicating his guilt included selection of his photograph by the victim from a photo array, apparently as one of the two or three photos most closely resembling her assailant. The morning after the arrest, a policeman accompanied the victim to the courtroom where petitioner was to appear for his preliminary hearing to determine whether there was probable cause to bind him over to the grand jury. Before the petitioner appeared in court, the policeman informed the victim that she was going to view a suspect and should identify him if she could. He also had her sign a complaint that named petitioner as her assailant. At the hearing, petitioner's name was called and he was led before the bench. Petitioner was told by the judge that he was charged with rape. The judge then called the victim, who had been in the courtroom waiting for the case to be called, to come before the bench. The State's Attorney stated that the policeman had found evidence linking petitioner with the offenses charged. He then asked the victim whether she saw her assailant in the courtroom; she pointed at petitioner. The State's Attorney then requested a continuance of the hearing because more time was needed to check fingerprints; the judge granted the continuance and set bail. Petitioner was not represented by counsel at this appearance and the court did not offer to appoint an attorney. At a later hearing, petitioner was bound over to the grand jury, which subsequently indicted him for rape, deviate sexual activity, burglary and robbery. Defense counsel was appointed and made an unsuccessful motion to suppress the victim's identification testimony on the ground that it would be fatally related to a pretrial confrontation at which petitioner's right to counsel had been violated. At trial, the victim testified as part of the prosecution's case-in-chief that she had, at the preliminary hearing, identified petitioner as the man who had raped her. She also made an in-court identification, testifying from present memory that petitioner was her assailant. Petitioner presented a defense of alibi, which was rejected by the jury; he was convicted of all charges. The conviction was affirmed by the Illinois Supreme Court, which did not reach the question of whether petitioner had a right to counsel at the confrontation which occurred during the preliminary hearing. Assuming that such a right existed and was violated, the court held that this did not affect the admissibility of the victim's testimony because there was an "independent source" for this testimony in the victim's previous selection of petitioner's photo from the array. Petitioner's claim concerning the identification procedure was rejected on federal habeas corpus by the District Court and the Seventh Circuit.

The Supreme Court reversed. Writing for the Court, Justice Powell concluded that the case was governed by Gilbert v. California. Although the identification confrontation had occurred prior to his indictment, petitioner's Sixth Amendment right to counsel had attached because the "prosecution in this case was commenced under Illinois law when the victim's complaint was filed in the court." The State had committed itself to prosecute. Further, the State had conceded that the preliminary hearing marked the initiation of adversary judicial criminal proceedings against petitioner within the meaning of *Kirby*. 434 U.S. at 228, 98 S.Ct. at 464–65, 54 L.Ed.2d at 433. The Court rejected arguments that the right to counsel does not apply to one-on-one identification procedures and that the right is inapplicable to confrontations that occur in the course of judicial proceedings. Responding to the state court's conclusion that the victim's testimony was nevertheless admissible, the Supreme Court applied the "strict" rule of *Gilbert*. Rejecting the "independent source" rationale relied upon by the state court, the Court held that under *Gilbert* the prosecution is prohibited from using, as part of its case-in-chief, evidence of a pretrial confrontation and identification conducted in violation of the defendant's Sixth Amendment right to counsel, even if it can prove an "independent source." Consequently, there was constitutional error in petitioner's conviction. The case was remanded, however, for inquiry into whether this error might be harmless. The Supreme Court further indicated that on remand the lower courts were free to consider other arguments advanced by petitioner, including his assertion that the victim's in-court identification was tainted by the prior uncounseled identification, and that the in-court identification should have been excluded under the Due Process Clause as the unreliable product of an unnecessarily suggestive identification procedure.

4. To what extent does the right to counsel apply at investigatory procedures that do not involve a physical confrontation between the defendant and a potential prosecution witness? In United States v. Ash, 413 U.S. 300, 93 S.Ct. 2568, 37 L.Ed.2d 619 (1973), the Court held that counsel is not required at a post-indictment photo array. Witnesses to a bank robbery had been shown five color photographs shortly before trial and long after Ash had been indicted. Finding no violation of the right to counsel, the Court distinguished *Wade* and *Gilbert*. The opportunities for suggestion and the difficulty of reconstructing a suggestive lineup were used in *Wade* only to address whether—assuming a right to counsel at the lineup existed—providing counsel only at trial would be sufficient. Whether the right to counsel attached at the lineup in the first place was determined in *Wade* by the Court's conclusion that the lineup constituted a "trial-like confrontation" requiring the assistance of counsel to counterbalance any "overreaching" by the prosecution. The initial question, therefore, must be whether a photo showing is such a "trial-like confrontation." Addressing this, the Court noted that since a defendant has no right to be present at the showing of a photo display and most likely will not be present, the showing is not a "trial-like adversary confrontation" and there is no possibility that the defendant might be "misled" by his lack of familiarity with the law or overpowered by his professional adversary. 413 U.S. at 317, 93 S.Ct. at 2577, 37 L.Ed.2d at 631. Both sides have equal access to witnesses for purposes of showing them photographs. The traditional counterbalance in the American adversary system for the prosecution's ability to interview witnesses and to show them photographs is the equal ability of defense counsel to seek and interview witnesses himself. While this does not remove all potential for abuse, "it does remove any inequality in the adversary process itself and thereby fully satisfies the historical spirit of the Sixth Amendment's right to counsel guarantee." 413 U.S. at 319, 93 S.Ct. at 2578, 37 L.Ed.2d at 632. Apparently acknowledging that requiring the presence of counsel would tend to encourage better pretrial identification procedures, the Court noted that the primary safeguard against abuses of pretrial identification is the ethical responsibility of the prosecutor. "If that safeguard fails, review remains available under the due process standards." 413 U.S. at 320, 93 S.Ct. at 2579, 37 L.Ed.2d at 633. The majority then concluded, "We are not persuaded that the risks inherent in the use of photographs are so pernicious that an extraordinary system of safeguards is required." 413 U.S. at 321, 93 S.Ct. at 2579, 37 L.Ed.2d at 633. If the Court had reached an opposite result in *Ash*, would it later have been able to distinguish interviews between prosecutors or police officers and witnesses that did not involve the showing of photographs? Do not such interviews create a danger of suggestiveness that might affect trial testimony? But would it be possible or acceptable to make all such interviews part of the adversary process at which the right to counsel applies?

## B. DUE PROCESS REQUIREMENTS INDEPENDENT OF THE COUNSEL REQUIREMENT

The third case of the 1967 identification trilogy, Stovall v. Denno, 388 U.S. 293, 87 S.Ct. 1967, 18 L.Ed.2d 1199 (1967), involved an attack upon a husband and wife in the kitchen of their home about midnight, August 23, 1961. The intruder stabbed both; the husband died but the wife, stabbed 11 times, survived. On the basis of evidence found at the scene, Stovall was arrested and arraigned on August 24. The wife had undergone surgery on that date for her wounds and there was still substantial question as to whether she would survive. About noon on

August 25, Stovall was brought to the wife's hospital room. He was handcuffed to one of five police officers who accompanied him; two prosecutors were also there. Stovall, the only Black in the room, was required to repeat a few words for voice identification; no one could later recall what words were used. After a police officer asked if Stovall "was the man," the wife identified him. At Stovall's later trial, the wife testified to her identification of him as her assailant and that of her husband. Stovall was convicted. The Supreme Court held that the right to counsel announced in *Wade* and *Gilbert* would not be applied retroactively, so the failure to accord Stovall the right to assistance of a lawyer at the confrontation did not entitle him to relief. The Court then turned to Stovall's claim that "the confrontation conducted in this case was so unnecessarily suggestive and conducive to irreparable mistaken identification that he was denied due process of law." This, the Court commented, "is a recognized ground of attack upon a conviction independent of any right to counsel claim." 388 U.S. at 302, 87 S.Ct. at 1972, 18 L.Ed.2d at 1206. Whether a violation of due process of law took place, however, depends upon "the totality of the circumstances" surrounding the confrontation. Stressing that the victim's condition made the confrontation "imperative," the Court found no due process defect. Id.

In a number of subsequent cases the Court considered claims that the suggestiveness of pretrial procedures rendered witnesses' testimony unavailable to the prosecution as a matter of due process. It generally found such claims without merit. See Neil v. Biggers, 409 U.S. 188, 93 S.Ct. 375, 34 L.Ed.2d 401 (1972); Coleman v. Alabama, 399 U.S. 1, 90 S.Ct. 1999, 26 L.Ed.2d 387 (1970); Simmons v. United States, 390 U.S. 377, 88 S.Ct. 967, 19 L.Ed.2d 1247 (1968). Only in Foster v. California, 394 U.S. 440, 89 S.Ct. 1127, 22 L.Ed.2d 402 (1969), has the Court found a violation of the due process standard. Foster was arrested for the late-night robbery of a Western Union office; the only employee present when the two robbers entered was Joseph David, the late-night manager. The following then occurred:

> David was called to the police station to view a lineup. There were three men in the lineup. One was [Foster]. He is a tall man— close to six feet in height. The other men were short—five feet, five or six inches. [Foster] wore a leather jacket which David said was similar to the one he had seen underneath the coveralls worn by the robber. After seeing this lineup, David could not positively identify [Foster] as the robber. He "thought" he was the man, but he was not sure. David then asked to speak to [Foster], and [Foster] was brought into an office and sat across from David at a table. Except for prosecuting officials there was no one else in the room. Even after this one-to-one confrontation David still was uncertain whether [Foster] was one of the robbers: "truthfully—I was not sure," he testified at trial. A week or 10 days later, the police arranged for David to view a second lineup. There were five men in that lineup. [Foster] was the only person in the second lineup who had appeared in the first lineup. This time David was "convinced" [Foster] was the man.

394 U.S. at 441–42, 89 S.Ct. at 1128, 22 L.Ed.2d at 405–06. At trial, David identified Foster as one of the robbers and testified to his identification of Foster at the second lineup; Foster was convicted. Finding that the suggestive elements in the identification procedure "made it all but inevitable that David would identify [Foster] whether or not he was in fact 'the man' ", the Court concluded that the procedure "so undermined the reliability of the eyewitness identification as to violate due process." 394 U.S. at 443, 89 S.Ct. at 1129, 22 L.Ed.2d at 407.

In dissent, Mr. Justice Black found the majority opinion ambiguous on a key point:

> The Court, however, fails to spell out exactly what should happen to this defendant if there must be a retrial, and thus avoids the apparently distasteful task of specifying whether (1) at the new trial the jury would again be permitted to hear the eyewitness' testimony and the in-court identification, so long as he does not refer to the previous lineups, or (2) the eyewitness' "tainted" identification testimony must be entirely excluded, thus compelling Foster's acquittal. Objection to this ambiguity is the first of my reasons for dissent.

394 U.S. at 445, 89 S.Ct. at 1130, 22 L.Ed.2d at 408.

## MANSON v. BRATHWAITE

Supreme Court of the United States, 1977.
432 U.S. 98, 97 S.Ct. 2243, 53 L.Ed.2d 140.

MR. JUSTICE BLACKMUN delivered the opinion of the Court.

This case presents the issue as to whether the Due Process Clause of the Fourteenth Amendment compels the exclusion, in a state criminal trial, apart from any consideration of reliability, of pretrial identification evidence obtained by a police procedure that was both suggestive and unnecessary. This Court's decisions in Stovall v. Denno, 388 U.S. 293, 87 S.Ct. 1967, 18 L.Ed.2d 1199 (1967), and Neil v. Biggers, 409 U.S. 188, 93 S.Ct. 375, 34 L.Ed.2d 401 (1972), are particularly implicated.

### I.

Jimmy D. Glover, a full-time trooper of the Connecticut State Police, in 1970 was assigned to the Narcotics Division in an undercover capacity. On May 5 of that year, about 7:45 p. m., e.d.t., and while there was still daylight, Glover and Henry Alton Brown, an informant, went to an apartment building at 201 Westland, in Hartford, for the purpose of purchasing narcotics from "Dickie Boy" Cicero, a known narcotics dealer. Cicero, it was thought, lived on the third floor of that apartment building. Glover and Brown entered the building, observed by back-up Officers D'Onofrio and Gaffey, and proceeded by stairs to the third floor. Glover knocked at the door of one of the two apartments served by the stairway.[7] The area was illuminated by natural

---

[7] It appears that the door on which Glover knocked may not have been that of the Cicero apartment. Petitioner concedes, in any event, that the transaction effected "was with some other person than had been intended."

light from a window in the third floor hallway. The door was opened 12 to 18 inches in response to the knock. Glover observed a man standing at the door and, behind him, a woman. Brown identified himself. Glover then asked for "two things" of narcotics. The man at the door held out his hand, and Glover gave him two $10 bills. The door closed. Soon the man returned and handed Glover two glassine bags.[8] While the door was open, Glover stood within two feet of the person from whom he made the purchase and observed his face. Five to seven minutes elapsed from the time the door first opened until it closed the second time.

Glover and Brown then left the building. This was about eight minutes after their arrival. Glover drove to headquarters where he described the seller to D'Onofrio and Gaffey. Glover at that time did not know the identity of the seller. He described him as being "a colored man, approximately five feet eleven inches tall, dark complexion, black hair, short Afro style, and having high cheekbones, and of heavy build. He was wearing at the time blue pants and a plaid shirt." D'Onofrio, suspecting from this description that respondent might be the seller, obtained a photograph of respondent from the Records Division of the Hartford Police Department. He left it at Glover's office. D'Onofrio was not acquainted with respondent personally but did know him by sight and had seen him "[s]everal times" prior to May 5. Glover, when alone, viewed the photograph for the first time upon his return to headquarters on May 7; he identified the person shown as the one from whom he had purchased the narcotics.

The toxicological report on the contents of the glassine bags revealed the presence of heroin. The report was dated July 16, 1970.

Respondent was arrested on July 27 while visiting at the apartment of a Mrs. Ramsey on the third floor of 201 Westland. This was the apartment at which the narcotics sale had taken place on May 5.[9]

Respondent was charged, in a two-count information, with possession and sale of heroin, in violation of Conn.Gen.Stat. (Rev. of 1958, as amended in 1969), §§ 19-481a and 19-480a (1977). At his trial in January 1971, the photograph from which Glover had identified respondent was received in evidence without objection on the part of the defense. Glover also testified that, although he had not seen respondent in the eight months that had elapsed since the sale, "there [was] no doubt whatsoever" in his mind that the person shown on the photograph was respondent. Glover also made a positive in-court identification without objection.

[8] This was Glover's testimony. Brown later was called as a witness for the prosecution. He testified on direct examination that, due to his then use of heroin, he had no clear recollection of the details of the incident. Tr. 81-82. On cross-examination, as in an interview with defense counsel the preceding day, he said that it was a woman who opened the door, received the money, and thereafter produced the narcotics. On redirect, he acknowledged that he was using heroin daily at the time, that he had had some that day, and that there was "an inability to recall and remember events."

[9] Respondent testified: "Lots of times I have been there before in that building." He also testified that Mrs. Ramsey was a friend of his wife, that her apartment was the only one in the building he ever visited, and that he and his family, consisting of his wife and five children, did not live there but at 453 Albany Avenue, Hartford.

No explanation was offered by the prosecution for the failure to utilize a photographic array or to conduct a lineup.

Respondent, who took the stand in his own defense, testified that on May 5, the day in question, he had been ill at his Albany Avenue apartment ("a lot of back pains, muscle spasms * * * a bad heart * * * high blood pressure * * * neuralgia in my face, and sinus,") and that at no time on that particular day had he been at 201 Westland. His wife testified that she recalled, after her husband had refreshed her memory, that he was home all day on May 5. Doctor Wesley M. Vietzke, an internist and assistant professor of medicine at the University of Connecticut, testified that respondent had consulted him on April 15, 1970, and that he took a medical history from him, heard his complaints about his back and facial pain, and discovered that he had high blood pressure. The physician found respondent, subjectively, "in great discomfort." Respondent in fact underwent surgery for a herniated disc at L5 and S1 on August 17.

The jury found respondent guilty on both counts of the information. He received a sentence of not less than six nor more than nine years. His conviction was affirmed *per curiam* by the Supreme Court of Connecticut.

Fourteen months later, respondent filed a petition for habeas corpus in the United States District Court for the District of Connecticut. He alleged that the admission of the identification testimony at his state trial deprived him of due process of law to which he was entitled under the Fourteenth Amendment. The District Court, by an unreported written opinion based on the court's review of the state trial transcript, dismissed respondent's petition. On appeal, the United States Court of Appeals for the Second Circuit reversed, with instructions to issue the writ unless the State gave notice of a desire to retry respondent and the new trial occurred within a reasonable time to be fixed by the District Judge. 527 F.2d 363 (1975).

In brief summary, the court felt that evidence as to the photograph should have been excluded, regardless of reliability, because the examination of the single photograph was unnecessary and suggestive. And, in the court's view, the evidence was unreliable in any event. We granted certiorari. 425 U.S. 957, 96 S.Ct. 1737, 48 L.Ed.2d 202 (1976).

\*    \*    \*

## IV.

Petitioner at the outset acknowledges that "the procedure in the instant case was suggestive [because only one photograph was used] and unnecessary" [because there was no emergency or exigent circumstance]. The respondent, in agreement with the Court of Appeals, proposes a *per se* rule of exclusion that he claims is dictated by the demands of the Fourteenth Amendment's guarantee of due process. He rightly observes that this is the first case in which this Court has had occasion to rule upon strictly post-*Stovall* out-of-court identification evidence of the challenged kind.

Since the decision in *Biggers*, the Courts of Appeals appear to have developed at least two approaches to such evidence. The first, or *per se* approach, employed by the Second Circuit in the present case, focuses on the procedures employed and requires exclusion of the out-of-court identification evidence, without regard to reliability, whenever it has been obtained through unnecessarily suggested [sic] confrontation procedures.[10] The justifications advanced are the elimination of evidence of uncertain reliability, deterrence of the police and prosecutors, and the stated "fair assurance against the awful risks of misidentification." 527 F.2d, at 371. See Smith v. Coiner, 473 F.2d 877, 882 (CA4), cert. denied sub nom. Wallace v. Smith, 414 U.S. 1115, 94 S.Ct. 848, 38 L.Ed. 2d 743 (1973).

The second, or more lenient, approach is one that continues to rely on the totality of the circumstances. It permits the admission of the confrontation evidence if, despite the suggestive aspect, the out-of-court identification possesses certain features of reliability. Its adherents feel that the *per se* approach is not mandated by the Due Process Clause of the Fourteenth Amendment. This second approach, in contrast to the other, is ad hoc and serves to limit the societal costs imposed by a sanction that excludes relevant evidence from consideration and evaluation by the trier of fact.

Mr. Justice Stevens, in writing for the Seventh Circuit in *Kirby*, supra, observed: "There is surprising unanimity among scholars in regarding such a rule [the *per se* approach] as essential to avoid serious risk of miscarriage of justice." 510 F.2d, at 405. He pointed out that well-known federal judges have taken the position that "evidence of, or derived from, a showup identification should be inadmissible unless the prosecutor can justify his failure to use a more reliable identification procedure." Id., at 406. Indeed, the ALI Model Code of Pre-Arraignment Procedure §§ 160.1 and 160.2 (1975) (hereafter Model Code), frowns upon the use of a showup or the display of only a single photograph.

The respondent here stresses the same theme and the need for deterrence of improper identification practice, a factor he regards as pre-eminent. Photographic identification, it is said, continues to be needlessly employed. He notes that the legislative regulation "the Court had hoped [*United States v.*] *Wade*[, 388 U.S. 218, 239, 87 S.Ct. 1926, 1938–1939, 18 L.Ed.2d 1149 (1967),] would engender," Brief for Respondent 15, has not been forthcoming. He argues that a totality rule cannot be expected to have a significant deterrent impact; only a strict rule of exclusion will have direct and immediate impact on law enforcement agents. Identification evidence is so convincing to the jury that sweeping exclusionary rules are required. Fairness of the

---

[10] Although the *per se* approach demands the exclusion of testimony concerning unnecessarily suggestive identifications, it does permit the admission of testimony concerning a subsequent identification, including an in-court identification, if the subsequent identification is determined to be reliable. 527 F.2d, at 367. The totality approach, in contrast, is simpler: if the challenged identification is reliable, then testimony as to it and any identification in its wake is admissible.

trial is threatened by suggestive confrontation evidence, and thus, it is said, an exclusionary rule has an established constitutional predicate.

There are, of course, several interests to be considered and taken into account. The driving force behind United States v. Wade, 388 U.S. 218, 87 S.Ct. 1926, 18 L.Ed.2d 1149 (1967), Gilbert v. California, 388 U.S. 263, 87 S.Ct. 1951, 18 L.Ed.2d 1178 (1967) (right to counsel at a post-indictment line-up), and *Stovall*, all decided on the same day, was the Court's concern with the problems of eyewitness identification. Usually the witness must testify about an encounter with a total stranger under circumstances of emergency or emotional stress. The witness' recollection of the stranger can be distorted easily by the circumstances or by later actions of the police. Thus, *Wade* and its companion cases reflect the concern that the jury not hear eyewitness testimony unless that evidence has aspects of reliability. It must be observed that both approaches before us are responsive to this concern. The *per se* rule, however, goes too far since its application automatically and peremptorily, and without consideration of alleviating factors, keeps evidence from the jury that is reliable and relevant.

The second factor is deterrence. Although the *per se* approach has the more significant deterrent effect, the totality approach also has an influence on police behavior. The police will guard against unnecessarily suggestive procedures under the totality rule, as well as the *per se* one, for fear that their actions will lead to the exclusion of identifications as unreliable.

The third factor is the effect on the administration of justice. Here the *per se* approach suffers serious drawbacks. Since it denies the trier reliable evidence, it may result, on occasion, in the guilty going free. Also, because of its rigidity, the *per se* approach may make error by the trial judge more likely than the totality approach. And in those cases in which the admission of identification evidence is error under the *per se* approach but not under the totality approach—cases in which the identification is reliable despite an unnecessarily suggestive identification procedure—reversal is a Draconian sanction.[11] Certainly, inflexible rules of exclusion that may frustrate rather than promote justice have not been viewed recently by this Court with unlimited enthusiasm.

We therefore conclude that reliability is the linchpin in determining the admissibility of identification testimony * * *. The factors to be considered * * * include the opportunity of the witness to view the criminal at the time of the crime, the witness' degree of attention, the accuracy of his prior description of the criminal, the level of certainty demonstrated at the confrontation, and the time between the crime and the confrontation. Against these factors is to be weighed the corrupting effect of the suggestive identification itself.

[11] Unlike a warrantless search, a suggestive preindictment identification procedure does not in itself intrude upon a constitutionally protected interest. Thus, considerations urging the exclusion of evidence deriving from a constitutional violation do not bear on the instant problem. See United States ex rel. Kirby v. Sturges, 510 F.2d 397, 406 (CA 7 1975).

## V.

We turn, then, to the facts of this case and apply the analysis:

1. The opportunity to view. Glover testified that for two to three minutes he stood at the apartment door, within two feet of the respondent. The door opened twice, and each time the man stood at the door. The moments passed, the conversation took place, and payment was made. Glover looked directly at his vendor. It was near sunset, to be sure, but the sun had not yet set, so it was not dark or even dusk or twilight. Natural light from outside entered the hallway through a window. There was natural light, as well, from inside the apartment.

2. The degree of attention. Glover was not a casual or passing observer, as is so often the case with eyewitness identification. Trooper Glover was a trained police officer on duty—and specialized and dangerous duty—when he called at the third floor of 201 Westland in Hartford on May 5, 1970. Glover himself was a Negro and unlikely to perceive only general features of "hundreds of Hartford black males," as the Court of Appeals stated. 527 F.2d, at 371. It is true that Glover's duty was that of ferreting out narcotics offenders and that he would be expected in his work to produce results. But it is also true that, as a specially trained, assigned, and experienced officer, he could be expected to pay scrupulous attention to detail, for he knew that subsequently he would have to find and arrest his vendor. In addition, he knew that his claimed observations would be subject later to close scrutiny and examination at any trial.

3. The accuracy of the description. Glover's description was given to D'Onofrio within minutes after the transaction. It included the vendor's race, his height, his build, the color and style of his hair, and the high cheekbone facial feature. It also included clothing the vendor wore. No claim has been made that respondent did not possess the physical characteristics so described. D'Onofrio reacted positively at once. Two days later, when Glover was alone, he viewed the photograph D'Onofrio produced and identified its subject as the narcotics seller.

4. The witness' level of certainty. There is no dispute that the photograph in question was that of respondent. Glover, in response to a question whether the photograph was that of the person from whom he made the purchase, testified: "There is no question whatsoever." This positive assurance was repeated.

5. The time between the crime and the confrontation. Glover's description of his vendor was given to D'Onofrio within minutes of the crime. The photographic identification took place only two days later. We do not have here the passage of weeks or months between the crime and the viewing of the photograph.

These indicators of Glover's ability to make an accurate identification are hardly outweighed by the corrupting effect of the challenged identification itself. Although identifications arising from single-photograph displays may be viewed in general with suspicion, see Simmons v. United States, 390 U.S., at 383, 88 S.Ct., at 970–971, we find in the instant case little pressure on the witness to acquiesce in the suggestion that such a display entails. D'Onofrio had left the photograph at Glover's office and was not present when Glover first viewed it two days after the event. There thus was little urgency and Glover could view the photograph at his leisure. And since Glover examined the photograph alone, there was no coercive pressure to make an identification arising from the presence of another. The identification was made in circumstances allowing care and reflection.

Although it plays no part in our analysis, all this assurance as to the reliability of the identification is hardly undermined by the facts that respondent was arrested in the very apartment where the sale had taken place, and that he acknowledged his frequent visits to that apartment.

Surely, we cannot say that under all the circumstances of this case there is "a very substantial likelihood of irreparable misidentification." Id., at 384, 88 S.Ct., at 971. Short of that point, such evidence is for the jury to weigh. We are content to rely upon the good sense and judgment of American juries, for evidence with some element of untrustworthiness is customary grist for the jury mill. Juries are not so susceptible that they cannot measure intelligently the weight of identification testimony that has some questionable feature.

Of course, it would have been better had D'Onofrio presented Glover with a photographic array including "so far as practicable * * * a reasonable number of persons similar to any person then suspected whose likeness is included in the array." Model Code, § 160.2(2). The use of that procedure would have enhanced the force of the identification at trial and would have avoided the risk that the evidence would be excluded as unreliable. But we are not disposed to view D'Onofrio's failure as one of constitutional dimension to be enforced by a rigorous and unbending exclusionary rule. The defect, if there be one, goes to weight and not to substance. * * *

The judgment of the Court of Appeals is reversed.

It is so ordered.

Mr. Justice Stevens, concurring [omitted].

Mr. Justice Marshall, with whom Mr. Justice Brennan joins, dissenting.

Today's decision can come as no surprise to those who have been watching the Court dismantle the protections against mistaken eyewitness testimony erected a decade ago * * *.

* * *

* * * [I]n determining the admissibility of the * * * identification in this case, the Court considers two alternatives, a *per se* exclusionary rule and a totality-of-the circumstances approach. The Court weighs three factors in deciding that the totality approach, which is essentially the test used in *Biggers*, should be applied. In my view, the Court wrongly evaluates the impact of these factors.

First, the Court acknowledges that one of the factors, deterrence of police use of unnecessarily suggestive identification procedures, favors the *per se* rule. Indeed, it does so heavily, for such a rule would make it unquestionably clear to the police they must never use a suggestive procedure when a fairer alternative is available. I have no doubt that conduct would quickly conform to the rule.

Second, the Court gives passing consideration to the dangers of eyewitness identification recognized in the *Wade* trilogy. It concludes, however, that the grave risk of error does not justify adoption of the *per se* approach because that would too often result in exclusion of relevant evidence. In my view, this conclusion totally ignores the lessons of *Wade*. The dangers of mistaken identification are, as *Stovall* held, simply too great to permit unnecessarily suggestive identifications. Neither *Biggers* nor the Court's opinion today points to any contrary empirical evidence. Studies since *Wade* have only reinforced the validity of its assessment of the dangers of identification testimony. While the Court is "content to rely on the good sense and judgment of American juries," the impetus for *Stovall* and *Wade* was repeated miscarriages of justice resulting from juries' willingness to credit inaccurate eyewitness testimony.

Finally, the Court errs in its assessment of the relative impact of the two approaches on the administration of justice. The Court relies most heavily on this factor, finding that "reversal is a Draconian sanction" in cases where the identification is reliable despite an unnecessarily suggestive procedure used to obtain it. Relying on little more than a strong distaste for "inflexible rules of exclusion," the Court rejects the *per se* test. In so doing, the Court disregards two significant distinctions between the *per se* rule advocated in this case and the exclusionary remedies for certain other constitutional violations.

First, the *per se* rule here is not "inflexible." Where evidence is suppressed, for example, as the fruit of an unlawful search, it may well be forever lost to the prosecution. Identification evidence, however, can by its very nature be readily and effectively reproduced. The in-court identification, permitted under *Wade* and *Simmons* if it has a source independent of an uncounseled or suggestive procedure, is one example. Similarly, when a prosecuting attorney learns that there has been a suggestive confrontation, he can easily arrange another lineup conducted under scrupulously fair conditions. Since the same factors are evaluated in applying both the Court's totality test and the *Wade-Simmons* independent-source inquiry, any identification which is "reliable" under the Court's test will support admission of evidence concerning such a fairly conducted lineup. The evidence of an additional, properly conducted confrontation will be more persuasive to a jury, thereby increasing the chance of a justified conviction where a reliable identification was tainted by a suggestive confrontation. At the same time, however, the effect of an unnecessarily suggestive identification— which has no value whatsoever in the law enforcement process—will be completely eliminated.

Second, other exclusionary rules have been criticized for preventing jury consideration of relevant and usually reliable evidence in order to serve interest unrelated to guilt or innocence, such as discouraging illegal searches or denial of counsel. Suggestively obtained eyewitness testimony is excluded, in contrast, precisely because of its unreliability and concomitant irrelevance. Its exclusion both protects the integrity of the truth-seeking function of the trial and discourages police use of needlessly inaccurate and ineffective investigatory methods.

Indeed, impermissibly suggestive identifications are not merely worthless law enforcement tools. They pose a grave threat to society at large in a more direct way than most governmental disobedience of the law, see Olmstead v. United States, 277 U.S. 438, 471, 485, 48 S.Ct. 564, 570, 575, 72 L.Ed. 944 (1928) (Brandeis, J., dissenting). For if the police and the public erroneously conclude, on the basis of an unnecessarily suggestive confrontation, that the right man has been caught and convicted, the real outlaw must still remain at large. Law enforcement has failed in its primary function and has left society unprotected from the depredations of an active criminal.

For these reasons, I conclude that adoption of the *per se* rule would enhance, rather than detract from, the effective administration of justice. In my view, the Court's totality test will allow seriously unreliable and misleading evidence to be put before juries. Equally important, it will allow dangerous criminals to remain on the streets while citizens assume that police action has given them protection. According to my calculus, all three of the factors upon which the Court relies point to acceptance of the *per se* approach.

\*    \*    \*

### III.

Despite my strong disagreement with the Court over the proper standards to be applied in this case, I am pleased that its application of the totality test does recognize the continuing vitality of *Stovall*. In assessing the reliability of the identification, the Court mandates weighing "the corrupting effect of the suggestive identification itself" against the "indicators of [a witness'] ability to make an accurate identification." The Court holds  \*  \*  \*   that a due process identification inquiry must take account of the suggestiveness of a confrontation and the likelihood that it led to misidentification, as recognized in *Stovall* and *Wade*. Thus, even if a witness did have an otherwise adequate opportunity to view a criminal, the later use of a highly suggestive identification procedure can render his testimony inadmissible. Indeed, it is my view that, assuming applicability of the totality test enunciated by the Court, the facts of the present case require that result.

\*    \*    \*

### IV.

Since I agree with the distinguished panel of the Court of Appeals that the legal standard of *Stovall* should govern this case, but that even if it does not, the facts here reveal a substantial likelihood of misidentification in violation of respondent's right to due process of law, I would affirm the grant of habeas corpus relief. Accordingly, I dissent from the Court's reinstatement of respondent's conviction.

## NOTES

1. Is the question whether "pretrial identification procedures are so impermissibly suggestive as to give rise to a very substantial likelihood of irreparable misidentification" one of fact or of law? A majority of the Court concluded that the issue was a factual one, at least for the purpose of deciding whether a federal habeas court must initially presume the accuracy of a state court finding on the issue under 28 U.S.C.A. § 2254(d). Sumner v. Mata, 449 U.S. 539, 101 S.Ct. 764, 66 L.Ed.2d 722 (1981). Mr. Justice Brennan, joined by Justices Marshall and Stevens, dissented.

> Plainly, the disagreement between the courts is over the constitutional significance of the facts of the case, and not over the facts themselves. Whether a witness's opportunity to view a crime is "adequate" for constitutional purposes, whether a particular course of conduct by state police raises a possibility of irreparable misidentification serious enough to violate constitutional standards, whether a witness's description is sufficiently detailed to dispel doubt about the procedures imposed, and whether the necessity for a photographic identification procedure is constitutionally significant are examples of questions of law, or at least mixed questions of fact and law. The questions addressed by the Court of Appeals for the Ninth Circuit required the "application of constitutional principles to the facts as found," and thus fall outside the limitations of § 2254(d).

449 U.S. at 556–57, 101 S.Ct. at 774, 66 L.Ed.2d at 737.

2. In Watkins v. Sowders, 449 U.S. 341, 101 S.Ct. 654, 66 L.Ed.2d 549 (1981), the Court held that the Fourteenth Amendment's Due Process Clause does not require a hearing out of the jury's presence on every contention that a witness's identification of the defendant was made by improper means. The Court said there might be special circumstances in which a determination out of the jury's presence would be constitutionally required, and that it would often be advisable to conduct such a hearing.

\*

# INDEX

References are to Pages

[1]

†